THE WOMEN WHO FLEW FOR HITLER

Also by Clare Mulley

THE WOMAN WHO SAVED THE CHILDREN

THE SPY WHO LOVED

CLARE MULLEY

THE WOMEN WHO FLEW FOR HITLER

A True Story of Soaring Ambition and Searing Rivalry

St. Martin's Press
New York

www.stmartins.com

The picture credits on p. 454 constitute an extension of this copyright page.

Map artwork by ML Design

Library of Congress Cataloging-in-Publication Data

Names: Mulley, Clare, author.
Title: The women who flew for Hitler / Clare Mulley.
Description: First U.S. edition. | New York : St. Martin's Press, 2017.
  | Includes bibliographical references and index.
Identifiers: LCCN 2017011483| ISBN 9781250063670 (hardcover) | ISBN
  9781250133168 (ebook)
Subjects: LCSH: Reitsch, Hanna. | Stauffenberg, Melitta, Grèafin,
  1903–1945. | World War, 1939–1945—Aerial operations, German. |
  World War, 1939–1945—Women—Germany. | Air pilots, Military—
  Germany—Biography. | Women air pilots—Germany—Biography.
  | Aeronautical engineers—Germany—Biography. | Iron Cross—
  Biography. | BISAC: BIOGRAPHY & AUTOBIOGRAPHY /
  Women. | HISTORY / Military / World War II. | BIOGRAPHY
  & AUTOBIOGRAPHY / Historical. | BIOGRAPHY &
  AUTOBIOGRAPHY / Military.
Classification: LCC D787 .M833 2017 | DDC 940.54/49430922—dc23
LC record available at https://lccn.loc.gov/2017011483

Our books may be purchased in bulk for promotional, educational, or business use. Please contact your local bookseller or the Macmillan Corporate and Premium Sales Department at 1-800-221-7945, extension 5442, or by email at MacmillanSpecialMarkets@macmillan.com.

First published in Great Britain by Macmillan, an imprint of Pan Macmillan

First U.S. Edition: July 2017

For my inspirational sister, Kate Mulley,

whose dry humour masks a warm heart.

Contents

Acknowledgements

One of the wonderful things about researching a biography is the sense you sometimes have of shaking hands – or joining a conversation – across history. Reading diaries and letters, or even less intimate material, can bring moments of profound empathy and a frequent sense of a meeting of minds, but also the sudden shock of finding inexplicable prejudice, or worse. It is important not to assume too much understanding, or forget what might be lost in translation across language, time or context. Occasionally there is a more literal shaking of hands when meeting veterans, survivors or other witnesses for interviews. Several times while researching this book I found myself just a couple of handshakes away from Hitler, bearing in mind that not everyone who took his hand did so enthusiastically. Meeting people in rooms displaying photographs of their parents decorated with the Iron Cross or conducting the Nazi salute has proved particularly interesting. Decisions and actions were rarely as clear-cut at the time as seventy years' distance might sometimes suggest, and reaching the many truths of any life, whether factual, moral or emotional, requires empathy as well as inquiry, criticism as well as care, and a respect for the absences from the record as well as for the traces left behind.

This book could not have been written without the very generous support of so many people who knew Melitta Schiller von Stauffenberg, Hanna Reitsch and their circles. In Germany, I was delighted to meet several members of Melitta and her in-laws' families. Her nephew Dr Reinhart Rudershausen, and his wife Elke, generously gave me full access to their collection of family papers at their beautiful lakeside cottage, and later sent me original family photographs. Heidimarie Schade recalled childhood memories, including the time she scoffed Melitta's Luftwaffe-issue chocolate, and her brother, Friedrich Berkner, also kindly shared all he knew. Major General Count Berthold von Stauffenberg, Claus von Stauffenberg's eldest son, spent a morning reminiscing about his family over and after a very fine breakfast. Thanks are also due to his sister, Konstanze von Schulthess-Rechberg, who recalled memories of her mother. Hendrik de Waal and his sister Katinka de Waal kindly shared a photograph of their uncle, Melitta's dear friend, Friedrich Franz Amsinck. Melitta's first biographer, Gerhard Bracke, who has his own fascinating childhood memories of the war, came to know Melitta's sister Klara well many years later. With extraordinary generosity, Gerhard gave me full access to his personal collection of recorded interviews, photographs and papers, including Melitta's handwritten 1943 and 1944 diaries, and some fascinating unpublished letters from Hanna.

Although unable to meet Hanna's family, I was lucky to interview several people who knew her. First among these was the remarkable officer and test pilot Captain Eric 'Winkle' Brown, the most decorated pilot in the history of the Royal Navy. Over a series of conversations, Eric described to me how he partied with Hanna before the war, formally identified her with the authorities during its closing days, and stayed in touch with her intermittently thereafter. Through the wonderful help of Margaret Nelson and Virginia Rouslin in Canada, I was also able to interview Luftwaffe Flight Captain Dietrich Pütter, who knew Hanna during the war. Lance Corporal Walter Rehling sent me his memories of her while I was visiting Peenemünde. The last person to meet Hanna among those I interviewed was BBC producer John Groom, who kindly recalled interviewing her for *The Secret War* series in the late 1970s, including watching her fall from her chair when carried away describing the flight arc of the rocket-powered Messerschmitt Komet. John Martin Bradley, who has spent years photographing veterans for his *Combat Pilots of WWII* collection, generously shared his interview with Hein K. Gering who once saved Hanna from a mouse, and James Holland kindly shared the many interviews with veterans he has conducted and posted on his *www.griffonmerlin.com* Second World War forum website. Very excitingly, Ian Sayer generously sent me scans of his important private collection of Hanna's unpublished post-war correspondence, which gave a fascinating new insight into her dogmatic character. Bernd Rosemeyer, son of the pilot Elly Beinhorn, and Barbara Pasewaldt, daughter of Luftwaffe Wing Commander Georg Pasewaldt, also kindly shared their parents' perspectives on both pilots.

I am also indebted to several veterans who talked to me about the context of the times, such as RAF Flying Officer John Alan Ottewell, my friend and neighbour Wing Commander Len Ratcliffe and, through Graham Cowie at the RAF Cosford Museum, Flight Lieutenant 'Rusty' Waughman and Flight Sergeant Jack Pragnell, who dropped bombs on Peenemünde during Operation Hydra while Hanna reportedly slept through the raid below. WAAF Intelligence Officer, Doreen Galvin, and both my parents, Gill and Derek Mulley, were also kind enough to share their wartime memories with me. I sincerely thank them all.

Among others who helped to shape this book are the historian Heiko Peter Melle, who took me round the Stauffenberg schloss, and author and curator Anne Voorhoeve, who showed me much of Melitta's Berlin. UCL's Professor Bernhard Rieger kindly shared his research on Hanna after the war; Caroline Esdaile the Kristallnacht memories of her father, Simon Reiss; and Chris Butler his family papers about Hitler's bunker in the first days of the peace. I must also particularly thank the historians and authors Nigel Jones and Paul Strong, conversations with whom led me to these women's stories, and Roger Moorhouse and Nick Jackson, who later generously helped to keep me on track in various archives and bars in London, Berlin and Munich.

My sincere thanks are also due to the archivists and staff at the British National Archives; the Imperial War Museum archives; the RAF Museum, Hendon; the British Library; the Deutsches Museum archive, Munich; the Technical University of Munich archives; the German Resistance Museum at the Bendlerblock, Berlin; the Plötzensee Prison Memorial Centre, Berlin; the Historical Technical Museum, Peenemünde; the US National Archives and Records Administration; Cornell University Law Library, Donovan Nuremberg Trials Collection; Alexander Historical Auctions; Hermann Historica International Auctions; Clint Daniel at the C. E. Daniel Collection; and the team at the Aerodrome de Gandalou, France, who bravely took me up in a glider and pretty quickly brought me back down again.

Ian Wolter and Kate Mulley – thank you for everything, you are both marvellous. Heartfelt thanks also to my brilliant editor, George Morley, Tania Wilde, Philippa McEwan and the rest of the team at Macmillan publishers, and my agent, Andrew Lownie. Also to all those who very kindly helped to locate and translate books, archive material and even at times rather torturous poetry: Marie Förg, Barbara Schlussler, Wolfgang Gehlen, Karin Fischer-Buder, Stephanie Holl-Trieu, Paul Skinner and Hans Fliri, as well as to my valiant readers, Alison Mable and Michelle Wheeler. Finally, it is with great pleasure that I thank my three daughters, Millie and Flo for pointing out appropriate references from their own reading of Anne Frank and Robert Harris, and Hester for much needed encouragement and distractions. Any errors are, of course, my own. Thank you all.

CLARE MULLEY, *February 2017*

Note on Spellings and Place Names

To assist the reader, whenever an unfamiliar German word is first mentioned, it will be in italics followed by an English translation. Thereafter, it will be in Roman. More anglicized German words, such as hausfrau and fräulein, appear in Roman throughout. German spellings use 'ss' rather than eszett for readability, so strasse rather than straße. Place names are as they were at the time, and within their contemporary borders, but with a footnote giving their modern equivalent and location when first mentioned.

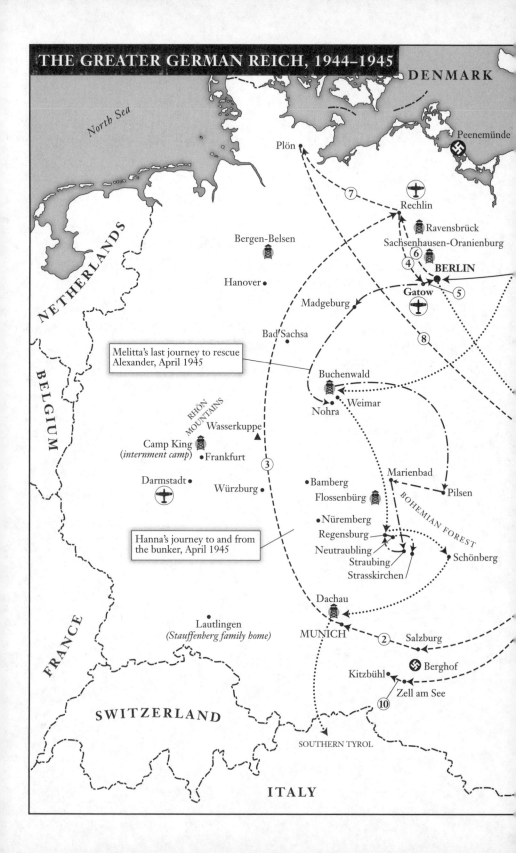

THE GREATER GERMAN REICH, 1944–1945

DENMARK

North Sea

Peenemünde

Plön

⑦

Rechlin

Ravensbrück

Sachsenhausen-Oranienburg

Bergen-Belsen

④

⑥

BERLIN

Hanover

Gatow

⑤

Madgeburg

NETHERLANDS

Bad Sachsa

⑧

Melitta's last journey to rescue
Alexander, April 1945

Buchenwald

Nohra   Weimar

BELGIUM

RHÖN
MOUNTAINS   Wasserkuppe

Marienbad

Camp King
(*internment camp*) •Frankfurt

③

•Bamberg

Pilsen

Darmstadt   Würzburg

Flossenbürg

BOHEMIAN FOREST

•Nüremberg

Regensburg

Hanna's journey to and from
the bunker, April 1945

Neutraubling

Schönberg

Straubing

Strasskirchen

Dachau

Lautlingen
(*Stauffenberg family home*)

MUNICH

②   Salzburg

FRANCE

Kitzbühl•   Berghof

Zell am See

⑩

SWITZERLAND

SOUTHERN TYROL

ITALY

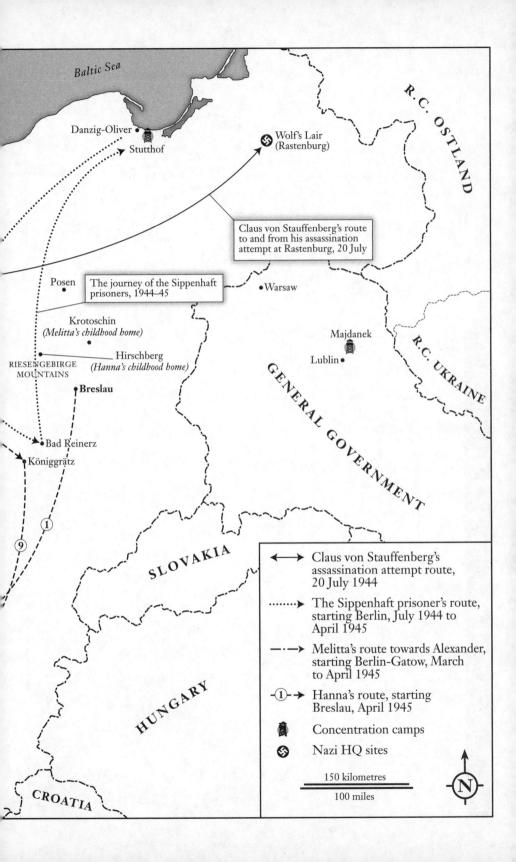

Baltic Sea

Danzig-Oliver

Stutthof

Wolf's Lair
(Rastenburg)

R.C. OSTLAND

Claus von Stauffenberg's route
to and from his assassination
attempt at Rastenburg, 20 July

Posen

The journey of the Sippenhaft
prisoners, 1944–45

Warsaw

Krotoschin
(Melitta's childhood home)

Hirschberg
(Hanna's childhood home)

RIESENGEBIRGE
MOUNTAINS

Majdanek

Lublin

R.C. UKRAINE

Breslau

GENERAL GOVERNMENT

Bad Reinerz

Königgrätz

(1)

(9)

SLOVAKIA

HUNGARY

CROATIA

Claus von Stauffenberg's
assassination attempt route,
20 July 1944

The Sippenhaft prisoner's route,
starting Berlin, July 1944 to
April 1945

Melitta's route towards Alexander,
starting Berlin-Gatow, March
to April 1945

(1) Hanna's route, starting
Breslau, April 1945

Concentration camps

Nazi HQ sites

150 kilometres

100 miles

N

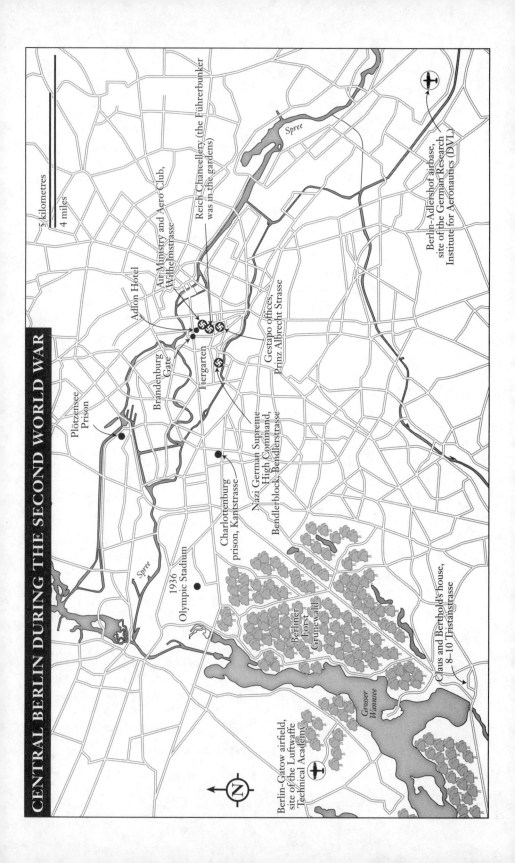

CENTRAL BERLIN DURING THE SECOND WORLD WAR

5 kilometres

4 miles

Spree

Reich Chancellery (the Führerbunker was in the gardens)

Air Ministry and Aero Club, Wilhelmstrasse

Adlon Hotel

Brandenburg Gate

Tiergarten

Gestapo offices, Prinz Albrecht Strasse

Berlin-Adlershof airbase, site of the German Research Institute for Aeronautics (DVL)

Plötzensee Prison

Nazi German Supreme High Command, Bendlerblock, Bendlerstrasse

Charlottenburg prison, Kantstrasse

1936 Olympic Stadium

Spree

Berliner Forst Grunewald

Claus and Berthold's house, 8–10 Tristanstrasse

Grosser Wannsee

Berlin-Gatow airfield, site of the Luftwaffe Technical Academy

N

The first thing Hitler did when he left his bedroom at the Berghof in the morning was to go straight to the magnificent terrace on the ground floor. There, at a particular time, he usually saw a wonderful and inspiring sight – two gigantic eagles sweeping in high circles through the sky; through field glasses he would eagerly watch the majestic flight of these rare but handsome birds. Then, one day, to his consternation, he saw but one eagle; what, he wondered anxiously, had happened to the other?

For days the subject was anxiously discussed among us, for we all saw how worried Hitler was at the disappearance of the second eagle.

A little later we decided to go again to Obersalzberg for his birthday, and a few days before the event our column set out from Munich. About thirty miles outside Munich we saw a fast-moving car approaching from the opposite direction, and in spite of the speed at which it passed us, Hitler noticed that some great bird with outspread wings was lying on the back seat. Immediately he halted the column. 'I do believe,' he said, 'that was my eagle!' and he forthwith ordered the Commando escort . . . to drive back and overtake the car.

'If I am fit, I promise you, gentlemen, that I shall mete out an exemplary punishment to those scoundrels! And not to them alone, but also to the recipient!' he said, and the black look on his face boded no good for the unfortunates who had roused his wrath.

About an hour later we saw the Commando car returning at full speed. We halted and Rattenhuber came running up.

'You were quite right, mein Führer,' he reported. 'It is the eagle from the mountains.'

'And the recipient?' asked Hitler in menacing tones.

Hesitatingly Rattenhuber continued. 'The eagle was delivered to your Munich residence . . . It is mounted on a marble plinth, which bears the inscription:

TO OUR BELOVED FÜHRER
FROM HIS MOUNTAINS
April 20th
From the Local Party Group
NSDAP Berchtesgaden.

HEINRICH HOFFMANN, 1955[1]

Preface: Truths and Lives

Hey, history this, history that . . . why should millions of viewers and readers of . . . films and magazines not be conned for the sake of drama? . . . If anyone had really wanted to tell the truth, they only needed to ask me.

HANNA REITSCH, 1973[1]

History doesn't develop following a concept; it follows its own, often random, path. You can't put either people or historical events into boxes that have been pre-prepared or constructed afterwards. People, events, and progress have their own dynamic.

NINA VON STAUFFENBERG, 1997[2]

Hanna Reitsch believed that she was an honest woman. Her American interrogator concluded his October 1945 report with the statement that her information had been 'given with a sincere and conscientious effort to be truthful and exact'. 'She claims that the only reason she remained alive is for the sake of the truth,' he added.[3] Having died six months earlier, Melitta von Stauffenberg never had the equivalent opportunity to add her voice to the historical record. Her surviving sister Klara, however, testified that Melitta would not have been 'capable of promoting anything against her better knowledge'.[4] Yet it is unlikely that, had Melitta been able to reflect on wartime events, the accounts of these two extraordinary women would have agreed.

The only female test pilots actively to serve the Nazi regime, Hanna Reitsch and Melitta von Stauffenberg were in many ways the mirror image of one another. One fair, fun, loud and irrepressible, the other dark, serious and considered; on the face of it there were few obvious similarities between them. Yet both were great patriots, with deeply held views on the importance of honour, duty and sacrifice, and both were to some extent misfits, whose love of sensation, adrenaline and personal freedom drew them to defy all social expectations.

Hanna and Melitta were born during the pioneering air age, when it was hoped that flight would bring nations together. The First World War changed that, giving pilots new roles in military reconnaissance and in combat, but the romance associated with flight persisted. Pilots prided themselves on their honour as well as their valour in the air, and aces including the 'Red Baron', Manfred von Richthofen, became legendary figures. Under the terms of the Treaty of Versailles, a defeated Germany was forced to demobilize its air force and destroy its military aircraft. The manufacture of engine-powered planes was also temporarily forbidden, but gliders were exempt. As a result, in the years immediately after the war, gliding became the aspirational sport for the country's youth, symbolic not only of peace and freedom but also of renewed national pride. Soon crowds of thousands were gathering to watch displays and competitions.

The Hirschberg valley, where Melitta went to boarding school and Hanna grew up, provided perfect conditions for gliding. As a result, both women learned to glide above the same green slopes, shocking their friends by risking their necks in fragile open-cockpit gliders made from wood and canvas. This was not the behaviour expected of young German fräuleins in the 1920s and early 1930s. What drove them was not just the adrenaline thrill of perilous flight, though that was a great lure for both women, but also the sense of freedom that gliding offered, taking them far away from the strictures and deprivations of Weimar Germany, and providing an opportunity to align themselves with the heroic restoration of their country's honour.

In 1922 Melitta, nine years older than Hanna and much more academic, threw herself into an aeronautical engineering degree at the Technical University of Munich, then the heartland of the Nazi movement. As soon as she was earning a living, she invested every spare pfennig in learning to fly engine-powered aircraft, and soon had every type of licence. Hanna skipped her college classes to learn to glide, astounding people with her natural ability. It was 1928 when Amelia Earhart impressed the world by becoming the first woman to fly across the Atlantic. Two years later Amy Johnson flew solo from England to Australia, setting another female first. This was the glamorous age of flight, when Earhart had her own fashion line and 'En Avion' was the perfume of choice. Soon Hanna and Melitta were making the pages of German society magazines, applauded for their beauty, as well as their skill and 'sensitivity' in the air.

During the mid-1930s, Hanna and Melitta's exceptional ability, courage and determination marked them as being of unique value to the new Nazi regime and both were awarded the honorary title of *Flugkapitän*, or flight captain, the first women to receive this distinction. Certain patriotic duties were now required of them. Both demonstrated their flying skills during the infamous 1936 Olympics, with Melitta performing aerobatics at the prestigious *Grossflugtag* ('Great Flight Day'). Two years later, Hanna, the first woman to fly a helicopter, would stun an international audience by flying one inside a building for the Berlin Motor Show.

When war returned in 1939, both women would also serve Germany. Their twin passions for their country and for flying had come together in the cockpit, and now both were being tested. Hanna flew a range of prototype gliders and approved pioneering flight equipment such as wing shields designed to slice through the steel cables of barrage balloons. In 1941 she became the first woman to receive the Iron Cross during the conflict. Less than two years later Melitta received the same honour for her pioneering work developing and test-flying dive-bombers like the Junkers Ju 87 Stuka. Although, as women, they were never technically employed by the Luftwaffe, from now on their stellar twin careers would be at the forefront of Nazi military aviation.

Having repeatedly risked their lives as pilots in the service of their country, Hanna and Melitta wore their decorations proudly. Both had made a significant contribution to the Nazi war effort, yet their views of their country and of the Nazi regime could hardly have been more different. Hanna felt that Germany was now truly alive, fighting proudly for its honour and rightful glory. Melitta was more circumspect. The traditional, conservative Germany that was her home was fighting for survival not only against Allied attack, but also against the brutal totalitarian Nazi regime. Although they sometimes flew from the same airfields and were both frequent visitors to the Berlin Aero Club, the two women avoided, ignored and belittled each other throughout the war. Their divergent political perspectives not only set them apart, but would lead them to make dramatically different choices as they developed their connections within the highest echelons of the Nazi regime.

After the war Hanna not only found herself famous in Germany, but also featured in numerous international books and films, with varying degrees of accuracy. Having been forced to reassess her values under US interrogation, she determined that honesty was one of her defining virtues and launched a campaign to set the record straight. 'Pitiless truth is necessary even though it may be hard to hear,' she told one interviewer fervently. 'It is of vital importance for the entire humanity.'[5] Eventually she published several versions of her memoirs in which she portrayed herself simply as a pilot and an apolitical patriot. These books were easy to write, she noted, 'since I only had to tell the truth and set it down frankly'.[6] Yet a former friend, British pilot Eric Brown, felt that at best Hanna was 'sparse with the truth'.[7] She never chose to address the criminal policies or practices of the Nazi regime, nor her own relationship with it.

Melitta, conversely, had all but disappeared from the record. In the mid-1970s her sisters, Klara and Jutta, began to ask Melitta's former friends and colleagues for their memories of her. Hanna was quick to put pen to paper. 'There is nothing that highlights Melitta's achievements as particularly remarkable,' she wrote to Klara when she heard that a biography might be in the offing.[8] Her

Iron Cross 'was not valid', Hanna asserted; her test flights 'couldn't possibly be considered risky'; and her ambition 'wasn't the normal, healthy kind of ambition but a temptation, maybe because of some kind of inner despair'.[9] 'It would be easier if you were here and we could talk about this because a written explanation can be even more hurtful than a spoken one,' she continued, adding, 'There are some things I would like to talk to you about in private which I can't write down.'[10] Whether constrained by a sense of decorum, or by concern not to leave a written record, Hanna later made some dramatic accusations about Melitta. 'Would it not be awful if these true events, known to several people, were to be described in detail . . . but falsehood certainly does come to light sooner or later,' she pressed on. 'I am sure that you will understand me correctly. I want to protect you, and Melitta's memory.'[11]

Hanna was *not* telling the truth. The question is, to whom was she lying about her and Melitta's past, and why? Klara responded by thanking Hanna for explaining her perspective 'so candidly'. 'We will, of course, accept any true version of events,' she ended their correspondence ambiguously. 'I assume that you too will be happy about this – for the sake of finding the truth.'

1

LONGING FOR FREEDOM
1903–1932

Seventeen-year-old schoolgirl Melitta Schiller stuffed her long dark hair into a tight-fitting leather flying cap and strode over to the glider she had finally been given permission to take up. Resting on the grass, its flimsy wooden frame was as light and fragile as a bird's skeleton, and yet full of promise. For months over the spring of 1920 Melitta had been a spectator, enviously watching young men learn to glide above the grassy valleys near her boarding school at Hirschberg in eastern Germany. At first she was largely ignored. It was assumed that a girl would do no more than stand at a safe distance and admire the brave men risking their lives for the thrill and the glory of flight. But Melitta was more interested in flying than social niceties. Soon she was helping to retrieve, mend and launch the gliders whenever an extra pair of hands was needed, and one warm day she was rewarded with the chance to attempt a flight herself. Perching on the centre of the plank that served as a seat, she found her balance, put both hands on the control stick, and looked up. Her 'fine, sensitive face' was torn between joy and concentration.[1] Then she gave a short nod. A moment later Melitta was powered into the air by two lines of young men in knitted jerseys, all pulling rubber-cord tow ropes as they charged down the slopes ahead of her. She pulled on the stick, released the tow, and soared above her ground team as they ducked or tumbled into the grass. Then she curved away from the contours of the world. She was gliding, observing every shudder of her machine as it responded to her hand on the stick or the shift of her weight. Melitta was mesmerized. Right from the start, she later confessed, 'Flying exerted an irresistible magic on me . . . I was dominated all along by the longing for freedom.'[2]

The first record of Adolf Hitler climbing into a cockpit also comes from the spring of 1920. Hitler's was a dramatic open-biplane flight from Munich to Berlin where he hoped to join the right-wing nationalist Kapp Putsch and witness the historic fall of the democratic Weimar Republic. Strapping a pair of goggles over his leather cap, Hitler composed his face, held onto his valise, and put his life in the hands of his pilot, the Great War flying ace Robert Ritter von Greim. 'In his tight, open seat, cramped between canister and oil, and buffeted by the wind, only one thought occupied his mind,' wrote the journalist Otto Dietrich. 'Will we make it to Berlin in time?'[3] Rough weather slowed them down, making visibility difficult and drenching both pilot and passenger. With no navigational aids, Greim had to make a stopover in Jüterbog where, according to Dietrich, the plane was surrounded by a hostile crowd of 'distraught Marxists'. By the time they reached Berlin, the putsch had failed. Hitler reportedly donned a false beard to make a discreet exit from the airfield, passing himself off as an accountant.[4] Yet despite the appalling weather, his airsickness, their late arrival and the failure of the putsch, he had been thrilled by the flight. For him the aeroplane was not just for sport or for the military; it was a political machine, and he was determined to align himself with this most modern form of travel.

The 'air age' had arrived in Germany at the turn of the twentieth century. It was 1900 when mighty Zeppelin airships had first fired the imagination of the German public, embodying age-old dreams of freedom and power. Three years later, less than twelve months after Melitta's birth on 9 January 1903, the Wright brothers successfully tested their pioneering engine-powered aeroplane in the USA. Within five years Germany was gripped by 'flight fever'. Over the next decade the country competed to set world records for altitude, distance, speed and endurance, and its successes generated a surge of patriotism. Flight had become the international measure of modernity and dynamism, and Germany was a country increasingly defined by its aspirations. Yet despite growing up during this craze for flight, as Melitta later acknowledged, 'The decision to devote her life to flying and thus to a job which . . . right from the start, appeared to be a specifically masculine one was, admittedly, unusual for a young girl.'[5]

Melitta was born in Krotoschin, a country town historically within the Kingdom of Poland but at that time in the Prussian province of Posen, near the Russian border.* The history of the town was reflected in its demographics. Almost two-thirds of the population were Polish but Melitta's family belonged to the privileged and conservative Protestant German community. Her father, Michael Schiller, was a civil engineer, architect and civil servant whose family, from Odessa, had become established through the fur trade. A proud local official, he liked his shirts to have high collars, his expensive coats to be double-breasted, and his fine moustache to be stiffly curled with wax. Her mother, Margarete Eberstein, came from similarly respectable roots, being the daughter of a schools inspector from Bromberg descended from a noble German family. She was almost twenty years younger than her husband, and a portrait by her talented sister Gertrud von Kunowski, who had studied at Breslau art academy, shows her looking effortlessly – almost carelessly – beautiful in her wedding dress, a coral choker echoing the deep red of the peonies resting in her lap.[6] Her daughters would remember Margarete's 'distinguished coolness', even as she struggled through two world wars.[7]

Settling in Krotoschin, the newly-weds developed a strong sense of national identity that chimed with the rising patriotism across their country. Firmly anchored in the values of upper-middle-class Germany, together they managed to instil a sense of both entitlement and social responsibility in their five clever children. Marie-Luise, better known as Lili, was the eldest, followed by Otto, the only boy. Melitta, called Litta by all who loved her, came next, and then her two younger sisters, Jutta and Klara. Although strict about their formal education, exercise and manners, Michael Schiller was also unusually keen to guide his children personally, especially when discussions turned to music, philosophy or science – the last of which fascinated Melitta. Margarete took them to the

---

* Now Krotoszyn, in central Poland.

theatre and to concerts, encouraging them to stage their own plays in an old horse-drawn carriage in the garden, and to swim, play tennis and learn dancing with other children of similar social status. Their aunt Gertrud set up easels and got them drawing, sculpting clay animals and cutting delicate silhouettes from paper. All of them were taught the importance of discipline, duty and noble endeavour, but all also had very active, independent natures. Escaping adult supervision whenever possible, they would play in the wreck of the family's first car, rusting away in a cloud of creepers and cornflowers at the end of the lawn or, as they got older, hike through the forests together to swim in the lakes, make camps and watch the stars come out.

Melitta was eleven when the First World War broke out in 1914. 'The days of my youth, where one can look for the origins and secret roots shaping a life, were a time when there was nothing but deep tribulation for Germany,' she later wrote.[8] At fifty-three her father was too old to fight, but as a reserve officer with a good knowledge of Russian he was assigned to a prisoner-of-war camp as a censor and interpreter. He eventually received the Iron Cross, Second Class, for his service. Margarete and her eldest daughter, Lili, volunteered as nurses: 'womankind's most noble and distinguished mission', as Melitta saw it.[9] Too young to join them, Melitta adopted animals to care for instead. She was not a natural nurse but after a favourite mouse died the family had it stuffed and she kept it in her bedroom.

When the front line came to within sixty kilometres of Krotoschin, the town began to fill with the wounded and Melitta, Jutta and Klara were sent to stay with their widowed grandmother in Hirschberg.* For Melitta, now twelve, the one advantage of this enforced evacuation was the chance to spend some time with her uncle, Ernst Eberstein. Already popular among his nieces and nephews for his jokes and easy manner, Uncle Ernst had gained huge cachet for being among the first to sign up as a combat pilot with the Imperial German Air Service. He served as a spotter in a

---

* Now Jelenia Góra in Lower Silesia, south-western Poland.

reconnaissance unit, taking aerial photographs and manning a mounted machine gun in a series of military biplanes. His role during one German victory against the Russians in August 1914 earned him the nickname 'Hero of Tannenberg'. That winter he received the Iron Cross, First Class. Family photographs show him in uniform but on leave, sitting beneath a tree, surrounded by children lapping up his tales of courage, skill and honour in the air.

As the war progressed, specialist air units were organized into fighter and bomber squadrons. The very image of the pilot was now being celebrated as the epitome of the courageous and honourable modern man, and Melitta proudly thought of her uncle whenever she heard 'aces' like the 'Red Baron', Manfred von Richthofen, Ernst Udet and Hermann Göring being lionized. One veteran, the philosopher Ernst Jünger, later argued that industrial mass warfare reduced most soldiers to the role of passive and rather pathetic victim. Pilots, by contrast, 'this ideal type in overalls, with a face hewn in stone under a leather cap', were part of 'a new and commanding breed . . . fearless and fabulous . . . a race that builds machines and trusts machines'.[10] This was the heroic ideal that inspired Melitta as she developed a passion for flight that was deeply bound to her wartime patriotism, her sense of honour and duty, and her love for both science and the adrenaline of action.

By November 1914 the Posen region had become less volatile and the three youngest Schiller girls returned home, still full of the adventures of their heroic uncle. Their mother's concerns were more prosaic: securing food and fuel as the British naval blockade held and the first refugees were billeted on the town. Dismissing her servants, Margarete started growing vegetables, and keeping rabbits and a goat in the garden. The house was freezing and the children often hungry over the next few winters. When the schools closed Melitta studied alone at home, working on her maths and Latin under a pile of coats and blankets, cocooned away from the material world while her mind continued to run free. When the weather improved she would drag her books up to the top of a tree in the garden, or climb to the roof to work on astronomy. Although irritable if interrupted, sometimes she invited her younger sisters to join her in charting the stars, and once, equipped with a pitcher of water, she and Klara scaled the high roof of their shed and lay on their stomachs to test the theory of drop formation. Physics became a lasting passion. 'At the moment I am particularly interested in the problems of flight and rocket dynamics,' a teenage Melitta told her friend Lieselotte. 'My father says that aged around eighteen, girls tend to lose their interest in science,' she added. 'So I have to make sure I get as far as possible before then!'[11]

In 1916 the Central Powers promised the reconstruction of historic Poland. The proposed boundary change included Melitta's home. At best, the Schillers saw this as a 'generous gesture' providing a buffer zone against Russia, but they were also concerned about growing Polish nationalism. Melitta and her sisters felt that the local Polish children were already 'triumphant', chanting that they didn't need 'your Wilhelm', while in town people marched with scythes and baling forks, calling for the German ruling classes to be driven out.[12] Two years later, the American president Woodrow Wilson reiterated the pledge to Poland. 'We all know that Posen is to be Polish,' Lili wrote angrily in her diary. It was, she felt, a 'humiliation', and a betrayal by the 'scoundrels and traitors to the Fatherland' sitting comfortably in Berlin.[13] No doubt her words echoed those around the family breakfast table. Polish troops arrived in Krotoschin soon after the Armistice, covering the town and garrison in white-and-red flags. While the majority Polish population celebrated, for Germans like the Schillers it felt like an invasion.

Despite the peace, Melitta's sixteenth birthday at the start of 1919 was a sad affair. Her brother Otto had been called up to serve in border security as a member of the German peacetime volunteers. Unofficially he hoped to help push back the boundary in favour of the Reich. Michael Schiller, briefly home after the German collapse, had been taken hostage by equivalent Polish volunteers, and deported to the very camp at which he had served as translator. 'You think the war is over,' Lili wrote that evening, 'and then something even worse happens!'[14] Michael returned after ten days, but the skirmishes continued until the borders were fixed on the ground, and later recognized by the Treaty of Versailles. Krotoschin and the surrounding mountains and forests were once again part of Poland, as they had been centuries before, and the Schillers no longer belonged to the social elite but to an unwelcome minority.

Melitta's German-speaking school was an early casualty of the Polish civic reorganization. In October 1919 she and Lieselotte set out for boarding school in Hirschberg, now across the border, with brand-new passports in their pockets and illicit food parcels for 'hungry Germany' hidden in their luggage.[15] If Melitta felt nervous during that long, uncertain journey, she hid it well. Lieselotte remembered there being 'something austere and disciplined about her' as she stood on the draughty station platforms, her sailor dress hidden beneath a thick navy coat with its collar thrown up, lace-up boots reaching almost to the hem of her skirt, and her long dark hair braided and tied with black ribbon.[16] Looking austere while taking bold action would remain Melitta's modus operandi throughout her life.

Melitta was more interested in studying than in making friends at her new school. For some time Lieselotte rarely saw her without a two-volume physics textbook at her side, and soon she had rigged up an electric light in the unheated attic room of her boarding house so she could read undisturbed through the night. When physics failed to satisfy Melitta's curiosity, she turned to philosophy.[17] One day Lieselotte found her 'immersed in Schopenhauer'. 'So, if it is not possible to live a happy life,' Melitta earnestly told her rather bemused friend, 'then the only way is to live a heroic life.'[18]

At first Melitta's 'heroism' was essentially sporting. Hirschberg was known as the gateway to the winter-sports paradise of the Riesengebirge mountains, and she spent every winter Sunday on her skis.* After two seasons she could compete with the locals.

---

* Melitta would have known them as the Riesengebirge, but they straddle what is now the south-west of Poland and the north of the Czech Republic, and are known as the Karkonosze or Krkonoše, which translates as the Giant Mountains.

'Oh, those dear boys,' she laughed when the young men who accompanied her grumbled about her recklessness. 'They always think everything's too dangerous for a girl.'[19] She would dismiss other men, among them an infatuated teacher, with similar brevity. The north slopes, facing Silesia, kept their snow the longest, and sometimes Melitta would still be skiing there when the flowers were already out in the valley below and her friends were playing tennis.

With summer came mountain walking, climbing, and swimming in quiet bays, sometimes by moonlight to see the forest silhouettes and watch the herons lift their grey bodies from the dark lakes. An early-morning start meant they could reach the Bober Reservoir at Mauer. Here the remnants of old farmsteads that once stood in the sunshine had been submerged when the dam was created shortly before the war. Melitta would wear her bathing costume under her dirndl, ready to plunge into the chilly water as soon as she arrived. 'Jumping from the dam wall was for suicides,' Lieselotte wrote bluntly, but one June, when the water level was still high, Melitta took the plunge. Her spectacular dive was soon legendary. As with skiing, you just 'have to know your limits and gauge the task accordingly', she told Lieselotte matter-of-factly. 'If you do that then all danger is reduced to chance, and if we were afraid of chance then we'd have to give up all car trips and horse riding, and we wouldn't be able to do any sports.'[20]

It was during Melitta's final year at school that enthusiasts started gliding in the Hirschberg valley. Under the humiliating terms of the 1919 Treaty of Versailles, Germany had been forced to dissolve its air force and destroy the remaining military planes: their bodies sawn apart, the engines smashed, while the construction of engine-powered aircraft was banned. Gliding was the phoenix that rose from these ashes, becoming not only a hugely popular national sport, but also a powerful symbol of the country's resistance and rebirth. Air shows became the rage, and thousands of spectators would regularly gather to watch German gliders soar above the tribulations of their country, bringing a sense of liberation as well as a new source of national pride.

As Hirschberg offered the perfect environment for gliding, veterans started to run courses there for interested local lads. Girls were excluded but, although it was a good hike from her boarding house, Melitta would often join the spectators at the edges of the fields. At first the crowds were mainly groups of men, sometimes with carthorses or the occasional bull to help tow a glider back up the slopes. Soon, however, whole families would turn out to watch, along with classes of schoolchildren trooping down in lines, the girls in white dresses with black woollen stockings. Melitta was one of the few girls to roll up her sleeves and get involved, and the only one recorded as taking up a glider herself. She had always enjoyed testing the limits of what was possible, whether through the exhilaration of skiing and diving, or the intellectual pleasure she gained from amateur scientific inquiry. These passions came together in the cockpit. Between the adrenaline rushes of take-off and landing, Melitta's modest first glide consolidated her fascination with every aspect of flight. Although she was proud of her achievement, it was against her nature to brag. Nevertheless, the news that a girl had flown in the Hirschberg valley quickly made 'considerable waves', Lieselotte noted.[21]

It was Easter 1922 when Melitta took her final school exams, achieving outstanding results. To celebrate, she and some classmates took a last skiing trip into the mountains. The gossip next morning was that Melitta had swum across the lake near the mountain peak, most of which was still frozen solid. But when Lieselotte went to congratulate her, Melitta was already focused on her next challenge – she had been offered a place at the Technical University of Munich. 'There it lies in front of you, your freedom,' Lieselotte sighed enviously. But Melitta saw things differently. 'You're wrong,' she said. 'Freedom is here. Here we were able to do whatever we wanted; they looked out for us and looked after us . . . all responsibility now lies with us.'[22] Melitta would chase freedom all her life, but she would never recapture the wonderful irresponsibility of her childhood.

One of the things that had attracted her to Munich was its reputation as a cultural centre, but by the time she arrived most artists were deserting a city that was rapidly becoming better known as a centre for the German extreme right.* As Hitler gained support, walls in the Schwabing area where Melitta had a room were plastered with bright-red National Socialist German Workers Party posters. Local and, increasingly, national newspapers filled their columns with reports of Nazi meetings in the city's traditional beer halls and rallies in the streets. Melitta may well have recognized the future Führer in his trilby and white-belted raincoat, perhaps sporting a whip; an affectation that he later dropped. She may even have heard some of his speeches and, like many, considered him too extreme to attract much lasting support.

The photograph on Melitta's university registration papers shows a fresh-faced young woman, her long hair pinned up, wearing an embroidered white peasant-style blouse.[23] The overall impression is of old-fashioned modesty, but her gaze is direct. Living in country towns during war and recession, Melitta had always worn simple clothes: soft pleated blouses with long sleeves buttoned at the wrist, dirndls and sailor dresses. On high days friends remembered her looking 'charming, in a dress of strong blue linen', sometimes with a few cowslips decorating her neckline.[24] The move to fashionable, urban Munich brought a radical new look. At some point Melitta must have decided that her long dark hair was too much trouble and she cut it off, or perhaps it was with a sense of liberation that she had it cropped into a fashionably sleek flapper's bob, shocking her parents as she marked her irreversible transition to adulthood and independence.† 'German youth no longer felt bound, in any way, by conventions and traditions,' she later wrote happily.[25] A natural 'new woman',

---

* When Melitta had her portrait drawn in Munich in 1924, it was Elk Eber who sketched her face in profile – always her preferred pose, her hair tucked into a bohemian velvet cap. Eber would become a draftsman for the Nazi press, and his war art was later collected by Hitler.

† Melitta's new haircut was not necessarily a political statement. Early on, conservative members of Hitler's National Socialist German Workers' Party (NSDAP) pleaded that women with short hair should not be admitted to Party gatherings but, according to his official photographer Heinrich Hoffmann, Hitler 'decided in favour of the bob'. See Heinrich Hoffmann, *Hitler Was My Friend* (Frontline, 2011), p. 142.

self-confident, athletic and ambitious, she soon took up smoking, and learned to ride the motorbike that provided her with an adrenaline rush as she hared through the city. But neither bob nor bike were as radical as the fact of being a woman studying engineering at the prestigious Technical University of Munich.

Surrounded by male students, it was not long before Melitta found her first romance. Wolfgang Schlotterer, a veteran of the German Imperial Navy during the war, had enrolled at the university a few years before Melitta, and shared her love of hiking, art – and mechanical engineering. The two quickly became close, spending weekends at the Schlotterer country home just outside the city. In 1923 they spent the summer break in Krotoschin where, despite the offence of failing to arrive in a hat, Wolfgang charmed Melitta's parents. He then wrote for permission to marry her. But, for reasons that have never emerged, there would be no wedding, and Melitta returned to college with a renewed sense of purpose. She now attended additional lectures on flight mechanics and aerodynamics, for which she would sit a special supplementary exam when she took her finals.

Having turned her studies towards aeronautical engineering, Melitta became determined to earn her pilot's licence. Since schools dealing with engine-powered aircraft did not admit women, she had to find creative ways to gain experience, 'exploiting every slightest opportunity', as she put it.[26] In 1923 she applied to join the fledgling 'Academic Fliers' Group', but was rejected on the basis that membership required service in the event of war. Melitta was quite happy with this condition; the Group's committee was not. Undeterred, she managed to cadge rides on local commercial ferry flights. A visit to the Udet aircraft works at Schleissheim gave her the opportunity to beg Ernst Udet, the greatest surviving fighter ace of the war and an acquaintance of Melitta's uncle Ernst, for a ride during his stunt flights. From then on Udet 'often took her with him to his daredevil flying displays', her sister Jutta wrote.[27] That year a monument to German pilots killed in action was erected at Wasserkuppe, the highest peak in the Rhön mountains, where annual gliding contests had been held since 1920. Over 30,000 people attended. Inspired, Melitta applied for a gliding course, but she had neither the time nor the money to take up her place.

Melitta's father, Michael Schiller, was now investing all his salary in the education of his youngest daughters, Jutta and Klara. Lili was training to be a radiographer in Berlin, and Otto was studying agriculture in Breslau.* Melitta, whose limited university grant was technically Polish, applied for scholarships and borrowed money from Otto, but she mainly paid her own way through college by tutoring fellow students. She never faced real hardship but was frustrated to find her horizons limited once again. At the same time, she watched with despair as war reparations, hyperinflation, economic stagnation and public protest forced the government to declare a state of emergency. One afternoon her mother and younger sisters were arrested and charged with smuggling some dollars and a butchered rabbit across the border as they travelled to a family wedding. Although they were released, the dollars were confiscated and the family felt utterly humiliated. 'It was too horrible,' Klara later recounted.[28]

In the autumn of 1923, members of Hitler's National Socialist Party, supported by many local students, failed in an attempt to overthrow the Bavarian government in Munich, an action that later became known as the 'Beer Hall Putsch'. Although Hitler was arrested and given a custodial sentence, the German chancellor was soon forced to resign after a vote of no confidence. The new coalition would last for less than a year. Things stabilized a little as foreign troops withdrew and economic treaties enabled some assistance, but anti-Semitism and both communist and nationalist movements were still on the rise. Melitta's parents now moved to a 'little pink house' in the pretty town of Oliva within the Free City of Danzig† where Michael could still draw his pension.[29] It was here, surrounded by woods and close to the Baltic coast, that

---

* Now Wrocław, the largest city in western Poland.

† The Free City of Danzig was a semi-autonomous city state that existed between 1920 and 1939. It is now Gdańsk in Poland.

Melitta wrote her dissertation in the summer of 1926, and immediately started to apply for work.

In October she was interviewed by the head of the aerodynamics department at the prestigious German Research Institute for Aeronautics, better known as DVL,* at Berlin-Adlershof airbase. Having temporarily closed its doors during the war, the institute was now aiming to restore Germany's international reputation in technology, and was keen to employ the brightest graduates. Invited to watch a test flight, Melitta was deep in conversation when the plane she was there to observe plummeted from the sky to crash only a hundred metres away from her. The entire crew was killed on impact. Although she was shaken, Melitta's resolve did not falter. The following year, aged twenty-five, she received her diploma and started work at DVL as a flight mechanic and mathematician in experimental aerodynamics research. Her initial brief was the operation of propellers, then known as 'airscrews', with particular focus on the sound and drag caused by high altitudes.

Although she had taken rooms within sound of the planes at Berlin-Adlershof, at first Melitta kept her distance from her colleagues. A woman's presence at DVL was a complete novelty for the men there. Her manager frequently ribbed her, and few colleagues gave her the recognition she deserved. Insulted, she began to gain a reputation for being 'dainty and reserved', and 'outwardly distant and cool, even aloof'.[30] Socially she was in any case monopolized by her current boyfriend, a possessive Danish student called Hendrik who, her sister Jutta felt, was 'jealous of everything close to her'.[31] But when Hendrik gave Melitta an ultimatum: flying or him, 'there was no doubt as to the outcome', as Jutta put it.[32] Free to focus on her work, over time Melitta's 'very meticulous and reliable' approach attracted growing approval until, as the engineer Paul von Handel noted, 'she was always consulted, and her advice sought, even by much older colleagues'.[33] As a result Melitta relaxed. She was soon taking part in the general chat, and sometimes even showing off her

---

* Deutsche Versuchsanstalt für Luftfahrt.

gymnastic abilities, using her office desk or a chair as a prop. Soon she was rubbing along well as a sort of honorary man, 'welcomed everywhere, liked by all', one colleague wrote, and she even started to make a few close friendships.[34]

Georg Wollé, another engineer, owned a magnificent motorbike that he would ride round the concrete perimeter of the airfield in his lunch hours. Caught admiring the machine, Melitta was soon making laps in its sidecar, and then riding it herself. After a while she also started to spend time under Georg's expensive sunlamp. Georg was intrigued by Melitta's 'delicate, attractive personality' and, aware of how reserved she could be, he was proud of their friendship. However, he had yet to manage first-name terms or use the more familiar *du* with her, 'although there were many suitable opportunities'.[35] Your soul is like a 'steep coast', he wrote to Melitta, trying to tease her out.[36] Although in time they became 'very close', Georg always saw their friendship as more 'comradely' than 'that of a trusted friend to whom she would open her heart'. He put her reserve down to 'her modest way of never drawing attention to herself'.[37]

Melitta and the rather scrawny and serious Paul von Handel developed a very different relationship, built on their shared fascination with the new basic problems of physics: 'the theory of relativity; quantum mechanics; the problems of causality, determinism and coincidence; and the probability of free will and biology'. As tenants in the same block, they often met to read together, 'always with a notepad lying at the ready', so they could test new theories as they went.[38] To Paul, Melitta was 'an extraordinary human being'.[39] Neither a typical engineer nor the usual flying type, he found her hard to categorize, and all the more interesting for it. They would become close lifelong friends.

Another colleague, Hermann Blenk, who would later head the Institute for Aerodynamics during the war, appreciated the breadth of Melitta's interests, and realized how frustrated she was, working at an airbase while tied to the ground. Melitta 'did not only want to know something', Blenk understood, she 'wanted to be able to apply that knowledge . . . it was her greatest wish to learn to fly'.[40]

Georg told her the idea was nonsense. Not only did he feel that, as 'a very sensitive person', she would make a hash of things, but flying was an expensive business, and Georg knew Melitta was earning as little as he was.[41] He would not be the last person to underestimate her.

In July 1929 Melitta enrolled at the flying school at Staaken, the airfield west of Berlin where the famous *Graf Zeppelin* airship had landed the year before. It was a two-hour journey from her apartment, but just possible to combine with her work, given a very early start and absolute commitment. Hastily scribbled postcards kept Georg up to date. One day Melitta reported that she had taken her first solo flight. Within two months she had earned her provisional licence for light aircraft, which – 'with an iron will', she later said proudly – she converted to a full licence the following spring.[42]

Over the next few years Melitta invested all her spare time and salary in flying lessons for every class of powered land- and seaplane. She was well aware that 'any basic mistake, any moment of failure, every lapse of concentration' could cost her not only her career but her life, but she also knew that she had to 'always achieve more than average results in my training, and as a result take more risks than male flying students, just to get through'.[43] Correspondingly, she 'grabbed indiscriminately at every opportunity', she admitted, 'whether it was in the most precious, untested or old aircraft, or under the worst weather conditions'.[44] Sometimes she flew demonstration flights or took people sightseeing to earn both flight hours and cash for her lessons. Georg helped to arrange events, for which she thanked him in notes addressed, 'Dear Impresario'. Her strong will and tenacity earned her the admiration and sometimes envy of her male colleagues, but her escapades did not always end well.

One December weekend, Melitta managed to get hold of a 'fast, open-cockpit fighter', in which she hoped to have some fun while building up her hours for her next licence.[45] The morning was thick with freezing fog, so she donned her fur-lined flying suit, gauntlets and goggles and flew from Berlin to Cologne. On arrival she decided to creep up the Rhine, keeping low over the surface of the water. As she took off again, a thick snow squall blew in, hiding even the cathedral from sight. She was soon caught in a violent gale that ricocheted between the cliffs flanking the river, tossing her machine about 'in a mad vortex'.[46] Hail and snow stuck to her windshield and goggles, and wiping her fur glove across them produced only 'a thin and completely opaque layer of ice'.[47] She was forced to remove her goggles, but her eyes were immediately pelted with 'sharp needles of ice'.[48] Ripping off a glove, Melitta desperately tried to scratch a hole in the ice on the windshield with her stiff fingers. Half blind, she was lucky to fly beneath a power line that stretched between the riverbanks.

Eventually she turned a bend in the Rhine and the winds died down. Thick snow clouds now forced her south-west until, running low on fuel, with no map and still limited vision, she spotted a small airfield and managed to land. It was only when the muffled figures she called out to for help failed to respond that she realized she had inadvertently entered the French border area – a feat that during the tense interwar years could mean her arrest and the confiscation of her borrowed machine. 'With a commanding gesture', she later reported, 'I waved the people away from my aircraft, gave it full power, and took off.'[49] She only just cleared the boundary fence. Shortly afterwards her engine failed and she was forced to land in a ploughed field on the German side of the border. As she touched down 'the undercarriage sank deeper and deeper into the very soft ground', pitching forward until it had completely upended.[50] Then, in one fell movement, 'the machine turned over and lay on its back'.[51] Melitta was lucky not to be decapitated in the process. Pinned in the cockpit between the control column and banks of mud, however, she could not move to release her harness and, to complete her humiliation, the last of the 'fuel was streaming over me'.[52] When she finally heard voices, it was two farmers wondering whether they should put out their cigarettes. 'It is not a pleasant feeling,' Melitta wrote, 'to be stuck helpless in a mouse hole, soaked in fuel, knowing there is a lit cigarette near you.'[53]

Eventually the farmers returned with spades and dug her out.

On seeing a woman emerge from the wreck they asked where the pilot was and, despite her explanations, a rumour soon spread that he must have bailed out. 'This impossible behaviour by the pilot of an aircraft seemed to them more likely than a woman flying a military machine,' Melitta wrote contemptuously.[54] It took even more effort for Melitta to dig herself out of the trouble she had landed in. The forced landing itself was faultless, and one of many on that stormy day. The French stopover, however, was unacceptable. Melitta was banned from further flights. In near-despair, she 'fought doggedly and bitterly', but friends in the Foreign Office, and even the French ambassador, failed to sway the decision. Eventually it was Ernst Udet who stuck his neck out for her and got the ban lifted.

Melitta was the first to admit that she had become 'thoroughly addicted to the enchantment of flying, in theory and practice' during her years at DVL.[55] Long days spent analysing the manipulation of airflow, and experimenting with power, wing shape and control mechanisms, led to the development and testing of various propeller types and other equipment. Eventually she started conducting her own test flights. She was popular among the pilots, most of them young men, 'not only because she was very pretty', Paul noted, but because they admired her courage and passion. Hers was not the bravado of the enthusiast, he appreciated, but bravery 'based on knowledge of the risks . . . real courage'.[56]

Even Melitta's free time revolved around flying, with hours spent on the road between airfields, events and training schools. Occasionally she relaxed with sport and clay sculpture, creating busts of her colleagues, but she had few other interests and rarely saw her family. By the early 1930s, however, even Melitta could not completely shut her eyes to what was happening outside the world of flying.

Up until 1928 it had been possible to believe that Germany was still on the road to economic recovery. The following year, the impact of the Wall Street Crash was quickly felt in Germany; industry ground to a halt, millions lost their jobs, and chaos once again gripped the country. To many Germans facing further national humiliation, unemployment and shortages of food, fuel and materials, Hitler began to look like a dynamic new type of leader: one able to restore not only their national, but their personal pride. Melitta was clever and naturally questioning. At work, Blenk remembered her as 'always ready to enter into wide-ranging discussions' about politics and economics, and he felt that 'she judged the rising National Socialism very critically and soberly'.[57] Rather than engage more deeply, however, Melitta preferred the distraction of flying. Seen from the air, the dramas below reduced pleasingly in both size and apparent significance.

Melitta took part in her first organized flying event in 1930, when she was twenty-seven. The advantage of there being so few female pilots was that they all met at such events, forming a strong and supportive community. A few years younger than Melitta, the talented Elly Beinhorn and Marga von Etzdorf were both wealthy enough to have enjoyed private flying lessons in their early twenties, although Elly had done so against her parents' wishes. Elly could not work up much enthusiasm for Melitta's interest in 'science and research', so when her money ran out she paid her way like the wartime aces Ernst Udet and Robert Ritter von Greim by giving aerobatic displays at weekends.[58] Inspired by Earhart and Johnson, Elly's great passion was for long-distance flying, and in the early 1930s she embarked on a series of increasingly high-profile expeditions to what were then Portuguese Guinea and Persia,* Indonesia and Australia. In the German press, flights such as these were presented as bringing countries and peoples closer together, and sometimes as reflecting Germany's potential mastery over territory and technology.

Marga von Etzdorf, the orphaned daughter of a Prussian captain, was the second woman to earn her licence after the war. In 1930 she bought her own plane, an all-metal Junkers Junior, which she had spray-painted bright yellow to compete in the first German Women's Aerobatic Championships that May. She and Melitta became firm friends. At weekends they and Georg Wollé would

---

* Now Guinea-Bissau and Iran.

drive to swimming resorts in the beautiful lakes south-east of Berlin. Marga, 'whose hair was bobbed' like Melitta's, Georg could not resist noting, 'behaved in a rather masculine manner'.[59] It was as though instead of female pilots domesticating flight, these women were seen as a modern new type of human, defined by their flying ability rather than their gender. Like Elly, Marga was increasingly drawn to long-distance flying and flew to Turkey, Spain, Morocco and Sicily. One weekend, while the friends were staying at her family's country estate, Marga confided her plans to attempt the first solo flight from Germany to Japan. The following year Georg checked the instruments in her little Junkers Junior before she left Berlin with minimal fanfare. By the time she touched down in Tokyo, twelve days later, she was famous. But Marga's plane was written off on the way back and, although she survived, she had to return rather shamefacedly on a commercial flight.

Melitta was proud of her friends, and of her own achievements, but she had no desire for the added pressures of public recognition.[60] Occasionally a Berlin illustrated weekly would print photographs of her with other female pilots at a dinner or social event but, although she had no qualms about flying, or even riding a motorbike around Berlin, being noticed in the papers did not, as she put it, 'readily coincide with my own views about female dignity'.[61]

Melitta's closest friendships, however, were with men. In April 1931, Paul von Handel had asked her not only to be a bridesmaid at his Berlin wedding to Elisabeth, Countess von Üxküll-Gyllenband, but also to fly in some of the guests. Among the bride's cousins was a tall young man with high cheekbones, brown eyes, a shock of thick dark hair and a keen interest in poetry and classical history. His name was Alexander von Stauffenberg. According to Paul, Alexander was 'very gifted', both 'artistically and poetically, a thinker and dreamer, not a "man of action"'. Melitta, he added slightly mischievously, 'could both think and dream' and 'was full of energy and enterprise'.[62] Photos show Melitta and Alexander standing on either side of the wedding group, Melitta for once in a dress that reached to the floor, and with a circlet of flowers in her hair. 'Her expression had retained a captivating naïve childishness around the mouth . . .' her sister Jutta recalled, 'supported by a proud bearing that one likes to attribute to those of noble spirit.'[63] Perhaps seeing Melitta gravitate towards the aristocratic Alexander who, friends noted, 'gave the impression of immediate significance', Jutta was deliberately painting them as equals.[64] In fact, as a graduate engineer, Melitta was already exceptional within upper-class circles, and as a pilot she was a sensation. Due to his height, Alexander had a sympathetic manner of holding his head bent forward, as though listening with amused but respectful attention. Melitta was impressed. But she, too, was charming, blessed with 'incredibly winning manners', and never less than fully focused on whomever she was speaking to while always 'remarkably modest' about herself.[65] Away from the other guests, over endless cigarettes, Melitta and Alexander slowly came to discover their shared love of endeavour, culture and their country, and to appreciate each other's views on everything from ancient history to aerodynamics.

Melitta was soon close to all three of the Stauffenberg brothers: the intellectual Alexander; his twin, Berthold; and the younger Claus. Belonging to one of Germany's most distinguished families, the boys had enjoyed privileged childhoods divided between a vast, turreted mansion in Stuttgart and an impressive country schloss in Lautlingen.* Educated by private tutors and inspired by some of the leading cultural figures of their day, they were deeply committed to the elitist, aristocratic traditions of monarchy, nobility, church and military. As young men they joined the inner circle of the influential and charismatic poet Stefan George. George was their first führer. His idealization of male heroism, loyalty and self-sacrifice deeply impressed all three of the brothers, but it was

---

* Alfred Schenk Graf von Stauffenberg, the boys' father, served as the last Lord Chamberlain in the court of King William II of Württemberg. Their mother, Karoline, Countess of Üxküll-Gyllenband, was a maid of honour for Queen Charlotte of Württemberg.

his concept of a secret elite, whose noble spirituality should set the tone for the nation, that they found most inspirational.

The Stauffenberg boys were all ambitious, and all brilliant, but George's preference for Berthold and Claus shook up their relationship. Alexander felt Berthold was the greatest among them, and could not but reflect on the intense bond between his own twin and their younger brother. He would always believe his brothers to be both cleverer and more heroic than himself, but he was sufficiently self-assured to admire them wholeheartedly while taking his own path. Soon he had found another mentor in the historian Wilhelm Weber, whose invitations to lecture tours around the ancient sites of Italy kindled new interests. Inspired by Weber, and Homer, Alexander pursued an academic career as a lecturer in ancient history at the University of Berlin. Berthold became a professor of law, eventually working at the Permanent Court of International Justice in The Hague that had been established through the League of Nations. Claus joined the famed Bamberg Cavalry Regiment of the German army, and appeared at Paul's wedding in full uniform.

Over the next few years Melitta would spend many of her weekends with Alexander, Berthold and Claus. She had quickly nicknamed Alexander her *Schnepfchen*, or little snipe – after the shy wading birds that fly in zigzags when startled and produce a bleating, drumming sound when courting. It was a highly affectionate, if slightly diminutive, term of endearment. Melitta's classical name, meaning bee, or honey-sweet, may have appealed to Alexander just as it was. Sometimes the sweethearts stayed at the Stauffenberg and Üxküll country houses, where Melitta soon felt at home, whether hiking up to a hunting lodge to go shooting and rabbit hounding, or dining in evening dress and discussing the issues of the day through a haze of cigar smoke.[66]

For many in 1932, Germany was a country in ruins. With six million unemployed, there was enormous public anger and regular clashes on the streets between supporters of Hitler's now flourishing National Socialist Party and organized communist activists. By the end of the year Paul von Hindenburg, the elected president of

Germany, would be negotiating the formation of another new government, this time with Hitler. The older Stauffenberg and Schiller generations were more interested in the 'cultural tides' than the sordid details of the fight for political power on the streets. 'The swelling of the ranks of support for the "Brown" and "Red" masses was registered and discussed as a distasteful product of the times,' Melitta's sister Jutta later wrote.[67] Like many right-wing intellectuals, they felt that the communists presented the greatest threat. The Nazis' methods might be unpleasant, but their rhetoric appealed to deep-seated feelings of nationalism – and were not all new regimes beset by teething troubles? Meanwhile, for Melitta, Alexander and their wealthy, well-connected friends, focused on their careers, their weekends and each other, these were, Paul said, 'wonderful, happy times'.[68]

Melitta was now in possession of almost every licence for motorized planes, and qualified in aerobatics, instrument flying and radio. Having helped the DVL staff flying club to win first prize in the German reliability flight contests that year, she returned to gliding, in many ways the purest form of flight. Her instructor was Peter Riedel, the head of the gliding research institute at Darmstadt, who would shoot to fame in 1933 when he won both the national gliding championships and the Hindenburg trophy.

Peter was about Melitta's own age and could not help but assess his new female student romantically, although she did not return his interest. She was an 'attractive woman', he wrote, 'but extremely reserved'.[69] They connected better discussing flight, and later, cautiously, the rise of Hitler. 'It was obvious the so-called democratic government had failed,' Peter later recalled. 'The country was going to hell, people starving . . . huge unemployment, lists every day in the papers of people who had killed themselves in despair.'[70] The communist talk was of revolution. The Nazis, he felt, stood for strong leadership, patriotism and the performance of one's duty. 'That sounded good.'[71] Nevertheless, Peter was concerned about the increasingly militaristic nature of the regime and, yearning for wider horizons, he was considering emigrating to Africa.

'In a way, she agreed with me,' he later claimed.[72] Melitta may have concurred about the threat of communism but, deeply patriotic, she would never have forsaken Germany or her work, which she saw as a form of national service as well as a source of personal pride. Freedom, for her, meant flying for her country, not flight from it. In any case, she was in love with Alexander.

'In the end', Peter decided, Melitta 'was too serious for me'.[73] Within a couple of years he would be sailing not to Africa but to South America, in the company of another female pilot. Hanna Reitsch's sympathies were rather different to Melitta's, and she and Peter would enjoy a more dramatic friendship. By then Melitta would have an unofficial agreement with Alexander von Stauffenberg, and Hitler, as the appointed chancellor of Germany, would have proclaimed the arrival of the Third Reich.

2

SEARCHING FOR THE FABULOUS
1912–1933

In 1920, while the teenage Melitta was sizing up gliders on the slopes near her boarding school, in a different suburb of the same town a spirited seven-year-old Hanna Reitsch was also turning her face to the sky. Pretty, petite, blonde and blue-eyed, Hanna lived in Hirschberg with her parents, her elder brother Kurt, her younger sister Heidi and a succession of maids, but she was already convinced she was destined for broader horizons. Family legend has it that Hanna first experimented with gravity when she was four years old, aiming to leap, with arms outstretched, from a first-floor balcony. Although frustrated on this occasion she never lost her fascination with flight, nor her desire to take to the skies. 'The longing grew . . .' she wrote, 'with every bird I saw go flying across the azure summer sky, with every cloud that sailed past on the wind, till it turned into a deep, insistent homesickness, a yearning that went with me everywhere and could never be stilled.'[1] Despite fracturing her skull after one particularly ambitious jump from the branch of a fir tree and literally being grounded by her parents, Hanna never doubted that, one day, she would fly. 'What child is there that lives, as I did, midway between Reality and Fairyland,' she would later ask at the beginning of her memoirs, 'who does not long sometimes to leave altogether the familiar world and set off in search of new and fabulous realms?'[2] Unlike Melitta, Hanna longed for more than freedom. In many ways she would achieve her dreams but she would, perhaps, never manage to live fully in reality, and somewhere during her all-consuming search for the fabulous she would lose the ability to distinguish between the two.

Born on 29 March 1912, Hanna was two years old at the start

of the First World War, seven at its close. Just old enough, perhaps, to absorb something of her nation's mood of hope, before the hardship and humiliation of the defeat. Most of her childhood memories, however, were not of the drama and despair of war, but of growing up during the depression that followed. It was the issues and impact of reparations, inflation and unemployment, civil unrest and anxiety, that coloured the Germany of Hanna's youth. Hers was a patriotic middle-class family, moderately well off, and all for God and Germany. Her parents felt that the Polish annexation of the eastern part of Upper Silesia, and the Allies' harsh war reparations under the Treaty of Versailles, were deep injustices. The violent rise of communism at home and abroad confirmed their patriotic, nationalistic world view. Besides 'respect for human dignity and a sense of honour', Hanna listed a love of 'the Fatherland' as the key moral value and principle instilled in her as a child.[3] She was brought up to believe that German national honour, and with it her family's pride, had been compromised, and that the integrity of her country was still somehow under threat. What seemed to be missing, under the Weimar Republic, was leadership strong enough to discipline, unite and rally the country.

Hanna's father, the strict and rather taciturn Dr Willy Reitsch, was a Protestant, a Prussian and a Freemason, who exercised 'uncontested authority' over his family.[4] He was also an eye specialist and the head of a private clinic. Hanna adored, but rarely impressed, him. An accomplished amateur cellist, at his most sociable Willy Reitsch would arrange musical soirées at their home. His standards were high, however, and although they were dutifully learning violin and piano, and singing traditional three-part Austrian yodelling songs, his children were rarely invited to perform. Medicine provided another opportunity for the children to bond with their father, and sometimes Willy would bring home pig or sheep eyes from the butcher, on which to demonstrate operations. On occasion Kurt and Hanna were even allowed to accompany him on his rounds, during which they gained a great respect for his dedication to his patients, but little enthusiasm for his daily routine. Not that this mattered to Hanna. 'In our family,' she later wrote, 'it was accepted as a principle, so obvious as to be unspoken, that a girl could only have one task in life, namely to marry and become a good mother to her children.'[5]

Hanna's own mother, Emy, was the eldest daughter of a widowed Austrian aristocrat. She quietly tried to imbue a sense of Catholic piety in her children while officially bringing them up in the faith of their father. Like her husband, Emy was a passionate patriot. Generally welcoming and tolerant, she nevertheless launched into occasional tirades blaming the government, various foreign nations or 'the Jews' for anything she felt was wrong with Germany. Deeply loving, but not deeply questioning, Emy was the rather unreliable moral compass upon whom Hanna relied. 'My mother and I lived in each other,' Hanna later wrote, 'each sensing the other's thoughts without need to confess or conceal.'[6] Emy saw her daughter's deep longing for something more than faith, motherhood and a gentle life contained in a pleasant country town, and it worried her. She cautioned Hanna not to give in to vanity or ambition.

Willy Reitsch was less empathetic than his wife. He found his daughter's school results disappointing and her high spirits trying. Her obsession with flight was to him not only unacceptable, but completely inexplicable. Hanna liked to spend hours watching larks hovering over the fields, buzzards circling in the summer air, and occasionally a glider crossing the skies. Sometimes, as Melitta once had, she insisted on doing her homework up a tree, and she regularly still spread her arms to leap from various windowsills. But Hanna's main problem seemed to be, as one of her school friends put it, that she was 'difficult to overlook'.[7] Bursting with energy and rather full of herself, Hanna was confident, loud and cheeky. With her wonky twin braids tied with broad ribbons and her wide, impish smile dimpling her cheeks, she laughed a lot and often inappropriately, was easily bored and 'always talked in superlatives', much like many young girls.[8] Her schooling was limited. History stopped at 1848, and discipline was deemed more important than debate. Although not ashamed to cheat in class, Hanna was highly sensitive to criticism and quick to perceive injustices. A natural extrovert, when she felt her personal honour had been besmirched she would plunge into overt misery, from which she often later appeared to emerge quite refreshed and reinvigorated.

At a time when many families faced crippling hardship, Willy Reitsch was fortunate that his livelihood was secure, and Hanna's early childhood was generally a happy one. Outside school, life was enlivened by family hikes, picnics in the mountains and tomboy escapades with her brother Kurt, as often as not with both of them dressed in lederhosen. But as Hanna grew up she felt increasingly restricted. Although never tall, with her blonde plaits now pinned up, her huge clear-blue eyes and brilliant smile, she was the very image of pretty, healthy 'Aryan' maidenhood. If Hanna yearned for more it was not just in reaction to forever having to make do and mend; she was quite happy in a plain corduroy dress and had never felt the despair of utter poverty. It was not material luxury she craved, but the luxuries of status, endeavour and aspiration. In winter she took pleasure in skiing and skating, in summer walking and cycling, but other sports were discouraged as unfeminine. Concerts and dances provided some entertainment, but trips to the cinema were vetted for the film's suitability and she was not allowed out at all without a chaperone. Not that Hanna was particularly interested in boys; it was the activities open to them that appealed to her. She now took a tram or cycled over to the gliding clubs outside the town almost every day, to lie in the grass at various vantage points and watch other people's dreams take flight.

As a teenager Hanna came up with a strategic plan: she would, she announced to her parents, become a doctor, 'not an ordinary one, but a missionary doctor . . . and above all, a flying missionary doctor'.[9] Her father was sceptical; her grades so far had failed to support such ambition, and he doubted whether she would have the sticking power. Meeting with unexpected persistence, however, Willy offered Hanna a deal: if she could refrain from mentioning flying at all for the two or three years until she passed her school-leaving examination, the dreaded *Abitur*, her reward would be a gliding course. Two years later Hanna's father marked her school graduation by presenting her with an antique gold watch. She had kept her side of the bargain so well that he had forgotten all about their pact. Hanna had not. She watched her father turn pale as she reminded him of his promise and, a man of his word, he agreed to honour it.

Hanna's parents hoped that medicine and flying would prove to be only a brief interlude before marriage and children. To prepare her for her domestic future, be it at home or abroad, Emy insisted that Hanna spend a year at the Colonial School for Women in Rendsburg before taking any gliding course. Germany's formal ties with African territories had been ended by the Treaty of Versailles, but a revanchist movement hoped to encourage ongoing connections. No doubt the colonial aspect of the school appealed to Hanna's parents, along with the presence of a naval training college not far away, ensuring an abundance of young men in the neighbourhood. Hanna was taught to cook and clean, keep animals, fix shoes, locks and windows, and to speak English, Spanish and one West African language. Her 'only notable success', she later wrote drily, was a private experiment with the sanitary training of pigs.

Hanna was nineteen, 'full of confidence and hope, shivering with excitement', when she finally cycled over for her course at the increasingly famous Grünau Gliding School. Like Melitta before her, she was the only girl among the boys, and she was set to soar above the same green slopes, but it was now a clear and cloudless day in 1931, eleven years after Melitta's first flight. 'With thumping heart', Hanna ignored the jeers of the young men around her and climbed into the open cockpit of her glider. First she had to learn to balance as it rested on the grass, quivering at the slightest movement, she felt, 'like a frightened bird'.[10] Then a bungee cord was attached to the nose of her machine, which was stretched out by one team of students while others held the tail. She was meant simply to let the glider slide forward along the ground, but on release she could not resist pulling on the stick a little. The next moment she 'could see nothing but sky, and then, sky again'.[11] Still only just over five feet tall and weighing less than seven stone, Hanna was too light for the team's powerful start, and with her nudge on the stick the glider had launched steeply upwards. 'For the first time in my life I felt invisible forces lifting and carrying me, higher and higher, until I was over the ridge and it receded away beneath me,' she later reported, her eyes shining. 'It felt like a fairy tale; wondrous.'[12] But there was no fairy-tale ending. The glider quickly fell back down to earth, ripping the safety straps and throwing Hanna from her seat. Miraculously, neither she nor the machine was seriously harmed; she could easily have been killed.

Hanna's recklessness was a disciplinary offence but she earned the nickname 'Stratosphere' from her fellow students, showing that they, at least, were grudgingly impressed. From one among them, the compliment was particularly meaningful. Wernher von Braun, the future pioneering rocket scientist, was less than a week older than Hanna. Inspired by the genius of Jules Verne and Georges Méliès, and encouraged by his parents' gift of a telescope to mark his confirmation, Braun's ambition was always to invade space. 'Don't tell me man doesn't belong out there,' he once commented. 'Man belongs wherever he wants to go.'[13] As a boy growing up in Berlin he had pressurized a prototype rocket with a bicycle pump, and was later cautioned by police after launching the world's first rocket-powered go-kart in the middle of the fashionable Tiergartenstrasse. Supremely confident, Braun was both brilliant and charming. He was 'handsome enough to be a film star, and he knows it', one reporter later noted, while female friends compared him to 'the famous photograph of Lord Alfred Douglas', better known as Bosie, the aristocratic young lover of Oscar Wilde.[14] Sadly, Hanna's impression of her fellow gliding student was not recorded, but he admired her courage and vivaciousness. 'Hanna has an unusually intriguing personality . . .' he later wrote warmly, 'she did all kinds of crazy things.'[15] Like Hanna, Braun would later claim to have had little interest in politics; what brought them together was their shared obsession with flight. 'Our minds were always far out in space,' one friend wrote.[16]

On the evening of Hanna's first flight and crash, Wolf Hirth, the head of the gliding school, was forced to consider expelling this apparently dangerous student for her own safety. Instead she was grounded for three days, for disobedience. She spent those days watching attentively as her peers did their exercises. In the evenings she practised manoeuvres in bed, with a walking stick to serve as her control column. On the fourth day the students were to take their 'A' test. When the most experienced among them went first, and failed to leave the slopes, Hanna was put forward next for her anticipated humiliation. As she was launched down the slope she noted her speed and balance, and directed the glider to lift. It was a perfect flight, nine seconds over the requirement, followed by a perfect landing. 'I did not stir,' Hanna wrote, as her classmates came whooping down the slope to meet her, 'but simply sat there in my beloved glider, caught in a blissful trance.'[17] When the course assessor put her achievement down to luck, Hanna happily flew again, passing with flying colours.

Wolf Hirth visited the school the next morning to assess this girl who had so spectacularly snatched victory from defeat. Hirth was one of the great pioneers of German flight. Having earned his pilot's licence in 1920, he and other enthusiasts founded the first Academic Flying Club – the society that would later refuse to accept Melitta among their ranks. Despite losing a leg in a motorcycle accident in 1924, Hirth went on to study engineering, toured the world to promote and demonstrate gliding, and designed and manufactured his own machines. A heavy smoker, his trademark cigarette holder was carved from the fibula of his lost leg. To Hanna, Hirth was 'a demigod'.[18] From his perspective, Hanna was pretty impressive too – a natural pilot, woman or not. After observing her faultless gliding, he arranged for her to fly every day under his personal supervision. Over the next few months she learned to turn and catch upwinds, sailing through her 'B' and 'C' tests.

In early 1932 Hanna was invited to try out the new glider design usually reserved for instructors. For once allowed to fly to her heart's content, she sang 'the loveliest songs I could remember' while in the air: the joyful response to flying that she would keep up all her life. Hardly noticing the rain and snow, Hanna returned to earth only five hours later when the wind dropped. As she touched down she was surprised to be met by an excited crowd; she had achieved a new world record for women's gliding endurance. That evening Hanna's name was broadcast on the radio, and flowers and congratulations arrived from around the country. 'I found it wonderful – I was young and overjoyed,' she wrote with winning honesty.[19]

Adolf Hitler was also back in the cockpit in 1932. His biplane flight to Berlin for the Kapp Putsch in 1920 had opened his eyes to the potential of flight, and over the next twelve years the Nazi Party had made good use of the symbolism of aviation, as well as the more practical opportunities it presented. Posters with illustrations of Zeppelins branded *NSDAP* helped to spread the word about growing Party membership and, during the 1932 election campaign, planes circling the main regional cities had sent leaflets drifting down with the message, *Unity, solidarity, peace, order and work, and below this, Give Adolf Hitler your vote and he will give you work and bread and freedom.*[20] Now Hitler was touring the country on his airborne hustings campaign known as 'The German Flight'; he was the first political leader to reach out to his electorate in this way.

The election tour was strenuous. Always the first up at this point in his life, Hitler discussed the precise programme for each day over morning porridge and a glass of milk. Coffee had been strictly prohibited, 'because of its revolting effect in the air'.[21] Once the itinerary was set, few changes were permitted. Hitler's personal pilot, Hans Baur, a veteran of the past war and early member of the Party, sometimes flew between five different mass rallies in one day. Confident in his destiny, Hitler would watch with excitement as Baur flew blind above heavy clouds – sometimes running low on petrol – and once through a hailstorm that had grounded all Luft Hansa flights.* 'We became "flying humans",' the journalist Otto Dietrich wrote, thoroughly enjoying his implicit membership of the super-race team. At every stop the plane would be met by crowds of enthusiastic followers shouting

---

* Deutsche Luft Hansa rebranded as Lufthansa the following year, 1933.

'Heil!' before Hitler was driven into the city in a motorcade. Then, after a speech and a short ceremony, they would set off again, 'the incredible exultation of the crowd . . . vibrating in us still'.[22]

Above all, Hitler liked to fly by night. A master of stage management, he would address the largest crowds at dusk so that they would be lit by a sea of torches, and would then rush back to the airfield where Baur would have the engines running and ready for take-off. As their plane curved around over the dwindling assembly below, Hitler would order the cabin to be lit up. 'At this moment, the crowd recognizes the glowing fireship up in the air which carries the Führer,' Dietrich powered on in elation. 'A deafening cheer starts up from hundreds of thousands of throats, so loud that it even drowns out the roaring of our motors, while the people wave their torches in salute.'[23] Hitler would look down over the spectacle in silence, 'while we experience something new, almost cosmic up here. It is beyond words.'[24]

It was in this electric political atmosphere, and as a qualified glider pilot, that Hanna dutifully started her first term at medical school in Berlin. Frustrated, and quickly bored in lectures, she immediately knew that she 'had only one desire – to fly again!'[25] With the money allowed by her parents for college expenses, she enrolled on a training course to fly engine-powered aircraft at Berlin-Staaken airfield.

Like Melitta, who had studied at Staaken two years earlier, Hanna had to rise early, setting off at five in the morning to get to the airfield in time. Once again, she was the only woman on the course, although there were now several other women flying from Staaken, including Elly Beinhorn who had just returned from her circumnavigation of the world, and with whom Hanna now also struck up a friendship. For Hanna flying itself was simple enough, and she quickly overcame the concerns of the men around her through her skill and dedication. More challenging was trying to understand the mechanics of the machines. At one point she dismantled an old engine under the supervision of the ground mechanics in the airfield workshops, and earned some respect by working through the night to reassemble it.

Turning to other engines, Hanna befriended the workmen responsible for the airfield vehicles. Soon she was not only learning to drive, she was learning about the men's war service, the bitterness that met them when they returned after defeat, and their periods of unemployment. Impressed by their stoicism, she promised to get them eye ointment from her father and, from her mother, dresses for their wives. 'But as soon as the men began to talk politics,' Hanna sighed, their fragile comradeship fell apart.[26] Few of the men belonged to the same party, and each wanted to win her round to his own viewpoint, arguing their case with such passion that they almost came to blows. Hanna was ill-equipped to follow the debates, 'for though naturally I had been brought up to be a patriot,' she wrote with youthful naivety, 'there had never been any question of political divisions in my home'.[27] Having automatically accepted her parents' conservative, nationalistic, racially conscious and casually anti-Semitic standpoint as the natural and neutral one, she did not consider that she already had a political position, or that politics might have any bearing on her own life. What horrified her now was not any particular belief or argument, but the dissent that politics, as a whole, brought to the group; 'how people who otherwise get on well together can become bitter and fanatical opponents as soon as politics are mentioned'. 'Depressed and thoughtful', she walked away not just from the men but, ironically, from the opportunity for learning from and engaging with the arguments.

If Hanna was apolitical, as she later claimed, it was through choice. Despite her fascination with everything to do with aviation, her memoirs mention nothing of Hitler's 'German Flight' campaign or the elections that took place that July, making the National Socialists the largest party in the Reichstag. And while she often visited her parents, she never commented on the growing anti-Semitism in their part of the country. Breslau, with its large Jewish community, was a stronghold of Nazi support less than two hours from Hirschberg. Here Jewish shops were already being boycotted, their owners legally restricted and socially ostracized. Later, Hanna would say only that she had been completely absorbed in learning to fly that summer.

Hanna's training plane was an open Mercedes-Klemm with dual controls, one of the few low-powered civil aircraft allowed under the terms of Versailles. Photos show her at the controls in a dark leather flying cap, her whole face lit up by a brilliant smile. After a few weeks she had progressed to an altitude of 6,500 feet, still in the Klemm but now in a fur-lined suit, with her face greased for protection against the sun and cold. Altitude removes a pilot from the world. Even during the group briefing before she took off, Hanna developed 'the strange feeling that I was no longer one of them'.[28] As she flew over the airfield workmen, she briefly wondered whether they were still arguing about politics, but checked herself: 'I had little time to think of that, for my ear was concentrated on the engine . . . soon the earth below dwindles into insignificance.'[29] For Hanna, flying at high altitude was a sublime experience, where 'the airman feels close to God' and 'all that hitherto seemed important falls away'.[30]

If Hanna had ever attached importance to her medical studies, it had only been as a means to escape. Now that flight was at hand, she rarely attended lectures and never opened the textbooks she had strapped to her bicycle when she first rode over to Staaken. In the summer recess of 1932, she returned home to resume her gliding training under Wolf Hirth. As an assistant in his workshop, she learnt to build and repair gliders. In the evenings she joined him and his wife at home, studying flight theory, including Hirth's pioneering work on thermals: the sun-warmed air above heat-absorbing terrain such as heath and roads, which rises naturally, creating currents in which a glider can circle upwards. Hirth had become Hanna's 'flying father': the first in a series of older male mentors to whom she turned for recognition and advancement. In September, Hanna's own father arranged for her to continue her medical studies at Kiel, a city that offered fewer distractions and had the added advantage of bringing Hanna close to her brother Kurt, now a midshipman in the Kriegsmarine stationed at the city. But Hanna had either lost interest in, or later chose not to comment on, anything but flight, and her memoirs pick up again only on her return to Hirschberg in May 1933.

By the start of 1933, with six million Germans out of work, people were losing faith in the entire political system. Three chancellors had come and gone within a year, and the simultaneous rise of Nazism and communism led to regular violent clashes on the streets, often deliberately provoked by the Brownshirts of the SA (*Sturmabteilung*). Along with many others, Hanna's parents were delighted by Hitler's nationalist platform, which promised the creation of jobs and the restoration of a sense of security and national pride. In January, after considerable backstage manoeuvring, Hitler was appointed Reich chancellor and immediately set about consolidating his authority. He was backed financially by key industrialists, and diplomatically by President von Hindenburg and the statesman and former chancellor Franz von Papen, who mistakenly believed they could manipulate this popular leader. The next month the Reichstag fire provided the Nazis with the opportunity to trade on the Bolshevik threat while imprisoning many communists, as well as the leaders of other parties and the independent press. On 5 May the Nazis won 44 per cent of the votes, providing enough seats to pass the Enabling Act that gave Hitler absolute power to set laws, abolish trade unions, make opposition political parties illegal, and effectively start a rule of terror enforced by the Gestapo.

Back home from Kiel that month, Hanna's thoughts were far from the appointment or policies of her country's latest chancellor. Dressed in sandals and a light cotton frock, she was strolling through the sun-drenched streets of Hirschberg one day, yearning only to be gliding across the clear blue sky, when she ran into Wolf Hirth. Hirth was also full of the joys of spring – he had invested in a Grunau Baby, the very latest type of sleek, single-seat training glider that he had helped to design. The Grunau Baby came with a rudimentary 'blind-flying' control panel: a pioneering set of six instruments to indicate airspeed, horizon, direction, climb or descent, turn or slip. Theoretically such tools could enable a pilot to fly safely through clouds or fog when visibility was limited. He wondered whether Hanna might like to take his impressive new glider up.

Within an hour Hanna was sitting in the enclosed cabin of the Grunau Baby without goggles or helmet, the parachute harness buckled straight over her frock. Hirth, in his engine-powered plane, towed her up to 1,200 feet before signalling to her to cast off. With not a breath of wind in the sky, Hanna began the gentle drift back down to earth. At 250 feet she was looking for a place to land when she felt the glider quiver. A moment later she was circling back up, swapping warm air currents until she coiled faster and faster to several thousand feet. Now she saw a huge black cloud overhead, formed by the rapid condensation of the thermals she was riding. 'The sight of this dark monster,' she wrote, 'filled me with glee.'[31]

Before Hanna had learned to fly, she had gazed up at glorious fluffy white clouds and longed to play among them. Now she knew that she could not reach such clouds without passing through them; they were spectral. Thunderclouds offered more tangible potential for enjoyment. Never one to err on the side of caution, Hanna saw this as the perfect opportunity for her first 'blind flight' through heavy cloud. Moments later her glider was completely wrapped in the grey mass and she had zero visibility. With all the confidence of the amateur, she watched her instruments, climbed to 5,500 feet – safely above the level of the nearest mountain peak – and relaxed. Later she spoke of feeling disconnected from the ground, 'humble and grateful in her heart', as this was 'when she knew there existed something, someone, greater, in whom she could trust, who guided and watched over her'.[32] It was then that the storm broke.

The first Hanna knew of the danger she was in was the 'frenzied staccato, an ear-splitting hellish tattoo' of rain and hail, drumming on the wings of the glider. With a cracking noise, the cabin windows began to ice over, and she focused again on her control panel. She was still climbing, and rapidly. At nearly 10,000 feet above the earth the instruments began to stick. Soon they were frozen solid. Hanna now had no direct visibility and no functioning instruments to guide her. She tried to hold the control column in the normal position, but without bearings this was impossible to judge. Then there was 'a new sound, a kind of high-pitched whistle', and she was pitched forward in her harness, the blood rushing to her head.[33] Caught in a downdraught in the turbulent centre of the storm, the glider was now diving vertically. Heaving on the stick, Hanna found herself momentarily hanging from her harness straps; she was soon performing a series of involuntary loops 'while the glider arrows down, shrieking'.[34]

Unable to see anything through the frosted mica of the cabin window, Hanna punched it out, but she was still enclosed by cloud, and now shivering all over, her hands turning blue as she sat in her summer frock, drenched in rain, hail and snow. Hoping that the Grunau Baby might retain some inherent stability, she abandoned the controls, 'no longer the pilot . . . but a passenger', and for the first time acknowledged the growing fear inside her.[35] Then the lightly built glider was carried up again, rising up through the towering pillar of cloud like a piece of paper sucked up a chimney. Fearing that she might lose consciousness, Hanna repeatedly screamed out her own name to keep her focus. Suddenly she was spewed down and out into the light, flying upside down but safely above the white peaks of the Riesengebirge mountains. Grateful still to be alive, she righted her machine and glided down until eventually she could make out the tiny dots of skiers returning home at the end of the day, and a safe place to land on the slopes beside a hotel restaurant.

Bedraggled and soaking wet, Hanna hauled herself out of the glider, its fuselage now perforated with holes punched by hailstones, and into the hotel to put a call through to Hirth. It was he who first realized that she had inadvertently entered the neutral zone, close to the Czechoslovakian border. Like Melitta landing without a permit in France, Hanna had committed a major offence that might result in the loss of her licence. Given the time and place, she might even have caused an international incident. Hirth told her to collect as many people as possible to help, and wait until he flew over – risking his own licence – to drop her a starting rope. Half an hour later two teams of hotel guests launched Hanna back into the darkening sky. Hirth, flying above, guided her down to the valley where a landing site had been floodlit for them with car headlamps.

Back on the ground again, for a while Hanna sat silently in her glider, letting her romantic mind reframe her adventure in the terms of the fabulous that she so loved. 'Earth and sky seem wrapped in sleep,' she wrote. 'My glider-bird slumbers too, gleaming softly against the stars. Beautiful bird, that outflew the four winds, braved the tempest, shot heavenward, searching out the sky.'[36] She would soon find even more to celebrate in her storm-cloud flight, when she learnt that she had unintentionally soared higher than any glider previously. Although not officially verified, her new world record was widely reported on German radio and in the national papers and, despite her discussions with her mother about humility, Hanna was soon giving a series of effusive talks and interviews. 'Gliding is a victory of the soul,' she gushed.[37] Hanna claimed not to fly from ambition, but simply for 'the immense pleasure it gave me', but hers was now a soul that yearned not only for the pleasure of flight, but for the adrenaline, recognition and honours that seemed to go with it.[38]

3

PUBLIC RELATIONS
1933–1936

'Women have always been among my staunchest supporters,' Hitler told the *New York Times* in July 1933. 'They feel my victory is their victory.'[1] While working to return women to their rightful and respected role, as he saw it, of hausfrau, Hitler had been keen to exploit any support for his National Socialist Party. At times this required rising above a tide of female fan mail and enduring more than one public display of adoration. 'He was often embarrassed' by such women, his friend and official photographer Heinrich Hoffmann later remembered, but he 'had no option but to accept their veneration'.[2] Hitler, Hoffmann felt, had 'a lovely appreciation of women as a political influence', and before the election he 'was convinced that feminine enthusiasm, tenacity and fanaticism would be the deciding factor'.[3] In fact, most women who supported the Nazis did so not for love of the leader or a desire to return to the home, but for the same reasons as men: the prospect of a strong government that could deal with the 'menace of communism', wipe out the shame of Versailles, and provide employment and a just redistribution of the nation's wealth. Nevertheless, appealing to women and harnessing their propaganda value were significant parts of Hitler's campaign before and after he assumed power. Hanna and Melitta would both soon duly play their part, and come to appreciate the vital importance of public relations under the new regime.

As Hanna spread her wings, the mood of the country seemed to lift with her. She had turned twenty-one in March 1933 and, for her, the last few years had been a wonderful adventure: leaving home, learning to fly, and setting new world records almost effort-lessly. In Hirschberg, as across Germany, there were frequent

patriotic marches and torch-lit parades with speeches, singing, and
copious flags and bunting. Hitler's speeches tended to deal with
grievances that were familiar to many working people, and had a
sort of evangelical simplicity that made them easy to follow. He
promised a higher standard of living with a car for everyone, beautiful homes, affordable holidays, marriage loans, respect for mothers
and a defence against Bolshevism. People seemed electrified, and
everywhere there was talk of 'the unity of the German people' and
the 'national uprising'.[4] With little interest in party politics or
current affairs, to Hanna it seemed simply patriotic to support
Hitler and his dynamic new regime. At last, the future looked
promising, and she was keen to seize every opportunity. When the
Führer called on the German people to 'awake to a realization of
your own importance' in his May Day speech of 1933, Hanna
might have been forgiven for imagining that he was talking directly
to her.[5]

Melitta followed the consolidation of Nazi power in Germany
from a more sober and critical perspective. She welcomed the
prospect of stable government, the pledges for greater safety on
the streets, job creation and the proposed investment in techno-
logical research, as well as the restoration of German pride and the
countering of communism on the international stage. However,
her doubts about the legitimacy and principles of the regime were
growing. Where Hanna saw parades and bunting, Melitta saw
Germany's constitution under attack. Hate-filled posters were
pasted onto walls, newspapers were thick with propaganda, and
trucks full of SA and SS troops were roaring through the major
cities, recruiting, collecting names, and occasionally breaking into
houses and apartments to arrest and remove not only communists,
who Melitta saw as a serious threat, but also social democrats,
union leaders and liberal intellectuals. The Nazi plan was to pre-
clude any attempt at organized opposition by removing potential
leaders and quietly intimidating the mass of the population. Like
many others, Melitta hoped such tactics would soon be replaced
by more benign policies. Then, in late May, personal tragedy overwhelmed her.

Melitta's closest female pilot friend, Marga von Etzdorf, had been attempting a record flight to Australia when her Klemm aeroplane was damaged in gales, forcing her to land at an airfield in Aleppo, in what was then the French mandate of Syria. Having asked for a quiet room in which to rest, Marga took out a gun and shot herself. She died instantly. It would later emerge that the French authorities had found leaflets for a German weapons manufacturer along with a model machine gun stowed on her plane. It seemed that Marga had been trying to supplement her sponsorship earnings by ferrying arms, in direct breach of the terms of the Treaty of Versailles. On hearing of their friend's death, the DVL engineer Georg Wollé immediately sought out Melitta. He found her in her office, 'in floods of tears'.[6] Marga's death 'hit her very hard', Melitta's sister Jutta recalled, adding that 'later, she had to mourn her colleagues all too often'.[7]

Hanna had also had to cope with personal tragedy. In the spring of 1933 she was working as an instructor at Wolf Hirth's gliding school when one of her students was killed in a crash landing. It was Hanna's first experience of losing a colleague, as it had been for Melitta. Although deeply shocked, she insisted on informing the man's family herself. His mother met her at the door, anticipating bad news. She told Hanna that the night before her son had dreamt that he would die. Whether it was a premonition, or just that a sleepless night had affected his concentration, Hanna felt a sense of relief; a little helpful distancing from the tragedy. A few days later she was due to compete in the annual Rhön-Rossitten gliding contests, and she wanted to be focused and show the world what she could do.

Organized by the meteorologist Walter Georgii, the first Rhön gliding competitions had been held on the Wasserkuppe mountain in 1920. Every summer since, thousands of sightseers had journeyed by train and foot up to the annual rallies held on the bare summit of the Wasserkuppe, the Rhön valley's highest point. According to contemporary German flight magazines, by the late 1920s the highest slopes of the mountain hosted a glider camp with its own water and electricity supply, hotels, bars and restaurants, a post office with special-edition stamps, and indeed everything, 'like in the big cities. Even dancing. Even bobbed hair!'[8] Perhaps their reporters had spotted Melitta up there among the crowds. Once a regular spectator, she had applied for a gliding course at Wasserkuppe in 1924 and, although not able to take up her place because of work commitments, she still visited when she could.

By the 1930s, over 20,000 people regularly travelled to the Rhön valley at weekends. On the day of the 1932 Reichstag elections, a temporary voting station had even been set up on the mountain, and Walter Georgii called on the people of Germany to 'do as the gliders have'. His message was clear – it was time to recognize the forces of nature and embrace a brave new future characterized by technical prowess, a love of freedom and a deep sense of national pride. With the Nazis securing over 50 per cent of the mountaintop vote, the Wasserkuppe fraternity's support for Hitler was considerably above the national average.* Here, with Wolf Hirth at her side, Hanna enjoyed feeling not only a part of the gliding community, but part of a brave, idealistic, almost moral endeavour, far removed from the partisan politics pursued in the valleys.

The Wasserkuppe rises 1,300 feet above the plains, and the air currents hitting it are swept forcefully upwards. Here there was 'wind in plenty', Hanna noted, and yet on her first competitive flight she failed to find an updraught strong enough to carry her now comparatively heavy and outclassed glider.[9] Forced to flop straight back down to earth, she had to wait, 'sitting in the ditch' as she put it, while the other contestants, including Hirth, continued to soar above her. A second attempt brought the same result and, whether it was the design of her glider, grief for her lost student, tiredness or just bad luck, so it continued throughout the day, and every day of the event. At some point Hanna lost heart, although not the resolve to keep plugging away. Before long she was seen as the comedy contestant, a subject for ridicule, and eventually she was unable completely to fight back her tears. It was with

---

* The NSDAP achieved 37 per cent of the vote nationally in 1932.

some surprise, then, that Hanna found her name on the rostrum for the final prize-giving. A sponsor had donated a meat-mincer and a pair of kitchen scales – what better to use as a booby prize, not only provoking 'uproarious laughter', Hanna noted ruefully, but also serving 'as a warning to any other forward little girls who might set their hearts on flying!'[10]

Melitta's former gliding instructor, Peter Riedel, was also at the Rhön contests that year, as every year. Peter, who had now applied for Nazi Party membership, was working with Walter Georgii at his gliding research institute,* experimenting with upcurrents and cloud-hopping to achieve spectacular heights and distances. As Hanna was presented with her kitchen scales, he was collecting the Hindenburg Cup, having established a new distance world record of 142 miles. Peter appreciated that Hanna's award was 'a crude sort of message that women should stay in the kitchen' and he was not impressed.[11] Already astonished by Melitta's skill in the air, he now openly admired Hanna's determination and refusal, as he saw it, to let 'this humiliation divert her from her dedication to flying . . . to her beloved Germany . . . and to Hitler'.[12] Peter was not alone in this assessment. In his final speech, Oskar Ursinus, gliding pioneer and the founder of the Rhön contests, pointedly declared that 'in soaring, it is not success but the spirit which counts'.

Walter Georgii noticed all the attention that Hanna had attracted. He was planning a research trip to study the powerful thermals in South America, and had already recruited Wolf Hirth, Peter Riedel and another of the Wasserkuppe competitors, a boyishly handsome pilot a year older than Hanna called Heini Dittmar, who was flying a glider he had built himself. Now Georgii invited Hanna to join the team as an extra pilot and, he quietly hoped, as a potential publicity hook for the institute and for Germany's reputation overseas. Hanna was thrilled – the only catch was that she would have to pay her own, considerable, travel expenses.

---

* Originally the Rhön-Rossitten Society, Professor Walter Georgii's organization was renamed the German Research Institute for Gliding in 1933, and became the German Research Centre for Gliding (DFS) in 1937. Hanna would start work there in 1934.

As a courageous pilot, with her vivacious personality, fashionable looks and brilliant smile, the truth was that Hanna had been attracting plenty of attention ever since she first stepped into a glider. After her record-setting storm cloud flight, the nationalist film studio, UFA, had invited her to act as a stunt double in a film about gliding. Now Hanna accepted the offer, on the proviso that they paid the 3,000 Reichsmarks required for her South American passage.

*Rivals of the Air** was an early Nazi propaganda film designed to inspire young men to become pilots, and was produced by Karl Ritter, a Great War veteran pilot and committed Nazi himself. The plot revolved around a young gliding enthusiast, played by Heini Dittmar, who persuades a female college friend to learn to soar with him. Failing the course, the female student is disqualified from entering the Rhön contests. However, 'being a small and rather energetic person', in Hanna's words, 'she has some ideas of her own'.[13] The young fräulein, clearly modelled on Hanna, borrows a glider and sets off in pursuit of the men, only to be rescued from storm cloud disaster by her older gliding instructor, in the form of Wolf Hirth. After much talk of courage, spirit and virility, the older instructor gets the girl, and the younger man wins national honours in the contest: everyone is happy – particularly Hanna who, apparently unconcerned by the politics behind the film, thoroughly enjoyed the chance to repeatedly 'crash' her glider into a lake, while getting paid for the privilege.

Hanna set sail for South America, her first venture out of Germany, in early January 1934. With four leading lights of the gliding scene – Walter Georgii, Wolf Hirth, Peter Riedel and Heini Dittmar – at her side, it was another dream come true. Perhaps encouraged by their on-screen romance, Heini flirted with Hanna, but she was not interested, and only complained to the tall, more brotherly Peter that their colleague was rather a nuisance. Perhaps bitterly, Heini later told a mutual friend that he was 'quite sure' that Hanna was a lesbian.[14] Peter had found romance elsewhere. He never found Hanna sexually attractive, 'too small, for one

---

* *Rivalen der Luft* (UFA, 1934).

thing', he joked, but he considered her, like Melitta, 'a great friend'.[15] In any case Hanna had no desire for a passionate romance that would inevitably curtail her freedom. Like her film double, her real admiration would always be reserved for older men, father figures like Wolf Hirth.

Everything else about the voyage, however, charmed her: the lights on the water; the captain's permission to climb the mast; 'the driving ice floes which broke up on the bow with a sharp tinkle like a toast from a thousand glasses'; and later dolphins, flying fish, and 'half-naked black boys, supple as fish', who dived for the coins they threw from the ship's rails.[16] Hanna, like many of her contemporaries, had absorbed – and helped to perpetuate – the casual racism of her times, often admiring from afar but at closer range finding the black men of the Spanish Canary Islands 'dark and sinister-looking, sending an involuntary shudder down the spine'.[17]

As soon as the expedition team arrived at Rio de Janeiro they embarked on a PR campaign, with a series of press conferences, dinners and speeches. Walter Georgii had been astute: pretty and petite, and typically dressed entirely in white from flying cap down to tights and shoes, Hanna made a striking figure and was soon generating considerable publicity. She was not just the only woman, but also the most junior member of the team. 'The presence of a girl . . .' she now realized, with rather mixed feelings, 'naturally increased . . . interest and curiosity.'[18] Every day 'hundreds and thousands' of spectators trekked over to the airfield to watch Hanna perform aerobatics, while the men took the lead in the cross-country flights that were the official raison d'être of their visit.

After a few weeks they moved on to São Paulo where Hanna had more opportunity to take part in the long-distance flights, guided by the cumulus clouds formed by warm rising air, or following the black vultures that soared the thermal upwinds.* One

---

* So adept were these birds at finding the currents that the team caged some to take back to Germany. Not surprisingly, once they had grown accustomed to being fed in confinement, they later refused to fly. Some were donated to Frankfurt Zoo, and one was reported as walking to Heidelberg.

Sunday morning she mistook a single 'thermal bubble', a small pocket of warm air, for a stronger rising column capable of taking a glider up and, with her usual mix of confidence and impatience, she cast off prematurely from her motorized tow-plane. To her dismay, she quickly found herself circling back downwards, forced to search for an emergency landing site. As she approached the only obvious field in the densely populated city below, she was horrified to see it was a football pitch with a match in progress, surrounded by crowds of spectators. In Hanna's account, it was only as she 'swooped clean through a goalmouth', screaming warnings in Spanish, that the players realized she was not able to pull up and ran or flung themselves to the ground. Fortunately no one was hit. Once down, her glider was mobbed by the crowd and she was only saved, she reported, by 'a German' who called the mounted police. Several people were injured, 'trampled beneath the horses' hooves', but instead of Hanna being reprimanded, the event turned out to be the most successful PR coup of the expedition, with many local newspapers covering the 'Strange and Marvellous Case of the Girl who Fell from the Sky!'[19]

Hanna spent several weeks in Brazil, and then soaring over the grassy plains of Argentina, where she landed twenty metres from the war minister after her opening display. 'Of course' the locals asked about Hitler, Peter wrote, as their planes 'bore the swastika above Argentina'.[20] By the time the team set off for home, in mid-April 1934, Hanna had been guest of honour at numerous events, and landed in several remote villages. She had stoically rebuffed not only Heini's advances but also the less unwelcome ones of a handsome young Spanish pilot, and she had collected the Silver Soaring Medal, the first woman ever to do so. Peter had set a new record for long-distance soaring, Wolf had achieved an unprecedented sixty-seven loops in succession, and Heini had broken the world altitude record. But 'more importantly', Hanna noted, 'we had built a bridge of friendship'.[21]

During their absence Germany had become increasingly unpopular overseas and, although their trip had not been an official goodwill mission, Hanna was delighted to have served as a voluntary ambassador for her country. At home, meanwhile, 'Hitler seemed to be carrying everyone along with him,' Peter wrote on his return. 'The economy was booming, the unemployment problem had almost disappeared, the country was becoming strong again after all those years of hopelessness.' Any earlier doubts he had harboured about the regime began to ebb away. 'I thought Hitler must be the right man for Germany,' he said.[22] Hanna emphatically agreed.

While Hanna had been away, courting publicity both for herself and for the Nazi regime, Melitta had been deliberately keeping a low profile at DVL, the German Research Institute for Aeronautics. A few years earlier, as a 'new woman' studying engineering, sitting astride a motorbike, or even just smoking a cigarette, she had been very visible in the Weimar Republic. But despite her unusual choice of career for a woman in 1930s Germany, as the Nazis gained support Melitta seemed discreetly to fade from view.

Melitta had always been a traditionalist at heart. Admittedly she still needed to fly as others need to breathe, but at thirty-one she was essentially socially conservative, keen on heritage, duty, and reward through hard work. She might have friends among working pilots and engineers, but now she also mixed with the aristocratic Stauffenberg brothers, rising figures in academia, law and the military, and her own siblings were flourishing in the very respectable fields of the civil service, medicine and business journalism. Melitta's statement bob was long gone, and if she still wore trousers to work they were now part of a well-cut suit and the look was carefully softened by a silk blouse and string of pearls. She was dressing to be practical, not provocative, and this seemed to reflect her whole approach to life. Jutta saw that her sister 'firmly declined to be dragged into the public eye', and Melitta herself declared that she would not be 'drawn into the shrill world of advertising in the press or radio'.[23] She may have been naturally reserved, but now she had another reason not to make unnecessary waves. While doors everywhere were opening for Hanna, Melitta had learned some family history that threatened not just her opportunity to fly, but also her professional life, economic well-being and even her personal relationships.

As a young man about to set out for university, Melitta's father, Michael, had been baptized as a Protestant. It was in this faith that he had been raised, and would later bring up his own children. Melitta's grandfather, however, Moses, had been a non-practising Jew. In the nineteenth century, when Posen had come under Prussian rule, a new synagogue had been built and the Jewish community developed close links with the German, mainly Protestant, population. Moses admired German culture, and when Michael was baptized, both father and son considered their Jewish roots to be behind them. They were German patriots, and either from a sense of shame, a wish to avoid discrimination or a belief in its irrelevance, the Schillers' Jewish ancestry was never discussed. None of Michael's friends knew that this young man was anything other than the model German Protestant that he both appeared, and considered himself, to be.

It is not known when Melitta first learned of her paternal Jewish ancestry: perhaps when she was confirmed, aged fourteen, or when Hitler came to power in 1933 and the fact became politically significant. That year the first wave of legislation came into force limiting Jewish participation in German public life, whether as students, civil servants, lawyers or doctors. She certainly knew by September 1935 when the Nuremberg Laws further codified the regime's anti-Semitism, stripping German Jews of their citizenship, depriving them of basic political rights and prohibiting them from marrying or having sexual relations with 'Aryans'. The Nuremberg Laws effectively ended any realistic hope the community might still have harboured for a tolerable existence within their country.

Close friends and colleagues knew that Melitta was already critical of Nazi policies. Perhaps while studying in Munich she had heard some of the early speeches in which Hitler referred to Jews as 'vermin', and insisted that 'the Jew can never become German however often he may affirm that he can'.[24] This 'Volkish' ideology, the belief that blood rather than faith or legal status determined the race to which any individual belonged, had been reiterated in the two volumes of *Mein Kampf*, published in 1925 and 1926.* Along with many others, at that point Melitta probably still doubted that Hitler would gain power. By 1933 'the Nazis were in the saddle, but no one dreamed that it would be for long', a Stauffenberg family friend wrote, before adding that 'it was amazing to watch the speed with which the paralysing power of dictatorship and tyranny grew'.[25] Two years later Melitta must have paid close attention to Hitler's introduction to the Nuremberg Laws, but here the Führer was uncharacteristically vague. In interviews afterwards he claimed that 'the legislation is not anti-Jewish, but pro-German. The rights of Germans are hereby protected against destructive Jewish influence.'[26]

Michael Schiller, now seventy-four, responded with a mixture of courage and caution. At the end of 1935 he submitted a three-page article to Germany's *Nature and Spirit* magazine, making the case for raising children to be 'fully human' by the cultivation of logical thinking and the exclusion of any belief in supernatural powers.[27] He was not making a stand for Jews, or for human rights in general, but simply for his own family. He could not understand how they could be defined by their 'blood' rather than by their obvious brains and abilities. On publication, he sent the article to his children; it would not be his last attempt to defend them.

In fact, at first, none of the Schiller family were directly affected by the Nuremberg Laws. In a painful attempt to discriminate systematically, the regime identified Jews as those who had three or four 'racially' Jewish grandparents, or two if they were practising Jews. Melitta and her siblings therefore fell outside the scope of the laws. Furthermore, initial exceptions were made for highly decorated veterans, people over sixty-five or those married to Aryans, meaning Michael was also exempt. There was no need for an anxious conversation about whether to register or try to

---

* In several high-profile cases it was not 'blood' but chance that determined race. In 1935 Hermann Göring personally selected the photograph to illustrate a perfect 'Aryan' baby for cards and posters that were circulated nationally. The child was Jewish. See the *Independent*, 'Hessy Taft: Perfect Aryan Baby' (02.07.2014).

disappear. Nevertheless, it was clear that the Schiller family were no longer quite the equal German citizens that they had once been, and now that the principles of racial segregation and discrimination were enshrined in German law, there could be no guarantee that they would not yet find themselves subject to persecution.

Before the end of 1935 new legislation further marginalized German Jews: Jewish officers were expelled from the German army; Jewish students could no longer take doctorates; German courts could not cite Jewish testimony; and some cities started prohibiting Jews from municipal hospitals. Soon 'Aryan certificates' were required for college, work and marriage. 'Luckily, we had all finished our studies,' Klara later remembered, but 'from that time on there was danger hanging over all of us like the Sword of Damocles.'[28] Lili, the eldest sister, had trained as an X-ray assistant in Berlin but, already married and quietly raising a family, she was unlikely to attract attention. Jutta was also married, to a senior Nazi official. For her these were peaceful years. However, Otto, Melitta and Klara all needed certificates for their workplaces. They decided to try to hide their ancestry. The fact that their father, Michael, was officially a Polish citizen following the border change helped to delay things. In an attempt to buy some time, 'we pretended to get our papers from Odessa,' Klara continued.[29] Later, they claimed nothing could be found. Otto was now an agricultural attaché at the German Embassy in Moscow. In 1932 he had visited Ukraine to gain an insight into the famine caused by Stalin's programme of farm collectivization, giving him unique value for the new regime. For now his position was secure. Klara had applied for and received German citizenship in 1932. That year she visited Otto in Russia, and stayed to study nutrition and then work in the north Caucasus. In 1935, probably in a deliberate strategy to keep her out of Germany, Otto helped find her work cultivating soya in Spain.

As a patriot Melitta continued to affirm her loyalty to Germany, but unlike Hanna she now saw a clear distinction between her adored country with its rich cultural heritage and the so-called Third Reich, from whom she suddenly had to hide her family history. Knowing that her aviation development work at DVL was of national importance, she focused on making sure she was regarded as an invaluable member of the team before her Jewish heritage could be revealed and her job called into question. She now spent long days on the airfield and in her office, talked a little less about politics, and very rarely mentioned her family.

Nazi interest in science and aviation had given Melitta's institute a much-needed boost. 'Suddenly there seemed to be an abundance of equipment, and plenty of funds for building up a new army and to carry out new scientific research projects, as well as for flying,' her friend and colleague Paul von Handel wrote.[30] Between 1934 and 1936, Melitta embarked on the first of a series of test flights with clear military significance. Previously, she had been experimenting with state-of-the-art wind tunnels to assess the impact of wing flaps, slats and adjustable propellers on aerodynamics, speed and efficiency. Her pioneering design solutions became standard for commercial airlines. In 1934, however, she focused on the performance of 'propellers in a nosedive'; test-flying, analysing and modifying designs that would later become essential for the Luftwaffe – and she was well aware of the implications of this work. Later that year when, as a woman, she was barred from participating in the German touring competition, Melitta flew the event route in an air ambulance, outside the official contest. She was the only pilot to incur no penalties. Melitta was not just making a point about her own ability, 'she simply didn't take seriously anything she disagreed with', one of her sisters commented.[31] She was also using the opportunity to gain some practice in case air ambulances should soon be in greater demand.

That autumn Hans Baur, Hitler's personal pilot, flew the Führer to the annual Nuremberg Rally. As his silver plane circled over the ancient city, thousands strained their eyes to watch him descend 'from the sky like a Teutonic god'.[32] In March he had announced the expansion of the Wehrmacht, the return of universal conscription and the official creation of the Luftwaffe. Public ceremonies were organized, with impressive aerial displays above and military parades below. According to Hanna, this was 'general peacetime conscription', but she admitted that the international atmosphere was 'extremely tense'.[33] Until this point, Winston Churchill later wrote, air sport and commercial aviation in Germany had hidden 'a tremendous organization for the purposes of air war'. Now, 'the full terror of this revelation broke . . . and Hitler, casting aside concealment, sprang forward, armed to the teeth, with his munitions factories roaring night and day, his aeroplane squadrons forming in ceaseless succession.'[34] Later that year, the flying ace Ernst Udet, who had served alongside Melitta's uncle in the Great War, demonstrated his chubby grey Curtiss Hawk and a Focke-Wulf dive-bomber at the Reich's party conference, paving the way for a full aircraft development programme. Melitta was soon busy not only undertaking blind-flying and radio courses, but also working on the development and testing of dive-brakes for bombers. With little safety equipment it was high-risk work; between 1934 and 1937, thirteen of her colleagues were killed in accidents at DVL.

Despite the growing investment in research for military applications, which Melitta welcomed, Paul felt that at DVL 'the influence of Nazi policies was, at first, barely perceptible'. Even in the army, he believed, 'there was little political interest'.[35] His – and Melitta's – friend, Claus von Stauffenberg, certainly considered himself an apolitical army officer in the best tradition of the military, although his family later said he would leave the room promptly should he hear Jews being insulted.[36]

Inside German universities the situation was quite different. Since the Nazis had assumed power, education at all levels had become strictly controlled and directed. For Melitta's flame, Alexander von Stauffenberg, a professor of ancient history at the University of Berlin and soon to be appointed both to the University of Giessen and as extraordinary professor at Würzburg, the imposition of a political agenda over academic history boded very ill. It was this, Paul believed, that made Alexander so 'much more critical of the political development of Hitler's Germany than Litta, Claus and I'.[37] Whether from a dreamy lack of social shrewdness or in deliberate angry defiance, Alexander repeatedly and publicly criticized the regime and its policies in a way that already few others would dare. His twin brother, Berthold, now a lawyer in The Hague, was also disturbed by the changing political climate. As early as July 1933, the Nazis had been declared the only legal political party in the country, and that October Germany left the League of Nations, prompting Berthold's return to Berlin to work at the Kaiser Wilhelm Institute. The regime's lack of legal principles and disregard for international law deeply disturbed him. Nationalist patriotism and even some level of racial distinctions he could accept, but not political tyranny or institutionalized racial persecution. Unlike many of their friends and relatives, none of the Stauffenberg brothers joined the NSDAP.

Alexander quietly moved in with Melitta in 1934. Although she did not introduce him to her family, both of them clearly considered their relationship permanent. The previous September, Claus had dutifully married Baroness Nina von Lerchenfeld, an 'extremely good-looking' member of the Bavarian aristocracy, 'with dark slanting eyes and glossy hair'.[38*] Berthold was engaged to the Russian-born Mika Classen, whom he would marry not long after the death of his father in June 1936. Mika's family had fled Russia during the revolution, but the old Count had been 'very much opposed' to the match because she did not come from an aristocratic German family.[39] Only Alexander was still officially single. It is unlikely that his father knew Melitta had Jewish ancestry, but he still had reservations about her social status.

Melitta's family was not immune from prejudice either, considering privilege not earned by personal merit to be vaguely ridiculous. 'How often she was teased, with a wink, by her brother and sisters when her mother joked, every now and then, about the

---

* Claus and Nina had honeymooned at Borne in Germany, where they enjoyed an exhibition celebrating Mussolini's first ten years in power. In doing so they missed the German elections of March 1933.

deeds of her own noble ancestors,' Jutta later recalled. Noticing Melitta's discomfort, her father maintained that coming from the once privileged classes 'contributed to the establishment of character based in reason and responsibility'.[40] Melitta's response is sadly not recorded but she had sufficient self-respect to see her prestige as a pilot as equal to that of the aristocracy. In any case, Alexander's classical understanding of what it meant to be noble meant he could never sit idle, resting on the family laurels. In fact he was as enthralled by his vocation as Melitta was by hers. However, there was another reason for Melitta and Alexander not to apply to get married – Melitta would have to provide an 'Aryan certificate'. Eventually she succumbed and formally applied for Aryan status for herself and her siblings, on the basis of her parents' wedding certificate listing both parties as Protestant. Then she waited.

Hanna had returned from South America in the late spring of 1934. 'We can't let you leave us now . . .' Walter Georgii had told her during the return journey, 'you belong to us.'[41] That June she joined Peter Riedel and Heini Dittmar at Georgii's internationally acclaimed gliding research institute based at Darmstadt, just south of Frankfurt. 'I could hardly imagine any greater happiness,' she wrote.[42] The timing was good. The Nazis were investing as much in gliding as in Melitta's aeronautical research institute, DVL, but Hanna needed training before she could become an official glider test pilot. Within a few weeks she established a new women's world record for long-distance soaring, covering a distance of over a hundred miles. On the back of this she secured a place at the Civil Airways Training School at Stettin, which usually took only male trainees.

Stettin was one of a number of thinly disguised military bases where the students' blue uniforms would turn out to be remarkably similar to those of the Luftwaffe, revealed the following year. 'The school was staffed,' Hanna said, 'by officers to whom a woman on an airfield was like a red rag to a bull.'[43] Despite causing much hilarity as she joined the morning drill line-up, her slight, feminine frame inevitably 'disturbing the splendours of the masculine silhouette', as she put it, Hanna quickly proved her capabilities and was accepted by her peers. Most of the flying suits were too large, and she needed cushions to boost her height in the cockpit, but she learned to fly loops, turns and rolls in a Focke-Wulf Fw 44, a two-seat open biplane known as the *Stieglitz*, or Goldfinch, and carefully concealed her initial sickness by throwing up neatly into one of her gloves. Back at Darmstadt, Hanna could now fly one of the six heavier Heinkels. These were military reconnaissance aircraft that had been stripped of their armaments and issued with civil registrations for use at flying displays, and for meteorological night flights at the institute. Since these machines had been issued first to DVL, it is likely that Hanna was now literally sitting in Melitta's old seat.

In 1935 Hanna officially became an experimental glider test pilot. The first aircraft she was required to test was a new glider being built at the institute known as the DFS *Kranich*, or Crane. All went well, and next followed the *See Adler*, or Sea Eagle, the world's first waterborne glider, whose gull wings were designed to stay high above the spray and waves. This didn't always work. After being dragged right under the surface of a lake by the weight of her tow rope during an early test, Hanna and the See Adler eventually lifted off only when pulled into the air by a Dornier flying boat.

Daily letters from her mother brought Hanna considerable comfort during these dangerous trials, reassuring her that she was in God's hands, if also slightly irritating her with constant warnings about 'the blindness of vanity and overweening pride'. Where they did see eye to eye was in their shared belief that Hanna's work was all 'in the cause of Germany and the saving of human lives'.[44]

According to Peter Riedel, Hanna quickly became 'a quite outstanding pilot' who, he could not resist adding, was 'capable of equalling or surpassing the best men'.[45] Apart from Melitta, who was keeping her head down at DVL, Hanna was the only other woman testing such exciting prototype aircraft. As a result, she started receiving invitations to represent Germany at flight events overseas. In Finland she performed gliding demonstrations to engage the country's young people in the sport. But en route to Portugal she caused controversy when bad weather forced her to land at a French military airfield without permission. The discovery of a camera on board led to accusations that Hanna was a spy. 'White with rage', she vociferously denied the claims, believing that not only she, but also her country, were being maligned.[46] Eventually the French Ministry of Aviation ordered her release. Delighted to leave 'the tensions of the outside world' behind her once again, she flew on to Lisbon, and happily abandoned herself to her 'one overmastering desire – to soar in the beauty of flight'.[47]

'Hitler wanted the Germans to become a nation of aviators,' the wife of Hanna's friend Karl Baur, a Messerschmitt test pilot, later wrote. 'If there was some kind of celebration in a city, an air show was a *must*.'[48] Karl worked with Hanna to develop an aerobatic programme, and she was soon busy on the demonstration circuit at regional flight days around Germany, performing aerobatics to entertain the crowds. Although his wife thought Hanna was 'a young fragile-looking girl', Karl was impressed by the energy she put into her performances, and recognized her as 'a very talented, enthusiastic pilot'.[49]

Hanna was now typically flying alongside other stars of the German aviation scene like Elly Beinhorn with her incredibly fast Me 108 *Taifun* (Typhoon), and Ernst Udet, who stunned the crowds with his sensational open biplane act of swooping down low enough to pick up a handkerchief from the ground with the tip of its wing. Since the Great War, Udet had made a career out of performing aerobatics and mock air battles with his friend and fellow veteran Robert Ritter von Greim, who he considered 'a splendid pilot'.[50] Having starred in several films, Udet was now a huge celebrity, 'but in all of this there was a secret longing to see the spirit which inspired us become a real power in the nation', he wrote in his 1935 memoir. 'We were soldiers without a flag' until 1933, when, he added, 'for old soldiers, life is again worth living'.[51]

Increasingly in the public eye, Hanna was herself becoming a minor celebrity. In 1934 she went from a few mentions in the gliding news to being the title story, and even the cover girl of magazines that featured her sitting in her open cockpit, grinning for the camera, her blonde curls tucked into her close-fitting flying cap, her goggles resting above. She even appeared, wearing a glamorous fur-collared flying jacket, on a gold-embossed Gabarty cigarette card for their collectable 'Modern Beauties' series, and no doubt in Germany she and Elly Beinhorn were the women most closely associated with Caron's 'En Avion' perfume, launched in 1932.* Hanna was a natural performer, and silent film footage from this time shows her looking relaxed and fabulous in her flying kit, shading her eyes from the sun and laughing as she gamely bats aside the feather duster being brandished by a handsome young man. With the duster propped in the nose of her glider, more men arrive to joke around with her. It all looks very jolly. In another scene, Hanna, now in a pretty white blouse and neck scarf, goofs about for the camera with a giant cuddly-toy dog dressed in jacket and trousers. Despite the constant sexism, Hanna can afford to laugh generously because she knows that she can fly all these men out of the sky. By the time she pulls her goggles down over her eyes and is strapped into her cockpit, around fifteen men – some in uniform – are gathered to watch her take off. Her elegant white glider dips out of sight and then rises, magnificently, above them all.

Hanna was publicly associating with the dynamic new regime, and beginning to rise with them, but she did not completely support all their policies. One of her flying friends, Dr Joachim Küttner, had been classified as 'half Jewish'. Küttner had joined Hanna on her official visit to Finland, and now they were both sent to Sweden with Peter Riedel to perform aerobatic displays. While there, Hanna asked Walter Stender, an aviation engineering friend, whether he could help Küttner find work overseas. Stender declined, commenting only that her desire to help a Jew was a 'noble and dangerous idea'.[52] In fact it is unlikely that Hanna was putting herself in great danger by canvassing for Küttner at this

* The perfumier behind Caron's 'En Avion' was Ernest Daltroff, a middle-class Jew whose family came from Russia. In 1941 he escaped Paris for America.

time, but her concern does show both that she was aware of growing, state-sanctioned anti-Semitism, and that it did not sit entirely comfortably with her. Nevertheless, she chose to make an exception to help a colleague rather than challenge the general rule. 'She didn't see these cases as symptomatic of anything,' a friend later argued. 'She saw them as isolated incidents that could be cleared up by a personal intervention . . . she wasn't able to see an evil principle in all of this.'[53]

In February 1936, Hanna was delighted to join Peter again, performing gliding aerobatics at the opening of the Winter Olympics held at Garmisch-Partenkirchen, a couple of small villages in the Bavarian mountains. It was a fun event, taking off and landing on the frozen lake where the figure skating would soon take place. Udet was also there, flying alongside Hitler's personal pilot, Hans Baur, and others, in a rally for engine-powered planes. Unfortunately for the Olympic competitors, Ga-Pa, as the site was soon known, had suffered from unseasonably light snowfall, but the towns were almost buried beneath an avalanche of swastikas on posters, flags and bunting. This new signage replaced the anti-Jewish notices that had been temporarily removed before the arrival of the international teams, press and spectators in tacit admission that other nations might not understand Nazi race policy. The Winter Olympics were being used to give the regime legitimacy. Despite attracting fewer foreign visitors than expected and some critical press reports from the likes of William Shirer, the bureau chief of the American Universal News Service, they would prove extremely effective. Had the games been officially boycotted internationally, or even had visitors left with a dim impression of the new regime, it is possible that Hitler might not have risked launching his expansionist foreign policy quite so soon. As it was, a month after the games opened, German troops marched into the demilitarized zone of the Rhineland in violation of the Treaty of Versailles.

That spring, back at the Darmstadt Research Centre for Gliding, Hanna started to test glider air brakes. These could be fitted to prevent a speeding glider from exceeding the structural limit of its frame, even when diving vertically, before the pilot could regain control. It was terrifying work as the whole glider would shudder when the prototype air brakes were used, and Hanna reported wedging herself against the sides of the cockpit in order to keep control. Modification and eventual success were an important aeronautical milestone. Perhaps not coincidentally, these air brakes were being developed at the same time as the Luftwaffe's research into the possibility of dive-bombing with Stukas was stepped up.

Here, for the first time, Hanna's and Melitta's work began to overlap. Melitta had already carried out experiments on adjustable propellers and their behaviour in 'headlong descent' – in other words, during dives – and Hanna was now testing dive-brakes. There is no question that by now these two exceptional women would have known of each other. Test pilots formed a close and supportive community and Hanna and Melitta were the only women at their respective institutes: a source of curiosity and gossip for the men, and of potential support for each other. Furthermore, they had several close friends in common, from Peter Riedel and Elly Beinhorn to the famous veteran Ernst Udet. However, neither Hanna nor Melitta made any public reference to the other, as if refusing to recognize another woman working in the same field.

In March, Hanna successfully demonstrated glider brakes to a number of Luftwaffe generals including Udet, who would soon be appointed chief of the Luftwaffe's technical office. Udet's friend, Robert Ritter von Greim, was also present. Greim was one of the very few people to have piloted a plane carrying Hitler. In 1920, he had flown Hitler through rough weather to Berlin for the Kapp Putsch. When the Luftwaffe was publicly launched in 1935, Göring named Greim as the first squadron leader and now, at forty-four, he was rapidly rising through the ranks. Both the new technology and the female test pilot made a deep impression on Greim and the other men.

Not long after, Hanna was notified that she was to be awarded the honorary title of Flugkapitän, or flight captain, the first German woman ever to be accorded such a distinction. Despite claiming to place 'no value on decorations', Hanna was thrilled.[54] Before the month was over, Göring had also presented her with a special women's version of the Combined Pilot's and Observer's Badge in gold with diamonds, along with a signed photograph of himself dedicated to 'The Captain of the Air, Hanna Reitsch'. As if not to be outdone, two days later, on Hanna's twenty-fourth birthday, Udet gave her a brooch in the form of a golden propeller overlaid with a swastika of blue sapphires, with his own dedication engraved on the reverse. Hanna was clearly the female pilot to know in the Third Reich, and both she and Melitta were fully aware of it.

The Winter Olympics had been a major date on the 1936 calendar, but the main event of the year would be the Berlin Olympics that August. The games had been awarded to Germany in 1931, but because of the severe economic depression nothing had been done at the Olympic site. Within three years of taking power the Nazis had built a monumental stadium to showcase their revitalized nation to the world. Sport in Nazi Germany, with its focus on physically 'perfect' young people, was inseparable from nationalism and the idea of racial superiority. Despite some international protest against Berlin as host city – the first time in history that an Olympic boycott was discussed – by July 1936 the German capital was draped not only in scarlet, white and black, but also with Olympic flags. Above the stadium the *Hindenburg* airship, its tail fins painted with swastikas, proudly trailed an Olympic banner from its gondola. New trees were planted along Unter den Linden, new rail links stretched beneath the city, and the National Socialist architectural style, designed to impress and inspire, was showcased in the massive new stadium as the capital geared up for the arrival of nearly 4,500 participants and 150,000 foreign spectators.* An estimated one million Berliners came out simply to watch Hitler's

---

* Among those boycotting events around the games was British scientist A. V. Hill. 'I have many German friends,' Hill wrote, 'but as long as the German government and people maintain their persecution of our Jewish and other colleagues, it will be altogether distasteful for me . . . to take part in any public scientific function in Germany.' See David Clay Large, *Nazi Games: The Olympics in 1936* (2007).

journey to the games. 'Berlin was ready for the festivities,' the film-maker Leni Riefenstahl noted in her diary, 'and the town burned with Olympic fever.'[55] Although Udet was banned from flying above the races to take film footage, Riefenstahl planned to get good aerial shots from cameras attached to hydrogen-filled balloons. Ironically, though, none of her footage captured the aerial elements of the games.

Germany had petitioned for gliding to be accepted as an Olympic sport but, after months of deliberation, the International Olympic Committee had rejected the proposal.* In order still to showcase German capabilities in the sky, an *Olympiade Grossflugtag* or 'Olympic Great Flight Day' was organized at Tempelhof airfield for 31 July, the day before the official opening of the games. There were to be tethered hot-air balloons; formation flying by glider pilots; the men's aerobatics championship finals; and aerial displays by different models of pre-war planes, light aircraft and other engine-powered planes; and it was Melitta – not Hanna – who was booked for the programme. Melitta was to perform a daring stunt flying in a Heinkel He 70 *Blitz* (Lightning), a plane once used as a light bomber and for aerial reconnaissance. Her display would follow a group of parachutists and some daylight fireworks, and come just before Elly Beinhorn was to wow the crowds in her Messerschmitt Me 108: a plane she had named the Taifun because it 'sounded international, powerful'.[56] All the aircraft were emblazoned with swastikas; this was political theatre at its most spectacular.

Melitta's thoughts on being involved in this huge public relations exercise are not recorded. However, hosting the games was a long-awaited honour for Germany and few people saw their country's impressive preparations in anything other than a positive light. Since Melitta regarded Germany as far greater than the current regime, she may have felt proud to have been selected,

---

* Gliding was officially accepted by the IOC in 1938 as part of an optional group of sports to be staged for the first time at the planned 1940 Tokyo Olympics. Hitler expected all subsequent Olympics to take place in Germany. However, the Tokyo Games were cancelled after the outbreak of the Finnish/Soviet 'Winter War'.

justifying her participation to herself in these terms rather than seeing the games for what they had become: a homage to Nazi Germany and the Führer, deliberately staged with an eye to world opinion. She must also have known that to refuse any such invitation could be seen as anti-German, and would have been extremely risky at a time when she was still waiting to hear about her personal legal status.

In the event, the weather was terrible. Heavy clouds hung overhead. It was wet, and an unseasonably fierce wind whipped summer hats off heads, set banners flapping and sent clouds of dust into watering eyes. Nevertheless, Hitler, square and stocky in his brown uniform, accompanied by Umberto II, the last king of Italy, attended the Grossflugtag, along with crowds in the tens of thousands. Events started badly. Forty of the 150 participating aircraft had to withdraw because of the weather or engine trouble. 'It was hell,' one of the pilots commented in an interview.[57] Yet Melitta's performance was spectacular. Her outstanding aerial acrobatics, control and accuracy generated huge applause and lasting admiration, as well as drawing considerable new attention to her.

Hanna was also expected to play her part during the Summer Olympics. Gliding had been accepted as a 'demonstration sport', and a display was scheduled for 4 August at Berlin-Staaken airfield. Although no official contest took place and no prizes were presented, the weather was better and pilots from seven countries took part, with Hanna a member of the strong German team. Unfortunately gliding proved to be the only sport that brought the games a fatality, when an Austrian sailplane crashed after damaging its wing.

Among those watching the displays was a seventeen-year-old Scot. Eric Brown was the son of one of the British air force veterans invited to the games by Udet and the German Fighter Pilots' Association for a 'shindig', as Eric put it, with their former enemies.[58] Udet would instil in Eric a lifelong love of flying. Taking him up for a spin, he only nonchalantly checked that Eric was well strapped in before rolling the plane onto its back as they started their approach to land. Eric, who momentarily thought 'the silly old fool's had a heart attack', was speechless, but Udet 'roared with laughter'.[59] Once back on the ground, Udet gave the teenager a slap on the back with the old pilots' greeting, 'Hals- und Beinbruch!' – 'Break a neck and a leg!' He then told him to learn to fly, and to learn German. He was 'a good mentor for someone who wanted an adventurous life', Eric said, and Hanna no doubt agreed.[60] Udet introduced them on the airfield. Hanna was a 'remarkable lady, tiny sort', Eric commented, adding that she 'flew a glider like an angel'.[61] Twenty minutes later he had her down as 'an intense, strong-minded woman, filled with ambition and determination'.[62] Like many others, however, Eric underestimated Hanna's ability. When he learned that she wanted to test-fly engine-powered planes he felt she had 'no hope', as she would never have 'the physical strength to take on a large aircraft'.[63] Hanna would soon prove him wrong.

It is hard to know which of these Olympic aerial events, the Grossflugtag or the gliding demonstration, was the more prestigious. Either way, there must have been some awkward moments at the parties and official receptions during the games, and later at Berlin's Haus der Flieger, or House of Aviators, established by Göring as a meeting place for flight officials and pilots. Hanna was soon talking derisively about Melitta's skills as a pilot, while Melitta, it was said, chose never to speak of Hanna, even refusing to have a cup of tea with her. It was perhaps inevitable that some gossips would define the relationship between two such brilliant female pilots as rivalry. But although there is no reason to think that Hanna knew of Melitta's Jewish ancestry at this point, there were many other reasons why the two might not have struck up a friendship. Hanna was vivacious, quick to laugh, and seemingly refused to take life seriously, and yet she had an eye for opportunity and a steely determination to succeed in her chosen career, whatever the obstacles. She could not bear Melitta's apparent sense of superiority and entitlement. The more considered Melitta was just as dedicated to her vocation, but believed in the old conservative virtues of modesty, study and hard work. For her, respect had to be earned, and she could not consider Hanna, who had no grasp of aeronautical engineering, as her peer. To see such rapid success go to anyone who had less knowledge and experience must have been trying, but to see it happen to someone who appeared so closely to represent and reflect the rise of the new regime must have been a particular challenge.

'This masculine Third Reich owes much of its success to its women athletes,' the New York Times reported from the Berlin Olympics.[64] Although the Nazis had initially opposed women's participation in competitive sport on the grounds that it was unfeminine and might damage their reproductive organs, the regime came to appreciate the propaganda value of female Olympians. Nevertheless, there was far less coverage of the women's events than the men's. As always, race was a very different issue. The selection of one part-Jewish German woman to compete in fencing, the 'honorary Aryan' Helene Mayer, who had previously fled to America to avoid persecution, was offered as evidence to the IOC that the regime selected athletes purely on merit. In fact, the only other German Jewish athlete they acknowledged, the track and field star Gretel Bergmann, was discreetly removed from the team at the last minute. Many people around the world cheered Jesse Owens' historic win as a victory over Nazi ideology, but few, even within Germany, realized that a woman of partly Jewish heritage had quietly starred in the opening Flight Day.

The 1936 Olympics proved an enormous success for Germany, both in terms of medal tally and for international relations. We are 'the premier nation in the world', Goebbels recorded with delight in his diary, while the Olympia-Zeitung asked more presciently, 'Must we not conclude that the biggest victor of the Olympic Games was Adolf Hitler?'[65] Most overseas commentators were positive. 'Only a determined deaf-and-blind visitor to any corner of this land could fail to see and hear the sight, the sound, of Germany's forward march,' the New Yorker reported.[66] Meanwhile the famous American pilot Charles Lindbergh, who had been Göring's guest at the games, noted that he had 'come away with a feeling of great admiration for the German people'. Although he added that, having been invited to tour the new civil and military air establishments, he still had many reservations about the Nazis, Lindbergh believed that the rumoured treatment of Jews in Germany must be exaggerated, and that German Jews must in any case accept some fault for having sided so much with the communists. 'With all the things we criticize,' he continued, Hitler 'is undoubtedly a great man, and I believe he has done much for the German people.'[67] His wife, Anne Morrow Lindbergh, the first American woman to earn a first-class glider pilot's licence, was even more enthusiastic, describing Hitler as 'a visionary, who really wants the best for his country'.[68] Despite the Nuremberg Laws, and despite the invasion of the Rhineland, this was a common conclusion.

Carving out careers in the competitive male world of aviation under the Third Reich had not brought Hanna and Melitta together. Despite her mother's concerns about pride and vanity, Hanna loved to perform and regularly demonstrated that she was more than willing to fly through public relations hoops for the Nazi regime. After one of her overseas visits, the German Aero Club wrote to thank her for having 'had an admirable political effect'.[69] She was becoming a very useful propaganda tool and, while she may not have recognized the full implications, if the pay-off was in her favour, Hanna was perfectly happy to be used in this way. The more publicity she received, the more secure she was in her role as a pilot in a country that was rapidly becoming militarized and had less and less need for glamorous female aviators. Melitta was also keen to serve her country but, for her, in 1935, 'public relations' under the Nazis had a very different connotation. The thought of having to expose her family to public scrutiny was distasteful at best. That they would eventually be discovered to have 'Jewish blood', and that this meant inevitable censure both socially and professionally, was appalling. From now on all Melitta's decisions and actions would be determined by the knowledge of her, and her family's, increasing vulnerability.

Hanna and Melitta had both been prepared to play their part in the pageant surrounding the 1936 Berlin Olympics. Their sensational performances would bring them new levels of fame and attention, but would also set them on increasingly divergent paths.

Soon both women would again be required to play public roles in support of their country. Like it or not, their reputations as brilliant female pilots were growing, and the way in which they positioned themselves in the new Germany was becoming more important than ever.

4

PUBLIC APPOINTMENTS
1936–1937

Just a month after the glamour and excitement of the Berlin Olympics, Melitta abruptly left the job she loved at DVL, the German Research Institute for Aeronautics. It was a shocking departure. She had spent the last eight years steadily earning the respect and friendship of her colleagues in defiance of every expectation of her as a woman. The pioneering concepts she had developed through theoretical and experimental investigations into aerodynamics as an engineer and test pilot had been widely adopted for both commercial and military applications. The official reason for her departure is not known, but descriptions in DVL's reference of an 'enthusiastic' and 'skilful' pilot who 'always carried out the work entrusted to her to a high standard' show it was not dissatisfaction with her work.[1]

Melitta's reference also states that 'she left her position at her own request'.[2] In a letter to her former colleague Hermann Blenk, however, she referred to certain 'difficulties' she had encountered at the institute, and talked of her 'dismissal'. 'I very much hope that you will not have any unpleasantness at all on my account,' she added.[3] Her sister Jutta felt that DVL was uncomfortable with what she called Melitta's 'independent nature and thoughtfulness'.[4] Blenk later admitted that Melitta was more critical of the regime than either himself or other colleagues. Similarly, another member of the team felt that 'after the takeover of power . . . she probably sensed Nazi intrigue' at work and inevitably 'suffered' under the regime's influence. Things came to a head after Melitta made an unauthorized flight to Budapest. 'In such a situation, incidents which under other circumstances have no lasting consequences,' one colleague commented cautiously, 'are enough to produce discord, and if the resentment reaches a certain level, it is only a question of time before a separation must come about.'[5] It seems that Melitta's 'independent nature' had been ringing alarm bells at a time when her application for 'Aryan' status drew official attention to her. Her unauthorized flight made a convenient pretext for her removal.

DVL was in effect a state institution, under the de facto control of the Ministry of Aviation. This was not a place where someone with questionable heritage could now be employed. Whether it was a pre-emptive resignation or an informal dismissal, Melitta's departure had been engineered. Struggling to find an alternative employer, for a while she turned back to clay sculpture, starting a very fine bust of Alexander. At the same time, her youngest sister, Klara, had been forced to give up her position at the University of Giessen, together with her doctorate, and was seeking work overseas. Otto also found himself no longer eligible for an embassy posting to Peking, and instead went into industry in Romania. The Schillers were on a list.

Hanna's career, conversely, had been going from strength to strength since her performance at the Olympics. Still working as a test pilot at the Darmstadt gliding research institute, she spent the autumn of 1936 completing a series of nosedives in a *Sperber* (Hawk) glider equipped with the air-brake flaps developed by Hans Jacobs along the lines that Melitta and others used for engine-powered aeroplanes. At the end of the year Udet arranged for her to give a demonstration to some Luftwaffe generals. They were so impressed that the Aviation Ministry agreed to confer the title of Flugkapitän, or flight captain, on test pilots; a rank previously used only to denote the senior civil pilots of Lufthansa after they had completed a series of test flights and exams.

Hanna was only twenty-five when she received the distinction of being named Germany's first female honorary flight captain in the spring of 1937, and found herself briefly presented to Hitler.* In private she later claimed to have been unimpressed by the

---

* In fact the female pilot Elfriede Riote, who had captained an airship in 1913, might already have received the title Flugkapitän, but this had somehow been lost from the record.

Führer, who, she noted, sounded uncultured, wore a crumpled suit and repulsed her by indiscreetly picking his nose.[6] The German press were equally bemused by Hanna. While applauding her courage and determination, they clumsily labelled her as 'a girl' who 'acted like a man'.[7] Hanna was certainly exceptional. Without her considerable skill and steely determination, as a woman she could never have enjoyed a career as a pilot. Even so, few male pilots would be considered for such a title before they were thirty, but Hanna also had more than 2,000 hours in the air, high public recognition and the support of Udet on her side.

Hanna's flight captain ceremony took place in one of the large hangars at the Darmstadt airfield. As symbols of her new rank, she was presented with a captain's cap and a sabre sheathed in a section of aeroplane wing. All the men of the research institute then had to march to her commands. It was a scene that 'ended in chaos', she wrote to a friend, and 'nearly resulted in the loss of my new rank' as she had no idea how to correctly word the commands.[8] Nevertheless, Hanna was immensely proud of her new honorary title and insisted on its constant use, much to the irritation of some of her colleagues who believed she had 'used her feminine wiles' to gain the rank, and would later claim that 'she used that title to death'.[9]

That March, Hanna fleetingly visited Hirschberg for her sister Heidi's wedding, but she could not stay for long. She was now sufficiently important to have a glider, a Sperber Junior, tailor-made for her by Hans Jacobs. This machine was so beautifully crafted that she alone could fit into the pilot's seat, and once there she felt such a part of it, she claimed, that 'the wings seemed to grow out of my shoulders'.[10] It was in this Sperber that, in May 1937, Hanna would make headlines once again.

Salzburg was warm and still, perfect flying conditions, when she set off as one of many competitors at an international gliding meet aimed at setting some long-distance and high-altitude records. It was a now familiar sensation when a jerk on her glider forced her backwards, and her machine swayed as the tow rope tightened and swung the glider in behind the straining plane ahead. Picking up speed, the noise of the wheels suddenly ceased as she lifted off, and soon there was only the drumming of the wind on the fuselage until she cast off her tow completely. Below her the valleys were filled with morning mist; above were occasional shreds of cloud. After a gentle start she felt the air currents grow stronger as the sun warmed the slopes, and she headed towards the snow-covered peaks to the south.

Gliding above the mountains a few hours later, so unexpectedly far from Salzburg that she had neither the map nor the warm clothes she needed, Hanna once again felt an almost transcendental connection. 'Suddenly I was a child again . . .' she wrote, 'weeping to see the glory of God.'[11] Shivering in her seat, she brought her mind back to the business in hand and turned her Sperber round to catch the upcurrents from the Dolomites. When she landed, she was over a hundred miles from Salzburg, on the Italian side of the Alps. Four other German gliders had crossed the Alps that day, a historic first that made the national papers. Hanna received plenty of attention as the only woman among them. A few weeks later she and Heini Dittmar took their gliders 220 miles to Hamburg during the International Gliding Contest at the Wasserkuppe, Hanna setting a new women's long-distance record while Heini collected the 'Hitler Prize'. Her position as one of the Third Reich's leading celebrities was confirmed.

Melitta would have been following the gliding news, but she did not have time to dwell on Hanna's rising star. Although forced to leave DVL, her skills and experience in aeronautical engineering were second to none and before 1936 was over she had secured work at a private company based in Berlin-Friedenau. Askania was one of the most respected names in aeronautical engineering, producing tools such as navigational and gyroscopic instruments for Lufthansa. Melitta was employed to work on the development of their autopilot flight system for transatlantic flights, initially tested on the twin-engine Dornier Do 18 flying boat, and the four-engine Blohm & Voss Bv 139 'float plane'.*

---

* Such technology enabled Germany to continue transatlantic flights during the winter months when no other nation could.

Askania's corporate mission, as outlined in their in-house magazine, was to work 'for peace and uniting peoples for the good of nations on both sides of the ocean'.[12] In experimental aeronautical engineering, however, the boundaries between civil and military research are porous. In early 1937, Sir Nevile Henderson, the British ambassador to Germany, reported that 'the building up of the German air force was . . . a striking achievement'.[13] Then, in late April, the Luftwaffe showed their capability when their dive-bombers destroyed the Basque town of Guernica, with horrific loss of civilian life, in support of General Franco's fascist campaign in Spain. Inevitably, both Melitta and Hanna would soon be drawn into the development of their nation's air force.

In June 1937, Udet was appointed to head the Luftwaffe's technical office. A great advocate of dive-bombers, one of his first actions on the day he assumed his post was to renew investment into developing the Junkers Ju 87 Stuka. The Stuka weighed about 7,000 pounds and stood nearly thirteen feet off the ground. To dive from high altitude and pull out at less than 1,000 feet needed considerable strength. Udet had undertaken four vertical nose-dives in late 1933, and was so physically exhausted afterwards that he could hardly climb out of his seat. Diving also required great courage. Stuka pilots experiencing extreme G-forces as they pulled up were at risk of losing consciousness. Nevertheless, Udet had long been convinced that Stukas were the way forward, and had used 'cement bombs' to demonstrate the accuracy of dive-bombing to the top brass of the Party. Despite some ongoing opposition, he secured the green light for a development programme. Askania's aim was to automate the process as far as possible. There was no question now that Melitta was employed in defence rather than civil aviation. 'You know, we only work for armament, war is already predetermined,' she told her fellow test pilot, Richard Perlia. 'When I started flying, I only worked with small planes and commercial aeroplanes and now it is the opposite. It will come to a terrible end.'[14]

Despite her concerns, Melitta was still dedicated to her career. An Askania colleague, Georg Zink, described her 'inexhaustible patience and reliability' as they developed the application of gyro-scopes through empirical research.[15] A series of test flights led to modifications in the Stuka's rudder and elevator angles and the recalibration of the pneumatic automatic course-changing device, until steep turns of up to eighty degrees of bank could be achieved without any pilot involvement. As flights of increasing duration were controlled, Udet and Erhard Milch, Göring's number two at the Reich Aviation Ministry, were invited to watch. Askania won the contract to develop automatic take-off and landing technol-ogies as a result, and Melitta was once again part of a development team and working directly for the Nazi regime. Although she was a test pilot as well as an engineer, there was no discussion of promoting her to the rank of honorary flight captain, but at this moment Melitta was more concerned about her other official status.

Following her application for 'honorary Aryan' status for her-self and her siblings, the German consulate in Russia had been trying in vain to secure Michael Schiller's birth certificate from Odessa. Now another complication emerged. The University of Würzburg, where Alexander lectured, was pursuing the state policy of encouraging single staff to 'marry someone desirable for the Third Reich'.[16] Although Alexander had volunteered with a cavalry regiment when he was eighteen, and had been a private in the reserves since 1936, he was pointedly not a member of the Party, and he was risking his career with his uncompromising, critical attitude towards the regime.

Alexander was 'against the Nazis from the very beginning', his nephew later wrote, 'and said so, many times – thoughtlessly, as was his way'.[17] He may have spoken carelessly at times, but his position was very considered. He refused to lend legitimacy to the Nazis, and when he started to disregard and deny the official line on ancient history, and to question the ideals of power-seeking emperors, his academic papers were censored. In July 1937, he used a public lecture to criticize the deliberate Nazi glorification of ancient Germanic peoples as a means to support their fanciful theories of racial supremacy. His younger brother

Claus, who read the paper while on military leave that summer, was impressed by his courage at a time when all public comments were scrutinized, and suspected anti-Nazi sympathies were already dangerous. The essay had caused quite a flutter, he wrote, and was 'the best piece of his I have read in a long time'.[18] Alexander was protected to an extent by his family name, but his refusal to marry might prove all the excuse the university needed to remove him. At best he might be regarded as unpatriotic; at worst, he was vulnerable to arrest and imprisonment as a suspected homosexual.

Melitta and Alexander loved and admired one another. They did not share all their interests, but they understood and appreciated the passion that each brought to their work. The differences between them were 'happily complementary', Paul von Handel wrote. 'She respected his talents and he respected hers.'[19] Furthermore, they shared a moral and political perspective, a sense of patriotism, and a belief that the best values of their country were under attack. To marry, they decided, would both celebrate their relationship, and be a quiet stand for decency and humanity. It might also hold more practical benefits. Melitta would become a member of one of Germany's oldest and most distinguished families, affirming both her national identity and her patriotism. Alexander could silence his critics, and would become eligible for the academic advancement open only to married men. But Alexander also knew that he was marrying a woman whose father had been born Jewish: a bold step in Nazi Germany. 'Of course it was brave for Alex to marry Litta,' Claus's eldest son later commented.[20] Under the Nuremberg race laws, it was also illegal.*

Melitta and Alexander married quietly on 11 August 1937, in the Berlin Charlottenburg-Wilmersdorf registry office. The story given to the registrar was that Melitta's family papers had been lost in Odessa. Within a year such excuses would no longer be accepted; the couple had seized the last possible moment for their wedding.

---

* The approximately 20,000 German Jews married to non-Jews before the Nuremberg Laws were enacted, were categorized according to their ancestry, gender and religious practice. A few were given 'privileged' status, but most would later be required to wear a yellow star or 'J' on their clothes.

Their witnesses were Melitta's sister Klara, and Paul von Handel. Klara was astounded to discover that she and Alexander had worked for a while at the same university, and Melitta had been visiting him without ever mentioning it. She was mollified, however, by having been asked to act as a witness. The rest of Melitta's family would only hear about her wedding some weeks later. 'Many thought this odd,' Klara later admitted, but added with some understanding that her sister 'probably just wanted to prevent a fuss'.[21]

Later Melitta and Alexander also had a small church ceremony on Reichenau, a monastic island on the Bodensee connected to the mainland by a causeway.[*] Although the island's ancient estates had long been secularized, three medieval churches decorated with beautiful wall paintings remained, testament to the importance of the site as an artistic centre in the tenth and eleventh centuries. Alexander and his brothers had often come here as young men, as part of the circle around the poet Stefan George. Now Alexander and Melitta retook their vows in front of what they considered to be the Stauffenberg altar in the minster. Then they went on to the *Haus am See*, the 'house on the lake', for a quiet evening celebration, with no photographs.[†]

Alexander's father had died in 1936. The rest of the Stauffenberg clan already knew and liked Melitta. Like Alexander, his mother 'didn't keep it a secret that she was absolutely against the regime', and she felt a natural empathy with her son's unconventional new bride, although she was sometimes surprised by what she considered Melitta's 'masculine logic'.[22] A comment about Melitta 'at least' having a 'classical profile' made by Claus's wife, Nina, was snobbish and may have been subconsciously anti-Semitic, but even these two strong women soon found much to admire in one another.[23] 'She has the brain of a man,' Nina liked to say, 'and the charm of a woman.'[24] But it was the head of the

---

* Bodensee is the German name for Lake Constance.

† The *Haus am See* had been a meeting place of the Stefan George circle. It would later be owned by the poet Rudolf Fahrner, an associate of the circle and member of the *Widerstand* resistance to Hitler. After the war, several Stauffenberg children would board at a school near the lake.

family, Alexander's uncle Nikolaus, Count Üxküll-Gyllenband, who was also opposed to the Nazi regime, who set the official tone by formally welcoming Melitta as a new member of the family. 'One for all, all for one!' the count closed his toast the night that Alexander brought home his new bride. 'That is, caught together, hanged together!' someone commented irreverently, compelling Melitta to add, 'One could say that!'[25] They would prove to be poignant words.

Alexander also had to inform his university of his marriage. Among the papers he signed was one stating that, to the best of his belief, he had no knowledge 'that my wife might be descended from Jewish parents or grandparents'.[26] He then fudged the information about Melitta's grandfather, altering his name, and the date and place of his birth. As a married man, Alexander was offered a chair at the University of Würzburg and began to earn a salary more than twice the national average.

Although she was now officially 'Melitta Schenk Countess Stauffenberg', Melitta continued to use her maiden name at work. At weekends she lived at her and Alexander's apartment in Würzburg, where she played the roles of both countess and competent housewife, donning an apron to cook a meal or writing up Alexander's academic notes for him between dealing with her own papers. A photograph, probably taken by Alexander, shows her working serenely at her desk, light flooding in from a nearby window and vases of spring flowers set on the tables beside her. 'It was probably in self-defence', Nina wrote, that Alexander 'emphasized that intellect came before technology, which has to be subordinated', a view that Melitta, apparently, 'accepted . . . with a smile'.[27] She now joined in energetically with all her husband's interests and 'gave him the appearance of only incidentally functioning in her own very intensive profession', Nina continued with wry admiration. In fact Melitta was happy to defer to Alexander in public because in private he supported her career with 'constant, understanding encouragement'.[28] In any case, Paul noted, 'in their daily married life, Litta took the lead. Not because she wanted to dominate . . . but because she was hoping to relieve him of the worries of daily life, and he was thankful for this.'[29] Each of them felt that, with the other's support, they could now relax a little, and focus once again on their demanding careers.

While Melitta's summer had revolved around her private life, Hanna had been constantly in the public eye. In July, Peter Riedel won a series of gliding awards at the Elmira contests in the USA. America, he told Hanna, was a country he was growing to admire in many ways. Despite rising tensions between Germany and Britain, in August Hanna flew first to Croydon aerodrome and then around the UK, attending soaring contests. British pilots generally welcomed their German counterparts, but some of the local papers were less than enthusiastic to see swastikas on their airfields. Hanna was surprised and dismayed by their criticism. She also visited Zürich, with Udet and others, for a gliding demonstration. While there, Udet got hold of a Swiss pamphlet criticizing National Socialism and showed it to several pilots including Heini Dittmar's brother. 'It was dangerous,' Edgar Dittmar later wrote. 'If one of us glider pilots had said a word in Germany, it would have cost Udet his head.'[30] If Udet showed the leaflet to Hanna, she wisely never mentioned it.

That September the crowds at the Nuremberg Rally numbered several hundred thousand. 'As a display of aggregate strength it was ominous,' Sir Nevile Henderson reported. 'As a triumph of mass organization combined with beauty it was superb.'[31] A few weeks later, Udet ordered 'Flugkapitän Hanna Reitsch' to report to the Luftwaffe testing station at Rechlin near Lake Mecklenburg for duty as a military test pilot. Hanna was delighted. Her brother, Kurt, was already serving on destroyers in the Kriegsmarine, and was sent to Spain twice in 1937 to support Franco's struggle. Now she too could serve her country.

Karl Franke, the chief test pilot at Rechlin, already knew Hanna and welcomed her to the team, but she felt many of his colleagues believed her very 'presence on the airfield was an outrage'.[32] Her insistence that she be addressed with her honorary title did not help her popularity but she refused to compromise, preferring to call in support from Udet rather than accept any-thing less than her due.

This was Hanna's first incursion into the military world, and the difference between the glider airfield at Darmstadt with its 'slim, silvery birds . . . light as swallows' and Rechlin's military bombers and fighters, which to her eyes 'seemed like lean arrows, straining towards their mark', made a deep impression.[33] 'To me, who naturally felt these things more strongly than a man,' she sighed, 'Rechlin had an air of grim and purposeful menace.'[34] Hanna knew that Germany was rearming, but wrote that she 'saw it with different eyes than the world'. She insisted that she did not want war, but having witnessed years of poverty and insecurity she accepted the Nazi rhetoric about the need for a 'just peace', and the 'right to self-protection'. It was in this patriotic light, she later claimed, that she considered the military planes she was to test as 'guardians at the portals of Peace'. Hanna hoped that 'through my own caution and thoroughness, the lives of those who flew them after me would be protected and that, by their existence alone, they would contribute to the protection of the land I saw beneath me as I flew . . . for it was my home. Was that not worth flying for?'[35] In this regard her stated views were similar to those held by many of her compatriots, including Melitta. The difference was that Melitta no longer knew how welcome she was as a citizen, rather than a subject, of Germany, or how long her contribution to her country's 'protection' might be accepted.

Hanna now flew various fighters and bombers at Rechlin, including the Junkers Ju 87 Stuka dive-bomber with which Melitta was also working, and the Dornier Do 17, which was being fitted with dive-brakes, and which she referred to as her 'most beloved bomber'.[36] One day, however, Karl Franke asked Hanna to fly him over to the Focke-Wulf factory at Bremen where he was due to take up one of the world's first helicopters, the precarious-looking Focke-Wulf Fw 61, for a test flight. Professor Henrich Focke's pioneering machine had overcome the two fundamental problems facing autogyro and helicopter designers: the asymmetric lift caused by the imbalance of power between the advancing and retreating 'air-listing screws', or rotor blades, and the tendency for the helicopter's body to rotate in the opposite direction to its rotors.[37] The solution was to use two three-bladed rotors, turning in opposite directions, which were fixed up on outriggers, like small scaffolding towers, in place of wings. An open cockpit sat below. It was not an elegant design; some papers described it as looking 'like a cross between a windmill and a bicycle', but it worked.[38]

According to Hanna, when she landed at Bremen with Karl Franke, Focke wrongly assumed that she was there to give him a second opinion. Seeing that she was 'brimming with joy' at the thought of taking the helicopter up, Franke was generous enough not to disabuse the great designer.[39] Franke flew the machine first, as a precaution keeping it tethered to the ground by a few yards of rope. Unfortunately this also trapped him in reflected turbulence, buffeting the helicopter about. Such an anchor did not appeal to Hanna. Before she took her turn she had the rope disconnected and a simple white circle painted on the ground around the machine to guide her.

As Hanna later recounted the story, with typical lack of false modesty, 'within three minutes, I had it'.[40] From now on Franke would argue that, in Germany, Hanna and Udet were the 'only two people who were divinely gifted flyers'.[41] The Fw 61's vertical ascent to 300 feet, 'like an express elevator', with its noisy mechanical rotors literally pulling the machine up through the air, was completely different from the long tows needed by gliders, or even the shorter runs required to generate lift by engine-powered planes.[42] To Hanna it was like flying in a new dimension. Despite the heavy vibrations that shook the whole airframe as she slowly opened the throttle, the revolutionary control of her position in the airspace at once fascinated and thrilled her, while the machine's sensitivity and manoeuvrability was 'intoxicating!' 'I thought of the lark,' she wrote, 'so light and small of wing, hovering over the summer fields.'[43] Hanna had become the first woman in the world to fly a helicopter.

Later that year Charles Lindbergh returned to Germany, visiting

Bremen, and winning 'all hearts, wherever he went', Hanna fawned.[44] She felt honoured to demonstrate the helicopter for him, rising vertically, hanging poised in the air, reversing and landing slowly, 'as easy as a bird'.[45] Even years later she would glow with pride when recounting how impressed Lindbergh had been. For his part, Lindbergh would describe shaking hands with Hanna, while she kept the helicopter hovering beside him, as 'one of the most amazing moments' in his entire career.[46] Udet then took him to look round the Luftwaffe's Rechlin test centre which, although closed even to foreign attachés, opened its doors for this American celebrity whose sympathy towards the Nazi regime was well known. 'Germany is once more a world power in the air,' Lindbergh duly reported.[47] Hanna's superiors were delighted. Not long afterwards she demonstrated the helicopter for an audience of Wehrmacht and Luftwaffe generals, after which she was awarded the Military Flying Medal, once again the first woman to receive such an honour.

Although her race status was still unresolved, Melitta's name was seemingly sufficiently cleared by her marriage into the Stauffenberg clan for her to be employed by the state again. It helped that Hanna had set a precedent, too, being appointed to the Luftwaffe test centre at Rechlin in September 1937. Melitta was not only a test pilot, she was also a brilliant aeronautical engineer. In October she was seconded from Askania to the Luftwaffe's Technical Academy at Gatow airbase on the edge of Berlin, set beside woods leading down to Lake Wannsee. Here she was charged with the development of bomb-aiming devices and dive-sights for Stukas, the planes in which Udet had invested all his hopes for the Luftwaffe.

German engineers had realized that the best way to achieve accuracy in bombing was for pilots to aim their whole aircraft at the target, and release their bombs only at the last moment. The future role of the Luftwaffe, essentially as long-range artillery able to knock out precise targets such as bridges, railway junctions and airfield hangars ahead of advancing troops, was beginning to crystallize. Much of the initial work was theoretical, but Melitta aimed to prove the validity of her extensive mathematical calculations by undertaking her own test flights. She did not trust any of the other pilots with this work, feeling that she alone would know each machine's history, its past repairs or usual performance, and so be able to 'notice the very subtle changes in the plane that were needed to find the solution' to any given technical problem.[48]

Although Melitta had the advantage of having already worked on dive-brakes at DVL, her determination to conduct nosedives was met with derision by her male colleagues. When she proved effective, there was reluctant admiration. In true Nazi fashion, Kurt Wilde, the usually brilliant head of the department, even looked to biology for an explanation, speculating whether 'the blood composition of women – perhaps the ratio of white to red corpuscles . . . is more favourable for such dives than that of males, so that actually women are better fitted for such tests than men'.[49] Others, conversely, felt that Melitta must be a very 'masculine' type of woman. One colleague, Dr Franks, even felt obliged to defend Melitta's femininity, describing her as 'a highly strung artist' in her private life.[50] This was a reference to Melitta's clay modelling, which she continued with as a way to relax after work, sculpting head-and-shoulder portraits of the pilots and engineers she admired. She showed the results to Alexander, and to Paul von Handel when he visited. 'They were very impressive,' Paul felt, 'of great impact and extremely lifelike.'[51] For Franks, such artistry provided another possible explanation for Melitta's success as a military test pilot. 'Maybe this has given her the sensibility to fly better than others,' he pondered. 'Not just the concentration, but a sixth sense for feeling the subtleties of the plane.'[52]

In late October 1937, Melitta was finally awarded the honorary title of flight captain by Göring, in recognition of her latest work. She was proud of her new rank, and sent the official photograph to several friends, including Peter Riedel. She looks pleased but rather modest in the picture, the lace collar of her dark dress and the small bows on her shoes emphasizing her femininity. A bunch of long-stemmed roses seem forgotten in her hands. Melitta's

colleague, Richard Perlia, who was also being honoured, understood that the title came with strings as well as flowers. 'If one
wanted to stay working in the wonderful field of aviation, one
needed the help of the Herr Reichsminister and supreme commander of the Luftwaffe, Hermann Göring,' Perlia wrote. 'It was
he who awarded the title Flugkapitän. Refusal . . . would probably
have led to immediate punishment with a flight ban, and no one
wanted to risk this. By awarding the title, they kept us in line.'[53]
For Melitta, however, the honour also seemed to show that, finally,
she had been accepted by the new regime.

Melitta now found herself profiled across the German press as
'no sports girl type, but indeed a scientist and a lady'.[54] Such a
blaze of publicity went against her nature, but according to her
sister Jutta, 'she bore these ordeals . . . with humour'.[55] The story
that must have rankled most was the one carried in Askania's own
in-house magazine. 'In Germany, this high recognition has only
been awarded to one woman previously,' the article opened, referring to Hanna in the first recorded comparison of the two women.[56]
'We are delighted to be able to number [Melitta] amongst our
staff,' the article continued, noting that, as a woman, she was still
officially a civilian employee on secondment from their company.
Although now 'entrusted with carrying out particularly complicated flying and applied mathematical special duties', they added,
the company hoped that Melitta would 'continue to be able to
work for us successfully for many years to come'.[57]

Richard Perlia now reluctantly recognized that, if he was to
continue flying, he had to join the Luftwaffe, 'no matter what I got
myself into'.[58] Melitta and Hanna, conversely, not only lived to fly
but also, as ardent patriots, ached to serve their country – however
differently they perceived it. Yet, as women, they could not become
official Luftwaffe pilots even though they were designated flight
captains, and were not entitled to wear uniform. Melitta usually
turned up at Gatow in a dark trouser suit and beret, riding a bicycle across the airfield to the research buildings or the latest plane
she was to test. Her new title was therefore an important mark of
her authority, but although Melitta preferred to be known as

Flight Captain Schiller, rather than Countess von Stauffenberg, she never insisted that either title be used. Her public endorsement by the regime was reassuring, but her self-esteem had never been dependent on such outward markers. Hanna, the only other female pilot working directly with the Luftwaffe, took the opposite approach. She designed a uniform-like dark-blue skirt suit for herself, and had another made in brown. Despite having claimed to despise honours just two years earlier, she was still adamant that she should always be correctly addressed as 'Flight Captain'.

In the 1930s all pilots were courageous. 'The planes were not reliable,' Elly Beinhorn's son admitted. 'Bits broke off, there were emergency landings.'[59] The great risks associated with flight meant that there was deep comradeship among pilots. Jutta knew that Melitta did not share the political views of many of her colleagues but understood that, despite this, 'she always felt very strongly connected to her fellow pilots'. Since so few women flew, this rule applied even more to them. 'She always had a good relationship with other female pilots, and never saw them as competitors,' Jutta continued. 'If she met with the opposite sentiment from them, she disarmed it with hearty laughter; to do otherwise was simply not in her nature.'[60]

Although based at separate institutes, Melitta and Hanna were both working on the development of Stukas and their paths inevitably crossed at their respective airfields. Sharing many close contacts in sporting aviation as well as in the Luftwaffe, they sometimes also found themselves invited to the same public and private events. Most of the time they ignored each other or, if pushed, exchanged polite nods or terse work conversations. In fact, they shared so little small talk that neither was aware they had spent much of their childhoods in neighbouring parts of Germany and had both gone to school in Hirschberg.

Hanna hated the fact that Melitta was the better-qualified pilot of the two of them, and a highly respected engineer to boot, and she bridled at Melitta's air of intellectual superiority – something probably not helped by Melitta's 'hearty laughter' when met with a difference of opinion. As a result, on occasion Hanna was 'heard to belittle' Melitta's achievements, and later told friends that Melitta 'developed instruments that were used to seek and shoot at targets from a flying plane, as she told me . . . She tested them by nosedives [but] she never had the job to test planes, only to test instruments.'[61] Hanna also resented Melitta's social status as a countess, and disliked the way that she seemed to prefer being treated as an honorary man at work in her trouser suits, and a countess at home, rather than carving a space for herself as a new type of professional woman. Completely missing the fundamental discrimination of the Nazi regime, to Hanna, Melitta embodied the old values, hierarchies and prejudices that she felt it was time to sweep away. With nine years between them, Melitta 'was much older than me, though', Hanna reflected more happily.[62]

Melitta, meanwhile, rarely mentioned Hanna in conversation, as if refusing to acknowledge her as in any way an equal. To her mind Hanna might have a good instinct for flying gliders and a degree of charisma, but she had no apparent scientific or political understanding. For Melitta, Hanna represented the blithe focus on self-promotion that had enabled the Nazis to cast aside the conservative traditions of her country. Above all, as Melitta 'made no secret of her oppositional views', Richard Perlia remembered, while Hanna was an enthusiastic supporter of the Nazi regime, neither woman wanted to spend much time, or be associated, with the other.[63]

At the close of 1937, Hanna celebrated the wonderful year that had seen her promoted into the previously all-male club of flight captains by presenting her parents with a finely sculpted bronze eagle with outstretched wings. A plaque on its green marble plinth informed them that this was a gift in gratitude for their patience and faith in her dreams, 'presented by their daughter, Flugkapitän Hanna'.[64] It must have weighed heavily on Dr Willy Reitsch's shelf, given his steady opposition to his daughter's chosen career, but to Hanna it was a joyful marker of her evident success. Melitta's family mantelpieces were laden with more traditional, and yet more personal, trophies: the handsome busts of Alexander, Claus, and other friends and relatives that she had sculpted in clay and cast in bronze.* For Hanna the public was personal, and recognition was the measure of her life; for Melitta the private was all too public.

On New Year's Eve 1937, Joseph Goebbels' propaganda machine produced a film entitled *Deutsche Luftgeltung*, meaning (German Air Retribution). Four beautifully shot reels presented aerobatic displays above military bands in glorious sunshine, and the sound of soldiers' formation marching echoing loudly as Hitler inspects his troops. Hanna appears in several scenes, dressed in a white shirt and pale trench coat, her hairband failing to control her windswept curls. All smiles, she holds a flight chart while a tanned young man in shirtsleeves and sunglasses walks beside her. The scene looks like an aspirational fashion shoot. Then there are gliders taking off in the countryside, their shadows crossing a lake, pine forests and snowy cloud-wreathed mountain peaks. Noble music plays. Here is Hanna again, laughing gaily. Hot-air balloons open reel two, which covers that year's Nuremberg Rally. Planes flying in formation cast the rippling shadow of swastikas over the contours of the crowds. 'Comrades!' Göring addresses the nation at the end of the film. 'The year 1937 was a year of building up our air force. I thank you for your willing sacrifices, your diligence and your faith, by which we have achieved our given goal. The year 1938 will bring new requirements of us all. We will fulfil these through our faith and devotion to the Führer, to our people and to the Fatherland.'[65]

---

* Among the bronze busts attributed to Melitta is a wonderful self-portrait in which her flying cap seems to meld organically with her hair, as if she herself is part-machine. A small plaque states that Melitta presented this sculpture to Claus in 1942, but its provenance is unconfirmed.

5

HOVERING
1938

After years of poverty and uncertainty, at the beginning of 1938 Germany was, in Hanna's words, a 'dynamic and prosperous nation', at last 'seeing bread and making progress'.[1] Five years into Nazi rule, the country was flourishing. Unemployment was down, exports were up, national pride had been restored, and Hitler was enjoying the adulation of the majority of the German people – as well as some rather more apprehensive admiration from overseas. Although presenting the German Führer as a 'grim figure' in his biographical volume *Great Contemporaries*, Winston Churchill, then a backbench MP, conceded that Hitler had 'succeeded in restoring Germany to the most powerful position in Europe'.[2] At the same time, the young John F. Kennedy, then motoring through Germany, jotted in his diary that 'the new autostradas . . . are the finest roads in the world', although rather wasted outside America, he felt. Kennedy went on to visit a 'terribly interesting' exhibition on the development of aviation at the Deutsche Museum in Munich, before exploring the local nightclubs, which were, he recorded cautiously, 'a bit different'.[3] Nightlife in the big German cities was no longer as politically uninhibited as it had been during the Weimar cabaret years, but was still impressive, with live music, troupes of dancing girls and an earnest sense of optimism that reflected the mood of the country as a whole.

Hitler claimed that his country's economic problems had been solved by motorization. Germany had not only invested in the autobahns, it was now a world leader in aircraft and general motor technology. Melitta and her colleagues had been showcasing German engine-powered aeroplanes overseas for several years. Now German auto-engineering had also gained a world-class reputation, and in 1938 the country's car exports, on their own, would exceed its entire car production levels for 1932. These were the years when Germany dominated the European Grands Prix with superstar drivers like Bernd Rosemeyer and Rudolf Caracciola. At the end of January 1938, however, a tragedy on the autobahn seemed to some like a bad portent. It was also an incident that would bring Hanna and Melitta together once more.

Three years earlier, Bernd Rosemeyer had met Melitta and Hanna's mutual friend, the acclaimed pilot Elly Beinhorn, at the Czechoslovakian Grand Prix. Elly had congratulated the new world champion, garlanded with a huge wreath of oak leaves, on his victory. They danced together that night, and were married the following year. Footage shows them laughing and kissing, him in pale overalls, her in a polka-dot dress, headscarf and sunglasses. A true celebrity couple, both handsome and talented, although 'not interested in glamour' they were the toast of Nazi Germany, and a reluctant Rosemeyer soon found himself ordered to join the SS.[4] 'He had to be in the Party to get a licence to race,' his son Bernd later claimed.[5] Ten weeks after young Bernd was born, Rosemeyer achieved a new world land speed record on the autobahn between Frankfurt and Darmstadt. Moments later he lost control of his beautiful custom-made Auto Union Type C car, which skidded and became airborne before crashing into a bridge embankment. Thrown from the car, Rosemeyer died at the roadside. Hanna and Melitta rallied around Elly as condolences from prominent Nazis, including Hitler himself, poured in. But Elly struggled to grieve for her husband in private, as Rosemeyer was not granted the simple, non-political funeral that she had requested. Instead, SS troopers carried his coffin and several Party members 'came to be seen', even giving public speeches at the graveside.[6] According to the accounts of some of the mourners, Elly walked away in protest.

A week after Rosemeyer's funeral, Hanna was required to perform another public relations exercise. That February, Germany was showcasing a range of Mercedes-Benz sports cars as well as revealing plans for the forthcoming 'Volkswagen' to an international audience at the prestigious Berlin Motor Show. 'The story of the Berlin exhibition since National Socialism came to power,' the national press fawned, 'has been an uninterrupted triumph.'[7] Hitler wanted to use the 1938 show as more than a trade fair. It was to be a demonstration of German engineering excellence for unprecedented numbers of visitors. For this he needed a star attraction. Hanna was booked to head the programme: she was to be the first person in the world to fly a helicopter *inside* a building.

The theme of the motor show was Germany's lost colonies: 'at that time a much ventilated grievance', Hanna noted. In preparation, the great Deutschlandhalle sports stadium, then the world's largest arena, had been furnished with palm trees, flamingos, a carpet of sand and, in Hanna's words, 'a Negro village and other exotic paraphernalia'.[8] This was the scene she was to rise above in the Focke-Wulf Fw 61 helicopter: a symbol of German power and control.

At first Hanna was scheduled to make only the inaugural flight, after which the chief Focke-Wulf pilot, Karl Bode, was to take over. During a demonstration for Luftwaffe generals, however, knowing that the helicopter's sensitivity meant any slight miscalculation could take him sweeping into the audience, Bode refused to risk rising more than a few feet above the ground. It was safe, but hardly impressive enough for the crowds who would be looking down from the galleries of steeply tiered seating. Then, through no fault of Bode's, one of the propellers broke. 'It was dreadful,' Hanna told Elly. 'There were splinters from the rotor blade flying around and the flamingos were all creating.'[9] Once the blades had been replaced, Hanna took her turn. With typical insouciance, she lifted the helicopter well above the recommended height and hovered in the gods. Göring quickly ordered that she was to make all the motor show flights. Bode never forgave her.

Hanna's delight at winning another promotion quickly turned to dismay, however, when she saw the publicity for the show. Huge, garishly coloured posters presented the list of attractions as *Dancing Girls, Fakirs, Clowns, Blackamoors and* – last item – *Hanna Reitsch will fly the helicopter*.[10] Hanna had no issue with the cultural agenda – even after she discovered, to her evident surprise, that the 'negroes' who sat around the helicopter reading newspapers between rehearsals spoke perfect German. 'Most of them had been born in a circus troupe,' she commented on this apparent absurdity, 'and knew less, even, about the jungle than I!'[11] However, although she could never be described as publicity-shy, Hanna resented the way that such 'variety hall'-style billing, as she saw it, presented her as part of some socially dubious sideshow rather than rightly affiliating her with the main act: the triumphant rise of National Socialism. Hanna felt that both she and the serious business of flying had been debased. The prospect of the show now 'appalled' her, she told friends bitterly, but with Göring watching and the reputation of German technology at stake, there was nothing for it but to give the performance of her life.[12]

Everything went well during rehearsals. Hanna circled the banks of empty seating closely enough to give the audience a good view of her sitting at the controls in her puffy white shirtsleeves, her fair curls tucked into her leather flying cap. Then, picking up on the 'atmosphere of almost solemn tension' as she stepped up to the helicopter on the opening night, she was struck by the name painted on its silver fuselage, the *Deutschland*, and her heart 'lifted in greeting to my country'.[13] But when Hanna revved up the rotors she was horrified to discover that the machine refused to lift. The reputation of the Reich, her own career and, Hanna must have realized, possibly even her liberty, hung stuttering in the spotlights just a few inches above the floor. Surrounding her, watching every manoeuvre of both machine and pilot through a growing cloud of dirt and sand, were some 8,000 spectators, including many representatives of the international press.

Hanna was certain that the problem was caused by the helicopter's normally aspirated engine being starved of air by the breathing of the vast audience. Painful minutes passed while the technicians debated, but then the great hall's doors were opened. Hanna and the *Deutschland* immediately 'shot up to about twenty feet' and slowly rotated on the spot.[14] At first 'the audience followed the flight intently', but such a controlled display held little drama and the applause grew desultory.[15] At the end of the demonstration Hanna neatly lowered the machine with her head held high, executed a perfectly timed, stiff-armed Nazi salute, and landed safely on her mark. She had practised this countless times for Udet while he sat comfortably ensconced in an armchair, puffing at a cigar.

Hanna was vindicated, but the helicopter performance was still not the outstanding success that Udet had promised, and that both Göring and Hitler had expected. Hanna herself felt that the audience had grown bored. Among the seated crowd was Eric Brown, the son of the British Great War pilot who had first met Hanna at the 1936 Olympics. Since then, the two of them had exchanged a few letters. Now the young Scotsman was studying in Germany and was one of Udet's guests at the motor show. Eric felt that Hanna 'did extraordinarily well' and claimed that her 'very mediocre reception' was chiefly 'because she had blown all the ladies' hats off and disturbed everyone's hair'.[16] Whatever the cause, Hanna was quick to distance herself from the event, claiming that Udet had 'grossly overestimated the capacity of the general public to appreciate a purely technical achievement'.[17] For a pilot and showman of Udet's experience it was damning criticism from his rather nontechnical young starlet.

That evening Hanna renewed her acquaintance with Eric at a lavish party in Udet's small but well-appointed apartment in the most fashionable part of Berlin. Since the Olympics, the Great War ace had taken Eric under his wing, often inviting him over for a glass of wine and to meet some of the Luftwaffe people who constantly seemed to drift through in a fug of tobacco smoke. Udet was a 'cigar-smoking, champagne-drinking sort of chap', Eric noted with evident admiration. He 'had many lady friends', and indeed, 'regarded the whole world as his friend'.[18] But watching the German hero with his petite young protégée, Eric saw that Udet was 'quite overcome' by Hanna.[19] To Eric, Hanna was 'pretty, but not beautiful'.[20] He decided that Udet was not so much romantically struck by her, more that he simply admired a kindred spirit, 'someone like himself, who was born to fly'.[21] Hanna, however, Eric increasingly came to believe, was very ambitious, calculating, even pushy, deliberately manipulating Udet, and 'wrapping him round her little finger' to further her own career.[22]

Eric later admitted that he had been superficially drawn to the Nazi Party. He admired Udet and found Nazi Germany exciting, with its passion for aviation, dynamic leaders and mass rallies.[23] Picking up on his apparent sympathy, when Hanna talked with Eric it was constantly about her support for National Socialism. 'She felt strongly that the Treaty of Versailles had stripped Germany of pride as a nation,' Eric recalled, 'and that the only way to get this back was to support Hitler.'[24] While Eric greatly respected Hanna's skills and courage, he began to realize that he 'did not care for her particularly as a personality, and certainly not for her politics'.[25] As he steered their conversations round to safer subjects, he noticed that Hanna never spoke about other women, and 'only cared for men as a tool to achieve her objectives'.[26] Although they would stay in touch, Eric would later coolly characterize his relationship with Hanna as 'a semi-professional friendship'.[27]

That night, however, Eric and Hanna shared sympathetic glances at the after-show party, when Udet announced his favourite party game: inviting guests to fire a small .22 calibre pistol over their shoulders at a round target fixed to the wall behind them, seen only through a mirror. According to Eric, 'Hanna regarded it all as a superfluous sideshow,' but she went along with it anyhow.[28] They both did; there was little else to be done with good grace. To add to the challenge, neither Eric nor Hanna was tall enough to make use of the mirror on the wall, so they had to take their turns using a hand-held shaving mirror. Udet, naturally, was a 'terribly good' shot, but both Hanna and Eric also managed to hit the fringes of the target. Several of the other guests were not so fortunate, plugging their bullets into the wall, laughing as if they were simply playing Pin the Tail on the Donkey. It was turning into a 'riotous evening' but there would be no complaints from the neighbours of a leading – and very popular – Nazi general.[29] 'Heady stuff', Eric remembered, but 'typical of the mood pervading Nazi Berlin'.[30]

That mood was no respecter of boundaries. On 12 March, Hitler announced the *Anschluss*: the unification of Austria and

Germany, or the German annexation of its neighbour. Austria's chancellor, Kurt Schuschnigg, had been planning a referendum, expecting the people to support Austrian independence, but before this could take place the Austrian Nazi Party orchestrated a coup d'état. Wehrmacht troops entered the country as power was officially transferred to Germany.

The German public response was mainly positive, encouraged by press reports of 'rapturous' Austrians greeting the German troops with flowers, and of a people hoping that the Führer would bring his economic 'miracle' to Austria. This was also the picture painted by Hanna's Austrian uncle, Richard Heuberger, in his letters to his sister Emy. Richard had joined the Nazi Party in 1934 and supported the annexation. His son, Helmut, was a keen member of the Hitler Youth and had spent the day among the cheering crowds. A plebiscite held the following month officially ratified the Anschluss, with an incredible 99.7 per cent of voters declared to be in favour. 'Although not achieved by those methods in which I believe, the Anschluss is now complete,' the first Austrian Federal President, Karl Renner, announced. It was, he added, 'true redress for the humiliations of 1918 and 1919', and as such to be greeted with 'a joyful heart'.[31] The unification of Germany and Austria had been specifically prohibited under the Treaty of Versailles, and yet Hitler's first step towards the creation of a greater German Reich was accepted with only mild statements of protest from foreign governments.

After the Anschluss, the situation for German and Austrian Jews, and others out of political favour, became increasingly difficult. It was now clear that Jews were no longer welcome in their country, but international borders were already closing against them. 'By the thousands, citizens of the civilized world . . . voiced sincere indignation at the persecution,' one Jewish resident of Berlin later wrote. 'But with few honourable exceptions, they fell silent when it came to rescuing the victims.'[32] In Germany itself there was a deeper silence still. Hitler had always faced some dissent, but after his leading opponents were arrested or killed, such voices had been largely hushed. That March, Fey von Hassell, the aristocratic daughter of the German ambassador to Rome, was struck by how visiting German friends would now always look over their shoulder before saying anything critical about the Nazis. It had become an automatic gesture, and even had a nickname, *der deutsche Blick*: the German glance. 'Only the people arrested are considered decent these days,' Fey learned.[33] Quietly, however, some members of the conservative opposition to the Nazi regime were already beginning to organize, and Fey's father, Ulrich von Hassell, was among them.

Hanna shut her eyes to what was happening to her neighbours who were Jewish or communist, or otherwise inferior *Untermenschen*. Brought up to accept both anti-Semitism and political disengagement as the norm, she felt that politics had nothing to do with her. Instead, she focused on her gliding, setting several records for altitude, speed and flight duration during May and June, which added to her international reputation.[34]

Melitta could not afford to be so cavalier, but neither did she wish to raise her public profile. Like thousands of others, Alexander was now enrolled in the volunteer reserves. Although honoured as a flight captain and working again for her country, Melitta's legal status was still uncertain. It is little wonder that fellow female pilots now referred to her 'excessive modesty'. Given her aviation skills, 'she is far too little known to the public', one friend wrote, 'as she likes to remain in the background as far as possible'.[35]

But Melitta could not stay out of the headlines altogether. In early July 1938, while Alexander was taking part in military exercises as a reserve, Melitta was nominated to participate in the German coastal reliability engine-powered flight competition, designed to test a pilot's ability to fly along coastal routes and deal with challenging wind conditions. It was the first time women had been allowed to compete in this event, albeit in a separate category from the men. Melitta was to fly a Klemm 25, a type of light leisure and training aircraft that Udet thought 'looked like a seabird' against the cliffs.[36] It was fun to fly but not very sturdy. Unlike many pilots Melitta was not superstitious, and she 'laughed heartily' when she saw her given competition number, 13, marked out on the nose of her plane, and even more at its call sign, *E-HIN*, which in the Austrian dialect means 'kaput'.[37]

When poor visibility delayed take-off, Melitta and her fellow competitors took refuge in black humour as they sat chatting around a half-empty coffee pot in the clubhouse. As it was humid as well as overcast, they even managed a quick swim in the lake beyond the airfield. When they were finally given clearance, Melitta and her navigator were the last to start, and saw the 'whole flight of pretty yellow aircraft swarming in front of us'.[38] Nevertheless, fuelled largely on coffee, cake and acid drops, the crew of 13 came in first at every stage. 'Victory was ours!' Melitta wrote triumphantly for the *Askania* magazine.[39]

Like Hanna's, Melitta's heart was more in flying than politics, and in the event she could not resist the chance to shine. After dinner that evening the leader of the National Socialist Flying Corps 'spoke about the higher purpose of this type of national competition', but Melitta admitted only to being 'very proud' as she received her roses and the winner's silver plaque.[40] Flying was her raison d'être, but she still had no wish to draw any more attention to herself than was necessary.

The following month, the Nazis announced that residency permits for all foreign nationals in Germany, including German Jews of foreign origin, were being cancelled, subject to reissue. More than 250,000 German Jews had already left Germany and Austria, and a further 300,000 were actively seeking asylum, causing an immigration crisis across Europe. The Nazi state, meanwhile, was profiting from the seizure of Jewish property and businesses. Hitler had helped millions of Germans back into work, but while miraculous economic growth was being celebrated, German Jews were struggling to survive. 'What everybody is striving for, in despair and often beyond that . . .' a typical letter stated starkly in one of the last issues of the German-Jewish journal *Der Morgen*, was just 'to be able to continue living'.[41]

As 1938 progressed, international opinion turned further against Germany. Peter Riedel found a tense atmosphere when he represented his country at the Elmira gliding championships in

New York that July. He had been the darling of the USA the year before when, sponsored by the International Soaring Society of America, he became the world gliding champion. But in 1938 he was sponsored by the German Aero Club and his glider sported the 'national markings', a red and black swastika, on either side of its vertical tail stabilizer.[42] It was rather a shock for Peter, now serving as assistant air attaché in Washington, to discover that he was regarded by many as 'a dedicated Nazi'.[43]

Peter had joined the Party in 1933, arguing that he could see no alternative. 'The Republic seemed so weak and helpless,' he contended. 'It was obvious that the democratic government had failed . . . the country was going to hell, people were starving.'[44] Despite his conversations with Melitta, when what he perceived as national duty had gone hand in hand with personal promotion it had been enough to win his backing for the Nazis, regardless of their less than palatable policies.

Hanna had also found duty and career conveniently aligned, and was keen to see the best in the regime that was rewarding her so well. 'Never before had the welfare of the masses been so effectively catered for, nor the working man made to feel such a vital part of his country,' she wrote, apparently unaware or unconcerned that working German Jews, Roma and others were specifically excluded from such care.[45] The 1938 Nuremberg Rally showed how many of her compatriots had reached a similar conclusion; a powerful mixture of enthusiasm and fear seemed to coexist in the Fatherland. 'I saw the spirit of Nazi Germany flowing through the ancient streets of Nuremberg like a river that had burst its dams,' the American journalist Virginia Cowles reported. 'A million red, white and black swastikas fluttered from the window ledges, and the town, swollen to three times its normal size, resounded to the ring of leather boots and blazed with a bewildering array of uniforms.' In a stadium packed with 200,000 spectators, Cowles watched as the crowd responded to their Führer, 'swaying back and forth, chanting "Sieg Heil" in a frenzy of delirium . . . tears streaming down people's cheeks'. It was only when she heard the 'sudden whine of a silver-winged fighter' that she found herself 'jerked back to the grim reality of 1938'.[46]

Like Peter before her, Hanna soon found that overseas perspectives on National Socialism were very different. It was September when she travelled to the USA, to give an aerobatics demonstration at the famous Cleveland Air Races in the new German *Habicht*, or Hawk: a glider designed by Hans Jacobs. If the name of her glider seemed ominous, Hanna refused to see it, claiming it was more 'like the true dove of peace, rather than the hawk after which it was named'.[47] Representing Germany at this event some years earlier, Udet had been photographed shaking hands with Colonel Rickenbacker, the most successful American pilot of the Great War, showing the world that 'honourable opponents can be honourable friends'.[48] Now, Hanna was disconcerted to find what she called 'strong anti-German feeling' in the United States.[49]

Peter came to meet Hanna when her ship docked at New York. 'She was like a sister to me,' he wrote, and he wanted to be there to discuss the changing political atmosphere and lend his support.[50] Used to being fêted, Hanna did not like her cool reception, but she was now an experienced ambassador, friendly, enthusiastic and 'full of sparkling energy'.[51] Her wonderful gliding performances and warm impromptu speeches soon won her American audience round. 'Tiny, blonde, blue-eyed and addicted to tea at breakfast', the *New York Times* reported, Hanna had gesticulated towards a skyscraper with a piece of toast as she promised, in her best English, 'I am come over here next year with a machine and land on a building.'[52] Hanna was impressed by American directness and good humour, their appreciation of effort rather than just results, the elegance of the women and the chivalry of the men, as well as the general level of gender equality she found. Nevertheless, although she favourably compared the USA to a Europe 'intellectually overburdened with centuries-old cultural legacy', she still had some reservations.[53] 'The American's uncomplicated acceptance of life-as-it-comes,' she decided, 'exposes him to the dangers of absorbing uncritically the opinions served up to him by press and radio.'[54] Her own thoughts, she claimed, without apparent irony, belonged to 'the wind, the clouds and the stars, where the game of political intrigue is unknown'.[55] Hanna may have believed herself above politics, but the Cleveland Air Races ended 'amid disturbing news from Czechoslovakia', as she put it, when a telegram ordered the gliding team to return without delay.[56]

While Hanna was competing in the USA, Neville Chamberlain was flying to the Bavarian Alps to hear Hitler's concerns about the security of the German minority in the Czech Sudetenland. Although Chamberlain considered Hitler's attitude 'unreasonable', the British prime minister was still hoping to prevent conflict in Europe.[57] 'It might be possible . . . to write up Hitler as an apostle of Peace,' Britain's ambassador Nevile Henderson had written the week before, cautioning that 'We make a great mistake when our press persists in abusing him.'[58] Despite some hostility in the papers, there were many more appeasing editorials, however, and the Führer was not unaware of potential British sympathy. Even among those opposed to fascism, many people could not bear to contemplate the possibility of another conflict just twenty years after the horror of the Great War, in which nearly every family had lost a husband, a brother or a son. A week later Chamberlain and his entourage returned for a second meeting. On arrival at Cologne aerodrome, a band greeted them with 'God Save the King', and at their beautiful hotel on the banks of the Rhine the bedrooms and bathrooms had been filled with the products of Cologne: 'scent and soap, bath salts and shaving requisites'.[59] But although Hitler came to meet Chamberlain personally, it quickly became clear that he was in 'an uncompromising mood'.[60] Once the British leader had confirmed that he would negotiate the peaceful transfer of Sudetenland to Germany, Hitler extended his claim to Hungarian and Polish territory and 'declined flatly' to consider alternative proposals.[61]

While Chamberlain was soaking in a cologne-scented bath, Melitta was facing her own small diplomatic crisis. Some days earlier, at next to no notice, the National Socialist Flying Corps had suddenly nominated Melitta and Elly to be the two German representatives at the 'grand opening' of Chigwell aerodrome, in

Essex. They packed that evening and prepared to fly out. Melitta would later sardonically call her report on the event 'Flight to England, with Incidents'.[62]

Chigwell airfield was being placed at the disposal of the British Women's Air Reserve. That July the British air minister, Sir Kingsley Wood, had invited the country's thousands of amateur flying clubs to join the newly created Civil Air Guard, and so form Britain's third line of air defence in the event of war. Within a month over 20,000 would-be pilots had enrolled for courses, and women were encouraged to sign up on equal terms with men. 'The menace is the woman who thinks she ought to be flying a high-speed bomber, when she really has not the intelligence to scrub the floor of a hospital,' one critic wrote indignantly in the *Aeroplane* magazine.[63] Even when the publicity was positive, it was still steeped in the casual sexism of the day. 'Beauty Queen joins Civil Air Guard' was the headline that followed the sign-up of Veronica Volkersz, who admittedly always flew with her powder compact to hand but was also a highly skilled pilot and became the first British woman to ferry a jet.[64] The following year these women would be among the first female pilots of Britain's Air Transport Auxiliary, or ATA, delivering RAF and Fleet Air Arm aircraft between factories and airfields.

Keen to show off both German planes and German female pilots, Göring selected Melitta and Elly for their skills as aviators as well as their evident attractiveness, to take part in the celebratory Chigwell aerial displays. Melitta was to fly over in a Klemm 35 open sports monoplane, which she considered a 'nice little touring aircraft', and Elly in her Messerschmitt 108 Taifun, both emblazoned with a swastika on the tail. Their mission was officially to extend the hand of friendship among the international community of aviators and, unofficially, to show British women how it was done.[65] Tired of her latest studies, Melitta was pleased to exchange her exams at the ministry for an opportunity to fly overseas but, fully aware of what she described as 'the highly charged political situation', she also steeled herself for 'unpleasant surprises'.[66]

Things started badly when Melitta's plane was reported overdue.

She had left Berlin punctually, 'like a shot out of a gun', she claimed, stopping at Düsseldorf and Brussels, and by noon the next day she had landed in Romford. Unfortunately she had failed to complete the required customs formalities at Croydon or Heston en route. 'One only gets to understand a foreign country gradually,' she later wrote, 'especially if everything goes wrong at first.'[67] It took five hours to sort out the necessary papers, by which time the press had had a field day with facetious reports that Melitta might be swimming the Channel, and of signals sent to passing shipping to search for 'a small German plane with swastika markings' and fish her out.[68] 'There must be some people who like to read about themselves in the newspapers. Yet others feel particularly at ease in the company of reporters,' Melitta continued drily, perhaps thinking of Hanna. 'Both these pleasures had been prepared for me this afternoon. It is an effort to smile in spite of this.'[69]

Later Melitta considered how selflessly event organizer Gabrielle Patterson had waited all afternoon for her arrival, despite not being able to contact her husband. Did this show her 'remarkable spirit', Melitta mused, or, thinking of Alexander, 'are English husbands so much more patient than others?'[70] She was relieved when she finally found Elly, who helped her to see the funny side of things. But Elly had caught sight of Chamberlain at Heston airport, on his way to Germany, and had noticed how restrained the public applause for him had been. Both women knew that good relations between their country and Britain were crucial at this moment, and Melitta, with her mind on the noble Junker ideals and traditions, was determined to bring honour to a Germany she still saw as greater than the Nazi Reich.

The next day the crowds and press alike were hugely impressed by the German performances. Melitta included several loops in her routine, despite the fact that her plane was not designed for aerobatics, and Elly gave 'an excellent display', particularly impressing the British female pilots, who 'had never seen a woman fly such a powerful aircraft before'.[71] On landing, both women answered questions about 'every detail' of their planes, and then posed for photographs, carefully leaning against the flank of the Taifun, where the huge 'D' for *Deutsche* was painted, rather than beside the swastika on the tail. 'It is no exaggeration to say that the world is awaiting with anxiety the message which Hitler has to deliver,' ambassador Henderson had written earlier that month.[72] In the absence of any news from the British PM's latest meeting with the German Führer, however, what better photo opportunity could there be than Mrs Gabrielle Patterson in a floral dress, founder of the British Women's National Air Reserve, chatting away to two pretty young German pilots in cotton skirts and light woollen cardigans, Melitta still wearing her trademark leather flying cap.

What followed next was 'an interesting example of how rumours get about', the British press later reported.[73] Stories were circulating that Melitta and Elly had been ordered to call their embassy and, should they not be able to get through, to report there in person immediately. The telephone having been cut off since that morning, the two German aviatrixes quickly prepared to leave for London, giving rise to enormous press speculation about the international situation. Might the women's recall be sympto-matic of degenerating relations between the two nations, and the disconnected telephone line symbolic of a wider breakdown in communications? Nervous excitement grew around the possibility of being the first to hear the news, and break the story, that the whole country was dreading. Reporters rang their offices ahead in anticipation of further updates.

In fact, it was Alexander's eagerness to arrange a date with his wife before she flew home that had inadvertently almost caused an international incident. He had been temporarily seconded to London on academic work and had been surprised to read about Melitta's unexpected visit to Chigwell in the British papers, whose subsequent reports wryly concluded, 'We trust that the dinner went off satisfactorily.'[74] Melitta bit her tongue and spent a long day with Alexander touring London architecture and art galleries. He 'spares me nothing', she wrote, betraying her desperation to satisfy what she called her 'natural need for tranquillity' after the press storm surrounding her visit.[75] It was with some relief that she left Britain for what she called 'the borderless sea of the air' the following day.[76]

Less than a week after Melitta flew back to Germany, the British, Italian and French heads of government formally agreed to Nazi Germany's annexation of the Czech Sudetenland, under what became known as the Munich Agreement. Chamberlain famously declared that the arrangement guaranteed 'peace for our time'. The following day, 1 October 1938, German troops marched into their new territory. Claus von Stauffenberg was among them. An imminent war seemed to have been averted, but at the cost of Czechoslovakian national security, Soviet faith in the Western powers, and the potential overthrow of Hitler by rebellious senior German army officers who had been relying on a broader European show of strength. Five days later Winston Churchill told the House of Commons that the settlement was 'a total and unmitigated defeat'. 'You were given the choice between war and dishonour,' he continued prophetically. 'You chose dishonour, and you will have war.'

6

DESCENT
1938–1939

Within a fortnight of the Munich Agreement, it became clear that Hitler wished not only to embrace those ethnic Germans living abroad within the expanding borders of the Third Reich, but also to exclude anyone insufficiently 'Aryan'. Melitta was still waiting for confirmation of her legal status and that of her family, and it was clear that the rules were getting tighter following Germany's declaration that Jews deemed to be of foreign descent were to have their residency permits revoked. Many countries were already panicking about the mass influx of Jewish refugees, and Poland's government announced that after the end of the month they would no longer accept German Jews of Polish descent as citizens. As a result, on 26 October 1938, 12,000 such Jews were arrested across Germany, stripped of their property, and herded onto trains for the border. Poland refused to admit them and, although the Polish Red Cross provided some humanitarian aid, conditions in the makeshift camps were soon squalid. Among the deportees were the parents of Herschel Grynszpan, a young German Jew who was living in France without papers. A few days later, distraught at this latest persecution of his family and community, Grynszpan bought a gun. Asking to speak to an official in the German Embassy in Paris, he shot dead the third secretary, Ernst vom Rath.* Grynszpan's act provided the pretext Hitler had been waiting for

---

* As Ernst vom Rath was well known to be gay, it has been suggested that Grynszpan acted after a lover's quarrel. Fears of a scandal prevented a Nazi show trial. Grynszpan insisted his motive was to raise awareness of the persecution of German Jews. Although vom Rath had expressed regret for Jewish suffering, he had maintained that anti-Semitic laws were necessary.

to encourage a massive pogrom against Jews across Germany and Austria.

On 9 November, out-of-uniform SA paramilitary thugs started to smash and loot Jewish homes and shops, identifiable by the white-painted names on their windows. The police and fire authorities stood by, making no attempt to intervene unless non-Jewish properties were threatened. More than a thousand synagogues were set on fire and 7,000 businesses attacked. The smashed glass that littered the streets led to the event becoming known as *Kristallnacht*. By evening Jewish families were being dragged from their homes. Between 90 and 150 people were killed, with many others badly beaten, threatened and spat on.

Hanna was on the annual Darmstadt Institute work outing that day, and she witnessed an elderly couple 'protesting and struggling' as they were forced out of their home, still in their nightclothes. She was shocked. 'People were jeering at them,' she recalled. A moment later she witnessed shop windows being smashed, and then 'some children coming noisily down the street, dragging behind them a Jewish hearse', which they 'chopped to bits with an axe, and then pushed into the river'.[1] Hanna's immediate thought was that this must be a 'Bolshevik uprising' and she shouted for the police. When she realized the truth, she called for restraint, asking the children's parents to stop the destruction, and loudly declaring that 'the Führer would weep if he knew such things were being done in his name'.[2] One of her more sympathetic colleagues, the glider designer Hans Jacobs, bundled Hanna away through the smell of burning, the ashes and rubble, before the growing crowd could turn against them. Later, she told friends that she had been attacked and 'could hardly escape'.[3] She had been with over a hundred Darmstadt employees that evening, but only half a dozen had shown any distress and some, Jacobs noted with disgust, 'were even excited and approved of the violence'.[4]

Hanna was appalled by the events she had witnessed. Soon afterwards she and Jacobs were taken before a committee of local Party officials to explain their apparent sympathy for the Jews. Risking their careers, both refused to retract their condemnation of the violence, but they were released nevertheless. Aircraft designers and test pilots of their skill and status were not easy to replace. It was a relief for Hanna when her 'adored' uncle, Friedrich von Cochenhausen, a lieutenant general in the Luftwaffe, assured her that the horror of Kristallnacht had not been planned.[5] An order by Goebbels for an isolated and discreet attack on one subversive synagogue had been misunderstood, he told her, and the violence had escalated as the German people spontaneously vented their anger against their Jewish neighbours. As the country's leader, Hitler was reported to be quietly shouldering the blame.

Hanna's sympathetic support of her Jewish friend, Joachim Küttner, shows that she was not ignorant of the Nazi state's growing anti-Semitism, but she was happy to accept her uncle's defence of the regime despite having witnessed the worst pogrom in Germany's history. Her refusal to retract her condemnation of the Kristallnacht violence was brave, but it was also a testament to how secure she felt personally in the Third Reich. She simply refused to believe that Hitler or other Party leaders had known about or condoned – let alone incited – such mob violence, and she chose not to question too far. Hanna had aligned her honour with the Führer, and she could not countenance the idea that he was unworthy. Fortunately for her, life offered pleasant distractions such as the Paris Air Show, and a reception held in her honour by the American–German Gliding Association later that month. A visit to Libya, then still under Italian colonial rule, followed. It was easier to study thermal wind currents in North Africa than disquieting political trends at home.* For Hanna, life continued much as it had before but, from this point on, her belief in the moral authority of the Nazi regime was a matter of active choice against a growing body of evidence.

---

* Although delighted by the Libyan children, the hospitality, and the 'dreamy tenderness' of the women, Hanna's racism made her fear the men. Her 'imagination was busy with blood and the glint of curving steel', and when she accepted a local invitation, she wrote, she found the 'animal smell, which the Arab carries with him, particularly disturbing'. See Hanna Reitsch, *The Sky My Kingdom* (2009), p. 173.

For many others, Kristallnacht would prove a turning point, opening their eyes to the true nature of National Socialism. In early 1938 many German Jews had chosen to hope that the worst persecution was over. Jewish contributions to popular culture, the press, the law and much business had been eliminated. Jews knew they were no longer equal citizens, but beyond that, one Berliner later recorded: 'Hitler's threats were so utterly implausible that we regarded them as unreliable guides to future conduct. They were literally incredible.'[6] After 9 November, however, the situation for Jews inside Germany became much worse. An estimated 30,000 Jewish citizens were arrested and sent to the concentration camps of Sachsenhausen, Dachau and Buchenwald where, one survivor later testified, they were 'frozen, starved, humiliated'.[7] Release was conditional on emigration. Over 2,000 would die while still interned. The Jewish community as a whole, meanwhile, was required to pay a collective fine of one billion Reichsmarks to cover the costs of the Kristallnacht damage: damage which had been inflicted upon them. Not long after, Jews were forbidden access to the theatre, cinema and cultural events, and were segregated on trains; they were being isolated and dehumanized. Some later asserted that 'the violence of [Kristallnacht] conditioned the German people to condone brutality', leading directly to the Holocaust.[8]

Melitta had never considered herself to be Jewish but she knew that the state might, and Kristallnacht had shown that it was not only her career or even her citizenship that was at stake; she and her family faced the risk of being deported and possibly murdered. Melitta never considered leaving her country; that would have gone against her deep patriotic belief in a Germany greater than the Third Reich, a Germany to which she felt she owed allegiance. Unlike Hanna, however, she knew she was in no position to publicly express her horror about the pogrom.

Alexander and his younger brother, Claus, did not feel so constrained. Alexander felt that the patriotism and sense of personal honour he held dear were being misused to create a climate that encouraged division, hatred and violence, while any dissent was interpreted as potentially treasonous criticism of the regime. Above all, he was disgusted at being surrounded by people who perpetuated Nazi lies, either through their own warped convictions or from fear of speaking out and the very real risk of indefinite detention. Determined to resist such intimidation and coercion, he again began to voice his opposition, particularly in regard to the Nazis' view of history and their racial doctrine. 'He was not careless,' his daughter later stated, but rather deliberately committed to affirming his resistance wherever possible.[9]

Claus took a different approach. He had never approved of the democratic Weimar Republic and, not in principle opposed to dictatorship, he had welcomed Hitler's strong leadership. He also supported many early Nazi policies, such as the reintroduction of conscription and the fight against communism. Casually anti-Semitic, he had not objected to limiting Jewish control of the arts and publishing, or the expulsion of non-German Jews. Yet he had doubts about the regime, too. Claus did not believe in what he considered to be 'the lie that all men are equal', and felt that natural hierarchies should be respected. In his opinion, the jumped-up 'petty bourgeois' Hitler had 'exceeded all bounds of hubris'.[10] Knowing that the sort of 'so-called society people' typified by Claus presented a potential conservative resistance, at the 1938 Nuremberg Rally Hitler had described them as having 'old and decadent blood'. 'These people are sometimes called, by those who don't understand, "the upper classes",' he continued. 'In fact, they are simply the result of a sort of miscarriage, of bad breeding. They are infected by cosmopolitan thoughts and have no backbone.'[11] Now Claus defied Hitler, condemning the Kristallnacht violations of law and decency that had 'shocked and disgusted him'.[12] He felt his doubts about the regime and its leader had been confirmed.

The responses of the wider world to Kristallnacht were mixed. Having witnessed 'frenzied Nazis' destroying much of Jewish Berlin, the American journalist Louis P. Lochner attended a Propaganda Ministry press conference the next morning. There he was incensed to hear Goebbels announce that 'all the accounts that have come to your ears about alleged looting and destruction of Jewish property are a stinking lie. Not a hair of a Jew was disturbed.'[13] Few people believed such statements. Britain's ambassador, Nevile Henderson, felt that the 'disgusting exhibition' had 'shocked all decent Germans as much as it did the outside world'.[14] In the USA, a horrified Peter Riedel wrote that 'the reaction of Heinrich Himmler and Joseph Goebbels made me ashamed for the first time of being German . . . I hated them and their brutal, organized bullies.'[15] Ulrich von Hassell, the German ambassador in Italy, also recorded his disgust at the 'vile persecution', noting in his diary that 'there is no doubt that we are dealing with an officially organized anti-Jewish riot . . . truly a disgrace!'[16] His daughter, Fey, called the attacks 'true barbarism!'[17] Hassell would spend the next six months scurrying between Henderson, who was pro-appeasement, and various Nazi chiefs, trying to prevent war. The brutality of Kristallnacht had changed the political climate but few could predict the horrors that lay ahead. It is 'unimaginable' that Jews in Germany 'will all be lined up against the wall one day . . . or that they will be locked up in giant concentration camps', the Italian Embassy in Berlin reported, tacitly recognizing the violence of Nazi German anti-Semitism.[18] Yet not one country broke off diplomatic relations with Germany, opened its borders to refugees, or imposed sanctions. While peace was still a possibility, no country wanted to provoke a political crisis.

That autumn Winston Churchill famously argued that 'the prime factor of uncertainty in the world today is the menace from the air'.[19] Germany was now so confident in its renewed air power that a 1938 Berlin music-hall joke claimed, 'the English may have so many planes that the sky is black with them, and the French ones are so numerous that you can't see the sun for them; but when Hermann Göring presses the button, the birds themselves have got to walk.'[20] But the skies were also a source of vital intelligence. It was a German, General Werner von Fritsch, then commander-in-chief of the Wehrmacht, who predicted that 'the military organization with the best aerial reconnaissance will win the next war' – which was ironic, given that it was the British who would lead the field.

The British chief of air intelligence at MI6, responsible for gathering information from overseas, was the charmingly named yet 'superbly anonymous' Frederick Winterbotham, better known to his colleagues as 'Cloak and Dagger Fred'.[21] A regular visitor to Germany throughout the 1930s, where he posed as a Nazi sympathizer, Winterbotham had been secretly monitoring the country's rearmament programme. In November 1938, a week after Kristallnacht, he appointed a tall, 'wolfish', middle-aged Australian pilot called Sidney Cotton to his team. After the First World War, Cotton had answered an advertisement in the *Aeroplane* magazine for pilots to fly over Newfoundland, spotting seals for culling.* Later he took aerial photographs for a map-making firm, using his legs to hold the stick steady while pointing a large plate camera over the side of his open cockpit. Over the next few years he and his photographer girlfriend, Patricia Martin, improved the technique until they were expert.

Winterbotham and MI6 now set Cotton up as an entrepreneur, providing him with a beautiful, state-of-the-art Lockheed aircraft in 'exquisite duck-egg green'. The colour was unusual in an era when most private aircraft were silver, but it ensured that the plane was practically invisible against the sky from below.[22] After some practice flights over France and North Africa, it was in this plane that Cotton started regular visits to Berlin, ostensibly on behalf of his aeronautical and colour film businesses. Having caused quite a stir with his elegant plane, he was introduced to some senior Nazis, leading to an invitation to photograph Göring at his country house. Cotton wrote that Göring was dressed like Robin Hood with his 'velvet knickerbockers, shoes with gold buckles and a sleeveless leather hunting jacket'.[23] He bit his tongue,

---

* While in this role, Cotton made friends with an eccentric fur-trapper and his family. Eating in his remote Newfoundland cabin, Cotton asked how his host managed to serve fresh peas. The trapper explained that he filled his baby's washbasin with salt water and peas, and let the Arctic winds freeze it over. His name was Clarence Birdseye.

however, as Göring showed him round his house and art treasures, even demonstrating his enormous model railway, which, Cotton noticed, had small Stuka aeroplanes on a track overhead, able to release wooden bombs at the flick of a switch.* Disappointingly, however, they did not dive.

In January 1939, a Party memorandum was issued, stating that Nazi policy towards the Jews was one of emigration. Less than a week later Hitler's so-called 'prophecy speech' to the Reichstag directly proposed the 'annihilation' of European Jewry. Still without news about her 'Aryan' status application for herself and her siblings, Melitta was keeping her head down at work while throwing herself into the enjoyment of every spare moment with Alexander. 'Due to the bleak backdrop,' her sister Jutta later wrote, these months were 'lived more intensely and as a result were happy.'[24]

Melitta usually made her weekly commute from her work in Berlin to see Alexander in Würzburg by plane, but now she also bought a car: a beautiful two-seater, four-cylinder-engine Fiat 500 *Topolino*, or Little Mouse. It was not exactly a convertible but it had a folding canvas top. Sometimes she and Alexander would drive to the Stauffenberg family residence at Lautlingen in the beautiful Swabian Alps for weekends of field sports and country walks in the richly wooded hills. Whenever possible they tried to coincide their visits with Claus and Nina, Berthold and Mika and their growing families. Claus and Nina already had three sons, the eldest of whom, another Berthold named after his uncle, was six years old. Melitta loved giving him exhilarating rides in the back of her Topolino, 'sitting on nothing', as he remembered it, while she tore round the country roads at speeds 'typical for a pilot'.[25] The young Berthold dutifully loved his uncle Alexander who was 'remarkably cordial' and 'of a poetic nature', but he adored his rather wilder aunt. Melitta did not just have a car, unusual though this was for a woman: she was also a pilot and an artist, she went

---

* Although Göring's house was an Allied target, it was Göring himself who eventually blew it up, on 28 April 1945.

hunting, sailing and could fire a gun. She was, her nephew felt, 'a woman who could do just about anything!' and he 'admired her completely'.[26]

All the children loved Melitta, not only because she was exciting to be around, but also because 'she treated children like people and not like babies', one of her nieces would later say.[27] But when Nina asked Melitta whether she and Alexander were planning a family of their own, Melitta blushed, lowered her face and said softly only that that was the plan. There was already enormous state pressure on 'Aryan' women in Nazi Germany to have babies. The first *Mutterkreuz* (Mother's Cross of Honour) for a woman who had raised four or more children was awarded that May, and Hitler would later become official godfather to every tenth child in such families. Still in legal limbo, Melitta and Alexander may not have wished to start a family, or they may not have been able to. In any case, Melitta was committed to her flying career and could not countenance giving it up. 'I just can't stop flying,' she told friends. 'I can't help it.'[28] This was something Hanna understood. 'Hanna was a fanatical aviatrix,' a fellow female pilot recorded, 'and could not bear to spend a day without flying.'[29] Melitta and Hanna were both exceptional women, and children were just not on their radar. When male pilots took out their wallets and showed her photographs of their wives and children, Hanna would tell them 'it was hard, very hard, to deny myself this fortune', but stoically explained that she 'had to do it, to completely dedicate myself to flying'.[30]

Alexander was also absolutely dedicated to his career, and increasingly obsessed by the poems of late antiquity. In March, while the Wehrmacht marched further into Czechoslovakia, in pursuit, it was said, of justice rather than war, Alexander's Würzburg University exempted him from military service, and sent him to Greece on a study trip. With his crisp white shirts and pale trousers, windswept hair and earnest face, Alexander was the epitome of a classics lecturer removed from the action and set down among ancient ruins. Although anxiously following events with the Luftwaffe, when Melitta could secure some leave she joined her husband on the Greek mainland. Unlike Germany's desperate Jews, she had no problem securing her travel documents to leave the country. A photograph taken by Alexander shows her smiling brightly in the spring sunshine but well wrapped up in tights and scarf, her short chestnut hair now curled and set – it must have felt strange not to have to force it under a flying cap every day. Perched on top of a stony outcrop in the mountains, she seems to be surveying the landscape below, map in hand, like a true navigator.

Melitta must have spent many hours studying maps that spring. Back at home, the state-controlled news was once again portraying the invasion of a neighbouring country, this time Czechoslovakia rather than Austria, as a welcomed intervention. Soon there was talk of restoring parts of Poland to the Fatherland, including the areas of Silesia where Melitta had grown up and which had been ceded to Poland in 1921. Danzig, where Melitta's parents, Michael and Margarete Schiller, were now living as part of the German majority in the city, was also being considered.* For once Melitta fully approved of Nazi policy, welcoming what she hoped would be the restoration of her childhood home to German governance. Few outside Germany saw such expansionist ambitions in such a positive light.

At the end of June, Sidney Cotton and his British co-pilot descended into Berlin's Tempelhof airport to find it bedecked with black and crimson Nazi flags, and the airfield surrounded by anti-aircraft guns. Watching a dozen armed soldiers running across the tarmac towards them, Cotton thought, 'Christ, we've had it,' but they were merely being greeted by a guard of honour.[31] The next month they flew to the international Frankfurt Air Rally, which was packed with Luftwaffe officers in their grey dress uniforms, including Udet, Erhard Milch, the deputy head of the Luftwaffe, and his chief of administration, Albert Kesselring, a friend of Hanna's popularly known as 'Smiling Albert'.[32] Despite his nickname, Kesselring had a taciturn, almost rude manner, and bluntly asked Cotton for a flight in the magnificent Lockheed

---

* Danzig was claimed as part of Germany on 1 September 1939.

with its painted, all-metal fuselage and heated cabin. Cotton, professionally charming, was delighted to oblige, even offering Kesselring the controls. Once up, he reached beneath his seat and activated the hidden German Leica cameras, the best on the market, focused down on the land below. When Kesselring asked about the unfamiliar green light flashing on the control panel, Cotton explained that it showed the petrol flow to the engines. Soon Cotton was taking a series of generals and colonels on joy-flights a couple of thousand feet 'above airfields and ammunition dumps, factories and fortifications', while his hidden cameras clicked away, taking some of the first aerial reconnaissance photographs of the coming war.[33]

By the time that Cotton was flying over Frankfurt, neither he, Melitta nor Hanna were in any doubt as to where their countries were heading. Even while signing the Munich Agreement the year before, Chamberlain had agreed to a huge increase in British armament spending, and production levels in German aircraft manufacturing had soared. Britain and France had guaranteed Poland's independence in March 1939. In August the Greater German Reich and the Soviet Union agreed a mutual non-aggression pact, Nazi German foreign minister Joachim von Ribbentrop flying to Moscow with Hitler's personal photographer to record the historic moment. Europe was dividing.

As the prospect of war looked ever more likely, Germany was gripped by a renewed sense of patriotism. By now both Alexander and Claus had taken part in military exercises, in different capacities. Despite his political dissent, Alexander had been brought up to value the honourable fulfilment of his duty to people and state above all else. As a result, although he considered himself 'unsuited to being a soldier', he had served voluntarily in a cavalry regiment as early as 1923, becoming a keen horseman.[34] Until March 1934 Alexander had even been a member of the SA, the paramilitary wing of the Nazi Party, although he was never a Party member. In 1936 he became a corporal in the Reserve, and it was as such that he participated in military exercises over the summer of 1938. Unlike his brother, Claus was a passionate soldier. Having already seen service in Czechoslovakia, he was now awaiting new orders. Nevertheless, 'the mass of German people . . .' Nevile Henderson wrote, 'were horror-struck at the whole idea of the war which was thus being thrust upon them'.[35]

Sidney Cotton finally returned to Britain with the dubious honour of being the last civilian to fly out of Berlin in late August 1939. He carefully photographed the German fleet congregating at Wilhelmshaven as he went over, with Hitler's personal yacht, the *Grille* – 'the cricket' in English – clearly distinct as a white fleck among the grey. Days later, although officially still a civilian, Cotton flew back to film the fleet again for the British Admiralty, showing which vessels had departed. Soon he was busy establishing a special unit to pioneer military aerial reconnaissance during the coming conflict, eventually accepting a commission with the RAF.*

Inside Germany, it seems that only the young and then politically naive British pilot Eric Brown, who had partied with Hanna at Udet's apartment after the Berlin Motor Show, was not anticipating the coming conflict. On the morning of Sunday 3 September 1939, he was 'shaken' to be arrested by the SS at the small Munich inn where he was staying.[36] Although he had been studying in Germany for several months, Eric had 'never once felt any real likelihood of war', he later claimed.[37] After an interrogation that lasted three days, he was pushed into a car and driven away. Thinking he was bound for a Gestapo cell or the firing squad, he was surprised to see his own beautiful MG Magnette sports car being driven behind, with the entire head of the large SS sergeant who was behind the wheel sticking up above the windscreen. To his astonishment, both he and the Magnette were deposited at the Swiss border, where he was told to drive on. His arresting officer 'was standing with a . . . hand machine gun pointing at my back, and the Swiss were standing with one pointing at my front,' Eric later recounted. 'I wasn't feeling too confident at this stage.'[38] Within a few hours, however, he was racing across

---

* Cotton's Lockheed had a long post-war career, and ended up starring in a number of films and television programmes, including *Doc Savage* and *The A-Team*.

Switzerland for France, his immediate fears of a bullet having been replaced by a nagging worry that everything would be over 'before I could get into uniform'.[39] He was lucky not to have been interned. Britain and Germany were officially at war.

7

WOMEN AT WAR
1939–1941

The invasion of Poland in September 1939 was known within Germany as the 'Defensive Campaign', and accepted by most of the population in this light. As directed by Goebbels' Ministry for Propaganda, the press had been railing against territorial losses for years, while the early critics of military intervention had long been silenced. Deeply patriotic, and keenly confident in their own abilities, both Melitta and Hanna volunteered for their country the moment war was declared. Hanna's brother, Kurt, was already serving with the Kriegsmarine. Otto, Melitta's brother, was an agricultural expert in the Foreign Service. Although still at the University of Würzburg, Alexander reported for duty as a non-commissioned officer in a reserve battery at Ansbach, but was soon released. Claus was on active service during the invasion, as an officer with the 6th Panzer Division. Had they been men, there is no doubt that both Hanna and Melitta would have enlisted with the Luftwaffe, but the only roles for women in the service were in office administration, releasing men for combat duty.

Undeterred, Hanna immediately petitioned General von Richthofen, whose Luftwaffe commands included the Glider Unit, to be accepted for direct military service. Her request was rejected. Instead, she was retained as a test pilot at the Glider Research Institute at Darmstadt. Melitta's first instinct was to request a transfer from research and development for the Air War Ministry to flying air ambulances with the German Red Cross, a 'more helpful and healing role', as she saw it.[1] She had been inspired both by her mother's and her elder sister's work as volunteer nurses in the First World War, and later by learning of the role played by Alexander's aunt, Countess Alexandrine Üxküll-Gyllenband, who

was one of the few women to visit German POWs in Russia under
the banner of the International Red Cross. As a result, Melitta had
been practising air ambulance flights since at least 1935. At the
outbreak of hostilities, however, 'the only thing that counted', her
niece later commented, 'was her qualifications'.[2] Melitta's request
was also declined. She was seconded instead as an engineer-pilot
to develop targeted dive-bombing at the Luftwaffe testing centre
at Rechlin, the remote airfield near Lake Mecklenburg that served
as the German equivalent of Farnborough. Although not assigned
active combat roles, both women would spend the war risking their
lives on a daily basis in the service of their country, and sometimes
at the same airfields.

Albert Speer, Hitler's architect and, as such, responsible for
erecting military buildings, later recalled that, from the start of the
war, 'the most pressing task was the Ju 88 programme for the Luftwaffe, which was to turn out the new two-motored medium-range
Junkers 88 dive-bombers'.[3] The Luftwaffe bombing strategy called
for pinpoint targeting rather than area bombing, but hitting precision targets from the air was difficult. Dive-bomber pilots were
expected to aim their whole plane at a target and they had only a
few seconds' margin in which to release their load before turning.
Existing guides included such handy advice as 'Fly onto target
exactly,' and 'If there is a strong headwind . . . dive more deeply!'[4]

Melitta's new assignment was to perfect the aircraft technically,
to eliminate as much risk as possible. The main task was to evaluate
and improve the targeting devices, and in particular the dive-sights
for the two-man Junkers Ju 87 Stuka, with its distinctive gull-wing
shape, and the popular four-man Ju 88 dive-bomber developed for
larger-scale strategic air war. This involved registering the contin-
uously changing angle of the dive, speed and dropping altitude, all
without modern instruments. She also worked on developing
dive-visors, ensuring that the autopilot levelled off the aircraft
automatically when a bomb had left its cradle so as not to put too
much strain on the machine's airframe, and that the automatic pull-
out sequence functioned at 6G – the point at which most pilots
suffered G-force-induced loss of consciousness. As well as Junkers,

Melitta flew a range of Messerschmitt and Focke-Wulf planes, and the lighter Fieseler *Storch*, or Stork. These aircraft were designed to support military invasion but Melitta enjoyed piloting them, she said, 'quite simply because they are particularly interesting from a flying point of view'.[5] She was constantly striving to attain peak performance from herself as a pilot, as well as from the machines she flew.

Testing dive-bombers was work that required not only patience, precision and considerable physical strength, but also great courage. Every morning Melitta cycled across the airfield from her dorm on her heavy-framed pushbike, before swapping her beret for her leather flying cap, donning her overalls and clambering into a Junkers' cockpit. She would take her machine up to 4,000 metres before rolling sideways and tearing down again at speeds of up to 350 mph, the engines howling and the surfaces of the plane whistling as the dive angle steepened until it was at least seventy-five to eighty degrees – not far from vertical. As Melitta plunged towards earth, her gloved hands tightly gripping the steering column, the whole frame of her plane would be shaking with the mounting pressure. The vibrations made it difficult to read her instruments accurately, so many of her dives were filmed to provide the detailed information required to enable incremental improvements to the targeting devices. Sometimes she would also release between four and ten cylindrical cement bombs to test her work. At between 150 and 200 metres, just as correction seemed impossible, Melitta would lift her plane's nose and skim low across the fields before circling back to land.

After several such tests over the course of a morning, her colleagues would heave her from her cockpit, unclip her parachute harness and help her out of her flying suit, so that she could return to her engineering role. Over desk and drawing board she would now conduct a precise evaluation of the dives, often working late into the night 'without making any fuss about it', her colleagues noted, to calculate the alterations required before testing could begin again.[6] Undertaking a few such dives without any of the engineering work had been enough to exhaust Udet some years earlier. Even with automatic dive-brakes, trainee Stuka pilots were often sick, and sometimes plunged into the sea. Yet Melitta might complete fifteen such test dives in one day: a performance unmatched by any pilot in history.

This punishing routine was, Melitta admitted, 'completely inadmissible from a medical point of view'.[7] Not only was she mentally exhausted by the intense concentration required, but enormous physical stresses were also being placed on her body. By 1940, Allied pilots would have the benefit of an 'anti-gravity flying suit' which used fluid pumped through tubes and pads to squeeze their legs and abdomen in a kind of auto-tourniquet, preventing their blood from dispersing to their extremities under G-force.* Melitta had no such pressure suit. When she turned her plane into a fast dive, her blood was forced up into her head. As a result, her vision would turn pink, a phenomenon known as 'red-out', and the pressure was sometimes enough to cause blood vessels in her eyes to rupture. As air closer to the ground is denser, aircraft will automatically slow as they approach the earth. Combined with the use of automatic dive-brakes, this would allow Melitta's blood flow to normalize, enabling her to reassert control in time to pull out of a dive. But pulling up too quickly would cause the blood to rush away from her head, towards her legs and feet. With her brain temporarily starved of oxygen, she regularly lost her vision, literally 'blacking out', and may even have temporarily lost consciousness on occasion.

Like most pilots, Melitta was extremely fit, exercising daily and avoiding alcohol. Already physically suspect as a woman, she was not prepared to risk any doubts about her ability, and she repeatedly denied that she was much affected by G-forces. 'In me, the disturbance of vision occurs only at very high acceleration,' she claimed, before suggesting, optimistically, that her 'intense concentration' might help to prevent the flow of blood away from her

---

* The suit was the brainchild of Canada's Wilbur Franks, a cancer researcher who had prevented his experimental test tubes from smashing when subjected to intense centrifugal force by placing them in stronger, liquid-filled containers.

brain.[8] More perilous work was hard to imagine, but Melitta refused to let other pilots conduct her tests. Not only did she want to feel every nuance of the aircraft's performance for herself but 'above all', she said, 'it seems to me simply more decent not to pass the dangerous part of one's work on to other people'.[9]

Dive-bombing proved extremely effective in the campaign for Poland, becoming synonymous with the *Blitzkrieg* in the process. Some of the Polish air force was effectively destroyed on the ground before it could be mobilized, but Polish fighters based in secondary airfields later shot down over 170 German planes. It was not enough. Having gained air superiority, the Stuka then acted in effect as long-range precision artillery. The planes' chilling screams, produced by sirens fitted to the wheel covers, would create terror among the infantry and tanks below before they were even within firing range. Perhaps Melitta sometimes thought of Claus with his panzer unit on the ground, supported by the planes she had helped to develop. Perhaps she also thought about the Polish neighbours from her childhood. Once it was safe, Hitler made a flying visit to the front, escorted by several fighters. En route he 'gazed from the windows without emotion', his pilot Hans Baur noted, as they flew over 'still-smoking villages, shattered bridges, and other evidence of the destruction of war'.[10] 'Our air victory is the Führer's great joy,' Goebbels wrote the following month.[11]

Claus, like Melitta, found satisfaction in doing his job well. With traditional military detachment he saw this as distinct from supporting the Nazi regime, but during his six weeks on active duty in Poland he also came to respect Hitler's then highly effective military strategy. Like many German nationalists, Claus believed that the invasion of Poland, like that of the Czech Sudetenland, was justified by the need to protect German populations from discrimination. Nor was he without racial prejudice. He described the Poles as 'an unbelievable rabble' of 'Jews and mongrels', who were 'only comfortable under the knout' – a vicious type of whip.[12] It is not known how much Claus knew about the murders being committed behind the advancing front line by the *Einsatzgruppen* – SS task forces specifically charged with killing Jews or other 'undesirable' people, as well as 'eliminating' the Polish intelligentsia as a preventative strike against resistance. By the end of 1939, an estimated 65,000 civilians had been killed, and few German officers could have been completely unaware of the policy. By November, even the American journalist William Shirer was reporting that 'Nazi policy is simply to exterminate the Polish Jews'.[13] Not surprisingly, however, Claus's letters home, which his wife Nina dutifully typed up and circulated among the family, made no reference to such horrors.[14]

By the following spring, stories of atrocities were widely circulating within diplomatic circles. 'The SS had taken 1,500 Polish Jews, including many women and children, and shuttled them back and forth in open freight cars until they were all dead,' Fey von Hassell wrote. 'Then about 200 peasants were forced to dig immense graves. Afterwards, all those who had taken part were shot and buried in the same place.'[15] Fey's father, Ulrich von Hassell, the former German ambassador to Italy, had been working in vain to keep unofficial diplomatic channels open with Britain, and was already secretly involved in plans to overthrow Hitler. When Claus returned to Germany, Nina asked him whether he too was 'playing conspirator'.[16] He told her he was. Since late 1938 Claus had stopped writing to Nina about what she called 'his inner conflicts'.[17] Instead he kept a notebook in which he scribbled down his thoughts to share with her whenever they met. Meanwhile he and his brother Berthold both tried to keep their mother and Alexander from being too open about their antipathy towards the regime. Claus also continued to serve in the military.

Hanna's hunger to see action alongside the men could not have been more different from Melitta's initial desire to place her skill as a pilot at the service of the German Red Cross, but their motivations were similar. 'When the war finally came . . .' Hanna's uncle later testified, 'she felt the moral duty not to forsake her Fatherland . . . it wasn't possible for her to see that the war had been started by Germany in the first place.'[18]

For some time before the war Hanna had been test-flying large prototype gliders at the Research Institute at Darmstadt. These had been designed to gather meteorological data and transport mail, and she had tested their viable load by methodically adding sacks of sand over a series of flights. It was not long before Ernst Udet recognized the potential military applications for such a glider to bring supplies to the front line, or reinforcements to a unit that had been surrounded. Furthermore, as Hanna put it, 'being noiseless in flight and able to dive at steep angles', the gliders seemed to 'offer an excellent means of landing bodies of infantry by surprise behind an enemy's lines'.[19] The institute had soon received a military contract to design a troop-carrying glider, able to transport ten fully equipped infantrymen, plus their commander. The resulting DFS 230 would become the war's first 'assault glider', with a wingspan of seventy-two feet and a top speed of 130 mph under tow.[20]

In the autumn of 1939 Hanna was selected to demonstrate the fully loaded glider to an audience of high-ranking officers including Udet, Robert Ritter von Greim, 'Smiling' Albert Kesselring and Erhard Milch. Once above 30,000 feet she cast off the cable to the transport Junkers Ju 52 that had towed them up, and put the glider into a steep dive. She landed just a few yards from the officers on the ground and within seconds the troops had tumbled out and dispersed, conclusively proving the military potential of the machine. 'The speed and precision of the whole manoeuvre so fired the Generals' enthusiasm', Hanna recorded proudly, that a repeat performance was requested – only with the generals as passengers.[21] It was a daunting request for any pilot, but the enthusiastic Hanna claimed she nearly fainted at the 'truly awe-inspiring responsibility that had been thrust upon me'.[22]

Hans Jacobs, the glider's designer, was equally unnerved. After Hanna had landed her 'precious passengers' safely back on earth, she caught Jacobs prising himself out from the glider's tail space. Knowing that, should disaster strike, 'I might as well be finished too', he had been unable to resist joining the historic flight.[23] It was a ruse that Hanna would remember later in the war. For now, her successful demonstrations further confirmed her standing with the senior military men of the Third Reich.

A German glider assault unit was formed almost immediately, which was intended to support an invasion of France in November 1939. However, the officers in charge of the operation had no gliding experience and while Germany's leading glider pilots had been recruited, they had no military status or training. Once briefed, these pilots were kept in strict isolation. Hanna pressed General von Richthofen to allow her to join the team, or at least arrange training, but as a woman she was flatly refused. When the invasion of France was postponed to later winter, she and Jacobs again worked together as designer and test pilot, developing brakes to enable the gliders to land on ice. Hanna then demonstrated the solution – lever-operated ploughshares – to the glider unit. It was only when she and the pilot Otto Bräutigam, an impressive man in Hanna's eyes, 'radiating with confidence, courage and humour', made a concerted appeal for better training that Greim consented to the request.[24]

Hanna had admired the highly decorated Greim, a friend of Udet's from the Great War, for several years. At nearly fifty, he might not have Bräutigam's physical magnetism, but he had gravitas, was an excellent pilot and officer, and was greatly admired by his men. Having served in the invasion of Poland, Greim now commanded the Luftwaffe research department. Hanna took the opportunity to secure a private meeting. Her enthusiasm for both the Nazi cause and for flying had made her extremely popular with the Propaganda Ministry and senior generals, but some of her younger colleagues still found her presence at the airfield offensive. Hanna wanted Greim's support to help her challenge 'those officers to whom the maintenance of masculine privilege', as she put it angrily, 'was more important than the needs of the hour'.[25] Greim was not concerned about gender equality but he was interested in Hanna and he supported her requests. Her need to be at once equal and special, however, along with her increasing tendency to appeal to Udet or Greim 'to smooth my path', as she put it, would do little to endear her to her less well connected colleagues.[26]

It was not until May 1940 that glider assault troops were eventually deployed, and then it was not in France but Belgium, in an attack on the reputedly impregnable fort of Eben-Emael near the Dutch border. Swooping down in a silent dawn raid, eleven gliders delivered sufficient paratroopers, Bräutigam among them, to destroy the fort's defensive armaments before any counter-attack could be launched. They had defeated a force ten times their own number. This decisive action cleared the way for German ground forces to enter Belgium. Rumour had it that it was Hanna who had planted the seed for the spectacular operation in Hitler's mind when, at an event in 1935, she had commented on how noiseless gliders were. Whatever the truth, Hanna's personal stock now rose to new heights, and features on her began to appear in everything from the national papers to *The Colourful Young Girls' League Book*, where she was somehow presented as a role model for German womanhood between articles on child-rearing and hand-icrafts.

Hanna was posted to Rechlin, where Melitta was based, in the spring of 1940, but the intensity of the two women's work schedules left little time for frosty meetings or even reconciliation between them in the busy canteen or corridors, and they chose not to actively seek each other out. Despite her equally important and dangerous work, Melitta was not considered suitable role-model material. Her father, Michael, had already been informed of his designation as a 'Jewish half-breed' when, on 23 May 1940, Melitta received her own letter from the Reich's German Genealogical Research Board. Their report, dated 7 May, classified her as a 'half-Jew' with 'two racially full-blooded Jewish grandparents'.[27] Melitta had known that the letter was coming. One week earlier the Ministry for Education and Culture had informed Alexander's university that his appointment as professor should be deferred until it was clear 'whether he would hold on to his marriage . . . or annul it'.[28] As he had married after the introduction of the Nurem-berg Laws, the ministry had assumed Alexander must have been unaware of Melitta's Jewish ancestry. He was in effect being given an escape route, on condition that he divorce and disown his wife. Instead he bravely stated that it was the Genealogical Research Board who must have made a mistake.

Over the following months Melitta appealed to Udet for support. Udet's friendship with her uncle during the First World War had led him to support her when she first started flying, and he had helped to dig her out of trouble when she had briefly landed on the wrong side of the border in 1929. Now she told him about the vital importance to the war of her current work. Alexander applied directly to Göring himself. When his university pressed him, he informed them that 'the Reich Ministry of Aviation (Colonel-General Udet) sent an appeal to the Reich Minister of the Interior, concerning the indispensability of my wife for the Luftwaffe's war-important Stuka testing, to order the Bavarian State Ministry of Education and Culture to refrain from taking any further steps at this point'.[29] Three months later, in December 1940, Alexander curtly informed the head of the university that 'the matter is considered closed'.[30] With no official paperwork, however, they did not see it that way.

All Melitta could do was keep her head down, and continue working to the highest standard in the hope that this would help her case. Colleagues now noted that 'she worked quietly and modestly', the section head even commenting on her 'aura of unapproachability'.[31] Inevitably stories were already circulating about what Hanna referred to as Melitta's 'racial burden'.[32] Melitta, Hanna felt, had 'some kind of inner despair . . . which she meant to keep hidden from work, and in general from everyone'.[33] Hanna reluctantly recognized Melitta's achievements but, irritated, she chose to attribute these to an 'unhealthy ambition' caused by concern about her ancestry.[34]

Not surprisingly, Melitta actively avoided Hanna at Rechlin. When they met by chance, Melitta 'didn't want to be included in any conversation', Hanna wrote with apparent pique, and seemed intent on 'harshly declining every well-intended offer of help from my side'.[35] Above all, Hanna thought it highly suspicious that Melitta 'avoided the company of certain colleagues', while 'on the other hand, she was frequently seen with such colleagues who meant to spoil the atmosphere by constantly teasing and complaining about the government'.[36] It seems that Melitta was still critical of the regime among close friends. Hanna, with her dogged loyalty to the state and her vivid imagination, could not help but wonder among her own circle whether there was 'something wrong'. 'Does she have a foot in both camps,' Hanna mused, 'or does she work for the enemy?'[37] Such insinuations were the last thing Melitta needed, and she threw herself ever more furiously into her test flights and engineering work.

France fell in June 1940. 'We had marvellous support from the Luftwaffe,' one Wehrmacht officer recalled. 'Our Ju 87 Stukas terrified the French just as they had terrified the Poles . . . Many soldiers simply ran away as if the banshees were after them.'[38] In the German popular imagination, Stukas now symbolized both the technical and the tactical superiority of the Luftwaffe; their pilots had a particular air of glamour and were lauded as heroes in the Third Reich. When Hitler returned from his victory tour of Paris, crowds lined the streets of Berlin to welcome him, troops paraded through the Brandenburg Gate and church bells pealed across the country. It was now clear that Melitta and Hanna had already made significant contributions to their nation's victories.

The year had begun well for Hanna. While she was still work-ing on troop-carrying gliders in February, her elder brother Kurt's wedding had provided an opportunity for the Reitsch family to get together. In April, however, Kurt was posted to the campaign for the north Norwegian port of Narvik, to safeguard the supply of iron ore to Germany. Within weeks Norway had fallen, but Kurt's ship had been sunk and he was reported missing.

Hanna, like Melitta, now threw herself into her work with ever greater intensity. The success of the glider attack on Eben-Emael had convinced the German Air Ministry to consider a similar stealth approach for the invasion of Britain. For this operation, however, not just men but considerable quantities of arms, ammu-nition, vehicles, including 200 tanks, would need to be transported across the Channel to form a bridgehead. The proposed solution came in the form of a new wood-and-steel Messerschmitt Me 321 high-wing monoplane glider, appropriately named the *Gigant*, or

Giant.* The wheels alone on the disposable undercarriage of this monster were almost as tall as Hanna, and the cockpit was fully sixty feet above the ground. With doped fabric stretched over its steel-tubing frame, it looked unhealthily bloated compared to the tiny, almost skeletal early gliders in which Hanna had learned to fly.

The Gigant needed three engine-powered planes working in perfect formation to tow it into the air, in addition to eight liquid-fuelled rockets attached to its own wings. 'What a spectacular affair it was!' Isolde Baur, the wife of Messerschmitt's chief test pilot Karl Baur later wrote. 'Three tow planes in front and a cloud of smoke from the rockets trailing behind.'[39] On landing, the Gigant's clamshell doors would burst open, and 200 armed men could emerge, or a fully equipped tank juddering into action.

Although Hanna was increasingly being selected for the sort of prestige projects that would showcase her talents, it was never expected that she should fly such an enormous glider. Just a few days after the initial test flight, however, she began lobbying to take her turn. Baur resisted. He was 'immensely worried' that, with her 'fragile build', she would not have the strength for the heavy controls.[40] Eventually, however, orders came through to make the necessary adjustments for Hanna to take the Gigant up.

When Hanna finally sat perched in the Gigant's narrow cockpit, her feet rested on wooden blocks installed to raise the rudder pedal height for her, and a cushion was sandwiched between her and the pilot's seat. As an extra precaution, the crew flying with her were briefed to keep a close watch. According to the slightly jealous Isolde Baur, 'sure enough, after she had handled the controls with great difficulty in flight, she yelled for help to the engineers when they approached the field for landing'.[41] Hanna did not later mention it, but reportedly one of the tallest men reached over, took the controls, and landed the massive glider for her.

---

* Junkers' proposed solution was an entirely wood-built Mammoth glider. Unable to leave the ground successfully, the prototype Mammoth quickly became extinct, and was eventually used only to stoke the boilers of German trains.

Hanna was not impressed. She knew the Gigant was designed to be expendable, but to her mind it was 'primitively built', as she claimed damningly in the Nazi-influenced language she was increasingly adopting.[42] Many of Hanna's criticisms were valid. Above all, the manual controls were so stiff that they were almost impossible to manoeuvre. Willy Messerschmitt dismissed her feedback because it came from 'too small a little girl, not a strong man fit for fighting', Hanna later paraphrased him angrily.[43] 'What is hard for me in a five-minute flight,' she retorted, 'is too hard for a strong man in a one-hour flight'.[44] Later twin pilot seats would be installed, so that two people could wrestle the controls together.

Hanna faced more problems on her next test. Two of the three tow-planes released their cables early, but the Gigant's rocket engines could not be shut down, leaving her 'hanging on one bomber, that was like a little fly compared to my giant!'[45] Having dropped the remaining tow she managed to coast back down, her heavy landing not only kicking up a cloud of dirt, but also breaking both legs of one passenger and sending another into shock. Few pilots were keen to let her have another attempt. She missed two more opportunities when Otto Bräutigam flew the Gigant without her, unwilling, she thought crossly, to share his experience. On the second occasion she was so furious, frustrated and humiliated that she burst into tears. A few moments later the Gigant crashed, killing the pilots of all three tow-planes along with its own six-man crew, including Bräutigam. Not long afterwards another test ended in disaster when the rocket assists on one side of the Gigant failed to fire, throwing it off balance. Again all the pilots were killed, along with the 110 troops being carried.

The Gigant would never be deployed as originally conceived, nor at all against Britain.* From July 1940, Luftwaffe bombers started to attack British shipping, and over the summer RAF airfields, aircraft factories and general infrastructure were targeted, in

---

* Eventually the Gigant evolved into a six-engine transport aircraft, employed to ferry freight to the Eastern Front and evacuate the wounded. Heavy and slow, it proved all too simple to shoot down.

an attempt to gain air superiority over the south of England. British bombers were also penetrating German airspace, mainly by night, as earlier daylight raids had suffered too many losses. Aerial reconnaissance showed that their bombing was far from accurate. Hitler, incensed, ordered Göring to take countermeasures. On 7 September London was bombed for the first of fifty-seven consecutive nights. Despite the deaths and devastation, towards the end of a 'grim week' in that first month of what became known as the Blitz, a 'numb laugh' was caused when the storerooms of Madame Tussauds were hit. 'Heads, arms and legs were strewn around,' the Daily Express reported. 'Flying glass had stuck into some of the models' faces . . . Hitler's nose was chipped and Göring's magnificent white uniform was covered in black dust.'[46]

As the Blitz continued, the Luftwaffe began to suffer heavy losses. Their bombers had inadequate defensive armament and their fighter escorts did not have the range to remain long over Britain, and were frequently intercepted by the RAF using radar. The Stuka's great strength now became its vulnerability. 'Once the pilot had started coming down, he was committed to his dive,' one RAF officer explained. 'You could see where he was going . . . they were sitting ducks.'[47]

Distraught at the mounting losses among Luftwaffe pilots, Melitta became yet more committed to her work. 'She was hoping that with the development and testing of these weapons . . .', her sister Jutta explained, she might 'restrict the war to military targets', and so reduce civilian casualties as well as the need for repeat raids by German pilots.[48] Furthermore, she was in no doubt of German victory and hoped that more effective precision bombing might help to hasten the end of the conflict and so 'shorten the slaughter' altogether.[49]

Melitta now regularly undertook ten or more nosedives a day, as well as watching trials, talking with mechanics, considering the worst scenario and possible chain reactions, before calculating potential performances and going back to prove the theory with another test. One afternoon, her old friend and colleague Georg Wollé, whose motorbike she used to ride before the war, bumped into her unexpectedly near the Aviation Ministry in Berlin. He was in uniform and hurrying to an appointment so they only had a few moments, but Georg was 'appalled to see how the extreme physical and mental efforts of aeroplane test flights had dug deep furrows into her once pretty, smooth and regular features'.[50] Although Melitta was almost permanently exhausted, it was a comment that perhaps spoke more about Georg than Melitta herself.

Melitta's reputation within aviation circles continued to grow. Despite her wish for a low profile, she was increasingly photographed on the airfield, cycling across the grass or in discussion with her observer, gloves in one hand, the arc of an anticipated flight traced with the other. She annotated the back of one picture with the simple possessive, 'My Ju 88'. More photographs show her working at her drawing board, checking the film of her latest test flight or calculating the adjustments needed, a female assistant hovering behind. As word about her work spread, even Göring came to admire 'the precise evaluation of the measured nosedives [that] were led by Countess Stauffenberg herself'.[51]

After the Gigant, Hanna was employed in testing a series of different prototypes. A pilotless glider had been developed for use as a petrol tanker, to enable refuelling in mid-air. Sitting with the controls locked, her function was to observe the glider's inherent stability as it was towed behind its parent plane. It had very little. Rocked around violently with no means of control, Hanna found herself subject to 'the most primitive and hateful fear', she said.[52] The tanker was abandoned. She then tested warship deck landings, descending into a dangerous mesh of cables. Again the Luftwaffe would eventually abandon the idea, but only after Hanna had narrowly avoided decapitation.*

Her next role was no less dangerous. She was required to fly a Dornier Do 17 bomber, 'my most beloved bomber', as she called it, and later a Heinkel He 111, directly into deadly anti-aircraft

---

* Eric Brown, with whom Hanna had partied in 1938, also carried out trial deck landings. Brown became Britain's most decorated Fleet Air Arm pilot, and held the world record for aircraft carrier landings. In total he flew 487 different types of aircraft, more than any other pilot in history.

barrage balloon cables.[53] The iconic silver hydrogen-filled balloons now formed an airborne barricade of 'grey silhouettes or silver blobs, depending where the sun was', over Southampton, parts of London and other cities, and sections of the English countryside.[54] Trailing lethal steel cables like industrial Portuguese men-of-war, these floating blockades had to be navigated by returning RAF planes and British ATA ferry pilots – all flying in radio silence – as well as by enemy aircraft. If forced to fly above the balloons, German bombers had no hope of accuracy, and crashing into one might cause a plane to be 'tipped up', even knocking the bombs back into their bays.[55] Below the balloons, however, the heavy steel cables that tethered them to the ground were hard to spot at speed, and invisible at night. They could easily, and often did, shear through propeller blades, or even slice the wing from a fast-moving plane, sending it spiralling down to earth.

To combat this threat, Hans Jacobs designed heavy fenders that were riveted onto the nose section of the bombers, and secured with straps to their wing spar. His plan was to deflect any cables down to the wing tips where sharp steel blades would cut them.* It was Hanna's job to test the prototype cutting devices against cables of various widths. Sometimes these were British cables. When the wind was strong, an unmanned barrage balloon could float to 2,000 metres and occasionally one would find its way to enemy territory where it might be 'captured', as Goebbels put it smugly in his diary, and redeployed for test purposes.[56] Instruments on board Hanna's plane would record the results of the impact, so that improvements could be developed. If the fenders did not work, it was feared that broken fragments of propeller might be hurled through the cabin, so a second set of controls was built into the rear gun turret, near to the escape hatch. Although Hanna could neither take off nor land using these supplementary controls, once

---

* As Germany also used barrage balloons, certain British bombers were fitted with similar devices. Wing Commander Leonard Ratcliff found flying into a cable 'required much skill, and a steady nerve'. See Sean Rayment, *Tales from the Special Forces Club* (2003), p. 173.

in the air she could maintain her course with them, and parachute out with her co-pilot if necessary.

Flying deliberately into a balloon cable required considerable courage but, typically, once in the air on her first test run, Hanna's imagination was caught by the beauty of the lethal lines 'gleaming silver in the sunlight against a backdrop of blue sky'.[57] She then swung her aircraft round, staggered down to the rear cockpit, felt the calm of intense concentration descend upon her, aimed, and flew directly towards her target. There was a sudden jerk as the cable hit the fender, and then the Dornier swept on. Although the design needed improvement, these first trials were encouraging. Greim asked for all the planes fitted with the fender to be transferred to his command, and pilots whose aircraft had been saved began to send back their thanks. Hanna would later present the aim of her work as 'the saving of human lives'.[58] Each test 'brought us a step nearer to overcoming some of those perils which pilots and aircrews had daily to face in operations against the enemy', she wrote with pride.[59]

Hanna was so committed to her work that she continued flying even when she developed a raging temperature towards the end of 1940. Diagnosed with scarlet fever, then a potentially lethal disease, she was forced to spend three months in a darkened hospital isolation ward, seething with frustration at her enforced inaction. By Christmas, Luftwaffe losses had risen significantly, and production levels were scarcely enough to maintain the fleet. Hitler's priority was now the Wehrmacht and he blithely accepted Göring's unsupported promises that such weaknesses would be overcome.

Hanna returned to work immediately after her discharge from hospital in the spring of 1941. Jacobs' fender design had now been replaced by a lighter strip of razor-sharp steel, fixed to the leading edge of the test plane's wings. Udet was en route to a conference with Hitler when he stopped off to watch the tests. That day Hanna was due to fly into a short length of cable attached to a balloon that had drifted over from England. To connect with this cable she had to fly at low level – too low to bail out should anything go wrong – so this time she flew alone. It was a blustery day,

and the balloon was twisting on its moorings, dragging the straining cable at an awkward angle. Had Udet not been watching, the
test might have been aborted. As it was, nobody wanted to disap-
point a general.

When Hanna's bomber hit it, the cable simply ripped apart,
whipping through the air and slicing the edges from two of her
propeller blades. Metal splinters shot through the cockpit, and the
starboard engine began to race, threatening to tear itself loose
from the wing. 'Hearing the crack of the parting cable and seeing
the air filled with metal fragments', Udet watched as the crippled
plane disappeared behind the treetops, and waited for the inevitable and all-too-familiar sound of exploding fuel tanks.[60] Nothing
happened. Incredibly, Hanna, who was uninjured, had managed to
switch off the crippled engine and perform an emergency landing.
When Udet reached the scene he stood transfixed while she
climbed out of the damaged plane and even managed a weak smile.
Having flown on to his conference, Udet described the incident in
vivid detail to Hitler.

A few weeks later, on 27 March 1941, Hanna found herself
invited to visit Göring at his lavish Berlin home. Dressed in his
famous white uniform, replete with gold braid, buttons and
medals, the commander-in-chief of the Luftwaffe was all set to
present Hanna with a special women's version of the Military
Flight Badge in gold with diamonds, for her courage and service.
This was the first time that Göring had given much consideration
to Hanna's person, and when she entered the room he continued
to stare over her head towards the doorway. After a few moments
Udet drew his attention to the fact that the guest of honour had
already arrived. 'Göring's amazement was great,' Hanna laughed in
her memoir. 'He planted his bulk squarely in front of me, his hands
resting on his hips, and demanded, "What! Is this supposed to be
our famous *Flugkapitän*? Where's the rest of her? How can this
little person manage to fly at all?"' Insulted, but evidently quite
comfortable in the company of the senior Nazi leadership, Hanna
made a sweep of her hand roughly corresponding to Göring's girth
and asked the Great War ace and Nazi Reichsmarschall, 'Do you

have to look like that to fly?'[61] Fortunately for her, Göring and his entourage laughed. Hanna proudly wore the golden wreath, through which a diamond-encrusted eagle carries a swastika, on her tunic for the rest of her life.

The following day, 28 March, Hitler himself was to receive Hanna in the Reich Chancellery, to confer on her the Iron Cross, Second Class, in recognition of her act of valour beyond the normal fulfilment of her duty. She was the first woman to be so honoured during the Second World War.* An adjutant led her down the long marble hall, 'polished like a mirror', towards the Führer's study.[62] Hitler's 'manner of walking was always measured, almost ceremonial', his secretary Christa Schroeder reported, knowing that he used such personal restraint, like the length of the hall, to intimidate.[63] But Hanna wrote that 'Hitler greeted me with friendly warmth', while Göring stood beside him, 'beaming', she felt, 'like a father permitted to introduce a prettily mannered child'.[64] She was then invited to sit between the two Nazi leaders at a large round table, the surreal nature of the moment enhanced by the vase of early sweet peas set in front of them.

Technical subjects were known to 'enthral' Hitler and, with little preamble, he began to question Hanna about her work.[65] It seems the Führer was in a cordial mood that day. At such times his eyes were often described as expressive and searching, and his conversation as animated. 'Undoubtedly he knew how to charm a person under his spell during conversation,' Schroeder wrote. 'He could expound even the most complicated subjects clearly and simply . . . he fascinated his listeners.'[66] Hanna was pretty charming herself. When she talked about planes her eyes lit up and she bubbled with enthusiasm, waving her arms around to illustrate her anecdotes. Later she cautiously wrote that 'it was impossible to gain any deeper insight into Hitler's personality and character', as

---

* Two women had already been awarded the Iron Cross. Disguised as a man, Friederike Krüger had served in the Wars of Liberation under the name August Lübeck. She was awarded the Iron Cross, Second Class, in 1813. Lonny Hertha von Versen, a nurse in the First World War, was decorated in 1915. Twenty-seven women would receive the Iron Cross, Second Class, mostly for courage while nursing.

they only discussed aircraft, but his technical knowledge and 'the searching pointedness of his questions' struck her as 'remarkable for a layman'.[67]

Over the next few weeks Hanna was delighted to find herself the subject of numerous articles in the German and international press.[68] She received so many congratulatory letters that she was assigned a part-time secretary to help manage her correspondence. She would grumble rather proudly about her 'mountains, mountains, mountains' of post ever afterwards.[69] At the start of April she returned to her home town of Hirschberg to be welcomed as a heroine, and as a rather unlikely role model for German womanhood under the Nazi regime. 'As soon as we reached the Silesian border, the villages were decked with flags, people at the roadside threw flowers or waved . . .' she wrote triumphantly. 'We had to stop several times while the schoolchildren sang songs, shook hands . . . and presented me with gifts.'[70] At the town hall she was presented with a Scroll of Honorary Citizenship, a distinction previously only bestowed on the poet and playwright Gerhart Hauptmann, a founder member of the 1905 German Society for Racial Hygiene. That afternoon, at her old school, she was amused also to be given a bound volume of those pages from the school class book that recorded the 'rich harvest of black marks' against her own name – at one stroke these had been neatly removed from the school's own records.[71] Above all, Hanna wrote, she was touched to look into 'the sparkling, eager eyes of the girls' in which she seemed 'to catch a reflection of my own youth'.[72] That evening she received another gift, a Grunau Baby glider, which she named 'after the unforgettable Otto Bräutigam' and donated to the local gliding school.[73]

Although she could not visit often, Hanna felt deeply connected to Hirschberg. Her mother, Emy, wrote almost every day, encouraging Hanna in her patriotic duty to her country while optimistically exhorting her to remain humble, and finally, lovingly, entrusting her to God. Emy prayed constantly for Germany, and for protection for those advancing the German cause, as she saw it. Like her mother's, Hanna's belief in God and the Fatherland was absolute.

'She herself thought she was a Nazi,' her uncle later testified, but she never joined the Party, perhaps because, as a Freemason, her father would not have been admitted.[74]

Hanna now saw how much her parents had aged. Emy's hair was grey and twisted back into a bun at the nape of her neck, and they both looked exhausted by worry. Hanna's brother, Kurt, had survived the sinking of his ship but was already back on active duty. Emy and Willy must have known that the odds of both, or even either, Kurt or Hanna surviving the rest of the conflict were slim. They found strength in their belief in the honour of their country, and the cause for which their children were fighting. It was their younger daughter, Heidi, who was their greatest source of comfort, however. The summer before, Heidi had given birth to twins, a boy and a girl, to keep their three-year-old brother company. Now she was pregnant again. Hanna loved playing with the children, often singing the Austrian songs that her mother had taught her and Heidi as children.

While Emy and Willy Reitsch were enjoying a rare family moment with both of their daughters at home, Melitta's equally proud and patriotic parents, like hundreds of thousands of German Jews, were facing the very real prospect of transportation to an unknown land or camp in the east. The first deportation of German Jews had taken place in January 1941. Initially Michael and Margarete were protected by the fact that Margarete was not Jewish, along with the influence of a close friend with the right connections, but they knew they could not rely on such support. In March, Goebbels noted that 'Vienna will soon be entirely Jew-free . . . now it is to be Berlin's turn.'[75] As their situation grew yet more precarious, ironically it was the suggestion that Melitta should be dismissed from Rechlin that would provide her entire family with a lifeline.

Melitta's extraordinary work with dive-bombers had not only proved her worth; she was increasingly considered to be irreplaceable. 'This woman's achievements . . .' Dr Georg Pasewaldt from the Aviation Ministry later testified, could 'scarcely have been performed by anyone else'.[76] Although officially her racial heritage was never discussed at Rechlin, not only the ministry but Göring himself now personally intervened to ensure Melitta's work was defined as 'war-essential', and her position was secure. As a result, on 25 June 1941, less than a month after Hanna had received her Iron Cross, Second Class, Melitta received something even more valuable – her *Reichssippenamt*, a certificate from the 'Reich Kinship Bureau', to confirm both her 'German blood' and her official status as 'equal to Aryan'.

'This special position saved her life,' Melitta's niece, Konstanze, later asserted, but Melitta was not satisfied.[77] Reasoning that if her work was considered war-essential, her requirements should be as well, she immediately risked everything she had gained by applying for 'equal to Aryan' status for her father and siblings. Lili was still fairly safe at this point, being married to a high-ranking Party official. Otto, an expert on Soviet agriculture, had gained almost unique value to the regime after the invasion of the Soviet Union a week earlier, although now rumours about massacres of Russian Jews began to filter back to Germany. Michael Schiller, and Melitta's younger sisters, Jutta and Klara, were all still extremely vulnerable.

Between 1935 and 1941, some 10,000 German descendants of Jewish families applied for 'equal to Aryan' status. Fewer than 300 would be successful, and all knew that their status could be revoked at any time.[78] In 1942, Martin Bormann, Hitler's fanatically racist personal secretary and head of the Party Chancellery, decided that only exceptional new applications would even be considered. None of the family could feel 'completely secure', Klara wrote, 'until the decision was made'.[79] Melitta's timely application may well not only have saved her family from deportation but, although she did not yet know it, ultimately prevented their murders. From this point on, Melitta knew that her Rechlin work was of vital importance not just for her fellow pilots, or even her country, but directly for the safety of her own family. She could not afford to take any unnecessary risks, but neither could she afford to be anything less than exceptional.

Among the pilots serving on the Eastern Front was Dietrich

Pütter, a lieutenant in a long-distance reconnaissance unit based at the historic city of Berdichev in northern Ukraine. Pütter flew a Ju 88, 'a pilot's aircraft', as he described it, 'the best in the world at the time', high above the Caucasus Mountains, providing aerial photographs of the passes in preparation for the German advance.[80] On a morning when he was the highest-ranking officer at the base, he spotted the Führer's sleek four-engine Condor approaching to land. Hitler had arranged to meet Mussolini at Berdichev and sat on Pütter's desk waiting for his guest, swinging his legs while the young lieutenant answered his questions about injection pumps, and the best routes through the mountains.* 'Hitler was impressive . . . he was so normal . . . and relaxed in the presence of his soldiers,' Pütter later recalled. And 'his political view was not so wrong'.[81] Berdichev had only been occupied since 7 July. At that point about a third of the Jewish population, including many Polish Jewish refugees, had managed to get out. Within a few months a ghetto had been established for the rest. Four hundred male 'specialists' were removed to provide labour. Between the summer of 1941 and June 1942 the remaining Jewish population was massacred.

In August 1941, Pütter returned to Berlin to deliver a box of Black Sea caviar to Göring, who he knew quite well, having trained with his nephew. Pütter was staying at the luxurious five-storey Adlon Hotel at the top of Unter den Linden, then *the* hotel in Germany and just round the corner from the Ministry of Aviation.† At breakfast, to his great delight, he found himself sharing a table with the now famous Hanna Reitsch. Hanna was dressed in one of the outfits she had designed for herself, and which reflected her position so appositely: 'like a kind of uniform, but not a uniform',

---

* Eventually Mussolini's Junkers Ju 52 arrived and Il Duce descended, desperate for the toilet. Pütter showed him the way, and one of his reconnaissance team quietly photographed Mussolini relieving himself. A few weeks later the SS arrived to confiscate the pictures.

† The Adlon had inspired Greta Garbo's 1932 film, *Grand Hotel*. It remained the social centre of Berlin throughout the war. For senior Nazis, however, the Kaiserhof was closer to the Reich Chancellery.

as Pütter saw it.[82] Both of them also wore their Iron Crosses. At nearly six foot, Pütter towered over the tiny Hanna, and the two of them were soon laughing at how she sometimes had to take a cushion into the cockpit.* 'She was very charming . . . with a winning smile,' he later remembered, but when he mentioned his coming appointment Hanna was suddenly appalled. 'Give me your jacket,' she said urgently, 'you can't go like that to the Reichsmarschall!' One button was hanging loose. Hanna searched in her handbag and found needle and thread. Then she deftly sewed the button on, still sitting at the breakfast table. It was 'very motherly', Pütter laughed.[83]

Back with his squadron a few days later, 'we all talked about Hanna', Pütter admitted. 'She was a hero, of that there's no doubt. She was very, very well known and we all admired her hugely.'[84] A few weeks later he was shot down over Russia and taken prisoner of war.† As his colleagues helped the front move east, the killing of Russian Jews became a large-scale enterprise with more Einsatzgruppen murder squads sent in behind the front-line troops, specifically to annihilate the Jewish populations in newly conquered territories. Tens of thousands would be executed. 'Intoxicated by their victories in Europe . . .' Clementine Churchill, wife of the British prime minister, wrote, 'the calculated cruelty and barbarism of the Nazis were carried to new excesses in the invasion of Russia.'[85] At the same time, in a villa on Berlin's Lake Wannsee, plans for the 'Final Solution' for all Europe's Jews were quietly being finalized.

By the autumn of 1941, Udet saw that Germany was no longer winning the war. The Stuka dive-bombers he had championed, which had been so effective during the blitzkrieg, had never been a strategic weapon and ultimately proved all too vulnerable to enemy attack. After the Battle of Britain had exposed the

---

* Britain's Eric Brown also carried a (green) cushion around, to raise his height in the cockpit.

† Dietrich Pütter returned to Germany in 1948. He never met Hanna again but continues to admire her.

Luftwaffe's weaknesses that September, Udet had repeatedly emptied his revolver into his apartment wall in a sad echo of the party games he had held before the war. A year later the Luftwaffe was suffering heavy losses on the Eastern Front and there was still no satisfactory four-engined bomber able to reach the Soviet production centres in the Urals. Under-resourced and poorly directed, Nazi German mass aircraft production was now far behind that of the Allies. Udet was ill and exhausted. His relationships with both Göring and his deputy, Erhard Milch, whom he had once taught to fly, were in crisis. He had also heard about the mass killings of Jews in the east. Above all, Udet knew that the Luftwaffe would face overwhelming odds within a few months, and he could see no viable way forward.

On the morning of 14 November, Udet woke and put on his red dressing gown, the same type he had worn ever since the Great War. He loaded his revolver, poured himself a brandy and returned to bed. Lying very still, he aimed the gun not at the wall, but against his own head. Then he pulled the trigger.

Hitler was 'much affected' by the news of Udet's death, his valet recorded. 'Pity,' the Führer said after some reflection. 'That was not the correct thing. Udet should not have given in, but fought for his ideas.'[86] Three days later, the tragic death of Colonel-General Udet 'while testing a new weapon' was announced.[87] Göring gave a tearful eulogy at the state funeral, but commented privately that he was glad 'that Udet dealt personally with his own case'.[88] Goebbels felt similarly. 'Far and away the greatest blame for [the failure of the Luftwaffe] falls on Udet,' he later noted in his diary. 'He tried to atone for this by committing suicide, but of course that didn't change things . . .'[89] Hanna had a more balanced view on the death of her former friend and mentor. It was Udet's 'inevitable failure' in his appointed role, along with 'Hitler's evident disgust with that failure, and the personal denunciation of Göring' that drove him to kill himself, she later wrote.[90] It was not long before the truth about Udet's death leaked out, causing a minor crisis in morale within the Luftwaffe, where the Great War hero had been immensely popular.

Hanna and Melitta had both admired Udet, and each had turned to him in confidence when they needed an ally. His willingness to support both women perhaps reflected the ambivalence Udet had felt towards the regime and its policies. Neither Hanna nor Melitta would talk about his death, however, 'which was puzzling', Peter Riedel wrote. 'As a rule, any serious accident is talked about and the details gone over again and again ... especially when a close friend has been killed. Here was a complete blank. Ernst, I thought, must have been flying some very secret aircraft.' Yet Peter could not help but notice that 'there was something odd about Hanna's manner'.[91]

The next month the Wehrmacht reached the outskirts of Moscow, but they were exhausted and ill-equipped for winter warfare. Their rapid advance meant they had outrun their own supply lines, and they were now expected to live off the land in the middle of winter, while the local population starved. In mid-December, following the Japanese attack on Pearl Harbor, Hitler declared war on the USA, naming himself commander-in-chief of the Wehrmacht a week later.

Few women in Germany had risked their lives more regularly for the Third Reich than Melitta von Stauffenberg and Hanna Reitsch. Yet few better represent the different and sometimes conflicting motivations behind support for the regime's war effort. Melitta was no reactionary. At a time of war she wanted to support her country, just as her father had twenty years earlier. There is no question that her contribution was significant. By the end of 1941 she had completed more than 900 almost vertical precision dives, testing various new sighting devices and other equipment. Melitta, however, was under no illusions about the moral authority of the regime she served, or about her family's precarious place within the country they called their own. Making herself indispensable to the regime gave her a way to protect her family. However naively, she also hoped that her work might help minimize losses among young Luftwaffe pilots, and civilians overseas. Hanna may not have fully appreciated the darker side of Nazi policy, but she had witnessed Kristallnacht and the cover-up around Udet's death, and she could hardly have failed to understand the general ethos of the super-race. Yet with her world records, diamond badges and Iron Cross, this was a 'race' to which she felt she belonged. Thrilled by her country's early military successes, and delighted to be part of the elite, at the close of 1941 Hanna was proudly signing photographs of herself wearing her Iron Cross to hand out as Christmas gifts.

8

DEFYING GRAVITY
1942–1943

'Flying ladies . . .' Colonel Dr Georg Pasewaldt at the Ministry of Aviation wrote dismissively, 'generally used the profession more or less to further their own publicity.'[1] As a rule, he 'paid no particular attention' to them.[2] At the end of 1941, however, Pasewaldt was undertaking an inspection at Rechlin when he spotted a Junkers Ju 88 twin-engine bomber streaking down out of the sky, straight towards the earth. The colonel demanded to know the name of the pilot at the controls, and what purpose was served by this high-risk manoeuvre, 'which appeared to me to far exceed the limits of the permissible, even at a test centre'.[3] It was just 'Melitta, doing her dive trials', he was told by the ground crew, who were amused by his surprise at what was to them so familiar.[4] Pasewaldt stared in disbelief as the bomber straightened out. Then he drove to the hangar to wait for Melitta.

A veteran of the First World War, and squadron commander of two Bomber Wings in the Second, Pasewaldt knew that taking a plane into even a moderate nosedive was 'something many male pilots already regarded as an act of heroism'. Melitta's work, repeatedly flying 'in the most extreme dive configurations' to develop equipment herself, was absolutely astounding.[5] From the moment Pasewaldt watched her 'climb out of her aircraft, fresh and light-hearted', he was captivated by Melitta's 'almost unique outlook on life . . . far removed from even the slightest hint of egotism'.[6] That day he 'firmly resolved to make sure that this exceptional woman should receive special distinction'.[7] Pasewaldt as yet 'knew nothing' about Hanna's flight trials. Before 1942 was out, however, he would find himself discussing 'what special, exceptional honour' could be awarded for her service as well.[8]

Melitta and Hanna were both transferred away from Rechlin at the beginning of 1942. Hanna left in January, returning to the glider research institute at Darmstadt. There she faced a terrible start to the new year. Within a month of Udet's death, the husband of her sister, Heidi, was killed in action, leaving his widow with three small children and heavily pregnant with their fourth. Two weeks later Kurt was reported missing for a second time. Heidi's baby died within a few months of birth, and Hanna's father, Willy Reitsch, slipped inexorably into depression. Hanna's work was going badly, too. At Darmstadt she was testing more of Hans Jacobs' designs, but these gliders no longer inspired her. With Udet gone, she needed a new mentor. An instinctive hero-worshipper, Hanna had adopted Wolf Hirth as her first 'flying father' until Walter Georgii and then Udet had taken over the role, easing her career path and generally promoting her to the Nazi leadership. Now she appealed again to Udet's fighter ace friend from the First World War, Robert Ritter von Greim.

Greim was an enthusiastic Nazi who had joined the Party early. It was he who had taken Hitler on his first flight, in an open biplane, to the Berlin Kapp Putsch of 1920. When the coup failed, Greim had performed aerobatics for a living, before accepting work with Chiang Kai-Shek's government helping to build a Chinese air force. Bluntly racist, he did not expect much from his Chinese students, and was pleased to return to Germany and lend his support to Hitler's Munich Beer Hall Putsch in 1923. Ten years later he was a key figure working with Göring to secretly rebuild the Luftwaffe. By 1942 he had supported the invasion of Poland, the Battle for Norway, the Battle of Britain and Operation Barbarossa, the surprise German invasion of the Soviet Union. His only son, Hubert, not far off Hanna's own age, was a Luftwaffe pilot. To Hanna, Greim embodied all the virtues she most admired: a love of flight, patriotism, honour, authority and absolute loyalty to the Third Reich. Now she began to lobby him for more exciting test work. Greim helped when he could. When he could not, Hanna started to claim that the Führer had given her licence to fly the best and most challenging aircraft the Third Reich had to offer. Not everyone believed her, but few wanted to get on the wrong side of Hanna Reitsch.

In February it was Melitta's turn to leave Rechlin. Pasewaldt's endorsement had helped secure her transfer to the Luftwaffe Technical Academy at Gatow, where some of the most advanced research in Germany was being carried out. Gatow was also the site of the Luftwaffe's most prestigious training school and, being on the outskirts of Berlin, it was the airport most often used by Hitler for his personal journeys. Set in beautiful deciduous woodland that ran down to the Wannsee, it was a surprisingly tranquil environment at the heart of Nazi air war operations. Melitta was allocated a room on the first floor of a guesthouse on the academy campus. From here she had fine views over the lake and the wooded shore beyond. Every morning she woke to birdsong, and she even befriended a squirrel, which allowed her to feed it from her window. In the evenings wild pigs would venture out, leaving tracks in the mud and, when it was cold, sometimes scavenging right up to the airfield hangars.

As time went on, 'the number of friends in her circle however diminished', Jutta realized, noticing that 'an increasing number of pictures of crashed, fallen and missing friends were hung on the wall'.[9] Melitta felt no allegiance to the Nazis, but these young pilots had been friends and colleagues, fighting and dying, she believed, for the honour and security of their country. Knowing that her work could reduce some of their risk, Melitta exploited every moment of good weather, walking or cycling over to the airfield early in the mornings and often managing twelve or more test-flight dives with Ju 88s and Ju 87s every day.

As an engineer–pilot, Melitta already had all the qualifications needed for a technical general staff officer so she now started work on a PhD. Her new work was focused on the development of a special night-landing device for single-engined night fighters. She was 'testing landings with fighter planes for unlit, improvised emergency airfields', and 'blind-flying' without any electrical landing systems, Jutta explained.[10] She also had to respond to various spontaneous demands and requests from the academy. Once, testing a powerful Ju 52 on a cross-country flight, her co-pilots were 'astonished by how precisely' she held the 'powerful central engine' even in squally weather.[11] 'During the flight, Countess Stauffenberg wore a grey or blue-grey suit and a hat with a broad brim which she did not remove during the whole flight,' one remembered noticing, before he was distracted when 'the frequent and full rudder movement due to the bumpy weather meant that she had to continually struggle with the skirt of her suit which tended to ride up'.[12] When, arriving back at the airfield, he expressed his amazement at the ability of this most feminine pilot, he discovered that 'the Countess's precise flying and holding of an exact course' were already well known and respected.[13]

The RAF and the Luftwaffe were now engaged in a sustained air war, with regular bombing raids on both sides. Although Britain was not yet undertaking saturation bombing, which was initially used to support ground operations, many residential areas in Germany were badly damaged and civilian casualties were high. The same was true in Britain. In May the House of Commons and Westminster Abbey received a direct hit during what the Nazi press called retaliatory action. 'The debating chamber of the House was wrecked . . .' *The Times* reported. 'Big Ben fell silent, its face blackened and scarred.'[14] 'Our ability to produce more and more [bombers] in spite of the air raids must have been one of the reasons that Hitler did not really take the air battle over Germany seriously,' Albert Speer later wrote.[15] But in 1941 Hitler had overextended his resources by embarking on the Russian offensive. As a result, he rejected Speer and Milch's proposals 'that the manufacture of bombers be radically reduced in favour of increased fighter-plane production', until it was too late.[16]

As the Allies invaded the airspace above Gatow, Melitta faced jeopardy not only from her own inherently dangerous work, but also from enemy engagement. Despite several attacks by Allied planes, which also strafed the airfield, Melitta's test rate never slowed. She would complete over 2,000 nosedives and patent many

innovative equipment designs during her time at Gatow.* 'I believe
I can say this much with satisfaction,' she later told an audience
when required to speak about her work. 'My efforts have not been
in vain.'[17]

As Gatow was on the edge of Berlin, Melitta often travelled in
to buy black tea and biscuits, or to meet friends for supper at the
Aero Club. She also relaxed by sailing on the beautiful Wannsee,
or sculpting fine busts of Alexander, his dissident uncle Nikolaus
von Üxküll-Gyllenband – now better known to her as Uncle Nüx
– and several of her colleagues.† Paul von Handel admired her
ability to catch a likeness and thought the portraits 'very impressive and powerful', but he wondered how she could find the time
for such work.[18]

Melitta was also trying to see more of her own side of the family.
Once she even managed to travel to Danzig for a party. Photographs
show her standing on the steps of her parents' house in a fashionable
satin summer dress, surrounded by Lili, Jutta, Otto and various
children. Most get-togethers were in Berlin, however. Otto's wife,
Ilse, was now living near Tempelhof airport at Manfred von Richthofen Strasse, named after the Great War fighter ace, and her
house became a hub for visiting family. Otto would sometimes
arrive in his long leather coat, with presents of clothes and hats from
Russia and Romania, or Delftware brought from the Netherlands.
No one asked how he had acquired them. Melitta brought gifts
too. Arriving for tea in one of her elegant trouser suits, she always
carried an incongruously large handbag. Ilse and Otto's two young
daughters, Ingrid and Hannalore, and their cousin, Heidimarie,
would pounce on the bag, knowing that their 'Tante Litta' brought
something more precious than textiles or ceramics. Melitta saved up
her rations of pilot's issue Scho-ka-kola chocolate for the children.
The round blue and white tins, featuring a swastika-laden eagle

---

* According to Jutta, Melitta had patented seventy-five of her inventions by 1943, but
no records have been found.

† Melitta sculpted Alexander on several occasions, looking increasingly imperious
over time. One version is kept with her bust of Nikolaus, and Frank Mehnert's busts
of Claus and Berthold, at the Stauffenberg schloss in Lautlingen, now a museum.

within a starburst, had become iconic when the brand was launched at the 1936 Olympics. Among other active ingredients, the chocolate contained Pervitin, a strong nervous-system stimulant that helped to keep pilots and other servicemen alert. No wonder the children loved it and would afterwards bounce around, particularly Heidimarie who, being the eldest, would always take 'the lion's share' of the chocolate when it was divided up.[19]

In February, Alexander was drafted into Artillery Regiment 389, known as the Rhine Gold Division, and sent to a former Czechoslovakian training garrison at Milowice.* Melitta missed him and worried about him terribly. Pulling a few strings, she managed to secure a work trip to nearby Prague, and Alexander took leave and travelled over to meet her with a close friend, Max Escher. Melitta was staying at the prestigious Hotel Ambassador and the men revelled in the chance to enjoy a bath and some good food before they all headed out for the evening. This was the first time Escher had met Melitta, and he was surprised to find a 'fine-limbed, delicate woman', who 'did not give the impression of a bold and daring pilot'.[20] Furthermore, Escher wrote, 'this objective woman with her incisive mind provided the greatest contrast to the imaginative, silent poet and academic, but also his best complement.'[21] Together, he felt, they were 'a quite amusing pair'.[22]

Melitta knew how much Alexander enjoyed a glass of really good wine but, having learnt that his camp was 'dry', she had been frustrated to discover that bottles of decent wine in Prague were impossible to buy. Instead, she made it her business to visit 'a string of wine bars' before he arrived.[23] At each venue, after sipping modestly at her drink, she covertly poured the rest of her glass into bottles hidden in her capacious handbag. When Escher feigned outrage at her duplicity, she laughed, telling him 'at first I wanted to wean [Alexander] off drinking – and in doing so I learnt to drink myself!'[24]

For a couple of days the three friends roamed through old Prague, exploring the cathedral, castle and palace like any pre-war

---

* Then occupied territory, Milowice is now in Poland.

tourists. They also visited the city's synagogue and Jewish cemetery. Melitta might not have considered herself Jewish, but her
appreciation of culture was not so narrow that she was uninter-
ested. At the sixteenth-century grave of Rabbi Löw, Escher told
the story of the Golem, which, he felt, 'suited our evening stroll
through the crooked, narrow lanes of the former ghetto quarter'.
Legend tells that Löw, a sculptor like Melitta, had created the
Golem of Prague from clay to defend the ghetto from the anti-
Semitic pogroms of the Holy Roman Emperor. When his work
was done, the Golem's body was stored in the attic of the old synagogue, in case he should ever be needed again.

It is not hard to imagine Melitta and Alexander's thoughts as
they listened to this story in the Prague of 1942. The first transports of Jews from the city to Łódź had taken place in November
1939. In 1941 Reinhard Heydrich had been appointed 'Protector' of annexed, occupied Czechoslovakia, and that October he
attended a meeting in Prague to discuss the deportation of a
further 50,000 members of the Jewish community. Heydrich had
been one of the minds behind Kristallnacht, and was directly
responsible for organizing the Einsatzgruppen, the task forces that
travelled behind the advancing Nazi German front line, murdering
Jews and others deemed undesirable. His round-up of Czechoslovakian Jews and the appalling reprisals exacted for any domestic
resistance had led him to be known as the Butcher of Prague. The
following January Heydrich chaired the secret Wannsee Conference, to discuss implementing the Nazi plan for the extermination
of the Jews through systematic genocide. Melitta, Alexander and
Escher would have known little of these events, but it must have
been notable how few Jews they encountered as they wandered
through old Prague, while any they had met would have been
wearing a yellow star and awaiting deportation to Theresienstadt
concentration camp, where 33,000 people would eventually die.*
'We warmed ourselves in a low dive off a gloomy lane,' Escher

---

* Two months later Reinhard Heydrich would die following an ambush by members
of the Czechoslovak resistance, supported by the British SOE, in Prague.

continued. 'A blind harpist sang Czech folk melodies. It almost confirmed the Yiddish romance of the place.'[25] He also commented that Alexander and Melitta 'sit together and cuddle a lot', but he did not say whether they clung together for romance, blithely unaware of the attacks on the community around them, or for consolation.[26]

Alexander came from an aristocratic conservative elite that had a history of anti-Semitism, and his brother Claus had certainly absorbed a good deal of racism – and displayed it. Yet Alexander was vehemently opposed to Nazi discrimination. Melitta had found herself aligned with a people she had never much considered previously, and with whom she now feared sharing an identity. Alexander once told Escher that 'in flying clothes and crash helmet', Melitta 'looked like the Archangel Michael himself'.[27] He had chosen an interesting simile. Michael is an archangel not only in Christian theology, but in Islam and Judaism, too, and he is widely considered a protector, a healer, and an advocate of the Jews, as well as the patron saint of the airborne.

The friends then found a bar and settled down to discuss their own likely futures. Escher wondered whether he and Alexander might volunteer for the Norwegian coastal artillery, but Alexander believed they would be sent to the Eastern Front. Although aware of the hardships there, he tried to keep their spirits up, laughing that 'we will have to see where the ancient Goths wandered about!'[28] Melitta said nothing to dissuade her husband from 'the Russian adventure', as Escher put it, but he noted that 'her anxiety showed itself as we parted: "Please keep an eye on Alexander",' she exhorted him; '"he is totally unmilitary!"'[29]

In early March, shortly before the men's transport left, Melitta managed to meet them again, this time at their camp in Milowice. Alexander had arranged for her to stay at a local guesthouse; he was so unworldly he did not realize that it also served as the troops' brothel. Word quickly spread about his faux pas, and new rooms were found at a farmhouse. It was clean but cold, so Escher arranged for two sacks of coal to be brought over from their own stocks. He and Alexander also liberated a heavy case of

French sparkling wine, which they dragged across the snow to the farmhouse.

The moon was already up when Alexander, Escher and Melitta met for a last night together before the men left for the front. In honour of the occasion, Melitta wore an evening dress with some old family jewellery. The farmhouse stove was glowing, and the painted furniture, woven chair covers and red-checked bedding made the room feel warm, safe and snug, but thoughts of death could not completely be chased away. Alexander read out some of his most recent poems, which were personal but also full of portent: 'Whoever thinks about the worst, about death, attracts it,' he had written.[30] Eventually, though, warmed and wearied by wine, they found themselves gripped by a 'lasting peasant-type jollity'.[31] Admiring Melitta's 'remarkable inner reserve', Escher decided that 'true serenity is the best protection for the soul, and the nerves'.[32] For all her 'robust attitude', however, it was clear to Escher that Melitta was struggling to 'overcome and forget the conflict between her gruelling service under a tyrant . . . and her growing insight into the criminality of his regime'.[33] Despite her 'shy smile', he wrote, 'she could not hide a slight, latent melancholy'.[34]

That spring was hard for Melitta. Alexander and the 389th Infantry Division saw action almost immediately after her return to Berlin. Casualty figures were high. Yet Melitta's work and day-to-day life had to continue much as before. Sometimes Claus's beautiful wife, Nina, would visit Melitta with her children in tow, and the two women would talk about their husbands away on active duty, the letters they sent back, and the direction of the war. As a distraction, Melitta also took Nina out sailing on the Wannsee, as was her habit with close friends. Once, a lady beside them on the same jetty dropped her handbag, which fell into the lake. Without a second thought, Melitta pulled off her jacket and dived in after it. Moments later she returned the bag to its owner, deeply impressing Nina's six-year-old son, Heimeran von Stauffenberg. It was typical of the spontaneous and slightly daring nature that made Melitta so popular with the children.

With Alexander now deployed, Melitta also started spending

more of her free time at Lautlingen, the Stauffenberg country home where Nina also liked to escape the air raids of Berlin. Melitta loved the grand old house and the surrounding hills, thick with forest, where she would go shooting with Alexander's uncle Nüx. She arrived not just with Scho-ka-kola for Nina's children but also model Junkers aircraft made from cast metal, precious gifts during wartime when chocolate and new toys were rare. Her nephews and nieces adored her and sat entranced by her flying stories, just as she had with her uncle Ernst during the previous conflict. They all found her much warmer than their academic uncle Alexander. When they were with Alexander, 'he was always writing poems which we children didn't read,' Claus's eldest son, Berthold, remembered. 'We liked him very much, but he was a bit unworldly.'[35] Not quite eight, but clever and mature for his years, Berthold had always enjoyed watching the adults and felt that, although they clearly loved one another, Melitta had tended to 'mother' Alexander.[36] His admiration for his aunt, however, was boundless.

On the rare occasions when Claus was home on leave, he and Melitta would also have long conversations at Lautlingen. Claus was serving in Vinnytsia, in Ukraine, where the mass graves of 10,000 men murdered by the Soviets just before the war had been uncovered in 1941. Later Nazi atrocities committed in the area included the murder of around 28,000 people, almost the entire Jewish population of the town. 'These crimes must not be allowed to continue,' Claus had reportedly sworn to officers at the General Staff headquarters.[37] Such words were worthless. Although seven-year-old Berthold did not know what his father and Melitta were discussing, he saw that 'they were close friends', and he understood that all was not right.[38]

While Melitta was developing aircraft technology at Gatow, and Alexander and Claus were on active service, Hanna was seconded from her glider research institute to work with the pioneering rocket-powered fighter plane, the Messerschmitt Me 163. Hanna had already tested several of Willy Messerschmitt's prototype gliders, including the Me 321 Gigant. Now Messerschmitt and his design team were focused almost exclusively on developing engine-less jet-powered aircraft. Their designs were revolutionary. The Me 262 *Schwalbe*, or Swallow, would become the world's first oper-ational jet fighter.* The stubby Me 163b *Komet*, a small egg-shaped machine with wings designed by Alexander Lippisch, would be the only operational rocket-powered aircraft.† Lippisch was also a vet-eran of the glider research institute, and had joined Messerschmitt at his base in Augsburg in 1939. His designs naturally reflected his experience. The Me 163 was made of fabric-covered wood, and while it flew at near sonic speeds under rocket propulsion, once its fuel was burned it coasted back down to earth as a glider.

From the summer of 1941 tests on prototypes of these incred-ible aircraft had been carried out both at Augsburg and at the top-secret proving ground at Peenemünde on the Baltic coast. Messerschmitt's chief test pilot was Heini Dittmar, the gliding champion who had travelled to South America with Hanna before the war to study thermal winds. Unfortunately he and Hanna had since fallen out. Hanna now had a reputation for demanding access to whichever aircraft she chose, sometimes delaying desperately needed trials. Furthermore, when she undertook test flights her reports were not always conclusive. 'She flies with her heart and not with her brains,' one pilot complained, or 'at least without critical understanding of her work'.[39] More than once, deficiencies were found in aircraft that Hanna had signed off. This 'was a little humiliating for her', noted Wolfgang Späte, the head of the oper-ational test unit.[40] Although 'not a very talkative person', Heini happily shared his blunt opinion of Hanna.[41] 'There are women who just can't stand it when there is a new man in town, and they

---

* The idea of jet-propelled aircraft was conceived by the RAF's Frank Whittle in 1929. Although he patented the idea in 1930 and built a prototype in 1937, he failed to gain financial backing. Germany's Hans Pabst von Ohain had a similar idea in 1936, and within weeks a vast development programme had been launched. Whittle went on to develop the British jet engine during the Second World War.

† The Me 163 was elegant in its own way. Test pilot Mano Ziegler described seeing it 'squatting in the twilight of the hangar, as graceful as a young bat'. See his *Rocket Fighter* (1976), p. 2.

haven't got him into bed yet,' he claimed. 'With Hanna it's the same, but about planes. Whenever there is a new prototype she becomes obsessed with it, and is not satisfied until she has flown it.'[42] Heini even threatened to leave the team, should Hanna be invited to join them. The other test pilots, including Rudy Opitz, a veteran of the Eben-Emael attack, supported him.

Späte was 'a dedicated Nazi', who had a reputation for arrogance.[43] He had known Hanna since their glider competition days when she had often outperformed him. Now he agreed that Hanna could be difficult. 'Her pride would neither tolerate accepting us as equal colleagues, nor even asking for our professional advice,' he wrote. 'She was number one, and she knew it!'[44] But Späte and Lippisch also recognized that Hanna had the support of Greim and other senior Nazis, and they hoped that her connections might draw extra funding to the project. Since Udet's death, the Me 163 had had to compete with rival super-weapon projects, such as the V-1 and V-2 rockets. 'Now and again, human nature and personal feelings tended to play a role,' Späte argued, 'and arousing the emotions of people in decision-making positions was one of Hanna's strong points.'[45] Späte negotiated a compromise. Heini and the team would continue their work at Augsburg, developing the aircraft as an interceptor to split up enemy bomber formations before attacking them individually. Hanna was sent to the Messerschmitt aircraft factory at Regensburg. Here she became the first woman to fly the rocket plane, undertaking at least four flights to test alternative landing equipment. To her intense frustration, however, none of her work required the use of rocket power; she was simply towed into the air and released to glide back down.

None of Hanna's colleagues at Regensburg doubted her courage or skill as a pilot, but a female flier was still a novelty. Although far from being the youngest test pilot at the base, Hanna had to work hard to maintain respect and generally keep the men in line. 'She was not an unattractive woman,' the pilot Hein Gering decided, but he understood that she was 'the girlfriend' of the Waffen SS's Otto Skorzeny.[46] Hanna did not yet know Skorzeny, although she would later work with him, and this may have been one ruse of several she adopted to keep men at bay.* Another was her habit of wearing a white angora sweater, 'so you could never put your arm around her because your uniform would be covered in white goat hair, and then everyone would know', Gering admitted.[47] But Hanna was not above appealing to the men for help when occasion demanded. 'There was one thing she was scared of,' Gering discovered, and it was not the Komet plane, the SS, or even the enemy.[48]

One evening a few of the pilots were sitting around in the officers' mess, chatting, when Hanna said she was hungry and headed to the kitchen to 'scrounge some food'.[49] 'All of a sudden we heard the most ear-splitting scream,' Gering remembered. The men immediately rushed into action, expecting to find someone trying to murder Hanna. 'Instead we saw her standing on the table in a state of great agitation, screeching at us to do something. Each of us looked at the other, not quite sure what to do . . .' Eventually they found the source of the commotion: 'a little mouse quivering in fear under the table'. Although it was quickly removed, 'no amount of reassurance would settle Hanna, and we had to make a bridge of chairs so poor Hanna could step from one to another before bolting through the door and into the darkness.'[50]

When the USA had entered the war in December 1941, Melitta and Hanna's gliding-champion-turned-air-attaché friend, Peter Riedel, was first interned, and then sent back to Germany via Lisbon. Arriving in Berlin with his American wife in May 1942, Peter feared he might be transferred to active service with the Luftwaffe.† In the hope that Melitta might be able to help him secure alternative work as an aeronautical engineer, he sought out 'the young Countess Stauffenberg', as he respectfully referred to her, and they arranged to meet at Gatow.[51]

---

* Gering may have had his dates confused, as Hanna and Skorzeny became closely associated in 1944.

† Helen Riedel arrived in Berlin within a month of the declaration of war between Germany and her native USA. She did not speak any German.

To Peter, Melitta seemed unchanged from 1932, when he had first taught her to fly gliders. 'The title of Flugkapitän, or similar honour, didn't seem to have gone to her head at all,' he noted with admiration.[52] Melitta had changed, however. She had learned to be suspicious of her colleagues, and to completely distrust the state she had been raised to feel so dutiful towards. Peter was bursting to talk. Having been based in Washington for some years, he felt he appreciated the extent of American air armament 'basically better than anyone else in Germany', and he had no doubt about the impending 'disastrous outcome of the war'.[53] Before he could say much more, however, Melitta suggested they take a boat out on the lake; it was only a short walk through the woods at the edge of the airfields, and the weather was too good to miss. Only when they were on the water and 'away from unwelcome witnesses' did Melitta start to ask questions.[54] This 'seemed to be the habit', Peter quickly realized, 'so that we could talk without fear of microphones'.[55]

Melitta and Peter talked for some hours. 'As I knew her and trusted her, I told her freely that I was very pessimistic about the outcome of the war,' he later recalled.[56] Melitta gave Peter a few work contacts but there was no obvious job for him at Gatow, so that very afternoon he and his wife visited another old friend doing well in the sector. Hanna 'had been like a sister to me in the past', Peter felt, not just on their 'wonderful soaring expedition to South America' in 1934, but also on her pre-war visit to the USA.[57] She had even helped to clear the way for Peter's marriage to Helen the year before, pulling a few strings with Udet and others.[58] Hanna now had a modest apartment in the Aero Club building, next to the impressive Ministry of Aviation in Berlin's Prinz Albrecht Strasse, which had once been home to Germany's upper house of parliament. Rather than meeting in one of the two beautifully furnished lounges at the Aero Club, under lifesize oil paintings of Hitler and Göring, however, Hanna kept their meeting to the privacy of her own small flat. Like Melitta, 'she was much more conscious of security than others I had met', Peter noted.[59]

'As usual, Hanna was full of energy,' he later wrote, and she was delighted to meet Helen. After the initial warm greetings, Peter mentioned that he had just come from seeing Melitta. To his shock, Hanna 'made an extremely rude remark'.[60] When he tried to interject, she carried on, using 'a very crude term', and even 'alleged that the Countess had made some sort of pass at her'.[61] Stepping back, Peter could hardly believe what he was hearing. Homosexuality was classed as a 'degenerate form of behaviour' in Nazi Germany, and lesbians were seen as 'antisocial' as well as being deemed 'non-Aryan'. Anyone found guilty of an 'unnatural sex act' was likely to be sent to a concentration camp, and trumped-up charges had been used to remove many people who had upset the Party hierarchy. But Hanna continued furiously, telling Peter that she had 'already rejected' Melitta twice and 'wanted nothing more to do with her'.[62]

It is unlikely that Melitta was attracted to Hanna. If she considered her at all, it would have been rather condescendingly as ill-educated, uncultured and politically naive – not the sort of person she would have invited sailing on the Wannsee, nor risked any close association with. Hanna may have felt patronized by Melitta, disdainful of her old-school conservatism and irritated by her cool lack of regard. She was certainly jealous of the respect generated by her work, and 'obviously furious', Peter realized, at her invasion of Hanna's space as *the* female pilot of note in the Third Reich.[63] Perhaps she did even feel rejected personally. Whatever the reasons, Hanna had taken offence, and the anger that stemmed from her keen sense of injustice and moral outrage at any perceived slight – a trait that had coloured her character from childhood – was now directed at Melitta.

Hanna did not stop there, however. According to Peter, she now used Melitta's Jewish ancestry 'as an opportunity to insult her in the nastiest way'.[64] 'This was the first time that Hanna Reitsch disappointed me as a person,' he later recalled. 'She spoke of Melitta in such a sharp and ugly way.'[65] Although Hanna's family had accepted and adopted the casual anti-Semitism prevalent in pre-war Germany, she herself had been horrified by the violence of Kristallnacht. But Hanna had not let this experience effectively challenge the fundamental racism with which she had grown up. Thoroughly attached to the Nazi regime that was providing her with both opportunities and honours, Hanna had willingly accepted both its propaganda and its policies, and allowed these to colour both her judgements and her friendships.

Neither Hanna nor Melitta knew about Nazi extermination camps, nor that the gas chambers quietly built and tested at Auschwitz, in annexed Polish territory, became fully operational that same month. The Third Reich now started to murder Jews, communists, Roma, homosexuals and other 'enemies of the state' on an industrial scale. While Heinrich Himmler, chief of the SS, spent part of his summer visiting Auschwitz to ensure that the system was running efficiently, Hanna and Melitta, like most German civilians, still felt that theirs was essentially a just war. The increasingly heavy bombardments of cities such as Berlin and Cologne reinforced the public mood of resistance and resolve.

That summer, Alexander's 389th Division joined the German offensive on the Eastern Front. Operation *Blau* (blue) aimed to capture Stalingrad on the Volga River supply route, and press on towards the Caucasus oilfields. The battle for Stalingrad was launched in late August, but the Soviet counteroffensive prevented the clean sweep round to encircle enemy troops that the commander of the 6th Army, Lieutenant-General Paulus, had planned. Alexander was serving in the middle of one of the bloodiest and strategically most decisive battles of the war. Within months he was seriously wounded and sent back to Berlin. He had been fortunate. His injuries were not life-threatening, but required some time to heal. Melitta joined him in Würzburg whenever she could, cooking him the best meals she could muster on their ration cards. Knowing these weeks were just a reprieve, they savoured every moment together. As he recovered, Alexander was even permitted to return to his academic work, and was appointed Chair of Ancient History at the University of Strasbourg, although he was not strong enough to take up the post.*

---

* Alexander would be sent back to the front before he could start at Strasbourg.

The incompetence of the military leadership, and the evident hopelessness of the situation that autumn, finally convinced Claus that Hitler had to be removed. From this point on, he worked actively towards the overthrow of what he now considered a criminal regime. At great personal risk, while he was stationed at Military High Command in Ukraine Claus contacted his brother Berthold, then advising Naval Command on the conventions of war and international law, as well as other trusted friends such as Helmut James von Moltke, Peter Yorck von Wartenburg, and even Paulus on the Eastern Front. '[Claus] was always keenly opposed to the [Nazi Party] business,' General Ritter von Thoma later remarked.[66] Now Claus drove around, urging officers to consider alternative ways forward. 'He opened his heart to us straight away,' one later admitted, at once impressed and shocked by Claus's courage, while another agreed, 'he was incredibly indiscreet'.[67]

In late October Melitta's father, Michael Schiller, now eighty-one, also rebelled, if on a more modest scale. Without consulting his daughter, he sent a handwritten plea to Göring, arguing that while Melitta's mathematical modelling and engineering work 'must definitely continue to be used in the interests of the Fatherland', she should be relieved of the nosedive test flights. 'According to medical opinion', he contended, these could 'prevent the possibility of issue'.[68*] With astounding audacity, he then suggested that a 'well-earned further honour for her services' might overcome any resistance from Melitta to the plan.[69]

If Michael had any concept of how Melitta was using the value of her work to protect herself and her family, he clearly felt it was not worth the daily risk to her life that came with the test flights. Melitta's mother, Margarete, however, was horrified when she discovered her husband was not only interfering in Melitta's affairs, but writing to the commander-in-chief of the Luftwaffe about their daughter's fertility. 'Reichsmarschall,' Margarete opened her

---

* Michael Schiller did not know that the enforced sterilization of 'half-Jews' had been discussed in Berlin earlier that year, so his chosen line of argument was unlikely to carry much weight.

own letter to Göring, 'As a result of his advanced age [my husband] overlooks the fact that parents should not involve themselves in the personal matters of their adult children . . .' Furthermore, she added, his belief that Melitta's work could have 'adverse effects, or even problems, in respect to children, I cannot understand at all'.[70] Having requested 'with the agreement of my husband' that Göring destroy and ignore the previous letter, she quickly signed off, 'Heil Hitler!'[71]

But the following year, Michael again petitioned Göring against Melitta's continued test flights. 'I submit . . . the most humble plea,' he wrote, prompted by his 'concern for her life'.[72] A pathetic last line begs Göring not to inform Melitta about this second letter. Presumably she had not been pleased to learn of his first. No doubt Michael hoped that Margarete might remain oblivious too. There is no record of any reply from Göring, but if neither Melitta's gender nor her 'Jewish blood' was enough to prevent her work for the Luftwaffe, then her father's letters stood no chance. Michael was only lucky that there were not greater repercussions.

While Michael was attempting to stop Melitta's test flights, Hanna continued her work without interference. Over the summer a military version of the Me 163 had been built. It was larger than its predecessor, and one test pilot felt it had 'the beauty of a mus-cular wrestler'.[73] This aircraft, the famous Me 163b Komet, was powered by extremely combustible twin fuels kept in tanks behind, and on either side of, the pilot's seat. The fuels were a mixture of methanol alcohol, known as *C-Stoff*, and a hydrogen peroxide mix-ture, or *T-Stoff*. Just a few drops together could cause a violent reaction, so they were automatically injected into the plane's com-bustion chamber through nozzles, where they ignited spontaneously producing a temperature of 1,800°C. Several test planes with unspent fuel blew up on touchdown. 'If it had as much as half a cup of fuel left in its tank,' one pilot reported, 'it would blow itself into confetti, and the pilot with it.'[74] Several simply exploded in the air. Hydrogen peroxide alone was capable of spontaneous combus-tion when it came into contact with any organic material such as clothing, or a pilot. To protect themselves, test pilots wore specially developed white suits made from acid-resistant material, along with fur-lined boots, gauntlets and a helmet. Nevertheless, at least one pilot would be dissolved alive, after the T-Stoff feed-line became dislodged and the murderous fuels leaked into the cockpit where they seeped through the seams of his protective overalls. 'His entire right arm had been dissolved by T-Agent. It just simply wasn't there. There was nothing more left in the sleeve,' the chief flight engineer reported. 'The other arm, as well as the head, was nothing more than a mass of soft jelly.'[75]*

On 2 October 1942, Heini Dittmar became the first person to fly faster than 625 mph in the Komet, reaching the edge of what was later called 'the sound barrier'. Although he was privately honoured for his achievement, because of its military significance the record was not made public. Hanna was impressed. She knew the Komet was a prestige project and, despite witnessing what she described as two pilots being 'blown to pieces when their plane exploded', she was itching to take her turn.[76] In fact, 'at least half of the test command is pushing to fly it', Heini laughed drily to Wolfgang Späte. 'And perhaps end up disintegrating in an explosion of T-agent!'[77] Later that month, after another Komet test, ground crew found Heini sitting in his cockpit paralysed with pain. His landing skid had not extended and the shock of impact had been transmitted through his seat. With a badly injured spine, Heini would be out of action for eighteen months. Hanna's opportunity had arrived.

'To fly the rocket plane, Me 163, was to live through a fantasy,' Hanna later wrote. 'One took off with a roar and a sheet of flame, then shot steeply upwards . . .'[78] Shortly after leaving the ground, the Komet reached a speed of 220–250 mph, blasting out what another pilot described as 'a violet-black cloud' behind it.[79] The

---

* Further dangers later faced Komet combat pilots. As forced labour was used in the planes' production, several examples of sabotage were discovered, including the use of contaminated glue, and stones wedged as an irritant between the fuel tank and its support. Inside the skin of one machine a brave French saboteur had written *Manufacture Fermée* ('Factory closed').

undercarriage, a wheeled dolly, then had to be jettisoned, as it could not be retracted and would otherwise create drag. The plane could then accelerate to 500 mph in the space of a few seconds, disappearing from sight as it reached an altitude of 30,000 feet in less than two minutes. 'It was like thundering through the skies, sitting on a cannonball,' Hanna raved, thinking of the cartoon of Baron Münchhausen riding on a cannonball that was the emblem of the test team. 'Like being intoxicated by speed . . . an over-whelming impression.'[80] After five or six minutes the fuel was spent, silence descended and the pilot had the momentary sensa-tion of swinging, suspended in mid-air, before sinking forward into their harness. The momentum of the aircraft carried it forward for a few more hundred metres, and then the speed started to fall away. The Komet glided back down to earth, landing on its retractable skid at a terrifying speed of between 100 and 150 mph.

'Bubbling with enthusiasm' even years later, Hanna would throw her head back and gesticulate expressively with her arms when describing the almost vertical ascent of the Komet, and once, in her eagerness, 'she slipped off the sofa and onto the floor'.*[81]

Späte still felt that Hanna was a liability. 'In my nightly prayers,' he confessed, 'I always include a little request that she doesn't show up again soon.'[82] Hanna, however, was nothing if not committed. Her fifth flight, on 30 October 1942, was again unpowered. Her Me 163b V5, carrying water ballast in place of fuel, was towed into the air behind a heavy twin-engined Me 110 fighter. But when Hanna came to release the undercarriage, the whole plane started to shudder violently. To make matters worse, her radio connection was also 'kaput'.[83] Red Very lights curving up towards her from below warned her something was seriously wrong. Unable to contact her tow-plane, she saw the observer signalling urgently with a white cloth, and noticed the pilot repeat-

---

* Although Hanna described flying the Me 163 under power, it has never been con-clusively verified that she did so. When Eric Brown later interrogated her about starting the rocket engine, she 'stammered and stuttered' and Eric became convinced that she had only ever flown the Me 163 while towed or as a glider. (Eric Brown, Mulley interview 18.03.2013.)

edly dropping and raising his machine's undercarriage. Clearly her own undercarriage had failed to jettison.

Down below, Hanna could see ambulances and fire engines rushing across the airfield. In such circumstances pilots were expected to bail out, but she was not prepared to abandon such a valuable machine should there remain any chance of bringing it safely back to earth. In any case, the stubby fuselage of the Komet meant that the fin was very close to the cockpit, so there was a high chance of her hitting it should she jump. Instead, her tow-plane circled her up to 10,500 feet. Then she cast off. Pulling out sharply, Hanna first attempted to shake the undercarriage free, but it would not move. Instead, with the plane still shuddering violently and time running out, she curved round and down to the airfield from a greater altitude than normal, aiming to side-slip the last few hundred yards to the edge of the field. As she did so, the plane dropped. 'I was struggling to bring the machine under control when the earth reared up before my eyes,' she later reported. As she hunched herself tightly together, 'we plunged, striking the earth, then, rending and cracking, the machine somersaulted over.'[84] The Komet had hit a ploughed field just short of the runway. It bounced violently, lost a wheel and slid to a halt after a 180-degree turn. Had she been carrying rocket fuel, Hanna would have been killed instantly.

To her surprise, the first thing she noticed when the Komet came to a stop was that she was not hanging in her harness, so she was probably right side up. She opened the rounded Plexiglas canopy. Feeling no pain, she cautiously ran her hand over her arms, chest and legs but found no injuries; it seemed miraculous. Then she noticed a stream of blood coursing down from her head, and moved her hand up to her face. 'At the place where my nose had been was now nothing but an open cleft,' she later recalled. 'Each time I breathed, bubbles of air and blood formed along its edge.'[85] Reaching for pencil and paper, Hanna managed to sketch the course of events leading to the crash before tying a handkerchief around her broken face to save the rescue party the sight of her shocking injury. Only then did she lose consciousness. Seeing her notes, even Späte was impressed. 'What a woman!' he commented.[86]

Hanna had fractured her skull in four places, broken both cheekbones, split her upper jaw, severely bruised her brain and, as one pilot put it, 'completely wiped her nose off her face'.[87] She had also broken several vertebrae. She was rushed to surgery but, knowing her arrival would cause a sensation, she insisted on travelling by car rather than ambulance, and on walking into the hospital through the quieter back entrance and up a flight of stairs before any members of staff were alerted.

After the operation, Hanna woke to find her head thickly bandaged, with just her swollen lips and 'the blue, bruised rims' of her eyes visible.[88] It still seemed unlikely that she would survive. Her mother joined her the following day, but her close friend Edelgard von Berg, who rushed to visit her, was killed in a car crash en route. It was another devastating blow, but as Hanna's condition remained serious there was nothing she could do but try to blank out her thoughts, for fear she would despair. 'I lay in pillowed stillness', she recorded, trying to cope with a 'new and passionless world'.[89]

'Our Me 163 had again attacked, like a stalking animal,' Späte wrote.[90] He conducted a thorough investigation, but was unwilling to take personal responsibility. His report emphasized that he had been 800 kilometres away at Peenemünde at the time of the accident and stressed that, despite the jamming of the landing mechanism, Hanna should have been able to manage a safe landing. Her injuries were largely her own fault, he implied, because she had not removed the gunsight that had smashed into her nose, while 'because of her short stature she had used a thick cushion behind her' and 'did not have her shoulder harness tight enough'.[91]

Hanna had needed the cushion and the loose straps to enable her to reach the controls in a cockpit designed for larger men. Späte had thought that wooden blocks to help her feet reach the rudder pedals would be ample modification. 'She must be able to do it in her sleep!' he had told himself. 'It would almost be an insult to give her advice.'[92] But the blocks had not been ready, and

Hanna would brook no delay. 'You can't accomplish much against her will,' one of the ground staff reported. 'She decided she would fly without the blocks. That was it. No discussion.'[93]

Letters, cards and gifts now poured in from around the Reich for the popular heroine. Späte was among many who arrived with flowers, but Emy Reitsch would not let him see her daughter. Even Himmler sent a bar of chocolate and some fruit juice, precious items in war-torn Germany, with his best wishes for Hanna's recovery. When Göring heard that Hanna had been critically injured during the course of her duty he felt that a public gesture should be made.

Georg Pasewaldt, from the Aviation Ministry, was with Erhard Milch when Milch decided to award Hanna the Iron Cross, First Class. Pasewaldt 'immediately expressed [his] strongest reservations', arguing that this was a military honour, to be earned in combat rather than through reckless misadventure.[94] He thought the War Service Cross, a decoration he already had in mind for Melitta, was more appropriate. His suggestion was quickly overruled. Milch wanted a 'special, exceptional honour' for Hanna Reitsch. Milch then placed a direct call to Hitler, described Hanna's accident and submitted his suggestion, pressing for an early announcement 'because of her imminent death'.[95] Reportedly 'deeply stricken and shocked', Hitler agreed at once.[96]

A few days later, in early November 1942, Hanna was officially awarded her second Iron Cross. She was the first woman to receive the First Class honour. It remained to be seen whether she would collect the medal in person or whether it would be presented posthumously, but her position as the great flying heroine of Nazi Germany was now unassailable.

While still in his meeting with Milch, however, Pasewaldt had taken the opportunity to request an honour for Melitta; something he had been wondering how to take forward for the best part of a year. Hanna's unexpected award had provided the perfect precedent. 'Countess Stauffenberg, with hundreds, more than a thousand experimental flights, beyond anything so far achieved in our special field, is most deserving,' he told Milch. She should, he said, 'be decorated with the Iron Cross, Second Class, at the same time'.[97] Milch had never heard of Melitta von Stauffenberg, but he knew of a modest aeronautical engineer called Melitta Schiller. His curiosity was piqued and he asked Pasewaldt for more details. 'This woman has sacrificed herself beyond description with her tireless practical trials for research in the service of the Luftwaffe,' Pasewaldt obliged. 'She has made technical and scientific evaluations and produced a complete report on each of her flights which include innumerable dives and night flights. This data is unobtainable by other means, and of unique value.'[98] Milch was suitably impressed.

On the morning of 22 January 1943 Melitta received a telegram from Göring. 'The Führer awarded you today with the Iron Cross 2,' it read.[99] Six days later she received another, which had been delayed. 'I will present you with the Iron Cross, awarded by the Führer to you, personally, on January 29.'[100]

Göring presented Melitta with her Iron Cross, Second Class, at his villa in Berlin's Leipziger Strasse, just along from the Ministry of Aviation. On arrival she was shown into a huge parlour, hung with tapestries and old-master paintings that the Reichsmarschall had collected. Presumably in deference to her gender, Göring's beautiful second wife, Emmy, her sister, niece and the female head of a theatre school joined Melitta first. Hitler was notably absent. Finally Göring arrived. Melitta was shown into his private office, where they talked for a while about her work. He 'absolutely can't believe that I fly heavy bombers, like the Ju 88, and even do nosedives with them', Melitta later reported to her family. 'He is also surprised by the number of my dives,' but he confirmed it all with his files.[101] Once satisfied, Göring led Melitta to his desk and pinned her medal on her. It had been intended that she should receive the Military Flight Badge in gold with diamonds and rubies as well, but the jeweller needed another eight weeks to complete it. Göring then expressed his 'deep, sincere admiration' for Melitta and her work, and joked with her that it would be easier to list the planes she could not fly, than the ones she could.[102] 'The thing was clearly fun for him,' Melitta wrote.[103]

At one point, Göring asked Melitta why she did not work directly for the Reich, rather than through a company secondment. 'After some thought, I answered that would be convenient in a way, because the other companies wouldn't see me as competition any more, as they sometimes do, even though I've been seconded from Askania since the beginning of the war.'[104] Scandalized that commercial interests were apparently still considered during wartime, Göring told her he would personally make arrangements for her release and transfer.

They then rejoined the other guests for a lunch of fish pancakes and wine. The talk was light-hearted, despite covering anticipated British air raids, and finally Göring asked about Melitta's 'strange husband, who let me fly like this', practically offering to promote Alexander to professor had he not already held the position.[105] It was only after 'coffee with cream and liqueur or brandy', that Melitta was finally offered a lift home. Even then, Emmy Göring held her back for a moment, forcing a package of coffee and tea on her, and inviting her and Alexander to use their box at the theatre, and to stay at their guesthouse whenever they wished. All in all, 'it was really cosy', Melitta told her family with some astonishment. 'The tone was pleasant and good-humoured, and you got the impression of an honest and touching heartiness.'[106] Göring even noted the event in his diary that evening: 'Gräfin Schenk (von Stauffenberg) awarded Iron Cross II'.[107] It was an extraordinary moment for a woman who the previous year had been under investigation as a 'Jewish *Mischling*' (half-blood).

The press covered the story over the next couple of days. 'Brave Woman Receives the Iron Cross' ran the typical headline, before summaries of Melitta's service for the Luftwaffe, the fact that the award was 'rare for a woman' and, sometimes, mention of her 'feminine grace'.[108] One piece even reported how her 'artistic sensibility' as an amateur sculptor served her well as a pilot, by providing an 'unerring sensitivity to the aircraft'.[109] 'Her name was on everyone's lips,' Jutta would later recall proudly.[110] Melitta's commemorative radio interview 'was a disappointment' to her superiors, however, 'as she was far too modest and spoke of simply carrying out her duty'.[111] As the news from Stalingrad continued to worry the population, her story was meant to be inspiring, but Melitta 'didn't want to be involved in propaganda such as this', Jutta wrote.[112]

Hanna Reitsch and Melitta von Stauffenberg were now the two most highly honoured women in Nazi Germany. But although officially both heroines of the Third Reich, and with their names prominently linked in the press, according to Peter Riedel, Melitta's award came 'much to the disappointment of Hanna'.[113]*

Hanna was still in hospital facing a series of operations, but off the critical list by the time Melitta received her award. Already livid at this further challenge to her status, Hanna believed that Melitta's part-Jewish heritage made the situation even more insulting. Even years later she would argue that Melitta's Iron Cross 'was not valid', but only something Melitta had bullied her superiors into agreeing to, and which was never correctly awarded.[114] It was probably a fear that her 'racial burden' might limit her career, Hanna claimed, that had led Melitta to call Professor Georgii in Darmstadt after Hanna had been promoted to Flugkapitän, 'not to congratulate me, there was not a word about that, but in order to ask Georgii, who was embarrassed by this, how to obtain such a rank'.[115] 'Even more embarrassingly', Hanna continued, after the award of her, Hanna's, Iron Cross, First Class, Melitta had visited Darmstadt to again lobby for her own honour. Udet had reported it to Georgii and herself, 'very excitedly', Hanna wrote, saying 'he had done something stupid. He had let himself be persuaded by Melitta's constant nagging to award her the Iron Cross, Second Class . . . to get rid of her.'[116] The head of Women's Affairs in the Reich, Frau Scholtz-Klink, had telephoned Udet 'scandalized', Hanna continued. 'She had been informed at Hitler's headquarters that the award had never been authorized. From then on everyone stayed silent, in embarrassment.'[117]

These were embarrassing claims indeed. Udet had been dead

---

* *Deutsche Luftwacht* (German Sky Guard) was among the publications to run an article featuring both Hanna and Melitta in early 1943.

for over a year before Melitta's award was even considered. Even had Hanna accidentally named Udet when she meant to refer to Milch or another general, there were other witnesses to Melitta's award proving its validity, as well as the reference made by Göring in his diary that confirmed the honour in writing. Furthermore, contemporary newspapers could not have published their reports, nor could Melitta have publicly worn her Iron Cross ribbon as she did, had the award not been legitimate. Ironically, while Hanna was intensely jealous of Melitta's honour, Melitta herself was ambivalent. 'She liked to wear the decoration,' Professor Herrmann, head of the Technical Academy at Gatow, wrote. It was reassuring for her to know she was valued, and she was proud of her work and that it should be recognized. But she wore it, Herrmann stipulated, 'in spite of her reservations which were becoming increasingly clear to those who were initiated into her personal thoughts'.[118]

9

UNDER ATTACK

1943

The Red Army launched a counteroffensive on the Eastern Front in November 1942. Since the Luftwaffe still had no fleets of long-range bombers capable of attacking Soviet factories or supply lines, the Russian advance seemed unstoppable. That winter, the German 6th Army in Stalingrad sat in their holes, anxiously listening for the drone of aircraft engines while trying to anticipate what limited supplies might be sent forward to them. They were in severe need of food, clothing, boots, artillery and fuel – indeed all essential supplies. With the December snows, conditions became unbearable. As the temperature dropped to 20° or 30° below freezing, it became increasingly difficult for any aircraft to fly. With the army unable to evacuate the wounded or those suffering from frostbite, mortality rates rose exponentially. Struggling on starvation rations, the men now supplemented their watery soup, one general recorded, with 'bones obtained from horses we dug up'.[1] 'Condition of the men is unfortunately shit,' another reported. The moment is coming 'when the individual says, "It's all the shit same to me whether I live or die" and simply allows himself to freeze to death or let the Russians overrun us.'[2] When Hitler's Luftwaffe adjutant, Nicolaus von Below, read out such 'pertinent extracts' from reports and letters, he noticed that the Führer only remarked on the 'profound duty in the struggle for the freedom of our people'.[3] Hitler preferred to lose the entire army in the fight, it seemed, than have them return defeated.

On 2 February 1943, Field Marshal Paulus, commanding the 6th Army in Stalingrad, surrendered to the Soviets in defiance of Hitler's orders. Hundreds of thousands of soldiers had died on both sides, and some 90,000 German survivors were now taken as

1. Cover of the commemorative book of Hitler's airborne election campaign, *Hitler über Deutschland*, by Heinrich Hoffmann and Josef Berchtold.

2. Hitler and his personal pilot, Hans Baur, studying a flight map beside their campaign tour aeroplane, April 1932.

3. Margarete Schiller with her children, 1912. From left: Klara, Otto, Jutta, Melitta (aged nine) and Lili.

4. Melitta's student ID photo from the Technical University of Munich, 1922 (*left*), and (*below*) with her statement bob, Munich, *c.*1923.

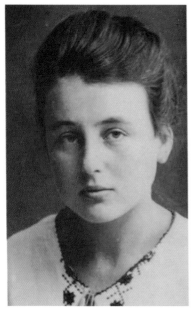

5. The von Stauffenberg family: Claus, Berthold and Alexander, sitting in front of their parents, Lautlingen, 1924.

6. Nina and Claus von Stauffenberg, Bamberg, 1933; the year they married.

7. Wedding of Paul von Handel and Elisabeth, Countess von Üxküll-Gyllenband, 9 April 1931. Melitta is second from right, front row, next to Claus in uniform. Alexander is on the far left.

8. Hanna as a child, *c.*1916, and on a Garbaty collectible cigarette card from their 'modern beauties' series, *c.*1935.

9. Hanna in a Motanol F glider, *c.*1934.

10. Hanna in a Sperber Junior glider, Wasserkuppe, August 1936.

11. Hanna flying a glider at the 17th Rhön gliding competition on the Wasserkuppe, August 1936.

12. From left to right: Wolf Hirth, Hanna, Dr Walter Georgii, Peter Riedel and Heini Dittmar, *c.*1933.

13. Melitta cycling across the airfield by a Junkers Ju 87 Stuka, Gatow, 1934.

14. Melitta in conversation with ground crew beside a Junkers Ju 88, Gatow, 1934.

15. Elly Beinhorn with Melitta at Chigwell aerodrome, Essex, September 1938.

16. Ernst Udet lighting Elly Beinhorn's cigarette on an airfield, date unknown.

17. 1936 Olympics poster advertising the 'Great Flight Day'. Melitta performed aerobatics at this prestigious event.

18. Hanna demonstrating the Focke-Wulf Fw 61 *Deutschland* helicopter inside the Deutschlandhalle stadium at the Berlin Motor Show, February 1938.

Soviet prisoners of war.* It was the greatest defeat in the history of the Wehrmacht and a turning point in the conflict. Germany was now on the defensive, no longer fighting to promote a political aim but rather to salvage some remnant of victory. Two weeks later Goebbels proclaimed the advent of 'total war', but as one pilot put it, 'after Stalingrad, the excitement in the Luftwaffe was over. The criticism, especially of Göring, became louder.'[4]

Melitta followed events from Gatow, desperately glad that Alexander had been injured and sent home before he could be killed or captured at Stalingrad. She regularly faced sleepless nights as Allied raids increased, and sometimes even came across British bombers when testing night-flying equipment above Berlin. Although 'tired and nervous', the 'destruction doesn't touch me', she wrote.[5] Melitta felt passionately that her own work 'could never be compared to the immeasurable suffering of the troops'; another reason she was so unwilling to blow her own trumpet in interviews when her Iron Cross, Second Class, was publicized.[6] Hanna heard the air-raid sirens from her hospital bed. Unable to do much more than listen to the radio, she noticed a faltering in what had once seemed to be the continual announcements of German victories, accompanied by fanfares and martial music. 'When the disaster of Stalingrad was announced . . .' she wrote, 'the shadows began visibly to descend over Germany, and in spite of official propaganda, which was still turned to victory, the feeling grew that the end was inexorably approaching.'[7]

Two weeks after Göring had presented Melitta with her Iron Cross, he ordered that she be given a 'government contract' with the Ballistics Institute.[8] As a woman, Melitta could never become military personnel, but over a series of lunches at the Aero Club she negotiated a remarkable arrangement with the Ministry of Aviation. She would be appointed as a professor, on a good salary, to an academic aeronautical institute. From there she could be seconded to the Technical Academy at Gatow for the rest of the

---

* Only an estimated 5,000 of those taken as POWs would ever return, and then only many years later.

war. The Nazi Party in Würzburg testified to her 'political reliability', and official photographs were taken. All that remained was
for her to complete her PhD.[9] She promptly suggested this be
awarded on the strength of two aeronautics projects that she had
already completed, and the doctoral thesis she was currently working on.

Melitta was now keeping a small appointments diary to help
her manage her hectic schedule. Her many brief but evocative
notes, scribbled in blunt pencil, hint at the strains that now characterized her official duties as well as her private life. Alongside
references to her dissertation and talks given for the Red Cross,
testing with Junkers continued. Her main focus was still Stuka
nosedives, but she was also working on adaptations for the Ju 88
to serve as a night bomber, and on cross-country flights over huge
distances between Berlin and, among other cities, Königsberg,
Dresden and Paris. Her test flights were not wholly without incident. Undercarriage doors got stuck, a canopy blew off during a
dive, there were problems with instruments and cameras, and a
crash while rolling to take-off. On one test she had to bail out
when her plane caught fire and on another, she noted simply,
'windscreen exploded'.[10] Once these might have been major incidents, but now they were almost lost among the broader dramas
of Melitta's life.

In addition to her own work, as Alexander recovered Melitta
was becoming ever more worried about his return to the front.
Surreptitiously listening to British and American radio to follow
the progress of the war – a crime now punishable by death – added
to her anxieties. The British public had first learned about Nazi
extermination camps from the BBC in December 1942, and
rumours about atrocities were now widespread within Germany.
Melitta was soon suffering from exhaustion, skin rashes and depression. When possible, she tried to unwind by taking Alexander to
leafy Lautlingen, and occasionally she took his mother to the
theatre. If she was stuck at Gatow, then Klara, Otto and other
family members would visit for tea – the Luftwaffe not only had
their own branded teacups and spoons but better rations than

civilians. But mainly Melitta went sailing on the Wannsee; a pilot's privilege to which few could aspire during the war.

Sailing also gave Melitta the chance to talk with Alexander, his brother Berthold, Paul von Handel and other trusted friends without risk of being overheard. All of them had learned to be cautious. Full names are rarely given in Melitta's diaries and there are no comments on the aims or direction of the war. She did not even mention events such as the much-publicized arrest and execution of Munich's 'White Rose' students, Hans and Sophie Scholl, who had distributed anti-war leaflets stating that 300,000 Jews had been killed in annexed Poland. The round-up and deportation of Berlin's Jews, even the extraordinary Rosenstrasse protest in February and March, which seemed to have secured the release from detention of the Jewish partners, mainly husbands, of 'Aryan' citizens – men in the same position as her own father – all passed without comment, although Melitta could hardly have failed to hear about and reflect on such events.*

In mid-March 1943 Melitta learned that Alexander was being sent on a training course in historic Jüterbog, in north-eastern Germany. Seizing this opportunity to avoid giving a Propaganda Ministry lecture in Sweden, she set out to visit her husband instead. Arriving late, in the dark Melitta stumbled on some filthy stairs, badly bruising her shin. 'Fainted, terrible, sick, crying fit,' she noted in her diary. 'Schn. very concerned.'[11] *Schn.* was shorthand for her pet name for Alexander, *Schnepfchen* or 'little snipe', although sometimes, she noted ruefully, with his dark army cape he now looked more like a black woodpecker. Melitta and Alexander managed to meet several times, heading out to bars and casinos. Once they even made use of Göring's box at the opera. Often Alexander was 'moody' when they met, but shared evenings made them both 'radiant with happiness', Melitta scribbled in her

---

* Although defending only so-called 'privileged Jews' married to 'Aryan' spouses, the Rosenstrasse protest is considered a rare moment when courageous civil disobedience resulted in defeat for Nazi racial policy and practice. However, it may be that these 'privileged Jews' were never intended for deportation at this stage, and their release was not related to the protest.

diary, before adding later, 'Schn. not that radiant any more, due to alcohol'.[12] At about the same time, news that not everyone at the barracks would be moving out caused elation: 'maybe some people will be spared!' Melitta wrote.[13] Alexander, however, received new orders before the end of the month.

Hanna spent five long months in hospital. After her condition stabilized, a series of pioneering operations included surgery to give her a new nose. Although she would always have a faint scar, and people who met her noted it was 'evident something had happened there', the reconstruction work was excellent.[14] Hanna was only ever matter-of-fact when mentioning her facial reconstruction, simply waving her hand towards her nose when words ran out, which took another kind of bravery. What she found harder to accept was the assumption, by both doctors and former colleagues, that her flying days were over.

In March, Hanna was discharged for a long period of convalescence. Although offered her choice of sanatorium, she chose instead to stay at a friend's isolated summerhouse, high up in the Riesengebirge mountains where she had hiked as a child, and above which she had often glided. 'She withdrew into a nutshell,' her colleague Wolfgang Späte wrote, 'and shut herself off from the rest of the world.'[15] But after a few days of 'timeless peacefulness', interrupted only by her mother bringing meals, Hanna set about planning her return.[16]

Still suffering from headaches and severe giddiness, her first priority was to recover her sense of balance, without which she knew she could not fly. The summerhouse had a flight of narrow steps running from the ground up to the steep, gabled roof. Hanna climbed them cautiously until she could sit astride the ridge of the roof with her arms firmly clinging to the chimneystack, and look around without losing her balance. After a few weeks her vertigo began to ebb and she risked letting go of the chimney. Within a month, through pure determination, she could ease herself along the entire length of the ridge without feeling giddy. She built up her strength by walking, then hiking, through the forest. Despite setbacks and some despondency, in time she began to climb the pines, branch by branch, ruefully recalling the days of her childhood when 'no tree had been too high'.[17]

Hanna's perseverance paid off. After a couple of months, the head of a local military flying school unofficially agreed to let her take up a plane. After managing a glider in a towed flight, she progressed to powered aircraft. Diving down on each flight from a greater height, she tested how much her head could tolerate. In time she practised steep turns, spins and, eventually, aerobatics. When she finally had a full medical check-up, the doctors were astounded at her recovery, 'but to me,' she wrote, 'all that mattered was – I was fit to fly again.'[18]

Hanna reported back for duty that spring. At first she was given public relations work. A 1943 propaganda film, *Hirschberger Fliegerjugend*, shows her glider arriving at her home town, where she is met by a froth of pretty girls, all blonde plaits and ankle socks, and strapping young lads who help her jump down. It was not long before she was back in the cockpit of an Me 163, however, testing the gliding descents. Hanna's fellow test pilots were much affected by her 'keenness and courage', but they knew that her safety was now a national concern.[19] Collectively, the pilots had an illicit store of eighty litres of brandy, which they kept in an enormous glass balloon protected by a wickerwork basket, hidden in Hanna's dorm cellar. When one of the team was killed or injured, they decanted a few bottles to give to the family with the bad news, as well as toasting them themselves. Hanna would help, sometimes laughing and joking with the men as brandy fumes gradually filled the small room. But everyone knew that it would take more than brandy to ease the news of any further accident that might befall Hanna. 'She was the one and only Hanna Reitsch,' as her colleague Mano Ziegler put it, 'a symbol of German womanhood and the idol of German aviation.'[20]

Given two theatre tickets one evening, Ziegler decided to offer one to Hanna but found her in her room, 'crying her eyes out'.[21] Wolfgang Späte had cancelled her first rocket-powered test flight. 'It's all so mean!' Hanna told Ziegler petulantly, in his account. 'He knows very well that I have longed for this take-off ever since my accident. And now he slams the door in front of my nose. It is so unfair!'[22] Hanna accused Späte of sexism, which was almost certainly true, but the fact still remained that she now held a unique position in the Reich. Späte was simply not prepared to take responsibility for her safety. According to Ziegler, Hanna's response was to stop her tears and start packing. 'I shall go straight away to see Göring – today, now!' she declared, and Ziegler believed her.[23] 'She had a will of iron and was not beaten yet,' he commented, 'even if she had to appeal to the highest in the land.'[24]

Whether by coincidence or design, Hanna soon received an invitation to join Göring and his wife, Emmy, at their Obersalzberg house in the Bavarian Alps near Hitler's own home, the Berghof. Over lunch they talked about her crash. To her horror, Hanna suddenly realized that Göring believed the Me 163 was already in mass production. 'I was astounded,' she later reported. 'I knew that at that very moment we did not have a single 163 ready for combat and, at the very best, we could not expect a single craft to be ready before the end of the year.'[25] Uncertain whether Göring was joking, or perhaps trying to reassure his wife, Hanna managed a half-laugh as she chipped in, 'That would be fine, if it were true.'[26] Göring demanded to know what she meant.

With 'stupefied amazement', Hanna started to give some realistic production figures to the commander-in-chief of the Luftwaffe. But 'Göring flew into a rage and, viciously pounding his fist upon the table, screamed that I didn't have the slightest idea . . . and strode angrily out of the room.'[27] Although Emmy eventually succeeded in calming him, it was clear that 'Göring did not want his comforting illusions to be disturbed.'[28] Now Hanna knew why no one dared to tell him the truth. Further attempts only confirmed that she had fallen from grace. She was, she later said angrily, 'never again called to see him or consulted on aeronautical matters'.[29]

Hanna was appalled and insulted by Göring's behaviour. She knew he was a morphine addict and now, with typical Nazi disgust at social deviance, she identified what she called his 'abnormal physical condition' as the source of his problems.[30] 'His feminine manner', she felt, was in stark contrast to his 'apparently iron commands', and 'his manner of dress, his use of cosmetics, his personal vanity, his perfume-drenched person and clothing, all created an actually decadent impression'.[31] A year earlier, Goebbels had been more forgiving. Göring's dress is 'somewhat baroque' and could strike one as 'laughable', Goebbels had written, but 'one must put up with his idiosyncrasies; they sometimes even have a charm about them'.[32] By 1943, however, with defeats in the east and the continued destruction of German cities from the air, Göring's star was on the wane. Milch argued that he had 'fallen asleep on the laurels won by the Luftwaffe in 1939 and 1940'.[33] Even Hitler was 'exceedingly angry' about the state of the Luftwaffe, expressing himself in the 'most furious and unrestrained language before the generals', and 'not even sparing the Reichsmarschall', Goebbels noted.[34] 'It appears that the Luftwaffe has lost much of its popularity,' he added with some relish.[35] Yet when confronted with uncomfortable truths, Göring 'would rant and fume', Hanna wrote, while continuing to delude Hitler with 'an entirely erroneous picture of his air strength'.[36]

For Hanna, Göring now became the scapegoat for all of the regime's misfortunes. Unable to contain herself, she rashly told her family about the parlous state of the Luftwaffe under the Reichsmarschall. Her Austrian cousin, Helmut Heuberger, had been invalided out of the army after being seriously wounded at Stalingrad. Once an enthusiastic member of the Hitler Youth, he was now the proud holder of the Iron Cross, Second Class.* Hanna's revelations forced him to take a long look at the Party leadership. Slowly he reached the difficult conclusion that his oath of loyalty should be towards the German Reich, rather than the Führer and his deputies. Not long after, Heuberger lent his support to the Austrian resistance through a distant relative. More

---

* Helmut Heuberger was the son of Hanna's mother's brother. The two families wrote regularly throughout the war and met when possible.

discreet than his cousin, he never discussed his changing views with Hanna, who remained blindly loyal to Hitler.*

Göring's 'gross incompetence', as Hanna put it bluntly, was certainly a key factor in the crisis facing the Luftwaffe, but Hitler's interventions had not helped.[37] Other factors included British air-warfare strategy and tactics. At the start of the war Sidney Cotton had been recruited into the RAF and given a team of specially modified Spitfires with which to conduct aerial reconnaissance. Two years later, this pioneering work had been significantly developed. RAF Medmenham, home of the British aerial intelligence 'central interpretation unit', had officially opened for business on 1 April 1941, at the 'hideous' former country home of 'a pickle millionaire', as one of the team, the future film star Dirk Bogarde, described it.[38] Humorists enjoyed the fact that this vital base for military intelligence was inaugurated on April Fools' Day, but ultimately the unit would prove as important to the British war effort as Bletchley Park. An estimated 80 per cent of British intelligence came from photographic reconnaissance and interpretation. 'At 30,000 feet you could take pictures of a man on a bicycle,' one pilot recalled.[39] Thirty-six million photographs were taken over the course of the war. Such a resource required a considerable team of interpreters, most of whom were WAAFs. 'Looking through a magnifying glass at minute objects in a photograph,' Cotton said, defending the recruitment of women, 'required the patience of Job and the skill of a darner of socks.'[40]

Photoanalysts were trained to recognize objects such as planes, roads or buildings from above, from their size, shape and features such as shadows. A small brass stand holding a pair of lenses, called a stereoscope, enabled analysts to obtain 3D images by simultaneously viewing two pictures taken from slightly different positions. 'Puzzling and tedious as it often was,' wrote the photo-interpreter

---

* After the war Helmut Heuberger became active in the increasingly violent South Tyrolean Liberation Committee. Although sentenced in absentia to thirty years in prison for involvement in bombings, he became a respected geographer and Alpine researcher, holding several academic posts. He died in 2006.

Sarah Oliver, daughter of British PM Winston Churchill, 'there were moments of terrific excitement and discovery.'[41]*

Photoanalyst Flight Officer Constance Babington Smith, a former journalist for both *Vogue* and the *Aeroplane* magazine, particularly enjoyed observing Rechlin. 'One never knew what one was going to find there,' she said, proving her point when she spotted an American B17 Flying Fortress on the enemy airfield, apparently being used for research.[42] Having been tasked with setting up the unit's dedicated aircraft section, then a unique appointment for a woman, Babington Smith identified the first image of a German jet aircraft by scorch marks on the grass airfield.† As her team hunched over their stereoscopes, it is highly likely that some of the dots emerging in 3D from the photos on their desks were Hanna and Melitta, walking to work across different airfields.

Appalled by Hitler's reckless military strategy at Stalingrad, when the battle was clearly lost Claus von Stauffenberg applied for a transfer. He was posted as a senior staff officer to the 10th Panzer Division in Tunisia. Here again, the situation for Germany was bleak. General Rommel had asked permission to retreat in November 1942, but had been ordered to hold out to the last man. Claus arrived to join the final days of the fierce battle for the Kasserine Pass through the Atlas Mountains. As he drove between units to supervise a tactical withdrawal, his car was strafed by enemy aircraft. Claus's head, back and arms were pitted with shrapnel as he dived for cover. His left eye was destroyed, and was later removed at the war hospital in Sfax. His right hand was amputated at the wrist, and he lost two fingers from his left. Evacuated to Munich, he underwent further surgery to remove shrapnel from his knee. Claus was determined not to be personally

---

* Oliver was popular not only for her hard work, but for her access to real coffee. 'She would share it round at midnight to keep us going,' a colleague, Doreen Galvin, revealed. (Mulley interview, Tempsford, 17.05.2015.)

† On one visit, Winston Churchill glowingly referred to her as 'Miss Babington Smith of Peenemünde'. (Churchill Archives Centre, Churchill College, Cambridge, CHUR 4/460A.)

defeated, however, and kept up his spirits by discussing a possible Bavarian–Austrian post-war solution with the operating surgeon.

Nina visited Claus immediately. In spite of his wounds, she found her husband full of vigour. At thirty-six, Claus, the quintessential soldier, could no longer use a gun, but friends noted that he was far from beaten, 'still handsome . . . [and] radiating a strong inner force and courage'.[43] Claus had a devoted wife, four young children and a strong sense of honour. 'In Africa they threw away my hand, even with my ring on it!' he told visitors with a wry smile.[44] His loyalty to his family and his country could not be tossed aside so easily. When his uncle Nüx visited, they talked about the limited German domestic resistance. 'If the generals won't do anything,' Claus told Nüx, 'then it's up to us colonels to take action.'[45] Later Claus whispered to his wife, 'It is time I saved the German Reich.' 'You are in the right condition for that now,' Nina laughed, assuming he was joking.[46] Later she would come to believe that this was 'the moment when he made the decision to actively involve himself'.[47]

Claus would not be discharged from hospital until early July. When he returned to Lautlingen, photographs show that he cut a gallant figure in his crisp white shirts and black eye-patch, playing with his children under the trees. 'He was essentially a brave man,' Nina felt, 'except when it came to wasps.' Whenever a wasp flew near him, 'he immediately disappeared under the table!'[48] His children remembered their father as 'absolutely wonderful' and 'extremely good-looking', but also very determined. He firmly refused any help with his bandages, joking that he was so dextrous, he did not know what he had done with ten fingers when he had had the full set.

Melitta greatly admired Claus, but she knew that her beloved Alexander was made from different metal. That spring, he had been transferred from Jüterbog for further training in northern France. Despite her hectic schedule, Melitta wrote every few days and flew over to visit every week. When planes weren't available she put on her thick coat decorated with her ribbon of the Iron Cross, and her standard look of implacable determination, and took overnight trains. By now the Allies had shown they could send bombers to Berlin, and there was a marked increase in the number of air raids. 'The English at present are making a sport out of driving as large sections of our population as possible out of their beds by air raid warnings . . .' Goebbels wrote irritably in his diary.[49] Melitta's journeys were often delayed by air strikes, and more than once she had to leave her train to take refuge in a trench. Coming back, if she couldn't make it to Gatow, she would stay overnight at Berthold's Berlin flat in Tristanstrasse. She was also lobbying friends, hoping to prevent Alexander's return to the front. When Claus heard of her efforts he wrote to her, 'shakily with the three fingers of his left hand', saying that neither she, nor their friends, should support such 'protective manipulations'.[50]

The next month, Melitta was assigned to supervise a twenty-four-year-old colonel, Friedrich Franz Amsinck, who had received the Iron Cross, First Class, and the Golden Wound Badge, having been injured in action. Franz had lost his right hand, like Claus, and had his left arm badly damaged, while serving on the Eastern Front. He had been lucky not to lose his life and was not expected to return to the front line, but he was still determined to serve his country. Having learned to glide as a boy, Franz was assigned to study mechanical engineering and aircraft construction, and slowly earned his pilot's licence. Melitta, now forty, was commissioned to train him, and directed all her frustrated protectiveness towards the injured but determined young man. That summer they worked together every day. Melitta taught Franz to fly a specially modified plane, eventually observing his nosedives and collaborating with him on technical problems.

Melitta and Franz also went sailing together, and often ate at the Aero Club in Berlin where she introduced him to friends like Paul von Handel, and in turn met his family. Occasionally the relationship hinted at something more than just comradeship. In July Franz gave her a copy of Antoine de Saint-Exupéry's *Wind, Sand and Stars*, a lyrical account of the celebrated French pilot's musings on heroism, camaraderie and life's meaning during his pre-war flights over Africa and South America. It was a poignant gift, and a rather daring one; Saint-Exupéry's books were already banned in Vichy France.* Not long afterwards, Franz flew aerobatics 'in front of my window', Melitta recorded in her diary, before repeatedly telephoning her. 'Says he wants to do something,' she scribbled cryptically. 'Think he can try to make someone else believe this.'[51] The next day, as if suddenly self-conscious, Melitta made her first diary reference to her clothes. 'Very bad mood, in old lady's suit in office, suddenly Franz . . . changed, ate together.'[52] She clearly enjoyed the young pilot's company, and cared about him and his good opinion.

A few days afterwards, the official photographs to mark the award of Melitta's Iron Cross were taken, rather late, at the studios of Hitler's personal photographer, Heinrich Hoffmann. For her equivalent portraits in 1941, Hanna had turned to the camera and smiled radiantly above her medal, delighted at the whole proceedings. Melitta chose to be pictured almost in profile, against a dark background. A pearl necklace emphasizes her aristocratic appearance, and the only view of the award itself is the official ribbon on her lapel, fashioned into a small ornamental bow as commissioned by Alexander. There is no visible swastika. This is a very considered portrait, in which Melitta wears her pride at her honour with great restraint.

That evening she attended a small party with work colleagues, including Franz. They drank sparkling wine and, after dinner, lit candles by which to keep talking. 'Very jolly,' she wrote before going to bed. 'Danced a lot.'[53] The following night Franz was round again, for a modest meal. 'Violent, almost unashamed,' Melitta wrote. They talked until the early hours, after which she wanted to lock her door.[54] It is not clear on which side of the door Franz was standing. Melitta saw him almost daily throughout the rest of July and August 1943, but now she more often sailed alone, or invited Paul and other friends to join her. She continued to visit

---

* Most famous as the author of *The Little Prince*, Saint-Exupéry flew with the French air force before his country's armistice in 1940, and later joined the Free French air force in North Africa. He disappeared over the Mediterranean on a reconnaissance mission in July 1944.

Alexander in France, and during his leave at Lautlingen they hunted fallow deer, but her diary mentions some anxiety before seeing him.[55] Perhaps Franz had simply mistaken Melitta's protective feelings towards him for something more, or maybe Melitta felt genuinely drawn to him. Either way, the two of them managed to maintain their friendship, but Melitta soon had more important concerns to occupy her.

That summer, British Bomber Command shifted its focus from the industrial Ruhr to German cities. The carpet-bombing of Hamburg near the end of July killed over 40,000 civilians and destroyed almost the entire city, including the radar defence system. Franz witnessed the attack and, appalled, determined to return to operational duties in the defence of his country. At the same time, Melitta's work developing 'blind-flying' techniques, to enable pilots to intercept without radar or directions from ground control, suddenly became a priority. The highly decorated Luftwaffe pilot Hans-Joachim 'Hajo' Herrmann had been working with Melitta since the spring, developing systems for his *Wilde Sau* (Wild Boar) unit of single-seater Me 109 fighters tasked with intercepting RAF bombers. Hajo and Melitta worked well together, both at the airfield and when discussing technical problems while out sailing. Impressed by her knowledge and ideas, Hajo kept copies of many of her reports as souvenirs. Their innovations were first tested during an RAF attack on Cologne, but the Wilde Sau had more success in August, when they brought down fifty-seven bombers during the biggest raid to date on Berlin.

Hanna was also making some important new contacts. Among the flowers and gifts she had received after her accident had been some chocolate accompanied by a personal note from Heinrich Himmler, exhorting her to deny herself nothing that might aid her speedy recovery.[56] It seemed that Himmler, a chief architect of the Holocaust and one of the most feared men in Germany, was an admirer. Over the next few months, more gifts appeared at regular intervals, always with a similar handwritten missive. Hanna found it slightly disconcerting. Himmler's atheism, his interest in the occult and his persecution of the traditional church had led her mother, Emy, to regard him as an enemy of Christianity. Yet his notes to Hanna were 'so simple and unaffectedly worded', Emy felt, that she began to doubt herself.[57] With Hanna's relationship with Göring now in tatters, Emy urged her daughter to thank Himmler for his kindness in person. Opportunity came in the form of an invitation to dine with him and his officers at his East Prussian headquarters one evening in July.

Apart from his black SS uniform, Himmler's appearance was unremarkable. Only his round glasses lent some definition to his face, sandwiched between an expanse of pale forehead and a weak double chin. Hanna's old gliding friend, now the respected aerospace engineer Wernher von Braun, thought Himmler looked more like 'a country grammar-school teacher than that horrible man who was said to wade knee-deep in blood'.[58] Disarmed by his mild appearance and good manners, and having enjoyed the camaraderie around the dinner table, Hanna happily joined Himmler in the privacy of his study. Here she confessed that his name 'had always aroused trepidation' in her family.[59] Himmler listened calmly before asking her whether she always formed her judgements so hastily. Pulling up an armchair for her opposite his own, he then 'delivered a sharp attack on the plausibility of the Christian doctrine, showing an intimate knowledge of the Bible'.[60] Only then, it seemed, did Hanna realize 'I would not be able to persuade Himmler to change his attitude,' but she urged him, nevertheless, to respect the views of others.[61]

Hanna then turned to another issue about which she felt strongly: not Nazi racism but Himmler's apparent attitude to women and the sanctity of marriage. Himmler supported Nazi 'bride schools', established to mould young women into suitable wives, and he also encouraged the fathering of both legitimate and illegitimate 'Aryan' children with the promise of support through the *Lebensborn* programme. Disconcerted by his 'purely racial and biological standpoint, considering woman only as a bearer of children', Hanna berated the head of the SS in a way few others would have dared.[62] She was clearly not intimidated either by the man or by the regime he represented. Himmler, she later reported, assured her that 'he shared my views entirely'.[63] His policy, he told her, had been 'misrepresented or misinterpreted . . . either unintentionally or from deliberate malice'.[64] At a time when Himmler was hoping to introduce a supplementary women's organization to the SS, he trusted that Hanna would challenge any such misconceptions in the future.

Although she 'did not fail to point out that, in spite of what he had said, appearances were in general against him', Hanna seemed satisfied and directed the rest of her attention towards Himmler's furnishings which were, she felt, in 'the utmost good taste'.[65] Her satisfaction that here, at least, Himmler bowed to her views, shines through when she noted that, after her criticism of the design of a Christmas platter, Himmler 'pursed his lips' and announced he would cancel the order for its manufacture.[66] Without apparently noticing, she had been diverted from women's rights campaigner to trusted adviser on tableware. She probably did not know that the porcelain factory, Allach, was exploiting slave labour from Dachau. Himmler then deftly thanked Hanna for her outspokenness, 'which he assured me was something new to him', and invited her to raise any future criticisms she might have, directly with him.[67] The next day she returned to work, rather relieved that Himmler had turned out to be so reasonable. Himmler went to Peenemünde, the Nazi secret weapons development and testing centre that Hanna now knew well from the Me 163 programme.

The Peenemünde facility had been established in the 1930s by Wernher von Braun. A political conformist brought up with right-wing, nationalist values, Braun had joined the Party in 1937, and the SS three years later. After graduating with degrees in mechanical engineering and applied physics, he persuaded the military to fund a development centre at Peenemünde: a location his mother had recommended, knowing it from her husband's duck-shooting holidays.*

Working with Braun was the older and somewhat paternalistic Major General Walter Dornberger, a leading proponent of the Nazis' V-weapon programme. The 'V' stood for *Vergeltung*, or

---

* In between his test flights, Wolfgang Späte still occasionally shot wild ducks at Peenemünde in 1943.

'vengeance'. It was 'an appellation', Braun wrote, 'that already betrayed an unspoken assumption, that their moral purpose was greater than their military effectiveness could ever be'.[68] These were Hitler's much-anticipated weapons of reprisal for the Allied bombing of Germany: rocket planes, like the Me 163; the V-1 flying bombs better known as the 'buzz bomb' or 'doodlebug' in Britain; and the V-2 rocket, the world's first long-range guided ballistic missile. These early 'weapons of mass destruction' were years ahead of Allied technology, but were needed because the Luftwaffe had never developed bomber capacity with range, payload and numbers similar to RAF Bomber Command and the US Eighth Air Force.*

Situated on the northernmost tip of Usedom Island on the Baltic coast, the once small fishing village of Peenemünde proved to be the perfect location for weapon research and development. Not only was the area relatively isolated; the 250 miles of open sea to the east provided a missile range, and thick forests supplied cover to hide power plants, workshops, test stands, housing and other facilities. Some of the technicians felt lucky to be posted to such an idyllic location, with its long stretches of sandy coastline. The more apprehensive, however, felt they were in a 'kind of ghetto for scientists', as one Peenemünde mathematician put it.[69]

At the end of 1942, Britain had dismissed Norwegian reports of enemy missiles as a hoax. Later these reports were corroborated by the secretly recorded conversations of captured German generals quartered in a British stately home, and intelligence reports from the Polish resistance. Peenemünde had been photographed earlier that year but, although the first ballistic missile had been tested there in October, the significance of the site was not at first appreciated.† By April 1943 the threat of V-weapons had been prioritized, and the 'Bodyline' organization was convened to develop

---

* Although Melitta never specifically worked on V-1s or V-2s, as these used complicated navigational systems, her work contributed to their development.

† According to Albert Speer, who witnessed an early missile test, the rocket 'rose slowly from its pad, seemed to stand upon a jet of flame . . . then vanished with a howl into the low cloud'. On that occasion the guidance system failed, and the rocket landed just half a mile away. See Albert Speer, *Inside the Third Reich* (1971), p. 495.

a response.* Peenemünde was now identified as the principal research facility. Working in shifts around the clock, and largely sustained by Spam sandwiches and coffee, Constance Babington Smith's team was on alert to look out for anything 'queer' that might be a long-range gun, a remotely controlled rocket aircraft, or 'some sort of tube . . . out of which a rocket could be squirted'.[70] Analysing photographs taken in June, Babington Smith found 'four little tailless aeroplanes . . . taking the air', which 'looked queer enough to satisfy anybody'.[71] They were prototype Me 163s, 'little white butterflies' that showed up relatively well on aerial pictures until the Luftwaffe painted them grey.[72] Among other equipment, two V-2 rockets were also spotted lying horizontally on transport vehicles near some elliptical launch sites. The operational importance of Peenemünde had been exposed.

Tuesday 17 August 1943 was long and hot. Walter Dornberger and Wernher von Braun were stuck in a meeting for most of the afternoon, arguing about the latest deadlines for V-2 production. Having won Hitler's enthusiasm for their work by screening the colour film footage of a successful test, the pressure was now on to deliver. Hitler was convinced that the V-2 was 'the decisive weapon of the war', and wanted 900 produced monthly.[73] The men were in mid-discussion when Hanna arrived at Peenemünde, ahead of some Me 163 test flights scheduled for the following day. Pleased not to be needed straight away, she took some time to stroll around the site, enjoying the breeze blowing in from the coast.

After dinner that evening, Hanna relaxed over drinks with the men, sitting around a glass-topped table in the panelled Hearth Room, which was lit by chandeliers. This was the same room in which Braun and Dornberger had entertained Himmler on his visit two months earlier, discussing Nazi racial policy towards the occupied Slavs until late into the night. On this August evening, however, they and Hanna were joined by one of Peenemünde's

---

* The code name 'Bodyline' was taken from the cricketing term, referring to something that 'was not only against the rules but certainly unsportsmanlike'. Ursula Powys-Lybbe, *The Eye of Intelligence* (1983), p. 192.

leading scientists, Dr Ernst Steinhoff, and Braun's younger brother, Magnus, a keen glider pilot who had been drafted into the Luftwaffe but managed to secure a transfer to Peenemünde. Hanna had dressed to impress, with her usual dark-blue unofficial uniform decorated with her Iron Cross, First Class, as well as the glittering diamonds of her Military Flight Badge. After a while, however, she curled herself up in a comfortable armchair, happily swapping old gliding stories as well as discussing more recent test work and new ambitions. 'Whenever anything brought her to Peenemünde, we were always glad to see her,' Dornberger wrote.[74] For him, 'listening to the laughter of these young people, who cheerfully took all the surprises of technology in their stride, with their eyes on the future, I felt less oppressed by the serious worries of the afternoon'.[75]

At some point during the evening Hanna slipped away, escorted by Braun to the car that was to take her to her dormitory for the night. Braun then strolled over to his own rooms. Dornberger was the last to leave, at about half eleven. All the facility's lights were already long out. Exhausted by the heat and excitement of the day, Dornberger was slowly walking the few steps that led to one of the residential houses when the air-raid siren sounded, as it quite often did. It was a full moon, but knowing that the RAF often flew over the Baltic en route to bomb elsewhere, he continued on his way and was quickly asleep in bed.

It was not long before Dornberger was woken by the sound of his windows rattling and gunfire outside. While cursing the anti-aircraft battery who were apparently disturbing his sleep with their tests, he slowly noticed the 'roaring, hissing double reports' of the heavy batteries firing along the edge of the airfield and down by the water, joined by the more muffled detonations of the posts on the opposite bank. More anti-aircraft guns barked from the roofs of the higher buildings. Braun had also been woken, but having quickly looked outside he assumed the bombers were headed straight over towards Berlin. Confident that it was not 'our night', he 'strolled back' to his quarters, but stopped short when he saw a targeting flare dropped by a British pathfinder.[76]

Peenemünde was soon being raided with wave after wave of bombers passing over the site without any aerial counter-attack. Leaping from his bed, Dornberger 'had breeches and socks on in record time'. He grabbed his tunic, trench coat, cap and gloves, even his cigar case, but his boots had been taken for cleaning so he made do with 'soft slippers' as he dashed outside.[77] At that moment a huge blast wrecked the building. As the doors were torn away, flying glass slashed through the air. Dornberger stood transfixed. 'The scene that met my gaze had a sinister and appalling beauty of its own', he later recalled. Through veils of 'fragile, cottony clouds' like a 'rosy curtain of gauze', he watched the moon light up the pine plantations, the road and bushes, the offices, works and canteen. Everything was covered in fine white sand, and much was already burning.[78] Above, the sky was now criss-crossed with the beams of searchlights, while waves of bombers smudged the black bursts of flak cloud that hung in the air. From all around, Dornberger continued, came 'the continual barking and cracking of the AA guns, the reports of the bursting shells, the thunderous impact of the bombs and the monotonous drone of the four-engined enemy bombers'.[79] 'My beautiful Peenemünde!' he was heard to moan.[80]

British Bomber Command had sent a massive assault force of 597 aircraft to drop between 1,500 and 2,000 tons of high explosives on Peenemünde in Operation Hydra. This was almost the entire bomber fleet – an enormous risk for one mission. Surprise was paramount to mitigate that risk. Once fed and briefed, the RAF pilots had been sworn to secrecy and locked into their hangars. Regular bombing raids on Berlin had been undertaken in the weeks before, in the hope that the Germans would assume this was still the target. A 'spoof attack' on the capital by British Mosquitoes was also planned; and fine strips of metal 'window' were dropped to blind the German radar.[81] Flying by the light of the full moon, many of the crew still felt 'pretty well naked' as they approached the German coast, but the preparations paid off.[82] 'They certainly weren't expecting us,' recalled Jack Pragnell, a Wellington observer in the first wave. 'The guns opened up only after we started work. Then we saw the searchlights come on in abundance.'[83] Paul Bland, the navigator inside a chilly Lancaster, agreed that 'they thought we were going to Berlin'.[84] Instead, the RAF's heavy bombs fell in ordered rows over Peenemünde, the smaller ones dropping together in groups, some waggling slightly on release. Pragnell was relieved to 'see the bombs hitting home'.[85] Smashing into the sandy earth from high above, they looked like boiled sweets dropping into a bowl of flour, but the crews all knew the importance of their mission and had been told that if the target was not destroyed they would be sent back repeatedly to finish the job.

Coincidentally, this was the first night that Hajo Herrmann's Wilde Sau unit was operating in force above Berlin, using the blind-flying techniques that he and Melitta had developed. One hundred and forty-eight twin-engined and 55 single-engined Luftwaffe fighters searched the night sky in vain for the anticipated bombers, exposing themselves to their own anti-aircraft guns below. It was only after the first wave of bombs had fallen on Peenemünde that the mystery became clear. The Messerschmitts raced north. At half past one they caught the last wave of RAF bombers, shooting down many of those that were still silhouetted against the flames and smoke from the burning buildings below. Altogether the British lost forty aircraft; 243 British aircrew died, and a further 45, who had bailed out, were captured. Those who made it home remembered how 'the fires of burning Peenemünde made an impressive view behind us'.[86]

'I am terribly ashamed to say that I slept through the whole night,' was Hanna's main comment on the raid.[87] She had been allocated a room in the officers' block in Peenemünde West, some distance away from both the scientists' and technicians' dormitories and the test facilities where the attacks had been focused. Even so, she could hardly have 'slept so deeply' as to have been undisturbed by the sirens, the sound and vibrations of more than 600 planes, or the 'thunderous impact', as Dornberger described it, of the bombing itself, which sent shock waves through the ground.[88] 'Unless she had consumed a good double whisky and was wearing earmuffs, she must have heard the crump of the bombs,' RAF pilot Pragnell later argued, before describing Hanna's claims as 'somewhat romantic'.[89] Nevertheless, according to her own account, on waking the next morning Hanna was rather surprised to find a heavy mist in the air, and only realized later that this was smoke.

When Luftwaffe chief of staff Hans Jeschonnek heard news of the destruction, he shot himself in the head with his service pistol. 'I can no longer work with the Reichsmarschall,' his last note read. 'Long live the Führer.'[90] 'Göring, grief-stricken, attended the funeral . . . with tears in his eyes,' Hanna later reported scornfully.[91] For many, Jeschonnek's suicide represented an admission of the Luftwaffe's defeat. Erhard Milch succeeded him, employing ever more draconian measures to grow aircraft production, including the increased use of slave labour.

In fact, although 'detailed plans of the experimental camp grounds' had been dispatched to London by Polish agents, the bomb damage was not as well targeted as first believed.[92] Several buildings that had been belching out smoke as the pathfinders arrived had made aiming difficult and some pilots had mistakenly dropped their markers two miles south. Later, as 'the target became a veritable inferno', according to one British officer, 'it became increasingly difficult to identify the various features'.[93] As a result, a number of the test fields and laboratories, the guidance control buildings and pioneering wind tunnel, were almost untouched while, tragically, many bombs hit the Trassenheide forced labourers' camp. Trapped behind barbed wire and with no shelters, an estimated 500–600 prisoners and forced foreign labourers were killed, including several Allied agents who had infiltrated the camp with workers from Luxembourg.*

An aerial reconnaissance sortie the next morning, however,

---

* While not responsible for the exploitation of forced labourers, Hanna would have been aware of the practice at Peenemünde. Wernher von Braun later claimed that he 'never knew what was happening in the concentration camps', but admitted he could have found out. He did not comment on the forced labour camps in the rocket programme. See Arthur C. Clarke, *Astounding Days: A Science Fiction Autobiography* (1990), p. 148.

showed that a substantial part of the main site *had* been damaged, including the experimental works, head office and design block. German casualties included the facility's chief engineer, Dr Walter Thiel, who died in a shelter with his family while their house remained undamaged. The use of delayed fuses meant that bombs continued to detonate for some days, hindering the German salvage operation. It was, one British pilot concluded, a 'major disaster' for the Nazis.[94] 'Nothing remained,' a German colonel of the V-1 launching regiment reported, 'other than a desert.'[95] 'The loss was irreparable,' Dornberger conceded, having inspected the damage while still covered in dust the next morning.[96]

Operation Hydra was not only a shock but an embarrassment to the Nazis. The net result was the enforced relocation of the rocket development facilities, causing a critical delay to the delivery of operational weapons. Rocket production moved underground, and some testing moved west – out of the reach of Allied bombers. 'If the Germans had succeeded in perfecting and using their new weapons six months earlier . . .' Eisenhower later wrote, 'our invasion of Europe would have proved exceedingly difficult, perhaps impossible.'[97] Certainly the Allied advance through Normandy would not have been possible in early June 1944 had it not been for the bombing of Peenemünde, and the war might have dragged on long enough to give the Nazis time to expand their development of jets and rocket technology even further.

Melitta had been in her room at Gatow, working late on her PhD dissertation, the night that Peenemünde was bombed. Before she turned out the light, she noted the Berlin air raid in her diary, perhaps wondering whether Hajo or Franz were engaged in intercepting the bombers. She subsequently added that she was late to work the next day, having overslept because of the sirens. Hanna had been present throughout the Peenemünde raid, but effectively dismissed it as almost insignificant in her memoirs. There is no evidence that either of them referred to the episode again, but as the aerial bombing of Germany intensified, civilian morale plummeted and the regime had to apply increasing oppression and compulsion to maintain order. Over the course of 1943, the

German courts passed more than a hundred death sentences every week on citizens deemed guilty of defeatism or sabotage. Melitta and Hanna were deeply affected by a growing sense that it was not just the Nazi regime, but their country as a whole, their colleagues, loved ones, and indeed themselves, that were under mortal attack. Both women now began to consider radical new ways to defend the different Germanys to which they had pledged allegiance. But while Hanna strove to find a significant new way to help win the war, Melitta's focus was increasingly turning to how she could help to end it.

10

OPERATION SELF-SACRIFICE
1943–1944

'Time,' Hanna decided a few days after the Peenemünde bombing, 'was not on Germany's side.'[1] With large parts of the Baltic proving ground now under rubble, ash and sand, Hanna returned to Berlin as soon as possible. She might have slept through Operation Hydra, but the implications of the raid weighed heavily on her mind. Domestic papers covering the bombing on 'the north German coast' focused on the number of planes shot down, but the foreign press reported that Himmler was investigating the operation personally to discover 'who had betrayed the position of the Peenemünde plant'.[2] British papers even claimed that Goebbels was 'feeding the wildest lies about Allied defeats to German listeners', while 'trying to hearten his own folks and scare ours with tales of terrible new Axis weapons now being mass-produced'.[3] 'There is no doubt that Hitler has been vehemently calling upon his scientific research experts to bring forth some salvation miracle,' they continued, slightly smugly, 'but the RAF raid on Peenemünde can not have helped that appeal much.'[4]

Unlike Melitta, Hanna had never doubted the aims of the Nazi regime. Even she, however, had now lost faith in the promised certain victory. 'One after another, towns and cities were crumpling under the Allied air attacks,' she wrote. 'The transport system and the production centres were being systematically destroyed . . . the death toll continually mounted.'[5] In late August, over lunch at the Berlin Aero Club, Hanna quietly discussed the adverse turn of events with two trusted friends, Captain Heinrich Lange of the special operations Luftwaffe squadron KG200, and the head of Rechlin's institute of aeronautical medicine, Dr Theo

Benzinger. Some radical new action was needed, they agreed, and Hanna believed that she might be the person to lead it.

Hanna reasoned that her Fatherland could only be 'saved from disaster' if the conflict could be brought to a rapid conclusion through a negotiated peace.[6] But Nazi Germany would not be able to secure favourable terms unless the military strength of the Allies could be considerably weakened first. 'This could only be done from the air,' Hanna, Lange and Benzinger agreed.[7] Together they sketched out secret plans for 'a rapid succession of devastating blows' at factories, power plants, water facilities and other infrastructure.[8] Crucially, naval and merchant shipping was also to be targeted should the Allies move to invade the European continent.

Hanna knew that the precision of these air attacks was critical to the success of her plan. Melitta's work with dive-sights and dive-bombing techniques had greatly improved accuracy, but Hanna had something more radical in mind. She wanted pilots, potentially including herself, to guide their missiles right down to the point of impact – without pulling out. With shipping targets, one paper outlined, 'the plane was expected to shatter upon impact with the water, killing the pilot instantly and allowing the bomb to tear loose from the plane to continue under the keel of the vessel, where it would explode'.[9] Although the pilots 'would be volunteering for certain death', Hanna added, 'it would be no task for mere dare-devils . . . nor for blind fanatics, nor for the disenchanted and the life-weary who might see here a chance to make a theatrical exit . . .' What was needed, she felt, were measured and honourable men, 'ready to sacrifice themselves in the conviction that only by this means could their country be saved'.[10] She named the fledgling plan 'Operation Suicide'.* Melitta was also having lunch with friends at the Berlin Aero Club a few days after the Peenemünde raid. She too was 'very pessimistic' about the war, she confided rashly to her diary.[11] Despite her work with Hajo Herrmann and his Wilde Sau group of interceptor fighters, Allied bombers were increasingly seen in the skies above Berlin. In September

---

* At this point Hanna was probably not aware of Japanese plans for suicide attacks.

Melitta gave Franz Amsinck an excellent reference to start night-fighter training. With so many close friends now deployed, she also began to record the details of those who had been killed in action. In early September she noted that 'bombs are close', and then 'bombs on the runway' at Gatow.[12] The raids deprived her of sleep, but were never enough to prevent her work. As a result she was permanently exhausted. Her allowance of pilot's chocolate, and the coffee that she found as 'welcome, as after a flight round the world', kept her going until she could collapse.[13] 'Slept like the dead,' she scrawled in blunt pencil.[14]

Like so many wives in wartime, Melitta was also suffering constant anxiety about the fate of her husband. Alexander was still on his artillery course in northern France, but expecting a new posting to the front at any time. Melitta's stress was soon manifested in stomach problems, renewed skin rashes and persistent headaches. She was also 'lonely', she recorded tersely.[15] The Aero Club was a good place to meet Franz, as well as old friends like Paul, and Alexander's brothers, Claus and Berthold, when they were in Berlin. 'I often talked to Litta about the conflict . . .' Paul later wrote. 'Should the individual carry on . . . to save the country from losing the war,' he asked her, 'or by contrast, was the possibility that Hitler could win a victory over Europe not the greatest evil that could happen – and in that case, was the fall of the Reich not a far lesser evil? In other words . . . shouldn't one contemplate the removal of the rulers of Germany and feel around for others who might think along similar lines?'[16] Such conversations were treasonous, punishable by death.

While Hanna and Melitta were quietly considering these questions at the Berlin Aero Club, work on Hitler's vengeance weapons continued. After the Peenemünde raid, the development and production of the V-2 rocket, the world's first guided ballistic missile, was transferred to Mittelwerk, a factory complex hidden inside the Harz mountains. Here slave labourers were set to work from the nearby Mittelbau-Dora concentration camp, established by the SS as a sub-camp of Buchenwald. This not only kept production costs down, but also helped to maintain secrecy about the site. By

October there were 4,000 prisoners, mainly Russian, Polish and French, labouring at Mittelwerk. By the end of November the number had doubled. There were no sanitary facilities and little drinking water. Overcrowded sleeping quarters were contaminated with excrement, lice and fleas. The dimly lit tunnels were cold and damp, and the workers' thin uniforms quickly disintegrated. Within months, epidemics of pneumonia, dysentery and typhus broke out, exacerbated by the prisoners' exhaustion and starvation. 'It was a pretty hellish environment,' Wernher von Braun later admitted, but he denied having witnessed any brutality and argued that 'war is war, and . . . I did not have the right to bring further moral viewpoints to bear.'[17] In total, up to 60,000 people forced to work on V-2 production died of disease, starvation and maltreatment, giving the weapon the dubious distinction of having killed more people during its production than in its application.*

Hanna would have seen the forced labour camps at Peene-münde, but if she was concerned, or heard rumours about the appalling conditions at Mittelwerk from Braun, Dornberger or anyone else, she did not record it. For a while she was busy touring airfields to demonstrate the Me 109 to trainee pilots. 'The impression of this new aircraft was really huge,' one recalled, but Hanna's heart was not in the work.[18] The testing of Me 163 Messerschmitt rocket planes had been moved west to Bad Zwischenahn, not far from the North Sea, and Hanna hoped that there she might still fly a prototype under full power. 'She intimated that the Führer and commander-in-chief of the armed forces had authorized, and if need be, ordered her to fly any plane in Germany that she wanted to,' Wolfgang Späte was informed on her arrival.[19] Späte did not believe a word of it but Hanna had set to work anyhow. 'Out on the runway, she's actually quite friendly and modest,' one of the ground crew reported, apparently 'shaking his head,

---

* Nicolaus von Below, Hitler's Luftwaffe adjutant, wrote that 'the prisoners seemed well-treated and were in good physical condition . . . but it was nevertheless a depressing sight to watch this forced-labour force, who hoped to purchase their lives by their industry'. He, too, must have known that few would survive. See Nicolaus von Below, *At Hitler's Side* (2010), p. 227.

somewhat surprised'.[20] Recognizing that his men 'were proud to be on the same footing as this famous female pilot', Späte sensed defeat.[21] Having secured authorization from Berlin, he finally gave her permission to fly whatever she chose, but whether she flew the Me 163 under power is not verifiably recorded. Her energies were increasingly directed towards promoting Operation Suicide.

At first Hanna had kept her discussions completely secret. Despite her talk of honour, the concept of suicide missions went against all European military tradition, and smacked of desperation, even defeatism. In the autumn of 1943, any talk that might be construed as undermining the morale of the people was already a serious crime. It would not be long before defeatist talk became punishable by death. Nevertheless, as word of Hanna's proposed suicide squadron spread, she began to receive discreet enquiries from other zealous pilots, enthused by the thought of sacrificing their lives for Hitler's Germany. Encouraged, Hanna sought out more volunteers. 'We found them everywhere,' she wrote with satisfaction. Most 'were married and fathers of families and were robust, uncomplicated individuals. As they saw it, the sacrifice of their lives would be as nothing compared with the millions, both soldiers and civilians, who would die if the war was allowed to continue.'[22]

As the number of people initiated into Hanna's plans grew, however, she also began to face objections. 'That we were often misunderstood is only to be expected,' she commented, before adding grandly, 'here was required nothing less than the complete conquest of the self'.[23] Nevertheless, it seemed wise to gain official sanction for the proposed operation before the criticisms grew more vocal. As Hanna was still persona non grata with Göring, and had in any case lost all respect for the Reichsmarschall, she approached his deputy, Field Marshall Erhard Milch. Milch knew that the Luftwaffe was already facing criticism for 'too much experimenting' instead of focusing resources on producing the planes and pilots that were desperately needed.[24] No doubt mindful of his personal position, as well as the potential waste of good pilots, he 'refused point blank' to consider the idea.[25] Bitterly disappointed, Hanna scornfully waved aside his moral objections, suggesting he leave these 'to the conscience of the individual volunteers, whom, after all, it primarily concerned'.[26] Milch was unimpressed, and curtly prohibited the use of any Luftwaffe aircraft or personnel for developing the project.

As Hanna wrestled with official rejection, Melitta was facing her own, more personal, heartache: Alexander had been sent back to Russia in mid-September. 'Grievous blow,' she confided to her diary.[27] Melitta begged Claus to discover her husband's route east, so that she might fly out and meet him on the way, but this time her efforts were in vain. 'Mentally very fragile,' she scribbled the next day, 'aching heart . . . all hope dashed.'[28] She knew that a posting to the Eastern Front was tantamount to a death sentence and, as the weeks passed with very few letters, she again became sick with worry. To distract herself, she took up sketching, went swimming, sailed a dinghy on the Wannsee with Claus and Berthold when they were around, drank lots more coffee and went on moonlit walks, picking mushrooms and shooting rabbits to supplement her wartime rations. Mostly, however, she just threw herself into her work. Despite occasionally snatching afternoon naps on a sofa, by mid-October she was 'very tired, depressed' and 'exhausted'.[29] By the end of the month she had tonsillitis and a fever, her rash was back and she was taking morphine. Soon her work was suffering, too. She was arguing with colleagues including Milch, and even found Franz irritating. He 'stretched it a little too far', she wrote tensely.[30] One 'black day', when she couldn't find her sunglasses, she had to brave going out with her eyes still puffy from crying.[31] Melitta was far from the typical hausfrau of the time but, as for so many women across the world, with her husband at the front and her home city under attack, daily life was becoming almost unbearable.

In November, Hanna was asked to undertake a morale-boosting visit to the men on the Eastern Front. Robert Ritter von Greim was commanding the air fleet in the central sector, but without sufficient aircraft he knew that the Wehrmacht had lost all initiative and there was little hope of them holding their positions, let alone advancing. Hanna was not only a national heroine, but also a symbol of courage and commitment above the call of duty. Attractive, highly decorated and seemingly unstoppable, she was still naturally light-hearted and Greim could think of no one better to rally the troops. Flattered, and inspired by the knowledge that Greim was 'engaged in a struggle of almost superhuman proportions', despite the great danger Hanna agreed at once.[32]

It was icy-cold when she reached Greim's headquarters in a forested area near the ancient city of Orsha, now in Belarus.* Although under Nazi-German occupation since July 1941, resistance in the area was infamous and several concentration camps had been established in response. An estimated 19,000 people would be killed in these camps. Hitler had given his soldiers free rein to act without restraint in the war in the east, and Jews, communists and other civilians were being murdered on a large scale. Greim would have been aware of these criminal developments, but it is unlikely that he discussed them with Hanna. If she saw any evidence of atrocities, or of the enforced movement of thousands of civilians by rail while she was travelling in the region, she chose not to record it. Six months earlier Greim had received the distinction of 'Oak Leaves' for his Knight's Cross, awarded for his service in Russia. Now morale was faltering but Hanna noted only that Greim was still greatly respected by his men, and indeed regarded almost as a father figure with his clipped white hair, furrowed brow and slightly sad, knowing eyes. 'I cannot convey to you the pleasure of the soldiers when the General appears,' she wrote enthusiastically to her parents and sister. 'They love and honour him greatly – and no wonder!'[33] As a mark of her personal respect, she never mentioned Greim without using his title and he, likewise, always referred to her as Flugkapitän.

Even the Berlin air raids had not prepared Hanna for the sense of unremitting threat she now experienced. 'Throughout the night, even in my sleep,' she later wrote, 'I could hear the ceaseless roll and thunder of the guns from the nearby front.'[34] At dawn, she

---

* Orsha was liberated by Soviet troops in June 1944.

and Greim set off in a small Fieseler Fi 156 *Storch* liaison and reconnaissance plane, flying low to avoid detection, towards the advanced anti-aircraft artillery positions. Although its cockpit was enclosed, the small, leggy aircraft was draughty and uninsulated, and Hanna was soon shivering despite her coat, thick gloves and fur-lined trapper hat. Once within sight of the front, they swapped the plane for an armoured car. The last stretch had to be undertaken on foot, 'working our way forward in short, crouching runs', Hanna tightly clutching the handbag she had brought from Berlin and carefully fastened to her sleeve with a safety chain and bracelet.[35]

No sooner had she reached the first German ack-ack position than the Russians started a heavy bombardment. 'Automatically everyone vanished into the ground, while all around us the air whistled and shuddered and crashed,' she wrote. After their own guns had pounded out their reply, a formation of enemy planes began to bomb the Wehrmacht position. 'I felt, in my terror, as though I wanted to creep right in on myself,' Hanna continued. 'When finally to this inferno were added the most horrible sounds of all, the yells of the wounded, I felt certain that not one of us would emerge alive. Cowering in a hole in the ground, it was in vain that I tried to stop the persistent knocking of my knees.'[36]

When the bombardment was over, Hanna emerged from her foxhole to help tend the wounded. Believing that 'the men's eyes light up at the sight of me', she insisted on visiting the forward gun sites.[37] 'Their astonishment and delight . . .' she later told her family with typical exuberance, 'was overwhelming.'[38] Over the next three weeks Hanna flew the Storch to most of the isolated Luftwaffe units in the area. From the cover of tanks and trenches, she watched as 'the earth heaved into the air' from exploding shells, and learned to distinguish between the sounds of German and Soviet fire. Meeting the men, and sometimes sharing a tin of sardines with them, she answered their questions as best she could. 'I tried hard not to raise false hopes,' she made a point of recording.[39] But whispering, so that the more senior officers would not hear, she also spoke about the secret 'wonder weapons', the V-1,

V-2 and Me 163. 'She actually glowed with optimism and encouragement,' one young soldier later reported.[40]

Hanna's visit to the front was certainly appreciated, but it was no substitute for the supplies or reinforcements that were desperately needed. For Hanna herself, the experience hardened her resolve to serve. 'I should like to stay out here, and be allowed to fight,' she wrote to her family.[41] She was being romantic. She knew her greatest contribution would not be made in the east, but the emotion behind her declaration was honestly felt. 'Flying beneath grey skies over measureless expanses of open country occupied by partisans, talking with weary and anxious men in huts and holes in the ground, the hand-claps of those from my own homeland, the agony, the endurance – and the cold,' she wrote, 'all this will not fade from my mind.'[42] A few weeks later, visiting her Austrian Heuberger cousins, she told Helmut that 'Stalingrad had been a disaster', and as the Luftwaffe was no longer in any state to defend Germany, 'more disasters were on the way'.[43] She then insisted on the family singing folk songs down a priority telephone line to Greim, who was still at the front. When the operator interrupted, questioning the importance of the call, the general insisted it was vital for morale.

Although also on the Eastern Front, Alexander was hundreds of miles from Orsha, serving as a front-line artillery observer on, 'or rather in,' Melitta wrote wryly, the Dnieper River, near Novo Lipovo, now in Ukraine.[44] At the end of October, she learned that he had taken part in a series of assaults against the encroaching Soviets. Touchingly, she spent that evening reading his essay on 'Virgil and the Augustinian state', as if his words could bring him closer. 'The losses were generally high,' she later wrote sparingly to her sister.[45] Indeed, the Germans were estimated to have lost at least 500,000 men and significant territory over the four-month operation. A week later a telegram arrived from Lublin. Alexander had been seriously wounded, his back ripped open by shrapnel from a grenade.

Despite his injuries, Alexander did not want to leave his unit and had to be forcibly moved back from the clearing station for transfer. Eventually he was sent to 'a very nice military hospital' in Würzburg, with Melitta calling in favours all the way.[46] As soon as she had leave, she cycled over early to the train station to visit him. It was dark by the time she returned, and with blackout in operation there were no lights to guide her way. When her bike hit a rut she was thrown from the saddle, hitting the ground hard and staying there, cursing the world while she caught her breath. 'All a bit much,' she later commented.[47] Alexander's injury 'was a grenade splinter which went deep into his back and is still there,' she wrote in anguish to her sister Lili a few days later.[48] But Alexander had again been lucky. The shrapnel had missed his ribs and lungs. Doctors agreed it could be safely left inside him, and the wound was healing well. As the hospital was near their apartment, soon he could even go home in the afternoons. Melitta joined him whenever possible; the rooms that she had found 'bleak' and 'depressing' without him were once again her home.[49] The only heating came from the stove and they no longer had a maid, but 'although we have come down a peg', she wrote, this had 'the comforting advantage of not always having a stranger in the limited space'.[50]

Occasionally Franz visited Melitta at the apartment for tea or dinner when Alexander was there, and sometimes he stayed until the early hours. She had now given her young admirer the pet name *Spätzchen*, or 'little sparrow', rather as she secretly called Alexander her *Schnepfchen*, or 'little snipe'. She clearly loved them both, although they occupied different places in her heart. Franz was certainly Melitta's friend, rather than Alexander's, but Alexander was 'okay with it', Melitta noted briefly, before grumbling about his occasional 'wallows'.[51] Whatever arrangement the three of them had come to, Alexander knew that his wife loved him deeply and, so long as her husband was out of danger, Melitta felt that everything else was somehow manageable.

Melitta yearned to stay longer with Alexander, but she was needed in Berlin. As well as her work at Gatow, she was due to be presented with the Military Flight Badge that Göring should have given her with her Iron Cross ten months earlier and which was finally back from the jewellers. The presentation was set for 19 November. Just before first light that morning, Melitta was woken by the deafening rumble of 440 four-engined Avro Lancasters flying in from the west. The RAF had arrived on their first major bombing offensive of the German capital. With the city hidden under heavy cloud, damage was limited, but the threat of further action was clear. Nevertheless, 'on the very afternoon of the first big attack', Melitta wrote to Lili, a private room was made available at the Gatow airfield mess and the commanding officer presented her with her honour.[52] A bottle of sparkling wine and a box of cigarettes were then passed around. When Melitta asked whether she might save her cigarette for her wounded husband, the whole box was quickly pushed her way. 'The cigarettes please me far more than the diamonds,' she whispered to the adjutant who had brought them.[53] A moment later the siren sounded again; the 'little celebration' was over and they headed to the cellar.[54]

A few days later the RAF made their most effective raid on Berlin, causing huge destruction to the inner city, including several residential areas. Many bombs also fell on the city zoo. One afternoon there were six female elephants and one calf doing tricks with their keeper; a few hours later all seven had been burned alive. Polar bears, camels and ostriches were all killed, while the snakes, whose enclosure was damaged, reportedly 'froze in the cold November air'.[55] The only comfort for the zoo's stricken staff was that at least these bombs had not fallen on housing. Between January 1943 and May 1945 350,000 Germans were killed by Allied bombing, as well as tens of thousands of forced foreign workers and POWs.* 'The longer the war lasted and the more fearful the air raids on the Fatherland became,' Hitler's photographer Heinrich Hoffmann recorded, 'the more intolerable grew the atmosphere in Führer headquarters, where the deepest pessimism reigned supreme.'[56] For Melitta, the scale of the terror and devastation was unbearable,

---

* Over 11,000 Germans had already been killed by Allied bombing between 1940 and 1942. British casualties from all forms of German air bombardment never exceeded 61,000 between 1939 and 1945. See Max Hastings, *All Hell Let Loose: The World At War 1939–1945* (2011), p. 480.

and she was proud of her part in developing the planes, equipment and techniques needed to intercept the bombers. She often showed her new decoration to friends like Claus's wife, Nina, who would hold it up for her 'very impressed' children to admire.[57]

Melitta spent the next few months commuting between Alexander, slowly recovering in Würzburg, and her work at Gatow. Her new employment contract with the Reich had finally come through, but she was not happy with the terms. Her salary had been pegged to Hanna's but she felt that any comparison of their duties or performance was misleading. 'Hanna Reitsch has not studied . . . [and] could only offer flying knowledge,' she told the ministry curtly.[58] She herself, being an aeronautical engineer as well as a test pilot, provided vital technical direction and should therefore be paid the same as 'officials or male employees of the Reich with equivalent previous knowledge for similar work'.[59] She was clearly feeling more secure personally, yet she still added the caveat that 'the work to be done is . . . so extensive that it will be years before it ends'.[60] Melitta's salary was eventually agreed at an initial 1,400 Reichsmarks, almost a third more than Hanna received, even given danger allowance, and three times Alexander's university salary. She was also promised a swift pay review, along with a research institute of her own the following year with a 100,000 Reichsmark start-up budget, plus the same again for running costs including salary for eight employees.

Claus and Nina's eldest son, Berthold, remembers overhearing a conversation between Melitta and his great-aunt Alexandrine, at around this time. Although just nine years old, Berthold was already 'a regular newspaper reader' and had often seen Hanna celebrated in the press as a heroine of the Reich, so his ears pricked up at the mention of her name.[61] It was with some surprise, then, that he realized 'it was obvious that [Melitta] did not like her'.[62] Melitta and his aunt then started caustically referring to Hanna by her nickname, *Heilige Johanna* – Saint Joan. The implication was not that Hanna was Germany's self-sacrificing saviour, but rather, Berthold thought, that Hanna 'thought herself to be so perfect'.[63]

The conversation also suggests that Melitta had now heard of Hanna's suicide-bomber plans.

Despite Milch's insistence that she drop the idea of suicide squadrons, after witnessing the situation at the front Hanna was more convinced than ever that this was the only way forward. Since her return to Berlin she had raised the idea with colleagues at the aeronautical research institute, and her persistence won unofficial support. That winter a group of naval and aeronautical designers, engineers and technical experts unofficially joined representatives from Luftwaffe fighter and bomber squadrons and medical specialists, to explore the feasibility of the idea.

Milch had expressly forbidden the experimental adaptation of existing Luftwaffe fighter planes, all of which were needed to intercept the growing numbers of Allied bombers. As a result, the informal project team proposed adapting a V-1 missile, soon to be known in Britain as the buzz bomb or doodlebug, for manned flight. But the Messerschmitt Me 328, a single-seater plane originally designed as a long-range fighter or light bomber, proved too appealing. Although it would still require considerable modification to avoid, as Hanna put it, 'entailing a frivolous and senseless destruction of life', it was both more suitable than the V-1 and, crucially, it was already in production.[64] The next challenge was to secure official approval for the production of a number of test Me 328s and the launch of a pilot training programme. With Göring already ruled out, and Milch unequivocally against the idea, the one authority to whom Hanna felt she could still turn was Hitler. Her Führer, however, was preoccupied.

According to his secretary, Hitler was 'full of enthusiasm for the V-1s and V-2s'. 'Panic will break out in England . . .' he told her. 'I'll pay the barbarians back for shooting women and children and destroying German culture.'[65] The bombing of Peenemünde had set the vengeance programme back several months, but since production had been transferred to underground sites like Mittelwerk, it was now protected from air attack. No longer able to destroy V-2 rockets at source, British aerial intelligence focused on finding the launch sites. They quickly had their first success. The concrete for the reinforced dome above a huge bunker had just been poured at Watten, in northern France, when the heavy bombers of the US Air Force attacked on 27 August. Ten days later the ruins had set hard in the concrete.* Many more sites were under development, however.

In October, all Nazi-held land within a 130-mile range of London was photographed and studied. The next month Constance Babington Smith spotted a tiny cruciform blur on a photograph. At less than one millimetre across, the image was hardly visible to the naked eye but Babington Smith had her pre-war German jeweller's magnifying glass. The V-1 was 'an absurd little object', she wrote, 'sitting in a corner of a small enclosure', but nevertheless 'a whisper went round the whole station. We were all very well aware that this was something fantastically important.'[66] British researchers now knew what they were looking for, and ninety-six V-1 launch sites were eventually identified in France, many with ramps pointing towards London. Estimates were that Germany would soon have the capacity to launch around 2,000 flying bombs every day. 'It seemed that the V-1 attacks, when they came, would be of appalling magnitude', Babington Smith continued. The sites 'had obviously got to be bombed'.[67]

While the Allies were photographing occupied northern France, Goebbels' Propaganda Ministry sent Melitta on a public relations mission to neutral Sweden. Apart from a few radio interviews, Melitta had largely avoided being used for Nazi PR. She had already won reprieves from visiting Stockholm on the pretexts that her husband needed her, and that she did not wish to look as though she were leaving Berlin from cowardice during the air raids. Now, however, Swedish students were demonstrating in support of their conscripted Norwegian counterparts. Needing someone to rally the Swedish establishment, the Reich pressed

---

* Asked to provide damage assessment, the eminent British engineer Sir Malcolm McAlpine commented that for the Germans 'it would be easier to start over again' than to salvage. See Constance Babington Smith, *Evidence in Camera: The story of photographic intelligence in the Second World War* (2004), p. 185.

Melitta, who reluctantly accepted that some public relations work had 'become unavoidable'.[68]

Her journey to Stockholm was an adventure in itself. Engine troubles prevented her flying from Würzburg, and the train to Berlin was delayed by three hours of air-raid warnings. In the capital, the Foreign Office had been bomb-damaged and the Swedish Embassy completely destroyed, making visas unobtainable. In any case, as a woman, she was told, she was ineligible for the reserved government seats on the only flight out. The official responsible for this decision 'gave way of course, within a minute, when he got a reprimand from on high', Melitta later reported with some satisfaction, but another air raid made her miss the flight anyhow.[69] Her phone calls to the Foreign Office went unanswered. 'The operators simply let me hang on,' she wrote, 'and, if I complained, snapped my head off because they took me for a secretary.'[70] Eventually she caught a flight to Copenhagen, in occupied Denmark, where she alighted without money or onward papers. 'Just as I was thinking that at last I had a night before me which would be undisturbed by air-raid warnings,' she wrote drily, 'there was a shooting a few steps away from me.'[71] A German sergeant had been killed by the Danish resistance: 'shot by an assassin', as Melitta reported it.[72] A moment later, she heard 'two big explosions' caused by sabotage inside nearby factories. Although well used to feeling under siege herself, she was shocked to witness such resistance to Nazi occupation.

Melitta eventually arrived in Stockholm by train the next day. She was received 'with an audible sigh of relief' by a representative from her embassy, along with a crowd of reporters, whom she tried to avoid.[73] Her phone did not stop ringing, however, until she walked out that evening in an elegant gown, quickly mended and ironed, to address an audience of almost 700 diplomats, Luftwaffe and Wehrmacht generals, scientists, academics and other dignitaries. Among them was her and Hanna's pilot friend Peter Riedel, who had managed to stay in diplomacy and been appointed air attaché to the German Embassy in Sweden a month earlier, as well as the two sisters of Carin Göring, the first wife of the Reichs-marschall.

Entitled 'A Woman in Test-Flying', Melitta's lecture provided a fascinating picture of her life and career, without going into the details of her current war work which was, she said, 'naturally of a secret nature'.[74] Although she was expected to champion the regime, at a time of great rhetorical flourish her carefully chosen words were telling in their modesty. 'I have tried to serve my country in both war and peace,' she began, framing herself as a patriot rather than a Nazi. Throughout the lecture, she avoided mention-ing Hitler and the National Socialist Party, and when she talked of her work as being 'a commitment to the Reich' she added the corollary that this commitment was one shared by all fighters and workers, men and women, 'and, therefore, I am not speaking to you in my own name . . .'[75] Rather, she said, she felt herself 'to be a representative of the thousands and thousands of German women who, today, are involved in fighting and danger, and . . . an ambassador of my "people in arms".' While Melitta did not overtly criticize the Nazi leadership or its policies, this was not the usual language of a proud spokesperson for the regime.

Perhaps the strongest rhetoric in Melitta's speech, however, was reserved for her thoughts on gender. Female pilots had long been a topic of press and public interest. Naturally conservative, Melitta knew she could speak from the heart on this subject with-out causing controversy at home. 'I believe I am able to say this in the name of all German female pilots,' she announced rather sweepingly. 'The values characteristic of all womankind have not been altered; for us flying has never been a matter of causing a sensation, or even of emancipation. We women pilots are not suffragettes.'[76] Although she had had to fight for her own oppor-tunities and equal pay, and never hid her irritation when she encountered sexism personally, Melitta saw herself not as an agent of change, but rather as the exception to the gender rule. Her argument that 'woman is no stranger at all to the most masculine activity and harshest self-denial in the service of higher values, while still safeguarding womanly worth and charm', was quite

sincere, and borne out by her own experience.[77] She had volunteered for a more feminine 'helpful and healing' role with the
German Red Cross, she said, and been rejected. Now she spoke of
her 'soldierly effort' in aircraft development, and test flights
undertaken even if they involved 'sacrificing my life'.[78]

Melitta's most poignant words, about the 'whirlwind' of war,
came as she wound up her talk.[79] 'War in our time has long outgrown the historical, initially incomprehensible, seeming futility of
its origins, and outgrown the question of guilt or cause – so that it
develops as if independent of every influence of the individual . . .'
she argued. 'Imperceptibly it has received its terrible objective
meaning, which we do not give it, but which towers threateningly
before us.' For Melitta, the horrors of the war, the injuries and
deaths of those fighting at the front or in the skies, and the bombing of civilians in their homes, had given the conflict an awful
meaning and momentum of its own. Whatever the causes, she was
not unaffected and could not stand passively by. 'Let me end,' she
said after a breath, 'not with such a pathetic picture, but with the
conviction that . . . we shall survive.'[80] Whether it was the Third
Reich in which she placed her faith, or simply 'the innermost sub-
stance of the people', as she put it, she did not clarify.[81]

'My lecture was exceptionally well received,' Melitta reported
boldly a few days later.[82] But despite the warm applause in the
room, there was little coverage in the Swedish press. A few days of
formal lunches, dinners and entertainment followed, hosted by
groups such as the Swedish Aero Club and the Women's Association. 'The Swedes were all extremely kind,' Melitta added,
although 'those who are friendly towards Germany lay themselves
open to attack'.[83] Before she left, one of Göring's sisters-in-law
sent Melitta 'a very touching letter' along with a woollen shawl and
two blocks of chocolate for her return journey.[84] A few days later
she arrived home exhausted, and headed straight back to work.

In mid-December Alexander was discharged from hospital for
two weeks' rest before redeployment. Melitta's sisters in the countryside sent them parcels of the food it was now impossible to buy
in Berlin: cake, vegetables and eggs, some of which survived the

journey to Würzburg in their cardboard trays. Not all the post was so cheering. There were funerals to attend, and one morning the shocking news came that Franz's plane had caught fire after its undercarriage failed to retract. Somehow he survived without serious injury, and Melitta breathed again. The approach of Christmas brought parties and presents to plan. In the evenings Alexander would sing in the kitchen, or recite poems to his wife. At work Melitta was surrounded by engineers and pilots, in front of whom she had to prove her worth. Alexander was different. Their time together gave her the safe space she needed to relax and express her own artistic side, and for this she loved him deeply.

Five days before Christmas, the US Eighth Air Force started to bomb the V-1 launch sites in northern France, to prevent a winter attack. Eventually they would obliterate every one. 'The first round of the battle against the flying bomb was an overwhelming victory for the Allies,' Babington Smith wrote with some flourish.[85] The bombing of the German capital also continued. Hanna was feeling under siege, but Melitta returned to Würzburg for the holiday. On Christmas Eve she put on a good brocade dress, and she and Alexander decorated a tree together before roasting potatoes for supper. Late that evening Franz knocked on the door. He ended up staying the night, and was still with them for a late breakfast the next day. After he left, Melitta and Alexander cooked a goose and enjoyed a 'cosy Christmas evening'.[86] The next few days were less snug. 'Freezing cold room,' Melitta recorded, but they still sang and laughed, and lit the candles on the tree.[87] Their best present arrived the next day, when Alexander learned his orders had not yet come through. 'Won some time together,' Melitta wrote happily.[88]

Despite Alexander's temporary reprieve, he and Melitta do not seem to have spent New Year's Eve together. Melitta drank sweet sparkling wine alone beside her Christmas tree that evening, and spent much of the next day in bed with a cold. She then headed back to work at various airfields. 'She was always very busy,' her sister Klara remembered.[89] Klara sometimes visited at weekends for a brief walk or sail on the lake, adding that 'as soon as we got back to her place she had to get back into urgent work'.[90] She would then help with the domestic chores that Melitta 'hated spending precious time on'.[91] This included preparing the rabbits that Melitta shot near the airfield. Klara found her sister's passion for hunting strange. 'She would not harm a fly – yet in Gatow she went rabbit shooting,' she remarked, adding that 'of course she always felt sorry for the rabbits, but her sporting ambition to hit a moving object would take precedence over sensitivity.'[92] Perhaps, Klara thought, this detachment was how Melitta managed to continue her work developing bombsights, while 'any thoughts about the target and the consequences of dropping a bomb' were 'pushed away'.[93]

Melitta was in fact now working more on the development of night interception technology and techniques – priority work, given the Allied bombing campaigns. 'One pitch-black night the Countess Stauffenberg . . . landed in a Ju 88 on the small airfield at Döberitz to explain her new night-landing technique to me,' Hajo Herrmann later recalled.[94] Night landing without ground guidance was still hazardous. Hajo's Wilde Sau group of interceptors were proving increasingly effective, but Hitler, he noted ruefully, did not like the name, 'preferring the beautiful word chosen by the Japanese for their fighter pilots: "Kamikaze" – the Divine Wind'.[95] Nevertheless, Göring rapidly promoted Hajo. At the start of 1944 he was a captain; he would end the year a colonel. Göring also 'put me up for a higher decoration, which I was then awarded by Hitler', Hajo later recounted proudly.[96] Much of his success and promotion was down to Melitta, and he knew it.

Over New Year Alexander visited his friend Rudolf Fahrner, a fellow academic and head of the German Research Institute in Athens. Fahrner had an isolated house by the Bodensee, where Alexander and Melitta had stayed after their wedding. This had once been the meeting house of the Stefan George circle, and it now proved the perfect setting for Alexander to finish his paean to the great poet, 'Death of the Master'.* George's seminal work, *Das*

---

* Fahrner sent a copy of Alexander's poems to Claus, who was impressed, staying up

Neue Reich (The New Empire), had been published in 1928 and was in part dedicated to Alexander's twin brother, Berthold. In it George had proposed a future Germany ruled by its aristocracy. This was no democratic vision, more a benevolent system of noblesse oblige that appealed to all three of the rather superior Stauffenberg brothers.* As a result, although many Party members claimed to have been inspired by the poet, by 1943 a significant number in the developing German resistance were also drawn from George's old circle, including Fahrner, and Claus and Berthold Stauffenberg. Alexander was back at the house again a week later discussing strategies for survival, and the possibility of resistance.

Less than two weeks into the new year, the commanding officer of the Gatow academies, Dr Robert Knauss, officially proposed Melitta for the Iron Cross, First Class. His paper cited her 'sublime achievements' and devotion to duty, specifying her 2,200 nosedives and other test flights to evaluate of the impact of wind, speed, height, angle and distance in the development of dive-sights and other innovations.[97] The proposal had already been discussed with Milch, who lent his full support.

On the day of her nomination, Melitta was testing a Ju 87 at Schleissheim airfield near Munich, the home of a night interceptor squadron. Unable to cope with the stresses she put it through, the armoured glass cockpit shuddered and cracked during her flight. 'Ju 87 window broken,' she noted prosaically. 'Organized repair, tea, toast, migraine.'[98] Melitta spent the next six days at Schleissheim, mainly working with Junkers. In the evenings she ate at the smartest local hotel. She was almost certainly with Franz, whose squadron was based at the airfield. She then flew to Lautlingen, where she met Alexander at the family schloss. Here there were still

---

late to discuss them with his house guests.

* Stefan George moved to Switzerland shortly after the Nazi seizure of power. His move was prompted more by illness than politics, and he died the following year. The poet had been ambiguous about the Nazi rise to power. He refused to join the Prussian Academy of Arts after it had purged anti-Nazi writers, but also disowned some of his Jewish followers who spoke against the anti-Semitism of the new regime.

luxuries to be enjoyed; morning walks in the sunshine, afternoon teas, sparkling wine and cosy evenings with her husband, but her visit was not entirely peaceful. 'A lot of fuss about Stockholm talk,' she noted irritably, and later 'evening tiff with Mika', Berthold's wife.[99] It seems that many in the family were not happy that she had eventually given way and let the Nazis exploit her for propaganda.

On arriving back at Würzburg with Alexander, Melitta telephoned the Schleissheim airfield to speak with Franz. His plane had crashed a few nights earlier, she was told. He had been killed immediately. 'Sp. dead, numb and no tears,' was all she wrote before taking the next train to Munich to learn more from the squadron commander.[100] 'Sp.' was short for *Spätzchen*; her 'little sparrow'. Melitta was devastated. Two days later she started taking prescription sleeping pills. Then her sisters Klara and Lili came to stay with her, taking care of the housework while Melitta worked, mourned, sheltered from air raids, swept up broken glass from her windows, watched a burning bomber crash, and still failed to sleep.

Franz's funeral was arranged for 3 February 1944. His family invited Melitta to visit a few days before and Anny, his sister, collected her from the station. They stayed up late that night, talking about Franz. His mother was calm, but his stepfather could not speak without choking up. He had started collecting letters and papers relating to his son, and Melitta transcribed some to keep for herself. As well as bringing a wreath with a stencilled ribbon, she had written a poem for the funeral. The second verse ran:

> *It is the wholeness within you that touched me,*
> *Your heart-rending courage, the love of your personal destiny;*
> *an unGermanic tradition,*
> *Gloriously reborn in you.*[101]

Melitta did not attend Franz's funeral, however. Perhaps it was not deemed appropriate that such a well-known woman, whose own husband was still on convalescent leave, should be seen there. Early the day before, she ate breakfast with the family and then quietly took the train back to Würzburg. The following morning she put on a black suit, noted the funeral in her diary, and tried to apply herself to finishing a flight logbook. But her work, and later a film at the cinema, failed to distract her. 'Useless,' she commented bluntly.[102] Alexander read out Franz's obituary to her two days later. That afternoon she started a new sculpture, a bust of Franz. She now rarely commented on her test flights in her diary, giving space instead to more personal details. She noted that a friend's son was missing in action, that an evening gown had arrived by post, and that she would wake up on a wet pillow to find she had been weeping in her sleep. One week later Alexander was posted back to the front. Melitta's world had fallen apart.

On 28 February 1944, Hanna was summoned to the Berghof, Hitler's chalet in the Bavarian Alps. She was due to be presented with a certificate by the Führer, to mark the award, over a year earlier, of *her* Iron Cross, First Class. Hitler was tired. There were already reports that he could no longer raise his arm to salute the people as he had always done.* His temper was short and his charisma waning. After the formalities were over, he invited Hanna to take tea in the large lounge that offered magnificent views over the Austrian scenery down towards Salzburg. The only other person present was his Luftwaffe adjutant, Colonel Nicolaus von Below.† Ignoring friends' warnings that any outspokenness could risk her life, 'I did not hesitate to take this opportunity of putting forward our plan,' Hanna later recounted. The conversation, however, 'took a somewhat unexpected course'.[103]

Recent developments with the war were not so serious as to justify such drastic measures as suicide missions, Hitler told Hanna. There was no precedent in German history and the German public would not stand for it. To her rising impatience, he then 'expounded his views on the subject in a series of lengthy monologues, supporting his arguments with numerous illustrations from the pages of

---

* Even in November 1943, Hanna's friend and former colleague, Karl Baur, had felt that the Führer 'looked tired and worn out. His hand had no strength and he could not raise his arm to salute.' See Isolde Baur, *A Pilot's Pilot: Karl Baur, Chief Messerschmitt Pilot* (1999), p. 151.

† Nicolaus von Below had been promoted to this role by Greim and Göring.

history'.[104] This was one of Hitler's standard tactics. 'The victim found himself muzzled,' one of his adjutants recalled. 'Hitler saw to it that he could not open his mouth, launching into long monologues which gave full rein to his own opinions.'[105] His stories 'were certainly recounted in compelling and memorable phraseology', Hanna noted politely, 'but on reflection I could see that, while superficially appropriate, they were, in reality, irrelevant'.[106]

Hanna had never been fond of lectures. Nor was she particularly good at controlling her temper. She knew there was no higher authority to which she could appeal, however, and that she had just this one chance to make her case. Intervening as politely as she could, she argued that Germany faced a situation 'without historical precedent', which 'could only be remedied by new and extraordinary methods'.[107] Sensing resistance from this brave woman, whose broken face now looked up at him, Hitler diverted onto the subject of jet aircraft, one of 'his favourite digressions'.[108] Hanna had been here before, with Göring, and the conversation had not gone well then. She knew better than anyone how premature Hitler was to pin his hopes on jets, which still needed many months of development, at the least. She had reached the end of her tether.* 'Hitler', she could see, 'was living in some remote and nebulous world of his own.' Momentarily forgetting to whom she was talking or the respect due to his position, Hanna cut him off in mid-sentence, loudly exclaiming: 'Mein Führer, you are speaking of the grandchild of an embryo!'[109]

In the 'painful silence' that followed, Hanna caught sight of Below's face, 'glazed with horror' at this unexpected exchange.[110] While secretly pleased that the Führer had heard of production delays from another source, his adjutant knew Hitler was 'convinced he was infallible' in military matters.[111] Moreover not even his most senior advisers spoke to him as Hanna had just done, and women were never 'allowed to hold forth or to contradict Hitler'.[112]

---

* In fact, production of the excellent Me 262 jet fighter had been delayed because of Hitler's demands that it be converted for use as a bomber.

Almost in panic, a moment later Hanna launched in again. It took a while before she realized that although he retained a conventional politeness, she had 'quite destroyed Hitler's good humour'.[113] The Führer had no more appetite for the facts than Göring had before him. 'His face wore a disgruntled expression', Hanna now saw, 'and his voice sounded peevish' as he told her she was ill-informed.[114] 'Totally distraught' that her interview was evidently at an end, she chanced one last request for permission to at least start experimental work so that, when Hitler decided the moment was right, suicide attacks could be launched without delay.[115] Wearily, Hitler gave what Below described as his 'grudging consent'.[116] His only proviso was that he should not be troubled with any issues that might arise during development.

Ten minutes later Hanna was on her way back to the aeronautical research institute. 'She left behind a long shadow,' Below commented.[117] Although Hitler refused to accept her word about Luftwaffe production delays, he 'set very great store by her personal devotion to duty'.[118] This was fortunate for Hanna. Had her ideas been 'expressed by a civilian on a Berlin tram', they could easily have led to denouncement, investigation and 'resettlement' in the east.[119] As it was, she returned to work beaming. Hitler had approved her plan in principle, and development work could start in earnest under the more acceptable code name of Operation *Selbstopfer*, or Self-Sacrifice.

Hanna was motivated partly by patriotism but, despite her misgivings about certain Nazi leaders, she also had an unshakeable faith in National Socialism. In proposing military strategy and engaging others to sacrifice their lives for the defence of the Third Reich, she became an active accomplice of the regime. Yet Milch, Göring, Goebbels, Himmler – and Hitler himself – had not shared her great passion for Operation Self-Sacrifice. According to Below, despite his apparent acquiescence, privately 'Hitler was completely opposed to the idea of self-sacrifice'.[120] On learning of Hanna's plan, Goebbels felt that she had 'lost her nerve'.[121] Hanna was 'a very energetic and feisty lady', he wrote, but in general, 'you shouldn't let women be the lead advocate dealing with such important questions. Even with

all their efforts, their sense of intelligence will fail, and men, especially of high calibre, would have difficulties allowing themselves
to follow the lead of a woman.'[122] For Himmler it was the waste
of good pilots that rankled, when the country had so few left. To
Hanna's horror, at one point he suggested recruiting her pilots
from 'among the incurably diseased, the neurotics, the criminals'.[123]
Göring, conversely, would later try to redeploy the volunteers she
had recruited, for Focke-Wulf suicide missions for which they had
no training.[124] For Hanna, without the perfect men, equipment or
training, the idea of sacrifice became 'repugnant'.[125] If, however, the
act was 'noble' rather than pragmatic, she was certain it was justified. 'We're no lunatics, throwing our lives away for fun,' she told a
friend, in what he called 'her emotional way'. 'We're Germans with
a passionate love of our country, and our own safety is nothing to
us when its welfare and happiness are at stake.'[126] Ironically, this last
sentiment was one that Melitta might have appreciated.

11

OPERATION VALKYRIE
1944

'Early call, Claus, Berthold, Haeften, finally came to an agreement,' Melitta scribbled in her little appointments diary on Sunday evening, 21 May 1944.[1] Her hair was wet, it was late and she was tired. She knew she had a busy week ahead and should get some sleep, but she wanted to record the moment. Melitta had spent a long day with Alexander's two brothers and their close friend Werner von Haeften, sailing a dinghy on the Wannsee at midday, sharing a bottle of wine in the afternoon, and then returning with more wine to wash down a rabbit picnic. That evening they had swum together in the dark waters of the lake before heading their separate ways, Melitta walking up through the woods to Gatow, Claus and the others heading back to Berlin on the other side of the Wannsee. Melitta did not expand on their conversation in her diary, but she later confided in Paul. 'Claus had spoken to her about his intention, and had asked her whether she would be prepared to make herself available to fly him to Hitler's headquarters,' he later reported.* There she was to 'fake an emergency landing', perhaps due to low fuel, and 'then wait for him until the deed had been done, and fly him back to Berlin'.[2] 'The deed' was Claus's proposed assassination of Adolf Hitler, and the rapid flight back to Berlin was crucial to the plotters' hopes of success. Although there were numerous potential problems with the plan, and failure would certainly mean the execution of the conspirators, Melitta did not hesitate. 'She had, of course, agreed to this,' Paul attested,

---

* In interview thirty years later, Paul von Handel referred to Hitler's HQ as being in East Prussia. In fact Hitler was then based at the Berghof.

sighing deeply before adding that he had tried every argument to dissuade her.[3]

By the spring of 1944, Claus, Berthold and Werner von Haeften were all key members of the clandestine German anti-Nazi resistance, *Widerstand*. Claus had first been approached to join a loose network of conspirators in late 1939 by his uncle Nüx. He had declined then, but did not report the incident. Six years earlier he had welcomed Hitler's appointment as chancellor. He had admired the Führer's strong leadership if not his middle-class roots, and supported many policies from investment in the military and the annexation of disputed territories, to the restoration of German national pride, as he saw it. A firm believer in 'natural hierarchies', Claus was willing to accept some racial prejudice and casual anti-Semitism, but he drew the line at state-sanctioned violence. The brutality of both the Röhm putsch in 1934, when Hitler had consolidated his power by organizing the extrajudicial execution of several SA leaders, and Kristallnacht four years later, had shocked him into questioning the legitimacy of the regime. Over the next year, while counselling Alexander and their mother, Karoline, to keep their criticisms to themselves, Claus had often found himself in sympathy with his brother's perspective. With the war, however, Nazi Germany's rapid victories in Poland, France and the Low Countries, combined with Claus's sense of military duty and oath of allegiance to Hitler, ensured his loyalty to the regime.

It was 1942 before Claus began to seriously question Hitler's military leadership, and with it his leadership of the country. The conduct of the campaign in the east had left German forces overstretched, under-resourced and vulnerable to both the enemy and the elements. By 1943 it was clear that the offensive was a disaster and the German position unsustainable. Slowly Claus realized that military strategy had been subordinated to ideology. Only a military coup, he now believed, could bring the leadership change needed to save Germany from the humiliating prospect of unconditional surrender. Claus had also witnessed mass executions, both of captured combatants and of Jewish and other civilians in the villages and densely wooded hillsides of Russia and Ukraine. Fellow officers would later testify that he had protested against these orders, but to no avail.[4] Claus was appalled by Hitler's seemingly insatiable appetite for conflict, his military incompetence, the atrocities being committed and the dishonour brought to himself, the Wehrmacht and the Reich. He finally lost faith in Hitler, and his loyalty to the regime was superseded by his sense of duty to his country. The enforced period of rest that followed his injuries in Tunisia had given him time to reflect. Claus had been in earnest when he had looked up at his wife, Nina, from his hospital bed, his head and hands still bandaged following surgery, and told her with a wry smile, 'It is time I saved the German Reich.'[5]

Able, energetic and charismatic, once Claus had made his decision he became a leading figure in the conservative military resistance. To commit high treason during the last phase of a struggle for what was widely perceived as national survival demanded great moral courage and mental fortitude. At first Claus hoped that a new German leadership would be able to agree peace terms with the west, while keeping their territorial gains in the east.[*] This required Hitler's removal but, as a Catholic, Claus clashed repeatedly with those who advocated assassination. 'Does not the thought torment you, that murder was not our destiny?' Alexander later imagined his noble-minded brothers asking one another.[6] But over time Claus's position hardened. Tentative discussions showed that many soldiers would feel released from their oath of loyalty only after Hitler's death. Simply arresting Hitler was not an option; they had to decapitate the Nazi regime.

Claus never considered advocating a return to complete parliamentary democracy. 'Leadership should be according to natural ranks (as there is inequality by nature)', was the way Alexander later summarized his brother's position.[7] But unless there was to be military dictatorship, the Widerstand needed to supply suitable

---

[*] The diplomat Ulrich von Hassell had sought to avert war through discussions at the British Embassy in 1939. Later he became a key figure in the German Widerstand, hoping to mediate with the Western Allies. Had the coup been successful, he might have become foreign minister in the transitional government.

men to take civil office in a transitional administration. Berthold was advising on legal issues to ensure legitimacy; others were trying to create consensus and momentum. In September 1943 Claus was appointed chief of staff of the Reserve Army under General Friedrich Olbricht. Together with Ludwig Beck, Carl Goerdeler and Henning von Tresckow, Olbricht had been developing plans to exploit the existing policy, code-named 'Valkyrie', for the Reserve Army to seize control of the state in the event of a civil emergency, such as Hitler's death.* Under the conspirators' direction, these reserve forces would not only arrest certain SS officers and other criminal elements in the Nazi elite across the Reich and occupied territories; they would also provide the stability required to push through a full revolution.

In October, Nina visited Berlin to attend a wedding. When she returned to Bamberg, the picturesque Bavarian town to which she had moved with her young family in order to be with Claus's mother, she brought a rucksack stuffed full of resistance papers that needed to be burned.† Understanding that the less she knew, the better, Nina did no more than glance at the documents, but one she later remembered was a leaflet by the 'National Committee for a Free Germany'.[8] She now knew that Claus was involved in a major conspiracy against the regime. Later they talked about 'the necessary assassination', but Claus never discussed the details.[9] Nina understood that Melitta also 'knew about the plan'.[10] 'The members of the resistance needed support from strong women,' Claus's daughter later wrote; women 'who stood behind them, no matter what'.[11]

On 23 December 1943, Claus travelled for the first time to the *Wolfsschanze*, or 'Wolf's Lair', the windowless mass of concrete that served as Hitler's military headquarters in the forests of Rastenburg, East Prussia.‡ His visit provided him with a clear

---

* Operation Valkyrie, or *Walküre*, was symbolically named after the Norse goddesses who carry the bravest fallen warriors to Valhalla in the absence of their leader, Odin.

† Claus could not burn the papers in Berlin because his house had no chimney, and he did not want to make the caretaker suspicious.

‡ Now Kętrzyn in northern Poland.

picture of the size of the site, its layout, meeting rooms and existing security measures. Then he travelled to Bamberg to join his family for Christmas. From now on, Nina felt the planned coup 'always hung over me, like the sword of Damocles'.[12] She was almost relieved when her father died at the start of January, as she felt it would have been terrible for him 'to discover that his son-in-law was at the centre of a conspiracy'.[13] Some weeks later, she decided to get rid of the 1938 notebook Claus had written for her, full of his early misgivings about the regime. 'This notebook seemed to me so explosive', she later related, that she gave it to a friend to hide, 'together with the post-revolution plans' that had been prepared.[14*] Except for Melitta, Berthold and his wife, Mika, there was no one to whom Nina could speak openly, and she was feeling increasingly insecure and isolated.

How far Alexander was aware of his brothers' involvement in the resistance is not known. There had never been much doubt about his political views. 'He was always openly against the regime and had to be cooled down a bit by his brothers,' Nina later recalled.[15] He may even have encouraged Claus and Berthold to resist, but Nina believed that they considered Alexander 'too much of a security risk' to include him in their plans.[16] In any case Alexander had few useful contacts, so there was little reason to endanger him or others through his involvement. 'When an overthrow is planned . . .' Paul later explained, 'it is a basic rule that nobody should speak, not even a brother to his brother, a son to his father, a husband to his wife, if these people are not active participants.'[17] Nina seems to have been an exception, as she had to burn key papers. It was better to get Alexander safely out of the way.

Melitta had been talking to Rudolf Fahrner, the head of the German Research Institute in Athens, since late 1943, to see if he could secure a position for Alexander, away from the front. Now

---

* When Nina's friend was arrested, family members quickly burned these documents before the house was searched. See Konstanze von Schulthess, *Nina Schenk Gräfin von Stauffenberg: Ein Porträt* (2009), p. 73.

she also involved the other Stauffenbergs. 'Conversation about Sch.',* she had noted in early March 1944, after sailing with Claus, Nüx and other close friends on the Wannsee, now their standard rendezvous for discreet discussions. 'Decided on next steps.'[18] The following day she met Berthold at the Aero Club. An Athens posting for Alexander was now definitely on the cards but causing 'a lot of fuss', she wrote.[19] Claus was far from happy about what he called Melitta's 'protective machinations' on behalf of her husband.[20] Perhaps it was a question of family honour, but he may also have been concerned about drawing any undue attention to the family; within the week an attempt was due to be made on Hitler's life by one of his circle.†

Eventually, halfway through April, Fahrner managed to secure Alexander a temporary position lecturing in Athens with immediate effect. The occupied city felt very different from the proud capital that Alexander and Melitta had visited in the spring of 1939. Greece was suffering terribly as the Nazis requisitioned food and other resources. Forty thousand civilians starved to death. Tens of thousands more were killed in brutal reprisals for acts of resistance. Lecturing on 'Tragedy and State in the development of Athens', Alexander could hardly have failed to reflect on the cycles of conflict and the fierce patriotism of the Greek people, as well as the commitment of his friends that had brought him there, so far from the Eastern Front.[21]

Melitta, still in Berlin, was now less safe than her husband, but she had stopped rushing to the cellars every time an air-raid siren sounded. Sometimes she even sat out raids in a friend's suburban garden. Once, her sisters reported, they stayed on a balcony, counting twenty-eight planes above the capital before watching

---

* 'Sch.' was another abbreviation for *Schnepfchen*, Melitta's nickname for Alexander.

† Military aide Eberhard von Breitenbuch had agreed to shoot Hitler with his 7.65 mm Browning pistol at a Berghof conference on 11 March 1944. The plan was aborted when SS guards blocked his entry under new rules that aides should not be permitted in the room. Melitta's diary reveals that she looked for Berthold unsuccessfully on 11 March, and the next day, 'very tired and nervous', she received a 'sad letter from Fahrner'.

'the downings'.[22] With Alexander out of immediate danger, Melitta felt able to breathe again. She kept up her all-important night-fighter development work with Hajo Herrmann, sat sadly with friends talking about Franz, went to the cinema, darned socks, smoked, and waited for Alexander to return to her.

On Hitler's birthday, 20 April 1944, German cinema newsreels broadcast uplifting footage to the nation, opening with a hand-some member of the Hitler Youth raising the Nazi flag by the Brandenburg Gate. Military bands march past, smiling women cheer, and huge banners and bunting are strung across the dam-aged buildings. Hitler, apparently in jovial mood, greets the crowds from his car. Later he meets Göring, inspects some troops and shakes hands with the injured. He is wearing his greatcoat, gloves in his hand, and his own salute is low and fast. A map then shows progress with the war in Russia. There are smiling, well-equipped troops; trucks; cattle and horses with a foal. Steam trains puff ahead, laden with arms and equipment; paratroops descend; men with binoculars nod sagely. In one scene, an injured Luftwaffe pilot bravely climbs into his plane, the propeller purrs and he lifts off to join a formation in the sky. The pilots all have beautifully sewn gloves, and their machines have handsome black dials in the cockpit. The triumphant music starts to crescendo as an Allied plane is hit, and finally the German Eagle fills the screen.

The war-weary citizens of Berlin must have known this was, at the least, an optimistic impression of the state of the country and the conflict in which they were still engaged. Perhaps to cheer or distract them further, a report on the concert to mark the Führer's special day was broadcast later. A row of highly polished Nazi top brass sit in a theatre box, their swastika armbands running like a single red ribbon woven through their bulk. The camera then pans down to the handsome young military heroes and celebrities in the audience below. There is no sign of Melitta, but Hanna is there, her pseudo-uniform decorated with the Iron Cross, First Class, her diamond Military Flight Badge catching the light. Hanna's hair is tightly curled, each strand commanded into place. Her face is soft and rounded, almost fat now, and her eyes look tired. She sits absolutely still as Goebbels gives his speech, which, we are told, is 'greeted with loud applause' including from 'a visibly moved Hanna Reitsch'.[23]

Once Hitler had given his approval in principle for Operation Self-Sacrifice, responsibility for development had been handed to the commander of the Luftwaffe's special duties combat squadron. Seventy pilots were required to sign the declaration: 'I hereby voluntarily apply to be enrolled in the suicide group as a pilot of a human glider-bomb. I fully understand that employment in this capacity will entail my own death.'[24] 'We were all crazy,' one later admitted. 'We would have done anything at all to do our part for German victory and prevent defeat. That included sacrificing ourselves.'[25] Hanna was among the first to sign, but 'was persuaded' by friends to delay her actual enrolment.[26] Not only did she lack combat experience, but remaining outside the Luftwaffe command structure protected her useful ability to appeal to any authority.

Technical preparations were placed under the control of the Reich Air Ministry, and Hanna was appointed as a test pilot for the prototype planes. She started with a small one-seater Me 328 at Hörsching, near Linz in Austria. At first, jet engines were added as power units, but this idea was soon abandoned in favour of an engineless version, to be delivered to the target zone on the back of a Dornier Do 217 bomber. The Me 328 pilot would then detach in mid-air, and glide down into the target. Tests were completed in April, and an aircraft factory in Thuringia was awarded the production contract. Not a single plane would be delivered. Despite ever longer working hours and the use of forced labour at many factories, production facilities were struggling to cope with existing Luftwaffe orders. 'International law cannot be observed here,' Milch announced grimly, as he approved the execution of foreign workers who were found to have committed sabotage, or who simply refused to work at aircraft factories.[27] Hanna's project was not a priority, and she came to believe that some sort of 'official sabotage' was also taking place, to delay or prevent the Me 328s from being delivered.[28] When the Thuringia factory suffered a direct hit, the project was postponed indefinitely. Hanna, however, did not give up.

Alexander's Greek lecture tour ended in April, and Melitta flew to Vienna to join him as he travelled back. For two days they walked around the old city, visiting the castle, cafes and theatre, and dining under the arches in the cellar of the famous Stadtkrug restaurant. Alexander had brought her presents of silk and other 'fabulous things', she scribbled in her diary, her writing now tiny so that she could fit more in.[29] When they were alone he read Homer to her, but mostly, she recorded, he 'speaks a lot about Athens'.[30] From Vienna, they flew back to Berlin together. Alexander's call-up papers had arrived before them. He was being sent back east. As soon as he left, Melitta collapsed. Her brother Otto and sister Klara rushed over to be with her. Litta is 'completely crushed . . .' Klara wrote to Lili, their eldest sister. 'She can't find any escape in her work, or in the little joys of spring any more . . . worries sap all her energy [and] she always has the darkest thoughts.'[31]

Melitta was depressed, but Hanna was angry. For some weeks now she had 'bitterly regretted' not having tested prototypes of a manned V-1 buzz bomb for Operation Self-Sacrifice.[32] The V-1 programme had its own budget line and production facilities, and its potential was now attracting the attention of several other committed Nazis. Towards the end of April, Hanna received a call from the notorious SS-Obersturmbannführer Otto Skorzeny.

An early recruit to the Austrian Nazi Party, Skorzeny had volunteered for the Luftwaffe soon after the Anschluss but, at thirty-one, found he was too old. Instead he joined the Waffen SS, forming his own special operations unit, *Jagdverbände* (Hunting Unit) 502, in April 1943. After the surrender of Italy, Hitler had personally selected him to rescue Mussolini from Allied custody in an isolated hotel in the Apennine Mountains. In a brilliant operation, Skorzeny led a surprise attack by glider-borne paratroopers who overwhelmed the defenders without a shot being fired. Keen to deliver the Italian dictator to Hitler personally, Skorzeny flew him out in a small Fieseler Storch observation plane – the same type that Melitta and Hanna often flew. The flare of publicity that greeted their arrival in Berlin won Skorzeny instant fame, decoration and promotion. Even Winston Churchill praised the mission for its 'great daring'.

Six months later Skorzeny was assigned to work on the development of special weapons. It was while he was admiring V-1 tests at Peenemünde that he heard of Hanna's proposals for a manned version of the missile. Innovative, and extremely dangerous, the idea immediately appealed to him. Hanna, he laughed, was 'as brave as a man', and he wasted no time in calling her to arrange a meeting.[33] Although rather surprised, Hanna invited the commando hero round to her Berlin flat.

Unlike most of the senior Nazis whom Hanna had met previously, Skorzeny was physically very powerful. His dark hair was swept back from a handsome face not only well weathered, but bisected from ear to chin by a duelling scar. At over six feet tall, in his black SS uniform and with the Knight's Cross at his throat, he cut an impressive figure. Hanna was not intimidated. She hated bravado and expected the famous man to be, in her words, a 'blind, ambitious political fighter'.[34] When he arrived at Hanna's flat, 'she surveyed me critically with her big, flashing blue eyes,' Skorzeny wrote, and 'gave me her views quite frankly.'[35] Skorzeny went out of his way to be accommodating and Hanna was soon won round, developing an almost unique perspective on the Nazi hero. He was, she said, 'an individual whose deeply warm-hearted soul and whose altruistic, kind helpfulness stood in strong contrast to his personal appearance'.[36] Skorzeny's tough, dark looks made a good foil for Hanna's fair slightness but, as the scars on both their faces testified, they had much in common beneath the surface. Both were immensely brave, impatient and determined, and they shared a passionate and unconventional approach to getting the job done. 'Otto was the male Hanna Reitsch . . .' the Scottish pilot Eric Brown, who had attended Udet's wild parties with Hanna before the war, later pronounced. 'Brash and brave', and both were 'dyed-in-the-wool Nazis'.[37]

Skorzeny and Hanna soon formed a deep and lasting friendship, and Skorzeny lent his considerable energy and influence to Operation Self-Sacrifice. Like Hanna, he had little respect for the protocols of the command structure. He glibly swept aside all objections to a manned V-1 test programme on the pretext that, as Hanna paraphrased it, 'Hitler had vested him with full powers and had expressly called for a daily progress report.'[38] Hanna did not mention that Hitler had explicitly told her not to trouble him with updates. Skorzeny's words, gender and status quickly had the desired effect. Within a week, a team of engineers had secretly converted a V-1 into a manned prototype with a single-seat cockpit, no engine but ailerons controlled by joysticks and foot pedals, and cushioned metal landing skids. It was designated the Fieseler Fi 103-R, the 'R' standing for its code name, Reichenberg. Hanna, Skorzeny recorded proudly, was 'overjoyed at my victory over bureaucracy'.[39]

Hanna's operation was back on track, but it was Melitta's work, developing the techniques and equipment to intercept Allied bombers, that had won the support of Göring and the Reich Air Ministry. Melitta had completed her PhD at the beginning of the year, and had since been working with Hajo Herrmann, Helmut Lent and several younger pilots to develop her ideas.* After she introduced her new night-landing procedures, the Luftwaffe was able to use single-engined night fighters as bomber-interceptors. Although they never had sufficient aircraft available, the results spoke for themselves. It may have been the greatest practical contribution either woman made to the German war effort.

In May, Melitta was appointed the technical director of a new Berlin-based 'Experimental Centre for Special Flight Equipment', with ten staff and a significant budget, as well as considerable equipment and vehicles. Her mandate was to further develop night fighters, with visual night-landing procedures, dive-sights, blind bomb releases and aiming devices for attacking large enemy bomber formations, among other 'pressing problems'.[40] Although there were six people on the board of the new centre, including

---

* Although Melitta became quite fond of several of the young pilots, none, she confided in her diary, compared with Franz. (Gerhard Bracke archive, Melitta's 1944 diary, 09.05.1944.)

Hanna's old gliding friend Professor Walter Georgii, Melitta's employment contract stated that she would 'retain complete freedom in the conduct of the duties and the planning of her work'.[41] She was to report directly to Göring. It was the pinnacle of the most extraordinary career for a woman in Nazi Germany.* 'They built a pilot test-station for her,' Klara wrote years later, still almost incredulous.[42]

The doors of the new centre officially opened on 23 May 1944, two days after Melitta had reached her most secret agreement with Claus, Berthold and Werner von Haeften. 'I have got my own little experimental centre,' she proudly told her sister Lili, happy to be able to write openly about something.[43] Among other distinguished guests, Walter Georgii, Hajo Herrmann and Paul von Handel arrived to sign the centre's statutes and, in Paul's case, have a coffee with Melitta. Paul was also in Claus's confidence and the two old friends had much to discuss. When Paul had to leave, Melitta accompanied him back to the station, prolonging their private conversation for as long as possible.

'Raids . . . constant phone calls . . . too much,' she wrote in her diary that evening.[44] The experimental centre was 'making a pile of work', but it was work directed primarily at improving the survival rates of the Luftwaffe pilots trying to intercept Allied bombers, and at preventing the destruction of German cities.[45] Melitta was proud of her contribution, and saw no contradiction in joining the clandestine fight against Hitler, the man who had led her country into such a desperate situation. 'With people whom she could trust not to pass on her dislike of Hitler, she didn't hold back on her opinion that he needed to disappear as soon as possible,' the test pilot Richard Perlia later wrote.[46] 'She didn't make

---

* Although female pilots had been able to join the British Air Transport Auxiliary (ATA) to ferry RAF planes where needed since 1940, it was only in the spring and summer of 1944 that their German counterparts, such as Beate Uhse and Liesel Bach, were enlisted as members of the Luftwaffe's aircraft ferrying units. Melitta and Hanna remained unique as female German test pilots, and Melitta was the only female aeronautical engineer.

a secret of her oppositional views; she had the best connections to "the top", to the head Nazis, who had "to be eliminated".[47]*

It was a warm, clear day when Hanna flew Skorzeny over to Lärz to watch the first manned V-1 test flight. They had to fly low, 'hedge-hopping' over the fields to avoid detection by any enemy aircraft prowling overhead, but Hanna was in fine spirits. 'I could hardly believe my ears when she began to sing, at the top of her voice, the folk songs of her native Silesia,' Skorzeny later recalled with amusement.[48]

Various test and training versions of the manned V-1 had now been developed. Some had twin seats and dual controls for instructor and student, while others were single-seaters. Most had power units and all had landing skids, but landing even an unarmed V-1 remained extremely hazardous. 'Pilots of an average ability could never be certain of surviving the attempt,' Hanna wrote bluntly.[49] The final, operational, model was powered by the standard pulse-jet engine housed just behind the pilot's head, and had almost 2,000 pounds of high explosives packed into the nose. This version had no flaps or skids, as it was not designed to land. 'Its first flight', as Hanna put it, 'would also, inevitably, be its last.'[50] At best, a pilot might hope to parachute out at the last moment, but essentially it was a suicide weapon, a manned version of an early cruise missile.

By the time that Hanna and Skorzeny reached Rechlin, a prototype V-1 was already 'nestled', as Skorzeny described it, under the wing of a Heinkel He 111 bomber, ready for take-off.[51] All went well as the Heinkel lifted from the ground and began its ascent. When the V-1 pilot detached his machine from the bomber, Hanna watched it 'drop away . . . like some small, swift bird'.[52] The V-1 flew at twice the speed of its Heinkel mother-plane, tearing away through the sky. After a few wide circles it began a smooth descent. Suddenly the pilot lost control. Moments later

---

* Perlia could not resist contrasting Melitta with Hanna, 'who was favoured by Hitler and could meet with him even if she had not been announced'. (See Richard Perlia, *Mal oben – Mal unten* [Sometimes Up – Sometimes Down] (2011), p. 194.)

the V-1 crashed to earth, its point of impact marked by 'a column of black smoke rising in the summer air'.[53]

While most of the observers still stood watching in horror, Skorzeny impatiently called for another test pilot, before striding off.[54] 'Always a gentleman . . .' Hanna later defended him: Skorzeny 'demanded more from himself than from his men . . . [and] won the hearts of the soldiers committed to his care'.[55] Incredibly, although badly injured, the V-1 pilot had survived. The crash was blamed on manual error. A second attempt, the next day, brought a similar result. According to Skorzeny, when the Air Ministry ordered an end to the programme, Hanna 'could scarcely hold back her tears'.[56]

She would later claim that her initial offer to test the V-1s herself had been rejected on the grounds that 'this was a man's job'.[57] Now that the men had failed, she volunteered again. Few pilots had her experience of landing dangerous high-speed gliders like the Me 163, she told Skorzeny, and the project engineers were prepared to let her fly without official clearance. 'Nothing doing, Hanna,' he told her. 'If anything happened to you, the Führer would tear me to pieces himself!'[58] But Hanna was determined and Skorzeny, the SS special ops hero, was shamed by her courage. The next day she was strapped into the V-1 cockpit, ready to be taxied into the air.* 'I do not think I was ever in such a fluster . . .' Skorzeny wrote, as when 'the airscrews began to turn'.[59]

Despite her rubber-lined leather helmet, Hanna must have been deafened by the noise of the Heinkel's engine and the battering of the slipstream on the V-1 as she was dragged into the air. Nevertheless, her release was perfect. As the V-1 engine began to stutter, Hanna dropped from her host and pushed the tiny missile to its cruising speed of around 375 mph. 'The handling of the machine and its beautiful circles soon showed what an amazing

---

* Despite the depiction of Hanna launching a V-1 from a catapult in the 1965 film *Operation Crossbow*, manned V-1s were launched from under the wing of a bomber. The G-force from a catapult launch, Hanna later explained, would have 'burst body organs, as we learned from experiments and dead pilots'. (Ron Laytner, *Edit International: A portfolio of some of Ron Laytner's greatest stories*, 2010.)

pilot this girl was,' Skorzeny noted in admiration.[60] Nevertheless he still broke into a cold sweat as Hanna brought the V-1 spiralling down. Since the missile was not designed to land, once the engine cut out she found it cumbersome, gliding down steeply, 'like a piano'.[61] Moments later she managed a fast but smooth touchdown on her skids, blowing up clouds of dust across the tarmac. 'Nothing wrong with it at all,' she proudly told the engineers who rushed up to meet her.[62] Milch reportedly 'turned pale' when told of the unauthorized test but, as Skorzeny emphasized, 'both the idea and the machine had been vindicated'.[63] 'Passed without incident,' Hanna recorded simply in her flight report.[64] She and Skorzeny were jubilant, and the project was given clearance to proceed.

Over the next few weeks Hanna completed another eight or ten test flights, although 'not without their awkward moments', she admitted.[65] Once, caught in sudden turbulence, the rear of her V-1 grazed the Heinkel as she pulled away, crumpling and twisting its tail with a loud rending noise. Fortunately the main fuselage was undamaged, and she managed to land safely. During another test, with the two-seater training version, the sack of sand providing ballast in the empty seat shifted as she dived, blocking the controls so that she could not pull up. Cutting the engine, she dived more steeply until the sack slumped aside and she could grab the controls to level out at the last moment. The hard landing splintered the skids and hull, but Hanna emerged unscathed. For later tests, a water tank was lodged in the hull to simulate the weight of a warhead. Theoretically, pulling a lever allowed the water to be jettisoned through a drain before landing, so that the weight would not smash the fragile skids on touchdown. At 18,000 feet, however, Hanna discovered that the drainage system had frozen solid. She was trapped in what was now an overloaded glider, heading towards the ground at more than 500 mph.* 'In a frenzy of desperation,' she wrote, 'I gripped and clawed at the lever until my fingers were bleeding.'[66] Only as the skids approached the landing

---

* Such high-speed descents were important to ensure that any enemy anti-aircraft fire would be practically useless.

strip did the lever finally connect, and the water gush out over the ground. Moments later she landed safely. She was, she confessed, 'extremely lucky'.[67] She was also very courageous and highly skilled. At least two other pilots in the development programme were killed.

Hanna's V-1 tests took the best part of the spring. It was the end of May before she was training volunteer pilots in the two-seater model. On 6 June 1944, the date known to the Allies as D-Day, almost 160,000 mainly British, American and Canadian forces landed on five beaches along a heavily fortified fifty-mile stretch of the Normandy coast. The action was so unexpected that Hitler was hosting the wedding of Eva Braun's sister in Austria. 'Enemy air superiority was clear-cut,' his Luftwaffe adjutant, Nicolaus von Below, wrote. 'Their aircraft patrolled the skies almost unmolested, and our troops were unable to move by day.'[68] Within a week, Operation Self-Sacrifice pilots were recalled for defensive duties. 'The invasion had begun . . .' wrote Hanna, and 'bore all our efforts into oblivion'.[69] Manned V-1 flying bombs would never be put into operational use as Hanna had envisaged. 'The decisive moment had been missed,' she wrote bitterly, blaming Göring and the Nazi leadership for failing to appreciate that the proposed operation 'was no stunt'.[70] 'And so', she concluded, 'died an idea that was born of fervent and holy idealism, only to be misused and mismanaged at every turn by people who never understood how men could give up their lives simply for an idea.'[71]

Alexander and Melitta woke together at their apartment in Würzburg on D-Day. They had arrived from Lautlingen the night before, with a side of venison from a buck they had shot in the beautiful wooded hills behind the family schloss. Fahrner had pulled off another small miracle: Alexander had been appointed as a National Socialist ideological education officer, based in Athens. At first he was loath to accept the post, knowing that strings had once again been pulled. On reporting for duty, he expressed his unsuitability, only to be told that the post was non-negotiable. With two free weeks before he had to leave, Alexander spent as much time as possible with Melitta. They hunted rabbits at Gatow, and deer at Lautlingen. In the evenings Alexander served a 'daily reading of Homer' to his wife, along with the venison.[72] But with news of the Allied landings, they were recalled to Berlin. Melitta flew them; Alexander was being dispatched to Greece and she was needed at the Air Warfare Academy. 'Invasion!' she wrote, allowing a rare exclamation mark to enter her diary.[73]

Despite the many demands upon her, on the evening of D-Day Melitta made time to ring Berthold. All but the most fanatical Nazi officers now concluded that defeat was almost inevitable, and Hitler's denial and ongoing mismanagement would only drag out the conflict, resulting in the complete destruction of Germany.* The Allies had refused to engage with requests from well-placed conspirators to negotiate a separate peace excluding Russia. Now they were approaching from the west, and Stalin's Red Army from the east. If the resistance were to act, it had to be soon. 'The assassination must be attempted at all costs,' Henning von Tresckow argued. 'What matters is that the German Widerstand will, before the eyes of the world and before history, have made the decisive step.'[74] The following day, Melitta was in touch with Berthold again, as well as Werner von Haeften and Friedrich Olbricht: all key conspirators. Claus, she noted without elaborating, was at Hitler's headquarters.

This was Claus's first military briefing in the presence of Hitler, and his first visit to the Berghof. He was not impressed. The Führer kept glancing around furtively. When he grasped Claus's hand between both his own, Claus felt him shaking involuntarily, and later his maps quivered as he shuffled them around. Himmler, Keitel, Speer and Göring were also present. Göring was clearly wearing make-up, Claus noted with distaste.

---

* As of July 1944, Otto Skorzeny believed 'no clear-sighted man could doubt that, from a purely military point of view, we had lost the war'. However, he felt officers should conceal this truth, arguing that 'our determination to resist [the enemy] with our last breath could be the only answer. No honourable man who loved his country could have done anything else.' See Otto Skorzeny, Robert Messenger, *Skorzeny's Special Missions: The Memoirs of 'The Most Dangerous Man in Europe'* (2006), p. 106.

The atmosphere was poisonous, he felt, and all the men, with the possible exception of Speer, were 'psychopaths'.[75] Speer felt that they had 'hit it off'*[76]. 'In spite of his war injuries . . . Stauffenberg had preserved a youthful charm,' he later wrote. 'He was curiously poetic and at the same time precise.'[77] At that moment Claus was interested in the precise details of the security arrangements around Hitler. Among his observations, he noted that 'in the Führer's immediate entourage, one had considerable freedom of movement'.[78]

That evening Melitta talked late into the night with Berthold. He left only at lunchtime the next day. Later she met Paul, who had just flown in from Rechlin. Together they walked along the quiet shoreline of the lake, deep in discussion, before heading in for a fortifying supper, coffee, cognac and vermouth. The Wannsee was the porous barrier that divided Melitta's two worlds. On one side she developed flight technology with the Luftwaffe; on the other, she conspired against the Nazi regime with her in-laws. Within a week she had sailed over again to meet Claus at Berthold's Tristanstrasse house where they both now lived and slept, and which had become a key meeting place for members of the conspiracy. Over supper, Claus gave Melitta his 'report from [Hitler's] headquarters'.[79] 'She was one of the very few people he trusted without reservation,' his daughter, Konstanze, later wrote.[80]

Klara, who was providing domestic help now that Melitta was running her own research institute, must have wondered how her sister made the time to keep meeting these friends. Melitta was too busy to see much of Klara and, when she thought about her at all, only vaguely worried that she was left 'at rather a loose end'.[81] On top of her work with Junkers, Melitta was now commissioned to consider the technical challenges of converting Germany's first operational jet, the Messerschmitt Me 262, into a fighter-bomber.

---

* Speer was probably right. Claus invited him to meetings, but he did not attend. Papers found later showed Speer's name listed as 'armaments minister' for a new government. The ancillary pencil note, 'if possible?' saved his life. See Albert Speer, *Inside the Third Reich* (1971), p. 527.

This was a pet project of Hitler's but the Me 262 was totally unsuitable and, in any case, mass production was still many months away. 'It was disturbing now to observe how [Hitler's] contact with reality was tending to slip away,' Nicolaus von Below wrote.[82]

On 16 June, Melitta recorded the 'use of vengeance weapons' in her diary.[83] The first unmanned V-1 buzz bomb had been deployed against London the day before, hitting a railway bridge as well as a number of houses, and killing six people.* In addition to the smoke and dust, for a moment it left a beautiful white semicircle in the sky above, a pressure wave, 'rather like a white rainbow'.[84] This was one of several range-finding tests, and a full assault followed. Although London was surrounded by 'a wall of balloons . . . to ward off the buzz bombs', as the strategically grouped blimps were described by one female ATA pilot, thousands of V-1s got through.[85]

One of the first destroyed the Aldershot house belonging to the Scottish pilot Eric Brown. Brown's wife was unhurt, but their cleaner lost an eye. After this Eric, now a test pilot at Farnborough, felt he had a 'special interest' in helping to improve the performance of RAF front-line fighters, so that they might intercept the low-flying V-1s.[86] They could not be shot down over built-up areas, and could not be blown up 'because you'd fly straight into the debris', Eric realized. Instead he helped to develop a booster system that could get a fighter alongside a V-1 for a short spurt, so that they could tip it off course by 'nudging its wings using air pressure and not actually touching'.[87†] Meanwhile, the Allied raids on Germany were stepped up. 'Many waves of planes flew very low,' the former diplomat, now conspirator, Ulrich von Hassell noted in his diary. 'The heaviest daylight raid yet . . . a number of barracks, an orphanage, several kindergartens, et cetera,

---

* The following day a faulty V-1 flew drastically off course, returning to explode close to the shelter occupied by Hitler and his aides. There were no casualties.

† On one attempt to tip a V-1, Brown was forced to bail out when his engine caught fire. He landed in a pond, beside a very angry bull. Eventually he was saved by the farmer, who led the beast away with the soothing words, 'Come on, Ferdinand.' (*Mail Online*, Robert Hardman, 'Hero who makes Biggles look like a wimp', 07.05.2013.)

were hit, with heartbreaking losses. This looks like an answer to the "robot" bombs.'[88]*

The day after the first V-1 hit London, a new refrain started to appear in Melitta's diary: 'Night flights Storch'.[89] Melitta's official work involved test flights with various Junkers at night, but she had never previously recorded night flights in her Fieseler Storch. She was evidently testing the machine, but as it was a low-speed observation plane, fun to fly but not used in combat, these flights cannot be explained by service requirements.† According to Paul, Melitta had already told him about her potential role providing return transport after an assassination attempt. Paul knew that Claus could trust Melitta 'absolutely'. Not only was she sympathetic to his political aims, she was also a brilliant pilot. Above all, were she to turn up somewhere unexpectedly, Paul believed that 'a woman of Litta's reputation would appear relatively harmless even in the highest Luftwaffe circles'.[90]

But Paul still had misgivings about Melitta's involvement. Planes were increasingly hard to get hold of. If Melitta were to fly to Claus without attracting attention, it would have to be in the Storch, the only plane she had free access to when not working. But a standard Storch could not fly the 300 miles from East Prussia back to Berlin without landing for fuel en route. After an assassination attempt, Paul argued, they were highly likely to be 'discovered and arrested' at any such stop.[91]

Melitta knew the capabilities of different aircraft better than Paul, and he felt that 'she was probably aware that the plan with the Fieseler Storch had almost no prospect of success'. He argued it was her duty to let Claus know, so that he could secure the use

----

* The destruction caused by the RAF and US Eighth Air Force far exceeded the impact of the V-1s.

† The Fieseler Storch was the plane Hanna had flown along the Eastern Front, and the one in which Skorzeny had flown Mussolini to Berlin. Britain's Wing Commander Leonard Ratcliff has described them as 'a toy really, a sort of little runabout' (Mulley interview, 12.12.2013). The French maquisards called them *mouches* (flies). See Paddy Ashdown, *The Cruel Victory: The French Resistance, D-Day and the Battle for the Vercors 1944* (2014), p. 98.

of a fast Luftwaffe communications plane instead. But Melitta 'was not prepared to tell Claus'. Instead, in Paul's dramatic retelling of their conversation, she insisted that 'when I am called, I'll be there. I am not afraid of death.'[92] Perhaps Melitta had modified the Storch, or added auxiliary fuel tanks, as between 17 and 26 June she recorded at least five night flights in it, without further explanation. She also undertook a 200-mile return flight to Rechlin, despite bad weather. On Tuesday 27 June, however, she met Paul again. 'Evening, Paul, late, depressing,' she recorded tersely.[93] The 'depressing' was not explained but, after this, there were no more night flights in the Storch.

Claus spent his last weekend at Bamberg with his family, between 24 and 26 June. Nina was packing to take the children to Lautlingen for the summer and was surprised that he seemed so unenthusiastic about their trip. 'It is no longer about the Führer, nor about the Fatherland, nor about my wife and my four children,' he told his fellow conspirators a few days later. 'It is now about the whole German nation . . .'[94] On 6 July, he was back at the Berghof, in his new capacity as chief of staff to the commander-in-chief of the Reserve Army. That day he sat at the round table in the main salon, keeping his 'remarkably plump briefcase', Speer noted, beside him.[95] Claus was carrying a bomb but did not prime it after it became clear that Hitler would not be joined by other senior leaders.

A week later Claus was pushing for another attempt. 'The aim is to preserve the Reich!' he argued. 'It is necessary to save Germany from unconditional surrender and from total occupation.'[96] On 11 July he was ordered to the Berghof to brief Hitler on the availability of replacement troops for the Western Front. As he walked towards his waiting plane at Rangsdorf airfield, near Berlin, Claus met Otto Skorzeny, who was on his way to board a flight to France. The would-be assassin and the ardent Nazi greeted each other politely, and stopped to talk for a moment. Later, Skorzeny reflected on how calm and friendly Claus had seemed. Claus had been carrying explosives, but again postponed the attempt when he learned Himmler would not be present. His aim was to eliminate

Hitler, Himmler and Göring in one operation, so as to better support the chances of the military coup that would follow under the Valkyrie plans.

The following day Claus met with members of the coup's proposed future administration. It was hot. The diplomat Hans Gisevius recalled that Claus pulled open his uniform jacket, and sat slumped with 'his arms dangling limply and his legs in their heavy top-boots sprawled out in front of him', while he 'wiped the perspiration from his forehead, brushing it back into his tangle of hair'.[97] Nevertheless, when he started to speak, Claus 'took over the conversation almost at once'.[98] Melitta was not present. It was better that she did not know any unnecessary details. Berthold was pessimistic about their chances of success. 'The worst thing is knowing that we cannot succeed,' he told Mika, 'and yet that we have to do it for our country, and for our children.'[99] For Berthold, Claus, Melitta and the others, just as much as for Hanna, the foreseeable future entailed high risk of self-sacrifice.

On Saturday 15 July, Claus flew back to the Wolf's Lair. At one point he was photographed standing to attention as Hitler greeted a colleague beside him, but that evening he was back in Berlin without having used his bomb. Nina knew that 'renewed attempts were always being made', and Melitta was also on tenterhooks.[100] Every day she went to work, determined to help the fight against the Allied bombers, while desperate for news of her brother-in-law's own bomb attack against the Nazi leadership. Her position was almost impossible. 'Miserable, exhausted,' she scrawled on the night of the 15th, her own meetings having run on until four in the morning.[101] A few hours later she was up and crossing the Wannsee by steamboat to meet with Claus and Berthold at their Tristanstrasse house. It was a Sunday, but Claus already had other visitors. He could only finally meet Melitta after dinner, and he left soon afterwards. 'Everything had to be done at night and by word of mouth, one could never make a telephone call or write a letter,' the wife of another resister later wrote. 'Everything was based on personal night-time contacts.'[102] By now Melitta had missed the last boat back, so she stayed at Tristanstrasse overnight, talking with Berthold. 'Bad,' she wrote simply in her diary.[103] Early the next morning, after seeing Claus once more, she raced back to Gatow, throwing herself into work meetings so she would not be missed.

On 18 July Melitta spoke with Paul again, arranging to meet him that evening. 'Storch organized etc.', she wrote, then, 'air-raid alarm, very late'.[104] The Allies were bombing Peenemünde again in their ongoing assault against the V-weapons, as well as other targets. Melitta saw Paul again twice the next day, in between her experimental-centre work. 'Tired,' she wrote sparingly.[105] It is not known whether she was yet aware that Claus had arranged another pilot through Eduard Wagner, Hitler's quartermaster general, who had joined the conspirators. That night Werner von Haeften called his brother to tell him that he had finally 'found an apartment for mother'.[106] It was their agreed code that the attempt was going ahead. At Tristanstrasse, Claus showed Berthold his plastic high explosives, which he then wrapped in a clean shirt and slid inside his briefcase. Later he tried to call Nina, but the phone lines were down following a bombing raid.

For Melitta, 20 July 1944 began with a Junkers Ju 88 workshop flight, followed by technical work on a Junkers Ju 87. It was another hot, sultry day, and she knew she would soon be sweating as she rushed between the workshops and the airfield. Claus and Berthold had been up since dawn. 'Even this early in the morning, the heat was unbearable,' Gisevius recorded.[107] Claus and Haeften, serving as his military aide, were needed at one of Hitler's daily conferences at the Wolf's Lair, now just fifty miles from the advancing Red Army. Their plane slipped in over the birch and pine forest later that morning, and was quickly camouflaged under grey-green nets by ground crew. Waved through the outer gates near the marshes by sentries wearing mosquito nets over their heads, they drove between minefields and past gun emplacements to a second gate in an electric fence. A final gate, a mile further on, led to Hitler's personal HQ, hidden inside the depths of the forest. As both men had passes, they were not searched.

It was now Claus learned that the conference had been brought forward to accommodate a visit from Mussolini later in the day. It had also been moved to a wooden guest hut, which was cooler than the underground bunker.* On the pretext of needing to change his sweat-stained shirt before meeting his Führer, Claus hurried to prime the bomb that was still hidden in his briefcase. Although he had a specially adapted pair of pliers, with only three fingers on his remaining hand it was a struggle to set the device and, having been interrupted once, he did not have time to prime the secondary explosives smuggled in by Haeften. At 12.35 Claus entered the claustrophobic conference room with his briefcase under his arm. 'He stood there quite erect,' one general later recalled, 'the picture of a classical soldier.'[108] Then he took the chair that Hitler motioned to, just one seat to his right, and placed his case under the table, as close to the Führer as possible. Moments later he excused himself to take a telephone call.

Not stopping to collect his hat, Claus headed straight to Haeften, waiting in the car. He was only halfway to the first gate when he heard the explosion, turned, and saw thick clouds of smoke, shot with yellow flames. 'No one in that room', he was certain, 'can still be alive.'[109] Bluffing his way through the checkpoints, he boarded the Heinkel 111 that had brought him in and was now waiting with its engines running, and headed for Berlin. It was still early afternoon when Claus landed, but to his anger there was no car ready to take him to the Bendlerblock, the main office of the Supreme High Command. When he finally arrived, Gisevius remembered that Claus 'stood breathless and bathed in perspiration', but 'somehow the massiveness of the man had been reduced; he seemed more spiritual, lighter'.[110] Claus had 'a smile of victory on his face', and radiated confidence and success.[111] He had not heard that Hitler had survived.

The Valkyrie plan depended on an immediate response to news of the assassination. 'The Führer, Adolf Hitler, is dead!' the conspirators' pre-planned radio announcement read, having been secretly typed up in the office by a secretary, Margarethe von Oven,

---

* The main bunker was also having repairs undertaken that day.

her heart thumping as she worked. 'The [new] Reich government has declared martial law in order to maintain law and order.'[112] But Margarethe's manuscript was still waiting in a desk drawer, martial law had not been declared, and the Reserve Army was not mobilized until four in the afternoon.* Without confirmation of the fatalities, Claus's fellow conspirators had hesitated, failing to secure the all-important radio station or persuade enough key military commanders to back the coup. To their perpetual dishonour, most senior officers placed their oath to Hitler, their military duties and personal reputations, above the interests of their nation. The plot crumbled that evening, when news spread that Hitler was still alive.

Hitler had been only six feet away from the bomb, but the thick conference table had shielded him from much of the blast. Thrown from his chair, he was concussed, his head and back struck by falling timber, his hair burned, ears ringing and thighs riddled with over 200 oak splinters, but he had sustained no serious injuries. He was lucky. Three officers and a secretary would later die from their wounds. Hitler's apparently miraculous survival fed his belief in his own inviolability. He greeted his secretaries 'with an almost triumphant smile', telling them, 'I have been saved. Destiny has chosen me . . .'[113] Later, after showing his shredded trousers to Mussolini, he sent them to Eva Braun, 'with the instruction that they should be carefully preserved' as evidence of providence.[114] On discovering that Stauffenberg was the culprit, however, he 'flew into a rage' and 'started cursing the cowards who wanted to get rid of him'.[115] Over tea that afternoon, Hitler once again 'leapt up in a fit of frenzy, with foam on his lips, and shouted that he would have revenge on all traitors'. Interrupted by a call from Berlin, he screamed orders 'to shoot anyone and everyone' before announcing, 'I'm beginning to doubt whether the German people are worthy of my great ideals.'[116]

---

* Henning von Tresckow sent Margarethe von Oven away from Berlin for the day of the coup. 'If we need you, I'll send a plane,' he told her. This precaution probably saved her life, and may also have explained why Melitta was still on standby. See Dorothee von Meding, *Courageous Hearts* (1997), p. 58.

After a brief gun battle in the first-floor corridors of Berlin's Bendlerblock, during which Claus was shot in the arm, he and his immediate clique were arrested. Their decorations and badges of rank were stripped from them, and tossed into an upturned helmet on the floor. Claus claimed personal responsibility for the attempted putsch, saying the others were under his command. Nevertheless, they were all summarily sentenced to immediate execution and led down the nearest staircase and out of the building. The front facade was floodlit by searchlights, and one side of the back courtyard was illuminated by the headlights of a truck. Set against a city in total blackout, 'it seemed as theatrical as a movie backdrop . . . inside a dark studio', Speer later recalled.[117] Just outside the glare, a firing squad was waiting. It was half past midnight, twelve hours since Claus had planted the bomb at Hitler's feet. Olbricht was the first to be led in front of the rifles, and was quickly cut down. Claus, his uniform sleeve now soaked with blood, was next, but some reports say that Haeften threw himself in front of the bullets intended for his friend. When his turn came, witnesses reportedly heard Claus shout out to the world, 'Es lebe heiliges Deutschland!' – 'Long live sacred Germany!'

12

IN THE CAMPS
1944

'Now, at last, things are going well! An assassination attempt has been made on Hitler . . .' one fourteen-year-old Dutch girl wrote effusively in her diary. 'And for once not by Jewish Communists or British capitalists, but by a German general who's not only a count, but young as well.'[1] Still hidden in her attic rooms in Amsterdam, Anne Frank believed that this was 'the best proof we've had so far that many officers and generals are fed up with the war and would like to see Hitler sink into a bottomless pit'.[2] Over 400 miles away, inside Nazi Germany, Melitta had also been confiding in her diary, but her entries were much more guarded. 'News of assassination', she pencilled neatly against 20 July, continuing without a pause: 'Night flights, Ju 87 doesn't work, due to loose contacts, repair and prepare installation Ju 88'.[3] The next morning Melitta went to work as usual. It was only after her assistant reported further news that Melitta allowed herself to note, 'apparently they have mentioned Col. Count St. [Stauffenberg] on the radio!'[4] The exclamation mark, like the use of Claus's formal name and title instead of the simple 'C' she usually wrote to denote him, put a discreet distance between herself and her brother-in-law. That evening she placed a call directly to Göring, whose adjutant eventually told her that no one had been critically injured in the attack. 'Doubt that', she risked adding to her account.[5]

For Otto Skorzeny, the first radio announcement on the afternoon of 20 July 'came like a thunderbolt'.[6] Quickly gathering some SS officers, he had arrived at the Bendlerblock around midnight. There he noted 'an atmosphere of hostile suspense', with several officers still armed with machine-pistols in the corridors.[7] He was too late to prevent the immediate execution of Claus but half an hour later he met with Speer and the head of the Gestapo to discuss next steps. 'When we greeted . . . no one clicked his heels,' Speer later recalled. 'Everything seemed muted; even the conversations were conducted in lowered voices, as at a funeral.'[8] Within a few hours, the machinery of the Nazi state was back in operation.

Skorzeny's take on the failed coup was that, 'with the exception of Colonel von Stauffenberg', the conspirators had been 'hopelessly irresolute and resigned to the worst, so that a slight push from a handful of opponents brought the whole set of cards tumbling to the ground'.[9] Even Churchill dismissed the attempt as simply part of 'a murderous internecine power-struggle'.[10] Skorzeny retained 'the greatest respect' for Claus, as a 'man prepared to give his life for his convictions', but he was incensed by the attempt to 'stab the German nation in the back when it was fighting for its life'.[11] Commissioned to hunt down the remaining conspirators, he applied a furious zeal to his work.

Hitler had addressed the nation just after midnight. At first he spoke slowly, hesitating, but his voice rose with passion as he attributed his survival to providence.[*] 'My heart stopped in shock,' the wife of one of the conspirators wrote, horrified to learn the attempt had failed, while another hurried 'to light a fire and burn papers'.[12] Outraged by the betrayal, the injured Führer was soon shouting into the microphone, swearing vengeance on the 'tiny clique of ambitious, wicked, and stupidly criminal officers' who had dared to oppose him. We will 'settle accounts . . .' he promised, 'in the way we National Socialists are accustomed to settling them'.[13]

'They will be murdered, wherever there's a hint of suspicion,' General von Thoma commented, listening to the broadcast as a POW in England. Stauffenberg's 'wife and children will probably have . . . long since been killed'.[14] Nina, however, was still asleep

---

[*] Hitler's photographer, Heinrich Hoffmann, swore that Hitler 'really believed' in providence, and that he himself had witnessed 'with my own eyes how often he escaped death by a hair's breadth'. See Heinrich Hoffmann, *Hitler Was My Friend* (2011), pp. 134–5.

in bed at Lautlingen. Having not heard from Claus for a few days, she had taken their children to the family schloss for the summer, where Berthold's wife, Mika, was already ensconced with her young family. On 20 July, the two women had been sitting in the garden when a maid ran out to tell them of a radio announcement about an assassination attempt. 'We only looked at each other', Nina later recalled, 'and said, "This is it!"'[15]

Early the next morning, Claus's elderly mother, Karoline, hurried into Nina's bedroom. Following Hitler's midnight broadcast, the Stauffenberg name was on everyone's lips. Neither Nina nor Mika yet knew the exact role their husbands had played, nor that Berthold had already been arrested, and Claus shot and buried.* Later that morning the Gestapo arrived at Bamberg to arrest Nina. Not finding her there, they arrested her mother, eventually sending her to Ravensbrück, the Nazi concentration camp built specifically for women, sixty miles north of Berlin. It would be two more days before they called for Nina and the others at Lautlingen.

For Nina, 'those two days were a gift from heaven'.[16] Claus had given her 'the order' not to stand by him, 'but to do everything to keep the children safe'.[17] Their eldest son, Berthold, was now ten. He read a newspaper every day, and had heard about the attempt on the radio. He wanted to know what was going on, but the adults would not discuss it. Instead, his great-uncle Nüx took all the children on a long walk, distracting them with stories of his adventures as a big-game hunter in Africa. The next day Nina took her two eldest boys aside and gently told them that their father had carried out the attack, and had been executed by firing squad late that same day. For Berthold, his mother's words were 'shattering . . . the end of my world'.[18] Like all the children, he had been brought up to venerate his Führer, but he also adored his father. 'He believed he had to do it for Germany,' Nina offered as she saw her son's confusion.[19] 'He made a mistake . . .' she added, reasoning that the boys might be interrogated. 'Providence has protected our

---

* Claus's body would later be exhumed and burned on Hitler's orders.

dear Führer.'[20] 'From that moment I was unable to think clearly,' Berthold later confessed. He simply steeled himself to absorb 'the blows that would fall on us'.[21] They fell quick and hard.

The Gestapo visited Lautlingen while the children were asleep that evening. The next day, both their mother and great-uncle Nüx were gone. Mika took a train to Berlin, hoping to find out what had happened to her husband, and to bribe the Gestapo to get the family released. Instead, she too was arrested. Nina had decided to 'play the stupid little housewife, with children and nappies and dirty laundry'.[22] Now she learned this would do little good. Hitler was invoking the ancient law of *Sippenhaft*, or 'kin detention'. 'This scum must be eliminated, exterminated root and branch,' he announced. 'It is not sufficient just to seize the culprits and bring them ruthlessly to account – the whole brood must be wiped out.'[23] Hitler's injuries were worse than he wished to admit. His hearing and the nerves in his left arm were damaged, his legs ached, and 'open sores' were visible on his hands.[24] He 'looked horrible', aides secretly admitted, 'a fat, broken-down old man'.[25] He was in no mood for mercy.

The night after Nina was arrested, Claus's mother Karoline, her sister, and many aunts, uncles and cousins were seized and detained.* Nina and Mika's children, the youngest of whom was just three, were left scared and bewildered in the care of their nanny and two Gestapo officials who quickly 'behaved like masters of the whole house'.[26] Margarethe von Oven,† the Reserve Army secretary who had typed out the Operation Valkyrie orders, was on a train back to Berlin on 21 July, carrying incriminating letters in her handbag. Suddenly she overheard people saying, 'Stauffenberg . . . assassination . . . providence . . . a small clique . . . all of them liquidated.'[27] Hurrying to the toilet, she tore up the letters and

---

* In December 1944, Karoline von Stauffenberg said that although she had not known the details, 'I knew of my son's deed and I approve of it.' See Peter Hoffmann, *Stauffenberg: A Family History, 1904–1944* (2008), p. 281.

† Margarethe von Oven was later arrested and imprisoned. 'I felt happy when . . . the door had shut behind me,' she said. 'At that point the tension was over.' Despite incarceration, she survived the war. See Dorothee von Meding, *Courageous Hearts* (1997), p. 58.

flushed them away. A week later, when she should have been keeping a low profile, she risked everything to visit the Stauffenberg children, still under house arrest. The name tags had been cut from their clothes, she noted, so that they could not be identified. In August the children were collected by the National Socialist Welfare Service. Before they left, their nanny took them to the local priest for his blessing. 'With tears in his eyes', he told them that whatever horrors lay ahead, they must never forget that their father 'was a great man'.[28] Only later did they realize how courageous these words were, at a time when the press and radio waves were filled with vitriolic reports about the conspirators. Then they were driven away in a black limousine. Such cars were now rare, and the children were torn between excitement and panic; their nanny was crying, and none of them knew where they were going.

Melitta had telephoned her family as soon as the first terrible reports began to come through, warning them to keep their distance from her, for their own safety. She hoped they would be overlooked because they were not blood-relatives of Claus.* 'The extent of the catastrophe was all too clear,' Klara said, immediately setting out for Gatow in spite of Melitta's caution. When she arrived, the sisters took their old walk through the woods and down to the lake. The water no longer glinted with possibilities. Melitta would never take the ferry over to Tristanstrasse again, or sail on the lake with Claus and Berthold. But the shoreline still provided the seclusion where she and Klara could talk without being overheard. Klara thought Melitta seemed surprisingly calm. She was 'under no illusion that she would avoid arrest', but believed that the importance of her work gave her a chance to 'come out unscathed'.[29] Expecting to be detained at any moment, Melitta avoided her rooms until, 'with a heavy heart', Klara left, promising to telephone every day.[30]

Melitta had also called Alexander in Greece. Although they couldn't discuss events, they tried to 'give each other courage'.[31] Melitta had already destroyed her husband's letters. Her main fear

---

* Neither Melitta's parents, nor any of her siblings, were arrested.

now was that she might be drugged during interrogation, and this might 'break her willpower'.[32] Although hundreds of miles away during the attempted coup, as the chief assassin's brother Alexander was still vulnerable. Nina thought the news had been 'a great shock' to him. Excluded from the plans, she felt 'he had been underestimated by his brothers' and 'undoubtedly sensed that they had not let him into the secret because he . . . was much too careless'.[33]* Alexander braced himself for news of the arrest and execution of his family, and probably his own detention. When friends offered him the opportunity to flee to Egypt, he honourably refused. 'If Schnepfchen must die for his brothers,' Melitta confided to her diary, 'then I am done with the whole thing here.'[34] Alexander was arrested the next day.

That afternoon Paul phoned Melitta. 'She was quite calm,' he reported, but let him know that, 'as a few gentlemen from the Gestapo were in her office, she probably would not be able to speak for some time'.[35] First her office was ransacked, and then her Würzburg apartment. She met the 'thugs' with 'such superior aplomb', Jutta proudly reported, that they did not dare smash her clay sculptures.[36] Melitta was then taken to the Gestapo offices on Prinz Albrecht Strasse.

Klara had kept her word, phoning every day. 'When . . . no one answered I knew they had come for her,' she wrote.[37] To her amazement, a few days later she received a letter from Melitta, reassuring her that she had already petitioned Göring, and was hopeful of a swift release. She made it clear that Klara 'should do nothing to intervene on her behalf'.[38] Melitta did not want any unnecessary attention drawn to her 'honorary Aryan' family.

Although Melitta was not allowed to see the other prisoners, she was bearing up well. Her prison bed was 'no worse than our Luftwaffe camp beds', she felt, and her food – thick cabbage soup, bread, jam and coffee, 'no worse than the mess'. She had been

---

* Alexander's stepdaughter, Dr Gudula Knerr-Stauffenberg, later argued that although he never talked about it, her father had known about the plotting, if not in detail, since 1943.

detained despite her 'proven innocence', she recorded neatly in the diary she had managed to bring with her, and was 'completely calm and quite collected'. This was not entirely true. 'Think a lot of the dead. Maybe I'll see them soon,' she wrote less carefully after her first interrogation. 'And the poor children. Will I be able to care for them?' As an afterthought she added, 'B. [Berthold] is supposed to be involved! Proceedings conducted very well.'[39]

To pass the time, Melitta developed a routine of gymnastics, washing, and cleaning her cell. She mended her socks and bra with threads pulled from other clothes, plugged the worst holes in the wall with squashed bread, and fed the sparrows at her window as she had once tamed squirrels at Gatow. Sometimes she jotted down her memories of Franz, her own lost 'sparrow'. After her 'frenetic daily round and night flights', however, she found her enforced inactivity hard to take.[40] She also knew that drawing attention to the importance of her work was her best hope for securing her release. Arguing that her technical innovations were 'indispensable', and could have a 'decisive influence' on the war, she requested permission to work from her cell.[41] Two days later Melitta's assistant brought in her papers, and took back news of her to her sisters. Other prisoners were soon roped in to type for her. If Melitta occasionally sighed to see 'two small Klemms' flying above the prison yard, now, as so often before, she found refuge and courage in her work.

The Gestapo commissioner in charge of the Sippenhaft prisoners was SS-Sturmbannführer Paul Opitz. 'A small, pale, tight-lipped man', Opitz at least had 'a kindly look in his eyes', one detained woman noted, unlike his hostile 'platinum-blonde' secretary.[42] A veteran of the Great War, like Melitta's father and brother Opitz had joined the post-war volunteer corps in Posen, fighting to push back the Polish border.* Most of his later career had been with the SS immigration and border police: work that involved administration for the Einsatzgruppen tasked with mass murder in Poland in 1941. After 20 July 1944, Opitz was appointed to the special commission

---

* Now once again Poznań, in west-central Poland.

formed to investigate the plot. Perhaps sensing that the tide of the war had turned, he allowed the women connected with the conspiracy to have visitors, and 'seemed to regard himself as a benevolent protector', one later wrote. 'I wish I could let them all go,' he once whispered. 'I don't want to have anything to do with the business.'[43]

Admiring Melitta's work ethic, Opitz made her an 'honorary prisoner'.[44] This meant she received more fresh water, and sweet rolls which she shared with other prisoners. 'She was so fabulous, never a word of complaint,' one recalled. 'When she entered a room, even if it was a prison cell, it was as if a being from another world had come in . . . I always called her the angel of the prisoners.'[45] Melitta also received a supply of menthol cigarettes and books. 'Very nice,' she wrote with typical brusqueness after reading *Jeeves Saves the Day*. 'Washed polo blouse and socks.'[46] In time she even gained some freedom of movement. Opitz told her she would soon be released. Instead, in early August she was transferred to Charlottenburg prison.* 'Depressing, no sparrows, darker, no loo, milk soup,' she wrote.[47]

While the Stauffenberg family was being rounded up, Otto Skorzeny had been busy tracking down the remaining conspirators, and anyone else the regime wanted rid of. Rumour was that it was 'risky even to look sad. A lot of people have been arrested just for saying "What a pity!"', one young journalist confided to her diary.[48] Eventually almost 7,000 people would be arrested, many disappearing into concentration camps. Others were shot immediately. Some military figures who had fallen from favour, like the popular Field Marshal Erwin Rommel, were forced to commit suicide. Many more were dragged in front of the infamous People's Court presided over by Judge Roland Freisler. The first trials were held in early August. Hitler, still 'dominated by the lust for revenge', as his personal valet put it, ordered those found guilty to be 'hanged like cattle'.[49] The 9th of August was a 'very black

---

* Charlottenburg became a female-only prison in 1939, mainly for women involved in some sort of 'political crime'. Several members of the Red Orchestra resistance group were held there in 1942, some before execution. In 2008, the cell scenes for *The Reader* were filmed there.

day', Melitta wrote, alone in her cell. 'Eight traitors hanged.'[50] Hitler, meanwhile, thanked Skorzeny personally for his efforts, telling him, 'You, Skorzeny, saved the Third Reich.'[51]

Berthold's trial took place the following morning. While Melitta silently washed her shirt in a prison sink, her brother-in-law, forbidden to wear uniform, tie, belt or braces, had to hold up his trousers as he entered the dock. Despite this attempt to humiliate him, Berthold kept his gaze level. He was resolved to meet his fate with dignity. Whenever he spoke, however, Freisler shouted over him so that his words would not make the record. Hitler had decreed that no martyrs were to be made that day.

Along with eight others, Berthold was sentenced to be hanged that afternoon. Taken to the execution shed at Plötzensee prison, he saw a bare, whitewashed room, furnished only with a guillotine and a steel girder lined with butcher's hooks for the prisoners, and a small table set with glasses and cognac for the executioners. Rather than being allowed to drop, he was then slowly hoisted into the air by a cord around his neck so that he could be hanged and revived several times before he died. These proceedings were photographed and filmed. 'Hitler put on his spectacles, eagerly grabbed the macabre images and gazed at them for an eternity,' one of his inner circle later wrote. 'The close-up shots of the victims' death throes were soon being passed from hand to hand.'[52]

Although spared such details, Melitta now suffered increasingly dark days. Against 11 August she wrote, 'Wedding anniversary, very sad.'[53] At some point she hid a lock of her hair in a folded page at the back of her diary, perhaps as a keepsake should she be condemned herself. Not long later, Nüx was sentenced to death, having refused to plead confusion due to his advanced age. Next it was the turn of Hans von Haeften, the brother of Claus's adjutant. Barbara von Haeften, who was also incarcerated in Charlottenburg, wrote that she 'almost drowned in my tears' after she heard of her husband's execution. Her only relief was that he had escaped more torture. Determined to 'live for my children', she passed the time in her cell patching Luftwaffe shirts 'with great zeal'.[54] Melitta knew that her value to the regime was the only hope she had of protecting herself, and perhaps to some extent also Alexander, Nina, Mika and the children. Working into the early hours, sometimes she would hear Barbara and other prisoners weeping. She offered comfort when she could, worked on, killed bed bugs, took sleeping pills, and was woken by air raids.

Melitta's dreams, when they came, were tortuous. She would be with Franz, and he would suddenly disappear. When she found him, in the cabin of a Lufthansa aircraft, he told her he wanted 'to go ahead alone'.[55] Understanding his meaning, 'I want to reproach him for his being so thoughtless,' she recorded, but up in the heavens 'he says quite brightly, "Just look", and shows me the new cut of a collar the tailor has designed for him. He is wearing a coarse, bright suit, just a design without its lining. I don't like the collar, say he should keep to his traditional heavy green jacket . . . I think it is certainly not worth making a new one, because he must die soon. When I asked whether I should go first, he kissed my hand sweetly and said we should go together, as that would be nicer than each of us having to find our way alone.'[56]

Opitz visited Melitta that evening, when she woke. After reassuring her that Alexander was well, he broke the news that, on Hitler's orders, she was 'not to be released at once'. 'Should [submit] another plea,' she wrote. 'Regard it as futile.'[57]

Unknown to Melitta, several colleagues at the Luftwaffe Academy and Ministry of Aviation were lobbying on her behalf. 'There was a special core of people all attached to flying, with a kind of team spirit,' one of her nephews later wrote. Melitta 'was known to every flier, to everyone who had anything to do with aviation. She had a number of personal friends in that crowd.'[58] Among them was Hajo Herrmann, leader of the Wilde Sau interception squadron and a close confidant of Göring. Hajo had been appalled by the assassination attempt. Although conceding that there had been 'failures' and 'weaknesses of the leadership', he felt it was 'our common duty to follow the path that history had marked out for us'.[59] Certain that Melitta could not have known about the plot, he remonstrated with Göring that her duty was also at her station. Her equipment was 'tremendous', he added, and he refused to fly without it.[60]

Opitz was also lobbying for Melitta's release.* She now added him to her mental aviary of close friends as her *Weisser Rabe* (White Raven), but she never added the sweet *-chen* that marked the affection of her nicknames for Alexander and Franz.† In late August, Opitz told her he had offered 'his own neck' as security for her release.[61] Under pressure from pilots and SS officers alike, as well as the continuing Allied bombardments, Göring finally endorsed Melitta's release. A week later, on 2 September, she was freed on the grounds of 'war necessity'.[62] She had spent six weeks in prison. Although distraught at leaving friends behind, Melitta now had hope: her release meant she was still of value to the increasingly desperate regime.

Two conditions were attached to her release. She was to return to work immediately, and she was no longer to use the Stauffenberg name. From now on she was officially known as Countess Schenk. Incredibly, Melitta also issued terms. She insisted on regular visits to all the detained Stauffenbergs, and the right to speak to Alexander at least once a month. Perhaps she had not forgotten Nüx's warm toast, 'All for one, one for all!' when he had welcomed her, half-Jewish under Nazi law, into the Stauffenberg family in 1937.[63] But Melitta was inspired not just by a sense of gratitude, but by love. Within hours of her release she had brought food to Alexander. He had written her a poem, 'Loving Memory', about the strength they had always found in each other.‡ Alone again that

---

* Aware that he might face prosecution after the war, Opitz recognized the potential value of Melitta's friendship. In 1946 he wrote to Alexander, offering to discuss all he knew about 20 July, and stating that he had always been 'in inner opposition' to the Nazi Party. In 1967, he was prosecuted in West Berlin for his role with the Einsatzgruppen mass murders in Poland, but was not found guilty of criminal conduct.

† In German, 'white raven' serves as the term for a 'rare bird', someone exceptional or unique.

‡ 'Know that even from a distance, your smile heals him who is unwell, who is enduring. A sad smile, which fills the empty cell, like sunset-lined clouds . . .' Alexander wrote. 'I feel your troubled mourning, and dull pain and torment. Persevere, hold out: we will survive, for that which our dreams have promised.' See Alexander von Stauffenberg, *Denkmal* [Monument] (1964).

evening, Melitta sat down with a bottle of red wine and started making phone calls.

She was back at work the next morning, within twenty-four hours of her release. That autumn Melitta worked with Junkers Ju 88s and Ju 87s, twin-engined Siebel 204s and Bücker Bestmann 181s, as well as training pilots in her night-landing technique. In November she took out a new Arado 96 in spite of heavy fog, and even flew the Messerschmitt Me 262 jet fighter, but her heart was no longer in her work. It was 'only a pretext for helping us', Alexander told a friend.[64] Klara was now officially seconded to serve as Melitta's assistant. Expecting to help with technical calculations, she was amazed when Melitta set her to work typing up Alexander's German translation of Homer's *Odyssey* instead. 'Thank goodness no one bothered me at my work station,' Klara laughed, 'so no one realized the nature of my "important-for-the-war-effort" work!'[65] 'By night she flies to test blind-flying equipment and in the daytime she rushes around from one office and Gestapo headquarters after the other, trying to help her husband and his relations,' another friend wrote, noting Melitta's thin frame and 'soft, rather weary voice'. 'I cannot imagine when she ever sleeps.'[66]

Melitta's first visit was to the Stauffenberg schloss at Lautlingen, which had been taken over by the Gestapo. Ostensibly she was going to collect her belongings, but Opitz had secured permission for her to contact Alexander's mother, Karoline, now living there under house arrest. Melitta suddenly appeared with family news, 'like a miracle, out of night and darkness',* Karoline wrote, 'like an impossible fairy-tale gifted by God'.[67] When she left, Melitta smuggled out her beautiful busts of Berthold and Nüx, among other things, so that they might be saved for posterity.†

Melitta had already lodged a petition for Alexander's release. Now, smartly dressed in a dark suit, with her diamond flight badge

---

* *Nacht und Nebel* [Night and Darkness] was Hitler's 1941 directive that political prisoners should disappear without trace.

† Melitta secretly hid these busts with Paul von Handel's family, without their knowledge.

pinned above the ribbon of her Iron Cross, she brought him suit-cases packed with clothes, food and books. She took parcels of warm clothing to Mika, who had no blankets and whose cell was freezing at night. Mika was terrified that her children might be used for medical experiments, but she still refused to cooperate during interrogations.* Nina, three months pregnant with her and Claus's fifth child, was being kept in isolation, in what she described as 'indescribably awful' conditions.[68] Melitta arrived with clothes, medicine, packages of fruit and vegetables, rabbit meat from ani-mals she had shot in the airfield park, and soya macaroons baked by Klara. While they were embracing, Melitta quietly confirmed to Nina that both Claus and Berthold were dead. Later, using her privileged pilot ration cards, she also brought Nina cod-liver oil, a maternity girdle, books, notebooks and a letter from her mother, now in Ravensbrück. Melitta was the only person outside the prison with whom Nina had any direct contact. Melitta also visited the older generation, and brought food parcels every week to other friends in detention but, try as she might, she could not find out where the Stauffenberg children were being held.

Bad Sachsa is a small town near Nordhausen in the Harz mountains, almost 200 miles from Berlin. In 1944 it was also a stronghold of support for the Nazi Party. Most of the children of the key conspirators, including all of Claus's and Berthold's chil-dren, had been taken to an orphanage on the outskirts of the town. Their older cousins, over thirteen, were sent to a concentration camp near Danzig. Travelling by car, truck and train, the younger children sang patriotic folk songs to keep up their spirits, and made friends with strangers, some of whom gave them buttered buns to share.

The orphanage itself comprised seven traditional wooden houses, each designed to hold thirty children segregated by age and gender. On arrival, Claus and Nina's eldest son, Berthold, had found himself the only child in one house, and from then on the

---

* Mika's file included a handwritten note to the effect that 'she knows more than she admits'. See Reinhild Gräfin von Hardenberg, *On New Ways* (2002), p. 155.

siblings and cousins met only 'occasionally, and by chance'.[69] A week later the children of other 'traitors' started to arrive. Many were traumatized, having been torn from their families. Without radio, newspapers, schooling or church, they had no contact with the outside world. 'It took us a while to trust,' young Berthold recalled. The strict director 'exuded authority', with her Nazi Party badge permanently pinned to her dress, and would organize 'parade drill'.[70] Other staff were warmer. Sometimes the children even played tricks on them, with surprise midnight piano recitals and bombardments of home-made clay pellets. Altogether, Berthold felt, they were 'well, even lovingly, treated'.[71] Away from the bombing raids, they spent long days reading, inventing games and exploring the estate.

Effectively, the children were in limbo, stolen from their families but their final destination still unknown. Their guardians' role was simply to keep them safe until they could pass on their responsibility. As a result they were adequately clothed, and fed with stewed beets, like those used for cattle feed. The children hated it, but it stopped their hunger. When they became ill with chickenpox or tonsillitis, they received good treatment. After some weeks Franz Ludwig, Claus and Nina's third son, picked up an ear infection. Taken to the local doctor, he refused to budge when a nurse called out 'Franz Ludwig Meiser'. The name 'Stauffenberg' was no longer acceptable, he was told, so a new 'neutral name' had been agreed 'to avoid any needless hostility'.[72]* 'But I am a Stauffenberg,' he insisted.[73] He was six years old.

Melitta kept up her visits to the adult prisoners as the weather turned colder. Alexander's cousin, Elisabeth zu Guttenberg, whose husband had also been arrested, visited Melitta at Gatow where she admired her friend's 'fine, sensitive face' and the sun 'shining on her lovely red-gold hair'.[74] 'There were high aviator's boots on her feet,

---

* The new name meant the children could be adopted anonymously by SS families after the 'final victory'. Hitler's belief was that 'eugenically a son nearly always inherits the characteristics of the mother': an argument he used to justify not having children himself, and which may have helped to save the Stauffenberg children. See Heinrich Hoffmann, *Hitler Was My Friend* (2011), pp. 146–7.

and a leather jacket thrown over her shoulders,' Elisabeth wrote. 'She had a gun in her hand, and I looked in astonishment at two dead rabbits, fastened to her belt.'[75] Seeing Elisabeth's surprise, Melitta explained that the rabbits 'make good eating for our prisoners'.[76] Together they then took more clothes and food to Nina. 'That day the temperature was far below freezing . . .' Elisabeth later recalled. 'The prison was like an ice-box, damp and without heat. Nina looked like death, but she was wonderfully calm.'[77] 'It is amazing what these days make of people,' Melitta said, shaking her head as they left. 'Heroes and saints!'[78]

A few weeks later, Nina was transferred to a Gestapo-run annex of Ravensbrück. She would spend the next five months in solitary confinement, in the windowless cells of the so-called 'bunker'. Sometimes her mother caught a glimpse of Nina through a crack in her door, but she could not get a message to her. In some ways Nina was privileged. Many pregnant prisoners were subjected to 'medical experimentation', and nearly all the women were brutally exploited as forced labour, many making components for aircraft, V-1s and V-2s, before being killed when too weak to continue. Nina was isolated but kept alive. With extraordinary fortitude, she filled her time darning socks, practising shorthand, making playing cards from cigarette boxes, and recalling literature and music. When given paper, she wrote to Melitta who sent fruit and vegetables, as well as larger, warmer clothes as Nina's pregnancy developed over the winter. It was here that Nina wrote her will. In the event of her death, she wanted her children kept together. Her new baby should be called Claus or Albrecht, if a boy, and if a girl, Konstanze. Alexander was to be the godfather and provide intellectual and religious education and, if their professional commitments allowed, he and Melitta were to take care of the children. Melitta had already given her word to do all she could to find them.

Alexander, Karoline, Mika and others were then suddenly transported out of Berlin. Left without news, Melitta was terrified that her husband had been sent to Plötzensee for execution, like his twin before him. In fact they had been sent to an isolated hotel in Bad Reinerz, a mountainous area in southern Silesia. Some Stauffenberg cousins and the wives and elder children of other members of the domestic resistance were already at the hotel, amazed at the luxury, having spent the months since July as prisoners in Augsburg and Nördlingen. One had arrived from the camp at Dachau. 'Nothing but skin and bones', his head had been shaved and he had been put to work at the camp's medical station, witnessing appalling atrocities.[79]

Although Gestapo officers patrolled the grounds, the prisoners were, temporarily, relatively free. Discussing the plot, they found that 'everybody's accounts were slightly different', Fey von Hassell noted, but 'the broad outlines were clear enough'.[80] As the former German ambassador to Rome, Fey's father, Ulrich von Hassell, had been an important member of the conspiracy in Berlin, and might have served as foreign minister in a post-coup government. Arrested at his desk in late July, he had been tried in September, and hanged two hours after sentencing. Fey, who had been forcibly separated from her young children during her arrest, 'felt instinctively close' to the Stauffenberg family and was particularly drawn to Mika, whom she described as 'a beautiful woman'.[81] The two mothers intuitively understood that, whatever the other might be doing, their thoughts were always with their missing children. 'The person I grew to admire most,' Fey wrote, however, was Alexander.[82]

Fey noticed Alexander as soon as he arrived, still in the officer's uniform he had worn to leave Athens. He was 'very tall, with hair that was never properly combed and a constant twinkle in his eye', Fey thought, 'full of charm and warmth . . . a most attractive person'.[83] Alexander was reading Dante's *Inferno* in Italian, using his knowledge of Latin and an English translation at the side of each page. Fey had lived in Italy when her father was the ambassador there, and had married an Italian. She now gave Alexander language lessons, shyly at first, because 'Alex seemed so much older and more cultured than I.'[84] Soon they were taking daily walks through the woods, talking in Italian. To Fey, Alexander personified 'the perfect German of my imagination: tall, manly, very much the gentleman'.[85] Their 'growing friendship became of inestimable value and consolation,' she wrote, 'certainly to me, but I think to both of us'.[86] Although he was at times melancholic, Alexander's courage in facing the future with optimism, the history lectures he gave for the prisoners, the poetry he could recite by heart, and his mischievous, 'boyish' sense of humour, often directed against the guards, were a source of strength to them all.[87] One of the teenagers among them, Eberhard von Hofacker, later testified that without Alexander's encouragement and example, he simply 'could not have survived'.[88*]

The deep bonds formed over their month at Bad Reinerz helped the Sippenhaft prisoners survive 'the long and painful months ahead', Fey wrote.[89] At the end of November they were transported by rail straight across the Russian front to Danzig. Sleeping on stone floors in icy-cold transit stations, with little to eat or drink, several of them fell ill. The cynical comments made by the 'grim-faced SS' officers escorting them led Fey to believe 'they were convinced that we would shortly be liquidated'.[90] Alexander and one of his uncles, still in their uniforms, were ordered to cut off their epaulettes, collar tabs and other marks of rank, suggesting that the SS did not want people to know that they were guarding German officers. When they refused, 'the SS men began screaming insults . . . ranting and storming about in almost hysterical rage'.[91] Later such scenes would become commonplace, but now they were all deeply shocked. Their fears proved correct. Their destination was the brutal Stutthof concentration and extermination camp where over the course of the war more than 65,000 prisoners would die of disease and starvation, be gassed with Zyklon B in the small gas chamber, or killed by lethal injection.

Peter Riedel had been serving as air attaché in Stockholm at the time of the July plot. 'The Swedish papers were full of the

---

* Eberhard von Hofacker was the elder son of the Luftwaffe colonel Caesar von Hofacker, a cousin of the Stauffenbergs who served as liaison between the plotters and was executed in 1944. (Caesar's father, a general in the First World War, was also called Eberhard.)

German generals' attempt on Hitler's life,' he recorded, and 'I was not the only person who could see where things were going.'[92] Soon Peter was concerned not only about the regime's ideological standpoint, but also its ability to make well-informed decisions. It was increasingly difficult, if not impossible, to report unpleasant truths through the embassy or Foreign Office, he noted, while 'any good news was inflated out of proportion'.[93]

In September Peter received a large, anonymous envelope. Propaganda and 'disinformation' were often sent over from the Soviet Legation in Stockholm, only to be thrown away, but this was different. Inside Peter found a leaflet with 'horrifying photographs' of Majdanek extermination camp, on the outskirts of Lublin in Nazi-occupied Poland.[94] Although initially established as a labour camp for POWs in 1941, Majdanek was later used for the industrial-scale killing of Polish Jews, as well as Russian troops and other prisoners. It became the first such camp captured by the Allies, just two days after the July bomb plot. The speed at which the Red Army advanced meant that much of the camp's documentation survived. Seven gas chambers had been put into operation in Majdanek in September 1942, and were never hidden from view. A year later, massacres by firing squad were also introduced under *Aktion Erntefest* (Operation Harvest Festival). At the height of the massacres, 18,400 Polish Jews were killed on a single day. The male and female inmates forced to bury, and later exhume and cremate the bodies, were later executed in turn. The killings continued until March 1944. The lowest estimate of the total number of men, women and children killed at the camp is almost 80,000, but a shed containing 800,000 pairs of shoes was later found, along with heaps of ash waiting to be used as crop fertilizer.

After capturing Majdanek, the Russians convened a Polish–Soviet commission to investigate and document the crimes against humanity committed there. This inquiry produced the leaflet sent to German embassies, as well as to the Allied press. Peter had heard rumours of atrocities in the east for two years, but had convinced himself that the one detailed eyewitness account of a mass shooting he had heard was an isolated mistake by fanatics, rather than evidence of official policy. 'If only the Führer knew, he would put it right,' was the common view among the people Peter knew.[95] Yet this leaflet contained evidence that atrocities were supported at the highest level, not just at the front, but in organized death camps. On the last page, the date of Himmler's visit to Majdanek was recorded. 'I knew now with awful certainty that the stories I had heard, the rumours of mass shootings, were far less terrible than the reality,' Peter wrote in despair.

Peter dared not discuss the leaflet at the embassy. As the story broke in the Western press, he wrote to an American general, to defend the honour of the 'misled, patient, hard-working and suffering German masses' who had been failed by their 'whole leading class'.[96] 'No decent German approves of these Gestapo crimes,' he wrote. 'Would it be fair to let the whole nation suffer as punishment for the crimes of some fanatics?'[97] His letter did not provide any new information on Nazi war crimes, and nor did it concern itself with the murdered victims of Majdanek. Furthermore, it was never sent. A few weeks later, on one of his monthly visits to Berlin, Peter smuggled in the Majdanek leaflet between the bottles and gifts in his diplomatic bag. He still had no idea what to do with it when, a few days later, he headed to the Air Ministry to meet Hanna for lunch. The once luxurious Berlin Aero Club had suffered considerable bomb damage. 'Pools of water stood about in the entrance hall,' Peter noticed, and 'water was dripping constantly inside as well as out'.[98] Hanna was waiting for him in the small room reserved for officers, 'the one bright spot in an atmosphere of deep gloom'.[99] Friends for more than a decade, the pair quickly started to catch up on news. 'Like everyone else, she was depressed,' Peter saw, but her spirits seemed to lift as they talked.[100]

Hanna's crash had not diminished her appetite for danger, nor had her tour of Russia dampened her belief in final victory. She was just back from a visit to the Wolf's Lair, she told Peter, accompanying Robert Ritter von Greim to a meeting with Hitler. Hitler had awarded Greim 'Swords and Diamonds' to go with his 'Knight's Cross of the Iron Cross with Oak Leaves' in August. Above his sparkling honours, Greim was looking more soft and grey than ever, but his ambition was unsated. Bitterly critical of Göring, he was keen to take over command of the Luftwaffe.* While he and Hitler were ensconced, Hanna had been delighted to bump into Otto Skorzeny, also getting some fresh air between the barbed wire and guard posts. That night she proudly introduced the two men she so admired. The younger Skorzeny was 'astonished by the energy and enterprise of which the General still showed himself capable', and was soon engaged 'in a serious and animated discussion' about the future of the Luftwaffe.[101] Hanna was in her element.

The next day, a bent and sickly Hitler appointed Greim as deputy commander-in-chief of the Luftwaffe, with a brief 'to take control of all military air operations in such a manner that [Hitler] would not have to remove Göring altogether'.[102] Humiliating as this was for Göring, it also left Greim impotent. Although disappointed that her favourite general had not secured the top position, Hanna was still delighted by his promotion. Skorzeny was more cynical. 'In view of the hopeless military situation I assume that Greim had declined to work anywhere near Göring,' he wrote.[103] Greim indeed requested a return to his old position.

That Hanna was incredibly well connected was no surprise to Peter, but he was disturbed to discover that she now counted Himmler among her circle. The chief of the SS and Gestapo was 'a kind, good-natured man', she told Peter, 'very correct in matters of etiquette and to her quite compassionate and charming'.[104] Peter was shocked into silence. Until then, he had always been able to talk freely with Hanna, whose honesty and frankness he much admired, so, despite some trepidation, a few hours later he called on her again, this time at her apartment. Throwing the Majdanek leaflet down on Hanna's table in what she called 'a state of considerable agitation', Peter told her, 'There's your friend Himmler for

---

* Göring held a Luftwaffe strategy conference in November 1944. As neither his leadership nor the Me 262 could be mentioned, little was forthcoming. He described the Luftwaffe's 'absolute failure' to Goebbels in December, blaming it on personnel and technical failures. (*Die Tagebücher von Joseph Goebbels: Oktober bis Dezember 1944*, Jana Richter and Hermann Graml (ed.), 07.12.1944, p. 371.)

you! See what he's been doing? Read that!'[105] As Hanna turned the pages she began to shake with rage. 'Do you mean to say you believe this rubbish?' she shouted. 'It is obviously enemy propaganda, not to be taken seriously.'[106] Hanna felt 'boundless fury' that Peter could give the account any credit at all, but her immediate dismissal of the leaflet made Peter's temper erupt in turn.[107] Where did the 800,000 pairs of shoes come from? he demanded furiously. Why should America's *Time* magazine, and the other Western press who had carried the story, toe a communist line? When their rage had finally exhausted itself, Peter looked steadily at Hanna. 'Prove that it's not true,' he urged her. 'Show it to Himmler, see what he has to say!'[108] Hanna agreed. Himmler was such 'an honourable and kindly man', she felt, there could be no danger.[109]

At their last meeting, Himmler had told Hanna that she might raise anything with him. Now, when she produced the Majdanek leaflet, he flicked through it without comment or any change of expression. 'What do you say to this, Reichsführer?' she prompted him.[110] In October 1943 Himmler had given a speech to Party leaders at Posen, in which he spoke frankly about 'the extermination of the Jewish people'. He had visited several camps since, reportedly handing out promotions after witnessing the use of the gas chambers at Sobibór. Avoiding Hanna's question, he now quietly asked her whether *she* believed it. She did not, she told him with impatient sincerity. Despite the growing rumours circulating after the introduction of forced camp labour, with the smell from crematoriums, and the lack of any letters back from deported Jews, Hanna had convinced herself that the leaflet was atrocity propaganda. Had she had any doubts, it would have been suicidal to confront the head of the SS with evidence of his crimes. Himmler, however, made no attempt to refute the veracity of the leaflet; he was more interested in judging Hanna. Unable or unwilling to consider this, Hanna ploughed on, urging him to counter the claims publicly. She seized on his agreement regarding counter-propaganda as if it were the comprehensive denial she was all too keen to hear. Then the meeting was over. She had been deeply shocked by the leaflet, Hanna later told Peter, but she had agreed to shed light on it, and their fears had been 'relieved' by her meeting with Himmler.[111]

In the first edition of her memoirs, Hanna wrote that it was only after the war that she knew the truth about Nazi concentration camps. In later editions, this statement was removed. The truth was clearly complicated. Perhaps she simply could not believe these unimaginable, unprecedented horrors. Perhaps the truth was too hard to process, demanding, as it would, the re-evaluation of her entire world view and her own moral worth, something she apparently had no desire to pursue. Yet Hanna had been disturbed enough by the Majdanek leaflet to ensure responsibility for dismissing it did not end with her. Himmler had not only reassured her; in some ways he had relieved her of her burden of knowledge. There is no question, though, that Hanna saw evidence of the atrocities at Majdanek. She chose both to disregard this, and to continue her active support for the regime.* Later that month she told an aviation friend that she did not agree with many things happening in Nazi Germany, but she was happy that she could raise issues that others would be executed for mentioning. That was 'her way to help', she said.[112] Her language not only implied moral righteousness, but also glossed over any reference to the appalling crimes she had seen reported.

A few days after Hanna's meeting with Himmler, the Majdanek reports were denied in a leading German newspaper, and across the Swedish press. Hanna was further reassured. Peter, however, returned to Stockholm with an impending sense of personal crisis. In mid-November he received two telegrams within an hour, summoning him to Berlin. Instead of returning, he asked contacts in the Swedish air force to arrange asylum. With his diplomatic

---

* The Canadian journalist Ron Laytner interviewed Hanna in the late 1970s. Asked about Nazi crimes, she reportedly replied, 'I asked Hermann Göring one day, "What is this I am hearing that Germany is killing Jews?" Göring responded angrily, "A totally outrageous lie made up by the British and American press. It will be used as a rope to hang us some day if we lose the war."' There is no corroboration of this story, so it may be an inaccurate account of her meeting with Himmler. (Ron Laytner, *Edit International*, 'Hanna Reitsch', 2010.)

immunity and passport both cancelled, he was officially stateless when he heard that German military intelligence, the infamous Abwehr, had abducted his wife from Switzerland and were holding her hostage for his return. Keeping his nerve, Peter checked with the Swiss Embassy, which was able to confirm that Helen was still safe in Davos. With the German Embassy making moves to extradite him for a court martial, Peter quickly dropped off the radar. Now he offered his services to the Allies. He hoped to give radio broadcasts telling the truth about SS war crimes to the civilians of Germany, but was told this would be 'of little use at this stage'.[113] He spent the rest of the war hiding in the Swedish countryside.*

As the goods train carrying the Sippenhaft prisoners approached Stutthof, just outside Danzig, Fey put her eye to a crack between the planks forming their carriage. They were passing 'an enormous net of barbed wire lit by huge searchlights', along which 'the outlines of watchtowers cut menacingly into the sky'.[114] She, Alexander and the others were lucky; their potential value as hostages meant they were transferred to a special 'VIP shed'. Here conditions were immeasurably better than in the rest of the camp, with several small rooms, a common bathroom and open toilets. Every day they were fed from an 'enormous barrel of thin soup', with a few vegetables and a chunk of black or grey bread. On Sundays they even got some meat.

The Sippenhaft prisoners' only work at Stutthof was chopping wood in a small yard, laundry, darning and cooking. 'Professors are obviously not good at certain practical things,' Fey wrote after Alexander nearly chopped off his toes with an axe.[115] While recovering, he showed Fey some of his poems. She was desperately in need of comfort, and confessed that 'even in his weakened state, Alexander was becoming more and more of a magnet for my wounded emotions'.[116] During daylight hours the group were allowed to move around their yard, but at night the building was

---

* Riedel was summoned back to Germany in May 1945. Fearing former colleagues might lynch him, he refused to go. After some time in a military prison in Casablanca, he lived with his wife in Venezuela. The relaxation of immigration laws eventually enabled them to move to the USA.

floodlit and the guards had orders to shoot. Escape was in any case impossible. They often heard patrol dogs, 'half-starved blood-hounds' as the elderly Clemens Stauffenberg called them, barking as a prisoner was being hunted down.[117] 'Pursued by these animals,' Fey continued, they 'would invariably be captured. A desperate, anguished scream would sometimes pierce the air as the dogs fell upon their victim.'[118]

Within weeks dysentery had broken out, soon followed by typhoid. Himmler had given orders that none of the Sippenhaft prisoners were to be allowed to die, 'at least not yet', so they were treated with drugs, and anyone with scarlet fever was put in isola-tion.[119] When two female Russian prisoners were detailed to nurse them, Mika spoke with them in their own language. 'Details of the grim life beyond the confines of our barrack emerged, and it made our lot seem like paradise in comparison,' Fey wrote. 'The women described how many of their companions had been tortured, then killed in the gas chambers and cremated in big ovens.'[120] No one doubted them. 'Day and night we saw the smoke from the crema-tory furnaces and smelled their sickish odour,' Clemens wrote.[121] Although privileged prisoners, their position seemed hopeless. 'Day and night,' Clemens added quietly, 'we waited for our own deaths.'[122]

Hitler left the Wolf's Lair for the last time in late November 1944. Arriving in the capital after dark, he 'had no chance to see Berlin's wounds as they really were', his secretary, Traudl Junge, recalled. 'The dipped headlights of the cars merely touched mounds of rubble to right and left of the road.'[123] His entourage knew he had deliberately avoided seeing the worst. 'The numerical superiority of the American Air Force,' Göring reported to him a week later, can 'no longer be overcome even by the supreme courage of our airmen'.[124] 'Hitler seemed to know that already,' Skorzeny com-mented, 'as he hardly took the trouble to listen.'[125] The RAF and USAAF were now treating German airspace almost as their own, with bombers going for pinpoint targets such as oil refineries, air-fields, aircraft works and supply facilities. A couple of months earlier, when Hitler had awarded Skorzeny the German Cross in Gold, he had talked excitedly about the country's 2000 rocket fighters, and the imminent bombing of New York by V-1 buzz bombs. Now Himmler mentioned just 250 rocket fighters, but Hitler took no notice, having 'apparently written off the Luftwaffe'.[126]

As the sixth Christmas of the war approached, the Sippenhaft prisoners began to hear artillery fire from the advancing front. Among others, Mika and Fey were both seriously ill with typhoid. Apart from the doctor among them, the only other prisoner to visit the sickroom was Alexander, bringing wood for the stove morning and afternoon. When he feared he might lose Fey, he wrote her a poem, which ended:

> Console me as we wander, pathless, starless,
> I cannot reach or touch you,
> But through the wall I hear your laboured breaths,
> So near, so near, through twelve sad nights of Christmas.[127]

Even with the stove working, 'the constant, bitter cold of that winter . . . was beyond belief', Fey later recalled.[128] Added to the prisoners' chill and hunger, their anxiety about typhoid, dysentery and scarlet fever, and their future in the hands of the SS, was now the fear of being bombed or overrun by the Red Army. Desperate to keep up morale, they folded scraps of paper into nativity figures and other decorations, and made a few stars from tin-foil to decorate a scrawny tree. On Christmas Eve, those who could stand sang traditional Christmas carols.

For the children still being held at Bad Sachsa, Christmas would hold a wonderful surprise. Melitta had met Opitz thirteen times since late September. Her petitions on behalf of Alexander had been 'found satisfactory', and Himmler had let her know he was 'well disposed' towards the case.[129] She was finally to be allowed to visit the children. The first few youngsters had been released in October, sent to grandparents or distant aunts, in part to stem rumours about the disappearance of 'pure German' children. By late December there were only fourteen children left, all Stauffenbergs and their cousins, brought together in one house.

They had still had no news from the outside world, and did not know whether their parents were alive.

After the obligatory appearance at her research institute's Christmas party, Melitta set out for Bad Sachsa by train on 22 December. Also travelling that day was Lieutenant Hans Wilhelm Hagen, who had just been discharged from military hospital where he had been receiving treatment for head injuries. Sitting in a carriage with more board than glass in its windows, and still wearing a bandage enveloping one eye, Lieutenant Hagen spent much of his journey in gloom. Only after some time was he surprised to notice 'a lady opposite me – in a military compartment, of all places'.[130] Hagen thought she must be lost, but as she removed her fur coat he noticed the Iron Cross, and below it the diamond pilot's badge, pinned to her jacket. 'Madam! May I introduce myself?' he asked Melitta, before adding gallantly, 'There is no need to say who you are, because there is only one lady in the world with these decorations.'[131] In fact there were two such ladies, but Melitta did not have half Hanna's celebrity. An awkward moment followed.

Perhaps it was Melitta's natural reserve and tact that prevented her from correcting the wounded lieutenant's mistake, especially after he praised her as 'the most famous and the bravest pilot' for her work with the V-1s.[132] But Melitta also had another reason not to disabuse Hagen. As her own diary entry, 'conversation with Lt. Hagen, Guards Battalion, 20 July' shows, Melitta knew exactly who it was she was talking with.[133] Hagen's Guards Battalion was the emergency force placed on standby with the enactment of Operation Valkyrie. In order to clarify the situation, Hagen had been tasked with contacting the battalion's patron, Joseph Goebbels. It was from Goebbels that he learned of the failed assassination attempt. He swiftly arranged for his commander to speak with Hitler by telephone. It was during this call that Hitler's command to 'squash this putsch by all means' was given.[134] Hagen's quick initiative was one of the key reasons the plot had failed. Over the next few hours Melitta quietly endured a conversation with the man whose actions had ruined all hope of overthrowing the regime, and led to the execution, detention and abduction of so many of her family, including her husband, and the children she was en route to visit. That she never revealed her true identity is borne out by Hagen's own memoirs, published after the war, in which he cheerfully recounted his encounter with 'Hanna' 'during the journey on my last Christmas leave of this war'.[135]

If it was with relief that Melitta finally bade farewell to Hagen, it was with trepidation that she eventually arrived at Bad Sachsa that evening with a small Christmas tree and an armful of presents. As their first visitor since the children had been abducted six months earlier, she had no idea how they had fared. In fact all were safe and happy. Some of the staff had even been reading them Christmas stories by candlelight, and there was an atmosphere of warmth, if not plenty. For their part, the children were thrilled to see their aunt. Even the youngest recognized her, and the news that their mothers, although in detention, were still alive, was 'the best Christmas present we could have wished for', young Berthold felt.[136]

Although it was freezing, the next day Melitta played outside with the children. Finding 'wonderful icicles' beside a stream, they 'built up a whole fairyland from them', before the chill sent them back in.[137] When Melitta struggled to carry four-year-old Valerie, Berthold took over, delighted to be of service. Later they decorated their rooms with pine branches, and clipped stubby candles onto the tree before singing Christmas carols. 'Sweet,' 'very sweet,' Melitta wrote repeatedly in her diary.[138]

She stayed with the children until Boxing Day. Although there was lots of fun and 'glorious games', sometimes they also stayed in bed for warmth, Melitta entertaining them with 'the most wonderful stories of her flying and her planes', Franz Ludwig, one of the younger boys, remembered.[139] 'We loved her,' he said. 'She was very exciting . . . Christmas was great with her that year.'[140] Although toys were hard to get, Melitta had managed to bring a fantastic number with her. There were construction kits to be cut out and glued together; toy cars, naval ships and rowing boats that really floated; paints; books; bows and arrows; dressing-up outfits and dolls. Somehow, she had even managed to appropriate a handful of war medals. Perhaps she had been thinking of those ripped from Claus and Berthold when they were arrested, and thrown into an upturned helmet on the floor. In any case, there was a poignant moment when she pinned the decorations on the boys' chests.* 'Of course we felt like real heroes,' Franz Ludwig later recalled warmly.[141] The girls were given pearls.

One of the children, Claus and Nina's second son, Heimeran, was being kept in isolation with scarlet fever. Before Melitta went to him, a nurse brought in a little tree, sat him up in bed, and blindfolded him. 'Straight away he felt my decoration and said immediately: "Auntie Litta",' Melitta wrote. 'Afterwards, to my pride, he assured me again and again, the best thing about Christmas was that I had come.'[142]

Above all, the children asked constantly about Nina, Mika and their grandparents. Melitta gently explained that their mothers could not visit just yet, as one was having a baby and the other looking after the sick, and they couldn't go home as there were bombed-out families living in their houses. On Boxing Day, after they 'lit up the tree again', she reluctantly had to leave.[143]

Melitta sent news of the children to Nina as soon as she got back. She could not reveal where they were being kept, as this would have resulted in her visiting rights being revoked, but she reassured her that they were healthy, happy and well looked after. It was the first news Nina had had of her children for five months. 'Berthold is really following in mummy's footsteps . . . He looks after and trains the younger ones touchingly,' Melitta wrote.[144] Franz Ludwig was 'sweet and loving as ever, red-cheeked, healthy and strong', while the girls were 'blooming and cheerful', 'self-possessed' but 'well-behaved'.[145] All were excited about meeting their new baby sibling. They 'think it will be a boy, and will be called Albrecht', Melitta wrote, before adding tactfully, 'but Heimeran would prefer a little sister'.[146] She told Nina all about their Christmas, enclosed

---

* Perhaps Melitta had also been inspired by the special 20 July Wound Badge Hitler had instituted for survivors of the bomb plot, which bore the inscription '20 July 1944' along with Hitler's signature.

a picture drawn by Heimeran, and said how much they missed their mother, but confessed they had 'played too many games' to have time for them all to write.[147]

As soon as she could get away again, Melitta visited Alexander and Mika at Stutthof concentration camp, letting them know that the children were fine. Then she took Nina a fur jacket that had once belonged to Claus, perhaps the one she had worn to Bad Sachsa, along with an emotional letter from the children to their 'faraway mummy', which Nina read, crying.[148] The children were well, they were together, and Melitta now quietly told her where they were being kept.* Nina was at once desperate and, for the first time since the failed coup, happy.

---

* Melitta also later told Karoline, the children's grandmother, where they were being held.

13

IN THE BUNKER

1945

Hitler looked sourly at the candles clipped to the branches of the small tree placed in one of his rooms. Towards the end of 1944 he had decamped to his Adlerhorst bunker complex in the Tanus mountains, from where he hoped to direct a great victory in the Ardennes. This 'wholly unexpected winter offensive . . .', one staff officer exclaimed, 'is the most wonderful Christmas present for our people.'[1] Few of the troops sucking at frozen rations while dug into trenches and foxholes along the Belgian front would have agreed. On Christmas morning a wave of Junker Ju 88s dropping magnesium flares led the German onslaught. They were soon answered by American fighter-bombers dropping napalm 'blaze bombs' and strafing with machine guns. In the long battle that followed there would be around 38,000 casualties, two-thirds of them German. The Führer's 'last gamble' was already faltering. On 26 December, Hitler talked about 'taking his own life, for the last hope of achieving victory had gone', his Luftwaffe adjutant, Nicolaus von Below, recorded. 'Thus ended 1944 in a mood of hopelessness . . . the Allies had almost total air supremacy.'[2]

Hanna spent her Christmas in the Luftwaffe hospital at the Zoo flak bunker in Berlin, recovering from concussion and an elbow injury sustained during an air raid. Although Berlin was under heavy attack she had refused to leave the capital, having heard an official radio broadcast in November: 'Stand fast. Hanna Reitsch endures this with you.'[3] The German airwaves were now full of such earnest morale-raising, but Berliners had developed their own 'Blitz spirit': 'Be practical,' they joked with gallows humour, 'give a coffin' for Christmas.[4] On Christmas Eve, 3,000 American aircraft bombed thirty-two towns and cities, including

Berlin, in one of the biggest raids of the war. One week later
Göring sent almost 1,000 planes to attack Allied airfields and
destroy their fleets on the ground. The Allies were ready for them.
Over a quarter of the Luftwaffe fleet was destroyed in the disastrous operation. Looking at the wounded servicemen in the cots
around her, Hanna was filled with a mixture of pride and anguish.
'I knew we were losing the war,' she admitted.[5] It was too late
for Operation Self-Sacrifice, but she wondered whether she could
still play a heroic role. 'I can still fly . . .' she whispered to Otto
Skorzeny, her commando friend, when he visited her after a conference with Hitler. 'I shall soon be in the thick of it again.'[6]

At the very least, Hanna decided, she could 'rescue' some of
the hospitalized servicemen before the Red Army arrived. With
the aid of Hans-Ulrich Rudel, a highly decorated Luftwaffe wing
commander and committed Nazi, recovering from the amputation
of his right leg, she mapped out evacuation routes. 'Flying in at
night and landing in the street beside the hospital' or, if she could
get a helicopter, on the flat roof of a nearby ack-ack tower, she
thought she could evacuate several loads of men.[7] Once discharged,
she flew round the city, memorizing the remaining landmarks
through the smoke and snow until she knew she would be able to
find the hospital from any direction, regardless of conditions, and
without radio guidance.

The war was now entering its final stages. Hitler retreated into
his Berlin bunker beneath the Reich Chancellery gardens on
12 January. Two weeks later the Red Army surged forward through
what had been Nazi-occupied Polish territory, taking the Wolf's
Lair at Rastenburg, and then liberating Auschwitz, 350 miles further south. Hanna followed the German retreat with helpless rage
and despair. Roads and railways were overflowing with returning
troops and thousands of civilian refugees, fleeing ahead of the
retreating front line. Reports of terrible atrocities at the hands of
the Russians were already circulating. Meanwhile 'the British and
the Americans flew over the western Reich more or less as they
pleased', von Below reported.[8] Wave upon wave of planes swept
across Berlin every day, sometimes twice a day. Many of the city's

exhausted population now lived in cellars and underground shelters, queuing at the few shops still open by day, and listening to the sirens and 'moan and crash of bombs' throughout the night.[9] There was as much danger of being hit by falling anti-aircraft shells as from Allied bombs, and occasionally whole buildings would collapse with a sickening crash, sending out sheets of flame and white-hot sparks through the burning wreckage. Clouds of smoke billowed up from the ruins.

Desperate to be of use, Hanna did not hesitate when the besieged city of Breslau, the capital of her native Silesia, sent a radio request for her to fly in to collect urgent dispatches for Berlin. Two weeks later, when Breslau was surrounded, she flew in again. This time she brought Nazi State Secretary Werner Naumann, an assistant to Goebbels in the Ministry for Propaganda, in an attempt to raise morale among the beleaguered citizens. Touching down for fuel and news en route, they received a telegram from Hitler, ordering them to turn back. With typical aplomb, Hanna decided that as a civilian employee of the Research Station at Darmstadt she was 'not subject to military orders', and ignored the message. Flying low to stay out of sight, she safely delivered Naumann to the last operational airfield before exploring the besieged city for herself. Seeing 'the pale, fear-ridden faces of the women and the old men', quietly awaiting their 'terrible fate' at the hands of the Red Army, she decided Naumann's job was hopeless.[10] Neither he nor Hanna spoke much as they flew back to Berlin.

Hanna's father, Dr Willy Reitsch, had been deeply disturbed by the stories of rape and violence he had heard while offering general medical help to refugees fleeing the Soviet advance. Fearing the worst, he and his wife, Emy, had abandoned their home in Hirschberg just seventy miles west of Breslau. Taking Hanna's sister Heidi, her three children and their maid Anni with them, along with as many possessions as they could carry, they headed south by train through occupied Czech territory and into Austria, where Emy had relatives. More fortunate than most of the refugees pouring in from the east, they found sanctuary in the attic rooms of Salzburg's Schloss Leopoldskron.* This elegant eighteenth-century mansion had been appropriated from its Jewish owners in 1938, to be enjoyed by senior Nazis as a summer residence and guesthouse.

The 20th of April 1945 was Hitler's fifty-sixth birthday. Although it was an established national holiday, there were few celebrations that year. Nazi flags were raised above the ruined centre of Berlin, and a group of Party leaders gathered in the echoing rooms of the Chancellery, many unable to sit down as the fine furniture had been packed away. After a few speeches, the Führer decorated a delegation from the Hitler Youth in the once handsome Chancellery gardens before returning to his bunker for the daily situation report. Four days earlier, citizens in eastern Berlin had been woken by vibrations 'so strong', one woman wrote, 'that telephones began to ring on their own and pictures fell from their hooks'.[11] The Red Army had arrived. Straight after midnight, on 21 April, their offensive on the German capital began. The bombardment left craters in the Chancellery garden, and the air filled with dust and smoke. Hitler's most senior officers recommended he leave while he could, and direct the war from a safer redoubt. Hitler dithered. His inner circle was more decisive. That evening Himmler, Speer and Göring all left Berlin. Only Goebbels insisted on staying, broadcasting to the nation that 'loyalty is the courage to face destiny'.[12]

Two days later Hitler exploded in a violent rage. Nuremberg, the Nazi Party's sacred city, had been overrun by American troops. In Berlin, the Waffen SS counter-attack Hitler had been depending on had failed to materialize. Soviet shells were raining down on the city and their troops were expected to move in any day. All was lost, Hitler screamed bitterly, he would meet his fate alone in Berlin. In fact Hitler was far from alone. He still had a retinue of military guards, liaison officers, secretaries, doctor,

---

* Schloss Leopoldskron is famous as the film location for *The Sound of Music*, although the von Trapp family in fact lived in a nearby villa in Aigen, appropriated by Himmler during the war.

cook and his private secretary, Martin Bormann, with him in the bunker. Recently his long-term mistress, Eva Braun, had also joined him, as had Joseph Goebbels with his wife, Magda, and their six children. Although he retained absolute authority, Hitler's nervous collapse was evident to all. When the Luftwaffe general Karl Koller reported Hitler's disintegration to Göring, the Reichsmarschall sent a telegram to his Führer. Göring had been nominated as Hitler's successor by decree in 1941. Now in Obersalzberg, he was better placed to direct the conflict, he wrote. Unless he received instructions that night to the contrary, he would assume that Hitler was dead or captured, and take over leadership of the Party and the Reich. Hitler, manipulated by Bormann, was incensed; to him it seemed the ultimate betrayal.

Hanna had been sent back to Breslau. Although her family had already left, this time she stopped at her old home town of Hirschberg. A few years earlier, when she had been given the freedom of the city, the streets had been lined with people waving flags, and the papers full of her gliding lessons with local schoolchildren. Now the school was empty and the streets deserted. Hanna suddenly felt lonely. Recalled to Munich to reconnoitre emergency landing grounds for hospital planes, she decided to visit her family at Salzburg first, just across the Austrian border. Her father was faltering, but her mother was stalwart, caring for them all, and Heidi was quietly talking of marrying again. 'Though overcast by the gathering clouds of the national tragedy,' Hanna wrote, 'we were as happy as ever in our reunion.'[13]

The next day, 25 April, as Soviet troops broke into the Berlin Olympic Stadium, Greim asked Hanna to report immediately to Munich for a special assignment. Greim and Koller had been summoned to a conference 'on a highly urgent matter' in the Führerbunker.[14] As Berlin was now surrounded Koller refused to go, instead defending Göring's actions. Greim, however, was determined to honour his Führer's command. In 1920 he had been the first pilot to fly Hitler, taking him into Berlin for the Kapp Putsch. Now, a quarter of a century later, he thought he might repeat the role, flying Hitler out of the capital.

The best way in, Greim decided, was to take an autogyro helicopter directly to the Chancellery gardens. Hanna knew how to fly a helicopter and, having practised the routes, she also knew the landmarks of the devastated city better than anyone. Aware that they were unlikely to survive such a dangerous mission, with the formality of a suitor rather than a commanding officer, Greim first asked Hanna's parents for their permission to deploy her. 'This they gave without hesitation,' she recorded proudly.[15]

It was midnight when Hanna pinned her Iron Cross onto her black roll-neck sweater, checked her hair, and went to say farewell to her family in their cellar air-raid shelter. She hugged Heidi first, and then each sleepy child in turn. Her proud parents followed her up to the waiting car, 'standing straight and motionless' as she climbed in and drove away.[16] Deeply moved, she resolved to keep a daily record of her personal impressions for her parents, 'so as to keep communicating with them in thought'.[17]

Hanna and Greim left Munich for Rechlin at half past two the next morning. Looking out into the clear, starlit heavens, Hanna saw that for once there was no sign of the enemy planes that had dominated the skies for weeks. They landed safely less than two hours later. The news at Rechlin was not good, however. The helicopter that Hanna and Greim had intended to land in front of the Chancellery had been destroyed in an air raid. If they were to continue it would have to be by plane. Gatow, the last of the capital's airports still in German hands, was surrounded and under continual artillery fire. No one knew whether there was sufficient good runway left for a safe landing. In any case, for forty-eight hours not a single plane had successfully penetrated the Russian defences.

Despite the huge risks, Greim ordered the Luftwaffe sergeant who had flown Speer into Gatow two days earlier to now repeat the journey with him. The same fast Focke-Wulf 190 was quickly readied. Although a single-seat fighter, this particular machine had been fitted with a second seat in its baggage space. The pilot was to deliver Greim to Gatow and return immediately, as the Russians were expected to take the airport at any moment.

Even should the plane reach Gatow, Hanna was worried about

how Greim would get from the airfield to the Chancellery building right in the ruined centre of Berlin. As he was getting ready, she quietly asked the pilot about the feasibility of joining the flight. When she was told that her weight wouldn't matter but there was simply no space for another passenger, even one as small as herself, she got the ground crew to thread her in horizontally, feet first, through a small emergency hatch in the rear fuselage of the little plane. There she lay in total darkness, wedged between the accumulators, oxygen cylinders and other gear. 'Compressed like a worm', as she put it, she could not even ease her arms or legs as they pressed painfully against the hard metal spars of the airframe.[18] If they were hit, she knew she had no means of escape, as the hatch could be opened only from the outside.

Hanna was not used to being utterly dependent on others. Momentarily terrified, she drew strength both from hearing the roar of the engines from their forty-strong fighter escort, and from the pistol in her hand. If forced to make an emergency landing in enemy-held territory, she was determined not to fall into Russian hands alive. Minutes later Greim took his seat. Only as they were about to take off did Hanna call out to him, 'Are you buckled in well?'[19] For a moment he was silent. 'I could feel how emotion and joy prevented him from answering,' she stated with her usual certainty.[20] Then she heard his voice, 'Kapitän, where are you?'[21] She barely had time to explain before they began to bump over the uneven runway, each jolt hammering her harder against the fuselage.

The regular flight time from Rechlin to Gatow was thirty minutes: Hanna counted down every one on the luminous dial of her watch. They were engaged by Soviet fighters as soon as they approached the outskirts of Berlin. Hanna thought she felt the impact of a few wing shots, before the Focke-Wulf suddenly pitched forward and, 'with screaming exhausts', plummeted vertically towards the ground.[22] Still tightly wedged into the tail, she was now rocketing down head first, 'tense in every fibre', as she waited for impact.[23] A few moments later she felt the pilot lift the Focke-Wulf's nose and they started to level off. They had not been hit, but had dived deliberately to avoid enemy attack. Most of their escorts were still engaged above them. In another few minutes Gatow emerged out of the smoke that billowed across the wreckage of Berlin, and they came in to land through a hail of bullets as Soviet fighters strafed the airfield.

Pulled from her hiding place as shells crashed around them, Hanna made a dash for the nearest shelter. There, while she stretched and rubbed her aching legs, Greim managed to place a call to the Führerbunker. Nicolaus von Below informed him that all the approach roads into the city were now in Soviet hands. The Führer still wished to see him 'at all costs', he added, 'but had not stated the reason'.[24] The only option was to fly a slow Fieseler Storch observation plane, designed for short take-off and landing, from Gatow to the avenue behind the Brandenburg Gate. Just before they were due to leave, their chosen plane was destroyed by artillery fire. At 6 p.m., making the most of the fading light, they took off again in the last remaining Storch at Gatow. They had not slept for thirty-six hours.

As Hanna had no experience of flying under fire, Greim insisted on taking the controls, keeping the little plane as low to the ground, roofs and treetops as its long, shock-absorbing legs would allow. Hanna was navigating from behind but, instead of strapping herself in, she chose to remain standing. A few minutes later they flew out over the lake at just a few metres' altitude. 'Beneath us, the waters of the Wannsee gleamed silver in the failing light,' Hanna saw, a scene of 'remote, idyllic peace'.[25] Then she looked ahead again, 'riveted with animal concentration', as she put it, in case they suddenly had to divert.[26] It was not long before a group of enemy fighters appeared, swooping up from the treetops of the Grunewald, the 'green forest' on the edge of Berlin, to attack from all sides. As Greim took evasive action, Hanna saw hundreds of Red Army tanks and soldiers below, 'swarming among the trees'.[27] For a moment she looked into upturned faces as they lifted rifles, machine guns and anti-tank weapons to aim at the precarious Storch. Then they began to fire. Immediately the air was filled with explosive puffs and haloes as bullets and shells flew at them from every direction.

Suddenly there was a rending crash, and Hanna saw a yellow-white flame streak up beside the engine. In the same moment Greim screamed that he was hit; an armour-piercing bullet had smashed through the fuselage, tearing the bottom out of the plane and shattering his right foot. 'Mechanically I stretched over his shoulder, seized the throttle and stick and struggled to keep the machine twisting and turning to avoid the fire,' Hanna wrote. 'Greim lay crumpled in his seat, unconscious.'[28] The noise was now deafening as the air exploded around them, and the Storch's fuselage was repeatedly hit. With 'a spasm of terror', Hanna saw dark streaks of petrol leaking from both wing tanks.[29] The cockpit soon reeked of fuel and she steeled herself for an explosion. More than once Greim opened his eyes and reached for the stick 'with convulsive energy', before losing consciousness again.[30] Neither of them expected to make it down alive and the thought that Greim might bleed to death was 'torturing' Hanna.[31] Miraculously, she remained unwounded and managed to keep control of the damaged machine.

They were now losing height. As the ground fire slackened, Hanna guessed that the area below was still in German hands. With smoke, dust and fumes swirling around them, visibility was almost nil, but remembering her coordinates Hanna headed for the ack-ack tower near the hospital. From there she could follow the main east–west thoroughfare through Berlin, leading to the Brandenburg Gate.

Hans Baur, Hanna's old friend and Hitler's doggedly loyal personal pilot, was supervising the creation of an emergency landing strip by removing lamp posts and chopping down the trees along the east–west axis. Hearing the failing engine of the Storch in the sky above, he sent out a search party. Hanna eventually landed just short of the Victory Column, with hardly a drop of petrol left in the tank.* Having hauled Greim from the bullet-riddled plane, she

---

* The Victory Column originally had three tiers to represent three military victories. In 1939 the Nazi regime increased its height, and relocated it from in front of the Reichstag to the Tiergarten, as part of a redesign for the future capital of the Reich.

tore the sleeve from her blouse and applied a makeshift tourniquet to his leg. When he came to, he was lying on the street between fallen trees, branches and pieces of concrete. Hanna realized that their only hope of reaching the bunker was to flag down a lift, but the whole area appeared deserted. 'A silent horror seeped from the jagged and gaping pillboxes that lay all around,' she wrote. 'The minutes dragged on funereally. Once, somewhere close at hand, came several sharp cracks – then a soundless desolation reigned once more.'[32] Eventually a military car appeared, Greim was lifted onto the back seat, and he and Hanna were driven under the gate, along Unter den Linden, through the Wilhelmstrasse and into the Vossstrasse. For Hanna it was hard to reconcile 'the devastation of rubble and charred wreckage' around her with the once proud buildings and avenues of trees that had until so recently lined these elegant streets.[33] At last she caught a hint of the feeling that so many had been living with for years: 'It was as if a drop-screen had been lowered,' she wrote, 'hiding the familiar reality.'[34]

All such thoughts were pushed aside as they reached the entrance to the bunker. For Hanna, who only felt truly alive in the sky, the descent into the shelter, 'encased', as Albert Speer put it, 'on all sides by concrete and earth', felt particularly unnatural.[35] 'It was . . .' she wrote, 'deeply depressing and quiet and still, like a tomb down there.'[36] On arrival in the cramped central corridor, she almost walked straight into Magda Goebbels. They had not met before but, as two of the most photographed women of the Third Reich, they immediately recognized one another. For a moment 'Frau Goebbels', as Hanna respectfully referred to her, stood staring in amazement, 'as if in wonder that anything living should have found its way there'.[37] Then, overwhelmed with emotion, she started to sob and clasped Hanna in her arms. A moment later Hanna saw Hitler standing further back in the narrow passage. One witness wrote that they 'greeted each other warmly', but Hanna recorded that Hitler's welcome was cool, his 'eyes were glassy and remote' and his voice 'expressionless'.[38] His 'head drooped heavily on his shoulders', she continued, 'and a continual twitching affected both his arms'.[39]

SS guards carried Greim straight to the underground operating theatre where Hitler's personal surgeon, Dr Stumpfegger, cleaned and dressed his wounds, and administered painkillers. He was still on a stretcher when Hitler arrived.* With some effort Greim partially raised himself, saluted, and reported the circumstances of his arrival. According to Hanna's emotional account, this seemed to lift Hitler's spirits, as he leant down to seize Greim's hands and then, turning to Hanna, exclaimed, 'Brave woman! So there is still some loyalty and courage left in the world!'[40]

Loyalty was Hitler's last obsession. He now produced Göring's final telegram, the uncontrolled shaking of his hands making it 'flutter wildly' as he handed it to Greim.[41] As Greim read, tears formed in Hitler's eyes. Then the muscles in his face began to twitch and 'his breath came in explosive puffs'.[42] Only with an effort did he gain sufficient control to shout, 'Nothing is spared me! Nothing! Every disillusion, every betrayal, dishonour, treason has been heaped upon me. I have had Göring put under immediate arrest, stripped him of all his offices, expelled him from all Party organizations.'[43] Hanna, who had long despised Göring as a grossly incompetent, physically 'abnormal', self-deluding morphine addict, was not surprised to hear of his 'shameful treachery'.[44] Himmler had often reported complaints against the Luftwaffe chief, and her resentment grew when Göring had 'not wanted to share the responsibility for, or command of, the Luftwaffe' with her hero, Greim.[45] When Hanna considered the travails of the Third Reich, she came to identify 'a long chain of injustice and evil, of which most could be directly traced to the guilt of Göring'.[46] Now Göring had deserted the Führer, while Greim was at his side. Hitler promoted Greim to the rank of field marshal with immediate effect, and charged him with the supreme command of the Luftwaffe. This was the great honour for which Greim had been summoned. It was a promotion that could have been conveyed by

---

* There are slight discrepancies in the accounts of the last days in the bunker. This account comes from Hanna's published memoirs. Her US interrogation report states, for example, that Hitler came to Greim in the operating room, but the gist is consistent.

telegram, and which left him in charge of an air force that had barely any planes.

Hanna had always been captivated by abstract concepts of honour, duty and loyalty, using these as excuses not to seek to question or understand the motivations of others, or the implications of her own beliefs. Hitler's 'may have been right or wrong leadership', she once told her brother; 'it is not my place to pass judgement or condemn'.[47] She knew that Greim shared the same values, and it bound her to him closely, in something more complicit than pure admiration. To Hanna, their shared sense of honour seemed almost spiritual, reaffirming their own righteousness. Watching him now, 'tight-lipped and motionless', she guessed that Greim's personal code of honour, so 'entirely immutable and selfless', as she saw it, meant that his promotion 'could only have one meaning – to stay here, in the Bunker, with Hitler, to the end'.[48] In that instant Hanna decided that, if Greim stayed, she would also ask Hitler for the ultimate privilege of remaining with him. Some accounts even have her grasping Hitler's hands and begging to be allowed to stay so that her sacrifice might help redeem the honour of the Luftwaffe, tarnished by Göring's betrayal, and even 'guarantee' the honour of her country in the eyes of the world.[49] But Hanna may have been motivated by more than blind honour. She had worked hard to support the Nazi regime through propaganda as well as her test work for the Luftwaffe, and there is no doubt that both she and Greim identified with Hitler's anti-Semitic world view and supported his aggressive, expansionist policies. Hanna 'adored Hitler unconditionally, without reservations', Traudl Junge, one of the female secretaries in the bunker, later wrote. 'She sparkled with her fanatical, obsessive readiness to die for the Führer and his ideals.'[50]

With Hanna's immediate audience with Hitler at an end, Magda Goebbels invited her to her room so she could wash. As the wife of Joseph Goebbels, Magda had elected to remain in the bunker with her husband and her Führer. She had also chosen to keep her young children with her. As Hanna stepped through the door, she found herself 'confronted with six little faces peering at me with lively curiosity from their double-decker bunks'.[51] Helga was twelve, quiet, tall and clever, and adored her father. Pretty eleven-year-old Hilde was known as Goebbels' 'little mouse'. These sisters were Hitler's favourites. Their only brother, Helmut, ten, had braces on his teeth and was considered a bit of a dreamer. Holde, 'like a little angel', her father wrote, was eight, while Hedda and Heidrun were aged six and four.[52] All three were even blonder than their older siblings, and had big sagging bows in their hair. Lively children, they played, joked and squabbled. Only Helga, the eldest, 'sometimes had a sad, knowing expression in her big brown eyes', one of the secretaries thought, and possibly 'saw through the pretence of the grown-ups'.[53]

All the children were delighted to see a new face, and they bombarded Hanna with questions. Although exhausted, she was happy to answer. Perhaps she was thinking of her sister's youngsters, whom she had hugged goodbye in their own shelter just two days earlier, or she may simply have been pleased to momentarily escape into the children's 'own lively little world', as she put it.[54] From then on Hanna often visited the children, teaching them Tyrolean yodelling, and part-songs which they later sang for Hitler. Like Melitta entertaining the abducted Stauffenberg children, Hanna also told fairy tales and stories about her own flying adventures and the 'strange lands and peoples' she had seen.[55] 'Each of them was a delight,' Hanna felt, 'with their open-hearted naturalness and bright intelligence.'[56] Most touching of all was their concern for each other. When the crash and thunder of the shells bursting above frightened the younger ones, their older siblings would reassure them that this was just the sound of their 'Uncle Führer' conquering his enemies.[57] The contrast between the children's 'little oasis of happiness and peace' and the crumbling world outside 'caused me more suffering than anything else', Hanna claimed.[58]

Magda told Hanna that every evening, when she put the children to bed, she never knew whether it might be for the last time. In response, Hanna started to sing to the children 'Tomorrow and it will be His Will, the Lord shall wake thee once again.'[59] Several staff members had already pleaded to accompany the children to a place of greater safety, but Magda was resolute that they should stay. Now Hanna added her voice, offering to fly the entire family out. Magda still declined, saying they preferred to die together. Hanna was impressed by her courage, self-control and cheerful manner in front of her children, and decided she could do no more.* She also admired Hitler's Golden Party Badge, which the Führer had taken off his jacket after fifteen years to pin on Magda's dress in recognition of her loyalty. In turn, Magda saw Hanna as an ally. 'My dear Hanna, when the end comes you must help me if I become weak about the children,' she told her. 'You must help me to help them out of this life. They belong to the Third Reich and to the Führer and if those two things cease to exist there can be no further place for them. But you must help me. My greatest fear is that at the last moment I will be too weak.'[60]

Over the next few days, the Soviet army pushed through Berlin until they were within artillery range of the Chancellery. Hanna spent much of her time in Greim's sickroom. Sometimes she dozed on the stretcher that had carried him in, but essentially she was a full-time nurse, washing and disinfecting his wound every hour, and shifting his weight to help reduce the pain. Any sustained sleep was now impossible as the bunker shook, lights flickered and even on the lower floor, fifty feet below ground, mortar fell from the eighteen-inch-thick walls. A stink from the blocked latrines, combined with the general body odour of around twenty exhausted staff and soldiers, polluted the air. The bunker had never fully overcome its teething problems with damp, diesel fumes and ventilation, and even without bombardments the atmosphere had been almost intolerably claustrophobic. Now, as shells and buildings crashed above them, Hanna heard 'deep sobbing' coming down the corridors.[61]

When she emerged from the sickroom, she met other residents

---

* Conversely, Hitler's secretary, Traudl Junge, said that Magda Goebbels 'hardly had the strength to face her children with composure now', and on leaving them usually burst into tears. See Traudl Junge, *Until the Final Hour* (2002), p. 174.

of the bunker. Nicolaus von Below, Werner Naumann and Hans Baur she already knew. Among the others were Hitler's long-term mistress, Eva Braun; Hermann Fegelein, Braun's brother-in-law and the long-standing liaison officer between Hitler and Himmler; the secretary Traudl Junge; and Martin Bormann who, Hanna noted, spent most of his time 'recording the momentous events in the bunker for posterity'.[62] Baur had flown alongside Greim in the last war, and the two talked at length. He and Below both liked and respected Eva Braun, at once so pretty and so brave; 'an example to us all in her conduct', Below asserted.[63] Hanna, however, considered Eva a pathetic figure, constantly bemoaning Hitler's lot while fussing over the state of her hair and nails, checking her face in her silver, swastika-embossed hand mirror, and changing her elegant outfit every few hours. The most theatrical resident of the bunker, however, was Joseph Goebbels. Hanna described him as incensed by Göring's treachery, 'muttering vile accusations . . . with much hand-waving and fine gestures, made even more grotesque by the jerky up-and-down hobbling as he strode about the room'.[64*] When not railing about Göring, Goebbels held forth on how his own death would be an 'eternal example to all Germans . . . that would long blaze as a holy thing from the pages of history'.[65]

One of those Hanna did not recognize was Bernd Freytag von Loringhoven, the staff officer responsible for preparing intelligence reports for Hitler. Freytag von Loringhoven's cousin, Wessel, had provided the detonator charge and explosives for Claus's assassination attempt. When the plot failed, he had committed suicide. Although not directly involved, Bernd Freytag von Loringhoven had only narrowly avoided being implicated and was keeping his head down. As Hitler's communications staff deserted the bunker, he secretly started to base his reports on information gathered from the BBC and Reuters. Unknown to Hanna, he

---

* Goebbels' right foot was deformed due to a congenital disorder, which childhood operations had failed to correct. Hanna's was a pathetic insult for a man guilty of so many crimes, but appropriately Nazi in its equation of biology and value.

thought it insane that Greim, that 'crony' of the Führer's, with such 'limited ability', had been brought in at enormous risk 'simply for the pleasure of receiving the halo of loyalty from Hitler'.[66]

Whatever their perspective, everyone in the bunker was 'on constant alert'.[67] Hanna believed that 'all of us knew, without a shadow of a doubt, that the end was coming hourly nearer'.[68] Traudl Junge felt the same. 'Those few of us in the Führerbunker know that Hitler withdrew from the battle long ago and is waiting to die . . .' she wrote. 'The Führerbunker is a waxworks museum.'[69] But as tensions mounted Hanna saw that Hitler and his inner circle increasingly chose to delude themselves that final victory might yet be possible. Hitler had not ventured above ground since his brief visit to decorate members of the Hitler Youth a week earlier. Now he strode round the bunker, waving a disintegrating road map in his sweaty, twitching hands, while directing the city's defence with an army that no longer existed. He and his closest advisers were 'living in a world of their own', Hanna told Greim, 'far removed from the reality outside'.[70]

Although unimpressed by Goebbels' tirades, Greim was not immune from his Führer's fantastic self-deception. As one of Hanna's Messerschmitt test-pilot friends, Mano Ziegler, later wrote, 'the "cause" and "final victory" had become a religion'.[71] When Hans-Ulrich Rudel,* the Luftwaffe wing commander with whom three months earlier Hanna had discussed the evacuation of wounded soldiers, telephoned offering to send a plane, Greim told him he had no intention of leaving. Greim then spoke with General Koller, astounding him with his optimism. 'Don't despair! Everything will be well!' Greim reportedly said. 'The presence of the Führer and his confidence have completely inspired me. This place is as good as a fountain of youth for me!'[72] Koller was dumbfounded. Hanna then took the phone, asking him to tell her family that she had had no choice in coming to the bunker, before giving

---

* Rudel had visited the bunker himself a week earlier. He survived the war, surrendering to US forces in May 1945.

such a 'colourful and spirited depiction' of her flight in, and listing her tribulations so thoroughly, that Koller eventually hung up on her, reasoning that the line should be kept free for more important calls.[73]*

Later, Hitler summoned Hanna to his study where he presented her with two small brass capsules, each concealing a fragile glass phial filled with half a teaspoon of amber liquid: cyanide. The bottles were designed to be broken between the teeth, and the poison quickly swallowed. News had come that Mussolini had been captured and shot, his body hung by the heels alongside that of his mistress in a public square in Milan.[†] If General Wenck did not make it through with the German 12th Army, Hitler told Hanna 'in a very small voice', he and Eva had decided to take their own lives rather than risk the humiliations of capture.[74] After her impressive display of loyalty, Hitler told Hanna that she belonged 'to those who will die with me'.[75] As Hanna understood it, she and Greim were being given 'freedom of choice'.[76] Taking the proffered capsules, she sank into a chair. With tears in her eyes, she asked Hitler to reconsider depriving Germany of his life. 'Save yourself, mein Führer,' she pleaded. 'That is the will of every German.'[77] Hitler refused. He had already rejected offers from Hans Baur to fly him out, insisting that he must stand by his post, ready should Wenck yet drive the Soviets back. Hanna felt it was only Hitler's conviction that his continued presence in Berlin was vital for the defenders' morale that was keeping him alive. Seeing, with some distaste, that his once famously expressive eyes were now watery and bulging, and his face was 'flaccid and putty-coloured', she secretly felt that, even should Wenck arrive, the Führer's 'vital energies were by now too depleted to sustain him'.[78]

That afternoon Hitler called a conference to ensure everyone knew how to use their cyanide, and had plans in place for the

---

* Koller disputed that Hanna had had no option, saying that Greim had not wanted her to join him but Hanna herself had insisted.

† Although the hanging of their bodies upside down was intended to humiliate, the petticoat skirts of Mussolini's mistress, Clara Petacci, were pegged together between her legs, so they would not fall and reveal her underwear.

destruction of their bodies. Despite this, Eva kept her phial in the pocket of her elegant dress, telling the women that she wanted to be 'a beautiful corpse'.[79] The meeting ended with spontaneous speeches of loyalty. Caught up in the collective hysteria, Hanna and Greim agreed that, should the time come, they would swallow their poison together, while pulling the pin of a heavy hand grenade held tightly to their bodies.

The next day, 28 April, Hanna learned that Hermann Fegelein, Eva's brother-in-law, had been accused of attempted desertion and summarily shot on Hitler's orders. Although she could accept the idea of voluntary death, Hanna was shocked by this execution of one of their company. 'Who was betraying whom? Who was against whom? That was the painful question that burnt inside me,' she wrote.[80] It felt as though 'the very ground beneath my feet was beginning to give way'.[81] That afternoon Rudel successfully sent a Junker Ju 52 to collect the new commander-in-chief of the Luftwaffe. To Hanna it seemed 'like a miracle', but Greim still refused to leave.[82]

By evening the Red Army had advanced block by block as far as Berlin's famous Potsdamer Platz, and the Chancellery building was under direct bombardment. With no sign of Wenck, central Berlin's defence depended on some 40,000 troops, a similar number of elderly members of the *Volkssturm*, and around a thousand members of the Hitler Youth.

Shortly after midnight Hitler arrived in Greim's sickroom and slumped down on the edge of the bed, clutching a telegram and map. His face was 'ashen-white', Hanna noticed, 'like a dead man's'.[83] 'Himmler has betrayed me . . .' Hitler stuttered, his voice unsteady as he spoke the name.[84] Having left Berlin one week earlier, Himmler had approached the Allies to discuss surrender terms without his Führer's knowledge or sanction. Hanna was appalled by the treachery of the man she had so admired. 'I wished I'd never been born,' she wrote. 'Where were loyalty and honour?'[85] For Hitler the answer was all too clear. Describing Himmler's negotiations as 'the most shameful betrayal in human history', he 'succumbed to a helpless paroxysm of rage, full of hate and contempt'.[86]

Hitler had also received reports that the Red Army was planning to attack the Chancellery in the morning. A two-seat Arado Ar 96 trainer monoplane had managed to get through. Hitler ordered Greim to fly out immediately, and organize a Luftwaffe attack on the most advanced Soviet troops. He hoped this would give Wenck a further twenty-four hours to arrive. For Hanna, the idea that any relief might still be possible was incredible. Below agreed, later writing that this was 'the high point of [Hitler's] self-deception'.[87] Greim was also charged with ensuring that Himmler should never succeed Hitler as Führer. These orders were given 'in a voice charged with uncontrollable hysteria', one army officer recorded, 'making it quite clear that Greim's best course would be to liquidate Himmler without delay'.[88]

In a volte-face, Hanna now protested against leaving, while Greim argued they had a duty to pursue their orders. While the new Luftwaffe chief made preparations, Hanna visited Hitler in his map room, petitioning him again to let them both stay. He looked at her for a moment, and said only, 'God protect you.'[89]

Half an hour later Hitler bade Hanna and Greim farewell with a cursory handshake. 'How hard it is to say farewell when one is leaving the other to certain death,' Hanna wrote. 'It is impossible to describe the feeling.'[90] Greim was carrying several official letters, and Eva passed Hanna a last note for her sister, Gretl Fegelein. For a moment everyone was silent. 'This pretty woman with her fresh, positive ways commanded the unqualified respect of all those assembled in the bunker,' one officer wrote of Hanna.[91] Then, as she turned to leave, Magda reached out for her, beseeching her to do everything she could to bring about the relief of the bunker. 'Regaining her wonderful composure,' Magda then also gave Hanna letters from her and her husband, to be delivered to her son from her first marriage, along with a diamond ring for Hanna to remember her by.[92] It was almost two in the morning, and the six Goebbels children were asleep; Hanna did not see them again.

When Hanna and Greim left the bunker, the latter half-carried, half-hobbling painfully on crutches, they were met not by fresh air but 'a billowing sea of smoke and yellowy-red flame', the distant but ceaseless drumming of gunfire and the 'wail and crash' of shells.[93] Requisitioning an armoured car, they drove through the Tiergarten, now a mostly treeless expanse of mud and rubble, and down to the Victory Column. The same remarkable pilot who had flown them into Gatow was waiting for them near the plane. Hanna crouched behind the machine's two seats, and they left immediately, while there was still enough good road to serve as an improvised airstrip.

Russian searchlights were now flooding the main thoroughfares as well as tracking across the skies above the burning city. Once airborne, the Arado faced a hail of fire as the troops of the Soviet 3rd Shock Army fired everything they had at it, fearing Hitler was escaping. As they passed the Brandenburg Gate, silhouetted against the beams, they were buffeted by explosions but never received a direct hit. From about 20,000 feet Berlin was a sea of flames, 'stark and fantastic', then the pilot swiftly climbed and the tiny plane was hidden in the clouds.[94] When they emerged again the sky was moonlit and clear. Looking down, Hanna saw 'the blackness threaded with silver-gleaming lakes and punctured with the red dots of the burning villages that everywhere marked the route of war and destruction'.[95]

With his last orders dispatched, the Führer turned to other matters. Still in his map room, but now with a minor local bureaucrat to officiate and Goebbels and Bormann as his witnesses, Adolf Hitler and Eva Braun signed declarations that they were of Aryan descent and free from hereditary disease. They were then officially married. After a brief champagne breakfast, the bridegroom dictated his last will and political testament while, above, Soviet artillery churned up the parkland around the Chancellery. Blaming the war on Jewish incitement, and defeat on the betrayal of his officers, Hitler ended his last statement with the injunction that his successors should 'above all else, uphold the racial laws in all their severity, and mercilessly resist the universal poisoner of all nations: international Jewry'.[96]

Despite the importance she always swore she attached to personal honour, at some point during their flight out Hanna read the last personal letters entrusted to her care. Joseph Goebbels was defiant. 'Alive or dead,' he told his stepson, 'we will not leave this shelter unless we leave it with honour and glory.'[97] Believing that his vision of a Nazi Germany would yet be manifest, Goebbels felt that the personal sacrifice being made by Hitler, and himself, would prove an inspiring example for future generations. 'The lies will one day break under their own weight and the truth will again triumph,' he had written with typical flourish. 'The hour will come when we will stand pure and undefiled as our beliefs and aims have always been.'[98] Magda Goebbels' sentiments were no less adamant, but she framed them as an expression of love for her children. 'To end our lives together with [Hitler] is a merciful fate,' she comforted her son. 'Is it not better, more honourable and braver, to have lived a short and happy life rather than a long one under disgraceful conditions?'[99]

Reading these declarations of honour, loyalty and sacrifice, Hanna understood they had been written not so much for Magda's son, as for posterity. She was not sure that she wanted to deliver either, but she kept the letters carefully. Eva Braun's last note, 'so vulgar, so theatrical', elicited less sympathy from her.[100] Although written to her pregnant sister, it did not mention the execution of Hermann Fegelein a few days earlier. Instead Eva had written that her life had 'already been perfect . . . With the Führer, I have had everything. To die now, beside him, completes my happiness.'[101]* Hanna and Greim considered the sentiment, like its author, immature; a pathetic bid for glory as a Nazi martyr that had no place, they felt, in the narrative history of the Third Reich. They had no idea that Hitler was now toasting his new bride, and Hanna later doubted any such marriage took place, commenting that 'the

---

* Hanna later recounted the contents of Eva Braun's letter, as she remembered it, to American intelligence officers.

circumstances in the bunker in these last days would have made such a ceremony ludicrous'.[102] Nevertheless, while Frau Hitler sipped champagne at her wedding breakfast, officially by the side of her Führer at last, Hanna was tearing up her last message and letting it fly out into the darkness.

14

FINAL FLIGHT
1945

A lone Fieseler Storch reconnaissance aeroplane circled in the sky, high above Buchenwald concentration camp and the surrounding beech woods after which it was named. Its stiff-legged silhouette was distinctive as it turned. Alexander, Mika and the other Sippenhaft prisoners arrested after the Valkyrie plot 'rushed outside' from their barrack into an enclosed yard, their fellow prisoner Fey von Hassell recorded, 'and waved with handkerchiefs and bed sheets'.[1] It was mid-March 1945, and Melitta was at the little plane's controls. Seeing the prisoners signalling to her through the foul-smelling smoke blowing across the camp from the crematory chimneys, she circled round once more, looking for a place to land her 'wing-weary little bird'.[2] The Storch's long legs splayed a little to absorb the shock of impact as she touched down in a neighbouring field. Her own shock at the sight and smell of this vast camp, with its thousands of starving prisoners, was cushioned only by a sense of relief at having finally found her husband.

Over two months had passed since Melitta had last seen Alexander. He had then been held in Stutthoff concentration camp, in East Prussia, and she had been able to pass on news of the children to him, Mika and their grandmother, as well as food and blankets. Four days later, the Soviets had launched their winter offensive, and Alexander and the other Sippenhaft prisoners were transported away from the approaching front line. None of them knew where they were being taken. Travelling in achingly slow, freezing train carriages, with huge drifts of snow blowing in through the broken windows, the group had to count themselves fortunate. Behind were open cattle cars packed with hundreds of less valued prisoners. At night, the temperature dropped to minus 30°. As people died from exhaustion and exposure, their bodies were pushed from the wagons to join the snow-blown corpses of horses and mules below. Stumbling along beside them were long columns of refugees, many leaving their own dead beside the tracks, the others 'silent and grim' as they pushed their way west.[3]

Melitta had been working at Berlin-Gatow airfield when her husband and his family disappeared. Despite desperately calling everyone she knew, she found that no one was willing to talk. Rumours had begun to circulate about Melitta's loyalties, always suspect, and even valued friends were now cautious about being seen to help her. 'When the news came that your sister-in-law had gone over to the enemy, I had to distance myself,' Paul Opitz, the Gestapo official who had helped Melitta so much in prison, later told Mika.[4] For weeks, the most Melitta learned was that the prisoners had likely fallen into Russian hands, and 'had probably not survived'.[5]

Officially Melitta's role was still to instruct pilots in the use of her optical night-landing equipment. She had also been commissioned to develop similar technology for the Messerschmitt Me 262, the world's first jet-powered fighter, and had been assigned a new young pilot to help with the test flights. Hubertus von Papen-Koeningen was the nephew of the former German Reich chancellor, Franz von Papen. He had lost both of his older brothers in Russia and, like Melitta, he was firmly anti-Nazi. Hubertus warmed to Melitta from the moment he knocked on her door, marked *Countess Schenk*, and realized she was not allowed to bear the Stauffenberg name 'because her brother-in-law was the assassin'.[6] They quickly came to trust one another, and often talked about the regime and the conflict behind closed doors. Neither of them believed the war could last much longer. While Hubertus carried out all the Me 262 tests, using a closed and concreted stretch of the autobahn as his runway, Melitta's energies were entirely directed towards finding and helping her family. 'Flying, as well as her technical development work, was completely in the background,' Hubertus later recalled. As far as he was concerned, 'one just had to win time until the end of the war'.[7] But Melitta knew that for Alexander and the other Sippenhaft prisoners, now witnesses as well as enemies of a desperate and brutal regime, the last days of the war were likely to be the most dangerous of all.

Melitta's one comfort was that she could still support Claus's widow, Nina. Until early January, the heavily pregnant Nina had been kept in isolation at Ravensbrück concentration camp. As her due date approached she was moved, under armed guard, over a hundred miles south to a Nazi maternity home in Frankfurt an der Oder. A few days later the home was evacuated, but a bed was found for Nina in a private Berlin clinic. Here, under the pseudonym of Frau Schank, Nina gave birth to her and Claus's last child, a daughter called Konstanze, on 27 January 1945.* As soon as she could get away, Melitta cycled over from Gatow with some roasted joints of rabbit and other smoked meat, a pair of men's trousers and some shoes. As she did not have the required Gestapo visitor's permit, she pinned the ribbon of her Iron Cross firmly to her jacket. Luckily the 'astonished' senior doctor had once served with the Luftwaffe and, recognizing Melitta as an aviation heroine, he let her in.[8] A power cut meant that the two women sat talking in the dark, but Melitta was delighted to meet her new niece and Nina gratefully stowed her gifts in the dilapidated hatbox that was now her only baggage. Eight days later both Nina and her baby had caught a raging infection and were moved again, still under guard. Unable to stand, Nina was 'bundled out like a crate of goods', and sent to a hospital in Potsdam.[9]

Unknown to Melitta or Nina, as the war ground interminably on, Himmler had come to regard Alexander and the other Sippenhaft prisoners as possible bargaining chips and ordered that, for now, they be kept alive. Their journey from Stutthof was soon broken at Danzig-Matzkau penal camp, built for Waffen SS officers charged with misconduct. Too weak to walk, they were dragged through the snow and into the yard by existing inmates, and fed on SS officers' rations. A few days later, they were told they

---

* 27 January 1945 was the same day that Hitler's Wolf's Lair in East Prussia fell into the hands of the Soviet army, and that Auschwitz concentration camp was liberated.

29. Melitta in the cockpit of a Junkers Ju 88, date unknown.

30. Melitta at the drafting table, 1943. The ribbon of her Iron Cross is clearly visible on her jacket.

31. One of Melitta's technical drawings, date unknown.

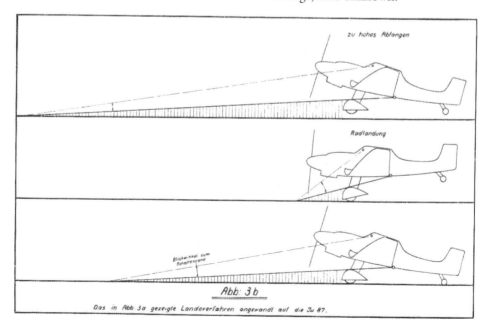

32. Claus with some
of the von Stauffenberg
children. From left:
Claus's daughter Valerie;
Berthold's children,
Elisabeth and Alfred; and
Claus's son Franz Ludwig.

33. Melitta's diary,
13–19 August 1944.
These pages, written while
in prison in Berlin, include
Melitta's dream about
Franz Amsinck.

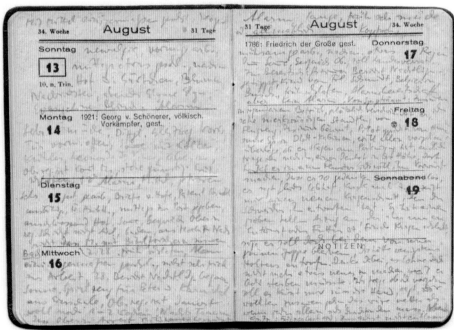

34. Fey von Hassell with her two sons, Corrado and Roberto, *c*.1943.

35. Otto Skorzeny during interrogation by the 307th Counter Intelligence Corps Detachment of the American Seventh Army, 1945.

36. Joseph and Magda Goebbels and their six children from top left: Helga, Hildegard (Hilde), Helmut, Holdine (Holde), Heidrun (Heidi) and Hedwig (Hedda). Harald Quandt, Magda's son from their first marriage, is on the right.

37. Wreckage of the Fieseler
Fi 156 *Storch* that Greim and
Hanna flew into Berlin on
26 April 1945. The Victory
Column can be seen in
the distance.

38. Nina and her children,
Berthold, Franz Ludwig,
Konstanze, Valerie and
Heimeran von Stauffenberg,
Lautlingen, summer 1947.

were to have hot showers. Ushered into an enormous room in a barracks at the far end of the camp, they were ordered to strip naked. Again they were spared. The doors were left open and searingly hot water poured from the taps; there was no gas chamber at Matzkau. Even so, it was here that the first of the group died.

Nina's mother, the courageous Anni von Lerchenfeld, had survived Ravensbrück, where she had briefly witnessed her pregnant daughter's solitary confinement. Nina had written to her mother, but had not known where to send the letter. Anni had then survived Stutthof, even though, as Fey von Hassell noted, being from the Baltics 'she was especially hated by the Nazis'.[10] Now the once noted society beauty walked around with her hair unbrushed, wearing shabby clothes and with huge slippers on her feet. 'People tended to avoid her,' Fey wrote, 'because she was so talkative.'[11] She finally died at Matzkau from a combination of pneumonia, typhus and dysentery.*

In February the prisoners were moved again. Carefully clutching their collection of blankets, nails, one pot, and a rusty stove that the men had dug from the floor at Matzkau, they travelled in turn by truck and cattle wagon, winding through a frozen Prussian countryside disfigured by burned-out vehicles, derailed trains and piles of rubble. Sometimes they heard the noise of gun battles nearby. As rumours came that the invading Soviets were killing SS officials, the dynamic between the prisoners and their captors began to change. Sensing 'the end coming', Alexander's cousin Otto wrote, 'they were often drunk, especially the women'.[12] One female guard 'took on the brittle expression of someone in a controlled but ever-growing panic', Fey added. 'Her sharp voice no longer resonated along the corridors. On the contrary, she became quite obsequious. Her fate was our fate, no better and probably worse.'[13]

Even at this point in the war, with Germany seemingly in chaos, refugees streaming between towns, and constant air raids,

---

* Anni von Lerchenfeld's body was buried at a nearby estate belonging to Melitta's family, almost certainly at the suggestion of Alexander.

soldiers were still being disciplined, trained and sent to the front, and the Sippenhaft prisoners were being transported hundreds of miles around the country. When they passed close to Sachsenhausen concentration camp, near Berlin, it became clear that Alexander's uncle, the increasingly weak Clemens, could no longer continue. He and his wife Elisabeth were forcibly taken from their three adult children, and left behind in the Sachsenhausen medical barrack. They knew they were unlikely to see each other again. As the size of the Sippenhaft group got smaller, so their individual hopes for survival also diminished.

Eventually, in early March, the 'stench from the crematory ovens', as Fey described it, told the remaining Sippenhaft that they were finally approaching Buchenwald concentration camp near Weimar, 170 miles south-west of Berlin.[14] Buchenwald covered an immense site, but its hundreds of barracks were overflowing with thousands of starving prisoners. The camp was 'indescribably filthy', one Stauffenberg cousin noted, and 'there was always an air of abject misery and cruelty'.[15] Female SS guards carried sticks and whips with which they frequently beat prisoners, especially if orders – given solely in German – were not obeyed immediately. Those prisoners who began to lose their sanity were locked into a single small room, the doors of which were opened only to allow in half-rations of food, or to bring out the dead. 'The whole attitude of the SS General Staff towards the prisoners was purposely inhumane and brutal. Prisoners were not regarded as human beings, but as something lower than cattle,' another Stauffenberg later testified.[16] At one point Fey watched a lorry drive past, 'filled to the brim with naked corpses'. The worst of it was that 'nobody seemed to notice', she saw with horror.[17] Rumour had it that between 200 and 300 people were dying at the camp every day. Certainly over 13,000 Buchenwald prisoners were registered as having died in the first three months of 1945, and that number did not include executions, arbitrary murders, or deaths from disease, exposure or starvation during transports.

Fortunately for the Sippenhaft group, they were again given exceptional treatment. On arrival at the camp they were pushed through to join other prominent prisoners being held in the 'isolation barrack', separated from the rest of the camp by a high wall covered in barbed wire. Foreign dignitaries being held there included the former French premier, Léon Blum, and his wife, who secretly waved to them as they arrived; Miklós Horthy Jr, the younger son of the regent of Hungary, who had been kidnapped by Otto Skorzeny in October 1944, forcing his father to resign; and the former Austrian chancellor, Kurt Schuschnigg; as well as a number of diplomats, church leaders and British POWs. It was here that Fey finally learned of her father's execution, as well as of his dignity during his trial, but there was no news of her young children. In these traumatic circumstances, the bond that had developed between her and Alexander grew stronger. His 'sympathy helped cushion my nerve-wracked mind', she wrote.[18]

While the Sippenhaft prisoners were being transported to Buchenwald, Melitta was preparing to leave Berlin. Germany's capital had endured 'incessant bombing' since February, her sister Klara wrote.[19] In response, Hitler had ordered the various schools of the Luftwaffe's Technical Academy to be dispersed to smaller, regional sites. Melitta was glad. For some time she and Hubertus had agreed that 'we must, on no account, fall into Russian captivity', and she and Klara had also quietly discussed fleeing westward on foot, if that were the only option.[20] Now Melitta arranged for her 'Experimental Centre for Special Flight Equipment' – namely herself, her prototype devices, work papers and a few staff – to be relocated to Würzburg. Klara agreed to drive Melitta's old Ford Alpha, loaded up with the heaviest equipment. She set out one foggy evening in mid-March, accompanied by Melitta's assistant with her dog. Melitta's official passes saw them through the many control points on the roads, and they arrived safely the next day. Melitta still had some work to attend to in Berlin-Gatow, and said she would follow by plane, having filed her travel cost claims and arranged transfer of her food coupons. In fact she was sending what coupons she could to Nina in Potsdam.

It was now Melitta finally learned that Alexander and his family had been sent to Buchenwald. Incredibly, she again managed to wring the required visitor permit from Gestapo head office. Then she packed her Storch with rabbit meat, fruit, vegetables and soya-flour biscuits, clothes with little notes hidden inside, even bed linen – anything she could find that might help keep the prisoners' bodies warm and their spirits strong. Her plane was unarmed, but perfect for the short-distance landing and take-off she might need to make. With a cruising speed of eighty miles an hour at low level, she could hope to arrive in under three hours, even if she took a circuitous route to skirt round the most dangerous areas. Above the clouds hanging over the city, it was a bright day and there was not an enemy plane in sight, but Melitta cautiously kept the Storch low as she headed south-west. Once out, flying over the country-side, the sunshine sparkled in the windows of the houses, and made the rivers and canals shimmer below her. For a couple of fleeting hours, it could almost have been a pre-war morning, and she once again thought of the plane as her 'little bird', for which she would have to find a 'suitable branch' to perch upon.[21]

Everything changed as she reached Buchenwald. Circling low above the rows and rows of barracks, straining to see some sign of where Alexander was being held and the best place to land, Melitta could not have missed the appalling reality of the vast camp, the purpose of the crematorium, or the dreadful stench hanging heavily in the air. Driven by personal desperation, she chose to close her mind to the horrific scale of the mass murder being committed and focus exclusively on the well-being of those she knew and loved. Touching down in a field, as close as she could to the far barracks where Alexander, Fey and the others had been signalling to her with bits of white cloth, she handed her papers to the guards. Then she waited, bracing herself to see the changes in her husband.

A few minutes later the gate to the privileged compound was unlocked and Alexander walked towards her. The handsome face she had so often carefully considered was tired and sallow. Alexander's skin had sunk around his chin and cheekbones. He was 'all eyes' and shadow. To Melitta he seemed, at best, a poorly sculpted ver-sion of himself, unfinished, the layers not built up, every contour incorrect. Even his uniform looked wrong, hanging from his reduced frame and still torn at the shoulders and collar where his marks of rank had been ripped away. Then he smiled at her, bending his head forward characteristically – a habit developed from being so tall, not the mark of a man who had been diminished. He was still her Alexander, her 'little snipe', and she longed to give him books, cigarettes and some bottles of good wine along with the bed sheets and dry biscuits. Instead Melitta gave him news about Nina and their friends, and the progress of the war. Alexander told her about their desperate journey, and the dramatic removal of Clemens and Elisabeth. When, all too soon, he went back through the gate, the others caught a brief glimpse of Melitta in the distance. She waved to them, silently pledging her support. A moment later they heard her plane's engines putter into life, the Storch circled once more over the woods, and she was gone.

Melitta knew she was in constant danger of being shot down by the Americans who now dominated the airspace over Germany, but this did not prevent her from flying over to Buchenwald and circling above the camp on eight separate occasions. Down below the prisoners nicknamed her the 'Flying Angel' and the 'Angel of the Camp', each visit giving them the vital hope that came with the knowledge they had not been forgotten.[22] Alexander was the only one permitted to speak with his wife, and then only twice. 'It was very secret,' Mika wrote, and rather miraculous.[23]

After that first visit, Melitta refuelled at Weimar-Nohra, an airfield a few kilometres from the camp, before flying on to Würzburg, only to find that her and Alexander's home had been obliterated. The RAF had firebombed Würzburg, like Dresden before it. Five thousand civilians had been killed, and the historic city left in ruins. Melitta and Alexander's home had taken a direct hit. All Melitta's art, saved since childhood, all her letters and photographs, all their crockery embossed with the Stauffenberg crest, Alexander's entire library, so carefully collected over the years: all was lost. What had not been destroyed or burned immediately was looted by their desperate neighbours. 'Everything . . . has been reduced to ashes,' Klara wrote to their sister Lili. 'Not even a pin or needle is left.'[24] At least no one had been at home.

Melitta rescued a few items from the rubble but admitted to Nina that she actually felt relieved by the destruction. It meant she could now focus all her efforts on the prisoners. She quickly arranged for her remaining research papers to be transferred to Weimar-Nohra. 'There was probably no lever that she did not use to help the prisoners,' Nina remembered. 'She employed her importance to the war effort and her personal charms (something which was not in accordance with her inherent, austere reserve) ruthlessly in order to obtain everything possible.'[25] Secretly, Melitta also began to organize a refuge within walking distance of the camp, in the hope that the prisoners might be released when the inevitable defeat was accepted.

A couple of weeks later, she flew over to Sachsenhausen to collect Clemens and Elisabeth von Stauffenberg. Clemens's heart was very weak, and Melitta had managed to negotiate permission to fly him home, thus preventing him from either dying while in Nazi custody, or falling into Russian hands. The stipulated condition was that she return Elisabeth, his wife, to the Sippenhaft group at Buchenwald en route. After another painfully brief exchange with Alexander at his barracks gate, Melitta flew on with her patient. Calling Elisabeth zu Guttenberg when she landed at Hof, she brought Clemens into the shelter of a wooden shack on the airfield. Elisabeth found Melitta sitting outside, exhausted, but enjoying the feel of the wind on her face. The first of Alexander's relatives was free. Together they lifted Clemens to his feet. He could barely stand, and 'looked as though he were dead', but they managed to get him into a car.[26] Melitta then turned to fly on. 'God be with you always,' she called. 'God bless *you*, dearest Litta!' Elisabeth yelled back.[27] Melitta waved from the cockpit, and her plane lifted off.

By the end of March the Red Army had penetrated deep into East Prussia. The city of Danzig-Oliva, where Melitta's parents, Michael and Margarete Schiller, lived, was under threat. Although most remaining telephone lines were reserved for military use, Melitta managed to call her parents, pledging to come and fly them out. But Michael, now eighty-four, could not be persuaded to leave his home, telling her that he 'trusted in the humanity of the victors', and Margarete would not leave without her husband.[28] Although she was desperately worried, there was little Melitta could do.

There were now only fourteen children left at the Bad Sachsa children's home, half of them Stauffenbergs, all living together in one villa. The home had been put under the auspices of military staff from a nearby base. At Easter the decision was taken to move these last children to Buchenwald.* Sent to pack their bags, they were told they were going to be reunited with their families at the camp. Ten-year-old Berthold had heard about concentration camps, 'if only in whispered tones', and knew enough to know he did not want to be sent to one.[29]

A few days later, the children were bundled into the back of a blacked-out Wehrmacht truck and driven to nearby Nordhausen, where they were to be put on a train for Buchenwald. As they reached the outskirts of the town, a siren howled. The truck pulled over, and the driver and two adults accompanying them threw themselves into a ditch beside the road. Sitting in complete darkness in the back of the truck, the children heard 'a terrific humming, then suddenly a whistling, and then a deafening crack'.[30] Some of them screamed, and a few of the younger ones began to cry. More bombs fell around them, and 'then it was quiet again'.[31] The air raid had destroyed the area around the station, and the station building itself had been reduced to rubble. 'The Nazis had no option but to take us back,' Berthold recalled, 'much to our relief.'[32]

In late March, Melitta's assistant pilot, Hubertus von Papen-Koeningen, had asked his commanding officer at Berlin-Gatow what action they should take in the event of enemy attack. 'See that you get home safely,' the general had answered, handing him three or four blank flying orders.[33] On Wednesday 4 April, Hubertus and

---

* The staff came from the top-secret Unit 00400, headquarters of the V-weapons programme. Bad Sachsa was close to the notorious Mittelbau underground rocket factory that produced V-2s after the bombing of Peenemünde.

Melitta decided that the moment had come. That morning she managed to telephone Nina, in Potsdam, telling her she had heard that the children were being transported away from Bad Sachsa, possibly to Buchenwald. She did not know that the Nordhausen aid raid had frustrated these plans, but promised to pass on more news once she had it. She also pledged to send Nina her heavy workers' food supplement ration cards for April, which she posted that afternoon. Amazingly, they arrived a few days later.

As soon as it grew dark, Melitta and Hubertus prepared the Storch for its final mission. Melitta was wearing a pilot-blue military-style suit under her dark coat, and had fixed the ribbon of her Iron Cross to the lapel. She carried a case packed with food, her washbag and pyjamas, as well as her capacious handbag full of personal possessions, both of which she kept close to her as she climbed into the navigator's seat. Hubertus was taking the first turn as pilot. He was hoping to rejoin his unit, but as yet did not know where they had been redeployed. The plan was to head first for Magdeburg-East, where the small pilot training school might have information, and then on to Weimar-Nohra and Buchenwald. Shortly before arriving at Magdeburg, however, the little Storch's engine failed. Hubertus was trained in forced landings. He brought them down gently over a freshly ploughed field, but in the darkness they could not tell in which direction the ruts ran. On touching down, the Storch's wheels caught in the furrows, flipping it onto its nose before it slowly toppled right over and came to rest belly-up, with both of them still strapped inside. 'Countess, are you hurt?' Hubertus asked after a moment. 'No, not at all,' Melitta replied, having automatically checked herself over.[34] Slowly, they clambered out of the broken plane.

Half an hour later they flagged down a passing military vehicle. Fortunate to find a lift so late, they hoped for a peaceful night at Magdeburg airfield. As they arrived, however, they were caught in an air raid. In the chaos Hubertus ran towards the silhouette of an anthill bunker, while Melitta found a narrow one-person shelter nearer by, cramming her bags in with her. They met at the airfield mess the next morning. There was no news of Hubertus's unit but, making the most of their open flight permits, they picked up both breakfast and an unarmed Bücker Bü 181 Bestmann two-seater aerobatic monoplane to fly on to Weimar. As they were now travelling in daylight, they stayed low, mostly only twenty metres above the ground, and hugged every corner of the forests to stay out of sight of enemy patrols. In fact the Americans were only flying over once every few hours, and they arrived in the Weimar valley without incident. From there they flew straight on to Buchenwald, Melitta following the routes she had taken in the Storch.

Usually, when flying over the camp, she could see people assembled or walking in the privileged barrack's yard, but this time there was no obvious movement. Flying lower, she saw with horror that the isolation compound was deserted. The main camp was still functioning in all its misery, but the Buchenwald crematorium had not been able to keep up with the death rate in these last weeks. There were growing piles of bodies stacked against some of the walls. All were stripped, and their skin had turned 'a dirty grey-green'.[35] Even from the air, Melitta could smell the 'thick and hanging' odour that clung to the camp.[36] She did not know whether Alexander was among the dead, finally executed like his brothers, or whether he had been transported on again. Landing back at Weimar-Nohra, she put through an urgent call to the Buchenwald administration office. The camp commander was not there but a young secretary answered. The prominent prisoners had all been moved, she confirmed, but she was unwilling to say more. Thousands of the prisoners from the main camp were still due to be evacuated before American forces could reach them. It was clear that many were too weak to survive these forced marches, and those who faltered were to be shot. Few people were willing to discuss such matters.

While Melitta was desperately trying to find out more, Hubertus was outside with some ground staff, rolling the Bestmann under cover. A pair of American bombers, on their way to attack Weimar, saw the activity in the airfield and decided to target the hangars as they passed. Hubertus was retrieving Melitta's bag and his own briefcase from the Bestmann, when he saw the two planes wheel round. They were Republic P-47 Thunderbolts, large single-engine fighter-bombers, with the American white star painted on their silver fuselage and one wing, and they were heavily armed. A second later the Thunderbolts dived, their Browning machine guns hammering at the Bestmann. The briefcase Hubertus was carrying was shot out of his hands and, with a deafening noise, bullets ricocheted off the stationary plane and around the inside of the hangar. In another moment the Americans had passed over-head. Pulling himself together, Hubertus ran for the relative safety of the airfield buildings as the pair of Thunderbolts started round for a second attack. Later that day he counted 137 bullet holes across the Bestmann's tubular steel cabin and wooden fuselage: although it had not exploded or even caught fire, it was no longer airworthy. Incredibly, Hubertus himself was unscathed, although two bullets had hit his briefcase, one slicing through the handle, the other lodging in his cigarette tin inside, still carefully wrapped in his pyjamas.

After this close call with death, Hubertus found a new deter-mination. Calling the Buchenwald administration office, he bluffed about his rank and told the secretary that he had urgent orders from Berlin, signed by Himmler himself, to be delivered to the camp commander. The secretary's resistance crumbled, and among other things Hubertus learned that the prominent prisoners had been sent to Straubing, a small town just south of Regensburg, three days before.

It had been almost dark, three nights earlier, when three grey Wehrmacht military buses had pulled up outside Buchenwald. Marching into the isolation barracks, SS troops rounded up the first groups to be pushed on board. Alexander, Mika, Fey and the other Sippenhaft prisoners were among them. A last group would follow in the back of a small blacked-out truck, powered by a wood-burning stove. Himmler was selecting prominent prisoners for possible release as a sweetener when negotiating terms with the Western Allies. Like many senior Nazis, including Hanna's friend Otto Skorzeny, he still believed that a reformed Germany, under new leadership, could join a Western anti-Bolshevik alliance against communist Russia. When it became clear this was hopelessly unrealistic, the prisoners' stock began to fall. As one of them, Sigismund Payne Best, a British MI6 officer who had already spent four years in Sachsenhausen, later wrote, they knew that 'at any moment an order might come for some or all of us to be gassed, shot or hung'.[37]

Alexander and the Sippenhaft group eventually arrived at Regensburg, eighty miles north of Munich, but the camp was too full to admit them. When one of the Stauffenbergs joked that friends in the neighbourhood had a castle and would be delighted to put them up, the guards lost their tempers. Eventually they were incarcerated on the second floor of the town's prison. After devouring some bread and a thin vegetable soup, they called to each other through the grilles on the cell doors. Later they were joined by other prominent prisoners including Dietrich Bonhoeffer, the Lutheran pastor famous as a vocal critic of the Nazi regime who had set up the defiant German Dissenting Church. The next morning the cell doors were opened so the prisoners could wash, and 'there was a great reunion in the corridors . . . introductions and exchanges'.[38] To the astonished warders, it seemed like a reception for the *crème* of German society. Bonhoeffer, in particular, was able to give several of the Sippenhaft prisoners news of their relatives from his detention at Prinz Albrecht Strasse prison. Like many, he thought that they had probably now escaped the worst danger.

Not wanting to risk another encounter with American fighter planes, Melitta and Hubertus stayed at Weimar until dusk. The airfield staff had told Hubertus that his unit was at Marienbad, about halfway to Straubing, so he and Melitta agreed to fly that far together.* As it grew dark they liberated an old Siebel Si 204, with a full tank, from the training school. This was a small transport plane with space for eight passengers, originally designed for civilian use but eventually produced for the Luftwaffe. By the time they had it ready, quite a crowd had gathered to watch. The last officers

---

* Marienbad is now the town of Mariánské Lázně in the Czech Republic.

from the school and the women from the weather station were anxious not to be left behind. Terrified by brutal stories emerging from the Soviet advance, and immersed in the racism of the time, the women pleaded, 'The Americans are coming; there are blacks among them and they'll rape us!'[39]

Half an hour later the Siebel took off with about a dozen passengers, their luggage crammed into its tail. Hubertus was again in the pilot's seat, with Melitta navigating beside him. The wind forced them to take off westwards, towards the American front. With so much weight, however, the tail dragged ominously as they taxied out. They only made it over the airfield's perimeter fence when Hubertus pressed his feet up against the control column to maximize his leverage, while Melitta furiously worked the elevator trim-wheel between their seats.

Once in the air they circled round to head south-east, flying as low as they dared in the overloaded Siebel. As night wore on, they reached the Bohemian Forest with its hundreds of single-track rail lines and small streams twisting through the trees: one of the most difficult landscapes to navigate without radio. As their fuel began to run low, they recognized the city of Pilsen on the far side of the forest. Hubertus fired up some red flares, requesting permission for an emergency landing, but was answered by more red flares from below, refusing them. All of Germany was on high alert, and without radio contact the airfield was nervous that theirs was an enemy plane. After a few tense moments and the deployment of several more flares, permission was given, the landing strip lit up, and the Siebel touched down. To celebrate their safe arrival Melitta and the female passengers shared a bottle of sparkling wine before the women slipped away. Then she let herself grab a few hours of much-needed sleep.

Melitta woke feeling anxious. Time was passing, nerves were fraying; it was now 6 April and she had still not found Alexander. She could not imagine what value he might still hold for the Nazis at this point in the war and increasingly feared that he was more likely to be quietly executed than released. By eight in the morning she and Hubertus had swapped their Siebel passenger plane for

another Bücker Bü 181 Bestmann. Melitta liked this small, respon-
sive aircraft with its good field of vision, which could fly very low,
even 'along every street, close to the ground', Hubertus felt, letting
them navigate by railway signs while staying as hidden as possible.
If they were seen by enemy fighters, the Bestmann was slow but,
being designed for aerobatics, it could spiral tightly down into any
forested area, fly and corner low, and only reappear again when the
enemy had sped past.[40]

They flew first to Marienbad, where Hubertus was to stay. The
flight took at most an hour and a half, and passed without incident.
In no mood for dawdling, Melitta quickly secured a signed and
stamped flight order from the airfield to go on to Straubing. This
document records, rather wonderfully, that the same Bücker Bestmann was to be made officially available to Melitta's Technical
Academy, 'for a special operation, important to the war effort'.[41]
This unspecified 'operation' was in fact a visit to the imprisoned
family of the most famous assassin in the Third Reich, and possibly
the rescue of Alexander. Melitta was finally looking ahead to the
restoration of peace and the rule of law in Germany, freedom for
her family, and fulfilling careers for herself and her husband. She
just had to keep him alive for a few more weeks, possibly just days,
bringing him food and courage and perhaps a way out, while
making it clear to the camp guards that these prisoners were valued
and under observation, until their surrender documents were
signed.

Hubertus sat beside Melitta in the cockpit as she taxied into
position, ready for take-off. As they said their farewells and wished
each other luck, she suddenly reached into her handbag and passed
him the first thing she found, a glass jar of honey. Hubertus
was deeply touched. He knew the gift must have been meant for
Alexander, but he may have missed the subtle humour it contained.
Melitta's name meant 'honey-sweet'. She was, symbolically, bringing herself to her husband. There could hardly have been a better
metaphor for her life-restoring goodness; it was just the sort of
clever gift a classicist and poet would appreciate. Carefully clutching the jar, Hubertus climbed down from the Bestmann. He now

wished he could travel on with Melitta, giving her the benefit of another pair of eyes on the sky, but he would have been taking up the precious second seat in her plane. Instead, he watched as she pulled up into the sky, waggling her wings in the fighter-style salute. All being well, by lunchtime or mid-afternoon she would be reunited with Alexander.

But Alexander was no longer at Straubing, or even in close-by Regensburg prison. While Melitta had been securing the onward use of the Bestmann in Marienbad, he and his fellow prisoners had been bussed to an empty school at Schönberg, a pretty village in the Bavarian forest. Here they were locked into classrooms – but the rooms were bright, with fine views down the mountain valley, and there were real beds set in rows, with coloured covers. Their spirits raised, the prisoners started talking again, even laughing. The men turned their backs while the women washed in a small basin. Some wrote their name above their chosen bed. A few managed to make contact with sympathetic villagers, with the result that some hours later a bowl of steaming potatoes arrived; the next day there were eggs, and a potato salad. None of them knew that they were now en route to Dachau concentration camp, about ten miles north of Munich. Orders for their 'liquidation' had finally arrived.

From Straubing, Melitta flew to Regensburg, where she discovered that she had missed her husband by just a few hours. Increasingly frantic, with single-minded determination she managed to secure a Gestapo permit authorizing her to contact the commander at Schönberg the following day. 'Countess Schenk came here today and was referred to the leader of the detachment in Schönberg,' this document records. 'There is no objection to her intended visit to her husband.'[42] She spent the night at the Regensburg-Neutraubling airfield, snatching what little sleep she could near the hangar.

The next morning, a Sunday, dawned clear and bright. At Schönberg, Pastor Bonhoeffer was leading a service in one of the classrooms. Suddenly a detachment of soldiers interrupted and, ignoring the protests of the others, bundled Bonhoeffer out, to be

taken to the camp at Flossenbürg.* Here he would be given a per-
functory and humiliating trial, and sentenced to death by hanging
along with Wilhelm Canaris, some men associated with the Valkyrie plot, and other enemies of the regime. The rest of the
prisoners were now guarded by members of the Gestapo execution
unit that travelled between concentration camps, 'liquidating'
those prisoners of no further value to the regime, 'like a pest
officer engaged in the extermination of rats', Sigismund Payne
Best observed.[43] Clearly they had not been forgotten by the state,
any more than by Melitta.

She was in the air again by seven. About twenty minutes later
she was hedge-hopping between the Danube River and a nearby
road, navigating south towards Schönberg by the Straubing–
Passau railway line. Down below, in the village of Strasskirchen, a
wounded serviceman on hospital leave was standing at the door of
his house, waiting for his wife to return from church. Intrigued by
the sight of Melitta's plane flying at a height of just ten metres, an
unusual sight on a Sunday morning, he stayed to watch a while. A
few seconds later, an American fighter roared along in the same
direction. Lieutenant Thomas A. Norboune of the US Air Force
15th Squadron reconnaissance unit, then tasked with sweeping
railway lines for trains, was also following the Straubing–Passau
line. Mistaking Melitta's unarmed Bücker Bü 181 Bestmann for a
Focke-Wulf Fw 190 fighter, and unwilling to miss such an unexpected opportunity, he quickly 'fired two salvos of about five to
eight shots'.[44†]

A retired railway foreman was dressing at his window, when
he saw the same encounter. Melitta was flying 'in a very leisurely
and peaceful manner', he reported, when 'suddenly, one or two
Me 109s [sic] thundered over and shot at the slow-flying machine.

---

* Dietrich Bonhoeffer first wrote his name in his volume of Plutarch, and left it with
the other prisoners. It was returned to his family after his execution.

† Lieutenant Norboune later reported his aerial victory in the region of Regensburg
at 7.40 a.m., 8 April 1945. The Focke-Wulf 190 has a similar airframe and rudder
shape to a Bücker Bü 181 Bestmann, especially when seen from behind, hence his
mistake. Norboune was later killed while serving in Korea.

A few seconds later, the slow-flying aircraft turned left a bit, and then spun into a field.'[45] There was no sound of an explosion, and no smoke. The railwayman grabbed his bicycle and pedalled over towards the site, joined en route by a French POW who had been working in some nearby fields.*

These two men were the first to arrive at the scene. To their great surprise, they saw a smartly dressed woman in her early forties sitting in the pilot's seat. Judging by her successful emergency crash-landing, the lack of obvious major wounds and her level of composure, the railwayman did not consider her condition to be critical. 'She just said, "please help me",' he reported.[46] Offering reassurances, he and the Frenchman freed Melitta from the wreckage and laid her on the ground. One of her legs seemed to be broken, and her other foot was lying, 'unnaturally twisted', to one side.[47] As they gently pulled her out, several items fell from her bag including chocolate, some tinned food, and her passport. Inside it read, 'Countess Schenk von Stauffenberg, Flugkapitän'.[48]

Leaving Melitta in the care of the French forced labourer, the railwayman cycled off to fetch a local doctor. He was pleased to notice some people from the neighbouring village were already walking over, and by the time he returned with the doctor, the local military had taken control of the site. Since Melitta was being tended to by a Luftwaffe doctor, the local men were dismissed. They watched her being lifted into an ambulance, and saw it drive off towards Straubing. The crash site remained under military guard.

Within a few hours of her emergency crash landing, Melitta was dead. The certificate issued by the medical superintendent of Straubing airbase gave the cause of death as a fracture at the base of her skull. Whether she died consciously fighting for life or fading more gently in the fields and the back of the ambulance is unrecorded. She was certainly weakened by blood loss. Further injuries listed include a 'severing of the left thigh, fracture of the

---

* Coincidentally, Melitta was only fifty miles from the site where Franz Amsinck had crashed the year before.

right ankle, left forearm, and minor head injuries'.[49] It seemed that Melitta had been directly hit by the American fire, before her forced landing. That she managed to control her descent at all is testament to her great personal determination and skill as a pilot.

At around ten that morning, the surgeon of Straubing hospital visited his workplace, having heard about Melitta's plane being shot down. There he watched as 'a female corpse in pilot's uniform was brought in by the Straubing ambulance crew'.[50] For a moment he could clearly see Melitta's face, which was unmarked. Her 'eyes were half open', he noted, and 'the facial features not distorted, but peaceful and serious, the mouth closed'.[51]

In just three more weeks, the war would be over. Against the incredible odds created by Nazi Germany, this official 'half-blood', female former prisoner, highly paid and decorated Luftwaffe engineer, test pilot and secret enemy of the regime, had been only hours away from achieving her final ambition. A few miles further south Alexander was comforting Fey as they were pushed back onto the military buses, talking with his fellow prisoners about their likely fate, wondering whether his extraordinary wife would find him again, and lifting his face to watch the clouds scud across the clear blue April sky.

15

LIBERATION AND DETENTION
1945–1946

The shocking news of Melitta's death reached Alexander four days later. With surprising sensitivity, one of the guards took him into a quiet corridor before informing him that Melitta had been shot down in aerial combat. It was clear that she had been heading towards him at Schönberg. When Alexander rejoined the other prisoners, 'his face was ashen', Fey recorded, and he seemed 'dazed, as if in a trance'.[1] She and his aunt Elisabeth sat with him as the reality of Melitta's sudden death sank in. Alexander had already lost his twin, Berthold, and his younger brother, Claus. The rest of his family was either imprisoned or under house arrest, and his home had been destroyed. His brilliant and courageous wife had been the one person with a good chance of surviving the war. Instead she had been killed while flying to his aid. With so little information, Alexander could only wonder whether she had finally been shot down by an Allied or German attack, whether she was planning a rescue, and whether she had suffered in her final moments.

Unknown to her husband, Melitta was buried the following morning, 13 April 1945. Her body was still dressed in the dark-blue suit she had chosen to put on almost ten days before, and which she had slept in more than once since. The ribbon of the Iron Cross was still on her lapel. Her possessions, including her passport, Gestapo permissions and other documents, a photograph album, and 4,000 Reichsmarks, amounting to all her and Alexander's savings withdrawn from their bank accounts, were given to the Straubing airbase commander's personal secretary, Bertha Sötz, for safekeeping. Surprised not to receive any of the jewellery said to have been found with Melitta, Sötz made enquiries and received her rings by return. Any other jewellery had disappeared.

Initially, with no one to claim her body or mourn her passing, Melitta was to be buried in a mass grave with local air-raid casualties. Perhaps out of respect for her contribution as an aeronautical engineer, however, or as the holder of the Iron Cross, Sötz arranged a private burial in the town's St Michael's Cemetery. A company from the flying school dug the grave themselves, and then attended the interment in the presence of their officers.

Just three days after Melitta was shot down, the US 104th 'Timberwolf' Infantry Division reached Nordhausen, the town near the Bad Sachsa children's home. Nazi-German resistance in the surrounding woods and hills was stubborn. There had been no further attempts to move the Stauffenberg children and their cousins during the confusion of the final weeks of the war, and now they found themselves on the front line. Allied fighters strafed not only the Wehrmacht vehicles in the woods surrounding their buildings, 'but also the strawberry patch in our garden', Berthold recalled.[2] As the house was exposed, the children took refuge in the cellar where the tools were kept, partially under and along one side of the property. This room reached ground level where there was no hedge or fence, so they found they could watch the planes, 'mostly American Mustangs or Lightnings – flying past and shooting'.[3]

Twelve hours later the children heard the sound of big guns, 'a deep thundering noise', as Berthold's younger brother, Franz Ludwig, described it, and knew the American line was advancing.[4] Soon they heard fighting nearby and the Wehrmacht soldiers stationed with them shouted that they were going to lose the war. Then, nothing. 'Finally the door was pushed open,' Franz Ludwig recalled, 'and a small soldier came in with his gun ready, looking about, and someone said that there were only children here, and then a second soldier came in and they seemed satisfied. That was it.'[5] The Germans had retreated and, after a thorough search, the site was occupied by American troops, staying in every house except the children's own. The soldiers were 'awfully nice, and they were all very young', Franz Ludwig added.[6] As well as playing games with the children, they brought them the first chocolate the younger ones had ever tasted, along with other sweets: 'a luxury for us beyond description'.[7]

The newly appointed Mayor of Bad Sachsa came to the home to tell the children that they were officially free, and to register them as local residents a few days later. Standing on a table, he also made 'a fiery speech' about how proud they could be of their fathers.[8] 'The words washed over us,' one of the cousins later wrote. For months they had been told that their parents were criminals, while their enemy had turned out to be the friendly American soldiers.[9] Although two nurses were delegated to look after the children, they were now largely left to their own devices. They plundered the stores and roamed the woods searching, like children everywhere, for spent ammunition, *Splitter* (or shrapnel), and other 'war booty', but essentially life continued at Bad Sachsa much as before. They had no idea how to contact their families, and they seemed to be nobody's priority.

The children had been abducted and detained, but they had never been held in a concentration camp. The Allies had received appalling reports for some time, ever since Soviet forces had reached Majdanek concentration camp in occupied Poland in July 1944. Later that summer, the remains of the camps at Bełżec, Sobibór and Treblinka were also overrun. Auschwitz had been liberated in January 1945, followed by Stutthof, Sachsenhausen and Ravensbrück, at times just weeks after the Sippenhaft and other prominent prisoners had been transferred elsewhere. American forces reached Buchenwald in early April, followed by Dora-Mittelbau, Flossenbürg and Bergen-Belsen two weeks later.

Travelling with the Americans to liberate Belsen was the Scottish pilot, Eric Brown. Now a decorated British test pilot, Eric had been sent to Germany with a team of scientists in the last stages of the war to locate pioneering aviation technology such as supersonic wind tunnels, along with examples of jet and rocket aircraft. He was also to interrogate Germany's top aeronautical designers, engineers and test pilots. His first lead was that two Luftwaffe pilots fleeing the Soviet advance had flown a pair of Messerschmitt Me 262s south towards Hanover. Eric was flown to Fassberg airfield, where he found the abandoned aircraft. He was 'immediately struck' by the 'complexity' and 'sensitivity' of the jet plane that both Melitta and Hanna had tested during development.[10]

The US Second Army that had captured Fassberg airfield was also detailed to take the camp at nearby Bergen-Belsen. Although it was not designed as an extermination camp, some 50,000 people had been killed or left to die at Belsen. Among them was Anne Frank, the Dutch teenager who had commented on Claus's assassination attempt in her diary the summer before. She and her family had been betrayed and arrested just two weeks later. Anne died a few days after her sister, probably of typhus, just weeks before Belsen was liberated. Mass murder was still taking place just days before the Allies reached the camp. Another 13,000 former prisoners were too frail to survive the weeks that followed.

As a German speaker, Eric was called in to translate. Arriving by jeep, he found former prisoners, 'silent, shuffling ghosts of men', pacing the yards or standing staring at the ground.[11] When he questioned them they were unable even to reply. Over 10,000 corpses lay between the barracks or in open graves. 'Bodies were piled high. Two-thirds of them were women,' Eric later testified. More 'had been bulldozed into pits . . . the stench was indescribable'.[12] Inside the huts, each built to house sixty people, on average he found 250 dying of typhus, dysentery and starvation. 'I had known the Germans, I had been happy in Germany,' he later wrote. 'In the war I had made excuses for them, blamed the Nazis. There could be no excuses for this.'[13] Eric then helped interrogate the camp commandants, including Josef Kramer and the twenty-three-year-old Irma Grese who refused to respond, but at one point 'leapt to her feet and gave the Heil Hitler salute'.[14] They, and almost two hundred other guards, were later court-martialled and hanged.

Eric then turned his attention back to locating and interviewing some of the engineers and pilots on his list, who included Wernher von Braun, Ernst Heinkel, Willy Messerchmitt, Focke-Wulf designer Kurt Tank, and Hanna Reitsch. His next lead came from overhearing some Germans in a Lübeck pub one evening.

Rumour was that Hanna, that 'fabulous creature', as Eric described her, had 'flown her Fieseler Storch on and off the roof of the German Air Ministry in the last days of the Third Reich', and was now hiding in Bavaria.[15]

The rumours were only a slight exaggeration. Hanna and Greim had avoided Soviet anti-aircraft fire on their way out of central Berlin, landing safely at Rechlin at three the same morning. 'Shivering, weary and oppressed' in the cold night air, Hanna stamped her feet to get warm while Greim had a conference with the remaining operations staff at the airfield and ordered all available aircraft to the defence of the capital.[16] From there they flew to Plön, close to the Danish border, to discover Himmler's whereabouts from Admiral Dönitz. Because of Greim's injury, Hanna was in the pilot's seat of their Bücker Bestmann, the same type of plane that Melitta had been flying over to Schönberg on her own final mission. Like Melitta, Hanna 'crept rather than flew', staying as low as possible along the edges of woods and 'almost brushing the hedges and fences as I passed over them'.[17] After the skies proved too dangerous, she drove the last thirty miles, occasionally pulling over to avoid being strafed by Soviet fighters flying overhead.

Hanna and Greim were still travelling when they heard the radio announcements of Hitler's death, and of the formation of a new German government under Admiral Dönitz. The Führer had died 'a hero's death', Dönitz announced. In fact Hitler and his bride had committed suicide as the Red Army closed in on the Reich Chancellery. Hitler's pilot, Hans Baur, and others ensured that their bodies were doused with petrol and burned. The dead Führer's 'untidy hair fluttered in the wind', his chauffeur later recorded, while Eva's dark-blue dress with white frills 'moved in the wind until finally drenched by the fuel'.[18] Other eyewitnesses reported the grisly detail that Eva's body slowly bent into a sitting position in the intense flames, while Hitler's shrivelled up in the blaze.

The next day, with the help of Dr Stumpfegger, Magda Goebbels had drugged her six children before they went to bed. Despite last-minute offers to escort the family out, she chose to kill each child in turn with cyanide while they slept. A few hours later, she and her husband left the bunker by the emergency exit leading onto the patch of earth and rubble that had once been the Chancellery garden. There they took their own lives. Their bodies were also burned. Hitler's Party badge, which Hanna had admired on Magda's dress in the bunker, was later recovered from her remains, rather melted round the edges. When the story emerged, Hanna would come to believe that the Russians would not have hurt the children she had visited in the bunker. 'Their lives were wasted,' she told a journalist, 'they were innocents'.[19]

Bormann, Stumpfegger, Below and Baur were among those who finally chose to flee the bunker for the 'confusion of cables, rubble and tram wires . . . ruins and bomb craters' that now formed Berlin.[20] Bormann and Stumpfegger bit their cyanide capsules when escape seemed impossible. Below was eventually arrested by the British, and held until 1948. Baur was captured by Russian troops, disappearing for a decade in Soviet detention.

When Hanna and Greim finally reached Plön, Dönitz was already at the helm. He greeted them with a speech on the pressing need to continue the fight against Bolshevism. No one remarked on the unspoken policy shift. Later Dönitz called a war council with the remaining ministers of the regime. When Greim spoke to Field Marshal Keitel about the best air tactics to support General Wenck's long-awaited advance into Berlin, Keitel informed him that Wenck's army had long since been destroyed. Capitulation was clearly imminent. Their only realistic goal was to contain the Soviet advance for as long as possible, allowing civilians to flee towards the Western Allies in the hope of better treatment.

Waiting outside the conference room, Hanna was shocked to see Himmler arrive. Later she recounted how she demanded to know whether he had indeed independently sued for peace. Himmler was happy to admit it. 'You betrayed your Führer and your people in the very darkest hour?' Hanna reeled. 'Such a thing is high treason, Herr Reichsführer . . . Your place was in the bunker with Hitler.'[21] Himmler reportedly laughed her off.

'History will weigh it differently,' he told her. 'Hitler was insane. It should have been stopped long ago.'[22] 'He died for the cause he believed in,' Hanna retorted. 'He died bravely and filled with . . . honour.'[23] When Himmler argued that his own actions had been 'to save German blood, to rescue what was left of our country', Hanna was dismissive.[24] 'You speak of German blood, Herr Reichsführer? You speak of it now? You should have thought of it years ago, before you became identified with the useless shedding of so much of it.'[25] In the heat of anger more truth had slipped out than Hanna usually chose to voice, but a moment later their tête-à-tête was cut short by an aerial attack.* Hanna would not see Himmler again.†

Berlin officially surrendered on 2 May. The last Operation Valkyrie plotters still imprisoned in the capital had been taken out and shot in the rubble a week before. Now exhausted Soviet troops arrived to find a ruined city engulfed in the smoke from persistent fires. The water and sewerage systems were wrecked; there was no fuel, electricity, transport or communications, and little food. The conquering soldiers stole bicycles, watches, bread and blankets. Many fell asleep in the streets, others in the ruins. The next morning many of the women in Berlin were raped, some receiving food or protection in return, others simply beaten. Hanna and Greim now flew on to Königgrätz where Greim belatedly ordered all remaining troops to hold out against the Soviets for as long as possible. He was now too ill to continue himself, lapsing in and out of consciousness, and Hanna had him admitted to hospital. When he took off his wire-rimmed glasses, the frames left a deep impression in his skin. With the heavy furrows on his forehead and the thin-lipped crease of his mouth below, his once full face looked almost folded and ready to be put away.

Temporarily grounded, Hanna and Greim discussed their

---

* Himmler had recently ordered the execution of all concentration camp inmates too sick to march away from the front line, but neither he nor Hanna was thinking of prisoners when they talked of the shedding of German blood.

† Himmler was captured on 21 May. Two days later he bit his cyanide capsule, dying within fifteen minutes.

possible future in a post-Nazi Germany, and decided they had none. They also cursed both Göring and Himmler for their weaknesses and ultimate lack of honour. At one point Greim confided he had associated doubts about Melitta. 'It wasn't just a suspicion of cooperating with Himmler,' Hanna later wrote, 'it is a fact that she was in contact with him.'[26] Himmler had mentioned Melitta in the spring of 1945, prompting Greim to wonder whether she was involved in 'espionage'.[27] Hanna had long seen how Melitta avoided certain colleagues and criticized the regime to others. 'The suspicion that Melitta was a spy was not viciously created by others,' she asserted, 'but tragically brought up by Melitta herself; for example by her way of avoiding me and harshly declining every well-intended offer of help from my side.'[28] Hanna also felt that Melitta's 'racial burden' made rumours that she 'had a foot in both camps' or was working 'for the enemy', more valid.[29] The fact that Hanna and Greim spent time discussing this in the final days of the war is more telling about their preoccupations and resentments than Melitta's connections and activities. There is no evidence that Melitta, whose sole concern by this point was the safety of her family, had been scheming with Himmler.

A few days later, news that capitulation was imminent spurred Greim on. With Hanna in attendance, on 8 May the injured field marshal was flown over the Alps to meet General Kesselring in Austria, to discuss last orders for the Luftwaffe. Kesselring was not in evidence. General Koller, chief of the Luftwaffe General Staff, was shocked by Greim's appearance. Even with two crutches, two officers and Hanna accompanying him, he could hardly be extracted from his car. He was clearly in pain, Koller noted in his diary. His face was 'saggy and almost yellow'.[30] Koller organized a quick breakfast with strong coffee. The two officers waited outside the room, but Greim insisted that Hanna stay with him at all times. 'It's not easy to speak frankly with the chief of the Luftwaffe . . .' Koller wrote plaintively, 'and it's made more difficult because I can't get Hanna Reitsch out of the room. I want to but Greim won't stand for it.'[31]

Greim and Hanna then recounted the story of their journey

from the bunker. Both stressed the pain of not being allowed to die with their Führer. By now in tears, Hanna added that 'she wanted to kneel at the altar of the Fatherland and pray'.[32] 'Altar?' Koller queried, unsure of her meaning. 'Bunker,' Hanna replied.[33] For Koller this was hysterical rubbish. In the published version of his diaries he claims to have told them that the bunker was 'a monument to the betrayal of Germany'.[34] When he proposed that Göring, who had done so much for Hanna, should be protected from the Soviets, Koller was again shocked by Hanna's retort that Göring was a traitor who should be dealt with. Koller, who had been trying to arrange a meeting between Göring and the Americans, did not find this helpful. Both Greim and Hanna then told Koller that if he were captured, he should shoot himself. 'You have to . . .' Hanna made her case; 'to be captured lacks honour.'[35]

That evening Greim received a telex informing him that the regime had signed an unconditional surrender and all hostilities were to cease, 'effective immediately'.[36] While most of the remaining senior leadership destroyed their paper records, Greim silently slipped his last orders into the pocket of his uniform jacket. His command was already at an end.

Two junior officers were now detailed to drive Greim and Hanna to the civilian hospital at Kitzbühel. Halfway there, Greim ordered the car to stop. His duties dispatched to the best of his abilities, he now planned to evade capture. In a meadow by the roadside, Hanna carefully helped him out of his uniform and into civilian clothes. It was a pathetic scene, and yet somehow also intimate. The last commander-in-chief of the Luftwaffe was badly injured and exhausted but nevertheless on the run. Instead of an officer, he asked Hanna, the only woman present, to help him change his clothes. Greim then told the officers to shoot him as a deserter. Later, Koller wrote that 'the situation for these young officers must have been extremely uncomfortable'.[37] Eventually they persuaded Greim back into the car, and deposited him and Hanna at the hospital. Even now Greim refused 'to take anyone with him, except Hanna Reitsch', who remained by his side.[38] He was still being treated when American troops entered the town and, as Hanna put it, 'we saw the final collapse of all our hopes'.[39]

Amid 'the chaos of defeat', Hanna later said, she had drawn strength from the knowledge that her family were nearby, at the Schloss Leopoldskron just outside Salzburg.[40] Now she asked for a pass to visit them. Instead, Koller reported that her parents, her sister and her sister's three children had all been killed in the last bombing raid on Salzburg, in the very final days of the conflict. 'She took it stoically,' he noted.[41] Afterwards she lit candles and propped up some photographs of her family in Greim's room.

Hanna would later learn that her family had been killed in quite different circumstances. Once the Third Reich had fallen, rumours began to circulate that displaced families within Germany would be returned to their home towns. Hirschberg was in the Soviet zone. Goebbels had long exploited stories of violence, rape and looting by the Red Army to support national solidarity in the face of invasion, but Willy Reitsch knew there was some truth behind the propaganda. As a doctor, when providing medical assistance in regions recaptured by the Wehrmacht he had seen the suffering caused by Soviet soldiers. He was terrified that such brutal treatment would be inflicted on those he loved. In time Hanna would come to see and describe her father's motivations at this moment as 'an overriding duty to preserve his own family'.[42] Willy Reitsch had been traumatized by the presumed death of his only son, the loss of the war, the collapse of the regime he supported, and the fear of a brutal life and death under the communist enemy. In a terrible echo of Magda Goebbels' extreme beliefs, to the controlling Willy Reitsch it somehow seemed best to kill all the women and children in his family himself.*

When a friend dropped by on 4 May, she was told the Reitsch family was unwell. The next day, the same caller saw a cart outside the Schloss Leopoldskron, its load covered with old blankets. Inside were the bodies of Willy and Emy Reitsch, their maid Anni,

---

* Willy Reitsch was one of thousands of civilians from eastern Germany making the same choice.

and Hanna's sister Heidi with her three young children. Having failed to fatally poison his family, Willy Reitsch had shot them all before turning the gun on himself. In a final note to Hanna, he told his daughter she must find solace in the knowledge that they were all now safely with their Maker. Her father 'had seen no alternative', Hanna later wrote through the lens of self-preservation, 'but to take upon himself the heaviest responsibility of all'.[43]

Eric Brown had now heard from his American colleagues that there was a 'smallish, fair, petite' woman in her mid-thirties hiding in an American hospital near Kitzbühel, who they believed might be Hanna Reitsch. Eric was asked to find and identify her. When he walked round the women's ward, Hanna 'immediately recognized' him and started 'feigning a heart attack', he later reported.[44] 'You know, Hanna,' he told her, 'the game is up.'[45] Negotiating the right to question her after the initial interviews, Eric handed Hanna over into American custody. When he was finally given access to her again, their conversation provided an extraordinary insight into her beliefs.

'At first she was very suspicious,' Eric wrote, but he reassured her that he wanted to talk about aircraft rather than politics, and 'she began to talk freely'.[46] He was fascinated by Hanna's experiences with a wide range of German civil and military aircraft, including helicopters and the V-1 flying bomb. His priority, however, was to get her to talk about the Messerschmitt Me 163 Komet rocket fighter, a plane that he had developed 'an overwhelming desire to fly as soon as possible'.[47] 'Although she was reluctant to admit this,' he later wrote, it soon became evident that Hanna had never flown the plane under power, but only 'to make production test flights from towed glides'.[48*]

It must have been a relief for Hanna to discuss aviation with someone who shared her passion. Once she began to talk, however, she quickly digressed. Eric could see that she was in 'an emotional

---

* Full of self-confidence, Eric took up a Komet not long after this. Accelerating rapidly to 450 mph, he felt as though he were 'in charge of a runaway train'. Once he had touched back down safely, he and the ground crew went for a celebratory stiff drink. See Eric Brown, *Wings on My Sleeve* (2007), p. 112.

state'.[49] She had not long since learned of her father's 'slaying of all the females in his household', he bluntly recalled.[50] He decided to let her talk on. In any case, 'when she started talking you couldn't stop her', he said. 'It was a cascade.'[51] At one point Hanna 'gushed out' information about the key players in 'ODESSA', the affiliations of former SS officers who she was sure would eliminate anyone they believed had committed high treason against the Third Reich.[52] She was more worried about having said too much to the Americans, she told Eric, than she was about being accused by them of cooperating with the regime. Eric was convinced she had many more contacts than she later chose to make clear; she never mentioned ODESSA again. She also 'spoke of Udet dispassionately, without any sign of loyalty', Eric felt, and then told him of her journey into Hitler's bunker, 'a saga of pure courage'.[53] To Eric it was clear that Hanna's 'devotion for Hitler was total devotion'.[54] 'He represented the Germany that I love,' she told him.[55]

Hanna also denied the Holocaust. When Eric told her that he had been at the liberation of Belsen, and had seen the starving inmates and piles of the dead for himself, 'she pooh-poohed all this. She didn't believe it . . . She didn't want to believe any of it.'[56] Such denial was painful for them both, but Eric found that 'nothing could convince her that the Holocaust took place'.[57] Hanna was, he concluded, a 'fanatical aviator, fervent German nationalist and ardent Nazi'.[58] Above all, he later wrote, 'the fanaticism she displayed in her attitude to Hitler, made my blood run cold'.[59]

Hanna was now placed under house arrest in her family's old rooms at the Schloss Leopoldskron. At first Captain Robert Work, the sympathetic head of the US Air Force Intelligence Unit, and his colleagues, simply helped her sort through her family's possessions. She saved only some of her mother's poetry, family photographs and letters.[*] She was also allowed to cycle over to their graves. Once, on learning that her and Melitta's former colleague,

---

[*] By contrast, when Göring was captured on 9 May, he reportedly had sixteen matching suitcases with him.

Professor Georgii, was being held just across the German border, she made an illicit trip over to visit him. Not long after, she was moved for interrogation. Before she left, Hanna's occasional wartime secretary, Gretl Böss, managed to visit her. During their half-hour alone together, the two women exchanged watches so that Hanna's, a gift from Udet years earlier, would be kept safe. With it, Hanna also secretly handed over her cyanide capsule.

Hanna was then transferred to another well-appointed villa, where she was gently questioned by Work. She 'carefully weighs the "honor" aspects of every remark', he commented. 'The use of the word amounts practically to a fetish complex . . . and is almost an incongruous embodiment of her entire philosophy. Her constant repetition of the word is in no manner as obvious to her as it is to the interrogator, nor is the meaning the same.'[60] For Hanna, 'honour' had become the overriding virtue that exonerated any lapse of judgement, however serious, but at the same time it was reduced to a simple code of loyalty. Ironically, this was a code she had often chosen to defy during the war when it suited her, but which she now embraced to rescue her conscience.

Work also recorded that Hanna still 'held the Führer in high esteem'.[61] Shocked by her impressions in the bunker, she reasoned that Hitler must have suffered a personality disorder in his last months, as a result of medicines prescribed by his doctors. 'Hitler ended his life as a criminal against the world,' she told Work. 'But he did not begin it that way.'[62] Hanna had not lost her faith in the early ideals of her Führer. Nor did she condemn the Nazi regime's fundamental racism. All she conceded was that Hitler had proved a poor soldier and statesman. 'Strangely enough,' Work noted, 'she does not appear to hold him personally responsible.'[63] Instead she argued that 'a great part of the fault lies with those who led him, lured him, criminally misdirected him, and informed him falsely'.[64] Ultimately, Hanna argued, Hitler's unchallenged power turned him from 'an idealistically motivated benefactor to a grasping, scheming despot'.[65] In her analysis, it was essentially the system, and the advisers, who were at fault.

Hanna would later provide a damning condemnation of Göring

and his 'morphine-sickened egotism', as well as considerable information on her aviation test work.[66] Her declarations that 'the
people must know what sort of criminal Göring was, a criminal
against Germany and a criminal against the world', led Work to
hope she might become an ambassador for reconciliation in post-
war Germany.[67] She had, after all, never become a member of the
Nazi Party. As a result he treated her with kid gloves, leading Eric
Brown to comment that 'she made a fool out of him'.[68] In fact
Hanna's criticisms remained focused on Göring for misusing the
Luftwaffe and deceiving Hitler. She did not express any wider
disillusion with the regime. 'Every life lost on either side . . . is, in
her opinion, to be unquestionably chalked up against Göring,'
Work closed his report incredulously.[69] Even 'Hitler's crime, was
that he did not possess the necessary insight to realize the incom-
petency of Göring.'[70]

Above all, however, the Americans wanted Hanna to provide
confirmation of Hitler's death. Soviet intelligence had found the
charred remains of his body within days of taking Berlin. Stalin
was not convinced, however, and stories began to circulate that the
Führer had managed a last-minute escape. Hanna dismissed the
suggestion contemptuously. She believed he had been too ill to live
long anyhow. 'Hitler is dead!' she told Work. 'He had no reason
to live, and the tragedy was that he knew it well.'[71] Although
Hanna refused to provide a report on this, Work believed she
answered his questions 'with a sincere and conscientious effort to
be truthful and exact'.[72] His interrogation report on the matter
would later join the supporting documents at the Nuremberg war
crimes trials.*

Greim was officially arrested on 22 May. If it was a moment to
take stock, his position was not heartening. His foot had never
fully healed and his health was wrecked. His air force was destroyed, his country in ruins and his cause discredited. Two days

---

* Hanna later denied the accounts published from her testimony, claiming she had
never authorized or signed her interrogation reports. In fact it was not standard
practice for such reports to be signed or approved by their subjects.

later he bit on the cyanide capsule given to him by Hitler. He was dead within minutes.

Hanna believed that Greim took his life to avoid having to testify at the Nuremberg trials against Göring, the man who had blocked his career, and who he held responsible for the destruction of the Luftwaffe.* 'I am sure that Greim was not able to reconcile his honour as a soldier with giving the information he would have had to give regarding the despicable traits and blunderings of Göring,' she told Work.[73] Further motivation might have come from the fear he might be selected for a prisoner exchange with the Russians, and face torture and execution.

Greim and Hanna had planned a joint suicide when Hitler had given them their lethal cyanide capsules. Once they had left the bunker, however, Hanna feared that taking their lives together might imply a romantic relationship, besmirching the honour of both. Hanna's Austrian cousin, Helmut Heuberger, believed they had a 'friendship based on deep love, in my opinion the greatest love. But it was never physically consummated.'[74] Greim was married, and it is possible that his and Hanna's sense of honour might have either restrained them, or provided a convenient excuse. Either way, their esteem for each other was certainly absolute. 'Our gratitude, respect and loyalty to him know no boundaries,' Hanna later wrote to a friend. 'His whole being and personality had earned our reverence.'[75] Hanna was not with Greim when he chose to end his life, but neither was she surprised by his decision. With almost everyone she cared for gone, she was only waiting a decent interval, she told herself, to avoid the scandal of an apparent suicide pact.

A few days later, still in American custody, Hanna allowed herself to be driven to Greim's grave, in the same Salzburg cemetery where her family was buried. In the car, her escorting officers showed her photographs from Dachau concentration camp. Hanna's immediate response was not recorded. If she thought again of Peter Riedel's Majdanek leaflet, the labour camps at Peenemünde

---

* Göring would also later kill himself with cyanide, just hours before he was due to be hanged on 15 October 1946.

or Eric's testimony from Belsen, or if she questioned her own complicity with the regime responsible for such crimes, she did not publicly admit it. Later she again claimed not to believe in such atrocities. She then paid her last respects at the grave of the man she had most admired in life. It was a privilege denied many millions of others under the regime they had both supported so fervently to the end.

While in the Salzburg cemetery, Hanna recognized another woman at the gravesides. Leni Riefenstahl was the film director who had become Hitler's most famous chronicler of the Third Reich. Hanna had first met her at the Berlin Olympics in 1936 when Riefenstahl was making her remarkable film about the games. They had shared a growing status as Nazi female celebrities ever since. When Riefenstahl came over, Hanna took some crumpled papers from her pocket and pressed them into her hands. 'Read this letter,' she said. 'It may be taken away from me, and then no one but me will know what it says.'[76] It was one of the Goebbels' last letters from the bunker. Hanna was now determined to ensure that these made the historical record. Riefenstahl then asked whether Hanna, who she described as a 'small, frail woman', had really intended to be a suicide pilot.[77] Hanna proudly confirmed it. She then reported Hitler's objection to the operation as being that 'every person who risks his life in the battle for his Fatherland must have the chance for survival, even if it is small'.[78] Hanna was still defending her Führer's ideals. She could not accept that he and the regime had betrayed the German people, any more than that they had been responsible for war crimes.

Looking at Greim's final resting place, and talking with Riefenstahl about their country and the decisions and reputation of the regime, Hanna came to a decision. As she hugged Riefenstahl goodbye, she decided she would not, after all, take her own life. She had always believed herself to be part of a solution, a force for good. Now she decided she would give herself once more to Germany, to help restore some national dignity and pride in the weeks, months, even years after defeat. Hanna now told her US interrogators that she planned 'to tell the truth about Göring, "the shallow showman"; to tell the truth about Hitler, "the criminal incompetent"; and to tell the German people the truth about the dangers of the form of government that the Third Reich gave them'.[79] But Hanna was either incapable of telling the truth, even to herself, or she was cynically lying. When the Americans organized a press conference for her to publicly repeat her denunciation of Hitler's military and strategic leadership, she instead defiantly asserted that she had willingly supported him, and claimed she would do the same again.

Alexander's elderly mother, Karoline von Stauffenberg, had spent the last months of the war under house arrest at the family schloss in Lautlingen. French forces arrived in mid-April and, after some desultory fighting, the town surrendered. As the unofficial head of the local community, Karoline received the French commanding officer in her little dressing room, between the sink and a table. At his request, she agreed to a small clinic being installed at the house, and the Red Cross flag was raised above the roof. When more French troops arrived, shops were looted and there were reports of rapes, Karoline provided refuge for the terrified villagers. She was also required to host a large number of evacuated Gestapo families.

In early June, Karoline's sister, Alexandrine, the children's great-aunt and a former Red Cross nurse, persuaded the French military commander to lend her his official car with French number plates and a precious tank of petrol. She then drove over three hundred miles through two Allied zones to Bad Sachsa, the last place where Melitta had reported the children were being held. When she arrived, on 11 June, she found the home empty. It was only when she reached the last villa that she heard young voices. All fifteen of the missing children were there. They 'cheered and surrounded their [aunt] immediately', Konstanze later wrote.[80]

Bad Sachsa would soon be transferred to Soviet control. 'The Russians were the key word for terror,' Franz Ludwig recalled. 'They were a menace . . . a cause of absolute fright.'[81] The irrepressible Alexandrine quickly stowed Berthold, Heimeran and Franz Ludwig in the French car, and organized a bus, powered by methanol, to follow behind with the other children. A few hours after they left, the Soviets moved into Bad Sachsa, prohibiting any further movement.

Driving back, Alexandrine passed the notorious Dora labour camp and the Mittelbau factory where the V-2 rockets were assembled by prisoners forced into slave labour. Berthold would never forget the entrance to the underground works so close to where he had been living, where so many had died for the Nazi vengeance-weapon programme. Alexandrine then told the boys about the actions taken by their father, uncle, other family and friends. Berthold and Heimeran already had a vague idea, but for Franz Ludwig it was 'quite astounding'.[82] All the children were also astonished by the devastation of their country. This was not a Germany they could recognize. The following day, against all the odds, the children of Hitler's most famous would-be assassin arrived safely home, thanks to two aunts: one a determined elderly veteran of the Red Cross, the other a courageous part-Jewish holder of the Iron Cross.

A few months earlier, after the news of Melitta's death had reached Alexander in April, the Sippenhaft prisoners had been moved on again, eventually arriving at the gates, watchtowers and high-tension wire fences of Dachau. Here the men were lined up against the wall of a brick building to be drafted into the Volkssturm, the people's militia created in the last months of the war for civil defence. Several of the women cried as the men were taken away. It was obvious that such weak people could not form an effective fighting force and they feared they would simply be executed.

By the time Dachau was evacuated ten days later, the Sippenhaft prisoners had been reunited. Together they watched column after column of prisoners marching out of the gates in their wooden clogs. Some were too weak to walk and collapsed onto their hands and knees. If they did not get up when the guards shouted at them, they were shot through the back of the neck. The prisoners were then herded onto buses and driven in convoy across the Alps into Italy. Their SS guards had orders to shoot them should there be any risk of their falling into Allied hands.

Eventually they arrived in the southern Tyrol, where a delicate ceasefire had been negotiated. Here some of the prisoners managed to make contact with a few senior Wehrmacht officers, who sent a company of soldiers to disarm their SS guards and claim responsibility for them. 'At times it was not quite clear who was planning to shoot whom,' one of the prisoners later wrote. 'Would the SS shoot the prisoners, would the soldiers shoot the SS, or would the Italian partisans, who were beginning to appear along the ridges and hillsides, shoot the whole lot of us?'[83] A week later the first American troops arrived, and the SS disappeared in the night.* 'Within a short time the entire place was crawling with jeeps and young American soldiers in their clean uniforms,' and the prisoners were handed over.[84] It was 4 May. Their liquidation, they discovered, had been set for 29 April, and the last, oddly shaped vehicle in their convoy had been a mobile gas chamber, able to poison passengers with the carbon monoxide from its own exhaust fumes.

The Americans had little idea who it was they had saved, but they understood they were VIP prisoners of the Nazis, and 'showered us with cigarettes and chocolates and . . . hundreds of tins of good American food', Fey wrote.[85] 'We couldn't quite join in the victorious mood of our foreign friends and the American soldiers,' Anna-Louise Hofacker, another of the group, later recalled. 'At the same time we were free, and on the side of the defeated.'[86] Driven first to Verona in the bright May sunshine, they were then flown to Naples before being transferred to the Hotel Paradiso in Capri. Here they were kept under guard for over a month while their stories were verified.

Walking round Capri together, Fey felt that she and Alexander at last found 'a kind of inner peace'.[87] Towards the end of their enforced stay, Alexander suggested they visit the small chapel. As he sat playing the organ, Fey found she could not stop her tears.

---

* Some of the SS guards were reportedly later ambushed by partisans, and hanged.

She knew that she would soon be rejoining her husband, and she still hoped to find her sons, but 'the thought of leaving Alex, who was in many ways so helpless and who had lost so much, made me immensely sad', she wrote.[88] Fey later confided to a close friend that theirs had been a 'love affair', and Alexander had hoped to marry her.[89] When he said farewell, he gave her a last poem: 'You are mine, I shout it to the winds,' he had written.[90]*

Alexander and Mika eventually arrived in Lautlingen the day after the Stauffenberg children returned, astounding everyone by pulling up in 'a great Mercedes car' loaned to them by the cardinal of Munich.[91] Mika and her children were overwhelmed to be together again, and Alexander was deeply moved to see all his nephews and nieces. With him he brought the shocking news of Melitta's death. The children now grieved for their 'shot-down aviator aunt', as well as for their fathers, uncles and great-uncle Nüx, all executed by the Nazis.[92] It was only when they were at their peaceful Lautlingen home again that the reality of what had happened sank in. Perhaps worst of all for Berthold, Heimeran, Franz Ludwig and Valerie, there was still no news of their mother.

Nina was alive, but since July she had been stranded in a small town in Bavaria, near the Czech border. It was another month before she managed to reach Lautlingen. She walked up to the house dressed entirely in black, still with her battered hatbox but now also carrying her young baby, Konstanze, in her arms. She 'still possessed much of her exotic charm', a cousin wrote, but not surprisingly after the shocking death of Claus, her long months of imprisonment and lonely childbirth, 'she looked worn and far older than her years'.[93] Karoline was astonished that the Gestapo had not murdered her son's wife. Nina's survival was due not only to her potential value as a prisoner, but also to Melitta's support, her own impressive resilience, and luck.

In early April a rather reluctant military policeman had been detailed to collect Nina and her baby from hospital and transfer

---

* Fey was eventually reunited with her Italian husband and sons, all of whom had survived the war. They settled together in Italy, where she later wrote her memoirs.

them to Schönberg, to join the other Sippenhaft prisoners. Because they were travelling together, people often mistook them for a married couple: a misapprehension that both guard and prisoner 'denied vociferously'.[94] Endlessly changing trains, Nina was appalled to see what had become of her country. Cars labelled 'Flying Court Martial' were parked at the stations. Dead bodies hung from trees in courtyards, with placards below labelling them as deserters.[95] Eventually she refused to go on. Writing her guard 'a testimonial to the effect that he had done his duty to the end', she found herself and her child willingly abandoned in a village near Hof.[96] Shortly afterwards the Americans arrived and, by chance, Nina had become the first of the prisoners to be officially liberated, if with no means of contacting her family. For a few weeks she stayed with friends, using Melitta's ration cards and regaining her strength while she nursed her baby. One evening a pair of drunken American soldiers forced their way into her building, threatening to shoot her. In the end one showed her photographs of his family, before they both fell asleep.

Only after Germany's official capitulation did Nina judge it safe to travel again. She went first to Buchenwald, searching for her four older children. American forces had liberated the camp on 11 April, following a revolt by prisoners who had stormed the watchtowers, seizing control earlier on the same day. Some 28,000 prisoners had already been forced to march further into Germany, a third of them dying from exhaustion or being shot arbitrarily en route. Yet over 21,000 people had still been incarcerated at the camp. 'Buchenwald was like a bled out wound,' Elisabeth zu Guttenberg wrote after also searching for the Sippenhaft prisoners there.[97] She and Nina had missed each other by a few hours, both learning only that their families had been moved before liberation, and that there were no records as to where.

Nina returned to Lautlingen with little hope, except to find a quiet sanctuary where she might care for Konstanze. Instead she was met by her three sons, Berthold, Heimeran and Franz Ludwig, and her young daughter Valerie. Karoline and Mika were also at the schloss, and Alexander had come and left again, searching for information about Melitta's last days. The terrible confirmation of her death hit Nina hard, but she had known the silence from her sister-in-law did not bode well. Melitta had always been in touch, brought material support, news and comfort, or sent food coupons. Her absence had been palpable. Yet 'feelings were a luxury that nearly no one allowed themselves . . .' Nina's last child, Konstanze, later wrote. 'It was more important to think about the necessities after the war.'[98] The courageous Nina mustered her strength and threw herself into the work of looking after five children, reclaiming her property, and securing an income in postwar Germany. For her, as for so many of the family survivors, the priority was her children, 'a new generation in whom lives the hope of the future'.[99]

Hanna was still in American custody when the surviving Stauffenbergs were reunited. She was now being detained in a series of prisons by the American Counter Intelligence Corps. Forgetting her acceptance of political arrests, imprisonments and executions under the Nazi regime, Hanna considered this move an outrage. Even her journey by jeep to the first prison, 'over atrocious roads', as she put it, fed her resentment.[100] As Eric Brown saw it, she had grown accustomed to large rooms and fine meals during her earlier 'soft-hearted' treatment by the US Air Force Intelligence Unit.[101] Internment, by contrast, was hard, and conditions basic.

Sitting on her straw mattress, Hanna felt the cold October air blow in through the barred window of her cell. 'The degradation of captivity', she felt, 'living between narrow walls through a monotony of days, gazing longingly to where, high above my head, a patch of blue sky could be glimpsed', was a feeling that Melitta might have recognized.[102] Whereas Melitta had learnt of the execution of her family while in detention, however, Hanna was tormented by the murder and suicide of hers. In a sense they were both victims of the same regime, but Hanna could still not accept the truth that would have put her on the wrong side of history. Instead she complained that her guards were unnecessarily antagonistic, and that the Americans had deliberately employed Jewish staff to make life more difficult for the Germans in their custody. Entirely self-centred, 'I tried to live on,' she wrote bitterly, 'enduring the vicissitudes of a High Criminal Person. My offence? I was a German, well-known as an air-woman and as one who cherished an ardent love of her country and had done her duty to the last.'[103]

In October, Hanna was transferred to the first of the two internment camps where she would spend the end of 1945 and most of the next year. Camp King near Oberursel, north-west of Frankfurt, for a while contained many of America's most important Nazi prisoners including Göring, Dönitz, Keitel and Kesselring. During the day prisoners could mix freely, and lectures, literary evenings and singing were organized, but it was cold, there was limited food and blankets, and Hanna could only see a process of 'torment and degradation'.[104] The only woman among the leaders awaiting trial, she was soon particularly close to Lutz Schwerin von Krosigk, the regime's former finance minister. Having enjoyed long conversations 'about everything', she told him she could 'feel your thoughts steadily in me, stronger than any words'.[105] When she learnt that her brother Kurt had survived the war, she proudly wrote to him that for many months she had been 'sitting behind barbed wire, surrounded by the most worthy German men, leaders in so many fields. The enemy have no idea what riches they are giving me.'[106] 'How are you bearing all those terrible things that have happened to our Fatherland, and us personally?' she went on to ask, before expressing her concern that the 'degrading and false reports' of the final days of the regime, stemming from her interrogation, might have caused him 'shame or anger' or tarnished the honour of their family.[107] 'We are delivered into the hands of the enemy', she wrote, and 'are at their mercy and at that of all their dirty methods'.[108]

Alexander spent the late summer and early autumn of 1945 trying to find Melitta's family. After the official surrender, Klara had cycled over a hundred miles to Würzburg, where she found the ruins of Alexander and Melitta's home. Neighbours told her that her sister had visited after the bombing, and gave her the address at Lautlingen. It was through mutual friends that she later received 'the unexpected and devastating news' of Melitta's death.[109] She soon had more dreadful news. Facing the Soviet advance towards Danzig, Melitta's elderly father, Michael Schiller, had decided, unlike Willy Reitsch, to stay in his home and confront the Soviet soldiers. He died some weeks later, in circumstances that have never become clear. His daughter Lili believed he met his end either in a shelter, or in the cellar of their old house, and was buried 'somewhere in the garden'.[110] Ill and exhausted, Melitta's mother Margarete had then headed west with thousands of other refugees, hoping to reach Lili at Neumünster. The last trace of her to reach her family was a letter entrusted to a fellow traveller: she must have died somewhere on the road.*

Having spoken with Klara, Alexander returned to Straubing, where Melitta had been shot down. He had no doubt that his wife had been flying towards Schönberg to find him, and he hoped to find anyone who had witnessed her last moments. American records were not available, and several witnesses thought the aggressor had been a German Messerschmitt Me 109. Rumours had also spread that, having survived the crash, Melitta had been denied life-saving medical treatment. As a result, many in the family held the Luftwaffe responsible for her death. Melitta's sister Jutta found it hard to accept that an American plane would have strayed so close to an aerodrome 'bristling with anti-aircraft armaments'.[111] 'The possibility cannot be excluded that German anti-aircraft weapons had fired under the mistaken belief that a supposed enemy of the people was involved,' she argued.[112] Others went further. Clemens's son believed Melitta was 'most likely' shot down 'by a German who knew who was in the plane'.[113] Nina agreed that, as 'there was no warning of enemy aircraft in the area', it was certainly possible that Melitta, 'who was an embarrassment, was shot down' deliberately.[114]

Other speculation had developed around Melitta's last intentions. The wounded serviceman who had witnessed her crash had heard that she 'was removing important files belonging to the

---

* Margarete Schiller's body was never found, and she was officially declared dead in 1962.

resistance movement'.[115] More likely, given that she was carrying her passport and a large sum of money, Jutta felt she was undertaking a 'bold rescue attempt . . . planned long ago', to bring Alexander and his family across the border into neutral Switzerland.[116]

Needing answers, Alexander sought out Bertha Sötz, the airbase secretary who had arranged Melitta's funeral. The Gestapo had ordered Melitta's personal possessions to be sent to their head office in Berlin. Instead Sötz had kept them, and she now handed Alexander Melitta's money, passport, Gestapo permits, photograph album and other effects. For a while he sat quietly holding Melitta's wedding ring; nothing could be more familiar and yet seem more out of place.

Alexander later wrote that he was forced to conclude Melitta was shot down by the Allies. 'She was trying to find me,' he added, 'and would have tried to escape with me to Switzerland.' Whether this had been Melitta's intention can never be known. What is clear is that it demanded enormous courage to fly a slow, unarmed Luftwaffe Bücker Bü 181 Bestmann on a private mercy mission above territory under regular attack in April 1945, and Melitta's sacrifice, as Karoline later wrote, was evidence of 'her deep commitment to the family'.[117]

After months of work, Alexander eventually arranged for Melitta's body to be exhumed for return to Lautlingen. He then formally identified her remains. Her face was largely unchanged and perfectly recognizable, the children later overheard him telling their mother, Nina. Melitta was not an incorruptible saint or martyr, but she had been buried quickly and her body preserved naturally in the very dry grave. Only her nose had disintegrated; her beautiful profile lost.

That autumn, Melitta's coffin was placed on a trailer hitched to a pre-war Hansa 1100 sedan car, owned by the son of the Lautlingen grocer, and driven back for reburial. On 8 September 1945, there was a small service at the local Catholic church, organized in sympathy although Melitta was a Protestant. Few people attended. In the autumn of 1945 there was still no postal service to send news, and travel permits were required even for short distances. As a

result it was only Alexander and his closest surviving family: Karoline, Alexandrine, Nina, Mika and the children, who witnessed the
mortal remains of Countess Melitta Schiller-Stauffenberg being
laid to rest in the family vault.

16

REPUTATIONS

Hanna was sitting on the edge of the sofa in her Wiesbaden apartment, bored and fidgety. Not long released from US custody, she was once again answering questions, this time for a German-born American army private charged with confirming the authenticity of Goebbels' diaries. For all her brilliance as a pilot, her latest interrogator decided Hanna was 'politically naive' and still 'fanatically devoted to Hitler'.[1] Her self-serving mantra about honour and duty, as she struggled to reconstruct her realities rather than reconcile herself to the truth of the Third Reich, echoed the moral illusions that had prospered within the system during the war. Noticing her fingers playing with a brass 'cartridge shell' as she wearily answered his questions, the soldier asked to take a look at it.[2] Unscrewing one end, he found a delicate glass capsule containing liquid cyanide, typical of the type carried by the senior Nazis at the end of the war. It was Hitler's gift to Hanna from the bunker. When asked what she needed the poison for, she answered evasively, shrugging, 'Just in case.'[3]

Hanna had been thirty-four when given her 'unconditional release' in July 1946.[4] She was kept under surveillance for several months. According to US intelligence reports, she had quickly found a room in the same building as her former secretary, Gretl Böss.[*] Böss was already on their radar, having once worked as private secretary for Gertrud Scholtz-Klink, the fanatical leader of the Nazi Women's League. It was Böss who had looked after Hanna's watch and cyanide capsule when she was interned, and had now restored them to her.

---

[*] Gretl is short for Margarethe, and Böss appears as Margarethe Böss in the American papers.

The Americans seemed unsure how to classify Hanna. In December 1945 they had recorded that she was 'not an ardent Nazi, nor even a Party member'.[5] Other memos listed her optimistically as a potential goodwill ambassador or even 'possible espionage worker'.[6] Hanna's celebrity, and close connections with former Luftwaffe staff and others once high up in Nazi circles, made her a potentially valuable asset 'with the power to influence thousands'.[7] But her stated desire to promote 'the truth' was never translated into action. Eventually they decided to keep her under surveillance in an intelligence operation code-named 'Skylark'. The hope was that she might inadvertently lead them to former members of the Luftwaffe still wanted for trial.

Hanna started receiving her 'highly nationalistic and idealistic' friends as soon as she was released.[8] To pre-empt criticism, she cast herself as a victim. She 'had a worse time [in US captivity] than the people in concentration camps!' the pilot Rudi Storck wrote in a letter that was intercepted.[9] Storck was arranging an event 'for friends' at which Hanna was to give a talk. A few months later, British intelligence reported that she was 'earning a number of free dinners and parties' through such speaking engagements. 'She is undoubtedly a very potent propaganda factor,' they continued, 'and is almost openly queuing up for *der Tag*.'[10]*

American intelligence then followed Hanna as she toured their zone of Germany and Austria, wrapped up in a fur coat behind the wheel of her sports model Fiat with red-upholstered seats. Aware that she was being watched, she told friends 'she was tired of everything and everybody; she just wanted to be left alone'.[11] When her little car needed repairs, however, she happily asked US intelligence to supply another. Keen to enable her movement, they did. In Salzburg Hanna had her hair permed, visited Greim's mother, and lit candles at his grave and those of her family. She also visited her old friend and early gliding instructor, Wolf Hirth.

'Everybody who was formerly prominent in the German air

---

* *Der Tag* is German for 'the day', the implication being that this was 'the day' when National Socialism would rise again.

force and . . . air industry has visited Hirth's place,' the Americans noted.[12] This included Hanna's old friends Elly Beinhorn and Hans-Ulrich Rudel, both now regarded as 'fanatical Nazis'.[13] Hirth later reported that Hanna felt 'all prominent persons in German aviation were honour-bound to assist her in creating a secret organization which for the time-being would have to be completely undercover'.[14] Her aim was to secure Germany's future air force, at a time when anything other than scheduled civil flights was forbidden and many of Germany's surviving pilots and air experts were leaving the country.

Rudel was among those hoping to emigrate.* Claiming to fear a communist Europe, he hoped 'to build a nucleus of the German air force' with friends in Franco's Spain.[15] Hanna's name was on his list. Intercepted letters included lines such as 'it would indeed be fortunate if somebody could take mail across the border. I expect you understand what I mean, dear Hanna.'[16] The Americans concluded that not only was she a member of a covert organization of former Luftwaffe personnel, but that she was 'acting possibly as an organizer or courier'.[17] Hanna may have been sympathetic to Rudel's aims, but her own belief was that mobilization should take place on German soil. She often stated that now was not the time to leave the country 'in the hands of the crippled, the sick, the uneducated, the inexperienced, to those without morals . . . nor to the Communists who will surely remain'.[18]

While Hanna had been interned, the Allies had been running various 'denazification' programmes. These included the investigation and prosecution of individuals, as well as public talks, radio broadcasts and screenings of documentaries about the concentration and extermination camps. Hanna had missed much of this but, having been a prominent figure in the Third Reich, she was given her own denazification hearing. 'As my profession as a pilot made me move more above the clouds than on the ground, I have never

---

* Rudel went to Argentina in 1948, from where he organized support for fugitive Nazi war criminals including the former SS 'doctor' from Auschwitz, Josef Mengele. He also worked as a regional military adviser and arms dealer, and supported the German far right until his death in 1982.

belonged to any organization or party . . .' she wrote in her own defence. 'I have simply been the German Hanna Reitsch.'[19] Yet it was undeniable that she had courted and enjoyed a close association with senior Nazi leaders during the war. Before her hearing, Father Friedel Volkmar, the Catholic priest at the Oberursel internment camp, organized testimonies in support of her good character. Another friend, the later author and journalist Horst von Salomon, wrote of her 'absolute integrity, her enthusiasm, extreme modesty, her absolute love for the truth', and insisted that Hanna 'is and was apolitical'. 'For her,' he continued, 'National Socialism was a powerful concept that was successful for Germany externally, and united the great majority of all Germans domestically. She didn't see any context.'[20] Such statements were commonly known as *Persilschein*, or whitewash certificates, and largely discounted. The testimony that carried most weight came from Joachim Küttner, the Jewish pilot Hanna had helped find work overseas in the late 1930s. She had clearly been aware of state anti-Semitism, but her response in his case meant her name was cleared.*

By the late 1940s German public interest in Nazi crimes was waning, as much of the civilian population tried to let the shock and horror of the recent past sink into oblivion. For many, the priorities were still securing sufficient food rations and safe shelter for themselves and their families. Hanna, whose well-being was secure, chose not to face the truth. Like Hitler's former Luftwaffe adjutant, Nicolaus von Below, who later proudly asserted that 'I am not a member of that choir which now condemns vociferously what they once so admired,' she considered it more honourable to stick to her beliefs than to re-evaluate them.[21] She also remained deeply suspicious of efforts to establish civil society and democracy within Germany. She soon found she was not alone. Friends sent hand-drawn cartoons of 'Infant Democracy' soiling his sheets, and of Hanna being roasted on a spit by two devils and a witch drawn

---

* Joachim Küttner had a brilliant career at NASA in the USA. He remained friends with Hanna and, in 1972, attended her sixtieth birthday party in Germany.

to represent Jews.[22] 'We will somehow pull through,' Elfriede Wagner wrote more discreetly. 'I have not lost my faith in the things that matter.'[23] While 'perhaps, after all, opportunity will come to us who are left behind with broken wings . . .' Greim's nephew told her. 'You know that we would give up anything for our great love. It was, it is, and it will be like that forever, as long as there are human beings who have the same ideals.'[24]

Soon Hanna was offering support to defendants at ongoing military tribunals. She felt, as many did, that the trials were driven by revenge. Under the stated motive of working 'against mutual hatred', she argued that 'if military leaders are made accountable . . . for the sake of justice and not out of hatred, revenge and feelings of superiority over the powerless, the military leaders of other nations must be held responsible too.'[25] Although she attended several of the trials, she was disappointed not to see her friend Lutz Schwerin von Krosigk. She later learned he had been sentenced to ten years' imprisonment. 'The suffering! The injustice!' Hanna wrote to Luise Jodl, whose husband, an injured survivor of Claus's assassination attempt, would be found guilty of crimes against humanity, and later executed. 'Your pain and my pain are the most holy thing left to us,' Hanna continued, adding that most of the defendants, 'especially the most worthy of them, carried their martyrdom with pride – most heroically'.[26]

Among those to whom Hanna lent her support was the commando officer Otto Skorzeny. Calling for him to be helped rather than condemned, Hanna wrote a 'solemn declaration' that Skorzeny had suffered when the honest principles of the SS had been turned into dishonest crimes by their leaders.[27] Skorzeny was acquitted. Hanna also spoke up for the popular Luftwaffe field marshal 'Smiling' Albert Kesselring, whom she praised for 'his chivalry, humanitarianism and fairness', despite a war crimes record which included the exploitation of Jewish slave labour and massacres in Italy committed by troops under his command.[28] Kesselring was sentenced to death, later commuted to life imprisonment. Hanna sent him a signed photograph of herself with a letter presenting her life as 'one long struggle for truth and honour, for understanding, reconciliation and peace', despite all the 'terrible things [happening in] our homeland'.[29]

In May 1948, Hanna was herself arrested while attempting to cross into Austria illegally. Despite her oft-repeated passion for honesty, she lied to the border officials and signed her statement under a false name. When later questioned, she said she had no choice, given the potential damage to her reputation. She was kept in a cell overnight, with a straw sack to sleep on and an open bucket to share with seven 'vicious' female prisoners. Three of the women were pregnant, 'whores all of them', Hanna decided.[30] To win some goodwill, she shared out her cigarettes and sandwiches. When they began to talk, she noted earnestly that 'each woman recognizes the spark of the Madonna that God laid in each female being'.[31]

The next day, Hanna admitted her identity to the local police chief, whose 'good, clear, earnest eyes', she wrote, reassured her that he had been sent by God to save her.[32] She claimed she had been trying to visit her family's graves, helped by a 'heaven-sent' young glider pilot.[33] Later she decided she could also speak honestly with a judge, despite the 'strong Jewish element' she noted in his features, 'because his eyes expressed goodness and purity'.[34] She was now not only anti-Semitic, but also delusional. She wept at being told she could not return to her cell to 'save' her fellow prisoners. Then, having been allowed to visit the graves, she came back with food, toiletries and fifteen of her mother's religious poems which she recited through her tears. Eventually she returned home, happy in the belief that she had accomplished much good work planned by God.

American intelligence suspected Hanna might have been helping former Luftwaffe personnel flee to Austria, and arranged a sting to see whether she would aid their agent, who posed as having escaped from internment. Although she agreed to see the man, questioned him closely, gave him food and 'began to weep for the hardships which the imaginary escapees had to endure', the operational report recorded, when pressed for further help, she regretfully replied that she 'had no means to do so'.[35] The Americans could only speculate that despite being 'very suspicious', the 'plainly nationalistic' Hanna would have given any assistance in her power.[36] Nonetheless, her record was technically clear.

While Hanna was being closely monitored by Allied intelligence services, once they had been cleared and released home, very little official interest was shown in the family of Hitler's most famous would-be assassin. Because their Bamberg home had been badly damaged during the war, Claus's widow, Nina, lived at the Lautlingen schloss for several years. It was here that she nursed her baby Konstanze, and sat with her mother-in-law and the older children, listening to the Nuremberg trials on the radio. Klara managed to visit her sister's grave at Lautlingen in the autumn of 1945. Her in-laws embraced her into the family. The children knew Klara as 'Tante Pims', remembering her as 'charming, lovely' and, as an engineer and nutritionalist, 'very, very clever'.[37] For the next couple of years, Lautlingen 'became my second home', Klara later wrote. 'In this way, Litta continued to give me much inner strength, even after her death.'[38*]

At the end of 1945 Nina was granted a small pension by the German administration in the French occupation zone. In this she was luckier than most of the widows of those involved in the assassination attempt. Germany's post-war bureaucrats had unearthed a law according to which civil servants were only entitled to a pension if they had not been found guilty of 'a capital offence, such as murder'.[39] The enthusiastic application of this law was no mistake. For many years, members of the resistance were widely considered to have betrayed their country, and their children were often labelled 'a poor traitor's child'.[40] As a result, many of the women whose husbands had bravely opposed the criminal regime were forced to challenge their automatic disqualification from the pension lists.

Soon after Melitta had been reburied, Alexander joined Rudolf Fahrner at his estate on the northern shore of Lake Constance,

---

* Every year, on 20 July, Claus, Berthold and Melitta are remembered with a small ceremony at Lautlingen.

where he and Melitta had married. Alexander would often return here over the next three years, walking, talking with friends and writing poetry, invariably with cigarette in hand, until he felt able to face the world again. His poem 'Litta', unpublished in his lifetime, opens with the beauty of reflection, but ends on a note of bittersweet grief. Although the war was over, these were possibly the darkest and most difficult years of his life. Devastated by the death of his wife and brothers, he also felt that his personal honour had been tarnished. Although Alexander had been the first to speak against the regime, his family had shielded him while they risked their own lives. 'Litta' not only celebrated those Alexander loved; it was also, he wrote, 'my ripe song of anguish'. The poem closed:

> *'On the Field of Honour', the message was announced,*
> *And with the pair of brothers gleams*
> *Before us your victorious face . . .* [41]

Alexander's thoughts might linger with the dead, but he still had many friends who had also suffered and who now stood by him. As Nina had hoped, he became baby Konstanze's godfather, but they met only at occasional family reunions. Konstanze would mainly remember how kind, and how tall, her godfather was. For a while he and Klara were close, sharing their grief. When Alexander gave her one of his books, inscribed, *From the depths of my heart, Alex*, Klara found he had slipped a copy of his poem, 'Litta', handwritten in blue-black ink, in between the pages.

Alexander also wrote long letters to Fey, now reunited with her husband and two young sons in Italy. These were 'at first rather sad', Fey felt, reflecting on the 'terrible personal losses he had suffered', and expressing nostalgia for the days they had spent together after liberation, before real life had started again.[42] Rumours still occasionally surfaced about their relationship, mostly among the surviving former Sippenhaft prisoners, but Alexander never spoke of it. He remained, 'in spite of what had happened to him, a true romantic', Fey concluded.[43] He was also a true survivor.

In 1948 Alexander became professor of ancient history at the

University of Munich, moving to the city that had once been the Nazi heartland. The following year he married again. Marlene Hoffmann was a widow with two children, who had been among the circle of friends living by Lake Constance since 1938. A talented silversmith, Marlene was also a poet and translator of European literature. She was, moreover, brave. When Fahrner was arrested in 1944, she had accepted responsibility for preserving the only known copy of Claus's so-called 'oath of conspirators', the highly incriminating typed statement of their vision for post-Nazi Germany. Safely hidden, the document survived the war. Alexander and Marlene married in July 1949, Alexander adopting her two daughters. Konstanze felt that 'it was hard for her to be the second wife, especially when Melitta was so loved by the whole family'.[44] But Marlene proved to be just what Alexander needed, and the new family flourished.

Hanna did not find such contentment. Since her release from detention, she had been fighting press stories about the closeness, even intimacy, of her relationship with Hitler, and the rumour that she had flown him to Argentina. All 'fairy tales', she insisted, arguing that such lazy journalism would not only destroy her own reputation, but 'drag the truth and honour of all of us through the dirt by labelling real, loyal and true Germans as individuals without character'.[45] Soon she was also contesting revelations made by British intelligence-officer-turned-historian Hugh Trevor-Roper, in his famous book *The Last Days of Hitler*. Although he had not interviewed Hanna, Trevor-Roper had read her interrogation reports, among other documents. Incensed that these papers had been made public, Hanna vociferously condemned the publication.* 'Throughout the book, like a red line, runs an eyewitness report by Hanna Reitsch,' she argued. 'I never said it. I never wrote it. I never signed it. It was something they invented. Hitler died with total dignity.'[46] A painful correspondence with Trevor-Roper led him

---

* Ironically, the Zionist paramilitary organization known as the Stern Gang was also incensed by Hugh Trevor-Roper's book, threatening to assassinate him for placing too much emphasis on Hitler's charisma and too little on the German people's willing consent.

to condemn her 'incorrigible love of rhetoric', and her to claim she felt persecuted.[47] Various people weighed in on both sides. Some pointed out that, unlike witness statements, interrogation reports are not usually signed. Others came to her defence. The well-known journalist Thilo Bode wrote a fifteen-page document entitled 'How History Can Become Falsified', describing Hanna as 'nearly fanatically truthful' and 'a great idealist'.[48]

Often Hanna was her own worst enemy. 'You ought to thank the Lord every day on your knees that the Germans did not shoot you,' she recorded telling the French resistance fighter Yvonne Pagniez, who had escaped from a concentration camp during the war.[49] Pagniez recorded the encounter very differently, surprised to find Hanna 'not the Walkyrie I had imagined, but a modest-looking, physically fragile woman, wiping away tears of confusion'.[50] She would later translate Hanna's memoirs into French. In 1955 Hanna published another version in English, without reference to Pagniez, and carefully avoiding any overt political commentary. Not only did she apparently see no reason to critically examine her role in the Third Reich, she avoided even considering that working under such a regime might entail moral dilemmas. 'I am longing to fly again . . .' she closed her book firmly. 'There can be no better instrument for peace and reconciliation than our beloved gliding. Flying – that is my life.'[51]

For most Germans, the late 1940s had been dominated by the Soviet Berlin blockade, American and British airlifts of supplies, and the future governance of their country. With the end of the blockade in 1949, two independent German states emerged: the democratic Federal Republic of Germany in the west, and the smaller Soviet-aligned German Democratic Republic in the east. Among the national surveys that followed in West Germany, one from 1951 found that only 5 per cent of respondents admitted any feeling of guilt concerning the Jews, and only one in three was positive about the assassination plot. Rather than further soul-searching, the public mood was for peace, rehabilitation and the advancement of West German national interests. This served Hanna well. 1951 was the year that she first flew in public again, competing in the relaunched gliding competitions at Wasserkuppe. Her hand was back on the control column and she sailed through the skies on shimmering wings. The following year the German Aero Club was reinstated with Wolf Hirth as its president. Hundreds of clubs sprang up across West Germany over the next few months and Hanna felt the future brighten.

The Gliding World Championships were held in Madrid in 1952. Hanna was the only woman to compete. She won a bronze for her country and, in a postscript to her memoirs, wrote how moved she was when a French Jew who had lost a leg and an arm during the war took her hand in Madrid, telling her she had won everyone's heart. But when the German press covered her victory, they had a different human-interest story: speculating whether Hanna had visited Otto Skorzeny, now living as an exile in Franco's Spanish capital. Although acquitted in 1947, Skorzeny had been kept at Darmstadt internment camp to go through what he called 'the denazification mill'.[52] Hanna had been the first person he visited while on parole. Skorzeny escaped the following summer, eventually arriving in Madrid where he founded a Spanish neo-Nazi group. He and Hanna were in touch, his letters sometimes delivered through sympathetic intermediaries.[*]

While Hanna was in Spain, the trial of the officers who had crushed the attempted Valkyrie coup found that the conspirators had acted 'for the greater good of Germany'.[53] Claus's formal death certificate was issued later that year. Nina and the children returned to their Bamberg home in 1953. Nina worked hard to rebuild the house, petition for the family's stolen valuables to be restored, and raise her children, sometimes still in the face of considerable hostility. At least in isolated Lautlingen, her eldest son Berthold realized, 'we were not constantly confronted with our status as outcasts'.[54] In Bamberg there were sideways looks and

---

[*] Otto Skorzeny never publicly denounced Nazism, although it is now believed he may have worked for Mossad after the war, perhaps for self-preservation. He died of cancer in Madrid in 1975, and was buried in a coffin draped in Nazi colours by former comrades who gave the Nazi salute.

unsigned letters, 'quite a number of them, quite nasty in tone'.[55] Then, in 1954, Theodor Heuss, the first president of the Federal Republic of Germany, gave an address at the first official memorial service for Claus, Berthold and their fellow conspirators, ten years after the attempted coup. Attitudes were slowly starting to shift.

The Gliding World Championships of 1954 were hosted by England. 'Adolf's Flying Femme Back', the British *Overseas Weekly* reported when Hanna's name was listed among the German team.[56] After some controversy, Heuss's government instructed Hanna be dropped. Outraged, she argued that she had only ever done her 'obvious duty for her country, like every Briton and every British woman also'.[57] Hanna's fury subsided when, aged forty-three, she became the German gliding champion. Over the next few years she set records at home and abroad. In 1958, however, the World Championships were hosted by Poland. Unhappy at the ceding of her Silesian homeland to Poland after the war, Hanna at first withdrew her name. When she changed her mind, to her astonishment the Poles refused her a visa. Poland had lost more than six million citizens during the war, the vast majority during the Nazi occupation. As an apparently unrepentant apologist for the Nazi regime, Hanna was not welcome. Incensed, she petitioned the new head of the Aero Club, Harald Quandt, to withdraw the whole German team. Quandt was the oldest child of Magda Goebbels, the son to whom her last letter had been addressed. But although he submitted a complaint, Quandt still fielded the rest of the team. Hanna severed all connections, effectively ending her gliding career in Germany.

Her friends quickly rallied round. Elly Beinhorn, who had also returned to competitive flying, often invited her over.* Even the famous Australian pilot, Nancy Bird, sympathized with what she saw as Hanna's 'victimisation and suffering'.[58] The Alte Adler, the German veteran pilots' association, publicly supported her, and the

---

* Beinhorn did not fly during the war. Later she won several international medals. She was often a guest of Melitta's former boss, Georg Pasewaldt, although he reportedly 'did not have any closer contact' with Hanna because of her politics. Beinhorn died aged one hundred in 2007. (Correspondence Barbara Pasewaldt/Mulley, 2014.)

far-right Brazil Sudeten Club made her an honorary life member, sending her 'patriotic greetings' from their 'group bound by their fate'.[59]* She was still receiving mountains of fan mail, and would be signing collectable postcards in a fading felt-tip for the rest of her life. 'You must not overrate me,' she replied to one admirer. 'My love for the Fatherland is something absolutely natural, and it is likewise natural to campaign for something you fervently love.'[60] To another she railed about 'the wall of lies and tales that have been created and that are weighing down the German people vis-à-vis the rest of the world'.[61] She was still berating the fact that 'the *Heimat* [homeland] is in a bad way, devoid of all honour', two years later. Those of us 'with the same convictions', she argued, must tell young people 'the truth and implant it in their hearts'.[62]

Many of the younger generation were already drawing their own conclusions about their nation's history and planning their contributions to a new future. Nina's eldest son, Berthold, elected to become a soldier in the West German Bundeswehr, joining up in 1955.† He knew he would spend his career in his father's shadow but believed 'that the burden would be worth it'.[63] Years of awkward questions followed, but Berthold learned to live with 'plenty of outspoken mess-room discussions' about his family name.[64]‡ He was deeply proud of his father, and never forgot his courageous aunt. 'Litta was everything,' he told *Der Spiegel*.[65] His younger brother, Franz Ludwig, who had once refused to answer to the wrong surname while detained at Bad Sachsa, developed an interest in the law. All the children, now young adults, would visit their Uncle Alexander at his Munich flat in the afternoons. 'In my eyes,' Konstanze felt, often noticing that her godfather's buttons were

---

* Founded in 1933, the original Sudeten Party had been one of the largest fascist membership organizations in Europe. After the war, many former members fled to South America where there was considerable sympathy for Nazi ideology.

† Nina died in 2006. Just before her death, she told Konstanze she was bored, then smoked a last cigarette.

‡ Generalmajor Berthold Schenk, Count von Stauffenberg, served most of his military career during the Cold War. He retired in 1994.

misaligned or his socks mismatched, 'he was a real professor, very intelligent but sometimes not from this world.'[66]

Wine and cigarettes aside, Alexander had always been more concerned with the cerebral than the material. In addition to translating Homer, Aeschylus and Pindar, in 1954 he published a short biography of Claus, praising his brother's 'high spirituality', impressive oratorial skills and exemplary determination to act.[67] At the same time, his academic work was becoming increasingly political. Assigned to committees to discuss the prospects for a reunified Germany, and West Germany's greater potential involvement in Europe, he became instrumental in helping to secure his country's membership of the European Economic Community in 1958.* Later that year he appealed for the creation of a nuclear-free zone and campaigned against nuclear rearmament.

Still unable to fly competitively in Germany, Hanna was delighted to receive an invitation to India in 1958. The country had resisted German approaches while under British rule, but an independent India was now accepting West German loans and investment. Several gliding clubs had been established by the 1950s and, when the gliders in New Delhi were accidentally damaged, West Germany saw an opportunity to forge stronger ties. In the spring of 1959, the government in Bonn sent over a state-of-the-art glider accompanied by Hanna to give aerobatic demonstrations. Originally invited for two weeks, she stayed for two months. She loved the warmth of her reception, gave frequent talks on the spiritual experience of silent flight, and developed proposals for glider training with the Indian air force. She was also thrilled with what she called 'the lively interest in Hitler and his achievements' that she claimed to receive 'all over India'.[68] The cherry on the cake came when the 'wise Indian Prime Minister', Jawaharlal Nehru, requested she take him soaring.[69] Hanna and Nehru stayed airborne for over two hours, Nehru at times taking the controls. It was a huge PR coup, widely reported across the Indian press. The next morning Hanna received an invitation to

---

* A precursor of the EU.

lunch with Nehru and his daughter, Indira Gandhi. Her last few days in the country would be spent as their guest.

When Hanna left India, the German Embassy triumphantly cabled Bonn that, 'since the end of the war, no other German public figure has met with a comparable reception'.[70] She stayed in touch with Nehru for several years, asking after his family, and expressing her concerns about the spread of communism. When she learned that President Heuss had also visited India, she wrote to him too, requesting a meeting to discuss the country and its problems. A polite but regretful reply came back; Hanna would never meet Heuss.

In 1961 Hanna returned to the USA at the suggestion of her old friend, the aerospace engineer Wernher von Braun, who was now working at NASA.* She often claimed to have refused post-war work with the American aeronautics programme on the basis that it would have been the ultimate betrayal of her country.† Braun felt differently, and occasionally tried to persuade Hanna to change her mind. 'We live in times of worldwide problems,' he had written to her in 1947. 'If one does not wish to remain on the outside, looking in, one has to take a stand – even if sentimental reasons may stand in the way of coming clean. Do give it some thought!'[71] Over a decade later Hanna visited Braun's rocket test sites in Alabama, witnessing the launch of a Saturn rocket, and giving a talk at the National Space Institute with both an ageing von Braun and a young Neil Armstrong in the audience.

While in the States, Hanna also took the opportunity to join glider pilots soaring over the Sierra Nevada, and to meet the 'Whirly Girls', an international association of female helicopter pilots. As the first woman to fly such a machine, she found she had the honour of being 'Whirly Girl Number One'. It was with the Whirly Girls that Hanna was invited to the White House, meeting

---

* Wernher von Braun became a naturalized citizen of the USA in 1955. He died of cancer in 1977, eight years after Neil Armstrong walked on the moon.

† There is no evidence that Hanna was offered such a role. Eric Brown felt it unlikely, as she was a test pilot rather than an engineer like Braun or General Dornberger, both of whom joined the American programme.

President Kennedy in the Oval Office. A group photo on the lawn shows her in an enveloping cream coat with matching hat and clutch, standing slightly in front of her taller peers. Her smile is once again dazzling; she felt validated. In interviews she revealed that Kennedy had told her she was a 'paradigm', and should 'never give up on bringing flying closer to people'.[72]

On her return to Germany, Hanna was presented with a new glider and largely accepted back into the flying community. But she was not on every invitation list. Eric Brown remembered her absence from the unveiling of a refurbished Me 163b Komet at the German Air Museum in Munich because, he later wrote, 'the notoriety of her Hitler's Bunker episode was an acute embarrassment to the Germans at a time when they were feeling their way back to political normality'.[73]

In 1962 Kwame Nkrumah, president of newly independent Ghana, invited Hanna to promote gliding in his country. Nehru himself had reportedly recommended her.* Despite her oft-repeated fear of the spread of communism, with little to keep her in Germany, Hanna accepted Nkrumah's invitation to help with the work she chose to see as nation-building. Petite and well dressed in cream twinsets and pearls, the 'Woman Who Dares the Heavens' was surprisingly 'feminine in every way', the Ghanaian press recorded.[74] She quickly formed a close bond with the handsome and dynamic Nkrumah, embassy staff noting that 'as a woman' she was above suspicion of harbouring political ambitions.[75] When Hanna enthusiastically promoted gliding as an ideal way to train character, Nkrumah commissioned her to establish a national gliding school as part of his programme to modernize the country.

Delighted by Hanna's reception, in 1963 the West German

---

* Ironically, Hanna had been recommended to Nkrumah by an Indian economist with the UN who had studied in Germany until 1938 when, as he put it, the 'change in the ideological climate' diminished the country's appeal. Perhaps there was an anti-British accent in the suggestion that it was Nehru who had recommended her, however; here two former British colonies were cooperating with a famous Nazi pilot. (*History Workshop Journal*, issue 64, Maya Jasanoff, 'Border-Crossing: My Imperial Routes', Autumn 2007, p. 375.)

government provided training support and the gift of a glider. When Hanna delivered the aircraft, she stayed on for four years, throwing herself into the development of the gliding school. Regularly up at four in the morning and 'bursting with energy in long white trousers', she oversaw the conversion of a colonial airfield and the erection of some hangars.[76] The first students were selected from the ranks of the Ghanaian Young Pioneers, a boys-only political youth movement. She had no interest in training girls who, she felt, had 'numerous other important tasks in order to prepare themselves for raising children'.[77] Her aim, she told a British film crew, banging her fist on the arm of her canvas director's chair, was 'to form the character of the youth . . . you see you can't be a pilot without being disciplined'.[78] Despite a tight budget, she won support for the increasingly controversial project by staging aerobatic shows, and was filmed chatting and laughing with Nkrumah as they hand-launched model gliders.

Hanna had again aligned herself with a leader increasingly seen as a dictator. Some Ghanaians felt she was politically innocent. 'Hanna lives truly in the heavens,' one author wrote to Nkrumah. 'Her total ignorance about her own country was clearly indicated when she was with us. They completely fooled her!'[79] For others, especially many American-Ghanaians, her Nazi past made her a controversial figure. Nkrumah was not concerned. That year he told the West German ambassador that he 'could not understand why the German people focused so strongly on [Hitler's] negative aspects without acknowledging his historical greatness'.[80] By 1965 the gliding school was showing results. Hanna saw her work as a kind of 'humane charity', she wrote, helping 'Africans develop' and learn to escape from poverty.[81] Ghana had become a public stage for her moral self-representation.

After Christmas in Germany that year, she returned to Ghana in early 1966. A few weeks later there was a military putsch. Nkrumah was stranded overseas. The gliding school was closed and Hanna was quickly deported. 'The most beautiful task of my life', she wrote, was suddenly at an end.[82] Back in Germany, she was shocked by reports of the putsch. 'Everything I read in western newspapers and magazines about the personality of Dr Nkrumah, his political philosophy, and his political goals, was so disconcertingly wrong, that for the sake of the truth,' she wrote, as emphatic as ever, 'I held it my duty to write down my experiences during those four years I was active for Ghana.'[83] Although Hanna stayed in touch with Nkrumah, exchanging roses as well as affectionate letters, they would never meet again.

In many ways Alexander had thrived during these years. Melitta was rarely mentioned at family events, the Second World War was not taught in schools or much discussed socially, and if asked about the assassination attempt he would say little but emphasize 'the humaneness and the tragedy of the act'.[84] Alexander preferred to focus on the present: his family; his poetry, academic work and several published books; and his voice in the shaping of his country. Photos show him looking suave and handsome in the early 1960s, dressed in a well-tailored suit, with a thin, dark tie and crisp pocket handkerchief, his gaze direct but a slight smile playing round the corners of his mouth. They also show that his hair had turned grey, white in parts. A few years later Alexander knew he was seriously ill. Eventually he had to give up lecturing, but he continued to receive students at his home. He died of lung cancer in Munich on 27 January 1964. He was fifty-eight. Reflecting his own path in life, he was not buried at Lautlingen with Melitta and the memorials to his brothers, but in Upper Bavaria where he had lived so happily with Marlene.* She had helped give him twenty more years, and he had used them well.

After his death, a collection of Alexander's prose and poetry about Melitta, Claus and Berthold was published under the title *Denkmal* (Monument). As well as the poem 'Litta', the volume included a poignant re-imagining of Claus and Berthold's last conversation on the night before the assassination attempt, and an epic poem, 'On the Eve', inspired by the conspirators' oath. Much of the epilogue was devoted to Melitta's fine mind, attitudes and power, as well as her 'courageous acts of loving support' when she

---

* Marlene died in 2001, and was buried next to Alexander.

repeatedly risked her life for her husband and his family. 'Heroes wasted, man's virtues and people's happiness diminished by too much talk,' Alexander had written in the foreword. 'And we stood there, powerless . . . in front of the graves of our proud youth.'[85] Later that year Germany honoured Claus, among other heroes of domestic resistance, on a set of postage stamps to mark the twentieth anniversary of the plot. Their faces and names would, for a while, be the currency by which all communications in Germany were sent, infiltrating silently into homes and offices. Whether Hanna ever received one on her considerable correspondence is not recorded.

Now in her fifties, Hanna found herself living alone in a small flat in Frankfurt decorated with photographs of the Alps, gliders, her family and Greim. Her association with another dictator had tarnished her reputation and, with the Social Democrats in power, there was little likelihood of further diplomatic missions. 'My life is very turbulent,' she wrote plaintively to a friend.[86] She channelled her energy into gliding regionally. Soaring over to Austria in 1970, she set a new women's Alpine record. Later that year she was presented with the International Gliding Commission's Diamond Badge, and attended the Wasserkuppe's Golden Jubilee celebrations, afterwards dining with the now famous Neil Armstrong, among other guests of honour.

Although still banned from flying motorized planes, the following year Hanna took part in the first world helicopter championships. She won the women's class, and came sixth overall. Eric Brown, now heading the British Helicopter Advisory Board, met her at the event. Believing that she was not mixing well 'because of her notoriety', he joined her for coffee and they talked about Udet and life before the war.[87] 'I was not sorry for her,' he said. 'I had a love/hate relationship with Hanna. I loved her courage, and hated her politics.'[88] They kept in touch over the next few years, at events and through the post. Hanna's typed letters were never 'chummy', and Eric's replies mostly dutiful. 'Hanna was always absolutely sure that she had done nothing wrong. She felt that any patriot would have done the same,' he explained. 'She saw herself as a female knight in shining armour, not a wicked witch.'[89] Later, seeing her wearing her Iron Cross with its central swastika symbol in public, Eric went further. Hanna had always argued 'that the real reason she was distrusted after the war was her deep, deep love of the Fatherland', he commented. 'It is arguable whether this was different to love for the Nazi vision.'[90]

In the 1970s, Hanna's aviation achievements were once again celebrated in the international press. At domestic events, one journalist recorded that 'dozens of surviving German air force pilots and present day German NATO pilots literally shook with excitement to see her'.[91] She tactfully did not attend the 1972 Munich Olympic Games, and does not seem to have commented on the murder of the eleven Israeli athletes. The highlight of that year for her was a return to America, where she was honoured in Arizona, and installed as the first female member of the prestigious international Society of Experimental Test Pilots. She could hardly have been happier, sitting in a hall of 2,000 people, discussing a possible new 'Hanna Reitsch Cup' with Baron Hilton. Back in Germany, she was now receiving hundreds of letters and parcels from schoolchildren as well as veterans, and even became an ambassador for the German section of Amnesty International. 'There are millions in Germany who love me,' she claimed, before adding, 'it is only the German press which has been told to hate me. It is propaganda helped by the government . . . They are afraid I might say something good about Adolf Hitler. But why not?'[92]

For her sixtieth birthday, the Alte Adler association threw her a dinner. Guests came from all over Germany, Europe and even the USA and Brazil. The 'sensation of the evening' was Hanna's spirited yodelling, the association's president later wrote.[93] 'It isn't easy to talk about our Hanna,' he had eulogized on the night. 'She embodies a woman who we, as humans, have to pay deference to, who always enchants with her charm and who earned the highest recognition and admiration for her achievements . . . especially attracting attention again and again with her constant helpfulness, loyal attitude and her love for the Fatherland.'[94] Yet his speech was tempered with regrets that while Germany's former enemies now

celebrated Hanna, she was yet to be honoured by the current
German government. 'She is a model of German honour, to our
country, and to our people . . .' he finished, 'out of her deep love
for her Fatherland.'[95]

Hanna was delighted with her reception, but her reputation
never felt secure. The following year, 1973, saw the premiere of a
British film, *Hitler's Last Ten Days*, based on the memoirs of those
stationed in the bunker, and starring Alec Guinness as the Führer.
Livid that she had not been consulted during the film's production,
and at the portrayal of her as an infatuated Nazi, Hanna began a
campaign of public complaint. When she was not taken seriously, she
extended her scope to criticize the ongoing imprisonment of Nazi
war criminals, and the collective guilt that she felt the world still
expected Germany to shoulder. Even thirty years on, Hanna refused
to accept the truth about the Nazi regime. Nor could she understand
why the country that she had refused to abandon after the war did
not officially regard, or even venerate, her as an honourable patriot.

It was at this moment that Hanna saw a notice in the papers,
asking for reminiscences of Melitta for a planned biography. She
was appalled. Melitta was her antithesis: a brilliant, part-Jewish,
female test pilot who had, in Hanna's eyes, betrayed her country,
while Hanna had held true. If Melitta was represented as a heroine,
Hanna could only wonder what this meant for her own reputation.
She immediately got in touch with the prospective biographer, and
then with Melitta's sisters, Jutta and Klara. Their correspondence
would last four years and was at times as heated as, and much more
direct than, any exchange between Hanna and Melitta in life.

Hanna first met Klara in 1975, when Klara invited both her
and her sister, Jutta, to lunch to discuss the draft manuscript.
Ostensibly writing to thank Klara for her hospitality, Hanna
focused most of her letter on destroying Jutta's character – the two
of them clearly hadn't seen eye to eye. Hanna was 'shocked' that
Jutta had shown no interest in her own memoirs, she wrote, 'but I
also felt pity because I felt that there was something ill and twisted
inside her. What could have possibly happened in her life to make
her like this?' With a 'mindset like this', Hanna continued, she

feared that any biography would 'do your sister more damage than good. This is exactly what I wanted to prevent, for the sake of authenticity and documentation.'[96]

Hanna then repeated the list of 'errors' she had found in the manuscript. Melitta 'had never been a test pilot of dive-bombers or any other kind of aircraft', she wrote, adding, 'there is nothing that highlights Melitta's achievements as especially remarkable'.[97] She also denied the validity of Melitta's Iron Cross, suggesting that she had manipulated her way into receiving an award she did not merit. 'I am convinced that Melitta did not resort to such an action just because of pure ambition, but because of despair caused by her racial burden,' Hanna continued, her insincerity almost audible. 'For Melitta's sake, I would not want these details to be made public.'[98]

Swinging chaotically between insults and wheedling praise, Hanna claimed she was relieved that no one had witnessed 'Jutta's reaction about the disagreements I had, and the explanations I offered'. 'I know you were just as sad as I was,' she continued, 'because in your wisdom, you know what the consequences will be if your sister won't change these parts'.[99] The rest of her long letter reiterated her concern that Jutta's reaction was 'alarming', that 'falsehood certainly does come to light sooner or later', and that Klara was risking 'embarrassing discoveries' should the book go ahead.[100] 'I am sure that you will understand me correctly. I want to protect you, and Melitta's memory . . .' she drew to a close. 'I can only pray that you will take this letter in the right way and be able to influence your sister successfully.'[101]

The biography was put on hold while the correspondence continued. When Klara defended Melitta, Hanna wrote to her, 'I knew and I suffered from the knowledge of how hard it would be for you to hear all these unpleasant things from me.'[102] When Klara stated the facts about Melitta's work, Hanna retorted, 'it seems embarrassing and like showing off when you include it in a biography'.[103] At different times she wrote that dive tests like those Melitta undertook were not risky, and also that she herself had performed similar tests 'for several years at the risk of my life'.[104]

She suggested that Melitta was untrustworthy and might have been at 'work for the enemy'.[105] Above all, she focused on what she called Melitta's 'inner despair about her racial burden'.[106] Hanna had more, but felt she could not write it down, so she gave Klara her phone number.

Klara's forbearance was remarkable. She thanked Hanna for explaining her doubts 'so candidly', expressed how devastating it was to see her sister 'presented in such a shadowy way', and assured her that she would not rest until everything had been cleared up. 'We will, of course, accept any true version of events, even if it should become apparent there have been actual mistakes. No one is infallible and she, thank God, was very human.'[107] But Klara also insisted that Hanna accept Melitta 'would have been incapable of promoting anything "against her better knowledge"'; Melitta was nothing if not honourable and Klara was determined to discover the facts.[108] 'I am happy about every step with you to discover the truth,' Hanna responded.[109] Eventually Klara put an end to their correspondence. She had found a number of people who supported her own picture of her sister. Sending the details to Hanna, she told her, 'With this, this unpleasant chapter is finally closed for my family and me. I assume that you too will be happy about this,' she could not resist adding, 'for the sake of finding the truth.'[110]*

The following year the BBC filmed a still effusive and engaging Hanna, dressed in a uniform-like skirt suit decorated with her flight badges, for a television series, *Secret War*. Before the interview began, the producer had to ask her to remove a decoration containing a swastika and, whenever the cameras weren't rolling, he was shocked at how pro-Nazi she was. 'She worshipped Hitler,' he later recalled. It was clear that 'she was very much in awe of him'.[111] Publicly, however, Hanna still argued that she was not political; that her only concerns were flight, truth and her personal honour.

---

* After a career as a nutritional scientist, Klara, the longest-surviving Schiller sibling, died in 1996. Jutta had worked as a journalist, and Otto had become a professor of agricultural policy and sociology at the universities of Hohenheim and, later, Heidelberg.

Melitta's family were more overtly politically engaged. In 1976 Franz Ludwig, now an attorney, was elected to the Bundestag, the German parliament, representing the democratic centre-right Christian Social Union. He would serve for almost ten years, as well as for six as a member of the European Parliament. Hanna, meanwhile, focused increasingly on gliding again. She set several more women's records in fibreglass 'racehorses', as she called the modern gliders, over the next few years.[112] When in 1978, aged sixty-six, she set an Alpine time and distance record: 'ten hours' hard fighting, but a most wonderful experience', the new president of the German Aero Club wrote to congratulate her.[113] Their twenty-year feud was over, but Hanna was already courting new controversy.

As well as aligning herself with the establishment whenever she could, Hanna maintained her links with the far right. Her correspondents now included Edda Göring, the only child of the Luftwaffe chief Hanna had so despised, and Fritz Stüber, editor of the anti-Semitic, extreme-right periodical *Eckarbote*, which aimed, Hanna understood, to preserve 'the indestructible German soul'.[114] She also had a long exchange with Eleanore Baur: the only woman to have participated in the Beer Hall Putsch in 1923, and an unrepentant Nazi who had been sentenced to ten years for war crimes. 'The Führer, our Hitler, would have been delighted to know we two are writing to each other,' Baur told Hanna. 'I believe he is watching us from above.'[115] Later she sent a photograph of herself with Hitler, revealed her delight at finding they shared 'all the same friends', and waxed lyrical about Hanna's memoirs, which she hoped to help promote 'as a thank you to you, and for the truth, and for the spirit of Germany'.[116]

Hanna was also in touch with another, unrelated Baur: Hitler's former personal pilot, Hans Baur, who at almost eighty was another unapologetic racist and unreconstructed Nazi. 'Apart from those people who admire us for our successes as pilots, much of the rest of the world is against us,' he cautioned Hanna. 'We have to be careful about what we say, and how we say it.'[117] In 1978 he and Hanna joined a public event to honour the life of the first pilot to cross the Atlantic from Europe to America, in 1928. A devout

Catholic, Hermann Köhl had taken a stand against the Nazis in the 1930s, only to be banned from public speaking, lose his job, and die in Munich four years later. The German press did not respond well to Hanna and Baur's presence, and the resulting articles rekindled Hanna's feelings of persecution and victimhood. In an attempt to cheer her, Baur praised her 'attitude and loyalty towards our Fatherland and Führer', and spoke warmly of the 'brave old Germans', 'real Germans', now living in South America, who saw her as 'a model of perfection'.[118] Hanna responded that while she appreciated his support, 'for the sake of truth and duty' she needed to set the historical record straight, 'from a German perspective'.[119]

Nine years younger than Melitta, Hanna had scarcely known any Germany other than the Third Reich, and having aligned herself with the new regime she had continued to create her own exculpatory narrative regarding her actions as the war progressed. As the extent of the Nazi programme of genocide was exposed after the war, many Germans had distanced themselves from their previous support for the regime. Far from softening over time, however, Hanna was becoming increasingly belligerent. Refusing to concede any error of judgement or show any remorse, instead she grew ever more critical of post-war West Germany. In letters to a British friend, Hanna bemoaned the number of 'foreigners' among Frankfurt's schoolchildren, and hearing more 'Turkish, Yugoslavian, Italian and Greek' than German spoken on the streets.[120] Her friend sympathized, inspiring Hanna to go further. 'The Jew is with my country,' she replied. 'The most horrible lies the history had ever produced with "Holocaust" is spreading around the world with the purpose to hate Germany. The Jews have the most rare brains to invent hatress, hatress, hatress [*sic*] instead of peace. A Jewish movie-"industry" in USA . . . invented this to save themselves. They are earning millions and millions of Dollars and the Germans are so characterless and stupid as no nation of the world is – and believe this.'[121*] Her anti-Semitic rant

---

* Hanna's English was not perfect, but her meaning is clear.

not yet over, Hanna now clung desperately to the work of Holocaust deniers to validate her decades-long refusal even to consider the truth. 'Historians from UK, from France, from USA are giving all kinds of proofs, that this all, are the most perfidy of lies the world has ever experienced!!!' she shouted onto the page, ignoring the fact she had seen photographs of the Majdanek camp during the war, and had heard Eric Brown describe his own experience of the liberation of Bergen-Belsen. As Hanna refused to accept the facts, denial became a part of who she was, and her need to shift all blame became visceral. 'These is cowardness making money in producing hatress! That is their "purpose of life",' she continued. 'Oh I am deeply unhappy and ashamed that my nation and also many of my German pilot-comrades are only "opportunists" joining those "devils".'[122]

Later that year the American photojournalist Ron Laytner conducted what became an infamous interview with Hanna. Laytner reported her bitter disappointment in West Germany, 'a land of bankers and car-makers'. 'Even our great army has gone soft. Soldiers wear beards and question orders,' she told him. 'I am not ashamed to say I believe in National Socialism. I still wear the Iron Cross with diamonds Hitler gave me. But today in all Germany you can't find a single person who voted Adolf Hitler into power . . .' Hanna's most unguarded comment, however, came at the end of the interview. 'Many Germans feel guilty about the war,' she concluded. 'But they don't explain the real guilt we share – that we lost.'[123]

Towards the end of 1978, Hanna agreed to give a lecture at an event organized by the Stahlhelm Youth, a fascist movement inspired by the Hitler Youth.* The talk was scheduled for 8 November. Given the furore over the commemorative event for the pilot Hermann Köhl, she cannot have been unaware that this date was the fortieth anniversary of Kristallnacht. More than insensitive, the planning of the Stahlhelm Youth event was deeply

---

* The original *Stahlhelm* [Steel Helmet] was founded as a paramilitary force in 1918. Subordinated to the SA, it was dissolved in 1945.

provocative. The mayor of Bremen's condemnation eventually prompted her to pull out. Yet when a Bremen Christian congregation questioned some of her words about the gas chambers, she once again threw herself into a letter campaign, accusing them of slander. Telling Hans Baur about this 'defamation' of her character, she wrote, 'What we think about these horrific exaggerations [about the gas chambers] remains in our hearts. As yet, we cannot determine where the truth begins – and where the lies end. I am passionately trying to find the truth – and I am fighting wherever I am able.'[124] Hanna demanded a public apology, refusing to let the matter drop, on the grounds of honour. Honour was the badge that she had proudly pinned to her chest when no longer allowed to wear her Iron Cross in public. In the decades since the war, she clung to it with increasing desperation.*

The strain of public controversy eventually began to take its toll on Hanna. She was still conducting her letter campaigns and giving talks all over the country into the summer of 1979. That August she told friends that she was having chest pains. When Joachim Küttner telephoned to see if she would like to meet at the airport, their regular rendezvous, she asked him to visit her at home instead, adding, 'I really have a problem, I need you, I need your help.' Unable to rearrange his plans, Küttner told her he would come another time. The following morning, 24 August 1979, Hanna died at her home. She was sixty-seven years old.

No post-mortem report is available, but the cause of death was given as a heart attack. In accordance with Hanna's wishes, her surviving family announced her death only after a private burial. She was interred with her parents, sister, nephew and nieces, in the municipal cemetery in Salzburg. A large boulder engraved with all the family's names marks the plot. Alongside is a tribute from the Alte Adler association, in the form of an eagle in flight surrounded

---

* Hitler had coined the phrase *Meine Ehre heisst Treue* ('My Honour is Loyalty') in 1931. Himmler then used a modified version of the phrase as the official motto of the SS, engraved into their knives and belt buckles. Hanna had clearly taken to heart the message that only blind obedience was honourable.

by a laurel wreath; a design very similar to the Nazi pilot's badge but without the swastika carried in the eagle's talons.

In the months that followed, speculation grew as to whether Hanna had finally kept her promise to Greim twenty-four years after his suicide, and stood by her concept of an honourable death by biting on her glass phial of cyanide. The capsule was not listed among her final possessions but neither, despite Hanna's love of getting the last word, was there any record of a note. Perhaps her contempt for the last letters of Eva Braun, and of Joseph and Magda Goebbels, had saved her from this last temptation. Or Hanna's brisk dispatch of Braun's last note might have given licence, to those who found her, to discreetly remove her own. Or perhaps there was neither note, nor suicide.

There was at least one last letter, however: a brief page Hanna sent to Eric Brown a few weeks before she died. In it she mentioned that she had been suffering from ill health, and that she felt angry and depressed because 'nobody', Eric included despite their 'common bond in our love for flying and danger', seemed to understand her 'passionate love of the Fatherland'.[125] To Eric, the letter implied 'that she'd come to the end of her tether'.[126] Hanna's intriguing last words before signing off were, 'It began in the bunker, and there it shall end.'[127] After hearing the news of her death, he had no doubt that Hanna had finally taken her life with the cyanide Hitler had given her in the bunker. He sent the letter to Hanna's brother Kurt, whom he knew through a post-war secondment to the German naval air arm. Kurt, who died not long afterwards, never acknowledged it. 'To the bitter end Hanna Reitsch managed to surround herself with controversy,' Eric later wrote.[128]

There is no evidence that Hanna finally took her own life rather than simply suffering a fatal heart attack. Whatever promise she had once made to Greim, she had decided, decades earlier, not to take her cyanide.* Hanna had never lacked physical courage. She

---

* Hanna's British pilot friend, Barry Radley, later claimed: 'She did intend to marry, but he was killed during the war.' Greim was already married, but her relationship

had accepted the likelihood of dying when she volunteered as both a test pilot and a suicide bomber, and had told her brother that 'one's own death has little importance'.[129] She did not change her mind from fear; she chose to live to defend her 'honour', along with that, as she saw it, of the Nazi regime. But Hanna had no moral insight. She never expressed remorse about her association with the Nazi leadership, and refused to accept any alternative world view. It was not that she was incapable of telling the truth; rather, she was a fanatic, and could not see any truth other than her own. Any romantic thoughts she might once have nurtured about eventually taking her own life may ultimately have proved as whimsical as her plans to work for historic truth, honour and reconciliation.

Melitta had died in action, knowing that Hitler's Reich had been defeated, and that she had done everything possible to defend her colleagues and her family. She had longed for freedom all her life, and was killed in the pursuit of that dream. That her bravery was little known or acknowledged would not have concerned a woman who had always sought to avoid publicity. Hanna had lived on long after the deaths of most of her family and close colleagues. She slowly realized that, however much she hid her political convictions in public, neither her aspirations for a renewal of Nazi government, nor her hopes to have her name entirely cleared, would come about. Her fate was not to be killed in the war, but to live and see her Nazi beliefs utterly refuted. Ironically, for a woman who had spent her life searching for the fabulous, and whose courage in pursuit of her dreams was beyond any doubt, Hanna died in her own bed, in many ways a coward, defeated by the truth.

---

with him was probably the deepest of her life. (Ian Sayer Archive, anon. newspaper, Barry Radley letter, 27.11.1979.)

EPILOGUE: A TIME OF CONTRADICTIONS

A dictatorship is a time of opportunism, of not wanting to know, of looking away. By contrast, it is also a time of resolute action and of making fresh and careful judgements every day about good and evil for those who – in whatever way – find themselves at loggerheads with the government . . .

DOROTHEE VON MEDING, 1992[1]

Hanna Reitsch and Melitta von Stauffenberg were both born before the First World War, in neighbouring regions of Germany. Both became brilliant and courageous pilots, motivated by a love of flight and personal freedom, and a belief in the importance of patriotism, honour and duty. The women's responses to flight neatly reflected their approaches to life. Learning to glide over the same green slopes, they were intoxicated by their ability to sail through what Melitta called 'the borderless sea of the air'. Hanna more covetously referred to 'new and fabulous realms'.[2] Later, while Melitta dedicated herself to learning how to direct and control her aircraft, Hanna decided that 'gliding is the best thing in the world because . . . [one is] carried along by a force of nature'.[3]

Neither woman was as comfortable on the ground. Melitta was anchored both by her conservative Junker values, and by the unexpected discovery of her Jewish ancestry. Although determined to lead an active and 'heroic life', she never questioned the importance of tradition and security.[4] Hanna, conversely, nine years younger, was keen to embrace the winds of change and seize the opportunities brought by the Nazi leadership. 'Just like an alcoholic, everything that justified flying was convenient for her,'

Melitta's nephew, Berthold von Stauffenberg, has said of Hanna. 'Flying justified her attitudes and morals.'[5]

Their gender has meant that Hanna and Melitta were, and are still, seen through a specific lens. If this means that Hanna has perhaps attracted more criticism than that attached to her male colleagues, then she has also, elsewhere, received greater support in deference to her presumed innocence. 'Aryan' girls were educated to believe in patriotism, honour and racial discrimination, and to be devoted uncritically to their country and their Führer. Women in Nazi Germany lived in a man's world. They were encouraged to be domestic rather than political, and assigned duties without rights. It is because Hanna and Melitta were not men, and so neither welcomed into aviation nor later conscripted into national service, that their actions undoubtedly involved a degree of choice. It was their strength of character and determination, as well as their differing values, interests and decisions, that would place them on opposite sides of history.

Melitta's deep patriotism was shaped by her experience of the Great War and the terrible peace that followed. She believed in dutifully serving her country through courage, determination and hard work. Although addicted to the thrill of flight, she saw herself not as an agent of change but as an exception to the gender rule: an honorary man at work, a pilot in the sky, and a supportive wife at home. 'The values characteristic of all womankind have not been altered, for us flying has never been a matter of causing a sensation, or even of emancipation,' she argued. 'We women pilots are not suffragettes.'[6] Like her aristocratic husband, Melitta believed in a certain social order. She might have 'admittedly unusual' career ambitions, but she could no more support Hitler's Nazism than she would have backed anarchy or communism.[7]

Her pre-war discovery that her family was considered part-Jewish and were thus unwelcome subjects rather than equal citizens of Germany, confirmed Melitta's early antipathy to the regime. Instead of speaking out against the government's dismantling of democracy, growing anti-Semitism and persecution of ideological enemies, as the state threat increased she chose to quietly focus on trying to protect her family.

Melitta was deeply conflicted when war came. She was privately opposed to the regime, but a nation is not indistinguishable from its government. For her, patriotism meant loyalty to a Germany that was older and greater than the Third Reich. She felt a duty to serve her country, and saw an opportunity to prove both her loyalty and her value. Later she also hoped to help protect German pilots under attack, and citizens suffering under Allied bombardments. 'War in our time has long outgrown the historical, initially incomprehensible, seeming futility of its origins, and outgrown the question of guilt or cause . . .' she argued. 'Imperceptibly it has received its terrible objective meaning, which we do not give it, but which towers threateningly before us.'[8]

By the spring of 1944, Melitta found herself heading up technical research for the Nazi Air War Academy, an extraordinary position for a woman in the Third Reich. Her association with Claus von Stauffenberg, however, also gave her an opportunity to support the assassination of Hitler. Many of the leading conspirators played similarly ambiguous roles. Most were not primarily motivated by ending the atrocities perpetrated against Jewish and other minorities, although this was a factor, but by what they considered the betrayal of the German people and their armed forces through the continuation of an unwinnable war. As Claus expressed it, they were planning 'treason against the government. But what [the government is] doing is treason against the country.'[9] When the plot failed, Melitta's only aim became to protect Alexander and the wider Stauffenberg family in defiance of Hitler's extermination orders.

Hanna was Melitta's antithesis, engaged not by conservative tradition but by the revolutionary dynamism of the Third Reich. Thrilled by Hitler's strong leadership, the way he championed patriotism, apparently legitimized prejudice, and promised a route out of the post-war recession with a great national revival, Hanna saw opportunity where Melitta saw adversity. She was pleased to lend her face, name and skills to the Nazi regime and its propaganda machine, and profit from her collusion. Ignoring the questions and rumours surrounding the deportation of Germany's Jewish community, she accepted Himmler's blithe reassurances when a friend showed her evidence of the atrocities at Majdanek concentration and extermination camp. She did not want to know the awful truth and chose to look away. During the final stages of the war, Hanna even proposed and developed military strategy.

Unlike those sometimes considered 'bystanders', caught up in the rapid rise of National Socialism by their own inertia, as a woman in the masculine field of aviation in the Third Reich Hanna's fight for promotion and active service was far from passive, banal or unconsidered. Later she was felt by some to be a role model for 'the emancipation of women'.[10] At best, it might be argued that ideologically Hanna was blindly self-centred; at worst, as Eric Brown believed, she was 'a fanatical Nazi'.[11] Whatever her precise degree of complicity, her importance to the Nazi regime was incontrovertible. Had Hitler won the war, there is little doubt that she would have been lauded as a heroine. As Robert Harris has imagined it in *Fatherland*, his novel set in a world in which Nazi Germany won the war, 'At the Flughafen Hermann Göring, the statue of Hanna Reitsch was steadily oxidizing in the rain. She stared across the concourse outside the departure terminal with rust-pitted eyes.'[12]

Yet Hanna was never a member of the Nazi Party. After the war she claimed she had never been political, but was an idealist and patriot whose natural sphere was 'more above the clouds than on the ground'.[13] 'I have simply been the German Hanna Reitsch,' she asserted during her denazification process.[14] Her actions spoke more loudly than her words. Having internalized the rhetoric of the regime, Hanna used the language of honour, truth and duty as an unassailable defence against questioning the moral integrity of her own loyalties. Honour and truth are admirable when harnessed to the real world but, once detached as lofty ideals, they become conveniently pliable concepts for zealots. Hanna wrote several versions of her memoirs, but never critically re-examined her association with the Nazis or denounced their criminal policies. It takes great courage to face the past and express regret. Hanna found it easier never to do so, never to admit to any knowledge, nor accept the truth. While portraying herself as a victim, she denied the Holocaust until her death over thirty years later.

The Second World War, as Melitta's nephew Berthold von Stauffenberg has said, 'was a time of contradictions . . . not every Party member was a Nazi, and not every non-Party member wasn't'.[15*] Few of Melitta's colleagues could believe that this upright woman, a staunch conservative and patriot, risking her life every day in the service of her country, could have known about her brother-in-law's plot to assassinate Hitler. Conversely, Hanna was believed by many to have begged Hitler to let her fly him out of the bunker to safety. Even years later, rumours persisted that she had succeeded.

Although their very different choices took both women right to the heart of the Third Reich, neither Melitta nor Hanna directly perpetrated, or prevented, war crimes. Somewhere between complicit and culpable, they lived, served, compromised, resisted and defied, supported and enabled, suffered or celebrated under the perverting conditions of a terrifying dictatorship and a country at war. Hanna was blindly loyal, and opportunistic. Later she shielded herself with her bespoke sense of honour. Melitta resisted as best she could, while continuing to serve the war effort. Perhaps she subscribed to Claus's belief that 'he who has the courage to do something must do so in the knowledge that he will go down in history as a traitor. But if he does not do it, he will be a traitor to his own conscience.'[16] Whatever they told themselves, their decisions were not without political consequence.

Actively or passively, through belief, fear or ignorance, the majority of the German people consented to the Nazi project. Ultimately, however, the dramatic lives of Melitta von Stauffenberg

---

* Eva Braun never joined the Party. Nor did Himmler's personal adjutant, Waffen SS field officer Joachim Peiper, despite being a committed Nazi, as he was waiting for a low membership number to come up. Oskar Schindler, however, was a card-carrying Party member. Hanna's lack of Nazi Party membership therefore does not necessarily comment on her political or ethical standpoint.

and Hanna Reitsch show both that German civil society was still multifaceted even after the political purges, racial cleansing and imposition of terror and propaganda under Hitler, and also that some choices were still possible. While many people strove to live with honour, interpretations of what this meant varied greatly. Duty, loyalty and self-sacrifice all held ambiguous meaning. Truth was often appallingly, and sometimes willingly, denied. War brought out the worst in many, but in some it also brought out the best. It was not war, however, but the regime and its ideology that led to the worst crimes being committed. What these women's stories illustrate with absolute clarity is the criminal absurdity of a regime based on the biological premise that women had purely domestic value, and that Jews had no value at all, which then bestowed its highest honours on two women, one 'Aryan', the other a Jewish *Mischling*, for their skills and achievements in defiance of such 'natural' laws.

Notes

Epigraph

1 Heinrich Hoffmann, *Hitler Was My Friend: The Memoirs of Hitler's Photographer* (Frontline, 2011), pp. 194–5.

Preface: Truth and Lives

1 Hanna Reitsch in *Die Welt*, 'Wie klein Mäxchen such den Untergang des Dritten Reiches vorstellt' [How the Little Maxes Imagine the Downfall of the Third Reich] (02.08.1973).
2 Quoted in Konstanze von Schulthess, *Nina Schenk Gräfin von Stauffenberg: Ein Porträt* [A Portrait] (Piper, 2009), p. 208.
3 Cornell University Law Library: Donovan Nuremberg Trials Collection, Robert E. Work, Hanna Reitsch interrogation report, 'The Last Days in Hitler's Air Raid Shelter' (08.10.1945).
4 Gerhard Bracke archive, letter Klara Schiller to Hanna Reitsch (27.06.1977).
5 Deutsches Museum archive, 101B, anon., 'Conversation with Hanna Reitsch' (nd).
6 Hanna Reitsch, *The Sky My Kingdom: Memoirs of the Famous German World War II Test Pilot* (Greenhill, 2009), p. 261.
7 Eric Brown, Mulley interview (March 2013).
8 Gerhard Bracke archive, letter Hanna Reitsch to Klara Schiller (07.02.1975).
9 Ibid. (07.02.1975, 18.02.1975).
10 Ibid. (18.02.1975).
11 Ibid. (07.02.1975).

1: Longing for Freedom

1 Elisabeth zu Guttenberg, Sheridan Spearman, *Holding the Stirrup* (Duell, Sloan and Pearce/Little, Brown, 1953), p. 212.
2 Archive Reinhart Rudershausen, Melitta Schiller (von Stauffenberg),

'Vortag gehalten in Stockholm am 6.12.43: Eine Frau in der Flugerprobung' [A Woman in Test Flying], Stockholm lecture (06.12.43).

3 Otto Dietrich, *Mit Hitler an die Macht: Personliche Erlebnisse mit meinem Führer* [With Hitler to Power: Personal Experiences with My Leader] (F. Eher nachf, g.m.b.h., 1934), p. 83.

4 Richard J. Evans, 'The Life and Death of a Capital', review of Thomas Friedrich's *Hitler's Berlin*, in *New Republic* (27.09.2012); http://www. newrepublic.com/book/review/abused-city-hitlers-berlin-thomas-friedrich

5 Archive Reinhart Rudershausen, Melitta Schiller (von Stauffenberg), 'Vortag gehalten in Stockholm am 6.12.43: Eine Frau in der Flugerprobung' [A Woman in Test Flying], Stockholm lecture (06.12.43).

6 Archive Reinhart Rudershausen, Gertrud von Kunowski, portrait of Margarete Schiller née Eberstein (1906).

7 Archive Reinhart Rudershausen, Jutta Rudershausen, 'Frau über den Wolken: Ein Leben für Wissenschaft und Fliegen' [Woman Above the Clouds: A Life for Science and Flying] (unpublished manuscript, nd).

8 Archive Reinhart Rudershausen, Melitta Schiller (von Stauffenberg), 'Vortag gehalten in Stockholm am 6.12.43: Eine Frau in der Flugerprobung' [A Woman in Test Flying], Stockholm lecture (06.12.43).

9 Ibid.

10 Peter Fritzsche, *A Nation of Flyers: German Aviation and the Popular Imagination* (Harvard University Press, 1992), p. 63.

11 Archive Reinhart Rudershausen, Lieselotte Hansen, 'Memories of Lieselotte Hansen, née Lachman' (unpublished manuscript, nd).

12 Archive Reinhart Rudershausen, Jutta Rudershausen, 'Frau über den Wolken: Ein Leben für Wissenschaft und Fliegen' [Woman Above the Clouds: A Life for Science and Flying] (unpublished manuscript, nd), p. 26.

13 Marie-Luise Schiller, diary 1918, quoted in Thomas Medicus, *Melitta von Stauffenberg: Ein Deutsches Leben* [A German Life] (Rowolt, 2012), p. 35.

14 Ibid. p. 36.

15 Archive Reinhart Rudershausen, Lieselotte Hansen, 'Memories of Lieselotte Hansen, née Lachman' (unpublished manuscript, nd).

16 Ibid.

17 Ibid.

18 Ibid.

19 Ibid.

20 Ibid.

21 Ibid.

22 Ibid.

23 Technical University Munich archive, Melitta Schiller entrance records (1922).

24 Archive Reinhart Rudershausen, Lieselotte Hansen, 'Memories of Lieselotte Hansen, née Lachman' (unpublished manuscript, nd).

25 Archive Reinhart Rudershausen, Melitta Schiller (von Stauffenberg), 'Vortag gehalten in Stockholm am 6.12.43: Eine Frau in der Flugerprobung' [A Woman in Test Flying], Stockholm lecture (06.12.43).

26 Ibid.

27 Archive Reinhart Rudershausen, Jutta Rudershausen, 'Frau über den Wolken: Ein Leben für Wissenschaft und Fliegen' [Woman Above the Clouds: A Life for Science and Flying] (unpublished manuscript, nd), p. 37.

28 Gerhard Bracke archive, Klara Schiller, Gerhard Bracke interview, 'Erinnerungen' (09.10.1982).

29 Archive Reinhart Rudershausen, Marie-Luise (Lili) Lübbert, 'Zweig Otto Eberstein' [Otto Eberstein family branch].

30 Archive Reinhart Rudershausen, Hermann Blenk, 'Erinnerungen an Melitta Schiller' [Memories of Melitta Schiller] (13.09.1974); and Archive Reinhart Rudershausen, Georg Wollé, 'Memories of a Colleague of Melitta Schiller in the Versuchsanstalt für Luftfahrt [Institute of Aviation] (DVL)' (11.02.1974).

31 Archive Reinhart Rudershausen, Jutta Rudershausen, 'Frau über den Wolken: Ein Leben für Wissenschaft und Fliegen' [Woman Above the Clouds: A Life for Science and Flying] (unpublished manuscript, nd), p. 33.

32 Ibid. p. 38.

33 Archive Reinhart Rudershausen, Paul von Handel, 'Erinnerungen an Litta' [Memories of Litta] (nd).

34 Ibid.

35 Gerhard Bracke, *Melitta Gräfin Stauffenberg: Das Leben einer Fliegerin* [The Life of an Aviatrix] (Herbig Verlag, 2013), privately translated, p. 99.

36 Archive Reinhart Rudershausen, Georg Wollé, 'Memories of a Colleague of Melitta Schiller in the Versuchsanstalt für Luftfahrt [Institute of Aviation] (DVL)' (11.02.1974).

37 Gerhard Bracke, *Melitta Gräfin Stauffenberg: Das Leben einer Fliegerin* [The Life of an Aviatrix] (Herbig Verlag, 2013) privately translated, p. 99.

38 Archive Reinhart Rudershausen, Paul von Handel, 'Erinnerungen an Litta' [Memories of Litta] (nd).

39 Archive Reinhart Rudershausen, Paul von Handel, 'Erinnerungen an Litta [Memories of Litta] (nd).

40 Archive Reinhart Rudershausen, Hermann Blenk, 'Erinnerungen an Melitta Schiller' [Memories of Melitta Schiller] (13.09.1974).

41 Archive Reinhart Rudershausen, Georg Wollé, 'Memories of a Colleague of Melitta Schiller in the Versuchsanstalt für Luftfahrt [Institute of Aviation] (DVL)' (11.02.1974).

42 Melitta Schiller, CV (1943), quoted in Thomas Medicus, *Melitta von Stauffenberg: Ein Deutsches Leben* [A German Life] (Rowohlt, 2012), p. 78.

43 Archive Reinhart Rudershausen, Jutta Rudershausen, 'Frau über den Wolken: Ein Leben für Wissenschaft und Fliegen' [Woman Above the Clouds: A Life for Science and Flying] (unpublished manuscript, nd), p. 44.

44 Archive Reinhart Rudershausen, Melitta Schiller (von Stauffenberg), 'Vortag gehalten in Stockholm am 6.12.43: Eine Frau in der Flugerprobung' [A Woman in Test Flying], Stockholm lecture (06.12.43).

45 Ibid.

46 Ibid.

47 Ibid.

48 Ibid.

49 Ibid.

50 Ibid.

51 Ibid.

52 Ibid.

53 Ibid.

54 Ibid.

55 Ibid.

56 Archive Reinhart Rudershausen, Paul von Handel, 'Erinnerungen an Litta' [Memories of Litta] (nd).

57 Gerhard Bracke, *Melitta Gräfin Stauffenberg: Das Leben einer Fliegerin* [The Life of an Aviatrix] (Herbig Verlag, 2013), privately translated by Barbara Schlussler, p. 26.

58 Elly Beinhorn, *Premiere am Himmel, meine berühmten Fliegerkameraden* [First in the Sky: My Famous Aviator Comrades] (Malik National Geographic, Munich, 1991), p. 250.

59 Archive Reinhart Rudershausen, Georg Wollé, 'Memories of a Colleague of Melitta Schiller in the Versuchsanstalt für Luftfahrt [Institute of Aviation] (DVL)' (11.02.1974).

60 Gerhard Bracke archive, *Berliner Illustrierte Zeitung*, jg. 38, No. 42 (20.10.1929).

61 Archive Reinhart Rudershausen, Melitta Schiller (von Stauffenberg), 'Vortag gehalten in Stockholm am 6.12.43: Eine Frau in der Flugerprobung' [A Woman in Test Flying], Stockholm lecture (06.12.43).

62 Archive Reinhart Rudershausen, Paul von Handel, 'Erinnerungen an Litta' [Memories of Litta] (nd).

63 Archive Reinhart Rudershausen, Jutta Rudershausen, 'Frau über den Wolken: Ein Leben für Wissenschaft und Fliegen' [Woman Above the Clouds: A Life for Science and Flying] (unpublished manuscript, nd), p. 52.

64 Karl Christ, *Der Andere Stauffenberg: Der Historiker und Dichter Alexander von Stauffenberg* [The Other Stauffenberg: Historian and Poet Alexander von Stauffenberg] (C. H. Beck, 2008), p. 9.

65 Gerhard Bracke archive, Philippa Countess von Thun-Hohenstein (née von Bredow), filmed interview, 'Memories of Melitta: personal impressions of Countess von Stauffenberg' (07.07.2000).

66 Archive Reinhart Rudershausen, Paul von Handel, 'Erinnerungen an Litta' [Memories of Litta] (nd).

67 Archive Reinhart Rudershausen, Jutta Rudershausen, 'Frau über den Wolken: Ein Leben für Wissenschaft und Fliegen' [Woman Above the Clouds: A Life for Science and Flying] (unpublished manuscript, nd), p. 53.

68 Archive Reinhart Rudershausen, Paul von Handel, 'Erinnerungen an Litta' [Memories of Litta] (nd).

69 Gerhard Bracke archive, letter Peter Riedel/Mrs Hacker (25.08.1980).

70 Martin Simons, *German Air Attaché: The Thrilling Wartime Story of the German Ace Pilot and Wartime Diplomat Peter Riedel* (Airlife, 1997), pp. 11–12.

71 Ibid. p. 12.

72 Gerhard Bracke archive, letter Peter Riedel/Mrs Hacker (25.08.1980).

73 Gerhard Bracke archive, Peter Riedel interview (late 1980s).

2: Searching for the Fabulous

1 Hanna Reitsch, *The Sky My Kingdom: Memoirs of the Famous German World War II Test Pilot* (Greenhill, 2009), p. 1.

2 Ibid.

3 Ibid. p. 177.

4 Ibid. p. 178.

5 Ibid. p. 3.

6 Ibid. p. 3.

7 Quoted in Judy Lomax, *Hanna Reitsch: Flying for the Fatherland* (John Murray,1988), p. 5.

8 Ibid.

9 Hanna Reitsch, *The Sky My Kingdom: Memoirs of the Famous German World War II Test Pilot* (Greenhill, 2009), p. 3.

10 Ibid. p. 9.

11 Ibid.

12 *Hanna Reitsch: Hitlers Fliegerin* [Hitler's Pilot], Interspot Film (dir. Gerhard Jelinek and Fritz Kalteis, 2010).

13 Deutsches Museum archive, 130/18, Wernher von Braun obituary, unknown newspaper (June 1977).

14 Michael J. Neufeld, *Von Braun: Dreamer of Space, Engineer of War*

(Alfred A. Knopf, 2008), p. 147; Arthur C. Clarke, *Astounding Days: A Science Fiction Autobiography* (Bantam Books, 1990), p. 181.

15 Deutsches Museum archive, 130/18, Wernher von Braun to Harry Walker (6 January 1960).

16 Arthur C. Clarke, *Astounding Days: A Science Fiction Autobiography* (Bantam Books, 1990), p. 181.

17 Hanna Reitsch, *The Sky My Kingdom: Memoirs of the Famous German World War II Test Pilot* (Greenhill, 2009), p. 16.

18 Ibid. p. 18.

19 Ibid. p. 26.

20 Gerda Erica Baker, *Shadow of War* (Lion, 1990), p. 23.

21 Otto Dietrich, *Mit Hitler an die Macht: Personliche Erlebnisse mit Meinem Führer* [With Hitler to Power: Personal Experiences with My Leader] (1934), p. 74.

22 Ibid. p. 9.

23 Ibid. p. 86.

24 Ibid. p. 10.

25 Hanna Reitsch, *The Sky My Kingdom: Memoirs of the Famous German World War II Test Pilot* (Greenhill, 2009), p. 27.

26 Ibid. p. 31.

27 Ibid. p. 31.

28 Ibid. p. 32.

29 Ibid. p. 33.

30 Ibid. p. 34.

31 Ibid. p. 49.

32 Deutsches Museum archive, PERS/F/10228/1, *Alte Adler* member magazine, Friedrich Stahl, Alte Adler president, speech at Hanna Reich's sixtieth birthday party (Spring 1972), p. 8.

33 Hanna Reitsch, *The Sky, My Kingdom: Memoirs of the Famous German World War II Test Pilot* (Greenhill, 2009), p. 50.

34 Ibid. p. 51.

35 Ibid. p. 51.

36 Ibid. p. 56.

37 Quoted in Judy Lomax, *Hanna Reitsch: Flying for the Fatherland* (John Murray, 1988), p. 15.

38 *Hanna Reitsch: Hitlers Fliegerin* [Hitler's Pilot], Interspot Film (dir. Gerhard Jelinek and Fritz Kalteis, 2010).

3: Public Relations

1 Helen L. Boak, 'The "Frauenfrage" and the Female Vote': http://www.academia.edu/498771/Women_in_Weimar_Germany_The_Frauenfrage_and_the_Female_Vote, p.1.

2 Heinrich Hoffmann, *Hitler Was My Friend* (Frontline, 2011), p. 143.

3 Ibid. p. 142.
4 Bernt Engelmann, *In Hitler's Germany: Everyday Life in the Third Reich* (Schocken, 1986), p. 27.
5 Norman H. Baynes, *The Speeches of Adolf Hitler 1922–1939*, vol. 2 (OUP, 1942), p. 1021.
6 Archive Reinhart Rudershausen, Georg Wollé, 'Memories of a Colleague of Melitta Schiller in the Versuchsanstalt für Luftfahrt [Institute of Aviation] (DVL)' (11.02.1974).
7 Archive Reinhart Rudershausen, Jutta Rudershausen, 'Frau über den Wolken: Ein Leben für Wissenschaft und Fliegen' [Woman Above the Clouds: A Life for Science and Flying] (unpublished manuscript, nd), p. 44.
8 *Luftfahrt* (Aviation) 30 (20.08.1926), quoted in Peter Fritzsche, *A Nation of Flyers: German Aviation and the Popular Imagination* (Harvard University Press, 1992), p. 109.
9 Hanna Reitsch, *The Sky My Kingdom: Memoirs of the Famous German World War II Test Pilot* (Greenhill, 2009), p. 61.
10 Ibid. p. 64.
11 Martin Simons, *German Air Attaché: The Thrilling Wartime Story of the German Ace Pilot and Wartime Diplomat Peter Riedel* (Airlife, 1997), p. 88.
12 Ibid.
13 Hanna Reitsch, *The Sky My Kingdom, Memoirs of the Famous German World War II Test Pilot* (Greenhill, 2009), p. 66.
14 Eric Brown, Mulley interview (June 2014).
15 Martin Simons, *German Air Attaché: The Thrilling Wartime Story of the German Ace Pilot and Wartime Diplomat Peter Riedel* (Airlife, 1997), p. 88.
16 Hanna Reitsch, *The Sky My Kingdom, Memoirs of the Famous German World War II Test Pilot* (Greenhill, 2009), pp. 69, 71.
17 Ibid. pp. 69, 70.
18 Ibid. p. 72.
19 Ibid. pp. 76, 77.
20 Deutsches Museum archive PERS/F/102228/2, *Luftwelt* [Air World], 10, Peter Riedel, 'German Gliding in Argentina' (1934), p. 175.
21 Hanna Reitsch, *The Sky My Kingdom, Memoirs of the Famous German World War II Test Pilot* (Greenhill, 2009), p. 82.
22 Martin Simons, *German Air Attaché: The Thrilling Wartime Story of the German Ace Pilot and Wartime Diplomat Peter Riedel* (Airlife, 1997), p. 12.
23 Archive Reinhart Rudershausen, Jutta Rudershausen, 'Frau über den Wolken: Ein Leben für Wissenschaft und Fliegen' [Woman Above the Clouds: A Life for Science and Flying] (unpublished manuscript, nd), p. 40.
24 Norman H. Baynes, *The Speeches of Adolf Hitler, April 1922–August 1939* (OUP, 1942), pp. 52, 59.

25 Elisabeth zu Guttenberg, Sheridan Spearman, *Holding the Stirrup* (Duell, Sloan, Pearce/Little, Brown, 1953)

26 Norman H. Baynes, *The Speeches of Adolf Hitler, April 1922–August 1939* (OUP, 1942), p. 731.

27 Archive Reinhart Rudershausen, *Natur und Geist: Monatsheft für Wissenschaft, Weltanschauung und Lebensgestaltung* [Nature and Spirit: The Monthly Bulletin of Science, Philosophy and Lifestyle] 3.12 (December 1935).

28 Klara Schiller quoted in Gerhard Bracke, *Melitta Gräfin Stauffenberg: Das Leben einer Fliegerin* [The Life of an Aviatrix] (Herbig Verlag, 2013), privately translated, p. 39.

29 Ibid.

30 Archive Reinhart Rudershausen, Paul von Handel, 'Erinnerungen an Litta' [Memories of Litta] (nd).

31 Archive Reinhart Rudershausen, Jutta Rudershausen, 'Frau über den Wolken: Ein Leben für Wissenschaft und Fliegen' [Woman Above the Clouds: A Life for Science and Flying] (unpublished manuscript, nd), p. 54.

32 C. G. Sweeting, *Hitler's Squadron: The Führer's Personal Aircraft and Transport Unit, 1933–45* (Brassey's, 2001), p. 20.

33 Hanna Reitsch, *The Sky My Kingdom, Memoirs of the Famous German World War II Test Pilot* (Greenhill, 2009), p. 100.

34 Winston Churchill, *Great Contemporaries* (Odhams Press, 1947, first published 1937), pp. 206, 208.

35 Archive Reinhart Rudershausen, Paul von Handel, 'Erinnerungen an Litta' [Memories of Litta] (nd).

36 Konstanze von Schulthess, *Nina Schenk Gräfin von Stauffenberg: Ein Porträt* [A Portrait] (Piper, 2009), p. 71.

37 Archive Reinhart Rudershausen, Paul von Handel, 'Erinnerungen an Litta' [Memories of Litta] (nd).

38 Elisabeth zu Guttenberg, Sheridan Spearman, *Holding the Stirrup* (Duell, Sloan and Pearce/Little, Brown, 1953), p. 184.

39 Count Berthold von Stauffenberg, Mulley interview (05.11.2014).

40 Archive Reinhart Rudershausen, Jutta Rudershausen, 'Frau über den Wolken: Ein Leben für Wissenschaft und Fliegen' [Woman Above the Clouds: A Life for Science and Flying] (unpublished manuscript, nd), p. 52.

41 Hanna Reitsch, *The Sky My Kingdom, Memoirs of the Famous German World War II Test Pilot* (Greenhill, 2009), p. 83.

42 Ibid. p. 85.

43 Ibid. p. 91.

44 Ibid. p. 125.

45 Martin Simons, *German Air Attaché: The Thrilling Wartime Story of the German Ace Pilot and Wartime Diplomat Peter Riedel* (Airlife, 1997), p. 88.

46 Hanna Reitsch, *The Sky My Kingdom, Memoirs of the Famous German World War II Test Pilot* (Greenhill, 2009), p. 105.

47 Ibid. p. 109.

48 Isolde Baur, *A Pilot's Pilot: Karl Baur, Chief Test Pilot for Messerschmitt* (J. J. Fedorowicz Publishing, 2000), p. 27.

49 Ibid. p. 28.

50 Ernst Udet, *Ace of the Black Cross* (Newnes, 1935), p. 162.

51 Ibid. p. 243.

52 Deutsches Museum archive, 130/101, Walter Stender, 'Politische Erklärung' [Political Statement] (01.07.1947).

53 Deutsches Museum archive, 130/101, letter Horst von Salomon/ Kaplan Volkmar (27.04.1947).

54 Hanna Reitsch, *The Sky My Kingdom, Memoirs of the Famous German World War II Test Pilot* (Greenhill, 2009), p. 91.

55 Cooper C. Graham, *Leni Riefenstahl and Olympia* (Scarecrow, 2001), p. 75.

56 Bernd Rosemeyer, Elly Beinhorn's son, interview, *ZDF-History*, 'Himmelsstürmerinnen, Deutsche Fliegerinnen' [Sky-Strikers, German Aviators] (2011).

57 Isolde Baur, *A Pilot's Pilot: Karl Baur, Chief Test Pilot for Messerschmitt* (J.J. Fedorowicz Publishing, 2000), p. 72.

58 *Britain's Greatest Pilot: The Extraordinary Story of Captain 'Winkle' Brown*, BBC2 documentary (ed. Darren Jonusas ASE, Executive Prod. Steve Crabtree, 01.06.2014).

59 Eric Brown, James Holland interview, www.griffonmerlin.com (2012); and Eric Brown, *Wings On My Sleeve: The World's Greatest Test Pilot Tells His Story* (Phoenix, 2007), p. 4.

60 Eric Brown, Mulley interview, West Sussex (18.03.2013).

61 Ibid.

62 Eric Brown, *Wings On My Sleeve: The World's Greatest Test Pilot Tells His Story* (Phoenix, 2007), p. 3.

63 Eric Brown, Mulley interview, Chalke Valley History Festival (29.06.2013).

64 Helen Boak quoting the *New York Times, Women in the Weimar Republic* (Manchester University Press, 2013), p. 265.

65 David Clay Large, *Nazi Games: The Olympics of 1936* (W. W. Norton, 2007), pp. 290–91.

66 Janet Flanner, *New Yorker*, August 1936, quoted in Cooper C. Graham, *Leni Riefenstahl and Olympia* (Scarrow, 2001), p. 127.

67 A. Scott Berg, *Lindbergh* (G. P. Putnam's Sons, 1998), p. 361.

68 David Clay Large, *Nazi Games: The Olympics of 1936* (W. W. Norton, 2007), p. 210.

69 Judy Lomax, *Hanna Reitsch: Flying for the Fatherland* (John Murray, 1988), p. 33.

4: Public Appointments

1 Archive Reinhart Rudershausen, Melitta Schiller, DVL job reference (23.11.1936).
2 Ibid.
3 Gerhard Bracke, *Melitta Gräfin Stauffenberg: Das Leben einer Fliegerin* [The Life of an Aviatrix] (Herbig Verlag, 2013), privately translated, p. 40.
4 Archive Reinhart Rudershausen, Jutta Rudershausen, 'Flugkapitän Melitta Schiller-Stauffenberg' (nd), p. 54.
5 Gerhard Bracke, *Melitta Gräfin Stauffenberg: Das Leben einer Fliegerin* [The Life of an Aviatrix] (Herbig Verlag, 2013), privately translated, pp. 40–41.
6 Judy Lomax, *Hanna Reitsch: Flying for the Fatherland* (John Murray, 1988), p. 75.
7 *Leipziger Neueste Nachrichten* (1937), quoted in Bernhard Rieger, 'Hanna Reitsch: The Global Career of a Nazi Celebrity' in *German History: The Journal of the German History Society*, vol. 26, no. 3, p. 388.
8 Deutsches Museum archive, 130/111, letter Hanna Reitsch/Herr Stüper (07.02.1974).
9 Eric Brown, speech, Chalke Valley History Festival (29.06.2013).
10 Hanna Reitsch, *The Sky My Kingdom, Memoirs of the Famous German World War II Test Pilot* (Greenhill, 2009), p. 128.
11 Ibid. p. 132.
12 Gerhard Bracke, *Melitta Gräfin Stauffenberg: Das Leben einer Fliegerin* [The Life of an Aviatrix] (Herbig Verlag, 2013), privately translated, p. 48.
13 Nevile Henderson, *Failure of a Mission: Berlin 1937–1939* (Hodder & Stoughton, 1945), p. 84.
14 Richard Perlia, *Mal oben – Mal unten* [Sometimes Up – Sometimes Down] (Schiff & Flugzeug-Verlagsbuchhandlung, 2011), p. 194.
15 Gerhard Bracke, *Melitta Gräfin Stauffenberg: Das Leben einer Fliegerin* [The Life of an Aviatrix] (Herbig Verlag, 2013), privately translated, p. 49.
16 Thomas Medicus, *Melitta von Stauffenberg: Ein Deutsches Leben* [A German Life] (Rowohlt, 2012), p. 154.
17 Count Berthold von Stauffenberg, letter to Thomas Medicus (21.05.2012).
18 Peter Hoffmann, *Stauffenberg: A Family History 1904–1944* (McGill-Queen's University Press, 2008), p. 94.
19 Archive Reinhart Rudershausen, Paul von Handel, 'Erinnerungen an Litta' [Memories of Litta] (nd).
20 Count Berthold von Stauffenberg, Mulley interview (05.11.2014).
21 Archive Reinhart Rudershausen, Klara Schiller, 'Memories of Klara Schiller' (nd).

22 Konstanze von Schulthess, *Nina Schenk Gräfin Stauffenberg: Ein Porträt* [A Portrait] (Piper, 2009), p. 72; Gerhard Bracke, *Melitta Gräfin Stauffenberg: Das Leben einer Fliegerin* [The Life of an Aviatrix] (Herbig Verlag, 2013), privately translated, p. 223.

23 Heidimarie Schade, Mulley interview, Berlin (01.10.2014).

24 Konstanze von Schulthess, *Nina Schenk Gräfin Stauffenberg: Ein Porträt* [A Portrait] (Piper, 2009), p. 87.

25 Nina von Stauffenberg quoted by Gerhard Bracke, *Melitta Gräfin Stauffenberg: Das Leben einer Fliegerin* [The Life of an Aviatrix] (Herbig Verlag, 2013), privately translated, p. 223.

26 Papers in the Bavarian State Archives (Bayerisches Hauptstaatsarchiv), quoted by Thomas Medicus, *Melitta von Stauffenberg, Ein Deutsches Leben* [A German Life] (Rowohlt, 2012), p. 155.

27 Nina von Stauffenberg quoted by Gerhard Bracke, *Melitta Gräfin Stauffenberg: Das Leben einer Fliegerin* [The Life of an Aviatrix] (Herbig Verlag, 2013) (privately translated), p. 223.

28 Ibid.

29 Archive Reinhart Rudershausen, Paul von Handel, 'Erinnerungen an Litta' [Memories of Litta] (nd).

30 Judy Lomax, *Hanna Reitsch: Flying for the Fatherland* (John Murray, 1988), p. 46.

31 Nevile Henderson, *Failure of a Mission: Berlin 1937–1939* (Hodder & Stoughton, 1945), p. 71.

32 Hanna Reitsch, *The Sky My Kingdom, Memoirs of the Famous German World War II Test Pilot* (Greenhill, 2009), p. 137.

33 Ibid. p. 135.

34 Ibid. p. 135.

35 Ibid. p. 136.

36 *Aeroplane Monthly*, 'Flugkapitän Hanna Reitsch' (July 1985), p. 348.

37 Hanna Reitsch, *The Sky My Kingdom, Memoirs of the Famous German World War II Test Pilot* (Greenhill, 2009), p. 139.

38 *Angus Evening Telegraph*, 'Plane that Flies Backwards' (04.11.1937).

39 Hanna Reitsch, *The Sky My Kingdom, Memoirs of the Famous German World War II Test Pilot* (Greenhill, 2009), p. 139.

40 Hanna Reitsch in *The Secret War*, BBC (1977).

41 Deutsches Museum archive, 130/109, letter Karl Franke/Hanna Reitsch (1977/8).

42 Hanna Reitsch quoted in Blaine Taylor, 'She Flew for Hitler', *Air Classics* (February 1989), p. 68.

43 Hanna Reitsch, *The Sky My Kingdom, Memoirs of the Famous German World War II Test Pilot* (Greenhill, 2009), p. 140.

44 Ibid. p. 141.

45 *Angus Evening Telegraph*, 'Plane that Flies Backwards' (04.11.1937).

46 *Nottingham Evening Post*, 'Helicopter's Amazing Performance' (05.11.1937).

47 A. Scott Berg, *Lindbergh* (G. P. Putnam's Sons, 1998), p. 368.

48 Archive Reinhart Rudershausen, Jutta Rudershausen, 'Flugkapitän Melitta Schiller-Stauffenberg' (nd), p. 60.

49 Gerhard Bracke, *Melitta Gräfin Stauffenberg: Das Leben einer Fliegerin* [The Life of an Aviatrix] (Herbig Verlag, 2013), privately translated, p. 54.

50 Archive Reinhart Rudershausen, Jutta Rudershausen, 'Flugkapitän Melitta Schiller-Stauffenberg' (nd), p. 64.

51 Paul von Handel quoted in Gerhard Bracke, *Melitta Gräfin Stauffenberg: Das Leben einer Fliegerin* [The Life of an Aviatrix] (Herbig Verlag, 2013), privately translated, p. 101.

52 Archive Reinhart Rudershausen, Jutta Rudershausen, 'Flugkapitän Melitta Schiller-Stauffenberg' (nd), p. 64.

53 Richard Perlia, *Mal oben – Mal unten* [Sometimes Up – Sometimes Down] (Schiff & Flugzeug-Verlagsbuchhandlung, 2011), p. 193.

54 Archive Reinhart Rudershausen, anonymous press clipping.

55 Archive Reinhart Rudershausen, Jutta Rudershausen, 'Flugkapitän Melitta Schiller-Stauffenberg' (nd), p. 54.

56 Gerhard Bracke, *Melitta Gräfin Stauffenberg: Das Leben einer Fliegerin* [The Life of an Aviatrix] (Herbig Verlag, 2013), privately translated, p. 61.

57 Richard Perlia, *Mal oben – Mal unten* [Sometimes Up, Sometimes Down] (Schiff & Flugzeug-Verlagsbuchhandlung, 2011), p. 236.

58 Richard Perlia, *Mal oben – Mal unten* [Sometimes Up – Sometimes Down] (Schiff & Flugzeug-Verlagsbuchhandlung, 2011), p. 135.

59 Bernd Rosemeyer, son of Elly Beinhorn and Bernd Rosemeyer, Mulley interview (23.09.2013).

60 Archive Reinhart Rudershausen, Jutta Rudershausen, 'Flugkapitän Melitta Schiller-Stauffenberg' (nd), p. 44.

61 Judy Lomax, *Hanna Reitsch: Flying for the Fatherland* (John Murray, 1988), p. 47; Deutsches Museum archive, 130/111, letter Hanna Reitsch/Herr Stüper (07.02.1974).

62 Deutsches Museum archive, 130/111, letter Hanna Reitsch/Herr Stüper (07.02.1974).

63 Richard Perlia, *Mal oben – Mal unten* [Sometimes Up – Sometimes Down] (Schiff & Flugzeug-Verlagsbuchhandlung, 2011), p. 236.

64 AKG Images, 7-I1-34032602.

65 IWM, film archive, GWY 556, Deutsche Luftgeltung 1937 [German Air Retribution 1937] (1938).

5: HOVERING

1 Sophie Jackson, *Hitler's Heroine: Hanna Reitsch* (History Press, 2014), p. 70; Judy Lomax, *Hanna Reitsch: Flying for the Fatherland* (John Murray, 1988), p. 46.

2 Winston Churchill, *Great Contemporaries* (Odhams Press, 1947, first published 1937), pp. 204, 210.

3 Oliver Lubrich, *Travels in the Reich: Foreign Authors Report from Germany, 1933–1945* (University of Chicago Press, 2010), p. 160.

4 Bernd Rosemeyer, son of Elly Beinhorn and Bernd Rosemeyer, Mulley interview (23.09.2013).

5 Ibid.

6 Ibid.

7 www.omnibusarchiv.de 'A Historical Review: The International automobile Show' (IAA) and Mercedes-Benz (18.09.2010).

8 Hanna Reitsch, *The Sky My Kingdom, Memoirs of the Famous German World War II Test Pilot* (Greenhill, 2009), p. 146.

9 Judy Lomax, *Hanna Reitsch: Flying for the Fatherland* (John Murray, 1998), p. 53.

10 Hanna Reitsch, *The Sky My Kingdom, Memoirs of the Famous German World War II Test Pilot* (Greenhill, 2009), p. 144.

11 Ibid. p. 145.

12 Ibid. p. 144.

13 Ibid. p. 146.

14 Eric Brown, James Holland interview, www.griffonmerlin.com/ww2_interviews/captain-eric-winkle-brown

15 Hanna Reitsch, *The Sky My Kingdom, Memoirs of the Famous German World War II Test Pilot* (Greenhill, 2009), p. 147.

16 Eric Brown, Mulley interview (18.03.2013); Eric Brown in *Hanna Reitsch: Hitlers Fliegerin* [Hitler's Pilot], Interspot Film (dir. Gerhard Jelinek and Fritz Kalteis, 2010).

17 Hanna Reitsch, *The Sky My Kingdom, Memoirs of the Famous German World War II Test Pilot* (Greenhill, 2009), p. 148.

18 *Britain's Greatest Pilot: The Extraordinary Story of Captain 'Winkle' Brown*, BBC2 documentary (01.06.2014).

19 *Mail Online*, Robert Hardman, 'Hero who makes Biggles look like a wimp' (07.05.2013).

20 Eric Brown, Mulley interview (18.03.2013).

21 Eric Brown in *Hanna Reitsch: Hitlers Fliegerin* [Hitler's Pilot], Interspot Film (dir. Gerhard Jelinek and Fritz Kalteis, 2010).

22 Eric Brown, Mulley interview (June 2013).

23 Eric Brown, James Holland interview, www.griffonmerlin.com/ww2_interviews/captain-eric-winkle-brown

24 Eric Brown, Mulley interview (23.06.2014).

25 Ibid.

26 Eric Brown, Mulley interview (18.03.2013).

27 Ibid.

28 Eric Brown, Mulley interview, West Sussex (18.03.2013).

29 *Mail Online*, Robert Hardman, 'Hero who makes Biggles look like a wimp' (07.05.2013).

30 Eric Brown, *Wings On My Sleeve: The World's Greatest Test Pilot Tells His Story* (Phoenix, 2007), p. 6.

31 Gerhard Bracke, *Melitta Gräfin Stauffenberg: Das Leben einer Fliegerin* [The Life of an Aviatrix] (Herbig Verlag, 2013), privately translated, p. 69.

32 Peter Gay, *My German Question: Growing Up in Nazi Berlin* (Yale, 1998), p. 120.

33 Fey von Hassell, *A Mother's War* (Corgi, 1991), p. 56.

34 *Dundee Courier*, 'Girl Glider Beats Day-Old Record' (16.05.1938).

35 Thea Rasche, quoted in Gerhard Bracke, *Melitta Gräfin Stauffenberg: Das Leben einer Fliegerin* [The Life of an Aviatrix] (Herbig Verlag, 2013), privately translated, p. 63.

36 Ernst Udet, *Ace of the Black Cross* (Newnes, 1935), p. 229.

37 Gerhard Bracke, *Melitta Gräfin Stauffenberg: Das Leben einer Fliegerin* [The Life of an Aviatrix] (Herbig Verlag, 2013), privately translated, p. 65.

38 Ibid. p. 66.

39 Ibid. p. 68.

40 Thea Rasche, quoted in Gerhard Bracke, *Melitta Gräfin Stauffenberg: Das Leben einer Fliegerin* [The Life of an Aviatrix] (Herbig Verlag, 2013), privately translated, pp. 63, 69.

41 Sarah Fraiman, 'The transformation of Jewish consciousness in Nazi Germany as reflected in the German Jewish journal *Der Morgen*, 1925–1938', in *Modern Judaism* (OUP, 2000) vol. 20, p. 52.

42 Martin Simons, *German Air Attaché: The Thrilling Wartime Story of the German Ace Pilot and Wartime Diplomat Peter Riedel* (Airlife, 1997), p. 29.

43 Ibid. p. 30.

44 Ibid. p. 11.

45 Judy Lomax, *Hanna Reitsch: Flying for the Fatherland* (John Murray, 1988), p. 59.

46 Virginia Cowles, 'The 1938 Nuremberg Rally' in Jenny Hartley, *Hearts Undefeated: Women's Writing of the Second World War* (Virago, 1999), p. 12.

47 Hanna Reitsch, *The Sky My Kingdom, Memoirs of the Famous German World War II Test Pilot* (Greenhill, 2009), p. 161.

48 Ernst Udet, *Ace of the Black Cross* (Newnes, 1935), p. 217.

49 Hanna Reitsch, *The Sky My Kingdom, Memoirs of the Famous German World War II Test Pilot* (Greenhill, 2009), p. 159.

50 Martin Simons, *German Air Attaché: The Thrilling Wartime Story of the German Ace Pilot and Wartime Diplomat Peter Riedel* (Airlife, 1997), p. 40.

51 Ibid.

52 Judy Lomax, *Hanna Reitsch: Flying for the Fatherland* (John Murray, 1988), p. 57.

53 Hanna Reitsch, *The Sky My Kingdom, Memoirs of the Famous German World War II Test Pilot* (Greenhill, 2009), p. 157.
54 Ibid. p. 158.
55 Ibid. p. 160.
56 Ibid. p. 161.
57 Neville Chamberlain, BBC radio broadcast (27.09.1938).
58 TNA, FO 371/21737, letter from Nevile Henderson (06.09.1938).
59 Nevile Henderson, *Failure of a Mission: Berlin 1937–1939* (Hodder & Stoughton, 1940), p. 153.
60 Ibid. p. 154.
61 Ibid. p. 155.
62 Melitta Schiller, 'Flight to England with Incidents', *Askania* magazine, quoted in Gerhard Bracke, *Melitta Gräfin Stauffenberg: Das Leben einer Fliegerin* [The Life of an Aviatrix] (Herbig Verlag, 2013), privately translated, p. 71.
63 Judy Lomax, *Women of the Air* (Ivy, 1987), p. 167.
64 Ibid. p. 168.
65 Gerhard Bracke, *Melitta Gräfin Stauffenberg: Das Leben einer Fliegerin* [The Life of an Aviatrix] (Herbig Verlag, 2013), privately translated, p. 72.
66 Ibid.
67 Ibid. p. 73.
68 *Dundee Courier*, '"Overdue" Air Girl Lands' (24.09.1938).
69 Gerhard Bracke, *Melitta Gräfin Stauffenberg: Das Leben einer Fliegerin* [The Life of an Aviatrix] (Herbig Verlag, 2013), privately translated, p. 74.
70 Ibid.
71 Nancy Bird, *My God! It's a Woman: The inspiring story of Australia's pioneering aviatrix* (HarperCollins, 2002), p. 124.
72 TNA, FO 371/21737, letter from Nevile Henderson (06.09.1938).
73 *Aeroplane* magazine, 'Women's Day at Chigwell' (28.09.1938).
74 Ibid.
75 Gerhard Bracke, *Melitta Gräfin Stauffenberg: Das Leben einer Fliegerin* [The Life of an Aviatrix] (Herbig Verlag, 2013) privately translated, p. 75.
76 Ibid. p. 76.

6: Descent

1 Judy Lomax, *Hanna Reitsch: Flying for the Fatherland* (John Murray, 1988), p. 60.
2 Ibid.
3 Deutsches Museum Archive, 130/101, Walter Stender, 'Political Statement' (01.07.1947).

4 Judy Lomax, *Hanna Reitsch: Flying for the Fatherland* (John Murray, 1988), p. 61.

5 Deutsches Museum Archive, 130/101, Walter Stender, 'Politische Erklärung' [Political Statement] (01.07.1947).

6 Peter Gay, *My German Question: Growing Up in Nazi Berlin* (Yale, 1998), p. 111.

7 Bernt Engelmann, *In Hitler's Germany: Everyday Life in the Third Reich* (Schocken, 1986), p. 145.

8 Simon Reiss, 'Remembering Kristallnacht, 9 November 1938–1998', speech at Westminster Central Hall (09.11.1998).

9 Karl Christ, *Der Andere Stauffenberg: Der Historiker und Dichter Alexander von Stauffenberg* [The Other Stauffenberg: Historian and Poet Alexander von Stauffenberg] (C. H. Beck, 2008), p. 161.

10 Dorothee von Meding, *Courageous Hearts: Women and the anti-Hitler Plot of 1944* (Berghahn, 1997), p. 200.

11 Fey von Hassell, *A Mother's War* (Corgi, 1991), p. 58.

12 Konstanze von Schulthess, *Nina Schenk Gräfin von Stauffenberg: Ein Porträt* [A Portrait] (Piper, 2009), p. 71.

13 Louis P. Lochner (trans., ed.), The Goebbels Diaries (Hamish Hamilton, 1948), pp. xxxvi, xxv.

14 Sir Nevile Henderson, *Failure of a Mission: Berlin 1937–1939* (Hodder & Stoughton, 1940), p. 172.

15 Martin Simons, *German Air Attaché: The Thrilling Wartime Story of the German Ace Pilot and Wartime Diplomat Peter Riedel* (Airlife, 1997), p. 45.

16 Ulrich von Hassell, *The Von Hassell Diaries: The Story of the Forces Against Hitler Inside Germany, 1938–1944* (Westview Press, 1994), p. 14.

17 Fey von Hassell, *A Mother's War* (Corgi, 1991), p. 59.

18 Stiftung Neue Synagoge [New Foundation Synagogue], Berlin, exhibition: 'From the Outside to the Inside: the 1938 November Pogroms in Diplomatic Reports from Germany' (May 2014).

19 Winston Churchill, *Step by Step: 1936–1939* (Odhams, 1949), p. 264.

20 Nevile Henderson, *Failure of a Mission: Berlin 1937–1939* (Hodder & Stoughton, 1940), p. 85.

21 Jeffrey Watson, *Sidney Cotton: The Last Plane Out of Berlin* (Hodder, 2003), pp. 70, 71.

22 Constance Babington Smith, *Evidence in Camera: The story of photographic intelligence in the Second World War* (Sutton, 2004), p. 7.

23 Jeffrey Watson, *Sidney Cotton: The Last Plane Out of Berlin* (Hodder, 2003), p. 104.

24 Archive Reinhart Rudershausen, Jutta Rudershausen, 'Flugkapitän Melitta Schiller-Stauffenberg' (nd), p. 58.

25 Berthold von Stauffenberg, Mulley interview (05.11.2014); Berthold

von Stauffenberg quoted in *Der Spiegel*, Susanne von Beyer, 'Frau im Sturzflug' [Woman in a Nosedive] (05.03.2012).

26 *ZDF-History*, 'Himmelsstürmerinnen, Deutsche Fliegerinnen' [Sky-Strikers, German Aviators] (2011).

27 Konstanze von Schulthess, Mulley interview (25.11.2014).

28 Richard Perlia, *Mal oben – Mal unten* [Sometimes Up – Sometimes Down] (Schiff & Flugzeug-Verlagsbuchhandlung, 2011), p. 194.

29 Nancy Bird, *My God! It's a Woman: The inspiring story of Australia's pioneering aviatrix* (HarperCollins, 2002), p. 129.

30 Deutsches Museum archive, 101a, Report on Hanna Reitsch (anon., nd).

31 Jeffrey Watson, *Sidney Cotton: The Last Plane Out of Berlin* (Hodder, 2003), p. 91.

32 Ibid. p. 99.

33 Constance Babington Smith, *Evidence in Camera: The story of photographic intelligence in the Second World War* (Sutton, 2004), p. 9.

34 Karl Christ, *Der Andere Stauffenberg: Der Historiker und Dichter Alexander von Stauffenberg* [The Other Stauffenberg: Historian and Poet Alexander von Stauffenberg] (C. H. Beck, 2008), p. 167.

35 Nevile Henderson, *Failure of a Mission: Berlin 1937–1939* (Hodder & Stoughton, 1940), p. 287.

36 Eric Brown, *Wings On My Sleeve: The World's Greatest Test Pilot Tells His Story* (Phoenix, 2007), p. 6.

37 Ibid.

38 James Holland interview with Eric Brown, www.griffonmerlin.com (2012).

39 Eric Brown, *Wings On My Sleeve: The World's Greatest Test Pilot Tells His Story* (Phoenix, 2007), p. 6.

7: WOMEN AT WAR

1 Melitta von Stauffenberg quoted in Bracke, *Melitta Gräfin Stauffenberg: Das Leben einer Fliegerin* [The Life of an Aviatrix] (Herbig Verlag, 2013), privately translated, p. 164.

2 Konstanze von Schulthess, *Nina Schenk Gräfin von Stauffenberg: Ein Porträt* [A Portrait] (Piper, 2009), p. 88.

3 Albert Speer, *Inside the Third Reich* (Sphere, 1971), p. 261.

4 TNA, AIR 40/36, A.I.2(g), Report (un-numbered) BZA-1 Dive Bombsight - German (translated).

5 Gerhard Bracke, *Melitta Gräfin Stauffenberg: Das Leben einer Fliegerin* [The Life of an Aviatrix] (Herbig Verlag, 2013), privately translated, p. 163.

6 Ibid. p. 91.

7 Ibid. p. 167.

8 Ibid. p. 165.

9 Ibid. p. 167.

10 C. G. Sweeting, *Hitler's Squadron: The Führer's Personal Aircraft and Transport Unit, 1933–45* (Brassey's, 2001), p. 45.

11 Fred Taylor (trans., ed.), *The Goebbels Diaries 1939–1941: The historic journal of a Nazi war leader* (Sphere, 1983) (entry from 20.12.1939), p. 70.

12 Roger Moorhouse, 'A Good German? Von Stauffenberg and the July plot' in *History Today*, vol. 59, issue 1 (2009).

13 William Shirer, *Berlin Diary*, November 1939, quoted in Richard J. Evans, *The Third Reich at War* (Allen Lane, 2008), p. 57.

14 Peter Hoffmann, *German Resistance to Hitler* (Harvard, 1988), p. 131.

15 Fey von Hassell, *A Mother's War* (Corgi, 1991), p. 72.

16 Konstanze von Schulthess, *Nina Schenck Gräfin von Stauffenberg: Ein Porträt* [A Portrait] (Piper, 2009), p. 72.

17 Ibid. p. 73.

18 Deutsches Museum archive, 130/101, statement of Prof. Richard Homberger (07.07.1947).

19 Hanna Reitsch, *The Sky My Kingdom: Memoirs of the Famous German World War II Test Pilot* (Greenhill, 2009), p. 183.

20 Cajus Becker, *The Luftwaffe Diaries* (Macdonald, 1966), p. 97.

21 Hanna Reitsch, *The Sky My Kingdom: Memoirs of the Famous German World War II Test Pilot* (Greenhill, 2009), p. 184.

22 Ibid.

23 Judy Lomax, *Hanna Reitsch: Flying for the Fatherland* (John Murray, 1988), p. 66.

24 Hanna Reitsch quoted in Oscar Gonzalez, Thomas Steinke, Ian Tannahill, *The Silent Attack: The Taking of the Bridges at Veldwezelt, Vroenhoven and Kanne in Belgium by German Paratroopers, 10 May 1940* (Pen & Sword, 2015).

25 *ZDF-History*, 'Himmelsstürmerinnen, Deutsche Fliegerinnen' [Sky-Strikers, German Aviators] (2011); Hanna Reitsch, *The Sky My Kingdom: Memoirs of the Famous German World War II Test Pilot* (Greenhill, 2009), p. 190.

26 Hanna Reitsch, *The Sky My Kingdom: Memoirs of the Famous German World War II Test Pilot* (Greenhill, 2009), p. 191.

27 Karl Christ, *Der Andere Stauffenberg: Der Historiker und Dichter Alexander von Stauffenberg* [The Other Stauffenberg: Historian and Poet Alexander von Stauffenberg] (C. H. Beck, 2008), p. 52.

28 Thomas Medicus, *Melitta von Stauffenberg: Ein Deutsches Leben* [A German Life] (Rowohlt, 2012), p. 176.

29 Ibid. p. 179.

30 Ibid. p. 179.

31 Gerhard Bracke, *Melitta Gräfin Stauffenberg: Das Leben einer Fliegerin* [The Life of an Aviatrix] (Herbig Verlag, 2013), privately translated, p. 92.

32 Gerhard Bracke archive, letter Hanna Reitsch/Klara Schiller (07.02.1975).
33 Gerhard Bracke archive, letter Hanna Reitsch/Klara Schiller (18.02.1975).
34 Ibid.
35 Ibid.
36 Ibid.
37 Ibid.
38 Bob Carruthers, *Voices from the Luftwaffe* (Pen & Sword, 2012), p. 33.
39 Isolde Baur, *A Pilot's Pilot: Karl Baur, Chief Messerschmitt Pilot* (Schiffer, 1999), p. 125.
40 Ibid. p. 126.
41 Ibid. p. 126.
42 Hanna Reitsch in *The Secret War*, Episode 4: 'If . . .', BBC (1977).
43 Ibid.
44 Ibid.
45 Sophie Jackson, *Hitler's Heroine: Hanna Reitsch* (The History Press, 2014), p. 80.
46 Hilde Marchant, 'A Journalist's Impression of the Blitz' in Jenny Hartley, *Hearts Undefeated: Women's Writing of the Second World War* (Virago, 1999), p. 100.
47 John Alan Ottewell, DFM, Mulley interview (09.10.2014).
48 Archive Reinhart Rudershausen, Jutta Rudershausen, 'Peerless Pilot' (nd).
49 Ibid.
50 Archive Reinhart Rudershausen, Georg Wollé, 'Memories of a Colleague of Melitta Schiller in the Versuchsanstalt für Luftfahrt [Institute of Aviation] (DVL)' (11.02.1974).
51 Thomas Medicus, *Melitta von Stauffenberg: Ein Deutsches Leben* [A German Life] (Rowolt, 2012), p. 170.
52 Hanna Reitsch, *The Sky My Kingdom: Memoirs of the Famous German World War II Test Pilot* (Greenhill, 2009), p. 192.
53 Hanna Reitsch in *The Secret War*, BBC (1977).
54 Gill Mulley, Harpenden, Mulley interview (20.05.2013).
55 Hajo Herrmann, James Holland interview, www.griffonmerlin.com (04.06.2008).
56 Fred Taylor (trans., ed.), *The Goebbels Diaries, 1939–1941: The historic journal of a Nazi war leader* (Sphere, 1983) (entry from 11.10.1939), p. 17.
57 Hanna Reitsch, *The Sky My Kingdom: Memoirs of the Famous German World War II Test Pilot* (Greenhill, 2009), p. 195.
58 Ibid. p. 190.
59 Ibid. p. 196.
60 Ibid. p. 199.
61 Ibid. p. 201.
62 Christa Schroeder, *He Was My Chief* (Frontline, 2009), p. 48.

63 Ibid.
64 Hanna Reitsch, *The Sky My Kingdom: Memoirs of the Famous German World War II Test Pilot* (Greenhill, 2009), p. 202.
65 Heinrich Hoffmann, *Hitler Was My Friend: The Memoirs of Hitler's Photographer* (Frontline, 2011), p. 188.
66 Christa Schroeder, *He Was My Chief* (Frontline, 2009), p. 51.
67 Hanna Reitsch, *The Sky My Kingdom: Memoirs of the Famous German World War II Test Pilot* (Greenhill, 2009), p. 202.
68 *Aberdeen Journal*, 'A German airwoman receives the Iron Cross' (24.04.1941).
69 Gerhard Bracke archive, Hanna Reitsch letter to Klara Schiller (09.07.1975).
70 Hanna Reitsch, *The Sky My Kingdom: Memoirs of the Famous German World War II Test Pilot* (Greenhill, 2009), p. 203.
71 Ibid. p. 204.
72 Ibid. p. 204.
73 Ibid. p. 204.
74 Deutsches Museum archive 130/101, statement of Richard Homberger (07.07.1947).
75 Fred Taylor (trans., ed.), *The Goebbels Diaries 1939–1941: The historic journal of a Nazi war leader* (Sphere, 1983) (entry from 8.3.1941), p. 272.
76 Gerhard Bracke, *Melitta Gräfin Stauffenberg: Das Leben einer Fliegerin* [The Life of an Aviatrix] (Herbig Verlag, 2013), privately translated, p. 90.
77 Konstanze von Schulthess, *Nina Schenk Gräfin von Stauffenberg: Ein Porträt* [A Portrait] (Piper, 2009), p. 88.
78 Thomas Medicus, *Melitta von Stauffenberg: Ein Deutsches Leben* [A German Life] (Rowohlt, 2012), p. 180.
79 Ibid. p. 342.
80 Dietrich Pütter, Margaret Nelson/Mulley conversations (19.04.2014, 24.06.2014).
81 Dietrich Pütter, Margaret Nelson/Mulley private interview (29.07.2014).
82 Dietrich Pütter, Margaret Nelson/Mulley conversation (19.04.2014).
83 Ibid.
84 Ibid.
85 Clementine Churchill, 'My Visit To Russia' in Jenny Hartley, *Hearts Undefeated: Women's Writing of the Second World War* (Virago, 1999), pp.164–5.
86 Heinz Linge, *With Hitler to the End: The Memoirs of Adolf Hitler's Valet* (Frontline, 2009), p. 77.
87 Cajus Becker, *The Luftwaffe Diaries* (Macdonald, 1966), p. 232.
88 Ibid.
89 Fred Taylor (trans., ed.), *The Goebbels Diaries 1939–1941: The historic*

journal of a Nazi war leader (Sphere, 1983) (entry from 22.5.1943), p. 309.

90 US National Archives and Records Administration, Hanna Reitsch Personal File, RG319, 270, 84, 13, 7, box 633 (7362164, XE053525), US Forces report, Hanna Reitsch interrogation, 'Condemnation of Göring by Hanna Reitsch' (16.11.1945), p. 5.

91 Martin Simons, *German Air Attaché: The Thrilling Wartime Story of the German Ace Pilot and Wartime Diplomat Peter Riedel* (Airlife, 1997), p. 128.

8: Defying Gravity

1 Georg Pasewaldt, 'Erfahrungen und Erkenntnisse einer Fliegerlaufbahn' [Experience and Insights from a Flying Career], private papers of Barbara Pasewaldt.

2 Ibid.

3 Ibid.

4 Ibid.

5 Ibid.

6 Ibid.

7 Ibid.

8 Ibid.

9 Archive Reinhart Rudershausen, Jutta Rudershausen, 'Flugkapitän Melitta Schiller-Stauffenberg' (nd).

10 Gerhard Bracke archive, Jutta Rudershausen in *Die Zeit*, 'Fifteen nosedives a day: forty years ago Flugkapitän Melitta Schiller-Stauffenberg was a pioneer of flight' (05.01.1973).

11 Gerhard Bracke, *Melitta Gräfin Stauffenberg: Das Leben einer Fliegerin* [The Life of an Aviatrix] (Herbig, 2013), privately translated, p. 94.

12 Ibid.

13 Ibid.

14 Carole Seymour-Jones, *She Landed by Moonlight, The Story of Secret Agent Pearl Witherington: the real 'Charlotte Gray'* (Transworld, 2013), p. 74.

15 Albert Speer, *Inside the Third Reich* (Sphere, 1971), p. 409.

16 Ibid.

17 Gerhard Bracke, *Melitta Gräfin Stauffenberg: Das Leben einer Fliegerin* [The Life of an Aviatrix] (Herbig, 2013), p. 164.

18 Archive Reinhart Rudershausen, Paul von Handel, 'Erinnerungen an Litta' [Memories of Litta] (nd).

19 Interview with Heidimarie Schade, Berlin (01.10.2014).

20 Max Escher, *Kulturwarte* magazine (1970s), quoted in Gerhard Bracke, *Melitta Gräfin Stauffenberg: Das Leben einer Fliegerin* [The Life of an Aviatrix] (Herbig, 2013), p. 96.

21 Ibid. p. 95.

22 Ibid. p. 96.
23 Ibid.
24 Ibid.
25 Ibid. p. 97.
26 Ibid.
27 Ibid. p. 96.
28 Ibid. p. 97.
29 Ibid.
30 Ibid. p. 98.
31 Ibid.
32 Ibid. p. 99.
33 Ibid.
34 Ibid.
35 Berthold von Stauffenberg, Mulley interview (05.11.2014).
36 Ibid.
37 Peter Hoffmann, *German Resistance to Hitler* (Harvard University Press, 1988).
38 Berthold von Stauffenberg, Mulley interview (05.11.2014).
39 Wolfgang Späte, *Top Secret Bird: The Luftwaffe's Me-163 Comet* (Independent Books, 1989), p. 79.
40 Ibid. p. 82
41 Ibid. p. 86.
42 Ibid. pp. 62–3.
43 Eric Brown, Mulley interview (18.03.2013).
44 Wolfgang Späte, *Top Secret Bird: The Luftwaffe's Me-163 Comet* (Independent Books, 1989), p. 82.
45 Ibid. p. 81.
46 John Martin Bradley, 'Combat Pilots of WWII' collection, interview with Hein K. Gering (27.06.2009).
47 Ibid.
48 Ibid.
49 Ibid.
50 Ibid.
51 Gerhard Bracke archive, Peter Riedel, Gerhard Bracke interview (late 1980s).
52 Ibid.
53 Ibid.
54 Gerhard Bracke archive, letter Peter Riedel/Mrs Hacker (25.08.1980).
55 Gerhard Bracke archive, Peter Riedel, Gerhard Bracke interview (late 1980s).
56 Ibid.
57 Gerhard Bracke archive, letter Peter Riedel/Mrs Hacker (25.08.1980).
58 Martin Simons, *German Air Attaché: The Thrilling Wartime Story of the German Ace Pilot and Wartime Diplomat Peter Riedel* (Airlife, 1997), p. 128.

59 Ibid. p. 128.
60 Gerhard Bracke archive, Peter Riedel, Gerhard Bracke interview (late 1980s).
61 Ibid.
62 Ibid.
63 Gerhard Bracke archive, letter Peter Riedel/Mrs Hacker (25.08.1980).
64 Gerhard Bracke archive, letter Hanna Reitsch/Klara Schiller (07.02.1975); Gerhard Bracke archive, Peter Riedel, Gerhard Bracke interview (late 1980s).
65 Gerhard Bracke archive, Peter Riedel, Gerhard Bracke interview (late 1980s).
66 Sönke Neitzel, *Tapping Hitler's Generals: Transcripts of Secret Conversations, 1942–1945* (Frontline, 2007), p. 237.
67 Ibid. pp. 262–3.
68 Archive Reinhart Rudershausen, letter Michael Schiller/Hermann Göring (26.10.1942).
69 Ibid.
70 Archive Reinhart Rudershausen, Margarete Schiller/Hermann Göring (11.12.1942).
71 Ibid.
72 Archive Reinhart Rudershausen, letter Michael Schiller/Hermann Göring (04.09.1943).
73 Mano Ziegler, *Rocket Fighter: The Story of the Messerschmitt Me163* (Arms & Armour, 1976), p. 22.
74 Eric Brown, Chalke Valley History Festival talk (02.06.2013).
75 Wolfgang Späte, *Top Secret Bird: The Luftwaffe's Me-163 Comet* (Independent Books, 1989), p. 194.
76 *The Secret War*, Episode 4: 'If . . .', BBC (1977).
77 Wolfgang Späte, *Top Secret Bird: The Luftwaffe's Me-163 Comet* (Independent Books, 1989), p. 86.
78 Hanna Reitsch, *The Sky My Kingdom: Memoirs of the Famous World War II Test Pilot* (Greenhill, 2009), p. 205.
79 Mano Ziegler, *Rocket Fighter: The Story of the Messerschmitt Me163* (Arms & Armour, 1976), p. 1.
80 *The Secret War*, Episode 4: 'If . . .', BBC (1977).
81 John Groom, producer, *The Secret War*, BBC, Mulley interview (24.06.2015).
82 Wolfgang Späte, *Top Secret Bird: The Luftwaffe's Me-163 Comet* (Independent Books, 1989), pp. 62–3.
83 *The Secret War*, Episode 4: 'If . . .', BBC (1977).
84 Hanna Reitsch, *The Sky My Kingdom: Memoirs of the Famous World War II Test Pilot* (Greenhill, 2009), p. 209.
85 Ibid.
86 Judy Lomax, *Hanna Reitsch: Flying for the Fatherland* (John Murray, 1988), p. 84.

87 Eric Brown, Chalke Valley History Festival talk (02.06.2013).
88 Hanna Reitsch, *The Sky My Kingdom: Memoirs of the Famous World War II Test Pilot* (Greenhill, 2009), p. 210.
89 Ibid.
90 Wolfgang Späte, *Top Secret Bird: The Luftwaffe's Me-163 Comet* (Independent Books, 1989), p. 103.
91 Ibid.
92 Ibid.
93 Ibid. p. 104.
94 Georg Pasewaldt, 'Erfahrungen und Erkenntnisse einer Fliegerlaufbahn' [Experience and Insights from a Flying Career], private papers of Barbara Pasewaldt.
95 Ibid.
96 Ibid.
97 Ibid.
98 Ibid.
99 Archive Reinhart Rudershausen, Melitta von Stauffenberg, 'Abschrift' [Report].
100 Ibid.
101 Ibid.
102 Ibid.
103 Ibid.
104 Ibid.
105 Ibid.
106 Ibid.
107 Hermann Göring's appointment diary (1943), catalogued by Herrmann Historica International Auctions, 70th auction online catalogue, lot 6140 (03.05.2015).
108 *Der Adler* [The Luftwaffe magazine], 'The Iron Cross for a Gallant Woman Pilot' (06.04.1943).
109 Quoted in Gerhard Bracke, *Melitta Gräfin Stauffenberg: Das Leben einer Fliegerin* [The Life of an Aviatrix] (Herbig, 2013), privately translated, p. 117.
110 Gerhard Bracke archive, Jutta Rudershausen in *Die Zeit*, 'Fifteen nosedives a day: forty years ago Flugkapitän Melitta Schiller-Stauffenberg was a pioneer of flight' (05.01.1973).
111 Archive Reinhart Rudershausen, Jutta Rudershausen, 'Flugkapitän Melitta Schiller-Stauffenberg' (nd), p. 66.
112 Ibid.
113 Gerhard Bracke archive, letter Peter Riedel/Mrs Hacker (25.08.1980).
114 Gerhard Bracke archive, letter Hanna Reitsch/Klara Schiller (07.02.1975).
115 Gerhard Bracke archive, letter Hanna Reitsch/Klara Schiller (18.02.1975).
116 Ibid.

117 Ibid.
118 Gerhard Bracke, *Melitta Gräfin Stauffenberg: Das Leben einer Fliegerin* (Herbig, 2013), p. 129.

9: UNDER ATTACK

1 Friedrich W. von Mellenthin, *Panzer Battles* (Tempus, 1956), p. 173.
2 Nicolaus von Below, *At Hitler's Side: The Memoirs of Hitler's Luftwaffe Adjutant 1937–1945* (Frontline, 2010), p. 161.
3 Ibid.
4 Walter Rehling, letter to Mulley (20.06.2013).
5 Gerhard Bracke archive, Melitta's diary (04.03.1943, 02.03.1943).
6 Archive Reinhart Rudershausen, Jutta Rudershausen, 'Flugkapitän Melitta Schiller-Stauffenberg' (nd), p. 66.
7 Hanna Reitsch, *The Sky My Kingdom: Memoirs of the Famous World War II Test Pilot* (Greenhill, 2009), p. 220.
8 Gerhard Bracke, *Melitta Gräfin Stauffenberg: Das Leben einer Fliegerin* [The Life of an Aviatrix] (Herbig, 2013), privately translated, p. 136.
9 Thomas Medicus, *Melitta von Stauffenberg: Ein Deutsches Leben* [A German Life] (Rowolt, 2012), p. 211.
10 Gerhard Bracke archive, Melitta's diary (13.05.1943).
11 Ibid.
12 Gerhard Bracke archive, Melitta's diary (20.03.1943, 25.03.43, 26.03.43).
13 Gerhard Bracke archive, Melitta's diary (15.03.43).
14 John Groom, producer, *The Secret War*, BBC, Mulley interview (24.06.2015).
15 Wolfgang Späte, *Top Secret Bird: The Luftwaffe's Me163 Comet* (Independent Books, 1989), p. 105.
16 Hanna Reitsch, *The Sky My Kingdom: Memoirs of the Famous World War II Test Pilot* (Greenhill, 2009), p. 212.
17 Ibid. p. 213.
18 Ibid. p. 214.
19 Mano Ziegler, *Rocket Fighter: The Story of the Messerschmitt Me163* (Arms and Armour, 1976), p. 27.
20 Ibid.
21 Ibid. p. 39.
22 Ibid. p. 39.
23 Ibid. p. 40.
24 Ibid. p. 40.
25 US National Archives and Records Administration, Hanna Reitsch Personal File, RG319, 270, 84, 13, 7, box 633 (7362164, XE053525), US Forces report, Hanna Reitsch interrogation, 'Condemnation of Göring by Hanna Reitsch' (16.11.1945), p. 4.

26 Ibid.

27 Ibid.

28 Hanna Reitsch, *The Sky My Kingdom: Memoirs of the Famous World War II Test Pilot* (Greenhill, 2009) p. 220.

29 US National Archives and Records Administration, Hanna Reitsch Personal File, RG319, 270, 84, 13, 7, box 633 (7362164, XE053525), US Forces report, Hanna Reitsch interrogation, 'Condemnation of Göring by Hanna Reitsch' (16.11.1945), p. 4.

30 Ibid. p. 3.

31 Ibid. p. 3.

32 Fred Taylor (trans., ed.), *The Goebbels Diaries, 1939–1941: The historic journal of a Nazi war leader* (Sphere, 1983), p. 197.

33 Louis P. Lochner (trans., ed.), *The Goebbels Diaries* (Hamish Hamilton, 1948), p. 246 (entry for 09.04.1943).

34 Ibid.

35 Ibid. p. 204 (entry for 03.03.1943).

36 US National Archives and Records Administration, Hanna Reitsch Personal File, RG319, 270, 84, 13, 7, box 633 (7362164, XE053525), US Forces report, Hanna Reitsch interrogation, 'Condemnation of Göring by Hanna Reitsch' (16.11.1945), p. 3.

37 Ibid. p. 1.

38 Dirk Bogarde, *Cleared for Take-Off* (Chivers, 1996), p. 30.

39 Jimmy Taylor, *The Secret War*, Episode 4: 'If . . .', BBC (1977).

40 Constance Babington Smith, *Evidence in Camera: the story of photographic intelligence in the Second World War* (Sutton, 2004), p. 51.

41 Sarah Churchill, *Keep on Dancing: an Autobiography* (George Weidenfeld & Nicolson, 1981), p. 61.

42 *The Secret War*, Episode 4: 'If . . .', BBC (1977).

43 Elisabeth zu Guttenberg, Sheridan Spearman, *Holding the Stirrup* (Duell, Sloan and Pearce/Little, Brown, 1953), p. 185.

44 Ibid.

45 Nigel Jones, *Countdown to Valkyrie: The July Plot to Assassinate Hitler* (Frontline, 2008), p. 154.

46 Konstanze von Schulthess, *Nina Schenk Gräfin von Stauffenberg: Ein Porträt* [A Portrait] (Piper, 2009), p. 78.

47 Ibid. p. 79.

48 Dorothee von Meding, *Courageous Hearts: Women and the anti-Hitler Plot of 1944* (Berghahn, 1997), p. 202.

49 Louis P. Lochner (trans., ed.), *The Goebbels Diaries* (Hamish Hamilton, 1948), p. 305 (entry for 21.05.1943).

50 Peter Hoffmann, *Stauffenberg: A Family History 1904–1944* (McGill-Queen's University Press, 2008), p. 183.

51 Gerhard Bracke archive, Melitta's diary (09.07.1943).

52 Ibid. (10.07.1943).

53 Ibid. (12.07.1943).

54 Ibid. (13.07.1943).
55 Ibid. (06.08.1943).
56 Hanna Reitsch, *The Sky My Kingdom: Memoirs of the Famous World War II Test Pilot* (Greenhill, 2009), p. 215.
57 Ibid.
58 Michael J. Neufeld, *Von Braun: Dreamer of Space, Engineer of War* (Alfred A. Knopf, 2008), p. 168.
59 Hanna Reitsch, *The Sky My Kingdom: Memoirs of the Famous World War II Test Pilot* (Greenhill, 2009), p. 216.
60 Ibid.
61 Ibid. p. 217.
62 Ibid. p. 217.
63 Ibid. p. 217.
64 Ibid. p. 217.
65 Ibid. p. 217.
66 Ibid. p. 218.
67 Ibid. p. 218.
68 Richard J. Evans, *The Third Reich at War* (Allen Lane, 2008), p. 660.
69 Ruth Kraft, Peenemünde mathematician, Flashback Television (2001), quoted in Taylor Downing, *Spies in the Sky: The Secret Battle for Aerial Intelligence during WWII* (Little, Brown, 2011), p. 278.
70 Constance Babington Smith, *Evidence in Camera: the story of photographic intelligence in the Second World War* (Sutton, 2004), p. 180.
71 Ibid. p. 182.
72 Ibid. p. 215.
73 Albert Speer, *Inside the Third Reich* (Sphere, 1971), p. 297.
74 Walter Dornberger, *V-2* (Hurst & Blackett, 1954), p. 151.
75 Ibid.
76 Michael J. Neufeld, *Von Braun: Dreamer of Space, Engineer of War* (Alfred A. Knopf, 2008), p. 153.
77 Walter Dornberger, *V-2* (Hurst & Blackett, 1954), p. 152.
78 Ibid. p. 153.
79 Ibid. p. 153.
80 Michael J. Neufeld, *Von Braun: Dreamer of Space, Engineer of War* (Alfred A. Knopf, 2008), p. 155.
81 RAF Museum sound archive, 330161 'The Great Raids: Peenemünde', John Searby, side A.
82 Ibid. side B.
83 Jack Pragnell, 102 Squadron veteran, Mulley interview (29 June 2015).
84 *The Lancaster: Britain's Flying Past*, BBC2 (20 July 2014).
85 Jack Pragnell, 102 Squadron veteran, Mulley interview (29 June 2015).
86 RAF Museum sound archive, 330161 'The Great Raids: Peenemünde', John Searby, side B.
87 *The Secret War*, Episode 4: 'If . . .', BBC (1977).
88 Ibid.; Walter Dornberger, *V-2* (Hurst & Blackett, 1954), p. 153.

89 Jack Pragnell, 102 Squadron veteran, Mulley interview (29 June 2015).
90 Cajus Becker, *The Luftwaffe War Diaries* (Macdonald, 1966), p. 315.
91 US National Archives and Records Administration, Hanna Reitsch Personal File, RG319, 270, 84, 13, 7, box 633 (7362164, XE053525), US Forces report, Hanna Reitsch interrogation, 'Condemnation of Göring by Hanna Reitsch' (16.11.1945), p. 5.
92 Tadeusz Bór-Komorowski, *The Secret Army: The Memoirs of General Bor-Komorowski* (Frontline, 2011), pp. 151–2.
93 RAF Museum sound archive, 330161 'The Great Raids: Peenemünde', John Searby, side B.
94 Ibid.
95 Colonel, Max Wachtel, V-1 Launching Regiment, *Secret War*, Episode 3: 'Terror Weapons', BBC (1977).
96 Walter Dornberger, *V-2* (Hurst & Blackett, 1954), p. 161.
97 *The Lancaster: Britain's Flying Past*, BBC2 (20 July 2014).

10: Operation Self-Sacrifice

 1 Hanna Reitsch, *The Sky My Kingdom: Memoirs of the Famous World War II Test Pilot* (Greenhill, 2009), p. 224.
 2 *Gloucestershire Echo*, 'RAF Bombers Blast New Baltic Target' (18.08.1943); *Nottingham Evening Post*, 'Echoes From Town' (21.08.1943). These articles paraphrase the Swiss and Moroccan press.
 3 *Nottingham Evening Post*, 'Echoes From Town' (21.08.1943).
 4 Ibid.
 5 Hanna Reitsch, *The Sky My Kingdom: Memoirs of the Famous World War II Test Pilot* (Greenhill, 2009), p. 224.
 6 Ibid. p. 225.
 7 Ibid. p. 225.
 8 Ibid. p. 225.
 9 US National Archives and Records Administration, Hanna Reitsch personal file, 'The Wind of Heaven Goes West' (October 1946), p. 2.
10 Hanna Reitsch, *The Sky My Kingdom: Memoirs of the Famous World War II Test Pilot* (Greenhill, 2009), p. 225.
11 Gerhard Bracke archive, Melitta's 1943 diary (18.08.1943).
12 Ibid. (03.09.1943).
13 Ibid. (23.09.1943).
14 Ibid. (02.10.1943).
15 Ibid. (01.09.1943).
16 Archive Reinhart Rudershausen, Paul von Handel, 'Erinnerungen an Litta' [Memories of Litta] (nd).
17 Michael J. Neufeld, *Von Braun: Dreamer of Space, Engineer of War* (Alfred A. Knopf, 2008), pp. 161–2.
18 Walter Rehling, letter to Mulley (20.06.2013).

19 Wolfgang Späte, *Top Secret Bird: The Luftwaffe's Me-163 Comet* (Independent Books, 1989), p. 105.
20 Ibid. p. 183.
21 Ibid. p. 183.
22 Hanna Reitsch, *The Sky My Kingdom: Memoirs of the Famous World War II Test Pilot* (Greenhill, 2009), p. 226.
23 Ibid.
24 Fred Taylor (trans., ed.), *The Goebbels Diaries, 1939–1941: The historic journal of a Nazi war leader* (Sphere, 1983), p. 214.
25 Hanna Reitsch, *The Sky My Kingdom: Memoirs of the Famous World War II Test Pilot* (Greenhill, 2009), p. 227.
26 Ibid.
27 Gerhard Bracke archive, Melitta's diary (25.09.1943).
28 Ibid. (26.09.1943).
29 Ibid. (14.10.1943, 15.10.1943, 18.10.1943).
30 Ibid. (20.09.1943).
31 Ibid. (25.10.1943).
32 Hanna Reitsch, *The Sky My Kingdom: Memoirs of the Famous World War II Test Pilot* (Greenhill, 2009), p. 221.
33 Judy Lomax, *Hanna Reitsch: Flying for the Fatherland* (John Murray, 1988), p. 91.
34 Hanna Reitsch, *The Sky My Kingdom: Memoirs of the Famous World War II Test Pilot* (Greenhill, 2009), p. 221.
35 Ibid. p. 222.
36 Ibid. p. 222.
37 Ibid. p. 222.
38 Judy Lomax, *Hanna Reitsch: Flying for the Fatherland* (John Murray, 1988), p. 91.
39 Hanna Reitsch, *The Sky My Kingdom: Memoirs of the Famous German World War II Test Pilot* (Greenhill, 2009), p. 223.
40 Judy Lomax, *Hanna Reitsch: Flying for the Fatherland* (John Murray, 1988), p. 92.
41 Ibid. p. 91.
42 Hanna Reitsch, *The Sky My Kingdom: Memoirs of the Famous German World War II Test Pilot* (Greenhill, 2009), p. 223.
43 *Hanna Reitsch: Hitlers Fliegerin* [Hitler's Pilot], Interspot Film (dir. Gerhard Jelinek and Fritz Kalteis, 2010).
44 Gerhard Bracke, *Melitta Gräfin Stauffenberg: Das Leben einer Fliegerin* [The Life of an Aviatrix] (Herbig, 2013), privately translated, p. 132; Gerhard Bracke archive, Melitta's diary (14.10.1943).
45 Gerhard Bracke, *Melitta Gräfin Stauffenberg: Das Leben einer Fliegerin* [The Life of an Aviatrix] (Herbig, 2013), privately translated, p. 132.
46 Ibid.
47 Gerhard Bracke archive, Melitta's diary (14.11.1943).

48 Gerhard Bracke, *Melitta Gräfin Stauffenberg: Das Leben einer Fliegerin* [The Life of an Aviatrix] (Herbig, 2013), privately translated, p. 131.

49 Gerhard Bracke archive, Melitta's diary (05.10.1943).

50 Gerhard Bracke, *Melitta Gräfin Stauffenberg: Das Leben einer Fliegerin* [The Life of an Aviatrix] (Herbig, 2013), privately translated, p. 133.

51 Gerhard Bracke archive, Melitta's 1943 diary (16.11.1943, 27.11.43).

52 Gerhard Bracke, *Melitta Gräfin Stauffenberg: Das Leben einer Fliegerin* [The Life of an Aviatrix] (Herbig, 2013), privately translated, p. 132.

53 Ibid. p. 131.

54 Ibid. p. 132.

55 Max Hastings, *All Hell Let Loose: The World At War 1939–1945* (Harper Press, 2011), p. 489.

56 Heinrich Hoffmann, *Hitler Was My Friend: The Memoirs of Hitler's Photographer* (Frontline, 2011), p. 215.

57 Gerhard Bracke, *Melitta Gräfin Stauffenberg: Das Leben einer Fliegerin* [The Life of an Aviatrix] (Herbig, 2013), privately translated, p. 133.

58 Ibid. pp. 144, 145.

59 Ibid. p. 145.

60 Ibid. p. 144.

61 Berthold von Stauffenberg, Oppenweiler, Mulley interview (05.11.2014).

62 Ibid.

63 Ibid.

64 Hanna Reitsch, *The Sky My Kingdom: Memoirs of the Famous German World War II Test Pilot* (Greenhill, 2009), p. 226.

65 Traudl Junge, *Until the Final Hour: Hitler's Last Secretary* (Phoenix, 2002), p. 121.

66 Constance Babington Smith, *Evidence in Camera: The story of photographic intelligence in the Second World War* (Sutton, 2004), p. 194; Elizabeth Hick, photographic interpreter, *Operation Crossbow*, BBC2 (2013).

67 Constance Babington Smith, *Evidence in Camera: The story of photographic intelligence in the Second World War* (Sutton, 2004), pp. 199–200.

68 Gerhard Bracke, *Melitta Gräfin Stauffenberg: Das Leben einer Fliegerin* [The Life of an Aviatrix] (Herbig Verlag, 2013), privately translated, p. 162.

69 Archive Reinhart Rudershausen, Melitta von Stauffenberg, 'Typed up Stockholm trip' (19.12.43).

70 Ibid.

71 Ibid.

72 Ibid.

73 Ibid.

74 Gerhard Bracke, *Melitta Gräfin Stauffenberg: Das Leben einer Fliegerin* [The Life of an Aviatrix] (Herbig, 2013), privately translated, p. 158.

75 Ibid. p. 157.
76 Ibid. p. 159.
77 Ibid. p. 158.
78 Ibid. p. 157.
79 Ibid. p. 168.
80 Ibid. p. 169.
81 Ibid. p. 169.
82 Archive Reinhart Rudershausen, Melitta von Stauffenberg, 'Typed up Stockholm trip' (19.12.43).
83 Ibid.
84 Ibid.
85 Constance Babington Smith, *Evidence in Camera: The story of photographic intelligence in the Second World War* (Sutton, 2004), p. 200.
86 Gerhard Bracke archive, Melitta's diary (25.12.1943).
87 Ibid. (26.12.1943).
88 Ibid. (28.12.1943).
89 Archive Reinhart Rudershausen, Klara Schiller, 'Memories of Klara Schiller' (nd).
90 Ibid.
91 Ibid.
92 Ibid.
93 Ibid.
94 Hajo Herrmann, *Eagle's Wings: The Autobiography of a Luftwaffe Pilot* (Airlife, 1991), p. 223.
95 Ibid. p. 230.
96 Bob Carruthers, *Voices from the Luftwaffe* (Pen & Sword, 2012), p. 51.
97 *Schlesische Flieger Nachrichten* [Silesian Pilot News magazine] (5.1988), p. 5.
98 Gerhard Bracke archive, Melitta's diary (11.01.1944).
99 Ibid. (17.01.1944).
100 Gerhard Bracke archive, Melitta's diary (23.01.1944).
101 Thomas Medicus, *Melitta von Stauffenberg: Ein Deutsches Leben* [A German Life] (Rowohlt, 2012), p. 259.
102 Gerhard Bracke archive, Melitta's diary (03.02.1944).
103 Hanna Reitsch, *The Sky My Kingdom: Memoirs of the Famous German World War II Test Pilot* (Greenhill, 2009), p. 228.
104 Ibid.
105 Bernd Freytag von Loringhoven, *In the Bunker with Hitler: The last witness speaks* (Weidenfeld & Nicolson, 2005), p. 82.
106 Hanna Reitsch, *The Sky My Kingdom: Memoirs of the Famous German World War II Test Pilot* (Greenhill, 2009), pp. 228–9.
107 Ibid. p. 229.
108 Bernd Freytag von Loringhoven, *In the Bunker with Hitler: The last witness speaks* (Weidenfeld & Nicolson, 2005), p. 83.

109 Hanna Reitsch, *The Sky My Kingdom: Memoirs of the Famous German World War II Test Pilot* (Greenhill, 2009), p. 229.

110 Ibid.

111 Bernd Freytag von Loringhoven, *In the Bunker with Hitler: The last witness speaks* (Weidenfeld & Nicolson, 2005), p. 88.

112 Heinrich Hoffmann, *Hitler Was My Friend: The Memoirs of Hitler's Photographer* (Frontline, 2011), p. 148.

113 Hanna Reitsch, *The Sky My Kingdom: Memoirs of the Famous German World War II Test Pilot* (Greenhill, 2009), p. 229.

114 Ibid.

115 US National Archives and Records Administration, Hanna Reitsch personal file, 'The Wind of Heaven Goes West' (October 1946), p. 3.

116 Nicolaus von Below, *At Hitler's Side: The Memoirs of Hitler's Luftwaffe Adjutant 1937–1945* (Frontline, 2010), p. 194.

117 Ibid.

118 Ibid.

119 *Aeroplane Monthly*, 'Flugkapitän Hanna Reitsch', part 4 (September 1985), p. 496.

120 Nicolaus von Below, *At Hitler's Side: The Memoirs of Hitler's Luftwaffe Adjutant 1937–1945* (Frontline, 2010), p. 194.

121 *German History: The Journal of the German History Society*, Bernhard Riegen, 'Hanna Reitsch: The Global Career of a Nazi Celebrity', vol. 26, no. 3, p. 389.

122 Jana and Hermann Graml (eds.), *Die Tagebücher von Joseph Goebbels: Oktober bis Dezember 1944* [The Diaries of Joseph Goebbels: October to December 1944] (K. G. Saur, 1996), pp. 262–3 (23.11.1944).

123 Hanna Reitsch, *The Sky My Kingdom: Memoirs of the Famous German World War II Test Pilot* (Greenhill, 2009), p. 237.

124 Judy Lomax, *Hanna Reitsch: Flying for the Fatherland* (John Murray, 1988) p. 98.

125 Hanna Reitsch, *The Sky My Kingdom: Memoirs of the Famous German World War II Test Pilot* (Greenhill, 2009), p. 226.

126 Otto Skorzeny, *Skorzeny's Special Missions: The Memoirs of 'The Most Dangerous Man in Europe'* (Greenhill, 2006), p. 100.

11: Operation Valkyrie

1 Gerhard Bracke archive, Melitta's diary (21.05.1944).

2 Archive Reinhart Rudershausen, Paul von Handel, 'Erinnerungen an Litta' [Memories of Litta] (nd).

3 Ibid.

4 Peter Hoffmann, *German Resistance to Hitler* (Harvard, 1988), p. 131.

5 Konstanze von Schulthess, *Nina Schenk Gräfin von Stauffenberg: Ein Porträt* [A Portrait] (Piper, 2009), p. 78.

6   Alexander von Stauffenberg, *Denkmal* [Monument] (Stefan George Foundation, 1964), p. 23.

7   Ibid. p. 25.

8   Konstanze von Schulthess, *Nina Schenk Gräfin von Stauffenberg: Ein Porträt* [A Portrait] (Piper, 2009), p. 82.

9   Nina von Stauffenberg to Peter Hoffmann in Konstanze von Schulthess, *Nina Schenk Gräfin von Stauffenberg: Ein Porträt* [A Portrait] (Piper, 2009), p. 88.

10 Konstanze von Schulthess Rechberg (Nina's daughter), Mulley interview (25.11.2014).

11 Konstanze von Schulthess, *Nina Schenk Gräfin von Stauffenberg: Ein Porträt* [A Portrait] (Piper, 2009), p. 24.

12 Dorothee von Meding, *Courageous Hearts: Women and the anti-Hitler Plot of 1944* (Berghahn, 2008), p. 188.

13 Ibid.

14 Konstanze von Schulthess, *Nina Schenk Gräfin von Stauffenberg: Ein Porträt* [A Portrait] (Piper, 2009), p. 73.

15 Dorothee von Meding, *Courageous Hearts: Women and the anti-Hitler Plot of 1944* (Berghahn, 2008), p. 189.

16 Gerhard Bracke, *Melitta Gräfin Stauffenberg: Das Leben einer Fliegerin* [The Life of an Aviatrix] (Herbig, 2013), privately translated, p. 224.

17 Archive Reinhart Rudershausen, Paul von Handel, 'Erinnerungen an Litta' [Memories of Litta] (nd).

18 Gerhard Bracke archive, Melitta's diary (03.03.1944).

19 Ibid. (07.03.1944).

20 Thomas Medicus, *Melitta von Stauffenberg: Ein Deutsches Leben* [A German Life] (Rowohlt, 2012), p. 262.

21 Karl Christ, *Der Andere Stauffenberg: Der Historiker und Dichter Alexander von Stauffenberg* [The Other Stauffenberg: Historian and Poet Alexander von Stauffenberg] (C. H. Beck, 2008), p. 45.

22 Thomas Medicus, *Melitta von Stauffenberg: Ein Deutsches Leben* [A German Life] (Rowohlt, 2012), p. 273.

23 IWM, film archive, GWY 213, *Die Deutsche Wochenschau* [The German Newsreel] no. 712 (April 1944).

24 Hanna Reitsch, *The Sky My Kingdom: Memoirs of the Famous German World War II Test Pilot* (Greenhill, 2009), p. 230.

25 *Hanna Reitsch: Hitlers Fliegerin* [Hitler's Pilot], Interspot Film (dir. Gerhard Jelinek and Fritz Kalteis, 2010). Comment made by Fred Weinholtz.

26 Hanna Reitsch, *The Sky My Kingdom: Memoirs of the Famous German World War II Test Pilot* (Greenhill, 2009), p. 230.

27 Max Hastings, *All Hell Let Loose: The World at War, 1939–1945* (Harper Press, 2011), p. 486.

28 US National Archives and Records Administration, Hanna Reitsch personal file, 'The Wind of Heaven Goes West' (October 1946), p. 4.

29 Gerhard Bracke archive, Melitta's diary (04.05.1944).
30 Ibid. (02.05.1944).
31 Thomas Medicus, *Melitta von Stauffenberg: Ein Deutsches Leben* [A German Life] (Rowohlt, 2012), pp. 266, 265.
32 Hanna Reitsch, *The Sky My Kingdom: Memoirs of the Famous German World War II Test Pilot* (Greenhill, 2009), p. 232.
33 Otto Skorzeny, *Skorzeny's Special Missions: The Memoirs of 'The Most Dangerous Man in Europe'* (Greenhill, 2006), p. 100.
34 Deutsches Museum Archive, 130/101, Hanna Reitsch, 'Solemn declaration' (12.04.1948).
35 Otto Skorzeny, *Skorzeny's Special Missions: The Memoirs of 'The Most Dangerous Man in Europe'* (Greenhill, 2006), p. 100.
36 Deutsches Museum Archive, 130/101, Hanna Reitsch, 'Solemn declaration' (12.04.1948).
37 Eric Brown, Mulley interview (23.06.2014).
38 Hanna Reitsch, *The Sky My Kingdom: Memoirs of the Famous German World War II Test Pilot* (Greenhill, 2009), p. 232.
39 Otto Skorzeny, *Skorzeny's Special Missions: The Memoirs of 'The Most Dangerous Man in Europe'* (Greenhill, 2006), p. 103.
40 *Schlesische Flieger Nachrichten* [Silesian Pilot News magazine] (5/1988).
41 Gerhard Bracke, *Melitta Gräfin Stauffenberg: Das Leben einer Fliegerin* [The Life of an Aviatrix] (Herbig, 2013), privately translated, p. 180.
42 Archive Reinhart Rudershausen, Klara Schiller, 'Memories of Klara Schiller' (nd).
43 Gerhard Bracke, *Melitta Gräfin Stauffenberg: Das Leben einer Fliegerin* [The Life of an Aviatrix] (Herbig, 2013), privately translated, p. 181.
44 Gerhard Bracke archive, Melitta's diary (23.05.1944).
45 Gerhard Bracke, *Melitta Gräfin Stauffenberg: Das Leben einer Fliegerin* [The Life of an Aviatrix] (Herbig, 2013), privately translated, p. 181.
46 Richard Perlia, *Mal oben – Mal unten* [Sometimes Up – Sometimes Down] (Schiff & Flugzeug-Verlagsbuchhandlung, 2011), p. 194.
47 Ibid., p. 236.
48 Otto Skorzeny, *Skorzeny's Special Missions: The Memoirs of 'The Most Dangerous Man in Europe'* (Greenhill, 2006), p. 104.
49 Hanna Reitsch, *The Sky My Kingdom: Memoirs of the Famous German World War II Test Pilot* (Greenhill, 2009), p. 233.
50 Ibid.
51 Otto Skorzeny, *Skorzeny's Special Missions: The Memoirs of 'The Most Dangerous Man in Europe'* (Greenhill, 2006), p. 104.
52 Hanna Reitsch, *The Sky My Kingdom: Memoirs of the Famous German World War II Test Pilot* (Greenhill, 2009), p. 234.
53 Ibid.
54 Dennis Piszkiewicz, *From Nazi Test Pilot to Hitler's Bunker: The Fantastic Flights of Hanna Reitsch* (Praeger, 1997), p. 78.

55 Deutsches Museum archive, 130/101, Hanna Reitsch, 'Solemn Declaration' (12.04.1948).
56 Dennis Piszkiewicz, *From Nazi Test Pilot to Hitler's Bunker: The Fantastic Flights of Hanna Reitsch* (Praeger, 1997), p. 78.
57 *Aeroplane Monthly*, 'Flugkapitän Hanna Reitsch', part 4 (September 1985), p. 497.
58 Otto Skorzeny, *Skorzeny's Special Missions: The Memoirs of 'The Most Dangerous Man in Europe'* (Greenhill, 2006), p. 105.
59 Ibid.
60 Ibid.
61 Ron Laytner, *Edit International Articles: A portfolio of some of Ron Layther's greatest stories* (2010).
62 Otto Skorzeny, *Skorzeny's Special Missions: The Memoirs of 'The Most Dangerous Man in Europe'* (Greenhill, 2006), p. 105.
63 Ibid.
64 Hanna Reitsch, *The Sky My Kingdom: Memoirs of the Famous German World War II Test Pilot* (Greenhill, 2009), p. 235.
65 Ibid.
66 Ibid. p. 236.
67 Deutsches Museum archive, 130/111, letter Hanna Reitsch/Ull Schwenger (22.07.1977).
68 Nicolaus von Below, *At Hitler's Side: The Memoirs of Hitler's Luftwaffe Adjutant 1937–1945* (Frontline, 2010), p. 203.
69 Hanna Reitsch, *The Sky My Kingdom: Memoirs of the Famous German World War II Test Pilot* (Greenhill, 2009), p. 236.
70 Ibid. pp. 236–7.
71 US National Archives and Records Administration, Hanna Reitsch personal file, 'The Wind of Heaven Goes West' (October 1946), p. 7.
72 Gerhard Bracke archive, Melitta's diary (11.06.1944).
73 Ibid. (06.06.1944).
74 Nigel Jones, *Countdown to Valkyrie: The July Plot to Assassinate Hitler* (Frontline, 2008) p. viii; Margarethe von Hardenberg in Dorothee von Meding, *Courageous Hearts: Women and the anti-Hitler Plot of 1944* (Berghahn, 2008), p. 52.
75 Nigel Jones, *Countdown to Valkyrie: The July Plot to Assassinate Hitler* (Frontline, 2008), p. 174.
76 Albert Speer, *Inside the Third Reich* (Sphere, 1971), p. 509.
77 Ibid.
78 Peter Hoffmann, *The History of the German Resistance, 1933–1945* (McGill-Queen's University Press, 1996), p. 380.
79 Gerhard Bracke archive, Melitta's diary (13.06.1944).
80 Konstanze von Schulthess, *Nina Schenk Gräfin von Stauffenberg: Ein Porträt* [A Portrait] (Piper, 2009), p. 88.
81 Gerhard Bracke, *Melitta Gräfin Stauffenberg: Das Leben einer Fliegerin* [The Life of an Aviatrix] (Herbig, 2013), privately translated, p. 181.

82 Nicolaus von Below, *At Hitler's Side: The Memoirs of Hitler's Luftwaffe Adjutant 1937–1945* (Frontline, 2010), p. 200.

83 Gerhard Bracke archive, Melitta's diary (16.06.1944).

84 Derek Mulley, Harpenden, Mulley interview (20.05.2013).

85 Veronia Volkersz, *The Sky and I* (W. H. Allen, 1956), p. 87. 'ATA' stands for the Air Transport Auxiliary.

86 Eric Brown, *Wings On My Sleeve: The World's Greatest Test Pilot Tells His Story* (Phoenix, 2007), p. 77.

87 *Mail Online*, Robert Hardman, 'Hero who makes Biggles look like a wimp' (07.05.2013).

88 Ulrich von Hassell, *The Von Hassell Diaries: The Story of the Forces Against Hitler Inside Germany 1938–1944* (Westview Press, 1994), p. 355.

89 Gerhard Bracke archive, Melitta's diary (17.06.1944).

90 Archive Reinhart Rudershausen, Paul von Handel, 'Erinnerungen an Litta' [Memories of Litta] (nd).

91 Ibid.

92 Ibid.

93 Gerhard Bracke archive, Melitta's diary (27.06.1944).

94 Gerhard Bracke, *Melitta Gräfin Stauffenberg: Das Leben einer Fliegerin* [The Life of an Aviatrix] (Herbig, 2013), privately translated, pp. 187–8.

95 Albert Speer, *Inside the Third Reich* (Sphere, 1971), p. 509.

96 Gerhard Bracke, *Melitta Gräfin Stauffenberg: Das Leben einer Fliegerin* [The Life of an Aviatrix] (Herbig, 2013), privately translated, p. 188.

97 Hans Bernd Gisevius, *To The Bitter End* (Jonathan Cape, 1948) , pp. 501–2.

98 Ibid. p. 502.

99 Annedore Leber, *Conscience in Revolt: Sixty-four Stories of Resistance in Germany* (Westview Press, 1994), p. 140.

100 Dorothee von Meding, *Courageous Hearts: Women and the anti-Hitler Plot of 1944* (Berghahn, 2008), p. 188.

101 Gerhard Bracke archive, Melitta's diary (15.07.1944).

102 Dorothee von Meding, *Courageous Hearts: Women and the anti-Hitler Plot of 1944* (Berghahn, 2008), p. 14.

103 Gerhard Bracke archive, Melitta's diary (16.07.1944).

104 Ibid. (18.07.1944).

105 Ibid. (19.07.1944).

106 Dorothee von Meding, *Courageous Hearts: Women and the anti-Hitler Plot of 1944* (Berghahn, 2008), p. 155.

107 Hans Bernd Gisevius, *To The Bitter End* (Jonathan Cape, 1948), p. 529.

108 Walter Warlimont, *Witness: The Plot to Kill Hitler*, BBC World Service (18.07.2014).

109 Fabian von Schlabrendorff, *The Secret War Against Hitler* (Westview Press, 1994), p. 287.
110 Hans Bernd Gisevius, *To The Bitter End* (Jonathan Cape, 1948), p. 534.
111 Ibid. p. 535.
112 Nigel Jones, *Countdown to Valkyrie: The July Plot to Assassinate Hitler* (Frontline, 2008), p. 160.
113 *Blind Spot: Hitler's Secretary, Traudl Junge*, Sony Pictures Classics (directed and written by Andrew Heller and Othmar Schmiderer, 2002).
114 Christa Schroeder, *He Was My Chief: The Memoirs of Adolf Hitler's Secretary* (Frontline, 2009), p. 122.
115 *Blind Spot: Hitler's Secretary, Traudl Junge*, Sony Pictures Classics (directed and written by Andrew Heller and Othmar Schmiderer, 2002).
116 Hugh Trevor-Roper, *The Last Days of Hitler* (Papermac, 1995), pp. 28–9.
117 Albert Speer, *Inside the Third Reich* (Sphere, 1971), p. 521.

12: In the Camps

1 Anne Frank, *The Diary of a Young Girl* (Penguin, 2012), p. 332 (21.07.1944).
2 Ibid. pp. 332–3 (21.07.1944).
3 Gerhard Bracke archive, Melitta's diary (20.07.1944).
4 Ibid. (21.07.1944).
5 Ibid. (22.07.1944).
6 Otto Skorzeny, *Skorzeny's Special Missions: The Memoirs of 'The Most Dangerous Man in Europe'* (Greenhill, 2006), p. 113.
7 Ibid. p. 117.
8 Albert Speer, *Inside the Third Reich* (Sphere, 1971), p. 521.
9 Otto Skorzeny, *Skorzeny's Special Missions: The Memoirs of 'The Most Dangerous Man in Europe'* (Greenhill, 2006) p. 118.
10 Joachim Fest, *Plotting Hitler's Death: The German Resistance to Hitler 1933–1945* (Weidenfeld & Nicolson, 1997), p. 231.
11 Otto Skorzeny, *Skorzeny's Special Missions: The Memoirs of 'The Most Dangerous Man in Europe'* (Greenhill, 2006), pp. 118–19.
12 Elisabeth zu Guttenberg, *Beim Namen Gerufen: Erinnerungen* [Called By Name: Memories] (Ullstein Sachbuch, 1992), p. 180; Eva Madelung, Joachim Scholtyseck, *Heldenkinder – Verräterkinder: Wenn die Eltern im Widerstand waren* [Hero Children – Traitor Children: Children of the Resistance] (C. H. Beck, 2007), p. 37.
13 Nigel Jones, *Countdown to Valkyrie: The July plot to assassinate Hitler* (Frontline, 2008), p. 236.

14 TNA, WO 208/4168 (SRGG 961c), interrogation reports of German
    POWs, General von Thoma.

15 Dorothee von Meding, *Courageous Hearts: Women and the anti-Hitler
    Plot of 1944* (Berghahn, 2008), p. 192.

16 Ibid.

17 Konstanze von Schulthess, *Nina Schenk Gräfin von Stauffenberg: Ein
    Porträt* [A Portrait] (Piper, 2009), p. 25.

18 Berthold von Stauffenberg, 'A Childhood in the Third Reich – from
    System Conformist to Traitor's Child'. Lecture delivered to the AV
    Rheinstein Köln-Lindenthal (14.04.2008).

19 *Witness: The The Plot to Kill Hitler*, BBC World Service (18.07.2014).

20 Dorothee von Meding, *Courageous Hearts: Women and the anti-Hitler
    Plot of 1944* (Berghahn, 2008), p. 198.

21 Berthold von Stauffenberg, 'A Childhood in the Third Reich – from
    System Conformist to Traitor's Child'. Lecture delivered to the AV
    Rheinstein Köln-Lindenthal (14.04.2008).

22 Konstanze von Schulthess, *Nina Schenk Gräfin von Stauffenberg: Ein
    Porträt* [A Portrait] (Piper, 2009), p. 84.

23 Robert Loeffel, *Family Punishment in Nazi Germany: Sippenhaft, Terror
    and Myth* (Palgrave Macmillan, 2012), p. 123.

24 *Spying on Hitler's Army: The Secret Recordings*, Channel 4 (02.06.2013).

25 Sönke Neitzel, *Tapping Hitler's Generals: Transcripts of Secret
    Conversations, 1942–45* (Frontline, 2007), p. 118.

26 Gerald Posner, *Hitler's Children: Inside the Families of the Third Reich*
    (Mandarin, 1991), p. 181.

27 Dorothee von Meding, *Courageous Hearts: Women and the anti-Hitler
    Plot of 1944* (Berghahn, 2008), p. 58.

28 Konstanze von Schulthess, *Nina Schenk Gräfin von Stauffenberg:
    Ein Porträt* [A Portrait] (Piper, 2009), p. 143; Gerald Posner,
    Hitler's Children: Inside the Families of the Third Reich (Mandarin, 1991),
    p. 181.

29 Archive Reinhart Rudershausen, Klara Schiller, 'Memories of Klara
    Schiller' (nd).

30 Ibid.

31 Gerhard Bracke archive, Melitta's diary (23.07.1944).

32 Archive Reinhart Rudershausen, Klara Schiller, 'Memories of Klara
    Schiller' (nd).

33 Dorothee von Meding, *Courageous Hearts: Women and the anti-Hitler
    Plot of 1944* (Berghahn, 2008), p. 189.

34 Gerhard Bracke archive, Melitta's diary (23.07.1944).

35 Archive Reinhart Rudershausen, Paul von Handel, 'Erinnerungen an
    Litta' [Memories of Litta] (nd).

36 Archive Reinhart Rudershausen, Jutta Rudershausen, 'Flugkapitän
    Melitta Schiller-Stauffenberg' (nd).

37 Archive Reinhart Rudershausen, Klara Schiller, 'Memories of Klara Schiller' (nd).

38 Ibid.

39 Gerhard Bracke archive, Melitta's diary (27.07.1944).

40 Ibid.

41 Ibid. (end pages).

42 Ursula von Kardorff, *Diary of a Nightmare: Berlin 1942–1945* (Rupert Hart-Davis, 1965), p. 137.

43 Ibid. p. 139.

44 Gerhard Bracke archive, Melitta's diary (03.08.1944).

45 Gerhard Bracke archive, Philippa Countess von Thun-Hohenstein (née von Bredow), filmed interview, 'Memories of Melitta: personal impressions of Countess von Stauffenberg' (07.07.2000).

46 Gerhard Bracke archive, Melitta's diary (04.08.1944).

47 Ibid. (06.08.1944).

48 Ursula von Kardorff, *Diary of a Nightmare: Berlin 1942–1945* (Rupert Hart-Davis, 1965), p. 122.

49 Heinz Linge, *With Hitler to the End: The Memoirs of Adolf Hitler's Valet* (Frontline, 2009), pp. 161, 163.

50 Gerhard Bracke archive, Melitta's diary (09.08.1944).

51 Glenn B. Infield, *Skorzeny: Hitler's Commando* (St Martin's Press, 1981), p. 64.

52 Bernd Freytag von Loringhoven, *In the Bunker With Hitler: The last witness speaks* (Weidenfeld & Nicolson, 2005), p. 68.

53 Gerhard Bracke archive, Melitta's diary (11.08.1944).

54 Dorothee von Meding, *Courageous Hearts* (1997), pp. 156–7.

55 Gerhard Bracke archive, Melitta's diary (17.08.1944).

56 Ibid. (17.08.1944).

57 Ibid. (17.08.1944).

58 Gerald Posner, *Hitler's Children: Inside the Families of the Third Reich* (Mandarin, 1991), p. 184.

59 Hajo Herrmann, *Eagle's Wings: The Autobiography of a Luftwaffe Pilot* (Airlife, 1991), pp. 227, 231.

60 Gerhard Bracke archive, Melitta's diary (24.07.1944).

61 Ibid. (25.08.1944).

62 Robert Loeffel, *Family Punishment in Nazi Germany: Sippenhaft, Terror and Myth* (Palgrave Macmillan, 2012), p. 146.

63 Nina von Stauffenberg quoted by Gerhard Bracke, *Melitta Gräfin Stauffenberg: Das Leben einer Fliegerin* [The Life of an Aviatrix] (Herbig, 2013), privately translated, p. 223.

64 Peter Hoffmann, *Stauffenberg: A Family History, 1904–1944* (McGill-Queen's University Press, 2008), p. 279.

65 Archive Reinhart Rudershausen, Klara Schiller, 'Memories of Klara Schiller' (nd).

66 Ursula von Kardorff, *Diary of a Nightmare: Berlin 1942–1945* (Rupert Hart-Davis, 1965), p. 152.

67 Konstanze von Schulthess, *Nina Schenk Gräfin von Stauffenberg: Ein Porträt* [A Portrait] (Piper, 2009), p. 143.

68 Dorothee von Meding, *Courageous Hearts: Women and the anti-Hitler Plot of 1944* (Berghahn, 2008), p. 193.

69 Berthold von Stauffenberg, 'A Childhood in the Third Reich – from System Conformist to Traitor's Child'. Lecture delivered to the AV Rheinstein Köln-Lindenthal (14.04.2008).

70 Ibid.; Melitta to Nina von Stauffenberg (30.12.1944) quoted in Gerhard Bracke, *Melitta Gräfin Stauffenberg: Das Leben einer Fliegerin* [The Life of an Aviatrix] (Herbig, 2013), privately translated, p. 222.

71 Berthold von Stauffenberg, 'A Childhood in the Third Reich – from System Conformist to Traitor's Child'. Lecture delivered to the AV Rheinstein Köln-Lindenthal (14.04.2008).

72 Bundesarchiv Berlin, R58/1027, quoted in Robert Loeffel, *Family Punishment in Nazi Germany: Sippenhaft, Terror and Myth* (Palgrave Macmillan, 2012), p. 178.

73 Berthold von Stauffenberg, Mulley interview (05.11.14).

74 Elisabeth zu Guttenberg, Sheridan Spearman: *Holding the Stirrup* (Duell, Sloan and Pearce/Little, Brown, 1953), p. 212.

75 Ibid.

76 Ibid.

77 Ibid. p. 215.

78 Ibid. p. 215.

79 Anne Voorhoeve private archive, Berlin, Otto-Philipp von Stauffenberg, 'Memories of the time after 20 July 1944, the day of the attempted assassination of Hitler'.

80 Fey von Hassell, *A Mother's War* (Corgi, 1991), p. 158.

81 Ibid. pp. 161 and 163.

82 Ibid. p. 161.

83 Ibid. p. 161.

84 Ibid. p. 166.

85 Ibid. p. 168.

86 Ibid. p. 168.

87 Ibid. p. 163.

88 Karl Christ, *Der Andere Stauffenberg: Der Historiker und Dichter Alexander von Stauffenberg* [The Other Stauffenberg: Historian and Poet Alexander von Stauffenberg] (C. H. Beck, 2008), privately translated, p. 161.

89 Fey von Hassell, *A Mother's War* (Corgi, 1991), p. 166.

90 Ibid. p. 173.

91 Ibid. p. 174.

92 Martin Simons, *German Air Attaché: The Thrilling Wartime Story of the*

German Ace Pilot and Wartime Diplomat Peter Riedel (Airlife, 1997), p. 180.

93 Ibid. p. 75.
94 Ibid. p. 183.
95 Ibid. p. 146.
96 Ibid. pp. 185, 188.
97 Ibid. p. 189.
98 Ibid. p. 196.
99 Ibid. p. 197.
100 Ibid. p. 197.
101 Otto Skorzeny, *Skorzeny's Special Missions: The Memoirs of 'The Most Dangerous Man in Europe'* (Greenhill, 2006), p. 129.
102 US National Archives, Hanna Reitsch interrogation summary, 'Condemnation of Göring by Hanna Reitsch' (16.11.1945), p. 6.
103 Otto Skorzeny, *Skorzeny's Special Missions: The Memoirs of 'The Most Dangerous Man in Europe'* (Greenhill, 2006), p. 216.
104 Martin Simons, *German Air Attaché: The Thrilling Wartime Story of the German Ace Pilot and Wartime Diplomat Peter Riedel* (Airlife, 1997), p. 197.
105 Hanna Reitsch, *The Sky My Kingdom: Memoirs of the Famous German World War II Test Pilot* (Greenhill, 2009), p. 218; Martin Simons, *German Air Attaché: The Thrilling Wartime Story of the German Ace Pilot and Wartime Diplomat Peter Riedel* (Airlife, 1997), p. 197.
106 Martin Simons, *German Air Attaché: The Thrilling Wartime Story of the German Ace Pilot and Wartime Diplomat Peter Riedel* (Airlife, 1997), p. 197.
107 Deutsches Museum archive, 130/109, Hanna Reitsch letter to Peter Riedel (27.11.1972).
108 Martin Simons, *German Air Attaché: The Thrilling Wartime Story of the German Ace Pilot and Wartime Diplomat Peter Riedel* (Airlife, 1997), p. 198.
109 Ibid.
110 Hanna Reitsch, *The Sky My Kingdom: Memoirs of the Famous German World War II Test Pilot* (Greenhill, 2009), p. 219.
111 Deutsches Museum archive, 130/109, Hanna Reitsch letter to Peter Riedel (November 1972).
112 Deutsches Museum archive, 130/101, Walter Stender, 'Politische Erklärung' [Political Statement] (01.07.1947).
113 Martin Simons, *German Air Attaché: The Thrilling Wartime Story of the German Ace Pilot and Wartime Diplomat Peter Riedel* (Airlife, 1997), p. 208.
114 Fey von Hassell, *A Mother's War* (Corgi, 1991), pp. 175–6.
115 Ibid. p. 179.
116 Ibid. p. 179.

117 Elisabeth zu Guttenberg, Sheridan Spearman, *Holding the Stirrup* (Duell, Sloan and Pearce/Little Brown, 1953), p. 22.
118 Fey von Hassell, *A Mother's War* (Corgi, 1991), p. 182.
119 Ibid. p. 179.
120 Ibid. p. 185.
121 Elisabeth zu Guttenberg, Sheridan Spearman, *Holding the Stirrup* (Duell, Sloan and Pearce/Little Brown, 1953), p. 228.
122 Ibid.
123 Anthony Beevor, *Ardennes 1944, Hitler's Last Gamble* (Viking, Penguin Random House, 2015), pp. 80–81.
124 Otto Skorzeny, *Skorzeny's Special Missions: The Memoirs of 'The Most Dangerous Man in Europe'* (Greenhill, 2006), p. 162.
125 Ibid.
126 Ibid.
127 Fey von Hassell, *A Mother's War* (Corgi, 1991), p. 184.
128 Ibid.
129 Gerhard Bracke archive, Melitta's diary (05–06.12.1944).
130 Gerhard Bracke, *Melitta Gräfin Stauffenberg: Das Leben einer Fliegerin* [The Life of an Aviatrix] (Herbig, 2013), p. 217.
131 Ibid.
132 Ibid.
133 Gerhard Bracke archive, Melitta's diary (22.12.1944).
134 Gerhard Bracke, *Melitta Gräfin Stauffenberg: Das Leben einer Fliegerin* [The Life of an Aviatrix] (Herbig, 2013), p. 215.
135 Hans W. Hagen, *Blick hinter die Dinge – 12 Begegnungen* [Behind the Scenes – Twelve Encounters] (Türmer-Verlag 1962), quoted by Gerhard Bracke, *Melitta Gräfin Stauffenberg: Das Leben einer Fliegerin* [The Life of an Aviatrix] (Herbig, 2013), pp. 215–18.
136 Berthold von Stauffenberg, 'A Childhood in the Third Reich – from System Conformist to Traitor's Child'. Lecture delivered to the AV Rheinstein Köln-Lindenthal (14.04.2008).
137 Gerhard Bracke, *Melitta Gräfin Stauffenberg: Das Leben einer Fliegerin* [The Life of an Aviatrix] (Herbig Verlag, 2013), p. 219.
138 Gerhard Bracke archive, Melitta's diary (23–25.12.1944).
139 Melitta to Nina von Stauffenberg (30.12.1944), quoted in Gerhard Bracke, *Melitta Gräfin Stauffenberg: Das Leben einer Fliegerin* [The Life of an Aviatrix] (Herbig, 2013), p. 220; Gerald Posner, *Hitler's Children: Inside the Families of the Third Reich* (Mandarin, 1991), p. 184.
140 Gerald Posner, *Hitler's Children: Inside the Families of the Third Reich* (Mandarin, 1991), p. 184.
141 Ibid.
142 Gerhard Bracke, *Melitta Gräfin Stauffenberg: Das Leben einer Fliegerin* [The Life of an Aviatrix] (Herbig, 2013), privately translated, p. 220.
143 Gerhard Bracke archive, Melitta's diary (26.12.1944).

144 Melitta to Nina von Stauffenberg (30.12.1944) quoted in Gerhard Bracke, *Melitta Gräfin Stauffenberg: Das Leben einer Fliegerin* [The Life of an Aviatrix] (Herbig, 2013), p. 219.

145 Ibid.

146 Ibid.

147 Ibid.

148 Konstanze von Schulthess, *Nina Schenk Gräfin von Stauffenberg: Ein Porträt* [A Portrait] (Piper, 2009), p. 90.

13: IN THE BUNKER

1 Anthony Beevor, *Ardennes 1944: Hitler's Last Gamble* (Viking, Penguin Random House, 2015), p. 219.

2 Nicolaus von Below, *At Hitler's Side: The Memoirs of Hitler's Luftwaffe Adjutant 1937–1945* (Frontline, 2010), pp. 223–4.

3 Ron Laytner, *Edit International Articles: A portfolio of some of Ron Laytner's greatest stories*, 'Hanna Reitsch: Greatest Nazi Test Pilot and World's First Astronaut' (2010).

4 Anthony Beevor, *Ardennes 1944: Hitler's Last Gamble* (Viking, Penguin Random House, 2015), p. 219.

5 Ron Laytner, *Edit International Articles: A portfolio of some of Ron Laytner's greatest stories*, 'Hanna Reitsch: Greatest Nazi Test Pilot and World's First Astronaut' (2010).

6 Dennis Piszkiewicz, *From Nazi Test Pilot to Hitler's Bunker: The Fantastic Flights of Hanna Reitsch* (Praeger, 1997), p. 87.

7 Ron Laytner, *Edit International Articles: A portfolio of some of Ron Laytner's greatest stories*, 'Hanna Reitsch: Greatest Nazi Test Pilot and World's First Astronaut' (2010).

8 Nicolaus von Below, *At Hitler's Side: The Memoirs of Hitler's Luftwaffe Adjutant 1937–1945* (Frontline, 2010), p. 229.

9 Hanna Reitsch, *The Sky My Kingdom: Memoirs of the Famous German World War II Test Pilot* (Greenhill, 2009), p. 253.

10 Ibid. p. 240.

11 Anon., *A Woman in Berlin*, introduction by Antony Beevor (Virago, 2011), p. 1.

12 Otto Skorzeny, *Skorzeny's Special Missions: The Memoirs of 'The Most Dangerous Man in Europe'* (Greenhill, 2006), p. 195.

13 Hanna Reitsch, *The Sky My Kingdom: Memoirs of the Famous German World War II Test Pilot* (Greenhill, 2009), p. 241.

14 Cornell University Law Library: Donovan Nuremberg Trials Collection, Robert E. Work, interrogation of Hanna Reitsch, 'The Last Days in Hitler's Air Raid Shelter' (08.10.1945).

15 Hanna Reitsch, *The Sky My Kingdom: Memoirs of the Famous German World War II Test Pilot* (Greenhill, 2009), p. 241.

16 Ibid. p. 242.
17 Deutsches Museum archive, 130/123, letter Hanna Reitsch/Kurt Reitsch (1946).
18 Ibid.
19 Ibid.
20 Ibid.
21 Hanna Reitsch, *The Sky My Kingdom: Memoirs of the Famous German World War II Test Pilot* (Greenhill, 2009), p. 244.
22 Ibid.
23 Deutsches Museum archive, 130/123, letter Hanna Reitsch/Kurt Reitsch (1946).
24 Hanna Reitsch, *The Sky My Kingdom: Memoirs of the Famous German World War II Test Pilot* (Greenhill, 2009), p. 245.
25 Ibid. p. 245.
26 Ibid. p. 245.
27 Ibid. p. 245.
28 Ibid.
29 Ibid.
30 Ibid.
31 Deutsches Museum archive, 130/123, Hanna Reitsch/Kurt Reitsch (1946).
32 Hanna Reitsch, *The Sky My Kingdom: Memoirs of the Famous German World War II Test Pilot* (Greenhill, 2009), p. 247.
33 Ibid.
34 Ibid.
35 Albert Speer, *Inside the Third Reich* (Sphere, 1971), p. 631.
36 Hanna Reitsch in *Die Welt*, 'Wie klein Mäxchen such den Untergang des Dritten Reiches vorstellt' [How the Little Maxes Imagine the Downfall of the Third Reich] (02.08.1973).
37 Hanna Reitsch, *The Sky My Kingdom: Memoirs of the Famous German World War II Test Pilot* (Greenhill, 2009), p. 247.
38 Gerhard Boldt, *Hitler's Last Ten Days* (Coward, McCann & Geoghegan, 1973), p. 178; Hanna Reitsch, *The Sky My Kingdom: Memoirs of the Famous German World War II Test Pilot* (Greenhill, 2009), p. 248.
39 Hanna Reitsch, *The Sky My Kingdom: Memoirs of the Famous German World War II Test Pilot* (Greenhill, 2009), p. 248.
40 Ibid.
41 Cornell University Law Library: Donovan Nuremberg Trials Collection, Robert E. Work, interrogation of Hanna Reitsch, 'The Last Days in Hitler's Air Raid Shelter' (08.10.1945).
42 Ibid.
43 Hanna Reitsch, *The Sky My Kingdom: Memoirs of the Famous German World War II Test Pilot* (Greenhill, 2009), p. 248.
44 US National Archives, Hanna Reitsch interrogation summary, 'Condemnation of Göring by Hanna Reitsch' (16.11.1945), p. 1.

45 Deutsches Museum archive, 130/123, letter Hanna Reitsch/Kurt Reitsch (1946).

46 US National Archives, Hanna Reitsch interrogation summary, 'Condemnation of Göring by Hanna Reitsch' (16.11.1945), p. 3.

47 Deutsches Museum archive, 130/123, letter Hanna Reitsch/Kurt Reitsch (1946).

48 Hanna Reitsch, *The Sky My Kingdom: Memoirs of the Famous German World War II Test Pilot* (Greenhill, 2009), p. 248.

49 Cornell University Law Library: Donovan Nuremberg Trials Collection, Robert E. Work, interrogation of Hanna Reitsch, 'The Last Days in Hitler's Air Raid Shelter' (08.10.1945).

50 Traudl Junge, *Until the Final Hour: Hitler's Last Secretary* (Phoenix, 2002), p. 174.

51 Hanna Reitsch, *The Sky My Kingdom: Memoirs of the Famous German World War II Test Pilot* (Greenhill, 2009), p. 249.

52 Fred Taylor (trans., ed.), *The Goebbels Diaries, 1939–1941: The historic journal of a Nazi war leader* (Sphere, 1983), p. 13.

53 Traudl Junge, *Until the Final Hour: Hitler's Last Secretary* (Phoenix, 2002), p. 175.

54 Hanna Reitsch, *The Sky My Kingdom: Memoirs of the Famous German World War II Test Pilot* (Greenhill, 2009), p. 250.

55 Ibid.

56 Ibid.

57 Ibid.

58 Ibid.

59 Ibid.

60 US National Archives, Air Division HQ United States Forces in Austria, Air Interrogation Unit, interrogation of Hanna Reitsch: 'The Last Days in Hitler's Air Raid Shelter' (08.10.1945), p. 6.

61 Cornell University Law Library: Donovan Nuremberg Trials Collection, Robert E. Work, interrogation of Hanna Reitsch, 'The Last Days in Hitler's Air Raid Shelter' (08.10.1945).

62 Ibid.

63 Nicolaus von Below, *At Hitler's Side: The Memoirs of Hitler's Luftwaffe Adjutant 1937–1945* (Frontline, 2010), p. 233.

64 Cornell University Law Library: Donovan Nuremberg Trials Collection, Robert E. Work, interrogation of Hanna Reitsch, 'The Last Days in Hitler's Air Raid Shelter' (08.10.1945).

65 Ibid.

66 Bernd Freytag von Loringhoven, *In the Bunker with Hitler: 23 July 1944–29 April 1945* (Weidenfeld & Nicolson, 2005), p. 164.

67 Deutsches Museum archive, 130/123, letter Hanna Reitsch/Kurt Reitsch (1946).

68 Hanna Reitsch, *The Sky My Kingdom: Memoirs of the Famous German World War II Test Pilot* (Greenhill, 2009), p. 251.

69 Traudl Junge, *Until the Final Hour: Hitler's Last Secretary* (Phoenix, 2002), p. 179.
70 Hanna Reitsch, *The Sky My Kingdom: Memoirs of the Famous German World War II Test Pilot* (Greenhill, 2009), p. 251.
71 Mano Ziegler, *Rocket Fighter: The story of the Messerschmitt Me-163* (Arms & Armour, 1976), p. 137.
72 Dennis Piszkiewicz, *From Nazi Test Pilot to Hitler's Bunker: The Fantastic Flights of Hanna Reitsch* (Praeger, 1997), p. 98.
73 Karl Koller, *Der Letzte Monat: Die tagebuchaufzeichnungen des ehemaligen Chefs des Generalstabes der deutsche Luftwaffe vom 14 April bis zum 27 Mai 1945* [The Last Month: The Diaries of Karl Koller, Chief of Staff of the Luftwaffe, 14 April to 27 May 1945] (Mannheim, 1949), p. 62.
74 Cornell University Law Library: Donovan Nuremberg Trials Collection, Robert E. Work, interrogation of Hanna Reitsch, 'The Last Days in Hitler's Air Raid Shelter' (08.10.1945).
75 Ibid.
76 Hanna Reitsch, *The Sky My Kingdom: Memoirs of the Famous German World War II Test Pilot* (Greenhill, 2009), p. 251.
77 Cornell University Law Library: Donovan Nuremberg Trials Collection, Robert E. Work, interrogation of Hanna Reitsch, 'The Last Days in Hitler's Air Raid Shelter' (08.10.1945).
78 Hanna Reitsch, *The Sky My Kingdom: Memoirs of the Famous German World War II Test Pilot* (Greenhill, 2009), p. 252.
79 Traudl Junge, *Until the Final Hour: Hitler's Last Secretary* (Phoenix, 2002), p. 177.
80 Deutsches Museum archive, 130/123, letter Hanna Reitsch/Kurt Reitsch (1946).
81 Hanna Reitsch, *The Sky My Kingdom: Memoirs of the Famous German World War II Test Pilot* (Greenhill, 2009), p. 252.
82 Ibid.
83 Ibid. p. 253.
84 Ibid. p. 253.
85 Deutsches Museum archive, 130/123, letter Hanna Reitsch/Kurt Reitsch (1946).
86 Gerhard Boldt, *Hitler's Last Days: An Eye-Witness Account* (Arthur Barker, 1973), p. 170.
87 Nicolaus von Below, *At Hitler's Side: The Memoirs of Hitler's Luftwaffe Adjutant 1937–1945* (Frontline, 2010), p. 238.
88 Gerhard Boldt, *Hitler's Last Days: An Eye-Witness Account* (Arthur Barker, 1973), p. 170.
89 Cornell University Law Library: Donovan Nuremberg Trials Collection, Robert E. Work, interrogation of Hanna Reitsch, 'The Last Days in Hitler's Air Raid Shelter' (08.10.1945).
90 Deutsches Museum archive, 130/123, letter Hanna Reitsch/Kurt Reitsch (1946).

91 Gerhard Boldt, *Hitler's Last Ten Days* (Coward, McCann & Geoghegan, 1973), p. 178.
92 Hanna Reitsch, *The Sky My Kingdom: Memoirs of the Famous German World War II Test Pilot* (Greenhill, 2009), p. 253.
93 Ibid. p. 254.
94 US National Archives, Air Division HQ United States Forces in Austria, Air Interrogation Unit, interrogation of Hanna Reitsch: 'The Last Days in Hitler's Air Raid Shelter' (08.10.1945), p. 11.
95 Hanna Reitsch, *The Sky My Kingdom: Memoirs of the Famous German World War II Test Pilot* (Greenhill, 2009), p. 255.
96 Hugh Trevor-Roper, *The Last Days of Hitler* (Macmillan, 1947), p. 158.
97 Cornell University Law Library: Donovan Nuremberg Trials Collection, Robert E. Work, 'Last Letters from Hitler's Air Raid Shelter' (01.11.1945).
98 Ibid.
99 Ibid.
100 Hugh Trevor-Roper, *The Last Days of Hitler* (Macmillan, 1947), p. 152.
101 Cornell University Law Library: Donovan Nuremberg Trials Collection, Robert E. Work, 'Last Letters from Hitler's Air Raid Shelter' (01.11.1945).
102 Cornell University Law Library: Donovan Nuremberg Trials Collection, Robert E. Work, interrogation of Hanna Reitsch, 'The Last Days in Hitler's Air Raid Shelter' (08.10.1945).

14: FINAL FLIGHT

1 Fey von Hassell, *Niemals sich beugen: Erinnerungen einer Sondergefangenen der SS* [Never Bow Down: Memories of the Special Prisoners of the SS] (Serie Piper, 1995), p. 172.
2 Gerhard Bracke, *Melitta Gräfin Stauffenberg: Das Leben einer Fliegerin* [The Life of an Aviatrix] (Herbig, 2013), privately translated, p. 76.
3 Fey von Hassell, *A Mother's War* (Corgi, 1991), p. 187.
4 Gerhard Bracke, *Melitta Gräfin Stauffenberg: Das Leben einer Fliegerin* [The Life of an Aviatrix] (Herbig, 2013), privately translated, p. 258.
5 Fey von Hassell quoted by Gerhard Bracke, *Melitta Gräfin Stauffenberg: Das Leben einer Fliegerin* [The Life of an Aviatrix] (Herbig, 2013), privately translated, p. 240.
6 Gerhard Bracke archive, Hubertus von Papen-Koeningen interview (10.08.1989).
7 Gerhard Bracke, *Melitta Gräfin Stauffenberg: Das Leben einer Fliegerin* [The Life of an Aviatrix] (Herbig, 2013), privately translated, p. 239.
8 Gerhard Bracke archive, letter H. Schrank/Klara Schiller (14.03.1975).
9 Dorothee von Meding, *Courageous Hearts: Women and the anti-Hitler Plot of 1944* (Berghahn, 1997), p. 196.

10 Fey von Hassell, *A Mother's War* (Corgi, 1991), p. 163.
11 Ibid. p. 164.
12 Anne Voorhoeve archive, Otto Philipp von Stauffenberg, 'Der 20. Juli und seine Folge' ('The 20th July and its Consequences'), p. 20.
13 Fey von Hassell, *A Mother's War* (Corgi, 1991), p. 198.
14 Ibid. p. 205.
15 TNA, WO 328/37, Statement of Count Clemens von Stauffenberg, Capri (31.05.1945).
16 Ibid.
17 Fey von Hassell, *A Mother's War* (Corgi, 1991), p. 209.
18 Ibid. p. 167.
19 Archive Reinhart Rudershausen, Klara Schiller, 'Memories of Klara Schiller' (nd).
20 Gerhard Bracke, *Melitta Gräfin Stauffenberg: Das Leben einer Fliegerin* [The Life of an Aviatrix] (Herbig, 2013), privately translated, p. 243.
21 Ibid. p. 76.
22 Archive Reinhart Rudershausen, Marie-Luise [Lili] Schiller/Lübbert, 'Zweig Otto Eberstein' [Otto Eberstein branch of the family] (nd); Archive R. Rudershausen, Jutta Rudershausen, 'Flugkapitän Melitta Schiller-Stauffenberg' (nd).
23 Gerhard Bracke archive, Mika Stauffenberg, untitled account of Melitta Schiller (17.02.1962).
24 Thomas Medicus, *Melitta von Stauffenberg: Ein Deutsches Leben* [A German Life] (Rowohlt, 2012), p. 13.
25 Gerhard Bracke, *Melitta Gräfin Stauffenberg: Das Leben einer Fliegerin* [The Life of an Aviatrix] (Herbig, 2013), privately translated, p. 226.
26 Elisabeth zu Guttenberg, *Beim Namen Gerufen: Erinnerungen* [Called By Name: Memories] (Harper, 1996) p. 204.
27 Elisabeth zu Guttenberg, Sheridan Spearman, *Holding the Stirrup* (Duell, Sloan and Pearce/Little, Brown, 1953), p. 227.
28 Archive Reinhart Rudershausen, Jutta Rudershausen, 'Flugkapitän Melitta Schiller-Stauffenberg' (nd).
29 Berthold von Stauffenberg, Lecture for the AV Rheinstein Köln-Lindenthal, 'A Childhood in the Third Reich – from System Conformist to Traitor's Child' (14.04.2008).
30 Alfred von Hofacker quoted in Robert Loeffel, *Family Punishment in Nazi Germany: Sippenhaft, Terror and Myth* (Palgrave Macmillan, 2012), p. 181.
31 Alfred von Hofacker quoted in Eva Madelung, Joachim Scholtyseck, *Heldenkinder – Verräterkinder. Wenn die Eltern im Widerstand Waren* [Hero Children – Traitor Children: children of the resistance] (C. H. Beck, 2007), p. 35.
32 *WWII Magazine*, Nigel Jones, 'Claus von Stauffenberg: The man who tried to kill Hitler' (HistoryNet.com, 22.12.2008).

33 Gerhard Bracke, *Melitta Gräfin Stauffenberg: Das Leben einer Fliegerin* [The Life of an Aviatrix] (Herbig, 2013), privately translated, p. 243.
34 Gerhard Bracke archive, Hubertus von Papen-Koeningen interview (10.08.1989).
35 Harry J. Herder, 'Liberation of Buchenwald', http://remember.org/witness/herder.
36 Ibid.
37 Sigismund Payne Best, *The Venlo Incident: A True Story of Double-dealing, Captivity and a Murderous Nazi Plot* (Frontline, 2009), p. 187.
38 Eberhard Bethge's biography of Bonhoeffer, quoted by Gerhard Bracke, *Melitta Gräfin Stauffenberg: Das Leben einer Fliegerin* [The Life of an Aviatrix] (Herbig, 2013), privately translated, p. 253.
39 Gerhard Bracke archive, Hubertus von Papen-Koeningen interview (10.08.1989)
40 Ibid.
41 Gerhard Bracke, *Melitta Gräfin Stauffenberg: Das Leben einer Fliegerin* [The Life of an Aviatrix] (Herbig, 2013), privately translated, p. 250.
42 Ibid. p. 262.
43 The Ian Sayer Archive (unpublished at the time of writing).
44 Gerhard Bracke, *Melitta Gräfin Stauffenberg: Das Leben einer Fliegerin* [The Life of an Aviatrix] (Herbig, 2013), privately translated, p. 265.
45 Ibid.
46 Ibid. p. 266.
47 Ibid. p. 266.
48 Ibid. p. 266.
49 Ibid. p. 269.
50 Ibid. p. 269.
51 Ibid. p. 270.

15: LIBERATION AND DETENTION

1 Fey von Hassell, *Niemals sich beugen: Erinnerungen einer Sonder-gefangenen der SS* [Never Bow Down: Memories of the Special Prisoners of the SS] (Serie Piper, 1995), p. 181; Fey von Hassell, *A Mother's War* (Corgi, 1991), p. 220.
2 Berthold von Stauffenberg, Lecture for the AV Rheinstein Köln-Lindenthal, 'A Childhood in the Third Reich – from System Conformist to Traitor's Child' (14.04.2008).
3 Ibid.
4 Gerald Posner, *Hitler's Children: Inside the Families of the Third Reich* (Mandarin, 1991), p. 185.
5 Ibid. p. 186.
6 Ibid. p. 186.

7   Ibid. p. 186.

8   Robert Loeffel, *Family Punishment in Nazi Germany: Sippenhaft, Terror and Myth* (Palgrave Macmillan, 2012), p. 181.

9   Alfred von Hofacker, quoted in Konstanze von Schulthess, *Nina Schenk Gräfin von Stauffenberg: Ein Porträt* [A Portrait] (Piper, 2009), p. 172.

10 Eric Brown, *Wings On My Sleeve: The World's Greatest Test Pilot Tells His Story* (Phoenix, 2007) p. 100.

11 Ibid. p. 97.

12 Eric Brown, James Holland interview, www.griffonmerlin.com.

13 Eric Brown, *Wings On My Sleeve: The World's Greatest Test Pilot Tells His Story* (Phoenix, 2007), p. 98.

14 Eric Brown, James Holland interview, www.griffonmerlin.com

15 Eric Brown, *Wings On My Sleeve: The World's Greatest Test Pilot Tells His Story* (Phoenix, 2007), p. 114.

16 Hanna Reitsch, *The Sky My Kingdom: Memoirs of the Famous German World War II Test Pilot* (Greenhill, 2009), p. 255.

17 Ibid.

18 Erich Kempka, *I Was Hitler's Chauffeur: The Memoirs of Erich Kempka* (Frontline, 2010), p. 78.

19 Ron Laytner, *Edit International Articles: A portfolio of some of Ron Laytner's greatest stories*, 'Hanna Reitsch: Greatest Nazi Test Pilot and World's First Astronaut' (2010).

20 Nicolaus von Below, *At Hitler's Side: The Memoirs of Hitler's Luftwaffe Adjutant 1937–1945* (Frontline, 2010), p. 241.

21 US National Archives, Air Division HQ United States Forces in Austria, Air Interrogation Unit, interrogation of Hanna Reitsch: 'The Last Days in Hitler's Air Raid Shelter' (08.10.1945), p. 12.

22 Ibid.

23 Ibid.

24 Ibid.

25 Ibid.

26 Gerhard Bracke archive, Hanna Reitsch/Klara Schiller correspondence (18.02.1975).

27 Ibid.

28 Ibid.

29 Ibid.

30 Karl Koller, *Der Letzte Monat: Die tagebuchaufzeichnungen des ehemaligen Chefs des Generalstabes der deutsche Luftwaffe vom 14 April bis zum 27 Mai 1945* [The Last Month: The Diaries of Karl Koller, Chief of Staff of the Luftwaffe, 14 April to 27 May 1945] (Mannheim, 1949), p. 93.

31 Ibid.

32 Ibid.

33 Ibid.

34 Ibid.

35 Ibid.

36 *The Telegraph*, Rob Crilly, 'Rare German surrender order expected to fetch £20,000' (26.04.2015).

37 Karl Koller, *Der Letzte Monat: Die tagebuchaufzeichnungen des ehemaligen Chefs des Generalstabes der deutsche Luftwaffe vom 14 April bis zum 27 Mai 1945* [The Last Month: The Diaries of Karl Koller, Chief of Staff of the Luftwaffe, 14 April to 27 May 1945] (Mannheim, 1949), p. 98.

38 Ibid.

39 Hanna Reitsch, *The Sky My Kingdom: Memoirs of the Famous German World War II Test Pilot* (Greenhill, 2009), p. 256.

40 Ibid. p. 257.

41 Karl Koller, *Der Letzte Monat: Die tagebuchaufzeichnungen des ehemaligen Chefs des Generalstabes der deutsche Luftwaffe vom 14 April bis zum 27 Mai 1945* [The Last Month: The Diaries of Karl Koller, Chief of Staff of the Luftwaffe, 14 April to 27 May 1945] (Mannheim, 1949), p. 128.

42 Hanna Reitsch, *The Sky My Kingdom: Memoirs of the Famous German World War II Test Pilot* (Greenhill, 2009), p. 257.

43 Ibid.

44 *Hanna Reitsch: Hitlers Fliegerin* [Hitler's Pilot], Interspot Film (dir. Gerhard Jelinek and Fritz Kalteis, 2010).

45 Ibid.

46 Eric Brown, *Wings On My Sleeve: The World's Greatest Test Pilot Tells His Story* (Phoenix, 2007), p. 119.

47 Ibid. p. 109.

48 Ibid. p. 119.

49 Ibid. p. 119.

50 Ibid. p. 119.

51 Eric Brown, Mulley interview (23.06.2014).

52 Eric Brown, Mulley interview (18.03.2013).

53 Eric Brown, *Wings On My Sleeve: The World's Greatest Test Pilot Tells His Story* (Phoenix, 2007), p. 119.

54 Eric Brown, Mulley interview (23.06.2014).

55 Eric Brown, Mulley interview (18.06.2014).

56 Eric Brown, Mulley interview (23.06.2014).

57 James Holland, interview with Eric Brown, www.griffonmerlin.com

58 Eric Brown, *Wings On My Sleeve: The World's Greatest Test Pilot Tells His Story* (Phoenix, 2007), p. 119.

59 Ibid. p. 119.

60 US National Archives, Air Division HQ United States Forces in Austria, Air Interrogation Unit, interrogation of Hanna Reitsch: 'The Last Days in Hitler's Air Raid Shelter' (08.10.1945), p. 2.

61 Ibid. p. 8.

62 Ibid. p. 9.

63 Ibid. p. 9.

64 Ibid. p. 9.

65 Ibid. p. 9.

66 US National Archives, Air Division HQ United States Forces in Austria, Air Interrogation Unit, 'Condemnation of Göring by Hanna Reitsch' (16.11.1945), p. 6.

67 Ibid. p. 7.

68 Eric Brown, Mulley interview (18.03.2013).

69 US National Archives, Air Division HQ United States Forces in Austria, Air Interrogation Unit, 'Condemnation of Göring by Hanna Reitsch' (16.11.1945), p. 8.

70 Ibid.

71 US National Archives, Air Division HQ United States Forces in Austria, Air Interrogation Unit, interrogation of Hanna Reitsch: 'The Last Days in Hitler's Air Raid Shelter' (08.10.1945), p. 8.

72 Ibid. p. 14.

73 US National Archives, Air Division HQ United States Forces in Austria, Air Interrogation Unit, 'Condemnation of Göring by Hanna Reitsch' (16.11.1945), p. 5.

74 *Hanna Reitsch: Hitlers Fliegerin* [Hitler's Pilot], Interspot Film (dir. Gerhard Jelinek and Fritz Kalteis, 2010).

75 Deutsches Museum Archive, 130/123, letter Hanna Reitsch/Kurt Reitsch (1946).

76 Leni Riefenstahl, *Leni Riefenstahl: A Memoir* (St Martin's Press, 1993), p. 320.

77 Ibid. p. 321.

78 Ibid. p. 320.

79 US National Archives, Air Division HQ United States Forces in Austria, Air Interrogation Unit, interrogation of Hanna Reitsch: 'The Last Days in Hitler's Air Raid Shelter' (08.10.1945), p. 14.

80 Konstanze von Schulthess, *Nina Schenk Gräfin von Stauffenberg: Ein Porträt* [A Portrait] (Piper, 2009), p. 152.

81 Gerald Posner, *Hitler's Children: Inside the Families of the Third Reich* (Mandarin, 1991), p. 186.

82 Ibid. p. 187.

83 Fabian von Schlabrendorff, *The Secret War Against Hitler* (Westview Press, 1994), p. 333.

84 Ibid.

85 Fey von Hassell, *A Mother's War* (Corgi, 1991), p. 243.

86 The Ian Sayer Archive.

87 Fey von Hassell, *A Mother's War* (Corgi, 1991), p. 243.

88 Ibid. p. 245.

89 The Ian Sayer Archive, letter Fey von Hassell (Pirzio-Biroli) to Sigismund Payne Best (28.07.1946).

90 Fey von Hassell, *A Mother's War* (Corgi, 1991), p. 247.

91 Gerald Posner, *Hitler's Children: Inside the Families of the Third Reich* (Mandarin, 1991), p. 187.

92 Berthold von Stauffenberg, Lecture for the AV Rheinstein Köln-

Lindenthal, 'A Childhood in the Third Reich – from System Conformist to Traitor's Child' (14.04.2008).

93 Elisabeth zu Guttenberg, Sheridan Spearman, *Holding the Stirrup* (Duell, Sloan and Pearce/Little, Brown, 1953), p. 241.

94 Konstanze von Schulthess, *Nina Schenk Gräfin von Stauffenberg: Ein Porträt* [A Portrait] (Piper, 2009), p. 157.

95 Dorothee von Meding, *Courageous Hearts: Women and the anti-Hitler Plot of 1944* (Berghahn, 2008), pp. 196–7.

96 Ibid. p. 197.

97 Elisabeth zu Guttenberg, Sheridan Spearman, *Holding the Stirrup* (Duell, Sloan and Pearce/Little, Brown, 1953), p. 238.

98 Konstanze von Schulthess, *Nina Schenk Gräfin von Stauffenberg: Ein Porträt* [A Portrait] (Piper, 2009), p. 174.

99 Elisabeth zu Guttenberg, Sheridan Spearman, *Holding the Stirrup* (Duell, Sloan and Pearce/Little, Brown, 1953), p. 264.

100 Hanna Reitsch, *The Sky My Kingdom: Memoirs of the Famous German World War II Test Pilot* (Greenhill, 2009), p. 258.

101 Eric Brown, Mulley interview (18.03.2013).

102 Hanna Reitsch, *The Sky My Kingdom: Memoirs of the Famous German World War II Test Pilot* (Greenhill, 2009), p. 258.

103 Ibid. p. 257.

104 Judy Lomax, *Hanna Reitsch: Flying for the Fatherland* (John Murray, 1988), p. 133.

105 Alexander Historical Auctions, www.alexautographs.com, letter Hanna Reitsch/Herr von Krosigk (13.05.1946).

106 Deutsches Museum Archive, 130/123, letter Hanna Reitsch/Kurt Reitsch (1946).

107 Ibid.

108 Ibid.

109 Archive Reinhart Rudeshausen, Klara Schiller, 'Memories of Klara Schiller' (nd).

110 Archive Reinhart Rudershausen, Marie-Luise [Lili] Schiller/Lübbert, 'Zweig Otto Eberstein' [Otto Eberstein branch of the family] (nd).

111 Archive Reinhart Rudershausen, Jutta Rudershausen, 'Flugkapitän Melitta Schiller-Stauffenberg' (nd).

112 Archive Reinhart Rudershausen, Jutta Rudershausen, 'Flugkapitän Melitta Schiller-Stauffenberg' (nd).

113 Elisabeth zu Guttenberg, *Beim Namen Gerufen: Erinnerungen* [Called By Name: Memories] (Harper, 1996) p. 214.

114 Gerhard Bracke, *Melitta Gräfin Stauffenberg: Das Leben einer Fliegerin* [The Life of an Aviatrix] (Herbig, 2013), privately translated, p. 258.

115 Ibid. p. 270.

116 Archive Reinhart Rudershausen, Jutta Rudershausen, 'Flugkapitän Melitta Schiller-Stauffenberg' (nd).

117 Konstanze von Schulthess, *Nina Schenk Gräfin von Stauffenberg: Ein Porträt* [A Portrait] (Piper, 2009), p. 149.

16: REPUTATIONS

1 Patricia Kollander, John O'Sullivan, *I Must Be a Part of The War: A German American's Fight against Hitler and Nazism* (Fordham University Press, 2005), p. 179.
2 Ibid. p. 180.
3 Ibid. p. 180.
4 US National Archives, XE053525, HQ US Forces, European Theater, file D-53525, subject 'Operation Skylark, re. Reitsch, Hanna' (15.02.1946).
5 US National Archives, XE053525, HQ US Forces, European Theater PR Division, release no. 794 (05.12.1945), p. 1.
6 US National Archives, XE053525, memo US/16,464.
7 US National Archives, XE053525, HQ US Forces, European Theater, file D-53525, subject 'Operation Skylark, re. Reitsch, Hanna' (15.02.1946).
8 US National Archives, XE053525, HQ CIC, US Forces, European Theater, Region III (Bad Nauheim) (15.10.1946).
9 US National Archives, XE053525, 'Censorship Civil Communications', R. Storck to G. Rieckmann (21.08.1946).
10 TNA, XE053525, British intelligence report quoted in US memo (22.10.1946).
11 US National Archives, XE053525, HQ CIC, US Forces, European Theater, Region VI (Bamberg) (23.11.1946).
12 US National Archives, XE053525, HQ CIC, US Forces, Region 1, memo subject 'Operation Skylark' (19.12.1946).
13 Ibid.
14 Ibid.
15 US National Archives, XE053525, HQ 970th CIC, US Forces, European Theater, memo subject 'Reitsch, Hanna, D-53525' (11.01.1947).
16 US National Archives, XE053525, US Civil Censorship (Germany) (18.03.1947).
17 US National Archives, XE053525, HQ 970th CIC, US Forces, European Theater, memo subject 'Reitsch, Hanna, D-53525' (11.01.1947).
18 US National Archives, XE053525, HQ US Forces, European Theater, file D-53525, subject 'Operation Skylark, re. Reitsch, Hanna'(15.02.1946).
19 Deutsches Museum archive, 130/100, letter Hanna Reitsch/Dr Laternser (17.03.1947).

20 Deutsches Museum archive, 130/101, letter Horst von Salomon/ Kaplan Volkmar (27.04.1947).
21 Nicolaus von Below, *At Hitler's Side: The Memoirs of Hitler's Luftwaffe Adjutant 1937–1945* (Frontline, 2010), p. 11.
22 Deutsches Museum archive, 130/101, hand-drawn card (1947).
23 Deutsches Museum archive, 130/111, letter Elfriede Wagner/Hanna Reitsch (31.12.1948).
24 US National Archives, XE053525, US Civil Censorship (Germany) (07.03.1947).
25 Deutsches Museum archive, 130/100, letter Hanna Reitsch/Dr Laternser (17.03.1947).
26 Deutsches Museum archive, 130/100, letter Hanna Reitsch/Frau Jodl (1948).
27 Deutsches Museum archive, 130/101, Hanna Reitsch, 'Eidesstattliche Erklärung' [solemn declaration], affidavit for Otto Skorzeny (12.04.1948).
28 US National Archives, XE053525, US Civil Censorship, 'Hanna Reitsch pleads for General Kesselring' (01.04.1947).
29 Hermann Historica International Auctions, 70th auction online catalogue, lot 6017, letter Hanna Reitsch/Albert Kesselring (29.02.1948).
30 Deutsches Museum archive, 130/100–101, Hanna Reitsch statement (20.05.1948).
31 Ibid.
32 Ibid.
33 Ibid.
34 Ibid.
35 US National Archives, XE053525, 'Agent Report' (19.07.1948).
36 Ibid.
37 Konstanze von Schulthess, Mulley interview (25.11.2014).
38 Archive Reinhart Rudeshausen, Klara Schiller, 'Memories of Klara Schiller' (nd).
39 Charlotte von der Schulenburg, in Dorothee von Meding, *Courageous Hearts: Women and the anti-Hitler Plot of 1944* (Berghahn, 1997), p. 141.
40 Dorothee von Meding, *Courageous Hearts: Women and the anti-Hitler Plot of 1944* (Berghahn, 1997), p. xxii.
41 Alexander von Stauffenberg, 'Litta', in the collection *Denkmal* [Monument] (Stefan George Foundation, 1964).
42 Fey von Hassell, *A Mother's War* (Corgi, 1991), p. 291.
43 Ibid.
44 Konstanze von Schulthess, Mulley interview (25.11.2014).
45 Deutsches Museum Archive, PERS/F10228/2, Dortmund newspaper report, 'Hanna Reitsch, "Alles Schwindel": Sie soll Hitler nach Argentinien geflogen haben' ['Everything vertigo': you should have flown Hitler to Argentina] (22.03.1950).

46 Ron Laytner, *Edit International Articles: A portfolio of some of Ron Laytner's greatest stories*, 'Hanna Reitsch: Greatest Nazi Test Pilot and World's First Astronaut' (2010).

47 Hugh Trevor-Roper, *The Last Days of Hitler* (Macmillan, 1947), p. 164.

48 Deutsches Museum Archive, 101b, Thilo Bode, 'How History Can Become Falsified: The example of Hanna Reitsch' (nd), pp. 14–15.

49 Hanna Reitsch, *Hohen und Tiefen: 1945 bis in die Gegenwart* [Ups and Downs: 1945 to the present day] (F.A. Herbig Verlag, 1978), pp. 178–9.

50 Yvonne Pagniez, foreword to Hanna Reitsch, *Aventures en Plein Ciel* [Adventures in the Sky] (La Palatine, 1952).

51 Hanna Reitsch, *The Sky My Kingdom: Memoirs of the Famous German World War II Test Pilot* (Greenhill, 2009), pp. 259–60.

52 Otto Skorzeny, *Skorzeny's Special Missions: The Memoirs of 'The Most Dangerous Man in Europe'* (Greenhill, 2006), p. 220.

53 Heidimarie Schade, Mulley interview (01.10.2014).

54 Berthold von Stauffenberg, Lecture for the AV Rheinstein Köln-Lindenthal, 'A Childhood in the Third Reich – from System Conformist to Traitor's Child' (14.04.2008).

55 Gerald Posner, *Hitler's Children: Inside the Families of the Third Reich* (Mandarin, 1991), p. 190.

56 US National Archives, D-53525, the *Overseas Weekly*, 'Adolf's Flying Femme Back' (28.02.1954).

57 *Die Zeit*, 'Unrecht an Hanna Reitsch' [Injustice to Hanna Reitsch] (22.07.1954).

58 Nancy Bird, *My God! It's a Woman: The inspiring story of Australia's pioneering aviatrix* (HarperCollins, 2002), p. 130.

59 Deutsches Museum Archive, 130/136, letter Brazil Sudeten Club/Hanna Reitsch (14.01.1958).

60 The Ian Sayer Archive, Hanna Reitsch correspondence, letter Hanna Reitsch/Herr Petzoldt (08.04.1957).

61 The Ian Sayer Archive, Hanna Reitsch correspondence, letter Hanna Reitsch/Herr Brockmann (11.11.1958).

62 The Ian Sayer Archive, Hanna Reitsch correspondence, letter Hanna Reitsch/Herr Brockmann (June 1962).

63 Berthold von Stauffenberg, Lecture for the AV Rheinstein Köln-Lindenthal, 'A Childhood in the Third Reich – from System Conformist to Traitor's Child' (14.04.2008).

64 Ibid.

65 *Der Spiegel*, Hamburg newspaper (March 2012), quoted in Heiko Peter Melle, Ernst Probst, *Sturzflüge für Deutschland: Kurzbiografie der testpilotin Melitta Schenk Gräfin von Stauffenberg* [Nosedives for Germany: a short biography . . .] (Grin Verlag, 2012).

66 Konstanze von Schulthess, Mulley interview (25.11.2014).

67 Karl Christ, *Der Andere Stauffenberg: Der Historiker und Dichter Alexander von Stauffenberg* [The Other Stauffenberg: Historian and Poet Alexander von Stauffenberg] (C. H. Beck, 2008), privately translated, p. 45.

68 *German History: The Journal of the German History Society*, Bernhard Rieger, 'The Global Career of a Nazi Celebrity', vol. 26, no. 3 (Sage Publications, 2008), p. 398.

69 Hanna Reitsch, *The Sky My Kingdom: Memoirs of the Famous German World War II Test Pilot* (Greenhill, 2009), p. 263.

70 *German History: The Journal of the German History Society*, Bernhard Rieger, 'The Global Career of a Nazi Celebrity', vol. 26, no. 3 (Sage Publications, 2008), p. 395.

71 Deutsches Museum Archive, 130/18, letter Wernher von Braun/Hanna Reitsch (18.08.1947).

72 Deutsches Museum Archive, PERS/F/10228/2-, *Frau mit Herz* [Woman with Heart] magazine, 'The life story of the famous pilot Hanna Reitsch: Only up in the air could I feel free' (nd).

73 Eric Brown, *Wings On My Sleeve: The World's Greatest Test Pilot Tells His Story* (Phoenix, 2007), p. 266.

74 *Daily Graphic*, Edith Wuver, 'The Woman Who Dares the Heavens', quoted in *American History Review*, Jean Allman, 'Phantoms of the Archive: Kwame Nkrumah, a Nazi Pilot Named Hanna, and the Contingencies of Post-Colonial History-Writing' (February 2013), pp. 104–29.

75 *German History: The Journal of the German History Society*, Bernhard Rieger, 'The Global Career of a Nazi Celebrity', vol. 26, no. 3 (Sage Publications, 2008), p. 401.

76 Deutsches Museum archive, PERS/F/10228/2-, *Frau mit Herz* [Woman with Heart] magazine, 'The life story of the famous pilot Hanna Reitsch: Only up in the air could I feel free' (nd).

77 Jean Allman, 'Phantoms of the Archive: Kwame Nkrumah, a Nazi Pilot Named Hanna, and the Contingencies of Post-Colonial History-Writing', *American History Review* (February 2013), p. 111.

78 IWM film archive, *Roving Report – Ghana*, ITN 111 (October 1964).

79 *American History Review*, Jean Allman, 'Phantoms of the Archive: Kwame Nkrumah, a Nazi Pilot Named Hanna, and the Contingencies of Post-Colonial History-Writing' (February 2013), p. 122.

80 *German History: The Journal of the German History Society*, Bernhard Rieger, 'The Global Career of a Nazi Celebrity', vol. 26, no. 3 (Sage Publications, 2008), p. 401.

81 Ibid.

82 Hanna Reitsch, *The Sky My Kingdom: Memoirs of the Famous German World War II Test Pilot* (Greenhill, 2009), p. 264.

83 Deutsches Museum Archive, PERS/F/10228/1, Hanna Reitsch,

'Ich Flög für Kwame Nkrumah' [I Flew for Kwame Nkrumah] (nd, *c.*1968).

84 Karl Christ, *Der Andere Stauffenberg: Der Historiker und Dichter Alexander von Stauffenberg* [The Other Stauffenberg: Historian and Poet Alexander von Stauffenberg] (C. H. Beck, 2008), p. 161.

85 Alexander von Stauffenberg, *Denkmal* [Monument] (Stefan George Foundation, 1964).

86 Deutsches Museum archive, 130/110, letter Hanna Reitsch/Herr von Barsewisch (31.08.1971).

87 Eric Brown, Mulley interview (18.03.2013).

88 Ibid.

89 Ibid.

90 Ibid.

91 Ron Laytner, *Edit International Articles: A portfolio of some of Ron Laytner's greatest stories,* 'Hanna Reitsch: Greatest Nazi Test Pilot and World's First Astronaut' (2010).

92 Ibid.

93 Deutsches Museum archive, PERS/F/10228/1, Alte Adler club newsletter (Spring 1972).

94 Ibid. p. 7.

95 Ibid. p. 12.

96 Gerhard Bracke archive, letter Hanna Reitsch/Klara Schiller (07.02.1975).

97 Ibid.

98 Ibid

99 Ibid.

100 Ibid.

101 Ibid.

102 Gerhard Bracke archive, letter Hanna Reitsch/Klara Schiller (18.02.1975).

103 Ibid.

104 Ibid.

105 Ibid.

106 Ibid.

107 Gerhard Bracke archive, letter Klara Schiller/Hanna Reitsch (13.2.1975).

108 Gerhard Bracke archive, letter Klara Schiller/Hanna Reitsch (27.06.1975).

109 Gerhard Bracke archive, letter Hanna Reitsch/Klara Schiller (nd).

110 Gerhard Bracke archive, letter Hanna Reitsch/Klara Schiller (01.04.1977).

111 John Groom, producer, *The Secret War*, BBC, Mulley interview (24.06.2015).

112 The Ian Sayer Archive, Hanna Reitsch correspondence, letter Hanna Reitsch/Barry Radley (29.06.1978).

113 The Ian Sayer Archive, Hanna Reitsch correspondence, letter Hanna Reitsch/Barry Radley (05.06.1978).

114 Deutsches Museum archive, 130/111, letter Fritz Stüber/Hanna Reitsch (15.06.1978).

115 Deutsches Museum archive, 130/139, letter Eleanore Baur/Hanna Reitsch (01.09.1978).

116 Deutsches Museum archive, 130/139, letter Eleanore Baur/Hanna Reitsch (20.11.1978).

117 Deutsches Museum archive, 130/109, letter Hans Baur/Hanna Reitsch (10.02.1976).

118 Deutsches Museum archive, 130/109, letter Hans Baur/Hanna Reitsch (28.11.1978).

119 Deutsches Museum archive, 130/109, letter Hanna Reitsch/Hans Baur (05.12.1978).

120 The Ian Sayer Archive, Hanna Reitsch correspondence, letter Hanna Reitsch/Barry Radley (17.09.1978).

121 The Ian Sayer Archive, Hanna Reitsch correspondence, letter Hanna Reitsch/Barry Radley (23.11.1978).

122 Ibid.

123 Ron Laytner, *Edit International Articles: A portfolio of some of Ron Laytner's greatest stories*, 'Hanna Reitsch: Greatest Nazi Test Pilot and World's First Astronaut' (2010).

124 Deutsches Museum archive, 130/109, letter Hanna Reitsch/Hans Baur (05.12.1978).

125 Eric Brown, Mulley interview (18.03.2013); Eric Brown, *Wings On My Sleeve: The World's Greatest Test Pilot Tells His Story* (Phoenix, 2007), p. 120.

126 Eric Brown, James Holland interview, www.griffonmerlin.com/WW2

127 Eric Brown, Mulley interview (18.03.2013).

128 Eric Brown, *Wings On My Sleeve: The World's Greatest Test Pilot Tells His Story* (Phoenix, 2007), p. 120.

129 Deutsches Museum archive, 130/123, letter Hanna Reitsch/Kurt Reitsch (1946).

EPILOGUE: A TIME OF CONTRADICTIONS

1 Dorothee von Meding, *Courageous Hearts: Women and the anti-Hitler Plot of 1944* (Berghahn, 1997), p. xv.

2 Gerhard Bracke, *Melitta Gräfin Stauffenberg: Das Leben einer Fliegerin* [The Life of an Aviatrix] (Herbig, 2013), privately translated, p. 76; Hanna Reitsch, *The Sky My Kingdom: Memoirs of the Famous German World War II Test Pilot* (Greenhill, 2009), p. 1.

3 Deutsches Museum archive, PERS/F/10228/2, letter Prof. Walter

Birnbaum to *Süddeutsche Zeitung* recalling train conversation with Hanna Reitsch (15/16.09.1979).

4 Archive Reinhart Rudershausen, Lieselotte Hansen, 'Memories of Lieselotte Hansen, née Lachman' (unpublished manuscript, nd).

5 Berthold von Stauffenberg, Mulley interview (5.11.2014).

6 Gerhard Bracke, *Melitta Gräfin Stauffenberg: Das Leben einer Fliegerin* [The Life of an Aviatrix] (Herbig, 2013), privately translated, p. 159.

7 Melitta Schiller, 'A Woman in Test Flying', speech at the German Embassy in Stockholm (06.12.1943), quoted by Gerhard Bracke, *Melitta Gräfin Stauffenberg: Das Leben einer Fliegerin* [The Life of an Aviatrix] (Herbig, 2013), p. 159.

8 Gerhard Bracke, *Melitta Gräfin Stauffenberg: Das Leben einer Fliegerin* [The Life of an Aviatrix] (Herbig, 2013), privately translated, p. 168.

9 Peter Hoffmann, *German Resistance to Hitler* (Harvard, 1988), p. 135.

10 Deutsches Museum archive, PERS/F/10228/2, Evelyn Künneke quoted in *Frau mit Herz* [Woman with Heart] magazine, 'The life story of the famous pilot Hanna Reitsch: Only up in the air could I feel free' (nd), p. 2.

11 Eric Brown, Mulley interview (18.03.2013).

12 Robert Harris, *Fatherland* (Arrow, 1993), p. 299.

13 Deutsches Museum archive, 130/100, letter Hanna Reitsch/Dr Laternser (17.03.1947).

14 Ibid.

15 *Der Spiegel*, Susanne von Beyer, 'Frau im Sturzflug' [Woman in a Nosedive] (05/03/2012).

16 Joachim Kramarz, *Stauffenberg: The Life and Death of an Officer* (André Deutsch, 1967), p. 11.

Select Bibliography

INTERVIEWS AND CORRESPONDENCE*

Captain Eric 'Winkle' Brown, CBE, DSC, AFC, Hon. FRAeS, Royal Navy Officer and Test Pilot (2013, 2014)

Doreen Galvin, WAAF Intelligence Officer, RAF Tempsford (2015)

John Groom, BBC producer, *The Secret War* (2015)

Flying Officer John Alan Ottewell, DFM, Légion d'Honneur, RAF 115 and 7 Squadrons, Pathfinder (2014)

Flight Sergeant Jack Pragnell, RAF 102 Squadron, Bomber Aimer (2015)

Lieutenant Dietrich Pütter, Luftwaffe reconnaissance pilot (2014)

Wing Commander Len Ratcliffe, RAF 161 Special Duties Squadron (2013)

Lance Corporal Walter Rehling, Luftwaffe Night Fighter Squadron NJG101 (2013)

Professor Dr Bernd Rosemeyer, son of Elly Beinhorn and Bernd Rosemeyer (2014)

Dr Reinhart Rudershausen, son of Jutta Rudershausen, Melitta's sister (2014)

Dr Heidimarie Schade, niece of Ilse and Otto Schiller, Melitta's brother (2014)

Konstanze von Schulthess Rechberg, youngest daughter of Claus and Nina von Stauffenberg (2014)

Major General Count Berthold von Stauffenberg, eldest son of Claus and Nina von Stauffenberg (2014)

Flight Lieutenant Russell 'Rusty' Waughman DFC, AFC, Légion d'Honneur, RAF 101 Special Duties Squadron (2015)

---

* Dates in parentheses are when the interviews took place.

PUBLIC ARCHIVES AND MUSEUMS

BRITISH PUBLIC ARCHIVES

Churchill Archives Centre, Churchill College, Cambridge
CHUR 4/460A

Imperial War Museum, London

Film archive
MTE 291, *Focke Helicopter: The First Really Successful Helicopter* (1938)
ITN 111, *Roving Report – Ghana* (1964)
GWY 556, *Deutsche Luftgeltung 1937* [German Air Effect] (1938)
GWY 213, *Die Deutsche Wochenschrau Nr 712* [newsreel] (April 1944) I & V
GWY 223, *Die Deutsche Wochenschrau Nr 712* (June 1944) III

Photo archive
Various

The National Archives, Kew

Air Ministry
AIR 34/625 'Peenemünde' (1944)
AIR 40/7 'Kutonase Balloon Cable Cutters' (1942)
AIR 40/21 'German Troop and Freight Carrying Gliders' (1941)
AIR 40/36 'BZA-1 German Dive Bombsight' (nd)
AIR 40/115 'German Helicopters, the Focke-Achgelis 223' (1944)
AIR 40/205 'Me 323 "Gigant" Aircraft' (11/42–5/45)
AIR 40/2840 'Launching of the German Flying Bomb, V-1' (1944)
AIR 40/2834 'Flying the German Messerschmitt Me 262 jet-propelled aircraft: practical advice from former German test pilot' (1945)
AIR 41/7 'RAF Narrative: Photographic Reconnaissance', vol. 2 (1941–5)

War Office
WO 208/4168 (SRGG 961c), interrogation reports of German POWs, General von Thoma
WO 328/36 Statement of Alexandra von Stauffenberg (May 1945)
WO 328/37 Statement of Clemens von Stauffenberg, Capri (May 1945)
WO 328/38 Statement of Markwart von Stauffenberg (May 1945)

Foreign Office
   FO 371/21737, Nevile Henderson letter (06.09.1938)
   FO 954/10 vol. 10/Folio 391 (Ge/44/14/A), Letter Foreign Office/
   Churchill's Private Secretary (24.07.1944)

ROYAL AIR FORCE MUSEUM, HENDON

Sound archive
   330161: John Searby, Master Bomber, 'The Great Raids –
   Peenemünde' (nd)

GERMAN PUBLIC ARCHIVES

DEUTSCHES MUSEUM ARCHIVE, MUNICH

Melitta Schiller collection
   FB89, Melitta Schiller, 'Windkanaluntersuchungen von Luftschrauben
   im Sturzflug' [Wind Tunnel Studies of the Propeller in a
   Nosedive] (06.04.1934)
   FB106, Melitta Schiller, 'Auswertung experimenteller Untersuchungen
   über Verstell-Luftschrauben' [Analysis of Experimental Studies on
   Adjusting Propellers] (15.09.1934)
   FB506, Melitta Schiller, 'Windkanaluntersuchungen an einem Flügel
   mit Rollflügel and Vorflü' [Wind Tunnel Tests on a Wing with
   Roll-Wings and Slats] (09.01.1936)

Hanna Reitsch collection, NL 130
   18. Correspondence:
      — Hanna Reitsch/Wernher von Braun (1947–71)
      — Hanna Reitsch/Amnesty International (1973)
      Wernher von Braun obituary (unknown newspaper, June 1977)
   100. Correspondence:
      — Hanna Reitsch/Dr Laternser (17.03.1947)
      — Hanna Reitsch/Frau Jodl (1948)
      — Hanna Reitsch statement (20.05.1948)
   101. Correspondence:
      — Hanna Reitsch/Kurt Reitsch (nd)
      — Hanna Reitsch/Otto Skorzeny (1974)
      — Horst von Salomon/Kaplan Friedel Volkmar (27.04.1947)
      — Friedel Volkmar/Dr Kindermann (July 1948)
      — Various hand-drawn Christmas and Easter cards (1947)
      Mano Ziegler, 'Die ersten Raketenjäger der Welt' [The world's
      first rocket hunters] (nd)
      Walter Stender, 'Politische Erklärung' [Political Statement]
      (01.07.1947)
      Richard Homberger (07.07.1947)

Hanna Reitsch, 'Eidesstattliche Erklärung' [Affidavit for Otto
   Skorzeny] (12.04.1948)
101a. Correspondence:
— Hanna Reitsch/Hugh Trevor-Roper (1948)
— Alfred G. T. Wilheim, *Die Epoche*/Hanna Reitsch
   (07.08.1947)
— Hanna Reitsch/*Die Welt* editor (01.12.1947)
Political reports:
— Anon., report on Hanna Reitsch (nd)
— Hanna Reitsch, *An den Kommandanten* [Statement to Camp
   Commanders] (March 1946)
— 'Abschrift' [Transcript] (Nuremberg, 08.04.1947)
Die Welt, Hugh Trevor-Roper, 'Hitlers Letzte Tage' [Hitler's Last
   Days] (14.10.1947)
101b.
Anon., 'Conversation with Hanna Reitsch' (nd)
Captain Musmanno, 'Private Conversation between Captain M.
   and H. Reitsch' (01.02.1948)
Thilo Bode, 'How History Can Become Falsified: The Example of
   Hanna Reitsch' (nd)
109. Correspondence:
— Hanna Reitsch/Heini Dittmar (1934–53)
— Hanna Reitsch/Wolf Hirth (1952–77)
— Hanna Reitsch/Peter Riedel (1960–78)
— Hanna Reitsch/Günther Rall (1975)
— Hanna Reitsch/Hans Baur (1976–9)
— Hanna Reitsch/Carl Franke (1977–8)
— Hanna Reitsch/Nicolaus von Below (1978)
110. Correspondence:
— Hanna Reitsch/Karl Bode (1951–79)
— Hanna Reitsch/Herr Brockmann (1958–62)
— Hanna Reitsch/Fritz Edelhoff (1967–71)
— Hanna Reitsch/Herr von Barsewisch (31.08.1971)
— Hanna Reitsch/Gerhard Bracke (1973)
Karl Bode, 'Darstellung der Vorführungen der Focke 61 in der
   Deutschlandhalle durch Frl. Reitsch im 'Stern' Nr 43' [Report
   of the performances of the Focke 61 in the Deutschlandhalle
   by Miss Reitsch in 'Star' No. 43]
111. Correspondence:
— Hanna Reitsch/Walter Schauberger/Hanna Reitsch (1947)
— Hanna Reitsch/Ernst Straka/Blüm/Hanna Reitsch
   (29.07.1970)
— Hanna Reitsch/Friedrich Wackersreuth (18.09.1971)
— Fan mail/Hanna Reitsch (1974)
— Hanna Reitsch/Herr Stüper (07.02.1974)

— Hanna Reitsch/Rud. Hèdrich-Winter von Schwab/Hanna Reitsch (24.02.1976)
— Hanna Reitsch/Dr Elfriede Wagner (1976–77)
— Hanna Reitsch/Pater Karl-Theodor Wagner (1976–77)
— Hanna Reitsch/Ull Schwenger (1977)
— Hanna Reitsch/Fritz Stüber (15.06.1978)
123.
Letter Hanna Reitsch/Kurt Reitsch (1946)
136. Correspondence:
— Hanna Reitsch/Brazil Sudeten Club (14.01.1958)
— Hanna Reitsch/Theodore Heuss (1960)
— Hanna Reitsch/Erika Christl Greim (29.08.1974)
Wernher von Braun, 'Wir Haben Allen Grund – Zu Beten' [We have every reason – to pray] (nd)
139. Correspondence:
— Hanna Reitsch/Eleanore Baur (1978)
— Hanna Reitsch/Edda Göring (18.10.1978)
PERS/F/10228/1
Unknown publication, 'Hanna Reitsch soll nicht in England fliegen' [Hanna Reitsch should not fly in England] (13.07.1954)
Hanna Reitsch, 'Ich Flog für Kwame Nkrumah' [I Flew for Kwame Nkrumah] (nd)
Alte Adler member newsletter, Friedrich Stahl, Alte Adler president, speech at Hanna Reitsch's sixtieth birthday party (Spring 1972)
PERS/F/10228/2
Newsprint articles including:
— *Frau mit Herz* [Woman with Heart] magazine, 'The life story of the famous pilot Hannah Reitsch: Only up in the air could I feel free' (nd)
— *Luftwelt* [Airworld], Peter Riedel, 'Deutsche Segelflieger in Argentinien' [German Glider Pilots in Argentina] (1934)
— *Illustrierter Beobachter*, 'Segelfliegen! Reichsluftminister Generaloberst Göring hat Hanna Reitsch zum Flugkapitän ernannt' [Gliding! Reich Air Minister Göring has appointed Hanna Reitsch as Flight Captain] (1937)
— Alte Adler newsletter, 'Die Geburtstagsfeier Unseres Ehremitgliedes: Hanna Reitsch' [The Birthday Party of our Honorary Member: Hanna Reitsch] (18.04.1972)
— *Süddeutsche Zeitung*, letter from Prof. Walter Birnbaum (15/16.09.1979)
Unknown publication articles:
— Dortmund newspaper, 'Hanna Reitsch, "Alles Schwindel": Sie soll Hitler nach Argentinien geflogen haben' ['Everything

vertigo': you should have flown Hitler to Argentina]
(22.3.1950)
— 'Warum Hanna Reitsch nicht nach England fuhr, Erklärung
des Präsidenten des Deutschen Aero-Club' [Why Hanna
Reitsch is not competing in England, a statement by the
President of the German Aero-Club] (14.07.1954)

THE PEENEMÜNDE HISTORICAL TECHNICAL MUSEUM
Permanent exhibition

PLÖTZENSEE PRISON MEMORIAL
Permanent exhibition

SCHLOSS LAUTLINGEN
Permanent exhibition

TECHNICAL UNIVERSITY OF MUNICH ARCHIVE
TUM entrance record for Melitta Schiller (1922)
Correspondence Melitta Schiller/TUM Professor (nd)

US ARCHIVES

CORNELL UNIVERSITY LAW LIBRARY: DONOVAN NUREMBERG TRIALS
COLLECTION
US Forces report, 'Last Letters from Hitler's Air Raid Shelter'
(08.10.1945)
US Forces report, Hanna Reitsch interrogation, 'The Last Days in
Hitler's Air Raid Shelter' (08.10.1945)

NATIONAL ARCHIVES AND RECORDS ADMINISTRATION
Hanna Reitsch Personal File, RG319, 270, 84, 13, 7, box 633
(7362164, XE053525)
'The Wind of Heaven Goes West' (nd)
US Forces report, Hanna Reitsch, 'Condemnation of Göring by
Hanna Reitsch' (16.11.1945)
US Forces report, Hanna Reitsch interrogation (04.12.1945)
Various papers relating to Hanna Reitsch, including:
— Memos relating to Operation Skylark (1946–7)
— US Forces, European Theater PR Division, release no. 794
(05.12.1945)
— 'Censorship Civil Communications', R. Storck to G.
Rieckmann (21.08.1946)
— US Civil Censorship (Germany) (18.03.1947)

— 'Hanna Reitsch pleads for General Kesselring' at Nuremberg
     Trials (01.04.1947)
— 'Agent Report' (19.07.1948)
Newspaper cuttings, including
— *Stars & Stripes*, 'German Woman Arrested at Border'
     (24.05.1948)
— *Overseas Weekly*, 'Adolf's Flying Femme Back' (28.02.1954)

PRIVATE ARCHIVES

ARCHIVE GERHARD BRACKE, GERMANY

Melitta Schiller's diary (1943, 1944)
Correspondence:
— Melitta Schiller/Blenk (17.03.1935)
— Michael and Margarete Schiller/Hermann Göring (1942)
— Hanna Reitsch/Gerhard Bracke (1973)
— H. Schrank/Klara Schiller (14.03.1975)
— Hanna Reitsch/Klara Schiller (1975–7)
— Peter Riedel/Mrs J. Hacker (25.08.1980)
— Peter Riedel/Klara Schiller (1981–2)
Mika Stauffenberg, untitled account of Melitta Schiller
     (17.02.1962)
Philippa Countess von Thun-Hohenstein, 'Memories of Melitta:
     personal impressions of Countess von Stauffenberg' (07.07.2000)
Audio interviews:
— Klara Schiller, 'Erinnerungen' [Memories] (09.10.1982)
— Hubertus von Papen-Koeningen (10.08.1989)
— Peter Riedel and Klara Schiller (late 1980s)
Photos: various

JOHN MARTIN BRADLEY, COMBAT PILOTS OF WWII COLLECTION
(http://www.combatpilotsofwwii.com)
Interview with Captain Hein K. Gering (27.06.2009)

CAROLINE ESDAILE FAMILY PAPERS
Simon Reiss, 'Remembering Kristallnacht' (9.11.1998)

ARCHIVE H. P. MELLE / STAUFFENBERG, GERMANY
Alexander von Stauffenberg, *Denkmal* [Monument] (Stefan Georg
     Foundation, 1964)
Marie-Luise Lübbert, 'Chronik der Familie Lübbert' (nd)
Photos: various

BARBARA PASEWALDT, PRIVATE PAPERS, GERMANY
Alte Adler, obituary of Georg Pasewaldt (1988)
Georg Pasewaldt, 'Erfahrungen und Erkenntnisse einer Fliegerlaufbahn',
[Experience and Insights from a Flying Career] (nd)

ARCHIVE REINHART RUDERSHAUSEN, GERMANY
Correspondence:
— Michael Schiller/Hermann Göring (26.10.1942)
— Margarete Schiller/Hermann Göring (11.12.1942)
Melitta von Stauffenberg reports:
— 'Abschrift' [Report (on the presentation of her Iron Cross II)]
(January 1943)
— 'Vortag gehalten in Stockholm am 6.12.43: Eine Frau in der
Flugerprobung' [A Woman in Test Flying], Stockholm lecture
(06.12.43).
*Natur und Geist: Monatsheft für Wissenschaft, Weltanschauung und
Lebensgestallung* [Nature and Spirit: The Monthly Bulletin of
Science, Philosophy and Lifestyle] 3.12 (December 1935)
'Melitta Gräfin Schenk von Stauffenberg Lebenlauf' [Resumé],
DVL reference (23.11.1936)
Hermann Blenk, 'Erinnerungen an Melitta Schiller' [Memories of
Melitta Schiller] (13.09.1974)
Paul von Handel, 'Erinnerungen an Litta' [Memories of Litta] (nd)
Lieselotte Hansen, 'Memories of Lieselotte Hansen, née Lachman'
(nd)
Jutta Rudershausen, 'Frau über den Wolken: Ein Leben für
Wissenschaft und Fliegen' [Woman Above the Clouds: A Life
for Science and Flying] (nd)
——, 'Flugkapitän Melitta Schiller-Stauffenberg: Von keinem
Piloter erreicht' [Peerless Pilot] (nd)
Klara Schiller, 'Erinnerungen' [Memories] (nd)
Marie-Luise (Lili) Schiller/Lübert, 'Zweig Otto Eberstein' [Otto
Eberstein branch of the family]
Georg Wollé, 'Erinnerungen eines Berufskollegen, der mit Melitta
in der Versuchsanstalt für Luftfahrt angestellt war' [Memories
of a colleague of Melitta Schiller at the Institute of Aviation
(DVL)] (11.02.1974)
Alexander von Stauffenberg, 'Litta' (handwritten poem, nd)
Painting: Gertrud von Kunowski, portrait of Margarete Schiller
née Eberstein (1906)

THE IAN SAYER ARCHIVE
Correspondence:
— Margot Heberlein/Sigismund Payne Best (17.06.1946)
— Fey von Hassell (Pirzio-Biroli)/Sigismund Payne Best (28.07.1946)

— Hanna Reitsch/Herr Petzoldt (1957)
— Hanna Reitsch/Herr Brockmann (1958–62)
— Hanna Reitsch/Captain Barry Radley (1975–9)
Newspaper cutting, Barry Radley letter regarding Hanna Reitsch (27.11.1979)

STAUFFENBERG FAMILY ARCHIVE
Berthold Schenk Graf von Stauffenberg, Generalmajor a.D., 'A Childhood in the Third Reich – from System Conformist to Traitor's Child'. Lecture delivered to the AV Rheinstein Köln-Lindenthal (14.04.2008)
Correspondence with Thomas Medicus (2012)

ANNE C. VOORHOEVE PAPERS
Otto Philipp von Stauffenberg, 'Der 20. Juli und seine Folge' ['The 20th July and its Consequences'] (talk, nd)
Marie Gabriele 'Gagi' von Stauffenberg, 'Aufzeichnungen aus unserer Sippenhaft 20. Juli 1944–19. Juni 1945' (Notes from our Sippenhaft experience, 20 July 1944–19 June 1945) (nd)

PRESS, JOURNALS, FILM, TV AND RADIO

ENGLISH-LANGUAGE PRESS

Aberdeen Journal
'A German airwoman receives the Iron Cross' (24.04.1941)
'Pension for Widow of von Stauffenberg' (26.11.1945)

Angus Evening Telegraph
'Plane that Flies Backwards' (04.11.1937)

Daily Mail
Robert Hardman, 'Hero who makes Biggles look like a wimp' (07.05.2013)

Daily Telegraph
Guy Walters, 'The truth behind *The Odessa File* and Nazis on the run' (1.12.2010)
Rob Crilly, 'Rare German surrender order expected to fetch £20,000' (26.04.2015)

Derby Daily Telegraph
'Glider Pilots Fined: Speeding – in Motor Cars' (08.05.1936)

Dundee Courier
'Girl Glider Beats Day-Old Record' (16.05.1938)
'Overdue Air Girl Lands' (24.09.1938)

Gloucestershire Echo
'RAF Bombers Blast New Baltic Target' (18.08.1943)
'Himmler at Peenemünde' (25.08.1943)

Nottingham Evening Post
'Helicopter's Amazing Performance' (05.11.1937)
'Echoes From Town' (21.08.1943)

ENGLISH-LANGUAGE JOURNALS

Academia.edu
Helen L. Boak, 'Women in Weimar Germany: The 'Frauenfrage' and the Female Vote', p.1 www.academia.edu/498771/Women_in_ Weimar_Germany_The_Frauenfrage_and_the_Female_Vote

Aeroplane magazine
'Women's Day at Chigwell' (28.09.1938)
Barbara Schlussler, 'Melitta Schiller' (June 1999)
'Flugkapitän Hanna Reitsch, 1914–79' (June, July, August, September and October 1985)
Alexander Steenbeck, 'The Man Who Flew With Stauffenberg' (October 2011)

Air Classics
Blaine Taylor, 'She Flew for Hitler! The story of Flugkapitän Hanna Reitsch and her aerial adventures in Nazi Germany' (February 1989)

American Historical Review
Jean Allman, 'Phantoms of the Archive: Kwame Nkrumah, a Nazi Pilot Named Hanna, and the Contingencies of Post-Colonial History-Writing' (February 2013), 118 (1), pp. 104–29

Edit International Articles: A portfolio of some of Ron Laytner's greatest stories
Ron Laytner, 'Hanna Reitsch: Greatest Nazi Test Pilot and World's First Astronaut' (2010): http://issuu.com/edit_international/docs/ publication_hanna_reitsch?mode=embed&documen tId=090107212350-fe902db02968468fb93464edc07459de&layout= grey

German History: The Journal of the German History Society
Bernhard Rieger, 'The Global Career of a Nazi Celebrity', vol. 26, no. 3, pp. 383–405 (Sage Publications, 2008)

History & Technology: An International Journal
Margot Fuchs, 'Like fathers like daughters, professionalization strategies of women students and engineers in Germany 1890s to 1940s' vol. 14, issue 1–2 (1997)

History Today
    Roger Moorhouse, 'A Good German? Von Stauffenberg and the July
        Plot', vol. 59, issue 1 (2009)
    Edgar Feuchtwanger, 'I Was Hitler's Neighbour', vol. 62, issue 6 (2012)

History Workshop Journal
    Maya Jasanoff, 'Border Crossing: My Imperial Routes,' Issue 64
        (Autumn 2007)

JewishJournal.com
    Alan Abrahamson, 'Photos reveal anti-Semitism of 1936 Winter
        Games' (1 March 2011)

Modern Judaism
    Sarah Fraiman, 'The Transformation of Jewish Consciousness in Nazi
        Germany as reflected in the German Jewish journal *Der Morgen*,
        1925–1938,' vol. 20, pp. 41–59 (OUP, 2000)

New Republic
    Richard J. Evans, 'The Life and Death of a Capital', review of Thomas
        Friedrich's *Hitler's Berlin* (27.09.2012), http://www.newrepublic.com/
        book/review/abused-city-hitlers-berlin-thomas-friedrich

WWII Magazine
    Nigel Jones, 'Claus von Stauffenberg: the man who tried to kill Hitler'
        (HistoryNet.com, 22.12.2008)

GERMAN-LANGUAGE PRESS AND JOURNALS

Der Adler [Luftwaffe magazine]
    'The Iron Cross for a Gallant Female Pilot' (06.04.1943)

Askania-Warte magazine
    'Flight to England with slight problems along the way' (24.09.1938)

Berliner Illustriete Zeitung
    jg. 38, No. 42 (20.10.1929)

Der Speigel
    Susanne Beyer, 'Frau im Sturzflug' [Woman in a Nosedive] (October 2012)

Die Welt
    Hanna Reitsch, 'Wie klein Mäxchen sich den Untergang des Dritten
        Reiches vorstellt' [How the Little Maxes Imagine the Downfall of
        the Third Reich] (02.08.1973)

Die Zeit
    'Unrecht an Hanna Reitsch' [Injustice to Hanna Reitsch] (22.07.1954)

Jutta Rudershausen [Melitta's sister], 'Täglich funfzehn Sturzfluge – Zu Unrecht vergessen: Flugkapitän Melitta Schenk Schiller war vor vierzig Jahren ein Pionier der Luftfahrt' [Fifteen nosedives a day, falsely remembered: forty years ago Flugkapitän MSS was a pioneer of flight] (05.01.1973)

Nina Gräfin von Stauffenberg, 'Wie das Konzept der Männer des 20 Juli 1944 aussah: Sie wollten Hitler nicht mit Stalin tauschen' [Clarifying the concept of the men of 20 July: They did not want to replace Hitler with Stalin], no. 37, p. 26 (08.09.1978)

Schlesische Flieger Nachrichten 6 [Silesian Pilot News]
Klara Schiller, 'Melitta Gräfin Schenk von Stauffenberg, née Schiller, 1903–1945' in pp. 2–6 (05.1988)

BRITISH FILM, TV AND RADIO

BBC, *The Secret War* (1977)
BBC 2:
Operation Crossbow: How the Allies used 3D photography to thwart the Nazis' super-weapons (2013)
The Lancaster: Britain's Flying Past (20.07.2014)
Britain's Greatest Pilot: The Extraordinary Story of Captain 'Winkle' Brown (ed. Darren Jonusas ASE, Exec. Prod. Steve Crabtree (01.06.2014)
Channel Four, *Spying on Hitler's Army: The Secret Recordings* (2013)
Sony Picture Classics, *Blind Spot: Hitler's Secretary*, featuring Traudl Junge
Me-163 flown by test pilots Hanna Reitsch and Heini Dittmar
BBC World Service:
History Hour: The Death of Mussolini (03.05.2014)
Witness: The Plot to Kill Hitler (18.07.2014)
BBC Radio Four, *Desert Island Discs*: Eric Brown (14.11.2014)

German-Language Film, Tv And Radio

ZDF (Germany):
Fliegen und Stürzen – Porträt der Melitta Schiller-Stauffenberg, eine aussergewohnlichen Frau [Flying and Nosediving: a portrait of Melitta Schiller-Stauffenberg, an exceptional woman] (6 January 1974)
Himmelsstürmerinnen, Deutsche Fliegerinnen – Ihre Rekorde und Tragödien [Women who stormed the sky, German women pilots, their records and tragedies], ARTE film by Bertram von Boxberg and Karin Rieppel (June 2011)
Interspot Film (Austria), *Hanna Reitsch: Hitlers Fliegerin* [Hitler's Pilot] (dir. Gerhard Jelinek and Fritz Kalteis, 2010)
Im Toten Winkel: Hitler's Secretarin [Blindspot: Hitler's Secretary], a film by André Heller and Othmar Schmiderer (Traudl Junge interview)

MEMOIRS AND RECOLLECTIONS

Anonymous, *A Woman in Berlin* (Virago, 2013)

Constance Babington Smith, *Evidence in Camera: The story of photographic intelligence in the Second World War* (Sutton, 2004)

Gerda Erika Baker, *Shadow of War* (Lion, 1990)

Hans Baur, *I was Hitler's Pilot: The Memoirs of Hans Baur* (Frontline, 2013)

Isolde Baur, *A Pilot's Pilot: Karl Baur, Chief Test Pilot for Messerschmitt* (Schiffer, 1999)

Elly Beinhorn, *Premiere am Himmel, meine berühmten Fliegerkameraden* [First in the Sky: My Famous Aviator Comrades] (Langen-Müller, 1991)

——, *Alleinflug: Mein Leben* (Malik, National Geographic, 2011)

Nicolaus von Below, *At Hitler's Side: The Memoirs of Hitler's Luftwaffe Adjutant 1937–1945* (Frontline, 2010)

Sigismund Payne Best, *The Venlo Incident: How the Nazis Fooled Britain* (Frontline, 2009)

Nancy Bird, *My God! It's a Woman: The inspiring story of Australia's pioneering aviatrix* (Harper Collins, 2002)

Dirk Bogarde, *Cleared For Take-Off* (Chivers, 1996)

Gerhard Boldt, *Hitler's Last Ten Days* (Coward, McCann & Geoghegan, 1973)

Tadeusz Bór-Komorowski, *The Secret Army: The Memoirs of General Bór-Komorowski* (Frontline, 2011)

Eric Brown, *Wings on My Sleeve: The World's Greatest Test Pilot Tells His Story* (Phoenix, 2007)

Sarah Churchill, *Keep on Dancing: An autobiography* (Weidenfeld & Nicolson, 1981)

Winston Churchill, *Great Contemporaries* (Odhams, 1947)

——, *Step by Step: 1936–1939* (Odhams, 1949)

Otto Dietrich, *Mit Hitler an die Macht: Personliche Erlebnisse mit meinem Führer* [With Hitler to Power: Personal Experiences with My Leader] (F. Eher nachf, g.m.b.h., 1934)

Kurt Doerry & Wilhelm Dörr, *Das Olympia-Buch* [The Olympic Book], published on behalf of the German State Committee for Physical Exercise, with foreword by President von Hindenburg (Olympia-Verlag, Munich, 1927)

Walter R. Dornberger, *V-2* (Hurst & Blackett, 1954)

Bernt Engelmann, *In Hitler's Germany: Everyday Life in the Third Reich* (Schocken Books, 1986)

Anne Frank, *The Diary of a Young Girl* (Penguin, 2012)

Peter Gay, *My German Question: Growing Up in Nazi Berlin* (Yale University Press, 1998)

Hans Bernd Gisevius, *To The Bitter End* (Jonathan Cape, 1948)

Joseph Goebbels, *The Goebbels Diaries, 1939–1941: the historic journal of a Nazi war leader*, ed. Fred Taylor (Sphere, 1983)

——, *The Goebbels Diaries: The Last Days*, ed. Louis P. Lochner (Doubleday, 1948)

Elisabeth zu Guttenberg, *Beim Namen Gerufen: Erinnerungen* [Called By Name: Memories] (Harper, 1996)

——, Sheridan Spearman, *Holding the Stirrup* (Duell, Sloan and Pearce/ Little Brown, 1953)

Reinhild Gräfin von Hardenberg, *Auf immer neuen Wegen: Erinnerungen an Neuhardenberg und den Widerstand gegen der Nationalsozialismus* [On New Ways: Memories of Neuhardenberg and the resistance against National Socialism] (Stiftung Schloss Neuhardenberg, 2002)

Fey von Hassell, *A Mother's War* (Corgi, 1991)

——, *Niemals sich beugen: Erinnerungen einer sonder gefangenen der SS* [Never Bow Down: Memories of the Special Prisoners of the SS] (Piper, 1995)

Ulrich von Hassell, *The Von Hassell Diaries: The Story of the Forces Against Hitler Inside Germany, 1938–1944* (Westview Press, 1994)

Sir Nevile Henderson, *Failure of a Mission: Berlin 1937–1939* (Hodder & Stoughton, 1940)

Hajo Herrmann, *Eagle's Wings: The Autobiography of a Luftwaffe Pilot* (Airlife, 1991)

Heinrich Hoffmann, *Hitler Was My Friend: The Memoirs of Hitler's Photographer* (Frontline Books, 2011)

Traudl Junge, *Until the Final Hour: Hitler's Last Secretary* (Phoenix, 2002)

Ursula von Kardorff, *Diary of a Nightmare: Berlin 1942–1945* (Hart-Davis, 1965)

Erich Kempka, *I Was Hitler's Chauffeur: The Memoirs of Erich Kempka* (Frontline, 2010)

Karl Koller, *Der Letzte Monat: Die tagebuchaufzeichnungen des ehemaligen Chefs des Generalstabs der deutschen Luftwaffe vom 14 April bis zum 27 Mai 1945* [The Last Month: The Diaries of Karl Koller, former Chief of Staff of the Luftwaffe, 14 April to 27 May 1945] (Mannheim, 1949)

Heinz Linge, *With Hitler to the End: The Memoirs of Adolf Hitler's Valet* (Frontline, 2009)

Bernd Freytag von Loringhoven, *In the Bunker with Hitler: The last witness speaks* (Weidenfeld & Nicolson, 2005)

Hilde M., *Girls: Your World, The German Girls' Yearbook* (Zentralv., Franz E., Gmbh, 1944), article 'Hanna Reitsch: A Life for Flying'

Friedrich W. von Mellenthin, *Panzer Battles* (Tempus, 1956)

Richard Perlia, *Mal oben – Mal unten* [Sometimes Up – Sometimes Down] (Schiff & Flugzeug-Verlagsbuchhandlung, 2011)

Powys-Lybbe, Ursula, *The Eye of Intelligence* (William Kimber, 1983)

Hanna Reitsch, *Aventures en Plein Ciel* [Adventures in the Sky] (La Palatine, 1952)

——, *Höhen und Tiefen: 1945 bis zur Gegenwart* [Ups and Downs, 1945 to the present day] (Herbig, 1978)

——, *The Sky My Kingdom: Memoirs of the famous German WWII Test Pilot* (Greenhill, 2009)

Jana Richter and Hermann Graml (eds), *Die Tagebücher von Joseph Goebbels: Oktober bis Dezember 1944* [The Diaries of Joseph Goebbels] (KG Saur, 1996)

Peter Riedel, *Start in den Wind – Erlebte Rhöngeschichte 1911 bis 1926* [Take-off in the Wind: Rhön History Experienced 1911–1926] (Motorbuch Verlag Stuttgart, 1977)

Leni Riefenstahl, *A Memoir* (St Martin's Press, 1993)

Christa Schroeder, *He Was My Chief: The Memoirs of Adolf Hitler's Secretary* (Frontline, 2009)

William L. Shirer, *Berlin Diary: The Journal of a Foreign Correspondent 1934–1941* (Gallahad, 1997)

Otto Skorzeny, *Skorzeny's Special Missions: The Memoirs of 'The Most Dangerous Man in Europe'* (Greenhill, 2006)

Wolfgang Späte, *Top Secret Bird: the Luftwaffe's Me-163 Comet* (Independent, 1989)

Albert Speer, *Inside the Third Reich* (Sphere, 1971)

Ernst Udet, *Ace of the Black Cross* (Newnes, 1935)

Veronika Volkersz, *The Sky and I* (W. H. Allen, 1956)

Mano Ziegler, *Rocket Fighter: The Story of the Messerschmitt Me-163* (Arms & Armour Press, 1976)

SECONDARY SOURCE PUBLICATIONS

Norman H. Baynes, *The Speeches of Adolf Hitler, April 1922–August 1939* (OUP, 1942)

Cajus Becker, *The Luftwaffe War Diaries* (MacDonald, 1966)

Anthony Beevor, *Berlin: The Downfall, 1945* (Penguin, 2003)

——, *Ardennes 1944: Hitler's Last Gamble* (Viking, Penguin Random House, 2015)

A. Scott Berg, *Lindbergh* (G. P. Putnam's Sons, 1998)

Helen L. Boak, *Women in the Weimar Republic* (Manchester University Press, 2013)

Gerhard Bracke, *Melitta Gräfin Stauffenberg: Das Leben einer Fliegerin* [The

Life of an Aviatrix] (Herbig Verlag, 2013), privately translated by
     Barbara Schlussler
Bob Carruthers, *Voices from the Luftwaffe* (Pen & Sword, 2012)
Karl Christ, *Der andere Stauffenberg: Der Historiker und Dichter Alexander
     von Stauffenberg* [The other Stauffenberg: Historian and Poet
     Alexander von Stauffenberg] (C. H. Beck, 2008)
Arthur C. Clarke, *Astounding Days: A Science Fiction Autobiography* (Bantam, 1990)
Taylor Downing, *Spies in the Sky: The Secret Battle for Aerial Intelligence
     during World War II* (Little Brown, 2011)
Richard J. Evans, *The Third Reich at War, 1939–1945: How the Nazis Led
     Germany From Conquest to Disaster* (Allen Lane, 2008)
Joachim Fest, *Plotting Hitler's Death: The German Resistance to Hitler
     1933–1945* (Weidenfeld & Nicolson, 1997)
Peter Fritzsche, *A Nation of Flyers: German Aviation and the Popular
     Imagination* (Harvard University Press, 1992)
Oscar Gonzalez, Thomas Steinke, Ian Tannahill, *The Silent Attack: The
     Taking of the Bridges at Veldwezelt, Vroenhoven and Kanne in Belgium by
     German Paratroopers, 10 May 1940* (Pen & Sword, 2015)
Cooper C. Graham, *Leni Riefenstahl and Olympia* (Scarecrow, 1986)
Jenny Hartley, *Hearts Undefeated: Women's Writing of the Second World War*
     (Virago, 1999)
Max Hastings, *All Hell Let Loose: The World At War 1939–1945* (Harper
     Press, 2011)
Peter Hoffmann, *German Resistance to Hitler* (Harvard University Press, 1988)
——, *Stauffenberg: A Family History, 1905–1944* (McGill-Queen's
     University Press, 2008)
Glenn B. Infield, *Skorzeny: Hitler's Commando* (St Martin's Press, 1981)
Sophie Jackson, *Hitler's Heroine: Hanna Reitsch* (History Press, 2014)
Nigel Jones, *Countdown to Valkyrie: The July Plot to Assassinate Hitler*
     (Frontline, 2008)
Patricia Kollander, John O'Sullivan, *I Must be a Part of This War: A
     German American's Fight Against Hitler and Nazism* (Fordham
     University Press, 2005)
Joachim Kramarz, *Stauffenberg: The Life and Death of an Officer, 15
     November 1907–20 July 1944* (André Deutsch, 1967)
David Clay Large, *Nazi Games: The Olympics of 1936* (W. W. Norton, 2007)
Annedore Leber, *Conscience in Revolt: Sixty-four Stories of Resistance in
     Germany, 1933–1945* (Westview Press, 1994)
Celia Lee and Paul Edward Strong (eds.), *Women in War: From Home Front
     to Front Line* (Pen & Sword, 2012)
Robert Loeffel, *Family Punishment in Nazi Germany: Sippenhaft, Terror and
     Myth* (Palgrave Macmillan, 2012)
Judy Lomax, *Hanna Reitsch: Flying for the Fatherland* (John Murray, 1988)
Oliver Lubrich, ed., *Travels in the Reich, 1933–1945: Foreign Authors Report
     from Germany* (University of Chicago Press, 2010)

Eva Madelung, Joachim Scholtyseck, *Heldenkinder – Verräterkinder: Wenn die Eltern im Widerstand Waren* [Hero Children – Traitor Children: Children of the Resistance] (C. H. Beck, 2007)

Thomas Medicus, *Melitta von Stauffenberg: Ein Deutsches Leben* [A German Life] (Rowohlt, Berlin, 2012)

Dorothee von Meding, *Courageous Hearts: Women and the anti-Hitler Plot of 1944* (Berghahn, 1997)

Heiko Peter Melle, Ernst Probst, *Sturzflüge für Deutschland: Kurzbiografie der Testpilotin Melitta Schenk Gräfin von Stauffenberg* [Nosedives for Germany: a short biography of the test pilot Melitta Schenk Countess von Stauffenberg] (Grin Verlag, 2012)

Roger Moorhouse, *Berlin at War: Life and Death in Hitler's Capital, 1939–45* (Vintage, 2011)

Sönke Neitzel, *Tapping Hitler's Generals: Transcripts of Secret Conversations, 1942–1945* (Frontline, 2007)

Michael J. Neufeld, *The Rocket and The Reich: Peenemünde and the Coming of the Ballistic Missile Era* (The Free Press, 1995)

——, *Von Braun: Dreamer of Space, Engineer of War* (Alfred A. Knopf, 2008)

Robert E. Norton, *Secret Germany: Stefan George and His Circle* (Cornell University Press, 2002)

Dennis Piszkiewicz, *From Nazi Test Pilot to Hitler's Bunker: The Fantastic Flights of Hanna Reitsch* (Praeger, 1997)

Gerald Posner, *Hitler's Children: Inside the Families of the Third Reich* (Mandarin, 1991)

Sean Rayment, *Tales from the Special Forces Club: The Untold Stories of Britain's Elite WWII Warriors* (Collins, 2003)

Hugh Trevor-Roper, *The Last Days of Hitler* (Macmillan, 1947)

Fabian von Schlabrendorff, *The Secret War Against Hitler* (Westview Press, 1994)

Konstanze von Schulthess, *Nina Schenk Gräfin von Stauffenberg: Ein Porträt* [Nina Schenk Gräfin von Stauffenberg: A Portrait] (Piper Taschenbuch, 2009)

Carole Seymour-Jones, *She Landed by Moonlight, The Story of Secret Agent Pearl Witherington: the real 'Charlotte Gray'* (Transworld, 2013)

Leslie Earl Simon, *German Research in World War II: an analysis of the conduct of research* (John Wiley, 1947)

Martin Simons, *German Air Attaché: The Thrilling Wartime Story of the German Ace Pilot and Wartime Diplomat Peter Riedel* (Airlife, 1997)

C. G. Sweeting, *Hitler's Personal Pilot: The Life and Times of Hans Baur* (Brassey's, 2000)

——, *Hitler's Squadron: The Fuehrer's Personal Aircraft and Transport Unit, 1933–45* (Brassey's, 2001)

Jeffrey Watson, *Sidney Cotton: The Last Plane Out of Berlin* (Hodder, 2003)

Robert Wohl, *The Spectacle of Flight: Aviation and the Western Imagination, 1920–1950* (New Haven, 2005)

FICTION

Robert Harris, *Fatherland* (Arrow, 1993)

WEBSITES

www.20-juli-44.de
  '20 July 1944: Memories of a Historic Day'
www.aircrewremembered.com
  Aircrew Remembered
  'Hanna Reistch: Luftwaffe Test Pilot and Aviation Record Holder'
www.alteadler.de
  Alte Adler association official website
www.astronautix.com
  Encyclopedia Astronautica, 'Peenemünde'
www.ctie.monash.edu.au/Hargrave
  Monash University website, 'Hargrave: the pioneers', collection:
  Hanna Reitsch (1912–1979)
  Melitta Schiller (1903–1945)
www.griffonmerlin.com
  Griffon Merlin: James Holland's Second World War Forum
  Interviews with Eric Brown and Hajo Herrmann
www.historynet.com
  History Net, 'Hanna Reitsch: Hitler's Female Test Pilot'
www.hpmelle.de/stauffenberg
  Stauffenberg family memorial website
www.remember.org
  A People's History of the Holocaust and Genocide
  Harry J. Herder, 'Liberation of Buchenwald' (nd)
www.romanoarchives.altervista.org

MISCELLANEOUS

Flight in a Twin Astir II, F-CFYI glider at the Aerodrome de Gandalou,
Tarn & Garonne (August 2013)
Handwritten letter from Hanna Reitsch to Wernher von Braun's
NASA secretary, Julie Kertes, from collection previously owned by
Julie Kertes, and sold on eBay', accessed 30 April 2014
Stiftung Neue Synagogue [New Foundation Synagogue], Berlin,
exhibition: 'From the Outside to the Inside: the 1938 November
Pogroms in Diplomatic Reports from Germany' (May 2014)
Alexander Historical Auctions:
Letter Hanna Reitsch/Lutz Graf Schwein von Krosigk (13.05.1946)
Hermann Historica International Auctions (70th auction catalogue,
May 2015):
Hermann Göring's appointment diary (1943), lot 6140
Letter Hanna Reitsch/Albert Kesselring (29.02.1948), lot 6017

Picture Credits

1, 8 (left), 17, 34: Public domain.
8 (right), 29: Courtesy of the author.
2: © Heinrich Hoffmann/Hulton Archive/Getty Images.
3: Archive Reinhart Rudershausen.
4 (left): Courtesy of [Quellenvermerk]: TUM.Archiv der
   Technischen Universität München.
4 (right), 7, 33: Archiv Gerhard Bracke.
5, 13, 14, 25, 26, 28, 31: © Archive H. P. Melle / Stauffenberg and
   Archiv Gerhard Bracke.
6, 32, 38: © Konstanze von Schulthess, private collection.
9, 18, 30: © akg-images / ullstein bild.
10, 36, 37: © akg-images.
11, 21: © ullsteinbild / TopFoto.
12: © C. E. Daniel collection.
15, 27: © de Waal family, private collection.
16: © Prof. Bernd Rosemeyer / Agentur Karl Hoeffkes.
19: © IWM (A 31014).
20: © INTERFOTO / Alamy Stock Photo.
22: © Heinrich Hoffmann/ullstein bild via Getty Images.
23: © Bundesarchiv.
24: © Keystone/Hulton Archive/Getty Images.
35: © Robert R. Richards, The Ian Sayer Archive.

Index